T19003

HEAL
THE
HYPERACTIVE
BRAIN

*Through the New Science
of Functional Medicine*

Written and Illustrated by:

MICHAEL R. LYON, B.Sc., M.D.

FOCUSED
PUBLISHING

Calgary, AB
1-800-898-0374

Notice: This book is intended to increase your knowledge of the latest developments in the field of attention deficit hyperactivity disorder (ADHD). Because every individual is different, a physician must diagnose conditions and supervise the use of any treatment. This book is not intended to serve as a substitute for professional medical care under the supervision of a duly qualified healthcare professional. You are urged to seek out the best medical resources available to help you make informed decisions.

Focused Publishing, Calgary, AB

© 2000 Michael R. Lyon, MD

Book layout and production: Impact Visual Communications Ltd.
Cover Design: Collin Whitney, Pandell Technologies, Inc.
Illustrations: Michael R. Lyon, MD

Printed in Canada

Canadian Cataloguing In Publication Data

Lyon, Michael R, (Michael Robert), 1959-
    Healing the hyperactive brain : through the new science of functional
    medicine
        p.   cm.
    Includes biographical references and data
    ISBN 0-9685108-0-9 softcover
    l. Attention deficit hyperactivity disorder-Treatment 2. Hyperactivity-
    Treatment 3. Natural Healthcare I. Title

RJ506.H9196 1999   616.85'8906   C99-900414-X

2 4 6 8 10 9 7 5 3

THE FUNCTIONAL MEDICINE MODEL OF ADHD

To Mom and Dad:

Thanks for always believing in me;
for teaching me to set big goals;
to work hard,
and to finish what I start.

ACKNOWLEDGEMENTS

I would like to thank Dr. John C. Cline, M.D., Medical Director of the Cline Medical Center and the Oceanside Functional Medicine Research Institute. Without his leadership and support, this project would not have been possible.

I also owe a debt of gratitude to Dr. Jeffrey Bland, Ph.D., founder of the field of Functional Medicine. His brilliance and dedication is destined to impact the future of medicine more than any other single person.

This book is largely an integration of concepts that have originated in the minds of others. I especially recognize Dr. Leo Galland, M.D. for developing the concept of the "Patient Centered Diagnosis and Treatment" which is discussed so extensively in this book. As well, Dr. Sidney Baker, M.D. is largely responsible for integrating the concept of biochemical individuality into the field of Functional Medicine.

I am also grateful for the knowledge and inspiration provided by Dan Lukaczer, N.D.; DeAnne Liska, Ph.D.; Barb Schiltz, M.S., R.N.; Robert Lerman, M.D., Ph.D.; David Jones, M.D.; Eleanor Barrager, R.D. and all of the other clinicians and scientists affiliated with the Institute for Functional Medicine.

Thanks as well to Joanne Totosy de Zepetnek, Ph.D.; Jackie Shan, Ph.D., D.Sc.; Peter Pang, Ph.D., D.Sc.; Christina Benishin, Ph.D. and the other scientists at CV Technologies, HerbTech and University of Alberta for your imporant contributions to the development of scientific botanical medicine.

Special thanks to Stacey London, M.S. and Barb Schiltz, M.S., R.N. for their assistance with our research and to Ronald Penner, Ph.D. for his tremendous help and many insights.

Finally, my love and thanks to my wife, Sandra Lyon, for her editorial assistance and her patience through this endeavor.

PREFACE

This book represents the culmination of my life's work, first as a physician and more recently as a medical researcher studying attention deficit hyperactivity disorder (ADHD). On a personal level, this book is an organized, rational and sensible explanation for how I have been able to emerge from ADHD as a productive, happy, and healthy person with a wonderful wife, incredible children, and a rewarding career. Although ADHD has lead me through much grief and pain, I can now also say that it is has become a true asset – a friend and ally.

As a teenager, nearly twenty-five years ago, healing my own scattered brain and unhealthy body, became the major focus of my life. Someone handed me a book about natural medicine, and it seemed to open up a window in my mind. Natural medicine was a subject that empowered my wandering brain with an intensity I had never experienced before. Although the science of natural healthcare was rather primitive back then, many of the principles I learned worked well enough to transform my life. Within a year of radically changing my diet, beginning a running program, cleansing my body through saunas and fasting, and spending time every day in meditation and prayer, my attitude, health, and academic standing had dramatically improved. I went from being an aggressive, longhaired, pot and cigarette smoking "party animal", to a serious, clean cut student who graduated as the top male student in my high school class. There was no doubt in my mind at all that natural medicine worked. It changed the whole direction of my life. Three of my tough-as-nails friends were not as fortunate. They, like so many kids with ADHD, ended their own lives. One of my other "hyper" buddies, a real confident big-shot at one time, put a gun to his head and still lives to this day in a psychiatric ward, completely blind.

After high school, my self-education in natural medicine took second-place to my vigorous pursuit of science and conventional medicine. Right out of high school, I jumped at the chance to begin working in research at the medical school of the University of Calgary. For the next several years, most of my vacation time, weekends and evenings were spent working with researchers in the departments of microbiology and pathology while I pursued my formal education in University. My lingering interest in natural medicine was a regular source of amusement for the professors who supervised my research work. Occasionally, I even received letters of exhortation from supervisors who, concerned for my otherwise promising career, strongly suggested that I lay aside such strange interests and focus instead upon "real" science. These exhortations gradually began to work and I became increasingly skeptical about many of the things I had come to believe about nutrition and natural medicine – principles which had turned my whole life around.

The lifestyle that accompanies medical school and residency provides such high doses of adrenaline that it's almost like being on Ritalin®. (After having spent a year on Ritalin® as an adult, I can rightfully compare the two experiences). I believe that it was the almost war-zone levels of adrenaline, as well my vigorous pursuit of bicycle racing, that kept me strong, focused and successful through those very difficult years of medical training. In fact, I flourished in that highly structured, pressure cooker environment. However, once I got out into the relative humdrum of medical practice, I became a sedentary workaholic and it wasn't long before my health began to deteriorate. Soon, I was overweight, exhausted, forgetful, depressed, full of allergies and asthma, and my marriage was on the rocks. To the outside observer, I had reached what appeared to be the pinnacle of my career. I was an Olympic team physician with a teaching appointment at the university and I was placed in charge of a prestigious sport science committee affiliated with the International Olympic Committee. I had climbed to the top of my professional mountain but I was sick and tired and bored out of my increasingly foggy mind. It was at this crisis point, about seven years ago, that I made a deep and spiritual commitment to rebuild my life and renew my pursuit of more natural, safe and cause-oriented forms of medicine. Later, I made a giant leap of faith when I decided to leave medical practice completely to pursue full-time research and teaching.

My first renewed exposure to medicine outside of the mainstream came through a chiropractor, Dr. Jeff Cameron. I had come to respect him as a fellow who was, in my mind then, quite scientific for a chiropractor. I had been taught in medical school that chiropractic was a "medical cult", an opinion which many in the ivory towers of medicine continue to uphold. After several conversations with Dr. Cameron regarding patients we were both treating, I was quite astounded at his level of knowledge and the depth of his clinical skills. Likewise, he was quite thrilled to come across a medical doctor who showed some interest in complementary medicine. Since then, I have come to realize that Dr. Cameron is not alone in his quest to combine the best of science with the best of complementary medicine. He is part of a whole new breed of chiropractors, naturopaths, scientists, complementary medical doctors and other "alternative" health care practitioners who are riding an enormous scientific wave that is about to sweep away much of the old medical paradigm. Powered by the information revolution and directed by some of the top scientists and physicians in the world, this great wave is called **Functional Medicine**, a term that will become increasingly familiar throughout the course of this book.

I can thank my friend for first opening my eyes to the world of Functional Medicine. I remember the day that he handed me a set of tapes from a scientific symposium he had attended. The tapes were from a day-long series of lectures given by Dr. Jeffrey Bland, Ph.D., a world renowned nutritional biochemist and founder of the field of Functional Medicine. Driving down the road, listening to the first cassette, I was skeptical that I could even find the time to fit these tapes into my extraordinarily busy schedule. I arrived home a few minutes later but sat in my parked car for the next hour, glued to my seat, while absorbing the words of Dr. Bland like a dry sponge. That day, it felt like my mind had come back to life. So much that I had learned about natural medicine as a teenager, and then later discarded as a skeptical physician, started to make a great deal of scientif-ic sense. Finally, someone had begun to explain concepts from natural and nutritional medicine in logical, scientific terms. Although I didn't realize it that day, the whole direc-tion of my life had begun to point toward the *Functional Medicine Revolution*.

Table of Contents

INTRODUCTION – ADHD and the Functional Medicine Revolution   13

SECTION ONE
What's going on inside the hyperactive brain? (Neurotransmitters and Other Symptom Mediators)

Chapter 1: The Boss of the Brain is on Vacation   23

Chapter 2: The Craving Brain   33

Chapter 3: The Undependable Brain   41

Chapter 4: ADHD and the Brain-Body Connection   47

SECTION TWO
Setting the Stage (Risk Factors for the Development of ADHD)

Chapter 5: A "Chip Off the Old Block" – the Genetics of ADHD   53

Chapter 6: Environmental Neurotoxins and the Hyperactive Brain   63

Chapter 7: Building Blocks of a Healthy Brain – Essential Fatty Acids   83

Chapter 8: Other Brain Critical Nutritional Factors   101

Chapter 9: Psychosocial Factors at the Heart of ADHD   123

SECTION THREE
Sick Cells, Sick Molecules, Sick Brains (Physiological Triggers of ADHD)

Chapter 10: The Gut-Brain Connection   133

Chapter 11: Food Allergies and Other Adverse Reactions to Foods   153

Chapter 12: The Universe Within
– Bacteria, Yeast and Parasites in ADHD   189

Chapter 13: Debilitated Defenses;
– Immune System Impairment in ADHD   213

SECTION FOUR
Solving the ADHD Puzzle through the Functional Medicine Method

Chapter 14: The Patient Centered Diagnosis   227

Chapter 15: Clinical Assessment of the ADHD Patient   237

Chapter 16: Functional Testing in the Assessment of the ADHD Patient   253

Chapter 17: An Intelligent Approach to Food Allergies and Intolerances   291

SECTION FIVE
Functional Medicine Approach to the Treatment of ADHD

Chapter 18: Patient Centered Treatment of ADHD   323

Chapter 19: Why Worry About Ritalin®, Dexedrine®
and Other ADHD Drugs?   333

Chapter 20: God's Pharmacy – Therapeutic Phytochemicals in ADHD   345

Chapter 21: Gastrointestinal Rehabilitation – The 4-R Program™   365

Chapter 22: Restoring Strength to the Battered Immune System   387

Chapter 23: Feeding the Hyperactive Brain
– Nutritional Management of ADHD   419

Chapter 24: Purifying the Toxic Brain   437

Chapter 25: Empowering the Hyperactive Brain through
Physical Exercise   455

Chapter 26: Focusing the Hyperactive Brain through Biofeedback,
Meditation and Prayer   463

Chapter 27: Keys to a Productive Life – ADHD as Friend and Ally   481

SECTION SIX
Functional Medicine Approach to ADHD
– Referenced Overview for Healthcare Professionals   497

REFERENCES   557

INDEX   589

Introduction

THE COMING STORM

Throughout history, catastrophic changes in society have often occurred suddenly and have taken the majority of people by surprise, even though coming calamity was often predicted by forward thinking individuals. Take for example, the Great Depression of the 1930's. The majority of the population was swept away by poverty and despair even though thousands of people were predicting it's inevitable arrival. Many who had the foresight to make preparations were left relatively untouched through the "dirty thirties". In fact, it is often said that more millionaires were made during the Great Depression than any other time in history. I believe our society is presently at another turning point where the storm clouds of change are just over the horizon. In fact, for ever-increasing millions of people, the storm has already begun to blow into their own lives. Those who are knowledgeable and prepared may avoid tremendous personal pain and may even find opportunity for achievement and success.

This growing storm consists of "invisible disabilities" such as chronic fatigue syndrome, fibromyalgia, and attention deficit hyperactivity disorder (ADHD). The incidence of all of these mysterious and potentially devastating diseases appears to be rising at an explosive rate and has now begun to impact society in a very serious way. So far, medicine has provided no real or lasting solutions for these often horrible afflictions. In fact, many doctors remain cold and scornful toward those who suffer with these conditions, often brushing them off as merely "psychosomatic cases". In the case of ADHD, the medical community generally considers the prescription of powerful symptom-suppressing drugs to be an adequate and responsible way to deal with this problem. Unfortunately, little effort is made to identify and appropriately deal with the underlying causes of ADHD or these other invisible disabilities.

If the incidence of chronic fatigue syndrome and fibromyalgia continue to rise at their current rate of growth, the very fabric of our productive society is threatened. However, of even more grave concern is the astounding increase in the rate of prescriptions for ADHD. The number of prescriptions written for Ritalin® has increased by several hundred percent over the last ten years. Does this trend simply reflect an increased recognition of ADHD amongst physicians? This is not easily determined from just examining statistics alone. However, anyone who deals with children; either teachers, day care workers or physicians, will tell you clearly that the number of completely unruly or severely inattentive children has dramatically increased in just a few years. If the incidence of the ADHD continues to rise at such an alarming rate, we are all in big trouble. What if ADHD eventually affects 20 or 30 or even 70 percent of our children? If this occurs, no magic drugs will be sufficient to prevent this coming storm from sweeping across our land destroying countless lives in the process. We need better answers and we need them soon!

A REVOLUTION IN THE MAKING

Many have said that medicine has lost its soul. The price we have paid for incredible technology is the industrialization and dehumanization of what was once just a gentle and helping profession. This is not to say that there still aren't many doctors who are kind, compassionate, and who sincerely desire the best for their patients. However, even the most compassionate physician is still part of an enormous industrial machine which has groomed and educated its members to efficiently carry out the tasks required to keep that machine growing in size and sophistication. Studies have shown that a growing number of physicians are disgruntled with the way their lives have gone. Many are frustrated and feel reduced to prescription-writing robots and slaves to managed-care organizations, or inefficient government health plans. It is largely this system which forces doctors to see patients every five to ten minutes to make ends meet.

A growing number of physicians are are now aware that many natural alternative remedies are just as effective or even superior to drug treatments and are cheaper and far safer. As well, a rising tide of physicians now yearn to fully use their intelligence and talents and to treat patients as whole persons rather than as impersonal cases. Many of these same physicians are tired of just covering over symptoms with drugs when the underlying causes of disease are being ignored. What so many physicians and other scientifically minded healthcare professionals are really looking for can be found in the revolutionary new science of Functional Medicine.

THE BASIC PRINCIPLES OF FUNCTIONAL MEDICINE

Functional Medicine is not a new medical specialty. In fact, Functional Medicine is practiced by a wide range of health-care professionals and can be considered, in its most basic form, a medical philosophy or an intellectual method which uses important principles as a guide in the assessment and treatment of patients. Most medical treatments are considered satisfactory if they simply reduce or eliminate the symptoms of a disease, or even just alter the results of a laboratory test. In many instances, little consideration is given for the overall quality of a patient's life or their ability to function as productive members of society.

In contrast, Functional Medicine is defined as patient-centered, science-based health care that identifies and addresses underlying biochemical, physiological, environmental and psychological factors to reverse disease progression and enhance vitality. Rather than depending on single, powerful treatments such as drugs or surgery, Functional Medicine relies more upon intelligent and individualized combinations of treatments or protocols.

To be considered as consistent with the principles of Functional Medicine, a treatment method must fulfill four important criteria. It must:

· Carry no risk of doing harm and should be free of unpleasant side effects.

· Improve symptoms as well as the overall function and quality of life.

· Help to correct the underlying causes of the disorder.

· Improve the long-term prognosis for the patient.

GETTING TO THE ROOT OF THE PROBLEM

When dealing with complex, multi-factorial conditions such as ADHD, a healthcare provider versed in the principles of Functional Medicine practitioner will approach the patient in an organized, systematic fashion. This process begins by a thorough historical interview and physical examination and is often followed by selected laboratory tests to help better define the set of problems unique to that individual. In a sense, the practitioner is a skilled detective in search of clues to piece together the mystery of why that individual patient suffers from their particular set of signs and symptoms. To those practicing Functional Medicine, it is not sufficient to randomly prescribe a treatment for ADHD.

ANTECEDENTS, TRIGGERS, MEDIATORS

The Functional Medicine practitioner begins to assemble an orderly list of problems suspected to be at the heart of ADHD in that particular patient. In most cases, ADHD is multifactorial, that is, it is the result of a collection of underlying medical problems, which have additive effects and may lead to ADHD symptoms. This problem list is divided into antecedents, triggers and mediators, which lead to the signs and symptoms of ADHD. **Antecedents** are risk factors which precede the onset of symptoms and which predispose the individual to the development of ADHD. These are factors that can often begin at conception, during pregnancy or during infancy and early childhood. Common antecedents might include such things as genetic factors, environmental toxins, head injury or stresses within the family. In essence, antecendents set the stage for physical imbalances and internal disorders by weakening a person's basic physiological foundation.

As well, the Functional Medicine practitioner begins to consider the triggers present within each individual with ADHD. **Triggers** are physical or biochemical problems arising out of the weakened or susceptible physiology in a person with various antecedents that have been exerting stressful influences upon organ systems, cells, or molecules. Common triggers might include such things as food allergies, intestinal parasites, or chronic infections. In general, triggers are more likely to occur in an individual who already has certain antecedents. For example, food allergies (trigger) are much more common if a person has a genetic predisposition to allergies (antecedent).

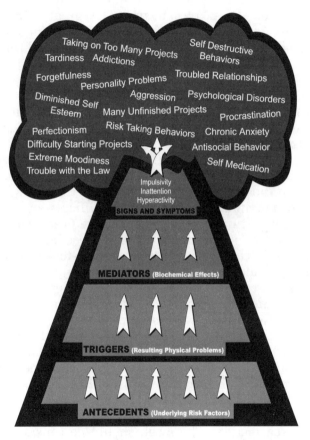

These triggers, in turn, lead to imbalances of other critical substances known as mediators. **Mediators** are those physical factors, which lead to or mediate the actual signs and symptoms of the disorder. The disturbed mediators in ADHD are primarily brain neurotransmitters such as dopamine, serotonin, and norepinephrine. Imbalance in these biochemical mediators then leads to the signs and symptoms of ADHD.

The search for antecedents, triggers, and mediators can involve repeated visits, sophisticated laboratory testing and extensive patient education. However, when these critical underlying factors are identified and dealt with effectively, the results are often extraordinary and the long-term prognosis for the ADHD patient may be greatly improved. Overall, this approach relies far less on symptom suppressing drugs and instead relies more on safe, natural therapies to address the underlying causes of the disorder.

BE EMPOWERED WITH KNOWLEDGE

First and foremost, this book seeks to empower the reader with knowledge. It is written with a minimum of jargon to communicate to the widest possible audience. The Functional Medicine approach is presented in a logical, systematic fashion. It is therefore advisable to read through the material in the order it is presented. Repetition is selectively used to maximize the learning of difficult and possibly foreign concepts. Laypeople or healthcare practitioners who have had no prior exposure to some of these ideas may have to read certain chapters more than once before the information really sinks in. Busy healthcare practitioners who would like a concise and more technical overview of the Functional Medicine approach to ADHD might consider reading Section Six before embarking on the more voluminous chapters. Every effort has been made to make the material presented as objective and as science-based as possible. Thousands of scientific references have been studied in preparation of this book. However, I must admit that I have also taken the liberty to add some of my own personal experiences, as well as observations that have been made in our research facility. This book should be considered as a pioneering work rather than a definitive treatise on the subject. However, although some skeptics will undoubtably criticize this approach as speculative or "unconventional" the elements of this program are already in widespread use and are helping thousands of people worldwide.

What's Going on Inside the Hyperactive Brain?
(Neurotransmitters and Other Symptom Mediators)

Taking on Too Many Projects

Tardiness   Addictions

Self Destructive Behaviors

Forgetfulness

Personality Problems

Troubled Relationships

Diminished Self Esteem

Aggression

Many Unfinished Projects

Psychological Disorders

Procrastination

Perfectionism

Risk Taking Behaviors

Chronic Anxiety

Difficulty Starting Projects

Antisocial Behavior

Extreme Moodiness

Self Medication

Trouble with the Law

Impulsivity
Inattention
Hyperactivity

SIGNS AND SYMPTOMS

Brain Neurotransmitter Dysfunction

MEDIATORS
(Biochemical Effects)

Chapter 1

The Boss of the Brain is on Vacation

THE MANY FACES OF ADHD

One of the first things I came to understand, as I became involved with ADHD research is that those with this condition are a highly varied group of people. They differ widely in their intelligence and capability to read and learn. ADHD can be found commonly amongst the intellectually challenged or those with various learning disabilities but, ironically, it is also reasonably prevalent amongst brilliant scholars, talented artists, and wealthy entrepreneurs. It crosses all boundaries, all races and all socioeconomic classes. I've frequently seen clear signs of ADHD amongst many of the hard-driving professional and Olympic athletes that I've worked with over the years and yet so many with ADHD are sluggish, clumsy and might not excel in sports if they spent their whole life trying. Although most people can recognize ADHD in a child or adult who exhibits extreme hyperactivity, few will identify the condition in the shy, silent daydreamer sitting in the back of the class. Many with ADHD are the warmest, most outgoing people you'll ever meet, yet the rate of ADHD amongst violent offenders is many times higher than it is amongst those who have never committed a violent crime. In spite of these vast differences, there is one thing, which seems quite certain. All those with ADHD suffer from characteristic problems with their brain function that will usually lead to significant disability or, quite commonly, catastrophic consequences in their lives. What is even more tragic is that few of those with ADHD will ever discover that they can improve their brain function remarkably and become stable, happy and productive citizens instead of suffering through a life of grief and despair.

SIGNS AND SYMPTOMS OF ADHD

The three cardinal symptoms of ADHD are inattentiveness, impulsivity and hyperactivity. According to the American Psychiatric Association, there are three sub types of ADHD:

- *primarily hyperactive type*
- *primarily inattentive type*
- *combined type*

According to this system of classification, all three forms are referred to as attention deficit hyperactivity disorder (ADHD). However, many people still refer to the primarily inattentive (non-hyperactive) form as attention deficit disorder (ADD). For simplicity we will refer to all types as simply ADHD. Beyond the three main symptoms of impulsivity, hyperactivity and inattentiveness, a multitude of problems can arise from the ADHD affected brain.

OUR AMAZING BRAIN

Through my years of work in the department of pathology, I would estimate that I have performed over two hundred autopsies. So many times I have held a fresh brain in my (gloved) hands and marveled that this rather simplistic looking blob of jelly is actually the most sophisticated technological marvel in the yet known universe. Far more than just a computer, the brain is actually a vast collection of separate microcomputers that are all networked together with a complexity that makes our current Internet seem rather laughable indeed. The simplest tasks, such as recognizing the face of an old friend, organizing our desk, or navigating our way through a busy shopping mall, requires such complex data input and information processing that even our greatest supercomputers are unable to compete successfully with just an average person's brain. The brain is a very critical interface between our inner soul and the outside world in which we live. Mess with the brain, and no matter how good your intentions, your life will be made more difficult or can easily be ruined.

OUR VULNERABLE BRAIN

The brain is the emperor over our body. Guarded in so many ways from the time of conception until the day we die, the brain maintains all-powerful authority over the rest of the body and yet, it is our most vulnerable member. Even the blood vessels which transport life giving nutrients and oxygen to the brain are different there than anywhere else in the body. The cells that line these blood vessels (called the blood brain barrier) are security guards lining the entryways to the brain and keeping out most threatening chemicals or microorganisms. The brain is also a glutton for energy and oxygen. This sedentary organ utilizes twenty-five percent of the body's supply of oxygen, almost as much as all of your muscles. The brain is also greedy for some of the rarest nutrients. For instance, one of the fats which makes up the majority of certain critical nerve endings is, in fact so rare that (apart from breast milk) it can only be found in any significant quantity in foods from the sea. The brain is also highly vulnerable to damage. One solid blow can render the brain useless for life. If the bacteria that causes minor childhood ear infections gains entry to the brain, it can cause death within hours or turn a previously healthy person into a permanent vegetable overnight. The brain is particularly susceptible to damage from our modern environment. Most naturally occurring toxins are water-soluble, not fat-soluble. These water-soluble toxins are prevented entry into the brain because of the properties of the blood brain barrier. However, most toxins from the industrialized world are fat-soluble and pass through the blood brain barrier quite readily. Since the brain is mostly made of fat, it soaks up these fat-soluble toxins like a hungry sponge. As you might well imagine, individuals with excessive exposure to neurotoxic chemicals, are sitting ducks for the development of brain problems, especially if events have taken place to damage the blood brain barrier.

THE BOSS IS ON VACATION

Research into the basic causes of ADHD has taken a dramatic leap forward in the last few years. Studies looking at the brain from several different perspectives have clearly demonstrated that ADHD is associated with significant problems of brain function. Magnetic resonance imaging (MRI), positron emission tomography (PET) scanning, electroencephalography (EEG) and various other technologies have all demonstrated significant problems in the frontal regions of the brain in those with ADHD. The part of the brain called the pre-frontal cortex (imbedded inside the frontal lobes) contains specialized zones called the executive centers. These are actually the most complex and sophisticated regions of the brain, the parts of the brain, which truly set humans apart from the animals. Within these executive centers the complex tasks of judgment, organization, moral thought, reasoning and other very sophisticated cognitive processes take place. As well, the executive centers as their name implies exert authoritative control over the rest of the brain. (Barkley, 1997b) Throughout the other regions of the brain, thoughts and feelings as well as impulses to move, to talk, and to act with aggression arise with great frequency. It is the job of the executive centers to reach back and inhibit all of those thoughts or actions, which are judged to be inappropriate. If the executive centers are damaged, sleeping or in some way functioning improperly, impulsivity, inattentiveness and hyperactivity are the result. Because of this loss of executive control, the brains of those with ADHD behave as though the boss is on vacation.

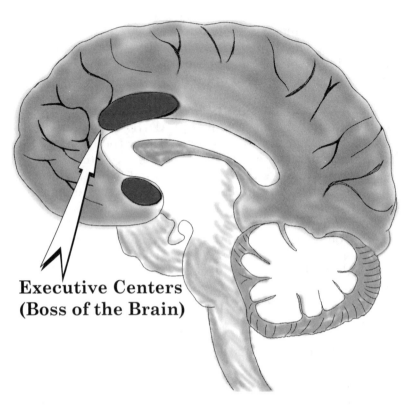

**Executive Centers
(Boss of the Brain)**

Unfortunately, of all the regions of the brain, the executive centers are the most sensitive to trauma, neurotoxic effects, stress and nutritional insufficiencies. Everyone has witnessed on one occasion or another, evidence of executive center problems in other individuals. For example, consider a shy, inhibited person who decides to have a few drinks of alcohol. Although they can still carry out basic functions such as thinking, walking and breathing, the very sensitive executive centers of their brain become depressed by the alcohol and are the first brain regions to be affected by this common neurotoxin. This alcohol-induced loss of executive center inhibition often results in the shy person "coming out of their shell" and becoming the most talkative, outgoing and even silly person at the party. Other persons, under the neurotoxic influence of alcohol, may instead, behave aggressively and commit impulsive acts which they will regret later. Besides alcohol, an extraordinary number of neurotoxic influences may also exert their primary affects upon the highly sensitive executive centers of the brain.

THE SECRET LIFE OF DOPAMINE

All nerves transmit information along the majority of their length through electrical impulses. However, once the electrical impulse reaches the end of the nerve, the information is then communicated through nerve endings to adjacent nerves through chemical messengers known as neurotransmitters. Numerous neurotransmitters have now been identified in various parts of the brain and nervous system as well as other systems throughout the rest of the body. Each of the brain's nerve cells or neurons release a different type of neurotransmitter depending upon that neuron's function. The neurons within the executive centers in the pre-frontal cortex of the brain are highly complex, each possessing many branches. At the ends of each branch, the neurotransmitter dopamine is stored in small packets. When an electrical impulse reaches the nerve ending, packets of dopamine are released into the space between the nerve ending and the adjacent nerve. The dopamine then quickly crosses this gap and sticks to complex proteins called dopamine receptors on the adjacent neuron. Once enough of these receptors are full of dopamine, an electrical impulse then begins to travel down this adjacent nerve. The dopamine receptors then quickly let go of their dopamine, which is then rapidly drawn back up into the nerve ending where it came from. Since the nerve ending prefers to use fresh dopamine, the recycled dopamine is quickly broken down and discarded. This whole cycle of dopamine release, attachment to receptors and re-uptake of dopamine takes place within a very tiny fraction of a second. If anything goes wrong with any part of this process, the whole computer system in that region can seriously malfunction.

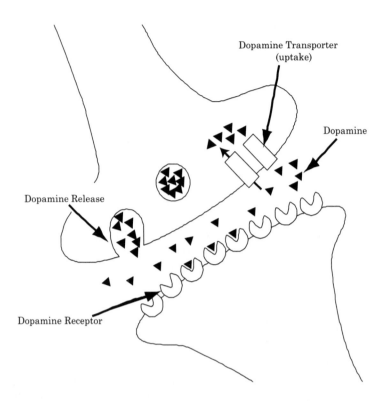

Dopamine Transporter (uptake)

Dopamine

Dopamine Release

Dopamine Receptor

In the parts of the brain which take care of automated functions, the neurons are less complex and are more resistant to injury, nutrient depletion or toxic stress. You can compare this to the stability of the tiny automated computer chips built into your wristwatch or VCR. However in the highly complex executive centers, the neurons are vastly more sophisticated and are highly sensitive to injury, nutrient depletion or toxic stress. This could be compared to the sensitive, unstable nature of the large computer networks that run big businesses.

Research has now demonstrated that the primary symptoms of ADHD arise largely because of a relative lack of dopamine activity in the neurons within the executive centers of the brain. The main reason why amphetamines like Ritalin® and Dexedrine® improve the symptoms of ADHD is that they increase the amount of dopamine activity in these critical regions. They do so largely by blocking the re-uptake or recycling of dopamine. This allows dopamine to "hang around" the dopamine receptors much longer thus increasing the amount of dopamine activity in the executive center regions.

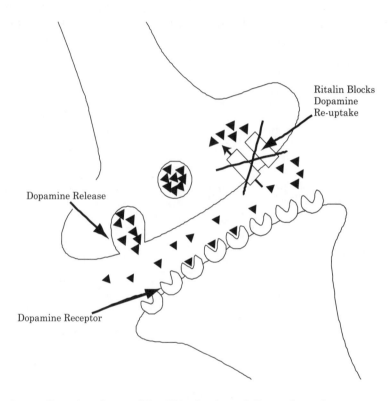

As well, stimulants like Ritalin® and Dexedrine® increase the activity or cause the release of several neurotransmitters as well as the stress hormones adrenaline and cortisol. These powerful drugs actually "rev up" the whole brain, the heart and the entire body. For example, they are virtually the same kinds of drugs ("uppers" or "speed"), that are illegally used by certain truck drivers to remain awake for long periods of time or that keep "speed freaks" up for days at a time. However, because these drugs awaken and activate the powerful and inhibitory executive centers, these regions are able to take back their rightful control over the rest of the brain kind of like having the boss come back from vacation. Thus, because they awaken the executine centers, the ADHD sufferer is able to sit still and focus when taking stimulant drugs. Wouldn't it be wonderful if the executive centers of the brain could be fully awakened through completely safe and natural means instead of powerful drugs? To a large extent, that is what this book is all about!

Chapter 2
The Craving Brain

Over the last few decades we have witnessed an incredible rise in the popularity of "extreme" sports of all kinds amongst our young people. During my years as a sports medicine physician, I saw a multitude of seriously injured kids and young adults who were willing to risk life and limb just for an incredible rush of adrenaline. In recent years, our nation has also experienced a dramatic increase in illicit drug use and violent crimes. Drug treatment centers are overflowing, and addictions to self-destructive behaviors such as gambling or promiscuous sex seem to be eroding the very fabric of our society. So many people seem willing to pay any price for a bit of fleeting ecstasy.

Parallel with this trend has been an incredible rise in the number of prescriptions written for the treatment of ADHD. Some might argue that this trend simply reflects an increase in the number of prescription-happy doctors. However, those on the front lines, the doctors, teachers and day-care workers, will tell you that the number of kids they see who are now very aggressive, pathological daydreamers, or hyperactive beyond control has risen immensely. Could there be a connection between the increase in addictions and the increase in ADHD? Many brain researchers would say most definitely yes!

One of the most astonishing new areas of brain research centers on discoveries related to the neurological basis of addiction. For most of history society has assumed that alcoholics and drug addicts are simply moral invalids who deserve all the punishment that they eventually get and more. While no one would argue that addiction has serious moral implications and generally involves a series of very wrong and avoidable decisions, it is now also very clear that there is a strong neurological basis to the problem of chemical dependency. In fact, it is quite likely that because of their unique brain structure and biochemistry, many people are literally sitting ducks for addiction.

Deep inside the frontal part of the brain is a small complex area known as the pleasure or reward center. Like the executive centers, the neurons in the reward center, when stimulated release the neurotransmitter dopamine. Once dopamine is released in this reward center, the individual experiences a sense of pleasure or satisfaction. It has now been shown that both animals and humans require a certain amount of pleasurable signals coming from this reward center every day in order to achieve a basic sense of contentment.

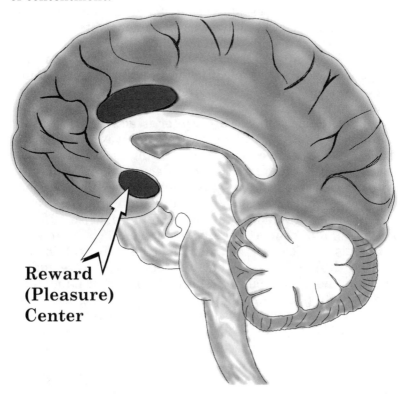

**Reward
(Pleasure)
Center**

Most people are able to achieve an adequate level of daily pleasure or reward through simple, healthy activities such as eating food, positive social interactions, normal sexual relations and recreation. However, both those with ADHD as well as those with addiction share one thing in common: a relative insensitivity of the brain's pleasure or reward centers. What this means is that these individuals have to work much harder to obtain an adequate amount of pleasurable stimuli and to achieve that basic sense of satisfaction. In the terms of brain researchers, both addiction and ADHD are now considered to be "reward deficiency syndromes". In other words, those with ADHD must, one way or another, learn to cope with a craving brain. (Blum, 1996)

Although it is possible to suffer from addiction and not have ADHD, it has been known for years that ADHD can be a setup for addiction. Studies conducted in chemical dependency treatment centers have clearly demonstrated that the incidence of ADHD amongst alcoholics and drug addicts is much higher than that of the general population. Several drugs, such as cocaine, nicotine and amphetamines stimulate the brain's reward center directly, leading to the release of dopamine which, in turn, brings about a sense of euphoria. As well, once the reward center is activated, a strong stimulus is then sent along neural pathways, awakening the brain's executive centers and bringing about a keen sense of focus. The drug cocaine effects the reward center explosively and dramatically creating a powerful experience of euphoria. Cocaine also powerfully stimulates the brain's executive centers and results in an intense sense of focus, alertness and control. These combined effects are why cocaine is so viciously addictive and help to explain why many with ADHD report that they knew they were addicted to cocaine after their first snort. On the other hand, nicotine and amphetamines (methamphetamine, Dexedrine®, Ritalin®) have a more subtle effect upon the reward center and result in a milder sense of euphoria. However, these drugs stimulate the executive centers more directly and result in a heightened sense of wakefulness and focus. Other drugs, such as heroin, marijuana or alcohol, stimulate the brain's reward center indirectly but still quite powerfully, resulting in a strong sense of euphoria with variable effects upon the brain's executive centers.

People with ADHD often gravitate into various forms of drug abuse because these substances seem to provide temporary chemical solutions for the pain and inner turmoil of their lives. In many cases, the only time a person with ADHD feels focused and satisfied is when they are "high" on drugs, alcohol, pornography or gambling. Others chain smoke or drink their way through the stresses of their life with little consideration for the long-term consequences of such behavior. Since the end result of drug abuse and addiction is usually despair, destruction and often death, those whose brains suffer from a "reward deficiency syndrome" urgently need to find better ways to fill their inner void and to find satisfaction and serenity without the use of drugs or other destructive influences.

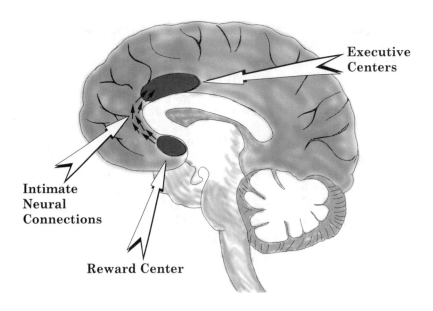

Many with ADHD aggressively pursue activities or behaviors that powerfully stimulate their brain's reward center without the use of artificial chemicals. Some of these activities, such as compulsive gambling or sexual promiscuity have the potential to be just as devastating or deadly as chemical dependency. For instance, gambling addiction is growing in epidemic proportions with far reaching consequences. Recent studies presented to the U.S. Congress by the National Gambling Impact Study Commission indicated that 16% of gambling addicts will eventually attempt suicide. (www.ngisc.gov) Dangerous sports or high-risk business ventures also run a fine line between great rewards and catastrophic loss. Many with ADHD become true "adrenaline junkies" who thrive on hazardous pursuits and who would never trade the thrill of staring danger in the face for a hum drum life of routines. Although our society almost worships the risk-taking entrepreneur, over 90% of new business ventures fail -- often resulting in devastated lives. How many of these failed businesses are the result of the impulsive, risk taking behaviors so typical of the ADHD adult? Even the more sedate ADHD sufferer will usually have a severe intolerance to boredom and may spend endless hours talking, worrying, watching TV, surfing the Internet, reading novels or playing video games all in the pursuit of that elusive sense of serenity.

In my own life I have run the gamut of almost every possible activity in pursuit of that elusive sense of satisfaction. In grade three I began to smoke and was a serious half pack per day puffer by the time I was in grade six. Throughout childhood, I was a compulsive overeater and was seriously overweight. In grade six, I was offered marijuana for the first time and I became a habitual "pot head" by the time I was in grade seven. By the time I was in high school, I had become an expert in motorcycle stunt riding and I found great joy in riding my dirt bike at sixty mph — front wheel high off the ground — past cheering kids in front of my school. After this era, I gave up the smoking, drugs and suicidal motorcycle riding and replaced them with the adrenaline of medical training and intense athletics. At one point, I became such a compulsive runner, that I developed stress fractures in both legs and knee problems eventually requiring three surgical operations. Once the intensity of medical training had ended and I settled into a busy, but routine medical practice, I became increasingly sedentary and bored out of my mind. In response to this intense restlessness, I became involved with several high-risk business ventures and began to pursue very dangerous commercial scuba diving. I even helped a friend build a submarine and almost lost my life on the bottom of a very cold lake while testing this dangerous invention. With all of the wild ventures I was involved with, I was soon bankrupt, my marriage was on the rocks, and my health had deteriorated to the point where I was chronically exhausted and continuously in pain. In the darkness and anguish of my unraveling life, I turned to prescription painkillers to get some relief from my suffering. Like so many others with ADHD, I found myself in the bottom of a deep, dark pit of despair, staring death right in the face. I am one of those fortunate ones who, by the grace of God, found the knowledge and strength to climb back out that horrible place and finally find peace and wholeness in my life. That was over seven years ago. I'm very thankful that today I'm very happily married to the same wonderful woman, have two incredible kids, an amazing and exciting career and I am healthier and happier now than I have ever been in my life. I use no alcohol or drugs, I'm not involved in any wild business ventures and, although I exercise daily, I am no longer an adrenaline junkie. I guess you could say that I have been bitten twice with the ADHD beast and have now grown in wisdom because of it.

Through research, study, practice and experience I have found a program that consistently provides deep and complete satisfaction for my craving brain. There's nothing magical or overly complex about this program. It is based on solid science, as well as natural and spiritual principles that have helped millions of people. This program begins by recognizing that the brain is a delicate organ made up of billions of highly sensitive cells intimately connected to every other cell in our bodies. This delicate organ is influenced tremendously by the adequacy or inadequacy of a wide range of nutrients, by a multitude of potentially toxic stresses and by the nature of our inner selves – our soul and our spirit. By combining principles of diet, lifestyle, psychology and spirituality even the most desperately craving brain can find focus, satisfaction, joy and serenity.

Chapter 3
The Undependable Brain

ADHD AND MEMORY FUNCTION

In spite of the clear association between ADHD and the brain, this condition is not, in and of itself, a learning disability. Nevertheless, many people with ADHD do suffer from learning disabilities and all suffer with nagging difficulties in some of their most basic thinking processes, particularly their memory function. In research conducted at our facility, fifty adults with ADHD were put through a lengthy test of their memory function. All but a small handful of these individuals had very significant deficits in various aspects of their memory. Interestingly enough, among the ADHD subjects with the most significant memory deficits were a few very successful professionals and business people. Our research findings are in no way unique. In fact there are numerous published research papers demonstrating significant memory problems in ADHD sufferers, both children and adults. (Benezra, 1988; Felton, 1897; Douglas, 1990)

WORKING MEMORY IS NOT WORKING VERY WELL

Perhaps the most important and consistent finding in this area of research involves the examination of working memory in those with ADHD. (Denckla, 1996; Barley, 1997) Working memory is that aspect of memory that enables a person to organize and efficiently complete the tasks that are right in front of them. For instance, if you have to sit down to organize and clean up a messy desk, your working memory becomes very important. To organize your desk, you must first quickly scan the desk visually to identify everything that is obviously just garbage. Once you have finished this scan for garbage, your working memory must store the identities of each piece of garbage until it has been discarded. Then, by quickly sorting through the piles of paper and all the various objects on the desk, you must begin to classify each document or object by category. At this point, your working memory must hold onto the basic categories of objects and documents until you decide where you're going to place them. You then have to begin filing the documents and place the objects in some organized fashion on your desktop or elsewhere in your office. All this time your working memory is holding onto a widely varied selection of items to keep you organized and on track. In a sense, working memory is kind of like a juggler who has to keep several objects in the air at once. Another person standing near the juggler keeps throwing new objects at the juggler. A person who does not have ADHD is like a juggler who can keep many items in the air at once. On the other hand, someone with ADHD is like a juggler who can keep very few things in the air before he begins to drop them.

In practical terms, problems with working memory can be very disabling. For instance, it is very common for those with ADHD to be slow readers. Occasionally, this is due to a true learning disability such as dyslexia. Far more commonly however, it is due to a problem with working memory. By the time they have finished the end of a sentence, they may have forgotten what they were reading at the beginning of the sentence. This is one of the main reasons why people with ADHD typically have to read things several times before they finally comprehend what they have read and are able to recall the material at all.

Problems with working memory can get people into all kinds of trouble. Without normal working memory, a person may have a very poor sense of time. Such individuals often have trouble keeping the various tasks and events of their day in focus and will commonly spend too much time on one task and not leave enough time for another. The same people are often chronically late for appointments or they may forget them altogether. In fact, some people with ADHD become so creative at making excuses for late or missed appointments that it becomes one of their most important life skills.

THE HYPER-FOCUSING PARADOX

ADHD sufferers adapt to problems with working memory in some very interesting and unexpected ways. Having poor working memory doesn't necessarily mean that the individual will have significant problems with other aspects of memory, particularly long-term memory. Many people with ADHD have come to realize that although they have trouble staying focused during most tasks, in other areas of particular interest or importance they are able to focus better than anyone else they know. This common feature of ADHD is known as hyper-focusing and it has the potential to be one of the most positive traits that often accompanies ADHD. The ability to hyper-focus may be due, in part, to poor working memory. When people with poor working memory focus upon something they are truly interested in, the rest of their life seems to literally vaporize from their consciousness. During the time that they are hyper-focusing, they can drift into an almost trance-like state where learning and productivity can become very efficient but where they may become oblivious to the rest of their environment. This may even explain, in part, the mystery of the "absent-minded professor syndrome".

Having worked in medical school research laboratories for several years, I will testify to the fact that there are indeed many "absent-minded professors"— brilliant individuals who can hardly remember to keep their own shoelaces tied. In the movie "Flubber", Robin Williams gives a somewhat exaggerated but hilariously accurate portrayal of a very typical "absent-minded professor". So many people with ADHD have traits like this professor. They have all the best intentions in the world but they just can't seem to get it together. They may be successful or talented in certain areas of their life, but in other areas they seem to fail again and again. Those who have succeeded in overcoming the major deficits that accompany ADHD are usually the ones who have developed their skills through hyper-focusing and have learned to build external structure and organization into their lives, making up for the abilities that they naturally lack. Only then, can a person's weaknesses – like poor working memory – become less serious and may even end up being a humorous part of their personality.

THE DARKER SIDE OF HYPER-FOCUSING

Unfortunately, not everyone with ADHD uses the power of hyper-focusing to develop life skills that will benefit themselves and the rest of society. In some cases, it might be that hyper-focusing is partly what enables an individual to become an expert criminal or a skillful con artist. In other cases, if the ADHD sufferer hyper-focuses on their worries or their physical afflictions they may eventually become a "bundle of nerves" or a chronic hypochondriac. It seems quite clear that hyper-focusing is a common and powerful companion of ADHD. Those who learn to harness and direct this dynamic trait in a positive way can eventually learn to soar high above their apparent disabilities and end up being very productive citizens. On the other hand, those who never gain control over this power, or who learn to use it in a destructive way, are likely to become another ADHD tragedy.

MORE PROBLEMS WITH THE ADHD BRAIN

It has been shown repeatedly that ADHD is often accompanied by other brain-related problems. Major depression, bipolar disorder (manic depression), anxiety disorders, oppositional defiant disorder (ODD), and Tourette's disorder (tic disorder) are all found more commonly in both children and adults with ADHD. (Biederman, 1993; Hornig, 1998) All of these disturbing conditions make the conventional diagnosis and drug oriented treatment of ADHD far more complicated than with ADHD alone. Drugs used in the treatment of ADHD potently increase or decrease the activity of very specific neurotransmitters. This may result in the improvement of some symptoms and no improvement of others. As well, drugs may improve certain ADHD symptoms but cause non-ADHD symptoms to be significantly worsened. For example, although Ritalin® improves behavior and attention in many kids with ADHD, if these kids have tic problems or Tourette's disorder, these symptoms may get significantly worse. In my own case, I had Tourette's disorder as a youngster. The symptoms of this were primarily a strange twitching of my neck muscles between my jaw and collarbone that caused my head to jerk to the side. This would go on all day long, especially when I was nervous or excited. If I concentrated quite hard I could suppress the symptoms but as soon as I began to think about something else the symptoms would return. This condition was embarrassing as a child, but would have been socially devastating as an adult. Fortunately, I was able to overcome this condition as a teenager through many of the the principles outlined in this book.

Unlike a drug approach to ADHD, which reduces only a few symptoms without ever addressing the underlying problems, Functional Medicine seeks to correct and resolve the underlying factors that have lead to the symptoms in the first place. Hyperactivity, inattentiveness, impulsivity, memory diffculties, depression, and a wide array of other problems may all improve or completely resolve when the principles of Functional Medicine are properly applied.

Chapter 4
ADHD and the Brain-Body Connection

ADHD IS MORE THAN A BRAIN PROBLEM

It has long been observed that children and adults with ADHD also commonly suffer from an assortment of physical complaints. In fact, physical symptoms are such a common element of ADHD that some authorities consider such complaints to be among the leading manifestations of this disorder. Considerable research has confirmed these observations and yet little effort has been made in research to address the underlying physical problems under the surface of the ADHD symptoms. Most practitioners will either treat the patient's physical complaints as a completely separate issue from their ADHD, or will classify their symptoms as being merely psychosomatic. Recurrent headaches, muscle aches and pains and abdominal pain are some of the so called "psychosomatic" problems commonly associated with ADHD. It has been largely assumed that individuals suffering from prominent physical manifestations of ADHD are neurotic, have weak personalities or are simply manipulative and doctors may dismiss their physical complaints as if they were "all in their head". These so-called psychosomatic problems are treated, for the most part, by reassurance. That is, parents and adult ADHD sufferers are supposed to ignore such psychosomatic symptoms for fear that focusing upon them may increase the individual's neurotic tendencies.

For example, children with ADHD commonly suffer from abdominal pain. Usually, the only treatment offered for such pain is to reassure the parents and the child that nothing is seriously wrong and to insist that they go to school. Little consideration is given for the possibility that the abdominal pain might actually be arising from significant physical problems within the stomach or intestinal tract. In some cases, a physician may offer false reassurance about the nature of the physical complaints after some type of limited test is performed. For a child with recurrent abdominal pain, the physician may order a barium swallow to look for stomach ulcers. If this test proves normal, he may conclude that the child's pain is psychosomatic without considering that he or she may actually have a bacterial infection of the stomach (e.g. Helicobacter pylori), intestinal parasites (e.g. Giardia), food allergies, or some other very physical cause for the abdominal pain.

PHYSICAL SYMPTOMS REFLECT REAL PHYSICAL PROBLEMS

Other physical complaints such as recurrent headaches, muscular aches and pains, or severe fatigue may also commonly accompany the symptoms of ADHD. Likewise, these may be dismissed as merely psychosomatic, when in fact, definite physical causes are usually at the root of such symptoms. In our research institute we have encountered a large population of ADHD sufferers of all ages. It has been our observation that physical complaints very commonly accompany the ADHD symptoms. Children with ADHD often suffer with allergic disorders and related conditions such as asthma or eczema. They may also have frequent muscle aches and pains, headaches and respiratory or ear infections. In some cases, few definite symptoms are reported but these kids seem grumpy, whiney and miserable much of the time -- they just don't feel good at all. In adolescent or adult ADHD sufferers, allergic or respiratory symptoms often become less predominant and physical symptoms can become increasingly difficult to define. Many of the adults suffer from nagging fatigue, frequent aches and pains and just a general sense of malaise or unwellness much of the time. We have also observed that many adults eventually suffer from fibromyalgia (a disabling condition of muscle pain and fatigue) or chronic fatigue syndrome (a disabling condition of severe fatigue and numerous other symptoms). We have also frequently noted that mothers with fibromyalgia or chronic fatigue syndrome often have children with ADHD. All of these associations between ADHD and various physical ailments are certainly not just coincidental. Yet, in conventional medical circles, the important connections between ADHD and physical illnesses are seldom made.

My own case is a typical example of the association between ADHD and physical ailments. Like many kids with ADHD, my mother suffers with fibromyalgia. She also has numerous allergies and had severe migraine headaches. I was a very colicky baby who demanded food almost constantly. I began having ear infections so frequently that I required surgical placement of tubes in my eardrums and I was almost completely deaf for over one year. I had eczema and various allergies and once I had be rushed to the emergency department because of a severe asthma attack. I also had frequent respiratory infections and, on one occasion, I developed pneumonia so severely that my doctor initially thought that I had tuberculosis. By the age of six, I had hay fever to the extent that, if I was exposed to grass pollen, my eyes would nearly swell shut and I couldn't breathe through my nose at all. I eventually had to have surgery to allow me to breathe through my nose. In addition, I was a compulsive overeater and was seriously obese. On top of all of this, I had a heart arrhythmia that caused my heart to skip beats or to race uncontrollably, sometimes for hours. I also had an insatiable thirst and I wet the bed until I was 11 years old. Although I was a pretty bright kid, I lived in a constant daydream. My mother used to aptly describe me as a "scatter brain" and indeed, my brain had a terrible time staying focused. Were all of my physical maladies completely coincidental to my scattered brain? Certainly not! I have long since learned through personal experience and years of scientific study, that the brain and the body are intimately connected and absolutely inseparable. I believe that the most important key in the management of ADHD lies not in the masking of symptoms, but rather in systematically uncovering and treating the underlying medical problems which are at the heart of this disorder.

Section Two

Setting the Stage
(Risk Factors for the
Development of ADHD)

Taking on Too Many Projects   Self Destructive Behaviors
Tardiness   Addictions
Forgetfulness
Personality Problems   Troubled Relationships
Diminished Self   Aggression   Psychological Disorders
Esteem   Many Unfinished Projects   Procrastination
Perfectionism   Risk Taking Behaviors   Chronic Anxiety
Difficulty Starting Projects   Antisocial Behavior
Extreme Moodiness   Self Medication
Trouble with the Law

Impulsivity
Inattention
Hyperactivity
SIGNS AND SYMPTOMS

Brain Neurotransmitter
Dysfunction
Brain   Immune Modulators,   Critical
Structural   Neuropeptides   Nutrient
Problems   and Neurotoxins   Insufficiencies
MEDIATORS (Biochemical Effects)

Impaired: "Leaky Gut"   Intestinal
Digestion,   Environmental Allergies   Dysbiosis:
Absorption,   Food Allergies/Intolerances   Parasites,
Liver   Chronic or Recurrent Infections   Bacteria,
Detoxification,   Fungi
Blood Sugar   Loss of normal gut flora
Regulation   Immune System Impairment
TRIGGERS (Resulting Physical Problems)

Environmental   Abuse, Neglect
Toxins,   Or Family
Brain Injury   Genetic   Nutritional   Stresses
Predisposition   Insufficiencies
ANTECEDENTS (Underlying Risk Factors)

Chapter 5
A "Chip off the Old Block" — the Genetics of ADHD

GENETIC ENGINEERING AND THE BRAVE NEW WORLD

Clearly we are in the midst of an information revolution. In no other field is this more evident than in the science of human genetics. Genetic research has advanced more rapidly in the last two decades than rocket science did in the years before men walked on the moon. This astounding new technology may usher us into a brave new world, a world where our strengths and weaknesses could be clearly identified at birth and a customized plan then devised to help ensure that we achieve our genetic potential. On the other hand, some of the potential implications of genetic research are truly frightening. Eugenics, the science of selective breeding for the development of a master race, and human cloning are no longer just in the realm of science fiction. These and other outgrowths from the science of genetic engineering pose some of the most difficult ethical questions ever to face humanity. However, many of the potential benefits of this astounding new science may be equally as great.

One of the true benefits of genetic science that will become increasingly available is the use of genetic technology for the early detection of disease susceptibility. This ability is coming about as medical genetics unravels the vast code within the human DNA and then identifies the specific genes, or sets of genes, that are associated with certain diseases. Numerous advances have already been made in this area and several practical applications of this knowledge are now available. The time might be just around the corner when parents could take their newborn baby to the doctor and request that genetic testing be done. Following this, a printout would be generated, which would list the child's strengths, weaknesses and their susceptibility to a wide range of illnesses. The doctor and parents could then work together and establish a plan to help the child avoid many illnesses to which they would have otherwise succumbed.

THE HUMAN BLUEPRINT

The identification of a person's genetic susceptibility to disease is certainly not just science fiction. The enormous Human Genome project is well underway and is likely to be completed within the first few years of the new millennium. Unraveling the code that identifies nearly every detail of our being, is a daunting task indeed. Every one of the trillions of cells in our body contains a vast database of stored information encoded in such a complex way that it makes our computer science look like kindergarten games. The nucleus of each cell is so minute that it is barely a speck when viewed under a microscope. Yet within these tiny structures is a collection of organized information so vast that if it were printed out on paper it would fill 200 volumes, each the size of Manhattan's telephone book. On paper, the total number of pages in the massive genetic database of a single human would be about 200,000 pages in all! That is why it is taking some of the most sophisticated supercomputers years and years to decode this genetic database. This vast information forms the basic blueprint for every aspect of our our body. What is even more astounding is the fact that there is a complete copy of this 200,000-page blueprint in virtually every one of our trillions of cells and the database is significantly different for every single person on the planet!

A few diseases such as cystic fibrosis, and muscular dystrophy result from a single abnormal gene. In some cases, the disease is programmed to occur and little can be done in modern medicine to prevent the full expression of the disorder. Gene therapy will eventually be a powerful treatment for those severe diseases caused solely by single defective genes. Using high-tech gene therapy methods, "bad" genes may be deleted and normal genes spliced in. Individuals with single gene diseases, which today are severe and eventually lethal, may someday lead completely normal healthy lives because of gene therapy.

GENETICS AND ENVIRONMENT

In spite of the powerful influence of our genetic background, the vast majority of diseases are not simply caused by defective genes. Behind most diseases are multiple genes that increase a person's susceptibility to certain health problems. However, in susceptible individuals most diseases only occur when certain lifestyle and environmental factors are present as well. In fact, a set of genes which gives a person great advantages in one environment may actually be highly detrimental in another. I saw a vivid example of this principle when I worked for several months as a resident physician at the Claremore, Oklahoma Indian Hospital, the largest native Indian hospital in North America. Adult onset diabetes is rampant amongst the First Nations people of the southern United States. Although they currently have the highest rate of diabetes of any single racial group on the planet, they are in no way a people with "weak genes". Diabetes is actually a very recent phenomenon for these people — an unfortunate byproduct of genetic susceptibility combined with an unsuitable industrialized lifestyle.

The inherited factors which allowed the First Nations people to become great endurance runners, powerful hunters and warriors, and to endure long periods of starvation no longer provide such advantages to these same people today. They store fat very efficiently and are naturally suited for living off that fat during periods of starvation or during lengthy hunting expeditions. These "warrior genes" are highly adaptive and purposeful in the traditional environment of the First Nations people. In fact, they can be thought of as "high-performance genes" rather than "weak genes" as long as these genes are exposed to the nutritional and environmental conditions most appropriate for their genetic makeup. Unfortunately, for many First Nations people who are immersed in a sedentary lifestyle and who are eating a westernized diet, their "warrior genes" are now at war with their own body. A return to the traditional values of discipline, athleticism, and dietary simplicity may be the only real hope that these people have of avoiding a genetic time bomb and, instead, living out their true inherited potential.

GENETICS AND THE ADHD BRAIN

It has been known for many years that inheritance plays a major role in the development of ADHD. It is now also certain that no single gene can account for all the manifestations of this disorder. In most cases it is probably a wide collection of genetic variables that lead to a high risk of an individual developing ADHD. It is clear that numerous nutritional and environmental factors exert tremendous influence upon the type and severity of symptoms that an individual will experience. Specific genes that have been associated with ADHD may also be purposeful "high-performance genes" under certain circumstances. For instance, it is known that individuals with ADHD have a high likelihood of possessing a gene that leads to increased activity of the dopamine transporter within certain nerve endings. (Blum, 1996; LaHoste, 1996; Cook, 1995) The dopamine transporter is like a little vacuum cleaner that removes dopamine from the space between nerves. If this dopamine transporter is overactive, there will be less dopamine activity in these brain regions. Lower dopamine activity within the executive centers of the brain will lead to reduced inhibitory influences from these executive centers. In times past, people with this type of genetic makeup might be revered for their bravery, quick thinking, creativity, deep contemplation and great endurance. Such an individual might have been chosen to be a leader, a great hunter or a warrior. In contrast, that same person today may be recognized as being impulsive, inattentive and hyperactive and then diagnosed with ADHD. Similarly, a significant percentage of people with ADHD have been found to have genes that lead to a decrease in the sensitivity of certain dopamine receptors in critical brain regions. Again, this state of decreased dopamine activity may be highly purposeful in certain settings, but will likely lead to a diagnosis of ADHD in our modern society.

ADHD AND THE HIGHLY SENSITIVE BRAIN

The genes which lead to decreased dopamine activity in critical brain regions may also lead to an increased brain sensitivity to various toxic influences, immunological stresses and nutritional insufficiencies. People with ADHD are also notorious for being "thin-skinned" and are commonly very sensitive people who are easily hurt by others and who seem to be worried about every little thing. The brain's executive centers are complex regions that are highly sensitive to toxic influences and other forms of stress. If a person has inherited a tendency towards decreased activity in these executive centers, any toxic or stressful influences upon these same brain regions will likely lead to more significant symptoms than would typically arise in a person with more normal executive center function. In other words, it takes a lot less to "rock the boat" in the brain of someone with the neurology of ADHD than in an unaffected person. Likewise, if an individual lacks certain nutrients that are critical to the function of the brain's executive centers (like the omega-3 fatty acid, DHA), symptoms are more likely to arise if that individual has inherited a tendency toward decreased activity of the brain's executive centers as well.

ALLERGIES AND INHERITANCE

Studies examining the genetic factors underlying ADHD have focused largely upon the direct impact of inheritance upon brain function. However, numerous other genetic influences may play a significant role in the risk of developing ADHD. It has been known for many years that individuals with ADHD have a much higher incidence of allergic-like illnesses (such as asthma) than that of the general population. (Marshall, 1989) It is also well understood that the risk of developing allergies can be passed from one generation to the next through genetic influences. As you will come to understand in forthcoming chapters, allergies may have a profound effect on brain function and behavior. In addition, allergies can have a widespread effect on nutritional status, and detoxification capabilities, which, in turn, can affect virtually every aspect of health.

NEUROTOXINS AND INHERITANCE

A number of highly common environmental toxins have the potential to have dramatic effects upon brain function. A person's susceptibility to most of these toxic agents is influenced tremendously by various inherited factors. According to some researchers, repeated exposure to even minute quantities of pesticides, heavy metals, PCB's, solvents or other neurotoxins may actually play a central role in the development of ADHD. The amount and frequency of various toxic exposures will determine, to a large extent, the degree of impact that such toxins will have upon brain function. However, recent research has revealed that individuals vary widely in their ability to excrete toxic substances. A vast selection of detoxifying enzymes within the liver and intestine, as well as antioxidant enzymes and metal excreting proteins, all work together at a feverish pace to effectively remove toxic molecules from our bodies every minute of our lives. A wide range of nutrients influence the efficiency of our detoxification systems. As well, every one of the hundreds of elements comprising our detoxification systems is inherited through a separate gene. The inherited differences between people's abilities to efficiently detoxify thousands of toxic substances are vast. For example, individuals may differ as much as 100-fold in their ability to excrete toxic metals. This would mean that two people could be exposed to the same daily dose of mercury or lead. One person may be able to efficiently excrete this amount of toxic metal and exhibit no ill effects, whereas the other person, with the exact same exposure, may be assaulted with 100 times their personal safe level of toxic metal and may experience serious toxic effects.

AWAKENING THE SLEEPING GENES

It has become widely accepted in recent years that ADHD is an inherited disorder. Because of this, many authorities in this field of research have taken a fatalistic attitude, assuming there is little that anyone with ADHD can do apart from taking medication, managing their behavior and simply accepting their disability. However, this attitude may actually be in direct contradiction to our current knowledge of medical genetics. One of the great surprises of genetic research is that a large majority of the genetic material within our chromosomes remains completely dormant and is rarely, if ever, used by the body. In fact, a very high proportion of the diseases passed along through inheritance only come to the surface after certain environmental influences have been present. Using the example of the southern American Indians, just 200 years ago the genes responsible for diabetes remained dormant throughout the lives of these individuals. Although some of these genes were partially activated in order to contribute to more efficient fat storage in preparation for periods of starvation, it was only following the "modernization" of these people that the genes for diabetes were fully activated, resulting in the cultural devastation that we see today.

Likewise, the genes that encode for many of the features of ADHD may only become fully activated or expressed under certain nutritional or environmental states. For example, the genes that encode for a tendency towards allergies may only be fully expressed if there is an insufficient supply of certain nutrients such as essential fatty acids, magnesium, zinc or bioflavonoids from the person's diet. Allergic responsiveness can also be markedly increased in genetically susceptible individuals if such persons also carry intestinal parasites such as Giardia or have overgrowth of the intestinal yeast organism, Candida albicans.

THE POWER OF ADHD GENES

In contradiction to the disease oriented perspective of most conventional medical practitioners, many of the genes that lead to negative ADHD traits may actually be very purposeful and beneficial if nutritional and environmental factors are optimized. Individuals with ADHD are more likely to have one or more genes that encode for decreased dopamine activity in the executive centers of the brain. Because these same executive centers are highly sensitive to any neurotoxic influence, this genetic blueprint can easily become a recipe for disordered brain function. On the other hand, if individuals with this same genetic blueprint experience optimal nutrition and have minimal neurotoxic influences upon their brain, they may never experience disordered brain function. In fact, the same genetic factors that often lead to ADHD may, under more optimal circumstances, be the recipe for a highly productive and successful life. Even amongst those who have been diagnosed with ADHD it is very common to find people who have adapted well to their condition and are energetic, intuitive, creative, quick thinking and highly persistent goal setters. It has been frequently pointed out that much of the progress in our world has come about through individuals with features typical of ADHD. Perhaps many of the world's great scientists, artists, musicians, broadcasters, explorers, teachers and political leaders actually have the genetic blueprint for

ADHD neurology, but they adapted to it and found ways to make the best of their genetic potential.

OPTIMIZING GENETIC POTENTIAL

One of the most exciting aspects of Functional Medicine is the concept that people can dramatically improve their quality of life and function by optimizing their genetic potential. The genes that we are born with are like a vast set of blueprints for a great city. If you were the overseer for the construction of this city, the blueprints that you were supplied with would only be one factor in determining the quality of your city. Other factors such as the contractors chosen to complete the construction, the building materials used and kinds of businesses invited to participate would greatly affect the function and quality of life within your metropolis. In a similar way, nutrients and toxic agents as well as social, spiritual and lifestyle factors all participate in a profound way to determine what your body does with its genetic blueprints. Except in the case of a few rare genetic diseases, your future is determined by far more than just your genes. People with ADHD have a unique opportunity to turn a disability into something that provides them with great strength and unique capabilities by optimizing their genetic potential. By improving physiology and brain function through the principals of Functional Medicine, individuals can tap the hidden power of their ADHD genes and lead lives that are stable, happy and productive instead of lives full of failure, disappointment and despair.

Chapter 6

Environmental Neurotoxins and the Hyperactive Brain

OUR TOXIC AIR

Since the beginning of the Industrial Revolution, the pollution of our planet has increased at an alarming rate. There is no longer any place on the Earth completely free from toxic chemicals. Air pollution, an unavoidable part of life in most cities, has become so severe in many parts of the world as to be nearly incompatible with life. Although pollution control measures have lowered the total quantity of smog in a few modern cities, most cities throughout the world have unacceptable and rising levels of air pollution. In a study published by the Environmental Defense Fund in April 1999, [www.edf.org/pubs/NewsReleases/1999/Apr] it was demonstrated that more than 220 million Americans currently breathe air that is 100 times more toxic than the goal set by Congress in the late 1980's. This study, based entirely upon data generated by the Environmental Protection Agency (EPA), also indicated that for 11 million Americans, the cancer risk from their neighborhood air is currently more than 1000 times higher than Congress's previous goal. Clearly, little progress has been made in a country where countless billions of dollars have been spent in an attempt to improve air quality. Much of the rest of the world is in far worse shape with little on the horizon to suggest that anything is likely to change this trend.

Even in those few regions where apparent smog levels have diminished, the variety of toxic chemicals in the air has increased dramatically. In some cases one pollutant is reduced through legislation only to be replaced by other pollutants with equal or even greater toxicity. For example, although leaded gasoline was removed from many world markets because of concerns about lead toxicity from car exhaust, some of the chemicals that were used to replace lead have been shown to be even more toxic to the brain and immune system. Many of these significantly neurotoxic components of car exhaust and other forms of air pollution may contribute to the development or worsening of ADHD. During the era of leaded gasoline, studies of violent offenders demonstrated higher than average levels of lead and cadmium in the hair of such individuals. Undoubtedly, a significant proportion of the lead exposure in these people came from breathing air polluted by car exhaust. More recently, with the advent of manganese containing gasoline additives, elevated levels of hair manganese are commonly found in violent criminals as compared to others. [Gottschalk, 1991] Although manganese is a necessary trace element when absorbed from the diet in minute quantities, when inhaled it is even more toxic to the brain than lead.

New variables have also entered into the air pollution picture. Global climactic changes have created unprecedented fires in many regions of the world. The fires that burned in the drought stricken forests of Indonesia turned many already polluted regions of Asia into smoke filled death traps for months. In addition, more greenhouse gases were generated from these fires during the 1998 El Niño than from all human activity in Europe in the last 20 years. How global climactic changes will impact future air quality is as yet uncertain, however, it is clear that humans will face unprecedented levels of toxic stress from air pollution in years to come. Although respiratory problems have been the primary focus of concern with regard to air pollution, many of these airborne toxins are readily absorbed by the brain and have significant negative effects upon this organ, which is so sensitive to toxic stress. It would certainly be wise for anyone with ADHD to try to avoid such neurotoxic stress by living in a region where air pollution is not unacceptably high. As well, people with ADHD should try to limit the time they spend in heavy traffic.

OUR TOXIC WATER
Perhaps the greatest health breakthrough in human history occurred with the advent of municipal water treatment. This important process dramatically reduced the risk of acquiring infectious waterborne illnesses, a major cause of human death and disease. Even today large proportions of the world's population have no access to microbiologically safe water and are thus subjected to unacceptable health risks from waterborne illness. However, those who have the good fortune of having access to municipally treated, microbiologically safe water should recognize that their tap water

might still be far from the perfect beverage. Even following municipal water treatment, tap water frequently contains a variety of toxic chemicals such as heavy metals, pesticide and herbicide residues as well as various industrial effluents. Most of these are usually present in only minute quantities. However, it is quite common for certain contaminants to be present in water at levels that could add significantly to an individual's level of toxic stress, especially over long periods of time. Ongoing research conducted by the Environmental Protection Agency (EPA) indicates that the quality of tap water throughout North America has diminished dramatically in the last few decades. Lakes, rivers, and groundwater are now all contaminated to such an extent that only a minority of the world's citizens now have access to reasonably toxin-free drinking water.

Furthermore, the water treatment process itself uses several chemicals, some of which are clearly toxic. For example, solid particles are removed from water during the treatment process by mixing aluminum sulfate into the raw water. The aluminum particles act like tiny magnets causing suspended solids to clump together. These clumps then quickly settle to the bottom of the holding tank or pond. This is the main process, which makes drinking water look crystal clear, and it removes the majority of disease causing bacteria, viruses or parasites. However, this same process leaves behind a significant residue of aluminum, often 100 mg or more per liter of tap water. When the municipal water treatment process was first developed, it was assumed that aluminum didn't absorb through the intestinal tract and it had absolute no toxicity. Today, this is known to be an entirely false assumption. The residual aluminum in drinking water has now been demonstrated to absorb through the intestine with reasonable efficiency especially under certain circumstances such as when an individual has a "leaky gut" or if they have ingested anything containing citric acid, a common component of both food and nutritional supplements. Once in the bloodstream, aluminum is a potent toxin of the brain and immune system.

Chlorination is another part of the water treatment process which is a "two edged sword". On one hand, chlorine effectively kills most microscopic contaminants in the water. On the other hand, it is a powerful oxidizing chemical, which places significant challenges upon the body's antioxidant systems. Chlorine also binds strongly to other molecules in the water forming toxic and highly persistent organochlorines, many of which are known carcinogens and others are neurotoxic and immunotoxic.

Overall, the lesson to be learned is this: be thankful for the benefits of municipal water treatment but don't ignore the potential health risks either. Purchasing and using a proven system for water purification may pay real dividends over the long haul. Reverse osmosis systems or distillers do the best job but may cost hundreds of dollars. Carbon filtration systems are not quite as good but are much less expensive and will provide healthier and tastier water that the whole family will enjoy as long as they are maintained appropriately. Drinking plenty of pure water is one of the basic principles of good health that simply cannot be ignored. Even people who dislike drinking water will often begin to enjoy it when offered delicious purified water. It is currently unrealistic to depend upon the government for the provision of completely pure water that is free from all chemical contamination. Concerned citizens will have to personally take on this responsibility and choose a reasonable means to provide truly clean water for themselves and their families.

OUR TOXIC SOILS

One of the most serious victims of industrial pollution is our soil. As the years go by soils accumulate numerous pollutants that do not biodegrade. Sites of industrial activity or chemical dumping are of course susceptible to soil contamination. However, agricultural soils are also quite likely to accumulate toxic material. Recent research has shown that commercial fertilizers now commonly contains significant residues of toxic metals such as lead or cadmium. In 1992, legislation was enacted to prevent the dumping of sewage as well as pulp and paper sludge (known as "biosolids") into the oceans because they contained unacceptably high amounts of heavy metals. Immediately after this, further legislation was pronounced which allowed this same sludge to be sold as fertilizer and dumped on agricultural soils. It seems ironic that a waste material which was too toxic for our oceans is now a profitable product promoted as beneficial for agriculture. Unfortunately, since the heavy metals in this sludge do not biodegrade, they tend to concentrate in soils over time and are taken up by food crops. These same toxic metals then end up on our dinner plates! Heavy metal contamination of our food supply is a very real and growing concern. In fact, recent research has indicated that unless farming practices change significantly, soils will eventually become so contaminated with heavy metal that most agricultural products will become unfit for human consumption. Heavy metals are a real threat to the health of our brains and especially the brains of our children.

Besides heavy metals, numerous other chemicals commonly contaminate agricultural soils. Organochlorine pesticides such as DDT and its close relatives, have largely been banned from North American agriculture but they resist breakdown and still heavily pollute many soils. These pesticides were once widely used because of their effectiveness and apparent low toxicity to humans. However, it has now been shown that these organochlorines are very toxic with low level, long-term exposure. These agents are highly carcinogenic and may currently be one of the leading environmental causes of breast cancer and other cancers. Some of these same substances are significantly neurotoxic and may be especially harmful to the brains of infants and children. In addition to that, many of the organochlorines have been proven to have hormone like properties. Researchers now believe that the dramatic increase in our exposure to hormone disrupting chemicals like organochlorines is the primary reason why the age at which puberty begins (particularly in girls) has decreased by several years during this past century. For many girls, puberty now begins at the age of nine or ten, a full four or five years younger than just a few generations ago. This change is having profound sociological implications and may be a major factor contributing to the epidemic of teenage pregnancy and sexually transmitted diseases. Unfortunately, organochlorines are very difficult to eradicate. Even if their use is banned, they do not biodegrade and they therefore remain in the environment for many decades. Recent studies have shown that certain vegetables harvested today may contain unacceptably high levels of DDT or other organochlorines even though such pesticides were last sprayed on the soils over 25 years ago! Although it may take hundreds of years for organochlorines to completely disappear from the environment, many countries continue to use these toxic chemicals extensively in agriculture and industry. A complete worldwide ban of organochlorines along with the widespread adoption of sustainable organic farming practices may be essential if we want to avoid an environmental catastrophe. In the meanwhile, choosing organically grown produce when possible may be one of the most practical ways to limit our exposure to organochlorines and heavy metals from contaminated soil.

OUR TOXIC FOOD

Besides heavy metals and organochlorines from toxic soils, a large number of toxic contaminants end up in our food supply through other sources. Because of increasing scientific awareness about the potential ill effects of pesticide residues in food, a bill known as the Food Quality Protection Act, was introduced in 1996 to more closely monitor foods for these toxic contaminants. Since the introduction of this bill, the United States Department of Agriculture (USDA) has conducted random testing on fruits and vegetables across the U.S. to determine the type and quantity of pesticides found on these foods. Based upon the enormous database that has now accumulated from the USDA, pesticide contamination of fruits and vegetables appears to be of far greater concern than was previously imagined. In a recent Consumers Union study, published in the March 1999 edition of Consumers Report Magazine, 27,000 samples of fruits and vegetables were purchased randomly from grocery stores throughout the United States and tested for the type and quantity of pesticide residues typically found in these products. Prior to testing, each sample of fruit or vegetable was washed and/or peeled in a fashion that would be typical of a consumer preparing the product for consumption. It was concluded in this report that pesticide residues were commonly present at levels far in excess of that which is known to be safe for children. In some cases, just one serving of certain produce could expose a child to quantities of pesticide over 100 times the known safe level! If a child eats a peach, for example, two out of three times he or she will have consumed a level of pesticide well in excess of that which is known to be safe. Apples and pears presented a similar risk. Fortunately, with many fruits or vegetables (such as apples, pears or peaches) simply peeling the product will significantly lower the pesticide content. However, with other produce (such as green beans, spinach or squash) the pesticide permeates the product completely and it cannot be washed or peeled away. In contrast, samples of organically grown produce consistently contained no measurable traces of pesticide residue.

Perhaps the biggest crime in this pesticide catastrophe is that extremely toxic pesticides continue to be marketed freely when far safer and yet effective pesticides or completely non-chemical pest control now exist for virtually all crops. This problem is all because of economics -- about cutting a few pennies per pound off the cost of commodities in a highly competitive marketplace. Dirty pesticides are not used because of a lack of cleaner technology. The worst toxic offenders amongst pesticides are the organophosphates. This group of chemicals originates directly out of research done in Nazi Germany in the 1930s. In preparation for war, Germany developed many innovative products to minimize their need for imports. One Nazi scientist, Gerhard Schrader, was assigned the task of finding new pesticides that could be manufactured in Germany. In the process of his research he became a recognized hero by discovering the deadly organophosphate nerve gases Tabin and Sarin. Although these lethal agents kill insects very effectively, they are far too toxic to be used in agriculture. While Tabin and Sarin continued to be manufactured and stockpiled as weapons of mass destruction, they also formed the prototypes for all currently used organophosphate pesticides. Malathion, Parathion and a wide range of other organophosphates have now been used for decades because of their potent ability to paralyze and destroy the nervous system of insects. Unfortunately, these agents are also highly toxic to the human brain and nervous system. Parathion, one of the most common pesticides in use today, is nearly one-fifth as toxic as Tabun, the deadly nerve gas which was being manufactured by the evil war machine of Saddam Hussein.

Although deaths from overt organophosphate pesticide poisoning are relatively uncommon, strong evidence has accumulated demonstrating that these poisons may have highly adverse effects upon the brain and developing nervous system of children even following minute exposures. Low level long-term exposure to these agents may have destructive and cumulative effects upon adult brains as well. Many of the more deadly pesticides have been around so long that they may have escaped appropriate regulatory controls through "grandfather" rules. Currently, the quantity of many pesticides legally permitted to remain as a residue on fruits and vegetables far exceeds the level that is known to be safe. In fact, some of the pesticides used widely today are so toxic that there may be no minimum safe level especially when ingested by infants, children or pregnant women. If parathion was developed today and presented to the FDA for approval for use in food crops it would be bluntly rejected because of its extreme toxicity. Yet, it continues to be a cheap and dirty solution to insect problems in a wide variety of food crops. In a sense, industrial agriculture is stealing from our future to increase their profits today.

Ironically, millions of children are put at risk every day by eating the very foods that are so necessary for the maintenance of good health. In the report entitled "Overexposed — Organophosphate Pesticides in Children's Food" [the Environmental Working Group 1718 Connecticut Avenue, NW, Suite 600; Washington D.C., 20009 (www.ewg.org)] it is stated, based on government data, that over 1 million American children consume an unsafe level of organophosphate pesticides each and every day! This same data suggests that every day over 575,000 children ingest more than the known safe levels of organophosphates from just apple products alone. Together, ingestion of apples, grapes, peaches and pears are estimated to result in 85,000 American children exceeding federal standards for safe levels of organophosphates by at least tenfold each and every day. Other foods such as nectarines, raisins, cherries, kiwi, green beans and spinach have also been frequently found to have unsafe levels of organophosphate pesticides. With many of these foods, children can exceed the daily safe level of organophosphates with just a few bites. In many cases organophosphate exposure probably creates very real and immediate symptoms in children and sensitive adults. (Remember, these poisons are just watered down nerve gases). After eating organophosphate contaminated food such individuals may experience mild to moderate flu-like symptoms of neurotoxic and immunotoxic poisoning including headaches, nausea, irritability as well as cognitive or behavioral problems. Even more worrisome is the very real potential for cumulative, long-term damage to the brain from regular exposure to unsafe levels of these deadly brain poisons. It seems ironic that the world has expended so much energy to crush Saddam Hussein's ability to produce organophosphate nerve gas when hundreds of tons of similar poisons are being sprayed on our food crops every day.

If agricultural and chemical industry lobby groups continue to reign supreme over our governments, it may be many years before these deadly poisons are removed once and for all from our food supply. Until that time, parents and adult ADHD sufferers should become aware of the most common sources of the most deadly pesticides. In some cases, new habits such as eating foods with the least likelihood of pesticide contamination may provide some protection against deadly brain poisons like parathion. The table on the following page illustrates some of the foods which are most commonly contaminated with very high levels of organophosphate pesticides along side the foods which are least likely to be contaminated with these neurotoxic contaminants.

Parents can reduce health risks to their children by feeding them fruits and vegetables with consistently low pesticide residues.

Most Pesticide Contaminated Foods		Least Pesticide Contaminated Foods	
Rank	**Food**	**Rank**	**Food**
1	Apples	1	Corn
2	Spinach	2	Cauliflower
3	Peaches	3	Sweet Peas
4	Pears	4	Asparagus
5	Strawberries	5	Broccoli
6	Grapes -- Chile	6	Pineapple
7	Potatoes	7	Onions
8	Red Raspberries	8	Bananas
9	Celery	9	Watermelon
10	Green Beans	10	Cherries -- Chile

Source: Environmental Working Group. Compiled from USDA and FDA pesticide residue data 1992-1997

Reproduced from the document "How 'Bout Them Apples? Pesticides in Children's Food Ten Years After Alar"; copyright 1999, Environmental Working Group, Washington, D.C., used by permission.

Another, even more ideal alternative, is to eat organically grown produce or to grow vegetables in a home garden or by hydroponics using organic methods. Most locations now have excellent organic produce markets and services that will deliver organic foods right to your home. Organically grown produce is not only free of pesticides, it is also higher in micronutrients and it is usually more flavorful besides. On top of that, organic farming is better for the environment and it supports the family farm more than giant industry.

Apart from pesticides, our food supply has been significantly altered through a wide range of food additives and the byproducts of food processing. Thousands of chemicals are used to increase the shelf life of food, to add or enhance a food's flavor, or to change the physical properties of a food product. Children or adults with ADHD may be particularly susceptible to adverse reactions from various food additives. One of the antecedents or predisposing causes at the heart of ADHD may be an inherited or acquired decrease in an individual's ability to adequately process and excrete certain types of chemicals. It is not uncommon to discover that someone with ADHD is hypersensitive to food additives such as benzoates, salicylates, caffeine, tartrazine, amines, sulfites, trans-fatty acids, or monosodium glutamate. These sensitivities are usually not true allergies but are often due to a diminished capacity of the liver or other systems of the body to detoxify these common chemical substances. This diminished detoxification capability allows high quantities of certain food-derived chemicals, or chemical breakdown products, to accumulate in cells -- leading to disturbances in cellular processes and the potential for adverse reactions. Although not everyone with ADHD will react in an obvious fashion to chemical additives, it is prudent to encourage those with ADHD to consume a diet composed primarily of fresh, whole foods with very few foods that are processed or have chemical additives. Some individuals on a whole -foods diet may still react to certain naturally occurring chemicals, such as salicylates, or they may experience various manifestations of food allergies or food intolerances. Identifying and eliminating specific chemicals and allergic or intolerant foods can be like solving a detective mystery. However, simply eliminating man-made pesticides and chemical additives in the ADHD diet may significantly reduce the total toxic load on the individual's brain and body and may pay valuable dividends in terms of health, cognitive performance and behavior.

In certain populations, other sources of toxic contamination from food can be very important. Individuals or populations who consume fish in large quantities may be at particular risk for exposure to high levels of neurotoxins. Fresh water fish and larger predatory fish are especially likely to carry unacceptably high levels of mercury (methylmercury) and organochlorines such as PCB's. (Gilbert, 1995) Recent research has demonstrated that pregnant women who consume contaminated fish at least twice per week are at very high risk of having a child with behavioral or cognitive problems. Children are also likely to suffer neurotoxic effects if they consume such fish. Even adult brains are very sensitive to mercury or PCB's and avid fish eaters of any age may likewise suffer neurological or psychiatric problems. (Bro-Rasmussen)

According to research by the Environmental Protection Agency (EPA), the number of lakes and rivers in North America populated by fish which are now inedible due to toxic levels of methylmercury has increased by over two hundred percent in just the past two decades. Mercury in fish is present because fish consume smaller aquatic organisms, which feed on mercury containing sediments. Because mercury is not biodegradable, it has been gradually accumulating in aquatic ecosystems during the past century. Mining activities, especially gold mining, as well as various industries such as pulp and paper mills release mercury directly into watercourses. However, at least eighty percent of all mercury in our lakes and rivers comes from coal burning power plants. Coal contains traces of mercury, which is released into the atmosphere when burned. Mercury then drifts around the world in wind currents and ends up in lakes and rivers as toxic fallout from rain. Because mercury, PCB's and numerous other non-biodegradable toxins travel easily in the upper levels of the atmosphere, there is now no place on earth, which has escaped the ravages of environmental pollution. Parents or adults with ADHD should be aware of the potential risks of neurotoxin exposure from fish. Non-fatty freshwater fish are most likely to contain mercury and should be generally avoided, especially by children or pregnant women. Large, older, predatory fish, both oceangoing and freshwater (e.g. swordfish, shark, tuna, pike and pickerel) are also best avoided. Smaller fish, especially oily fish such as herring, sardines and smaller salmon are generally safe in moderation and are also more likely to contain brain beneficial essential fatty acids.

OUR TOXIC HOMES

It has become well established that air quality within homes and buildings is often very poor and may contribute significantly to the overall toxic burden confronting our bodies. In fact, the air quality within many homes and buildings can be far worse than the outside air in most polluted cities. The so-called "sick building syndrome" has become widely recognized as a major cause of diminished productivity and chronic or recurring illness in office workers. Improved energy efficiency of newer homes or office buildings is often due in part to increased recirculation of inside air with minimal flow of fresh air into the building or home. Although minimizing the intake of outside air decreases heat loss and saves on energy bills, it may result in harmful particulates or gases being trapped inside the building. Carpets, furnishings, paints and household cleaners all release gases which are potentially toxic to the brain and immune system. Even in homes or buildings where ventilation is much better, new carpet, furnishings or paints can expose a child or adult with ADHD to enough neurotoxic chemicals that their brain function may be significantly affected.

As well, a wide range of seriously neurotoxic chemicals may be used quite commonly inside the home. Household cleaners, various solvents and glues, secondhand cigarette smoke and even certain air fresheners can have significant adverse effects upon the sensitive brains of those with ADHD, even when household ventilation is good. With certain other chemicals, such as bug sprays used for pest control, an individual who experiences even one significant overexposure may have some degree of permanent damage to the brain as a result. Parents should be vigilant to teach their children about the dangers of commonly used house, garage and yard chemicals and should be exceptionally cautious if any highly neurotoxic chemicals like bug sprays are ever used in the home. In some cases the use of chemicals is virtually unavoidable but a range of choices may still exist. For example, if household plants have bugs, special soaps can be sprayed on the plants instead of toxic insecticides. Much healthier alternatives to toxic household cleaners are now also widely available. Anyone with ADHD or who has a child with ADHD should become familiar with potential toxins in the household and if such chemicals must be used, they should become acquainted with proper ways to handle them. Also, healthier alternatives should be sought out and utilized whenever possible. These same principles apply to the school environment. Endemic behavioral problems in certain schools have been linked to contaminated school environments. (Thorn, 1998; Lundin, 1999) Toxic indoor fungi growing inside walls or under roofs because of roof leakage or flooding may also be a significant contributor to sick building or school syndrome, especially in more humid climates. (Cooley, 1998)

Of particular concern for children and adults suffering from learning or behavioral disorders is the age-old enemy of the brain – lead. This common heavy metal has found thousands of uses in industry and it continues to be of significant economic importance to the world. Although lead has been recognized as a serious toxin for over one thousand years, it is only in the last two decades that it has been identified as an important neurotoxin even with relatively miniscule exposure. Brains are particularly susceptible to lead during fetal development, infancy and childhood and recent evidence suggests that the number of children who are adversely affected by lead is far higher than previously imagined. Current estimates from the Environmental Protection Agency, the Center for Disease Control and Prevention and the American Academy of Pediatrics state that between one in five and one in eleven children currently have blood lead levels at or above that required to make the diagnosis of lead poisoning! Extensive research over the past two decades has clearly demonstrated that blood lead levels which were previously considered to be acceptable, actually result in behavioral problems like hyperactivity or oppositional behavior, as well as cognitive problems such as diminished IQ, learning disorders and attentional problems. Blood lead levels over the acceptable range (10 micrograms per deciliter) are actually so common that the American Academy of Pediatrics has stated that chronic, low level lead poisoning is presently the number one pediatric health problem in the world.

So where does all this lead come from? The burning of leaded gasoline was, of course, a significant source of lead contamination in the past and it continues to be a major source of lead contamination in some countries. Lately, it seems that lead keeps popping up in the most unexpected places. In recent history, toxic levels of lead have been found covering the tops of wine bottles, in plastic window blinds, in hair dyes, in children's vinyl chew toys, in the soils under and around playgrounds and schools and in herbal "medicines" from China and India. There are actually innumerable potential sources of lead but, far and above, most lead poisoning in children comes from leaded paint within older homes. The use of lead paint in homes was banned in North America in 1978. Houses built prior to this may contain lead paint, which eventually deteriorates and then children may ingest small paint chips. Paint chips are also gradually ground up and incorporated into the house dust, until eventually, such homes become heavily contaminated with lead. Sanding or removing walls during renovations are especially likely to contaminate a house with dangerous levels of lead.

Children are at particular risk in a high lead environment for several reasons. Firstly, children's intestines absorb ingested lead about five times more readily than that of adults. Because of this, a child only needs to swallow a single two-milligram paint chip in order to suffer from lead poisoning. Secondly, because small children frequently put unwashed fingers or small items into their mouth or nose, they tend to transfer more of their immediate environment into their bodies. Thirdly, children's brains are far more sensitive to the neurotoxic effects of lead than are adults. Lastly, children can easily suffer from some degree of nutritional inadequacy (especially iron, calcium, protein, vitamin C or B vitamins), which render them more susceptible to the toxic accumulation of lead. In essence, it is now clear that there are as many children with low-level lead poisoning as there are children who are left handed — it is an exceedingly common and serious problem. (Minder, 1994; Needleman, 1993; Needleman, 1995)

Parents of children with any form of cognitive or behavioral problem should have their child assessed for lead poisoning. Any physician can easily obtain a blood lead level on a child. Ideally, blood lead levels should be measured as soon as behavioral or cognitive problems are first detected. If blood lead levels are above current acceptable limits (10 micrograms of lead per deciliter in conventional units or 0.48 micromole per liter in SI Units) every effort should be made to determine all sources of the child's lead exposure. Home test kits are now readily available to test for lead in various places in a home. Windowsills, heating ducts and carpets are high probability sites for lead dust accumulation. Also, if the outside environment is contaminated with lead and people track outside shoes through the house, carpets can eventually become "toxic waste zones" even if there is no lead paint inside the home. Other sources of lead should be searched for diligently. Homes built prior to about 1990 will often have copper water pipes joined with lead solder. Water that has been standing in such pipes for more than six hours can have very high levels of lead. If tap water is used for drinking, all family members should be made aware that water should not be consumed until it is allowed to run for one or two minutes each morning. Children's toys, paint sets, school and play environments should also be considered as possible sources of lead. For a child whose blood lead levels are unacceptably high, numerous steps can be taken, apart from removing him from a lead-contaminated environment, to ensure that he is adequately detoxified from lead and other heavy metals. These measures will be reviewed in Chapter 24.

OUR TOXIC WORKPLACE

Vast numbers of people also encounter a wide range of toxic chemicals in their work environment, most of which have never been studied for their effects upon the brain, immune system or developing fetus. Many workplace chemicals are known to be severely toxic even in short-term exposure and should be handled with special equipment, procedures and ventilation. However, in many cases, workplace chemicals are handled improperly or, in some cases, accidental overexposures occur. Even when handled properly, many chemicals are eventually proven to be highly toxic with very low level exposures over the long-term.

Individuals with ADHD are particularly susceptible to neurological and immunological impairment from even the lowest levels of exposure to neurotoxic agents. Because of their peculiar neurological makeup, those with ADHD may have a brain that is more highly sensitive to an array of toxic influences than most other people. Children with ADHD should be encouraged to aim towards a career that will minimize their occupational exposure to neurotoxins. Auto body repair, welding, crop spraying or house painting are all examples of trades where exposure to significant amounts of neurotoxins is virtually unavoidable. Those with ADHD must be particularly careful to guard their brains from neurotoxic stresses and should steer clear from occupations where toxic exposure is an inevitable part of their job. Children with ADHD should also be instructed to carefully avoid toxic chemicals as far as possible in school shops or art class.

OUR TOXIC MOUTH

Of all the neurotoxic influences that have been imposed upon us by industrialization, there is none that is more widespread or more controversial than mercury from dental amalgam fillings. For over one hundred fifty years, the most popular material used to fill dental cavities has been so-called "silver amalgam". Although silver or gray in color, amalgam fillings are actually composed of fifty-percent mercury along with small amounts of silver, tin, copper and zinc. Just before the filling is placed, liquid mercury is vigorously mixed together with a powder containing all the other metals. A paste is formed from this mixture which is pressed into the drilled out cavity. It is then carved into the appropriate shape and it quickly solidifies forming a durable chewing surface. From a physical standpoint, dental amalgam is an ideal material. It is cheap, easy to work with and highly durable. For many years it was also assumed that mercury, which was a known toxic metal, somehow became stabilized through the amalgamation process and all risks of toxicity were thus eliminated. However, research over the last two decades has now clearly demonstrated that amalgamation does not stabilize mercury in any fashion. In fact, because mercury resides together in an amalgam with other dissimilar metals, it vaporizes quite readily through a process known as electrolysis. Research conducted at several different medical schools around the world has now established that mercury vapor is continuously emitted from dental amalgams in quantities which may very well be highly toxic over long-term in certain susceptible individuals. (Vimy, 1985) In fact, the World Health Organization (W.H.O.) now recognizes that dental amalgams are by far the major source of mercury in the human population (except for those few groups who eat large amounts of fish). (Friberg, 1991) According to the W.H.O., individuals with amalgam fillings absorb between three and seventeen micrograms of mercury vapor every day. Remarkably, the amount of mercury vapor that is currently considered safe is four micrograms per day for adults. This means that it is not uncommon for individuals to be exposed to mercury vapor at levels nearly five times higher than that which is considered safe just through the vapor emitted from their dental amalgams.

It is clear that developing fetuses, children and the elderly are far more sensitive to the neurotoxic effects of mercury and may more easily exceed safe levels even with relatively minimal exposure to mercury vapor. (Lorscheider, 1993) It is also quite clear that individuals may differ markedly in their ability to excrete toxic metals like mercury. Our bodies have several special mechanisms within cells and organs to bring about the excretion of mercury and other toxic metals, the efficiency of which may be determined genetically. (Gochfeld, 1997) According to recent research, genetic differences may account for a one hundred-fold difference between individuals in their capability to excrete toxic metals. As well, numerous nutritional and lifestyle factors can dramatically influence an individual's ability to eliminate mercury and other metals from the body.

Recent research conducted by Dr. Stephen Edelson in Atlanta, which looked at fifty-six children with autism, suggested that all of these kids had seriously elevated levels of toxic heavy metals as well as a diminished capacity for excretion of these poisons. (Edelson, 1998; Edelson, 1999) Is quite likely that children with ADHD have similar abnormalities at least in some cases, or on a lesser scale. Because mercury is such a potent neurotoxin, it would be wise to avoid amalgam fillings altogether -- particularly in children or pregnant women. There are now alternatives to amalgam that are durable, reasonable in cost and which appear to carry virtually no risk of neurotoxicity.

All in all, it is quite clear that we are all exposed to an array of unnatural chemical agents, which impose stress upon our brains. It is also clear that the degree of exposure to these various agents and an individual's susceptibility to their effects can vary drastically. These agents also never act alone but, instead, act together with all other neurotoxic influences. Identifying and reducing the total load of toxic stresses on the brain of an individual with ADHD is one of the foremost goals of the Functional Medicine approach to this disorder. This is one antecedent (risk factor) for ADHD which, if effectively addressed, may pay big dividends not only in improved brain function, but also in better health in most every way. Chapter 24 will cover these concepts in more detail and from a more practical perspective.

Chapter 7

Building Blocks of a
Healthy Brain -
Essential Fatty Acids

FATS AND THE BRAIN

On casual inspection the brain appears to be little more than a lumpy heap of glistening gray jelly. However, on a microscopic level the brain is a vast collection of specialized computer processing regions and data storage areas all networked together through an immensely complex communications architecture. Individual brain cells or neurons are the most specialized and complex cells within our body. It is now known that a single brain cell may actually be directly connected to as many as one hundred thousand other brain cells! On top of being the most complex cells of the body, they are also the most long-lived: almost every brain cell you possess at the end of your life was alive and functioning when you were two years old. Like all cells, brain neurons are fluid filled structures completely covered with a thin membrane composed mostly of various types of fats. These specific fats within the neuronal cell membrane can vary greatly between different brain cell types and even within different regions of the same brain cell. The brain neurons utilize a tremendous amount of food and oxygen for energy which is used mostly to create electrical impulses that travel along the length of the neuron at lightning speeds. The fatty insulating layer around the neuron keeps these electrical impulses from jumping across and creating short circuits with other neurons. So much of the brain is actually made up of this fatty insulation that, if dehydrated, the brain would be made of mostly just fat.

THE CRITICAL IMPORTANCE OF NERVE ENDINGS IN ADHD

At the very end of the neuron is a nerve ending, a critical switching station for the transfer of information from one cell to another. As explained in Chapter 1, it is nerve endings within the specialized regions of the brain known as the executive centers, which are of tremendous importance in ADHD. These are the nerve endings that rely primarily upon the release of the neurotransmitter dopamine. The normal function of these nerve endings depends upon very rapid processing capabilities. When a nerve impulse reaches the nerve ending, dopamine is released into the space between the nerve ending and the adjacent nerve. The dopamine then attaches briefly to receptors on the adjacent nerve, which then triggers a fresh nerve impulse in the adjacent nerve. The dopamine is then rapidly taken back up by the nerve ending where it originated by little vacuum cleaners known as dopamine transporters. The dopamine is then broken down in the antioxidant rich environment within the neuron. This whole cycle of dopamine release, attachment to receptors, reuptake back into the neuron and breakdown of dopamine all occurs at an extraordinarily rapid rate. The speed of this process depends largely upon the fats that compose these specialized nerve endings. Approximately eighty percent of these dopamine producing nerve endings are made up of the thinnest, lowest viscosity fat within the human body, known as DHA (docosahexaenoic acid). DHA is an omega-3 fatty acid — a highly polyunsaturated oil which gives the nerve ending extremely fluid properties enabling very rapid release of dopamine. If sufficient DHA is made available to the brain cells then the dopamine producing nerve endings are able to function efficiently and rapidly. However, if an adequate supply of DHA is lacking, especially during the critical period of brain construction (fetal development through early childhood), the body will substitute thicker fats (omega-9 instead of omega-3) in order to build these important brain cells. Thicker fats in this important region will mean that the nerve endings are less fluid and dopamine release may be much more sluggish. One might liken brain regions with adequate DHA to a fast computer processor – say a Pentium III, whereas brain regions deprived of DHA are more like a slow computer processor – say a clunky old 386.

DHA AND THE STRUCTURE OF THE NERVOUS SYSTEM

Deprivation of DHA may also explain a revealing discovery by researchers at the National Institutes of Mental Health. Using a high resolution MRI scanner, investigators were able to consistently demonstrate that children with ADHD have regions of the brain (executive centers) which are shrunken and underdeveloped. (Castellanos, 1996) Since these are also regions which normally possess rich quantities of DHA, this part of the brain may be underdeveloped because of DHA deprivation during fetal development or childhood. It has been clearly shown in animal studies that if the developing brain is deprived of DHA, inadequate brain development is almost certain. Also, since DHA is a highly fragile fatty acid and is consumed by normal cellular processes, it must be continually supplied to the brain throughout life in order to maintain adequate brain function.

Not only is DHA important in the brain, it is also of critical importance in the development and function of the eye. The back of the eye, or retina, is a complex and highly specialized collection of nerve tissue. The cells within the retina turn incoming light images into electrical nerve impulses that are transmitted to the brain. In order for the processing of light information to occur in an extremely rapid fashion, the membranes of retinal cells are composed of a very high percentage of the very fluid fat, DHA. If DHA supplies are lacking, especially during fetal development or childhood, it may contribute to significant visual problems.

THE BENEFITS AND DRAWBACKS OF DHA

If the dopamine containing nerve endings are rich in DHA their processing speed is extremely rapid. However, besides being the lowest viscosity oil in the body, DHA is also the most fragile of all the fatty acids. Saturated fats are thick (high viscosity) and highly resistant to becoming rancid or oxidized. However, polyunsaturated fats are oily liquids; they are low in viscosity but they become oxidized (rancid) very easily. Omega-3 fatty acids such as DHA are often classified as super-polyunsaturated fats. They are even lower in viscosity than other polyunsaturated fats (like canola oil or other vegetable oils) and are much more susceptible to oxidation. The brain, although it only makes up two percent of the body's weight, it consumes nearly twenty-five percent of the body's supply of oxygen. Thus, it is the most aerobically active region of the body and, therefore, anything within the brain will be very prone to becoming oxidized. Since DHA is so prone to becoming damaged through oxidation, anything that increases oxidation within the brain will also increase the need for DHA.

An extraordinarily wide range of agents or events will increase oxidative stress within the brain and will contribute to the depletion of DHA. For example, trauma or emotional stress will increase the quantity of circulating stress hormones such as adrenaline and cortisol. Inside the brain, stress hormones are rapidly broken down or oxidized. These oxidized byproducts must then be quickly removed from the brain because they can cause oxidation damage to brain cells. Thus, it has become clear that prolonged periods of excessive stress or trauma can actually cause molecular damage to the brain and accelerate the aging process. (Campbell, 1999; Seeman, 1997) Besides stress hormones, many neurotoxic chemicals are also known to increase oxidative stress within the brain. Heavy metals such as lead or mercury, pesticides, first or second-hand cigarette smoke and the breakdown products of amphetamines like Ritalin® or Dexedrine® are just a few examples of chemical substances that can increase oxidative stress in the brain. (Cadet, 1997) Chronic illnesses such as allergies or inflammatory disorders also increase oxidative stress and thus may increase the body's need for DHA. Therefore, individuals who are under stress, who are suffering from illness or who have significant exposure to neurotoxic chemicals all have an increased need for both DHA and antioxidants. Recent research at our facility examined fatty acid levels in the blood of seventy-five children with ADHD. In this study we found approximately eighty percent of these children had low levels of DHA. Are these children lacking omega-3 fatty acids in their diet? Are their brains under oxidative stress from neurotoxic influences? Or are they lacking other nutrients that should enable them to properly process and internally manufacture omega-3 fatty acids like DHA from common dietary fats? In actual fact, probably all of these factors are present to some degree in these children.

SOURCES OF DHA

Since DHA is such a critical nutrient it may be surprising to learn that most people have very little of it, if any at all, in their diet. In fact, DHA is a rather rare nutrient found only in certain fish and aquatic plants. Fortunately, under most circumstances the human body can manufacture DHA from a more readily available omega-3 fatty acid known as ALA (alpha linolenic acid). Although ALA is still not over abundant in most people's diets, it can be found in small amounts in several land based plant foods. Most people get all of their ALA from vegetable oils such as canola and soy, which contain tiny amounts of this important omega-3 fatty acid. Those who have gotten smart about the need for omega-3 fatty acids may also be consuming flax oil, the richest source of ALA. However, even though ALA is relatively common in the modern diet, there are several reasons why the body may not be able to manufacture sufficient DHA from the ALA in our foods.

First of all, there may simply not be enough ALA in a person's diet to manufacture sufficient DHA to meet the needs of the brain. As mentioned before, individuals with allergies or other chronic illness, as well as those under stress or exposed to neurotoxic agents, all have increased requirements for DHA. The amount of omega-3 fats in their diet may just not be sufficient in the absence of supplementation with ALA (flax oil) or DHA (fish oils or algae-derived DHA).

Secondly, the conversion of vegetable derived ALA into brain-critical DHA takes place in the body through a series of enzymes steps. To make DHA, the polyunsaturated ALA must be made even more unsaturated and the length of the molecule must be increased. One of the enzymes that is required for this process is highly sensitive and can be shut down very easily. This enzyme, known as delta-six desaturase, is blocked by a variety of toxic influences including excessive stress hormones, tobacco smoke, alcohol, chronic infection, heavy metals, trans-fatty acids, drugs and pesticides. Since these and many other toxic influences are so common during fetal development, as well as childhood and adult life, it is likely that DHA production is commonly impaired through toxicological effects.

Thirdly, the enzyme delta-six desaturase is also highly dependent upon certain nutritional factors. If cells containing delta-six desaturase do not have adequate quantities of zinc, magnesium, vitamin C, vitamin E, and certain B vitamins, conversion of vegetable derived ALA to brain-critical DHA will not take place. Studies have demonstrated improved behavior and cognitive performance in children with ADHD who are given supplements containing zinc, magnesium and certain B vitamins. Part of the reason for this improvement may be that these nutrients assist in more efficient production of DHA from the more readily available ALA in the diet.

Lastly, the ability to convert ALA to DHA may vary widely depending upon a person's genetic makeup. For example, certain cultures such as coastal Indians, Eskimos and those from northern Scotland and Scandinavian countries traditionally consume large amounts of cold water fish like salmon, which contains high amounts of DHA. These people may have a genetic requirement for high amounts of omega-3 fatty acids and their bodies may not be capable of efficiently converting ALA to DHA. If individuals with this genetic background move away from coastal areas and no longer consume a lot of fish oil, they may have significant problems from lack of omega-3 fatty acids.

DHA IN FETAL DEVELOPMENT AND INFANCY

There is clearly a special need for DHA during pregnancy, infancy and early childhood. Brain development begins very early on in fetal development. During this time nutritional adequacy and absence of neurotoxic influences are both of critical importance. If the fetus is deprived of sufficient DHA during this vital period, significant problems with brain and eye development may occur. During pregnancy it would be highly prudent for a woman to consider supplementing her diet with ALA through flax oil. It would also be wise to add additional DHA through certified, heavy metal free, fish oil or algae-derived DHA. Essential fatty acid supplementation during pregnancy can be thought of as "brain insurance" for the precious baby. Vitamin and mineral supplementation will also help the mother's body convert more ALA to DHA so that plenty of it is available for her baby's developing brain. Shunning cigarette smoke, alcohol, drugs and pollutants will also help to insure efficient DHA production.

Infants also need plenty of DHA. As everyone has heard, "the breast is best" and infants who are breast-fed are half as likely to develop ADHD. This may be due, in part, to the fact that breast milk contains DHA, unlike infant formulas, which have no DHA at all. (Uauy-Dagach, 1995) To obtain the maximum benefit from breastfeeding, it should be the infant's exclusive diet for at least six months. Secondly, the breastfeeding mother should supplement her diet with adequate amounts of omega-3 fatty acids such as ALA from flax oil and DHA from fish oil or algae to insure that her breast milk does indeed contain adequate amounts of DHA. Thirdly, mothers should be careful to avoid neurotoxic chemicals during breastfeeding. Mercury vapor from amalgam fillings has been shown to readily enter the breast milk. (Vimy, 1997) Therefore, nursing mothers should avoid having fillings removed or new fillings placed during this time. They should also avoid other sources of neurotoxins such as freshwater fish or larger predatory ocean fish, solvents or pesticides.

Once a child is weaned, parents should continue to be vigilant to insure that their child obtains adequate amounts of omega-3 fatty acids. Flax oil is an excellent food for children and can be easily incorporated into their diet. It would also be advisable to supplement the diet of infants and children (especially those with ADHD) with moderate amounts of DHA. Sardines and salmon are two good sources of DHA, which many children will accept. However, because it is a potential source of mercury, salmon should probably not be eaten by children more than once per week. Certified heavy metal free fish oil capsules are now widely available. Tuna oil is an excellent source of DHA and heavy metal free products are easily obtained. Tuna oil contains higher amounts of DHA than most other fish oils and has become the preferred fish oil for supplementation of children's diets. Canned tuna, on the other hand, is one of the worst offenders for mercury contamination and should not be eaten on a regular basis. Probably the purest DHA of all is that which is extracted from algae and is available in either capsule form or as an additive to other products. One main advantage of the algae derived DHA is the lack of a fishy taste.

Kids often refuse to take fish oil capsules as soon as they experience the first yucky fishy burp after taking these products. The fresher the fish oil, the less the fishy burps will be a problem.

ONE EASY WAY TO CONSUME DHA

One of the best ways to supplement a child's diet with DHA is through a product called Ultracare™ for Kids. This product is a medical food or functional food, which contains a wide variety of nutrients, designed to benefit children with allergies or ADHD. Ultracare™ for Kids is a hypoallergenic white powder made from rice protein and rice carbohydrate and can be used as the base for delicious "smoothie drinks". This product contains significant amounts of DHA derived from algae as well as high amounts of calcium, vitamins and minerals. It also contains FOS (fructooligosaccharides) which helps to restore normal bacteria to the child's intestinal tract. One or two scoops of Ultracare™ for Kids powder is put into a blender along with frozen fruit, a bit of honey or other natural sweetener (such as sugar-free stevia extract) and other nutritious ingredients as desired. Water is added and then the whole mixture is blended into a delicious smoothie. Research at our facility has demonstrated that children with ADHD readily except smoothie drinks made from Ultracare™ for Kids if it is prepared in a tasty manner with the right ingredients. Our research also showed that children on the Ultracare™ for Kids had significant increases in their blood DHA levels over a period of eight weeks. Drinking a delicious yet scientifically engineered smoothie is certainly an easy way to increase a child's nutritional status while decreasing their intake of unhealthy junk foods. Great-tasting smoothies can become a real favorite for kids as well as the whole family .

LEARNING TO MIND YOUR FATS

Another group of essential fatty acids, which must be obtained from the diet, are the omega-6 fatty acids. The brain contains large amounts of one omega-6 fatty acid known as AA (arachidonic acid), This fatty acid plays an essential role in the function of the brain and immune system. Fortunately AA is easily obtained from the diet and is abundant in animal fats and other common dietary sources. Lack of AA is relatively uncommon in the developed world and, in fact, excessive AA can be found quite frequently. Too much of this omega-six fatty acid might be associated with problems such as allergy, inflammation or muscle spasm. Another omega-6 fatty acid known as GLA (gamma linolenic acid) may also be of significant importance in brain and immune system function. Unlike AA, GLA is quite uncommon in the diet and is usually produced within the body through enzymatic conversion of the more common vegetable-derived omega-6 fatty acid known as LA (linoleic acid). LA is the primary fatty acid in most vegetable oils and thus very few people will suffer from a lack of LA. Recent research at our facility has demonstrated excessive levels of LA in many children with ADHD. On the other hand this same research identified inadequate levels of the omega-6 fatty acid GLA in one out of five children with ADHD. In these children, supplementation of their diets with GLA would probably be beneficial. GLA can be obtained from evening primrose oil, borage oil, or black current oil. Today, some of the most popular fatty acid supplements designed for individuals with ADHD contain a combination of GLA from evening primrose oil and DHA from tuna oil. Products containing this balanced combination of omega-3 and omega-6 fatty essential fatty acids provide a safe and sensible means of insuring optimal intake of essential fatty acids.

If you are completely confused by now with all of the strange letters representing various essential fatty acids just remember three important fats: ALA is the omega-3 fatty acid found in flax oil. DHA is the brain critical omega-3 fatty acid found in fish oils and aquatic plants and GLA is the important omega-6 fatty acid found in evening primrose oil, borage oil or black current oil. A prudent fatty acid supplement program for those with ADHD might include fresh flax oil added to foods as well as capsules containing a combination of tuna oil and evening primrose oil. As mentioned previously, another excellent source of DHA, as well as many other nutrients, are the delicious smoothies made from Ultracare for Kids.

OTHER BRAIN FATS WORTH THINKING ABOUT

The membranes of virtually every cell in the body contain large amounts of a special family of fats known as phospholipids. These large molecules have special properties that make them very important structural elements of cell membranes. Neurons in the brain depend upon the provision of adequate quantities of important phospholipids in order to function normally. One phospholipid, PS (phosphatidylserine) has received a fair bit of attention as a potential enhancer of brain function. Studies have now shown that supplementation with PS can improve memory and concentration in both normal and brain disordered adults. (Crook, 1991) In response to this research, several products have been developed which contain PS. Perhaps the most interesting supplement of this type is a combination product, appropriately known as PS-IQ, which contains high amounts of PS as well as the essential fatty acids DHA (from tuna oil) and GLA (from evening primrose oil). This combination of brain boosting fats may be an ideal mixture for those with ADHD.

BUILDING GOOD BRAIN FATS

Apart from ensuring that the diet contains adequate quantities of essential fatty acids, those with ADHD must also include sufficient quantities of the nutrients that are required for adequate processing of those fatty acids within the body. Eating a balanced, whole foods diet will provide a wide range of important micronutrients, many of which are important in fatty acid metabolism. In addition, it is reasonable to consider dietary supplementation with additional magnesium, zinc, B complex, vitamin C, and vitamin E. These nutrients are all critical in the function of enzymes which the body uses to manufacture fatty acids for the brain, immune system and organs.

GUARDING YOUR BRAIN FATS

During the normal, day-to-day operation of the brain, intense aerobic activity leads to "wear and tear" of the brain cells due to oxidation. Normal levels of oxidation within the brain leads to oxidative destruction of essential fatty acids like DHA. This is one of the reasons why there is an ongoing need for essential fatty acids throughout life. However, under conditions of emotional, physical, infectious or toxicological stress, the level of oxidation within the brain may increase dramatically. This could lead to a marked increase in destruction of the highly fragile essential fatty acids. To help protect against the ravages of oxidation within the brain, certain antioxidants can be of tremendous value. Although vitamin C and vitamin E are important antioxidants, other natural molecules known as bioflavonoids may play a far more important role in protecting the brain from oxidation. A healthy, whole-foods diet that is rich in fruits and vegetables, contains hundreds of different bioflavonoids, many of which have brain-protecting effects. In fact, several thousand bioflavonoids have now been identified; a few of which can enter the brain quite readily and exert powerful antioxidant effects. A group of bioflavonoids known as proanthocyanidins have been shown to be particularly effective as antioxidants for the brain. Because they contain high amounts of proanthocyanidins, grape seed extract, pine bark extract (Pycnogenol), and Ginkgo biloba extract are three common herbal substances that are highly useful as brain protecting antioxidants. Parents of children with ADHD commonly report that their children's behavior improve significantly following the administration of either one of these three antioxidant supplements. Recent research conducted at our facility supports this observation. Utilizing a combination product containing Ginkgo biloba and American Ginseng extracts known as AD-FX (Attention FX in the U.S.), we observed significant improvements in the behavior and cognitive performance in 90% of thirty-seven children with ADHD. This study helped to demonstrate that by providing potent antioxidant protection to brains under significant oxidative stress, numerous physiological improvements in brain function evidently take place.

AVOIDING NASTY FATS

It is clear that fat metabolism within the brain and body can be negatively influenced by the consumption of certain unhealthy fats and oils. Three main categories of unhealthy fats are commonly ingested in the standard North American diet: saturated fats, trans-fatty acids, and rancid fats.

Saturated fats are naturally occurring fats that come primarily from meat and dairy products as well as tropical oils (coconut and palm kernel oil). Moderate amounts of saturated fat are fine for most people, especially children. However, it is common for certain popular foods to contain enormous quantities of saturated fat; amounts that are very unhealthy for anyone. A typical fast food cheeseburger often contains fifty to one hundred grams of almost pure saturated fat. That's almost enough grease to lubricate the rear axle of a large truck! Excessive intake of this kind of fat can have serious implications for cardiovascular health. As well, high amounts of saturated fat have been shown to adversely affect cognitive performance and may significantly harm circulation to the brain over long periods of time. Moderation is the key word when it comes to saturated fat. Modest amounts of saturated fat can generally be part of healthy diet for individuals with ADHD.

Trans-fatty acids are a type of saturated fat that should be avoided altogether. (Ascherio, 1997; Carlson, 1997) These fatty acids are common constituents of processed foods and they are completely unnatural to the human diet. They are created when liquid vegetable oils are turned into solid fats through a process known as hydrogenation. In this process, polyunsaturated oils like soybean, canola, or sunflower oils, are exposed to hydrogen gas under high heat. Depending upon what degree of hydrogenation is utilized, the oil may thicken slightly or it may be completely solidified. Vegetable oil shortening is an example of a thick, greasy fat which has been created by a high level of hydrogenation. Before hydrogenation was utilized, when the food industry required fats which were solid at room temperature and which were stable at high temperatures for baking and deep frying, they had to utilize either lard (animal fat) or coconut oil. The process of hydrogenation was a great breakthrough for the vegetable oils industry. It allowed the industry to produce solid, saturated fats with the same physical properties as naturally saturated fats at a significantly lower cost. This powerful industry also engaged in a widespread "educational" campaign to promote their products as "health foods". Unfortunately, hydrogenated vegetable oils are not at all healthy. The trans-fats contained within hydrogenated vegetable oils have now been shown to be significantly toxic and have been completely banned in some countries. Trans-fatty acids have been associated with an increased risk of cardiovascular disease and cancer with long-term consumption. As well, they have been shown to be significantly toxic to the brain and gastrointestinal tract and may cause adverse symptoms almost immediately upon ingestion in some individuals. These unnatural substances interfere with the normal metabolism of fats and they may actually block the production of critical brain fats such as DHA.(Carlson, 1997)

Individuals with ADHD should probably avoid every trace of trans-fatty acids in their diet. This may take some real getting used to because the average North American consumes approximately fifteen to twenty five grams of trans-fatty acids every day! To get smart about trans-fatty acids one has to read labels. Many commercial baked goods including cookies, crackers, cakes and a wide variety of packaged, processed foods will be found to contain hydrogenated vegetable oils. Anything with hydrogenated, partially hydrogenated or modified vegetable oil, as well as vegetable oil shortening, should be completely avoided by people with ADHD. This also means avoiding certain foods when eating out. In almost every case, foods that are deep-fried are cooked in vegetable oil shortening. Giving up doughnuts, french-fries and the like may seem like a real sacrifice for some people but it's one of those simple steps which may pay big dividends in the long run.

Another group of fats, which should be avoided by individuals with ADHD, are rancid fats. Rancidity is a common term used to describe oils that have become spoiled through oxidation. Polyunsaturated vegetable oils are particularly susceptible to oxidation damage. Unfortunately, common methods used to process and store polyunsaturated vegetable oils generally lead to high levels of oxidation. Most commercial oils are extracted under conditions of extremely high temperature and in the presence of oxygen and light. Toxic solvents, such as hexane, are also used to maximize the amount of oil extracted from the oil seed. Even though the toxic solvent is boiled off, traces can still be detected in the oil. This aggressive combination of processing maximizes the yield and minimizes cost, making vegetable oils a more profitable product. Unfortunately, these polyunsaturated oils are very fragile and readily undergo oxidation under the conditions that are commonly used for commercial extraction. Furthermore, these oils tend to be stored in clear bottles and kept on store shelves at room temperature. This means that the oils continue to oxidize because of light and oxygen during storage. Even though they may not taste rancid, laboratory measurements will verify that significant portions of the polyunsaturated fatty acids in the oil are oxidized. These oxidized fatty acids, once ingested, will tend to create further oxidation of fatty acids within cell membranes adding significantly to the oxidative stress inside the body. People with ADHD should probably avoid using commercial vegetable oils, except extra virgin olive oil. This oil is processed at much lower temperatures and is more stable because it is primarily monounsaturated. Polyunsaturated oils can be obtained safely by eating fresh, raw nuts and seeds. Also, several manufacturers now offer vegetable oils, such as flax, canola and sunflower oils that are processed at very low temperatures in the absence of light and oxygen and without the use of solvent extraction. These oils are then stored in opaque bottles and kept refrigerated. Health food stores and many supermarkets now carry these special oils. But because the high temperatures of cooking will oxidize these oils, it is still not wise to cook with them. Instead, it is preferable to use small amounts of butter, olive oil or coconut oil and cook at the lowest temperature possible.

MANAGING YOUR BRAIN FATS

To summarize, it should be clear by now that improving brain physiology has quite a bit to do with managing the fats within the brain. Behavior and cognitive performance are so related to this important aspect of brain physiology that people with ADHD simply cannot ignore it. Managing brain fats should involve a combination of intelligent supplementation with fatty acids (and perhaps phospholipids like phosphatidylserine) as well as micronutrient support (magnesium, zinc, B complex, vitamin C, vitamin E) in order to enable the body to adequately process, manufacture and metabolize critical brain fats. In addition, antioxidant support using specific bioflavonoids (such as Ginkgo biloba) should be provided to help preserve and protect these vital molecules. Finally, managing brain fats should include a thoughtful search for causes of increased oxidative stress within an individual's brain. Many of these factors are the antecedents (underlying risk factors) and triggers (physiological disturbances), which are at the heart of ADHD and can be managed according to the Functional Medicine principles outlined in this book.

SOLVING THE PUZZLE OF ADHD

Hopefully by now you are beginning to grasp the amazing interconnectedness of these various factors within the complex systems of the body. In order to think in a manner consistent with the principles of Functional Medicine, it is necessary to stop looking for "magic bullets" or quick fix cures. Instead, you should begin to see the web-like connections in which healthy and unhealthy factors interact in amazingly complex and individualized ways. Finding real healing solutions for medical conditions like ADHD using a Functional Medicine approach is much like solving a jigsaw puzzle. At first the puzzle might seem impossibly complicated and none of the pieces may seem to fit. However, with persistence, the pieces will gradually begin to fit together until the puzzle is eventually solved. You don't have to be a rocket scientist to solve a jigsaw puzzle – you just have to be persistent and believe that if you keep working at it, one day, it will all start to come together. I have had the rewarding experience of witnessing numerous parents and adults with ADHD who persisted until they found answers to their personal jigsaw puzzle. The steps toward this personal triumph come largely through knowledge. Some of this information may seem confusing or irrelevant at first, but if you persist and study these principles, eventually it will all make sense and you may be empowered to play a very important role in the transformation of someone's life (perhaps your own or your child's). You should still seek the guidance of a qualified Functional Medicine practitioner but now you will be a key participant, not just a passive recipient of tests and prescriptions.

Chapter 8

Other Brain Critical Nutritional Factors

Perils of a Junk Food Diet

One of the most unfortunate things about modern life is how certain large corporations exploit people for their own profit. One clear example of this phenomenon is seen in the way food companies market their products to children. Junk foods, fast foods and convenience foods are all particularly appealing to children who have no understanding that such products lack vital nutrients and may contain harmful ingredients. The marketing campaigns associated with these profitable food products have been so aggressive and pervasive that is almost considered cruel or immoral to deprive your child of such pleasurable delicacies as sweetened breakfast cereals or deep-fried fast foods. However, children pay a high price for a diet in which junk foods play a significant role. Although the effects of such unnatural fare may not be immediately apparent, as time goes on, the impact of these foods upon the brain may be highly significant. Junk foods are largely empty calories. What this means is that they contain significant amounts of calories from macronutrients (carbohydrates, fats or proteins) but contain insufficient quantities of micronutrients (vitamins, minerals and accessory nutrients such as bioflavonoids). When an individual runs on empty calories, basic bodily processes continue to take place. However, without an array of micronutrients, cellular processes become increasingly inefficient, communication between cells become disordered, and cells become subjected to increasing levels of oxidative stress. This can lead to poor organ function and eventually to disease.

Junk Food Junkies

I am often amazed at the diet of many kids (and adults) with ADHD. Kids with ADHD are most often very picky eaters who may favor only a very narrow range of foods. Unfortunately, the foods that these kids prefer are very seldom healthy, whole foods. Instead, they crave junk foods and packaged processed foods and many parents feel powerless to change their children's tastes. Unwitting or not, parents all too often provide their kids with a regular selection junk foods. Candies, cookies, chips, pop and the like are well recognized junk foods and most people realize that they should be eaten in moderation because of their low nutritional value. However, a great number of foods are junk foods in disguise and may be equally as harmful as the more obvious ones. As an example, most packaged breakfast cereals are little more than sugar and starch. Some people are fooled into thinking that these are nutritious foods because they are "enriched" with a few vitamins and iron. Although this "enrichment" of junk foods may help to prevent overt vitamin deficiency diseases it certainly doesn't replace the vast array of important phytochemicals (medicinal plant chemicals), minerals and fiber found in whole foods.

MALNUTRITION IN THE MODERN WORLD

The kind of malnutrition that is so common in the Third World, starvation or protein-calorie malnutrition, is relatively uncommon in the developed world. However, micronutrient malnutrition is rampant. Even as the rate of obesity reaches an all-time high amongst children and adults alike, micronutrient malnutrition is an invisible plague crossing all socioeconomic barriers. Many of the micronutrients that lead to severe deficiency diseases are now added to commercially processed foods. This means that diseases like goiter (from iodine deficiency), rickets (from vitamin D deficiency), and scurvy (from vitamin C deficiency) are now relatively uncommon because these nutrients are common food additives. However, the range of micronutrients that are now known to be important for optimal health is far beyond that which can be added to commercial foods. Numerous minerals such as magnesium, zinc, selenium, chromium, manganese and molybdenum, known to be critical for optimal health, are not added to commercially processed foods. The thousands of phytochemicals found in fruits and vegetables are, of course, not usually obtained by eating processed foods. People who do not eat a rich diet of whole foods will clearly lack a wide range of important micronutrients. As well, individual needs for specific nutrients may be much higher than expected because of genetic differences, illness or stress. On top of all of this, genetic tailoring of food crops (for uniformity of taste and not nutrition) along with the depletion of trace minerals in soils from non-organic farming practices, has created a food supply which contains lower quantities of micronutrients than ever before.

SATISFYING A HUNGRY BRAIN

The brain is clearly the hungriest organ in the body. You can tie a tight tourniquet around your leg and cut off the blood supply completely for over four hours before permanent damage begins to occur. However, if you deprive the brain of oxygen for five minutes or blood sugar for ten minutes, you will most likely be dead. Not only does the brain have a voracious appetite for basic fuel (glucose) and oxygen; it is the most sensitive organ in the body to the adequacy of numerous other nutrients. Vitamins such as the B vitamins, thiamine (B1), pyridoxine (B6), niacin and vitamin B12 all have a tremendous impact upon brain function. Giving supplements containing high amounts of B vitamins has been shown to improve behavior and cognitive function in children with ADHD. This likely reflects the fact that these children have a need for B vitamins that may go well beyond the RDA and certainly beyond what they are getting in their diets.

PROTEIN AND THE BRAIN

One of the most tragic things about poverty is how it can imprison children and keep them in its grip for life. Poor families may not have the resources to purchase foods with enough protein to meet the needs of growing children. It has been well documented that children who are deprived of adequate protein early in life will suffer from a permanent reduction in brain size and a significant loss of intelligence. Although this phenomenon is seen in its obvious form in cases of desperate poverty or severe neglect, less extreme forms of protein deprivation can still have a significant impact upon behavior and cognition. Kids who skip breakfast, for example, or who eat breakfasts with inadequate protein will tend to be more irritable, easily distracted and hyperactive. Protein provides the amino acids needed to make neurotransmitters and it helps to smooth out rising and falling blood sugar levels, which can have an adverse impact upon brain function.

One of the most important contributions that protein provides to the brain are the building blocks for several important neurotransmitters — the chemical messengers that allow brain cells to talk to each other. If protein is efficiently digested, it will be broken down completely into amino acids. The amino acids tyrosine and phenylalanine are used to make norepinephrine and dopamine; glutamine is used to make GABA; and tryptophan is used to make serotonin. If protein intake is inadequate or if digestion of protein is inefficient or incomplete, the brain may not be able to make sufficient neurotransmitters and brain function may suffer. Poor breakdown of protein or inefficient absorption of amino acids may actually be a significant factor in both addiction and ADHD. Research conducted by Dr. Kenneth Blum at the University of Texas has demonstrated that individuals with various addictive problems, as well as those with ADHD show significant improvements when given supplements containing several of the above described amino acids. (Blum, 1996) Our research has also demonstrated that improved behavior and cognition accompany improvements in gastrointestinal function in children with ADHD. These improvements in brain function may be due in part to improved protein digestion and more efficient absorption of brain-critical amino acids.

IRON AND THE BRAIN

Other minerals may also have a significant role to play in ADHD. Several studies have shown that iron deficiency can lead to significant cognitive and behavioral problems in children. Iron is, of course, a critical constituent of red blood cells. This is why iron deficiency leads to anemia (reduced quantity of red blood cells within the bloodstream). Inside the red blood cell, iron is an important component of a protein called hemoglobin — which is used to carry oxygen throughout the body. Iron is also incorporated into important enzymes known as cytochromes. This family of enzymes includes some that detoxify drugs and poisons.

These types of cytochromes are located primarily within the gastrointestinal tract and liver. Other cytochromes are found in every cell and are used by the cell to generate energy. Cells that generate the most energy, such as brain cells, have high concentrations of cytochromes within the cellular energy generating stations called mitochondria. Because they are the most energy demanding cells of the brain, the dopamine producing neurons in the brain's executive centers contain the highest concentration of iron. (Youdim, 1983) Therefore, iron deficiency can lead to cognitive and behavioral problems in children because without adequate iron, brain cells simply cannot manufacture enough energy to perform adequately.

As children are growing, their bloodstreams are constantly expanding. Because the bloodstream is so vital, iron from the child's diet will go preferentially to build red blood cells. If iron intake is inadequate, brain cells may be deprived of sufficient iron to keep energy-generating cytochrome enzymes working properly. As has been mentioned previously, inadequate energy production within certain regions of the brain (executive centers) is a primary characteristic of ADHD. This may be due, at least in some cases and to some extent, to a decreased availability of iron within the brain. Some studies have shown, in fact, that iron supplementation in children with ADHD (even without anemia) can improve behavior and cognitive performance. (Sever, 1997) It should be noted, however, that iron supplementation in full-grown adolescents or adults with ADHD should be used only if they have measurable iron deficiency. In adults, excesses of iron are actually far more common than deficiencies, and in the absence of anemia, iron supplementation has never been shown to increase energy or cognitive performance.

MAGNESIUM AND THE BRAIN

Another trace mineral that is highly important in ADHD is magnesium. This mineral has a multitude of different uses within the body including the activation of several hundred different enzymes. As was mentioned before, magnesium is one of the necessary cofactors required by the enzyme delta 6 desaturase. This is the enzyme responsible for the conversion of vegetable derived omega-3 fatty acids to the brain critical fatty acid, DHA. Therefore, if levels of magnesium are less than ideal, DHA deficiency is very likely to exist. Magnesium is also a calming mineral that relaxes nerves and muscle and diminishes the effects of stress. On the other hand, if magnesium levels are low, muscle tension will increase, nerves will become hyperirritable and the effects of stress are magnified. Unfortunately, stress of all kinds will increase the loss of magnesium from cells and eventually from the body through the kidneys. Emotional stress, abuse and neglect can all lead to profound magnesium loss. Other, more physical forms of stress, such as recurrent infection, food or environmental allergies and gastrointestinal parasites also can result in excessive magnesium depletion. Also, various drugs like caffeine, cortisone, Ritalin® and Dexedrine® mimic stress and promote excessive magnesium loss. Thus, varied degrees of magnesium deficiency are very likely to be common in children with ADHD who all suffer from some or all of these psychological, pharmacological and physical factors which lead to the depletion of magnesium. Low levels of magnesium may be associated with hyperactivity due to hyperirritability of brain neurons. Studies have indeed shown that supplementation with magnesium can improve behavior and cognitive performance in children with ADHD. (Kozielec, 1997; Starobrat, 1997) Adults with ADHD are also likely to require a very high intake of magnesium and will benefit from magnesium supplementation. Avoiding stimulants like caffeine, nicotine or amphetamines (Ritalin, Dexedrine and methamphetamine), as well as learning to manage stress and addressing physical problems such as chronic infection, allergies and a "leaky gut" are all important factors which will help to decrease magnesium loss.

On a personal note, as a youngster, I suffered from many allergies, including allergies to foods that I ate every day. I also smoked and was quite overweight. For many years, I also suffered from an arrhythmia of the heart, in which my heart would suddenly begin beating at an enormous rate for no good reason at all. This would continue for minutes to hours and would often be quite exhausting. At other times, my heart would beat very irregularly. It would flip-flop in my chest and chug away for hours at a time (at one time I had atrial fibrillation). I also suffered from muscle tension problems and my neck and back seemed to always be in pain. As well, muscles throughout my body would twitch frequently (a symptom called fasciculations). All of these problems worsened during the year that I was on Ritalin until these and other side effects became intolerable and I stopped the medication. I eventually had my magnesium levels checked using a test developed by NASA and performed by Intracellular Diagnostics Laboratory. This test determined how much magnesium was actually in my body cells. The test revealed that I was severely magnesium deficient. I had probably been magnesium deficient all my life from a combination of poor magnesium intake combined with medical problems that resulted in magnesium wasting. Ritalin, because it mimics the effects of stress, only made the magnesium deficiency much worse. Once I began a regimen of magnesium supplementation, taking about one thousand milligrams of magnesium per day, and a few intravenous magnesium infusions, the heart arrhythmia disappeared, the muscle tension problems resolved, and the muscle twitching (fasciculations) went away. Since that time, as long as I keep my magnesium intake high, I rarely suffer from the symptoms suggestive of magnesium insufficiency. Many people with ADHD go through life with significant magnesium deficiency, which is never detected and treated appropriately. Not only does this likely lead to a worsening of the symptoms of ADHD, but it can increase the risk of developing allergies, heart disease, high blood pressure and a host of other problems. Magnesium supplementation is one of the safest, simplest and least expensive things that can be done to help a person with ADHD.

ZINC AND THE BRAIN

Zinc is another mineral that may be of primary importance in ADHD. Zinc is responsible for the activation of numerous enzyme systems within the body. Low-grade zinc deficiency will result in weakened immune system responses and diminished digestive system function. Decreased levels of zinc may also lead to a poor sense of taste and diminished appetite. Kids who are zinc deficient are often picky eaters who love junk food or who have strong preferences for only a few foods — which of course only worsens the zinc deficiency. They may also have recurrent respiratory and ear infections and end up on antibiotics repeatedly. These are kids who often have subtle digestive problems and are more likely to have intestinal parasites or suffer from overgrowth of undesirable bacteria and yeasts in their gut. Research has demonstrated that children with ADHD are more likely to have low tissue levels of zinc than the levels found in unaffected children. Studies have also shown that children with ADHD who are unresponsive to stimulant drugs are more likely to be zinc deficient than children who respond favorably to these medications. (Arnold, 1990) In addition, zinc is an important component of the enzyme delta 6 desaturase, which converts vegetable derived omega-3 fatty acids to the brain critical omega-3 fatty acid DHA. (Bekaroglu, 1996) This probably explains why children with low levels of zinc also have low levels of essential fatty acids in their blood.

Zinc also plays a key role in the body's ability to excrete toxic metals. It is the primary stimulus for the production of a protein within cells called metallothionein. This complex protein is produced to some extent by every cell and it acts like a metal cleanup service traveling throughout the cell, and capturing toxic metals. Once metals are captured by metallothionein, they can be transported to the outside of the cell and then be removed effectively by the body. In cases where zinc levels are inadequate, a person's metallothionein production is very low and cells tend to accumulate toxic metals much more readily. Studies have shown that zinc supplementation dramatically increases metallothionein production in humans. (Sullivan, 1998) Since neurotoxic metals like lead, cadmium, mercury, aluminum and arsenic may play a significant role in ADHD, ensuring adequate levels of zinc may be of critical importance. Overall, dietary supplementation with modest amounts of zinc in children and adults with ADHD is a safe and prudent measure that may bring about numerous physiological benefits.

CALCIUM, CHROMIUM, SELENIUM AND ADHD

People with ADHD must also be aware of the importance of several other minerals. (Chandra, 1997) Calcium is the most abundant mineral in the body and it is, of course, the key component of bones and teeth. Calcium also plays a lead role in muscle contraction, nerve conduction, enzyme activity and blood clotting. Children with ADHD are often allergic to dairy products and, as a result, they may be restricted from eating this major food group. Without careful substitution or supplementation, children who do not consume dairy products may easily become calcium deficient. In addition, individuals with food allergies, those who take stimulant drugs (caffeine, nicotine or amphetamines), those who eat excessive quantities of protein, and those who are under significant stress may have a tendency to excrete excessive amounts of calcium from their kidneys. If these individuals also abstain from dairy products they may be seriously calcium deficient unless they are given appropriate food substitution or nutritional supplementation. Cabbage family vegetables, nuts, seeds, legumes and canned fish with bones are all reasonable sources of non-dairy calcium. Tofu is an excellent source of calcium and protein with many versatile uses. In spite of years of opposition by the dairy industry, rice milk and soy milk and orange juice are now available with calcium and vitamin D fortification — a real breakthrough for those who are allergic to milk. Another excellent non-dairy source of calcium is the hypoallergenic medical food, Ultracare™ for Kids. Smoothies made with Ultracare™ for Kids provide an easy way to increase dietary calcium along with many other important nutrients.

It is important to note that calcium has a very close relationship with lead. Chemically, calcium and lead are quite similar even though lead is, of course, highly toxic. Once inside the body, lead and calcium tend to be in "chemical competition". If lead is present in the body, the atoms of lead will try to occupy the same places as are normally occupied by calcium — the bones and in regions of cells where calcium normally is present. Because of this, people who are calcium deficient are much more susceptible to lead poisoning. In keeping with the same principle, the most important treatment in helping a person detoxify from lead is to administer high amounts of calcium. Ironically, studies conducted by the FDA in recent years have demonstrated that calcium supplements are often heavily contaminated with lead. Calcium carbonate based supplements, including oyster shell, as well as most bonemeal, are likely to contain significant quantities of lead. Calcium citrate and microcrystalline hydroxyapatite, which is certified to be free of heavy metals, are acceptable sources of supplemental calcium. Ultracare™ for Kids and the microcrystalline hydroxyapatite manufactured by Metagenics are both lead-free sources of calcium.

Another mineral that may be a significant importance in ADHD is Chromium. Studies conducted by the USDA and other organizations indicate that insufficient intake of chromium is currently very common. Inadequate levels of chromium would be especially likely in individuals who consume significant quantities of processed foods and who shun whole grains. Chromium is thought to play a vital role in the regulation of blood sugar. It is the key component, in combination with niacin and certain amino acids, in the formation of a complex molecule known as glucose tolerance factor (GTF). It is now known that GTF has strong insulin-enhancing properties, which works by helping insulin to bind with receptors located within cell membranes. If a person has inadequate stores of chromium, his or her cells will be relatively insensitive to insulin. This may tend to create a situation in which excessive amounts of insulin must be released by the pancreas following meals to prevent blood sugar from rising too high. Later on, the high level of insulin would tend to result in an excessive drop in blood sugar and symptoms typical of hypoglycemia, e.g. weakness, shakiness, sweating, rapid heartbeat, irritability or moodiness, cognitive problems, hyperactivity or lethargy. This would be especially true after sugary foods, meals that are high in carbohydrate and low in protein, or if meals are skipped altogether. The hypoglycemic effects of chromium deficiency also tend to be worsened by caffeine intake.

It has been widely recognized that children who skip breakfast or who eat inadequate protein for breakfast tend to have behavioral and learning problems. In contrast, simply giving a child a good breakfast with adequate calories and protein has been shown repeatedly in research to improve behavior and school performance. Parents of children with ADHD commonly report that their children's behavior and cognitive capabilities tend to worsen two to three hours after meals and improve again once the child has eaten. Many parents and some researchers have also observed that ADHD children experience significant deterioration in behavior and cognition after eating sugary foods.(Conners, 1986) Although lack of chromium may not be completely responsible for these problems, chromium insufficiency can certainly promote significant disturbances in blood sugar control. Chromium supplementation and avoidance of sugary foods along with the provision of frequent meals which contain an adequate balance of protein, carbohydrate and fat, can help to smooth out "roller coaster" blood sugar levels and keep the brain on an even keel.

Another mineral that is worth considering in ADHD is selenium. This is another trace element that fulfills many vital roles within the body and yet, it is very common for people to have insufficient or marginal selenium intake. Selenium is a key factor in the activation of several highly important enzymes. The majority of the body's antioxidant protection comes from antioxidant enzymes generated within cells. The most important of these antioxidant enzymes is a selenium dependent enzyme known as glutathione peroxidase. If the body's selenium levels are inadequate, glutathione peroxidase activity will be markedly diminished. This causes the body to be highly susceptible to oxidative damage and leaves organs, like the brain, highly vulnerable to toxic stress.

Selenium also plays a major role in thyroid function. The thyroid gland primarily produces a relatively inactive hormone called T4. In order for T4 to become active it has to be converted in the liver and other cells of the body to an active hormone called T3. This conversion requires an enzyme called 5' deiodinase, which depends upon selenium for its activity. If a person has inadequate levels of selenium, the thyroid may function perfectly and release adequate quantities of T4 but the activation of T4 to T3 may be very inefficient. Since T3 is very difficult to accurately measure, this subtle thyroid problem will usually go completely undetected. It has been suggested for years that subtle thyroid problems may play a role in ADHD since inadequate T3 activity may result in profound diminishing of brain function. Ensuring adequate selenium intake is a harmless intervention that may help to avoid subtle thyroid problems.

Another important reason to be sure selenium intake is adequate has to do with the relationship between selenium and mercury. (Goyer, 1997) Within the body, the toxic metal mercury chemically competes with selenium. Mercury and selenium are quite similar chemically and they bind to similar sites on sulfur rich proteins. In essence, what this means, is that those who are selenium deficient are also highly susceptible to accumulation of toxic mercury. Similarly, those who have significant accumulations of toxic mercury will also suffer from diminished activity of selenium dependent enzymes. This means that mercury decreases the activity of the important antioxidant enzyme glutathione peroxidase, which leaves an individual highly susceptible to oxidative stress. As well, mercury toxic individuals will have decreased activity of the enzyme 5' deiodinase, which is used to convert the relatively inactive thyroid hormone T4 to the active thyroid hormone T3. Since mercury is such a potent neurotoxin, ensuring adequate selenium intake may be one of the most important things we can do to help to protect the brain and to assist the body in the excretion of this common pollutant.

Besides the minerals mentioned thus far, several other trace elements are known to be essential for human health and may play a role in ADHD. Copper, manganese, molybdenum, nickel, vanadium and cobalt are examples of metals that are known to be essential in trace quantities. Overall, the most important way to ensure an adequate intake of nutritional trace minerals is to eat a whole foods diet with plenty of whole grains, fruits and vegetables. Eating organically grown produce will help to reduce an individual's exposure to pesticides and herbicides. In addition, since organic farming requires the use of rich, natural fertilizers, it has been shown to yield foods with higher levels of nutritional trace minerals than those derived from conventionally grown crops. Although seaweeds are not a usual part of the North American diet, they are a rich source of trace elements and should be included in the diet if possible. If hidden in foods like soups, their unusual taste can be well masked. It is probably also prudent for those with ADHD to consider taking a good multi-vitamin with trace minerals supplement. Care should be exercised to ensure that the multi-vitamin and mineral supplement contains adequate quantities of the desired minerals in a highly absorbable form and it should supply an adequate quantity of B vitamins as well. Children should generally take a multi-vitamin with trace minerals supplement that contains iron whereas an adult's should be iron-free. Suitable multivitamins should be free of common allergens, artificial colorings, artificial flavors and artificial sweeteners. There is an extremely wide range of quality when it comes to multivitamins with trace minerals. It is wise to consult with your Functional Medicine practitioner for suggestions regarding the choice of a good multi-vitamin with trace minerals. Since calcium and magnesium are required in very high quantities, these additional supplements should be taken separately.

In general, is not wise to use colloidal mineral supplements instead of more conventional products. Colloidal mineral supplements are usually derived from either clays or from salt waters. Many of these have been shown to contain high amounts of aluminum and measurable quantities of other toxic metals. The premise behind these supplements is the suggestion that humans require trace quantities of dozens of very obscure elements such as strontium, and uranium. Evidence supporting the need for most of these rare elements is currently lacking and there are significant reasons to believe that colloidal mineral supplements may lead to an accumulation of toxic metals over time while providing insufficient quantities of the known essential minerals.

THE IMPORTANCE OF PHYTOCHEMICALS

Vitamins and minerals are all absolutely essential to the function of the body. Severe deficiencies of any vitamin or necessary trace mineral will cause serious illness. On the other hand, it is now recognized that there are thousands of naturally occurring chemicals from plants which are not absolutely essential and yet contribute greatly to optimal health and human performance. In fact, it is becoming increasingly clear that good health simply cannot be maintained without an adequate quantity and variety of phytochemicals.

One important group of natural plant chemicals or phytochemicals is the carotenoids. These plant pigments give color to many plants like orange and yellow vegetables. Carotenoids are classified as pro-vitamins. This means that they are not vitamins but they can be used by the body to manufacture a vitamin. In this case vitamin A can be manufactured from carotenoids. In addition, carotenoids have diverse antioxidant effects within the body and thus help protect against free radical or oxidation damage. Like all antioxidants, carotenoids do not work efficiently by themselves but should be used instead in combination with other antioxidants such as vitamin C, vitamin E, and bioflavonoids. Adults and children should be able to get plenty of carotenoids by eating colorful vegetables such as carrots, squash and sweet potatoes.

Another group of phytochemicals, which have already been mentioned, is the bioflavonoids. This is a vast family of chemicals with several thousand different forms now identified. Plants use bioflavonoids for their own purposes. Some bioflavonoids are natural insecticides while others are natural insect repellents. Bioflavonoids may also have significant antibacterial, antifungal or antiprotozoal properties, thus protecting the plant from infection. However, bioflavonoids have gained great fame for their potent and diverse antioxidant capabilities. It is probably the antioxidant properties of bioflavonoids that allow certain plant species to live for extraordinary periods of time. One example of this is the Ginkgo biloba tree, which contains hundreds of powerful antioxidant bioflavonoids. This is likely why the Ginkgo tree can resist aging and live over two thousand years. Humans cannot produce their own bioflavonoids and must consume these phytochemicals to obtain their benefits. Fortunately, most plant-derived bioflavonoids are free of toxicity and can be safely ingested by humans. Eating a wide variety of fruits, vegetables, herbs and spices will ensure that a person consumes significant quantities of bioflavonoids. Green tea has achieved the status of a medicinal wonder of late because of the wealth of research now demonstrating the healing power of its bioflavonoids and other components. In some cases, standardized herbal extracts are taken to obtain the benefits of certain medicinal bioflavonoids. For example, milk thistle extract contains bioflavonoids that provide antioxidant protection for the liver, assisting with detoxification. Turmeric, rosemary and ginger contain bioflavonoids with potent antioxidant and anti-inflammatory properties. In ADHD, bioflavonoids may be useful in providing antioxidant protection to the brain. Ginkgo biloba extract, grape seed extract and pine bark extract (Pycnogenol) all contain bioflavonoids that readily enter the brain and provide significant antioxidant protection.

Many other important phytochemicals can be found in the plant world. Chlorophyll, the green pigment in plants, is being increasingly recognized in research as an important phytochemical, having antioxidant effects and assisting in the removal of heavy metals by binding them within the gastrointestinal tract. Sulfur containing compounds found within vegetables of the cabbage family (cruciferous vegetables) are being recognized as extremely important phytochemicals. Cabbage, cauliflower, broccoli, Brussels sprouts, kale and kohlrabi all contain sulfur-rich phytochemicals that greatly assist the liver in its role as our major detoxifying organ. Since ADHD may be related, at least in part, to impaired detoxification, eating cruciferous vegetables as often as possible may be of great benefit and may reduce the risk of other diseases such as cancer over the long-term.

Carbohydrates are a group of phytochemicals, which have been proving to have a diverse array of medicinal benefits. Carbohydrates like sugar and starch are of course digested, absorbed and used by the body for energy. On the other hand, dietary fiber is composed of various types of carbohydrate, which the body cannot digest and absorb. Fiber has numerous important benefits for the digestive system and other parts of the body. Fiber will be discussed at more length in an upcoming chapter.

Oligosacharides are a special class of carbohydrates composed of short chains of rare and unusual sugars such as rhamnose, fucose, xylose and mannose. These interesting phytochemicals are particularly important in the function of the immune system. If certain oligosacharides are added to the diet, the immune system can become remarkably energized and it can fight infection with much greater efficiency. Oligosacharides exist to some extent in a many plants and vegetable foods. Certain extracts of the aloe vera plant, for example, contain abundant immune stimulating oligosacharides, which have been proven to be useful in several applications. Our facility has been involved in research looking at the effectiveness of an oligosacharide preparation, which was discovered at the University of Alberta in Canada. This extract, which is commercially known as Cold FX, is a concentrated oligosacharide preparation obtained from the root of the American ginseng plant. Cold-FX may very well be the most potent immune stimulating substance ever discovered. Research at University of Alberta has demonstrated that Cold-FX is actually 20 times more potent as an immune stimulant than Echinacea. Cold-FX appears to be particularly helpful in the prevention and treatment of respiratory infections like colds and influenza, and it shows promise as an agent to improve the function of the immune system of the gastrointestinal tract. Both of these applications may be of great importance in the treatment of ADHD since, as will be clarified in chapters 13 and 22, immunological problems play a significant role in this condition.

Each year, the list of important phytochemicals being recognized by researchers is growing remarkably. It is now quite clear that an adequate intake of phytochemicals is one of the most important factors in the maintenance of good health. Those with ADHD especially need an adequate quantity and variety of phytochemicals in their diet. Increasing the intake of both fruits and vegetables is of course the primary way to increase phytochemicals. As was stated previously, those who are seeking to increase their consumption of fruits and vegetables must also take measures to minimize their exposure to pesticides such as eating organic produce and choosing foods which are least likely to be contaminated with pesticides.

Another way to easily increase phytochemical intake is through dehydrated plant food powders, some of which are available in capsules or tasty fruit bars. Because these powders are highly concentrated versions of the original plant foods, small quantities can provide very generous quantities of phytochemicals. These powders can be easily added to smoothies without degrading the taste significantly. As long as one can get used to a smoothie with a strange green color this is certainly an easy way to increase phytochemical intake, especially in children who are very picky eaters.

SATISFYING A THIRSTY BRAIN

Perhaps no other dietary intervention is as simple and inexpensive as ensuring that an individual has an adequate intake of water. However, perhaps no other habit is as commonly neglected. Chronic, low-grade dehydration may, in fact, be one of the most widespread health risks facing our society. (Kleiner, 1999) Children with ADHD may be particularly at risk of chronic dehydration for various reasons. First of all, ADHD kids are often so busy that it is hard for them to slow down long enough to get a drink of water. They may also get so wrapped up in their play that they don't notice a gnawing sense of thirst. As well, they often have low levels of certain fatty acids in their blood and tissues.

Fatty acid deficiencies may have a significant diuretic effect upon the kidneys. This means that a child with fatty acid deficiencies can lose excessive amounts of fluid through the kidneys almost as though they were on a water pill or diuretic. Some of these kids will develop a tremendous sense of thirst and will drink copious amounts of water. In turn, the kidneys lose large amounts of fluid very rapidly and these kids can quickly become dehydrated if they don't drink enough to keep up with their fluid loss. Similarly, food allergies are associated with excessive thirst and excessive urination. These two factors may also be why these kids often wet the bed.

If dehydration occurs frequently, as it does in many kids with ADHD, the sensation of thirst can eventually become quite inefficient. Instead of feeling thirsty, many kids with ADHD will simply feel miserable when they become dehydrated. Even very minor degrees of dehydration may cause irritability, malaise, cognitive problems, lethargy or hyperactive behavior. Dehydration also causes very significant impairment of the immune system and can lead to a high degree of susceptibility to respiratory infections. As well, dehydration is one of the major causes of constipation, which is a very common accompaniment of ADHD. Finally, individuals who are chronically dehydrated will have very inefficient mechanisms for detoxifying and eliminating a wide range of toxic substances since detoxification requires optimal function of the liver, kidneys and bowel, all of which require good hydration.

Parents who have children with ADHD should be vigilant to ensure that their child learns the principles of good hydration. Firstly, they should ensure that their child drinks a good-sized glass of water upon arising each morning. In addition, it is wise to consider sending a child to school with a one-liter container of water. Insulated carrier packs for this size of bottle are now easily available. The quality of tap water from school water fountains is often marginal or poor. Recently, I was asked to speak about lead poisoning to a crowd of concerned parents and teachers after a random water sample taken from a school drinking fountain revealed levels of lead five times higher than acceptable standards. Apparently this is quite commonplace (perhaps in as many as one in three drinking fountains) and it usually results in no significant remedial measures when discovered. Sending a child to school with water from home gives parents control over the quality of the water and allows some degree of monitoring of the child's water intake. When the child returns home from school, the parent can inspect their water bottle and then make sure that they drink more water before the evening meal. The usual recommendation of six to eight glasses of water per day may be insufficient for active kids especially those who are involved in athletics or who have fatty acid insufficiencies or food allergies. Fruit juices should not be over-consumed because they add a great deal of sugar to the child's diet. Unsweetened fruit juices may be used in moderation if they are diluted with two to three times the amount of water recommended on the container. In general, it is best to use water that has been purified either through reverse osmosis, distillation or good carbon filtration.

FEEDING THE BRAIN FOR LIFE

The nutritional requirements of the brain are amazingly complex if we want our brains to function optimally. If the brain is deprived of crucial nutrients, particularly during fetal development, infancy or childhood, it can certainly help to set the stage for the development of ADHD. As well, the unique neurology of the ADHD brain tends to make it more sensitive to both toxic influences and nutritional inadequacies throughout the sufferer's life. Unfortunately, because many kids with ADHD are fussy eaters and tend to be oppositional when efforts are made to try to improve their diet, parents may become frustrated and give in to their children's tendency to remain on a nutrient poor, junk food enriched diet. In our research we have addressed the very real problem of how to improve the diet of very stubborn, junk food-loving kids, many of whom were addicted to the very foods to which they were later found to be allergic. This research proved successful and we were able to discover ways to significantly improve the nutritional status of these children and see many of these kids improve dramatically in terms of their health, behavior and school performance. One of the most important skills that children and adults with ADHD must learn is how to properly feed their own brains for life. Although all of this nutritional science may seem overly complex, my experience has convinced me that with the right tools, virtually anyone can become sophisticated enough in their knowledge of nutrition to successfully implement life enhancing dietary changes within a few weeks. Upcoming chapters will help to equip you with the knowledge to guide you through this nutritional maze.

Chapter 9

Psychosocial Factors at the Heart of ADHD

NATURE AND NURTURE

Thus far, our discussion has focused upon important physical antecedents or risk factors (genetics, toxicological influences, and nutritional factors), which may set the stage for the development of ADHD. Certainly, brain development and function may be profoundly influenced by many physical and biochemical factors. Nevertheless, social and psychological factors play an equally important role in brain development and may contribute significantly to the incidence or severity of ADHD. Neurobiological research has clearly revealed that normal brain development depends upon such factors as nurturing parental relationships as well as intellectual, social and sensory stimulation. (Joseph, 1999) It comes as no surprise that severe abuse or neglect in infancy or childhood often results in lifelong psychological or psychiatric problems. Studies have also shown that amongst those who have suffered from severe abuse there is a much higher incidence of ADHD than that found in the general population. Of course, ADHD is not always preceded by abuse or neglect. In fact, children with ADHD often come from the best of homes with some of the most dedicated and loving parents one can find. Nevertheless, there may an number of social and psychological factors, which shape the developing brain and may contribute to the neurological circuitry that is characteristic of ADHD.

SOCIAL AND PSYCHOLOGICAL NUTRITION

Proper social interaction is mandatory for normal human development to occur. The loving bond formed between an infant and its parents is like a critical nutrient, which feeds and brings order to the developing brain. (Nelson, 1998) Infants that are deprived of this vital interaction may suffer serious cognitive, behavioral and psychiatric problems. (Murray, 1996) Demonstrations of this phenomenon have been seen within understaffed orphanages in impoverished countries where infants have been left nearly unattended for months and end up severely retarded or psychiatrically afflicted. These extreme cases may also be similar to the degree of neglect experienced by some infants within homes where drug addiction or alcoholism prevails. In such circumstances, even if the infant's basic nutritional needs are met, their developing brain is essentially "malnourished" and hungering for the warmth and security of parental love.

It was explained in previous chapters that the highly developed executive centers within the frontal part of the brain are very sensitive to nutritional adequacy and to toxicological stresses. Likewise, according to animal studies, these sophisticated executive centers are also highly susceptible to deprivation of maternal affections. The creation of the maternal-infant bond is a deep and mysterious process, which begins soon after birth and is particularly apparent when the new mother breast-feeds her child. This bond continues to deepen and grow each day as the mother holds, caresses, nurses and talks to her baby. It forms a profoundly secure environment for the infant who lives protected from the hostile world within the consistent, serenity of her mother's love and provision. As the infant's reality begins to expand beyond the confines of herself, her mother and her immediate environment, the child's father and other caring individuals may also contribute to this loving brain "nourishment".

According to neuroscience research, the maternal-infant bond may provide stimulation and direction for the development of critical neuronal pathways and brain centers. The baby's first experiences of pleasure and attentiveness occur within the borders of this same loving relationship. Each time the infant stares into his mother's face, tastes her soothing milk, smells her familiar fragrance or hears her loving voice, his brain's pleasure center awakens and his executive centers are aroused simultaneously. Repeatedly, when the infant feels discomfort, the mother provides pleasurable relief from suffering. Whenever this experience occurs, neurological pathways grow stronger, connections between neurons become more abundant and critical brain regions are provoked into development. This is the time when the seeds of attentiveness, serenity and self-control are planted and nurtured to life. If this loving environment is disrupted through abuse or neglect, the effects may be significant and long lasting. In years to come, this individual may be more likely to express the symptoms associated with ADHD, anxiety disorders, depression or addiction.

Obviously, the majority of people with ADHD did not (or do not currently) suffer from severe maternal neglect. ADHD crosses all socioeconomic barriers and can be found commonly amongst individuals with loving and caring parents. Perhaps disruption of the maternal infant bond need not be as profound as would be experienced through severe abuse or neglect in order for brain development to be adversely effected. Research has demonstrated that infants who are breast-fed have less than half the risk of developing ADHD than infants who are not given this benefit. (Uauy, 1995) As we have previously discussed, breast milk has clear nutritional and immunological superiority over infant formula. However, in addition to its biochemical benefits, the process of breast-feeding may strengthen the process of maternal-infant bonding, which might, in turn, stimulate superior brain development. Other factors such as maternal depression or anxiety may also impair the process of maternal-infant bonding and may deprive the infant of necessary "psychological nutrition" during this critical period of brain development.

In his book, "Scattered Minds", Dr. Gabor Maté outlines research indicating that healthy parenting plays an important role in the development of the brain's executive centers. (Mate, 1999) According to Dr. Maté, positive emotional interactions between a child and her parents stimulate the release of reward chemicals such as dopamine and endorphins. These substances, in turn, encourage the growth of brain cells and promote vital connections between these cells. In contrast, stress hormones such as cortisol and adrenaline cause brain cells to disconnect to one another and important brain regions can actually shrink under their influence. Dr. Maté theorizes that family stresses may contribute significantly to the development of ADHD. According to his view, maternal anxiety or depression combined with the lack of a nurturing father influence is an important cause of ADHD. After working with the families of many individuals with ADHD he has noted that in such families it is common to find significant depression or anxiety in the mother coupled with a father who is demanding, aggressive and hard-driving. Although Dr. Maté does not acknowledge the tremendous importance of genetic, nutritional and toxicological contributions to ADHD, his theories and observations may add another importance piece to the ADHD puzzle.

AN ADHD BRAIN IN AN ADHD WORLD

We live in a helter-skelter world a world with fast paced, push button, instant answers for everything. Most people's days are so packed with activities and responsibilities that there just isn't enough time for everything. Today's businesses and organizations are lean and mean. Everyone has to do the work of three people and spare time is at an all time premium. On top of this, job security is a foreign concept to more and more people, as mergers, downsizing and cutbacks seem to dominate the workplace. Society as a whole is becoming fragmented as extended families become a distant memory and marriages tend to be a modern day battleground. In the midst of this whirlwind life, children often get brushed aside for "more important" matters. The typical child of today experiences meaningful interaction with her parents for just a few seconds each day. If family and social factors have any bearing upon brain development then it is little wonder that the incidence and severity of ADHD is growing explosively. In a sense, our society has ADHD and there is little indication that this trend will abate anytime soon.

STABILITY IN AN UNSTABLE WORLD

In many ways ADHD traits are promoted and encouraged by society. We live in a world where violence is glamorized by Hollywood, where people who risk their lives in extreme sports or their financial futures in risky businesses are heroes and where traditional family and spiritual values are scorned by the media. In our hectic world, busy parents may gradually feel that they are having little influence on their child's development. In more and more families, it seems clear that the primary forces working to shape the character and personality of children are external, artificial and market driven. Rock musicians, TV and movie stars, as well as peer pressure play an increasingly important role in child development as the influence of the family becomes less and less. Children with ADHD may gravitate to these potentially negative influences in order to compensate for areas which are weak or lacking in their own personality and character. For instance, a child with ADHD, and perhaps aggressive tendencies and low self-esteem, may strongly identify with violent television heroes and may develop and socially exploit his aggression. By becoming a school bully, he may gain self-esteem and may be regarded by his peers as a leader. However, if this characteristic is not reshaped and properly channeled through positive parental influence, this child is more likely to eventually end up in serious trouble with the law. In many other ways, parents may play a vital role in influencing whether their child's ADHD characteristics are minimized and properly channeled or maximized to become life destructive traits.

SCULPTING THE SOUL OF A CHILD

Parents can have a tremendous impact upon the "shape" of a child's character and personality. As described previously, the maternal-infant bond may play an immense role in the development of brain circuitry related to ADHD. Beyond infancy, both parents act as "sculptors of the soul". Wise parents will cherish this role and will expend considerable effort to impart positive traits to their child through a warm, and nurturing parent-child relationship. Parents also must set up clear borders of acceptable child behavior and develop reasonable and effective disciplinary strategies to help their child learn to live within the safe confines of these behavioral borders. Parents who choose not to expend this effort or who are unskilled in the process of positively sculpting a personality are knowingly or unknowingly handing over the sculpting process to the child's peers, advertising agencies and the entertainment industry. Children with ADHD may be especially sensitive to the shaping influence of the parent-child relationship. Although parental influences may not be able to create or prevent ADHD, such influences at least have a tremendous effect on the outcome of the disorder.

EFFECTIVE PARENTING AND THE ADHD CHILD

Societal changes have certainly contributed to changes in the structure of the family and the role of parents in today's children. According to the 1999 report of the Federal Interagency Forum on Child and Family Statistics, the percentage of children living with two parents has declined from 77 percent in 1980 to 68 percent in 1996. (www.ChildStats.gov) This certainly places a tremendous strain on the parent who must be both the primary breadwinner as well as the primary caregiver and likely is a contributing factor to the rise in prescriptions for ADHD. Such changes, along with increasing numbers of families in which both parents work full time have certainly given parents less time with their children and less ability to devote energies into effective parenting.

Parents under increased time and financial pressure are less likely to be effective in providing what is generally considered to be important parental contributions to a child's development. Traditionally parents have played a primary role in helping their children with goal setting and encouraging them to develop important skills. Parents have also been the most important influence, which enables a child to understand and respect rules, orderliness and politeness. Parents have traditionally been the primary force in promoting work values balanced with the need for appropriate recreation. They have also imparted moral and spiritual values into their child's life. The busier and more stressed parents become, the less likely they will be able to effectively convey these important life skills to their child. Since the stability of our culture has rested upon the foundation of the family, it is little wonder that we are now beginning to see the adverse impact of weakened families on our society. The role of parents, as a whole, has substantially changed in the last few years. It is probably not just a coincidence that the apparent incidence of ADHD has risen in parallel with these changes.

In some cases, having a child with ADHD is a wake up call to parents that their child needs to become a greater priority in their lives. The program outlined in this book is certainly not a "quick fix" approach and will require considerable study, time and, to some extent, a reallocation of financial resources – all invested in the ADHD child. Many parents who have decided to get to the bottom of their child's ADHD, and to find better and more lasting solutions to their problems than drugs, have found that the extra time and effort that they must invest in their child has an unexpected side benefit – greatly improved bonding with their child. Our family has certainly experienced this. Because my son has ADHD, I have been motivated to pour so much more of my life into him than I probably ever would have. We home school both of our children and I spend a good deal of my spare time with my son. Over the past two years, we have become great friends and we really enjoy the time we spend together. I have also helped him to become a champion bike racer and have shared the enjoyment of his personal victories over what could have been a serious disability. If my boy had not been recognized as having ADHD, I may have stayed on the sidelines of his life and watched him grow up from a distance as I furiously pursued my own goals and dreams. What started out as a curse has now, in many ways, become a blessing for our family. I am aware of many families who have similarly been brought closer together by taking a very proactive and positive approach to their struggles with ADHD.

Sick Cells, Sick Molecules, Sick Brains
(Physiological Triggers of ADHD)

Taking on Too Many Projects
Self Destructive Behaviors
Tardiness   Addictions
Forgetfulness
Personality Problems
Troubled Relationships
Diminished Self Esteem
Aggression   Psychological Disorders
Many Unfinished Projects
Procrastination
Perfectionism
Risk Taking Behaviors   Chronic Anxiety
Difficulty Starting Projects
Antisocial Behavior
Extreme Moodiness
Self Medication
Trouble with the Law

Impulsivity
Inattention
Hyperactivity

SIGNS AND SYMPTOMS

Brain Neurotransmitter Dysfunction

Brain Structural Problems

Immune Modulators, Neuropeptides and Neurotoxins

Critical Nutrient Insufficiencies

MEDIATORS (Biochemical Effects)

Impaired:
Digestion,
Absorption,
Liver Detoxification,
Blood Sugar Regulation

"Leaky Gut"
Environmental Allergies
Food Allergies/Intolerances
Chronic or Recurrent Infections
Loss of normal gut flora
Immune System Impairment

Intestinal Dysbiosis:
Parasites,
Bacteria,
Fungi

TRIGGERS (Resulting Physical Problems)

Environmental Toxins,
Brain Injury

Genetic Predisposition

Nutritional Insufficiencies

Abuse, Neglect Or Family Stresses

ANTECEDENTS (Underlying Risk Factors)

Chapter 10

The Gut-Brain Connection

INTIMATE CONNECTIONS BETWEEN THE BRAIN AND IMMUNE SYSTEM

Science is continuing to reveal how different organs and systems of the body are intimately connected together in fascinating and complex ways. A vast amount of information flows continuously through the body to regulate thousands of physiological functions. Although the brain and nervous system form the primary basis for this vast communications network, other systems contribute greatly to the information flow. In particular, the immune system functions like a "mobile nervous system", forming a vital component of the body's vast communications infrastructure.

The nervous system is primarily able to sense physical stimuli such as temperature or pressure and then transmit that information to the brain and other parts of the nervous system. The immune system, on the other hand, is able to sense and identify specific molecules, toxins or hostile cells and then communicate this data to the rest of the body by the release of information-containing molecules. In fact, the immune and nervous systems form a highly integrated and inseparable communications and defense network.

Research over the last few years has demonstrated that the immune and nervous systems continuously "speak" to each other back and forth through nervous impulses and the release of information molecules. (Pert, 1985) For example, neurotransmitters are molecules released by nerve endings, which communicate information to other nerve cells. Interestingly, receptors for every neurotransmitter can be found on the membranes of both nerve cells and immune cells. This suggests that anything "said" by the nervous system is "heard" by both the nervous and immune systems simultaneously. Likewise, receptors for the wide range of information molecules released by immune cells can be found on the membranes of both immune and nerve cells. This is part of the evidence demonstrating that when the immune system "speaks" the nervous system "listens".

The close and fascinating partnership between the immune and nervous systems can be seen in other ways. Precious and long-lived neurons of the brain live in intimate proximity to immune cells called microglia. Billions of these microglia inhabit the brain — each one living its life dedicated to the care and protection of a cherished brain cell. When events occur which threaten the health of the brain, microglial cells may be transformed into aggressive defenders ready to give their life to protect the beloved brain cells.

For example, when a person becomes infected with the "flu" virus, immune cells throughout the body sense the presence of the virus and release "alarm molecules" into the bloodstream. These alarm molecules (known as cytokines) speak to every other cell in the immune system alerting these cells to the presence of a potentially deadly virus. Even though the flu virus may never physically enter the brain, circulating cytokines cross the blood brain barrier screaming to the network of microglial cells, "EMERGENCY! EMERGENCY!" Then the microglial cells respond to this chemical message by releasing substances that serve to protect the brain cells from infection. These substances may include hydrogen peroxide, which functions to oxidize any virus in the area. Angry microglial cells may also release nitric oxide (NO), which will markedly decrease the metabolism of the adjacent brain cells placing them into a kind of protective hibernation state. All of these activities may significantly reduce the chance of a brain cell becoming infected with the flu virus. However, these immune system processes may markedly impact brain function resulting in a sense of "brain fog" with poor concentration, severe drowsiness and emotional irritability. It is important to note that it is not the influenza virus itself, which creates the symptoms experienced when one has the flu. All of the unpleasant symptoms accompanying the flu are the direct result of molecules of information and inflammation, which are released by immune cells in response to the war against the invading enemy.

There are actually a multitude of events besides infection with the influenza virus, which can activate the immune system and lead to vast changes throughout the body, including the brain. Like the flu, some of these events are quite temporary and last only a few days. Others events, such as HIV infection, chronic allergy or toxin exposure may go on for weeks, months or years. This may result in chronic changes within the immune system including the persistent over activation of the brain's own microglial immune cell network. In turn, chronic over activation of microglial immune cells leads to a marked increase in oxidative stress in the brain and altered brain metabolism. This phenomenon has been seen by prominent brain researchers to play a central role in many chronic neurodegenerative disorders such as Alzheimer's disease and Parkinson's disease. Over activation of the brain's immune cells may also contribute significantly to the changes in brain function seen in ADHD, chronic fatigue syndrome and other brain-related disorders.

INTIMATE CONNECTIONS BETWEEN THE DIGESTIVE AND IMMUNE SYSTEMS

Most people probably think that the immune system is composed primarily of white blood cells circulating around within the bloodstream. In fact, this is not the case. The majority of the immune system's cells are strategically located within tissues and organs. Some of these cells are stationed in one location throughout their whole lifetime, whereas other immune cells spend their life roaming about in certain regions, traveling wherever other immune cells command them to go. Even those immune cells that are official members of the bloodstream spend the majority of their life clinging tightly to the walls of blood vessels only entering circulation when an emergency command is given from other cells of the immune system. Even after this, they often circulate only briefly as they quickly penetrate into injured, infected or inflamed tissues where they carry out whatever work they are instructed to perform.

One of the most interesting facts about the immune system is that the majority of its cellular population (60 to 70 percent by weight) is located in and directly around the digestive system. This clearly reflects the immense importance of the immune system's relationship to the gastrointestinal tract. Not only are there vast numbers of immune cells associated with the digestive tract — this is also the most complex and organized collection of immune cells within the body. This population of specialized cells (known as the gut associated lymphoid tissue or GALT) is currently the focus of attention in hundreds of research labs around the world. Over the past few years, evidence has rapidly accumulated indicating that the GALT may play a central role in numerous disease processes. Recent research carried out in our facility strongly suggests that disruption in the normal function of the GALT may be of critical importance in the majority of children with ADHD.

IMMUNE CELLS SPEAK TO OTHER IMMUNE CELLS THROUGH

"MOLECULES OF INFORMATION"

Numerous mechanisms have been proposed in the scientific literature to explain how disturbances in gastrointestinal function could have an adverse influence upon brain function; in other words, how there could be a "gut-brain connection". Many of these mechanisms have gained strong support through clinical and experimental research. One of the most well understood mechanisms for a gut-brain connection begins with an over activation of the gut associated lymphoid tissue (GALT). Although the GALT is busy all the time, it can become over activated, or inflamed under several circumstances. For instance, when the intestine becomes infected with a parasite (like Giardia) or bacteria (like certain strains of E. coli), the GALT becomes activated and it goes into a state of high alert. Alarm substances, with names like tumor necrosis factor, interleukin-1, histamine and bradykinin, are then released from GALT cells and begin to circulate locally and throughout the body. Locally, these molecules of information speak to other GALT cells commanding them to join the battle. In other parts of the body, these circulating alarm substances warn immune cells of impending danger and command them to go into a state of high alert. In the brain, microglial cells hear the message being shouted from the GALT and they turn their attention from nourishment and repair of brain cells to angrily defending neurons against infection through the production of substances of inflammation such as hydrogen peroxide and nitric oxide (NO). In the short-term, this angry response of the microglia to messages coming from the GALT may be highly appropriate and may even prevent a devastating brain infection. However, if the intestinal infection persists, the GALT will continue to release alarm substances, which, in turn, over activate the microglia. This persistent over activation of microglia can adversely affect brain function and may cause significant harm to brain cells over time.

Recent research conducted at our facility was the first to demonstrate that various chronic gastrointestinal infections are indeed very common in attention deficit disorder. This research data adds credibility to the observation, made by numerous practitioners of Functional Medicine, that improving gastrointestinal function in individuals with ADHD often results in improved behavior and cognitive performance.

IMMUNE CELLS SPEAK TO NERVE CELLS

Other mechanisms have been described to explain how the GALT is involved in the gut-brain connection. As was explained before, the immune and nervous systems form a highly integrated and inseparable unit. Not only do immune cells speak to other immune cells (such as the GALT speaking to the microglia); they also speak to nerve cells through the same chemical messengers. Nerve cells, in turn, communicate to immune cells through the same molecules used to "talk" to other nerve cells. Under normal circumstances, the chemical dialog between these two integrated systems takes place throughout the body, at a rate of millions of "words" per second. Under conditions of stress, injury, infection or inflammation the chemical dialog between the immune and nervous systems changes dramatically in "loudness", and "emotional content".

When the GALT is activated by infection, allergy or stress, the same chemical messengers that activate the brain's microglial cells also have direct effects upon brain neurons. As well, information molecules released from the GALT can directly affect billions of nerve endings that reside within the tissues of the gastrointestinal tract.(Theodorou, 1996)

These nerves belong to a two-directional system of communication between the brain and internal organs known as the autonomic nervous system. When chemical messengers coming from the GALT stimulate certain autonomic nerve endings, signals are carried back to the spinal cord and brain, which may then translate into sensation, emotion or changes in various aspects of brain function. In turn, signals may return to the gastrointestinal tract through the autonomic nervous system, which may significantly alter digestive system function. (Weingarten, 1996)

NERVE CELLS SPEAK TO OTHER NERVE CELLS THROUGH MOLECULES OF EMOTION

One of the biggest surprises to emerge from medical research over the last few decades involves the discovery of chemicals naturally produced within the body, which have properties very much like commonly prescribed drugs. Many nerve cells and certain immune cells manufacture and release a class of molecules called neuropeptides (peptides are tiny bits of protein). One of these neuropeptides, known as beta-endorphin, is a natural painkiller with a potency fifty times that of morphine. This mysterious neuropeptide is released during times of stress or trauma and it helps to ease the pain, suffering and mental anguish associated with such events. Many people may recall the strange, dreamlike calm and the unexplainable lack of pain, which accompanied the first minutes or hours following a serious accident. This phenomenon probably occurs because of the sudden release of high levels of endorphins following the accident. Nerve cells may release a variety of "molecules of emotion" during other circumstances or within certain disease states. For instance, a peptide called substance-P can be found at high levels in the blood of individuals suffering from chronic pain. Unlike beta-endorphin, which decreases pain, substance-P greatly increases the sensation of pain. There is also a naturally occurring molecule produced by the human body which acts like Valium, and another which has effects identical to the street drug PCP or "angel dust". Clearly, these molecules of emotion serve important purposes in the body when they are present at the appropriate times and in the appropriate quantities. Unfortunately, the symptoms of many disease states may exist, at least in part, because of an imbalance in some of these critical chemical messengers.

FOOD AS A SOURCE OF INFORMATION

Everyone knows that food is a source of energy for the body. It is also common knowledge that the body uses food for the growth and repair of cells and organs. Science is now just beginning to recognize another important function of our food — the provision of information. As strange and fascinating as it sounds, after every meal, our food "speaks" to our digestive, immune and nervous systems with a complex dialog of molecular words. When you eat food derived from soybeans, specific molecules are absorbed which communicate to your liver cells telling them to decrease their production of cholesterol. This is a case where food provides energy, structural building blocks as well as information, which the body then translates into instructions to carry out specific functions. Information is, in fact, contained within virtually every food that we eat. Some of the messages in food speak loud and clear to our cells, whereas other messages may only be heard under certain circumstances. For instance, when cow's milk is partially digested, the proteins in the milk are broken down into smaller molecules known as peptides. Several of these peptides, known as casomorphins, have potent morphine-like properties. (Teschemacher, 1991) If casomorphins are directly injected into the bloodstream they can have a wide range of effects including lethargy, problems with memory and concentration as well as mood and behavioral changes.

Fortunately, in adults and children after the age of weaning, the healthy intestinal tract doesn't allow casomorphins to readily pass through into the bloodstream. Within the normal small intestine, protein digestion proceeds until these morphine-like peptides are fully digested into tiny amino acids. The healthy intestinal tract then absorbs the amino acids, which are subsequently used for energy as well as for the growth and repair of tissues and organs. In contrast, the normal intestinal tract of the infant is highly permeable (leaky) to larger molecules such as casomorphins. In other words it is quite normal for an infant to have a leaky gut. The primary purpose of a leaky gut in an infant is so that important molecules contained in the mother's milk can readily cross over into the infant's bloodstream before being digested. This means that when infants ingest milk, they may absorb significant quantities of morphine-like peptides such as casomorphins. There is actually a purpose to this strange phenomenon. Milk may naturally contain these mysterious molecules of information to promote infantile behavior and cognitive patterns where such behaviors are normal and desirable. Casomorphins may have a wide range of physiological and psychological effects, which are completely appropriate for the infant but quite undesirable at later stages of development. (Reichelt, 1996; Reichelt, 1994)

Many other information-containing molecules are now known to exist in all kinds of foods. (Schick, 1985) Most of these molecules are able to issue orders to the cells through drug-like, or hormone-like effects. For example, the partial digestion of wheat gluten (the main protein in wheat) results in the production of peptides with strong morphine-like activity. Many of these informational molecules are completely inactivated by the digestive process and do not end up in the bloodstream to carry on a "molecular dialog" with the body. However, if a child or adult suffers from inefficient protein digestion, or if the lining of their intestine has become damaged in some way, large quantities of food-derived, biologically active molecules may be inappropriately absorbed and may carry undesirable messages into the body.

ADHD AND THE "LEAKY GUT SYNDROME"

For several years it has been suspected that abnormal intestinal permeability (or leaky gut) may play a significant role as a causative factor in autism. (Reichelt, 1994) Research has repeatedly demonstrated that autistic children have high amounts of neurologically active peptides (protein fragments) in their blood, urine and cerebrospinal fluid. Studies have also shown that a high percentage of autistic children have a leaky gut. (D'Eufemia, 1996) Recently, it has also been found that autistic kids suffer from inefficient digestion of protein within their intestinal tract. The combination of poor protein digestion and a leaky gut may be the primary reason why these kids suffer from the effects of high amounts of neurologically debilitating morphine-like peptides.

Until recently, it was not known if children with ADHD shared any of these factors with autistic kids. Our research organization in cooperation with researchers from the Institute for Functional Medicine In Gig Harbor Washington, performed intestinal permeability testing on 66 children with ADHD. None of the children in this study had known gastrointestinal disorders. In spite of this, we were surprised to discover that 74 percent of these kids had increased intestinal permeability (leaky gut). This data strongly suggests that the majority of children with ADHD suffer from significant problems with gastrointestinal function and that these abnormalities may contribute significantly to their behavioral and cognitive problems. Children with a leaky gut, especially those consuming wheat (and perhaps other glutinous grains) and/or dairy products, will likely be absorbing significant quantities of neurologically active peptides which, in turn, affect brain function. I have recently learned, through personal communication, that researchers in England have accumulated data on large numbers of children with ADHD demonstrating that these kids, like autistic kids, have high amounts of neuropeptides in their urine. This provides further evidence of a significant gut-brain connection in ADHD.

THE NORMAL STRUCTURE OF THE SMALL INTESTINE

The small intestine is an amazingly complex organ with an immensely important role to play in the maintenance of health. This 20-foot long, multilayered tube has an inner surface so folded and complex that, if it were flattened out, its surface area would be equal to the square footage of two tennis courts. To the naked eye, the inner surface of the small intestine appears to be covered with small folds like the pleats in a curtain. Closer inspection with a magnifying glass would reveal a surface made up of countless millions of tiny finger-like projections known as villi. If a sample of these villi were placed under a microscope one would see that the surface of the villi are completely covered with a single layer of rectangular cells whose outer surfaces are covered by a layer of tiny projections called microvilli. These folds within folds, are what give the small intestine such a massive surface area for absorption of nutrients.

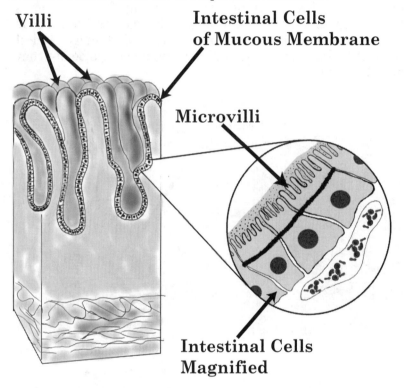

Villi

Intestinal Cells of Mucous Membrane

Microvilli

Intestinal Cells Magnified

A layer of cells called the mucous membrane forms almost the entire lining of the small intestine. The healthy mucous membrane is thinner than a sheet of cellophane, and yet, is virtually leak proof.

Each cellular member of the mucous membrane is glued to its neighbors by a thin belt called a tight junction. The leak proof nature of the mucous membrane is maintained largely by the integrity of these tight junctions. The intestinal cells expend a great deal of their energy in the maintenance of their tight junctions.

Another critical component of the small intestine's mucous membrane is a thin layer of mucous covering every cell. Within this mucous exists a variety of friendly bacteria with names like Lactobacillus acidophilus, Lactobacillus casei, and Lactobacillus rhamnosus. This living mucous layer is like the grass on the side of a hill; it protects the mucous membrane from infection, from chemical damage and it helps it to digest, process and identify molecules before they are absorbed.

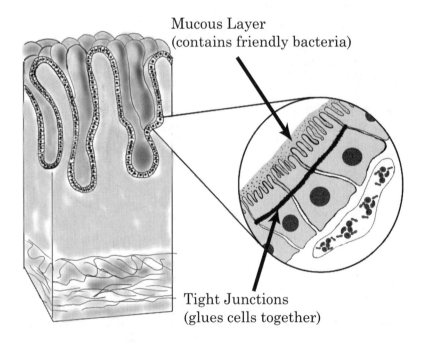

Mucous Layer
(contains friendly bacteria)

Tight Junctions
(glues cells together)

Mucous membrane cells are some of the busiest and most energetic cells of the body. They also face the most hostile environment of any cell in the body because they have to deal with stomach acid, digestive enzymes, a variety of microbes, food contaminants, and potentially hostile molecules. This may be why the small intestinal cells have the shortest lifespan of any other cells — none of them live any longer than three days. If stress on immune cells is too great, tight junctions will begin to break, and intestinal permeability increases, resulting in a leaky gut. Large molecules or even whole microbes will begin to pass through the openings between damaged cells. As well, a leaky gut is often accompanied by overgrowth of unfriendly microbes and damage to microvilli. Each of these changes brings problems of their own and causes further stress on the already stressed intestinal cells.

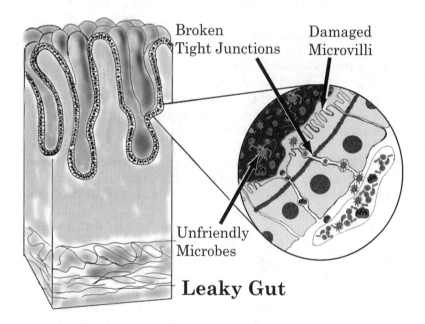

Broken Tight Junctions

Damaged Microvilli

Unfriendly Microbes

Leaky Gut

Interestingly, imbedded every few millimeters in this mucous membrane, a tiny collection of immune cells can be found peering into the inside of the intestine. These little groups of cells act like millions of eyes and ears for the immune system. More precisely, these immune cells form an advanced surveillance system which samples billions of molecules per second and then carries on a dialog with the components of the immune and nervous systems embedded within the deeper layers of the intestine. If these immune sensors detect danger in the form of disease-causing microbes, food allergens or chemical irritants, alarm molecules are released which alert the immune and nervous systems of impending danger.

WHAT CAUSES INCREASED INTESTINAL PERMEABILITY?

The cells of the small intestine's mucous membrane are almost constantly under some degree of stress from a variety of factors. Proper nourishment of the intestinal cells and a relative absence of irritating factors, along with a healthy mucous layer populated with plenty of friendly bacteria, are the primary first lines of defense against damage to the leak proof lining of the intestine. As well, under normal circumstances, the immune system of the gut (the GALT) constantly surveys the internal environment of intestine and provides defensive forces against invasion by hostile microbes or undesirable molecules. Many factors may weaken or overly stress the intestinal mucous membrane and can lead to a leaky gut:

- Deficiency or relative insufficiency of nutrients that are critical in the proper function of intestinal cells can lead to a weakening of intestinal cell function. This, in turn, can lead to breakage of tight junctions — the regions around the middle of cells that glue the intestinal cells together. If enough of these tight junctions are broken, gaps open up between cells and a leaky gut is the result.

The number one nutrient of the small intestinal cells is the amino acid (protein building block) known as L-glutamine. Most research suggests that the small intestinal cells use L-glutamine as their primary source of energy instead of the sugars or fatty acids used by most other cells. This important amino acid is found to some extent in nearly all proteins and it is released into the intestine during efficient protein digestion. (It is important to note that monosodium glutamate (MSG) is, in no way, a suitable replacement for L-glutamine.) For therapeutic purposes, L-glutamine may be prescribed in various forms to promote the healing of a leaky gut. This nutrient is found in especially high quantities in proteins derived from rice. The UltraClear™ line of products (sold in healthcare practitioners' offices and distributed by Metagenics) are easily digestible, low allergy-potential medical foods made from a base of rice protein with numerous other nutrients added. Functional Medicine practitioners often prescribe UltraClear™ products (or Ultracare for Kids™) to improve digestive function and to aid in the healing of a leaky gut.

Several other nutrients are also important in the function of intestinal cells as well as cells of the gut associated lymphoid tissue or GALT. These nutrients include certain essential fatty acids (omega-3 and omega-6), zinc, certain B vitamins (particularly, pantothenic acid) and various antioxidants (vitamin C, vitamin A, and vitamin E).

Overall, nutritional inadequacy is probably a very common contributing factor to the development of a leaky gut in many people. Children, adolescents or adults who are picky eaters, frequently skip meals or routinely consume foods which are largely "empty calories" (junk foods, snack foods or fast foods), probably do not consistently provide their intestinal cells with adequate quantities of the nutrients required to prevent a leaky gut.

- Food allergies or intolerances can be a significant source of irritation to the intestinal mucous membrane. This may, in fact, be the most common cause of a leaky gut, especially in children. Food allergies and other adverse food reactions will be covered fully in the next chapter.

- Direct or indirect damage to the intestinal mucous membrane can occur following the ingestion of various drugs and toxins.

Alcohol, cortisone (and cortisone derivative drugs), aspirin and related anti-inflammatory drugs such as ibuprofen, are all well-known causes of a leaky gut.

Antibiotics can quickly destroy the friendly bacteria living within the mucous layer and can promote the growth of toxic or aggressive bacteria and yeast organisms. Studies have shown that a leaky gut can develop very rapidly after the ingestion of an antibiotic. Individuals with ADHD often have a history that includes repeated courses of antibiotics for ear infections or other problems.

- Common food contaminants such as pesticides, herbicides and heavy metals may all contribute to the biochemical stresses, which can lead to a leaky gut.

- Intestinal infection or overgrowth of certain parasites, bacteria, yeasts or viruses can cause significant harm to the delicate intestinal mucous membrane. Microorganisms produce a wide range of toxins, some of which directly injure or impair the function of intestinal cells. Other microbial byproducts may be toxic to the immune system or may provoke a significant inflammatory reaction. In all such cases, a leaky gut may be the result and it may only be possible to repair the gut when the undesirable microbes are reduced or eradicated.

- Severe stresses such as starvation, extremes of physical exertion, surgery, extensive burns, and significant trauma can all seriously weaken intestinal cells and lead to a leaky gut.

- Diseases of the intestine such as celiac disease or Crohn's disease lead to a state of chronic inflammation within the intestinal mucous membrane and are often accompanied by a leaky gut.

All of the above factors are highly stressful to the intestinal cells and will often lead to a widespread breakdown of the tight junctions which glue the cells together as a leak proof layer. Wherever tight junctions are broken, gaps will open up between the cells. These gaps allow massive molecules, fragments from microorganisms, and in some cases, even whole living microbes to cross the mucous membrane of the small intestine. This undigested debris poses a tremendous challenge to the immune systems of the gut (gut associated lymphoid tissue or GALT) and can lead to numerous adverse effects.

WHAT ARE THE EFFECTS OF A LEAKY GUT?

From a microscopic and biochemical point of view, the world within the intestine is potentially very hostile. Trillions of living microorganisms thrive within the gastrointestinal tract, most of which would cause speedy death if they gained entry and began to multiply within the bloodstream.

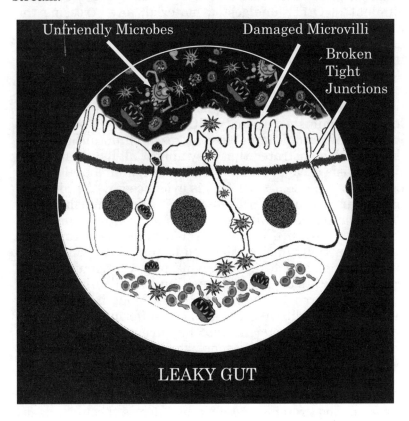

As well, undigested food is potentially toxic to the body. If you were to liquefy the healthiest lunch in a blender and then proceeded to inject this liquid lunch into your bloodstream, your immune system would react so violently that you would probably be dead in minutes. The thorough digestion of food into its most basic biochemical components is absolutely essential before the body can derive benefits fom and not be injured by food. The mucous membrane barrier of the intestine is the first line of defense to prevent this hostile world from invading the body. In the case of a leaky gut, significant quantities of undigested or partially digested food materials inappropriately cross over the mucous membrane barrier of the small intestine. Cells of the gut associated lymphoid tissue (GALT) quickly take up some of this material, which then has to be processed, digested and eliminated. Other undigested material, after crossing the mucous membrane of a leaky gut, bypasses the GALT and ends up in the bloodstream where it is then captured by immune cells within the liver.

Apart from an overburdening of the liver's immune system, one of the other consequences of this increased workload is a diminished capacity of the liver to carry out its critical detoxification duties. Recent research on autistic children has demonstrated that they almost all have a markedly diminished capability to detoxify environmental toxins. (Edelson, 1998; Edelson, 1999) This is evidenced by the high levels of various toxins in their tissues and diminished liver detoxification capability as measured by functional liver testing. Although decreased liver detoxification capability may be partially due to inherited factors, autistic kids also commonly have a leaky gut. This may contribute significantly to a state of exhaustion within their livers. Although similar research has yet to be carried out in those with ADHD, it is highly likely that those suffering from a leaky gut will also have a significant impairment in their ability to detoxify the various poisons, which we are all exposed to on a daily basis.

Quite clearly, the passage of undigested or partially digested food proteins and microbial debris through a leaky gut can provoke an inflammatory response by the immune system. In such cases, alarm substances are released by the immune system of the gut and liver. These molecular messengers of inflammation travel throughout the body setting off alarms in the brain, nervous and immune systems. The leaky gut also gives free passage to partially digested proteins (peptides), which have drug-like effects (such as the morphine-like peptides from milk protein and wheat gluten). Although research in this area is in its infancy, there are probably a host of other drug-like proteins and peptides, which can be absorbed through a leaky gut; some of which, undoubtedly, will be shown to have significant effects upon brain function.

To complicate matters even further, many of the changes, which accompany a leaky gut, can also make the brain more permeable to large molecules like neuropeptides. Under normal circumstances, the blood vessels of the brain are relatively leak proof. The cells of these blood vessels are highly selective in what they let through into the brain. This highly specialized circulatory system is known as the blood brain barrier. The relatively leak proof nature of the blood brain barrier is a critically important mechanism to protect the brain from potentially toxic molecules. Unfortunately, some of the alarm substances (cytokines) released by angry immune cells of the gut and liver cause an inflammatory change to occur within the cells of the blood brain barrier, resulting in increased permeability or leakiness of these vital blood vessels. (Wahl, 1985; Heyman, 1994) Thus, a leaky gut involves not only the passage of increased quantities of neuropeptides and other toxins into the bloodstream but potentially also into the brain through a leaky blood brain barrier. The brain-critical omega-3 fatty acid DHA is involved in the maintenance of the normal blood brain barrier. Therefore, if deficiencies in omega-3 fatty acids (especially DHA) occur, along with a leaky gut, then the blood brain barrier is even more likely to be leaky. (Hussain, 1994) Since our recent research has demonstrated that children with ADHD have a high likelihood of suffering from both a leaky gut and decreased levels of DHA, it is quite likely that these children also suffer from the effects of increase permeability (leakiness) of their blood brain barriers. Since there is currently no test available to check for a leaky blood brain barrier we can only speculate that a leaky gut and a leaky blood brain barrier might go hand-in-hand and may both be key components of the gut-brain connection in ADHD.

Finally, a leaky gut is also evidence that other aspects of intestinal function may be compromised. Depending upon the degree of damage accompanying a leaky gut there is likely to be some degree of malabsorption as well. What this means is that individuals with a leaky gut may also experience increased difficulty in absorbing certain vital nutrients from their diet. Unfortunately, some of the nutrients most likely to be affected by malabsorption are also nutrients, which have been proven to be important factors in ADHD. The absorption of essential fatty acids, magnesium, zinc, iron, calcium, selenium, chromium and many other nutrients may be significantly impaired in the state of poor intestinal health accompanying a leaky gut. All in all, science is now providing us with strong reasons to believe that there is indeed a gut-brain connection in ADHD.

Chapter 11

Food Allergies and Other Adverse Reactions to Foods

WHAT IS OUR BODY'S NORMAL RELATIONSHIP TO FOOD?

The processes involved in the digestion and absorption of food are highly complex. Undigested or incompletely digested food is foreign to the body and it must undergo extensive processing before it can circulate and be distributed to the cells of the body without causing serious problems. All food must be disassembled, through the process of digestion, until it is composed of only the simplest building blocks. Within the intestine, protein is digested into smaller peptides and then into amino acids; carbohydrates (sugars and starches) are digested into simple sugars; and fats are digested into fatty acids. Once fully digested, these nutrients can be absorbed without provoking a war with the immune system or creating biochemical havoc. Normal digestion also liberates vitamins, minerals and other important nutrients so that they can be readily absorbed.

ANTIGENS — THE UNIVERSAL IDENTIFICATION SYSTEM

Everything we eat or drink (other than water and salt) is derived from living organisms, which are, of course, made up of cells. Every living cell contains a certain amount of protein and it is the proteins within the cell that give that cell its individuality. Proteins are large, complex molecules made of as many as several thousand amino acids joined together in a long chain. The exact sequence of amino acids in each protein will determine how the chain will bend, fold and twist until it forms a highly complex three-dimensional structure. Just like larger objects, the structure of the protein is what determines its function. A saw, a hammer and an airplane wing may all be made of metal but their size and structural differences determine their function. Similarly, in living cells, proteins carry out a multitude of functions depending on the structure of each protein.

In addition to determining its function, a protein's exact structure gives it a specific identity. Its amino acid sequence and specific three-dimensional shape is an encoded identification system, which can be interpreted by various cells such as those of the immune system. For example, skin proteins from a human, a fish, and a chicken are similar enough that they perform most of the same functions for each organism. However, each organism's skin proteins have distinctly different molecular identities. If a surgeon was to graft a piece of chicken skin onto your arm, your immune system would recognize the chicken skin proteins as foreign and a violent rejection reaction would occur.

Whole protein molecules, as well as protein breakdown products (peptides) larger than just a few amino acids, carry distinctive identities, recognizable by the immune system — sort of like a molecular bar-code system. Any protein or peptide large enough to be recognized by the immune system is known as an antigen. The immune system remembers virtually every antigen it is ever exposed to, so that by the time a person has reached adolescence, their immune system can recognize millions of different antigens. This massive molecular database also contains details about how the immune system should respond when a specific antigen is encountered.

ANTIGENS — FRIENDS OR FOES?

Certain cells of the immune system spend their whole life examining and identifying antigens within the body. Antigens belonging to the body are known as "self". It is, of course, very important that the immune system clearly recognizes self-antigens and does no harm to them. During fetal development the immature immune system must become programmed to know that anything it encounters within the fetal body is "self". One by one, the immune cells learn the identity of every self-antigen in the fetal body so that by the time an infant is born, the immune system has a permanent record of each and every antigen. Although the immune system continues to sense and identify all antigens that reside inside the body, it is now programmed to have tolerance toward all self-antigens. In the science of immunology, tolerance toward an antigen means that the immune system recognizes an antigen but has specific orders to leave it completely alone. Of course, the development and maintenance of immunological tolerance toward all proteins and peptide antigens, which rightfully belong to the body is critical for ongoing good health. If the immune

155

system attacked self-antigens instead of having tolerance towards them then damage to the body would be the natural result. Loss of tolerance to certain self-antigens results in what are called autoimmune disorders. Lupus, rheumatoid arthritis, ankylosing spondylitis, juvenile diabetes, and rheumatic fever are just a few of the hundreds of autoimmune disorders which result when the immune system loses tolerance towards self-antigens and begins to attack body proteins as though they were hostile invaders.

It is equally important that the immune system recognizes foreign (non-self) antigens and destroys, neutralizes or eliminates any of those capable of doing harm to the body. Bacteria, for example, have distinctive protein or peptide antigens on their cell wall, which the immune system can use to identify the organism. When the immune system encounters a specific type of bacteria, it senses the foreign antigens on the bacteria's surface. If this is the immune system's first encounter with this organism, a permanent record is then made of those bacterial antigens. If it is a disease-causing bacterium, the immune system may react rather slowly to this initial encounter. This is why the first encounter with many disease bacteria or viruses is likely to result in more serious disease. However, if the immune system encounters these bacteria on a subsequent occasion it will immediately remember the specific bacterial antigens and will rapidly mount a powerful and highly focused immune response to wipe out the foreign invader. This learned non-tolerance to certain foreign antigens enables the immune system to effectively defend the body against hostile forces. The immune system must also be capable of learning non-tolerance to antigens from damaged or cancerous cells in order to weed out those cellular citizens that have become sickly or delinquent before they cause damage to the rest of the body.

FOOD ANTIGENS — FRIENDS THAT CAN LOOK LIKE FOES

Foreign antigens can enter the body through many different routes. The skin is largely an impenetrable barrier for antigens unless it is damaged. The mucous membranes of the eyes and respiratory tract are more permeable (leaky) to foreign antigens. This is why the surfaces of the eyes and respiratory system are prone to allergic reactions to foreign antigens such as grass pollen, dust mites or animal dander. However, the gastrointestinal tract is exposed to vast quantities of foreign antigens day in and day out. The massive surface area of the intestine combined with the delicate nature of its mucous membrane suggests that foreign antigens have easier access to the body through the gastrointestinal tract than through any other surface of the body. As well, the intestinal tract is just loaded with antigens. Vast quantities of potentially disease causing microorganisms within the gut, combined with the frequent intake of a wide range of food antigens (every food contains antigens), makes the intestinal immune system's job very challenging indeed.

As was mentioned previously, the majority of the immune system is located within the gastrointestinal tract and is comprised of a highly sophisticated army of immune cells known as the gut associated lymphoid tissue (GALT). (Brandtzaeg, 1998) The GALT devotes much of its energies to the work of "farming the intestinal flora". These immune cells are constantly scanning for the presence of potentially hostile microbes and, if any are detected, specific immune defenses are activated to weed out these foreign invaders. In contrast, the GALT tolerates the presence of beneficial bacterial flora and may even produce substances, which encourage their growth. The tolerance to antigens from friendly bacteria and the non-tolerance to antigens from potentially hostile organisms is learned and memorized by the GALT cells one antigen at a time until a vast database of antigens is collected. Your diet and your environment both have a tremendous influence on the content of this antigen database.

Although you have an intestinal tract loaded with trillions of bacteria, you can still be perfectly healthy because your immune system is capable of preventing hostile organisms from over-growing and causing disease. However, if you travel to a Third World country and indulge in the local cuisine, you may become deathly ill by ingesting microbes that are not found in your immune system's database. If your immune system is unfamiliar with the antigens in these hostile microbes it will not be programmed to take quick defensive action when these organisms are encountered. In such cases, the unfriendly microbes may be able to overgrow and cause diseases like the dreaded "Montezuma's Revenge". The people who are native to the area you are visiting are regularly exposed to these same microbes without any ill effects. This is because their immune systems have learned non-tolerance to these specific bacterial antigens and are able to rapidly generate highly targeted defensive strategies when needed. Clearly, this is one situation where the development of a strong immunological non-tolerance to certain antigens may even be critical for survival.

Food presents a very complex challenge to the immune system. Vast quantities of antigens are present within all food. It is up to the immune system to screen through every bit of food to determine what is safe (nutrients) and what is potentially hostile (toxins, microbes, parasites). Under normal circumstances very small quantities of intact or partially intact proteins (antigens) leak across the intestinal mucous membrane and are captured by immune cells. The immune cells then examine the antigens and determine whether these are friend or foe. If the immune system has learned tolerance towards these specific antigens, it will not react adversely. However, if the immune system is non-tolerant or hypersensitive towards certain food antigens, an adverse immune response will occur. An adverse or hypersensitive response of the immune system to a food antigen is the basis for food allergies.

Under normal circumstances the immune system develops and maintains tolerance for all food antigens. Tolerance toward food antigens is gradually learned as the immune system is exposed to foods throughout infancy and childhood. It is only under abnormal circumstances that the immune system becomes non-tolerant or hypersensitive to any food antigens. Food hypersensitivity, also known as food allergy, is a common malady, especially amongst children. Many authorities now believe that untreated food allergies may be a causative or contributing factor in many illnesses including ADHD.

What determines whether or not a person becomes hypersensitive to particular foods is not fully understood. A combination of high exposure and certain molecular properties of the food are both important factors. Only a short list of foods is responsible for over ninety percent of all food allergies. Dairy, wheat, soy, corn, egg, peanut, tree nuts, shellfish, fish, oranges, strawberry, and yeast are the most common allergenic foods in North America. Early and repeated exposure to these foods may play a significant role in determining the likelihood that an allergy will develop. For example, although peanut allergy is quite common in North America, where peanut butter is a childhood favorite, it is quite uncommon in Great Britain where peanuts and peanut butter are not often eaten. Similarly, although rice allergy is very rare in North America, it is the most common grain allergy in Japan where rice is consumed in large quantities on a daily basis. Instead, North American's, who consume wheat with almost every meal from the time of infancy, are most likely to develop an allergy to wheat rather than any other grain.

FOOD ALLERGY — CONSENSUS AND CONTROVERSY
No one doubts that food allergy is to blame when an individual eats a portion of a peanut and then rapidly develops hives, swollen lips and breathing difficulties. This kind of allergic reaction, known as anaphylaxis, is the most severe form of allergic response and can even result in death if not treated promptly and appropriately. Fortunately, severe anaphylaxis occurs in only a small minority of those with food allergies. However, it is also unfortunate that less severe forms of food allergy can easily go undetected and may never be properly treated.

The subject of food allergy has generated more controversy than perhaps any other topic in medicine. There are numerous reasons why this subject stirs up such heated debate between conventional allergy specialists and alternative or complementary health care practitioners:

· Laypersons and many alternative health care practitioners often refer to any adverse reaction to food as a food allergy even though many adverse reactions to food are not truly allergic in nature. This imprecise or inaccurate use of language has generated confusion and has contributed to cynicism toward the subject of food allergies by much of the medical profession.

· Lack of agreement in the scientific and healthcare community as to what actually constitutes an allergic response to food. This is due, in part, to the enormous complexity of the immune system and the relatively primitive nature of the science of immunology as it relates to food allergy.

· Lack of accurate general knowledge about the nature of food allergies amongst most medical doctors and other healthcare professionals. Most physicians have little or no training in nutritional science and have never studied any reputable material on the subject of food allergies.

· Lack of straightforward laboratory or in-office diagnostic tests, which can accurately prove the existence of food allergies and distinguish without doubt which foods are the perpetrators of the allergic symptoms.

· Difficulty in distinguishing between food allergies and other adverse responses to food, which are not allergic in nature.

· Extraordinary variation in the kinds of symptoms, which can be experienced or exhibited due to food allergy. Some of these symptoms are not easily recognized as the symptoms of allergy.

For these and other reasons, the majority of medical practitioners, registered dietitians and other conventional health care practitioners have largely ignored the subject of food allergy. If a patient is relying upon the advise of their family physician, internist, pediatrician, or even allergy specialist, their medical problems may never be correctly associated with food allergy unless they suffer from the classical symptoms of severe immediate type food allergy (anaphylaxis). This is particularly true for those with ADHD even though there is plenty of evidence that food allergies play a very important role in this condition. (Carter, 1993; Boris, 1994; Kaplan, 1989; Salzman, 1976; Egger, 1985; Schulte-Körne, 1996; Williams, 1978; Egger, 1992; Kitts, 1997)

WHAT SYMPTOMS HAVE BEEN ASSOCIATED WITH FOOD ALLERGIES?

Many decades of research concerning food allergies has now accumulated and the understanding of this complex problem is becoming clearer. Many authorities working in this field have come to accept that food allergies and other adverse reactions to foods can manifest in a multitude of ways. (Joneja, 1998) The following is a partial list of some of the most common symptoms or medical disorders which have been associated with food allergies or other adverse reactions to foods:

Respiratory System
- Non-seasonal runny nose, nasal congestion
- Allergic rhinitis (hay fever)
- Allergic conjunctivitis (red, itchy eyes)
- Recurrent serous otitis media (inflammation and fluid in the middle ear)
- Asthma
- Throat swelling (in serious anaphylactic reactions)

Skin
- Hives
- Eczema
- Swelling of mouth, eyelids and lips (angioedema)
- Itching skin

Digestive System
- Diarrhea
- Constipation
- Nausea and/or vomiting
- Bloating
- Burping
- Flatulence
- Upset stomach or indigestion
- Belly pain

Brain and Nervous System
- Dizziness
- Irritability or aggression
- Hyperactivity, agitation or anxiety
- Poor concentration
- Exhaustion
- Insomnia
- Migraine headache

Miscellaneous
- Dark Circles Under Eyes
- Paleness
- Excessive Sweating or Slight Fever
- Rapid Heartbeat
- Muscle Aches and Pains
- Bed Wetting
- Frequent Urination and Excessive Thirst

WHY ALL THE CONFUSION ABOUT FOOD ALLERGY?

To the scientist and scientifically oriented healthcare practitioner the correct use of language is very important. If terminology is not clearly defined or if medical terms are used incorrectly, science becomes inexact simply due to a lack of precise communication. On the other hand, medical science has also been weakened by a tendency to define complex medical conditions like food allergy within the boundaries of very strict and limiting terminology. The controversies surrounding the subject of food allergy have arisen to a large extent because of confusion in the language commonly used to describe this highly multifaceted process.

The first area of confusion results when all adverse reactions to foods are improperly called food allergies. Adverse reactions to foods, which are not caused primarily by the immune system, are known officially as food intolerances. For example, if an individual cannot digest milk sugar they may experience bloating, gas, cramps and nausea after drinking milk or eating dairy products. These symptoms result from undigested milk sugar reaching the colon where it is then fermented by bacteria into gas and acids. The immune system probably has very little to do with this type of adverse food reaction so it is therefore not properly classified as food allergy. Similarly, if a child becomes aggressive, hyperactive or moody after eating sugary foods this does not necessarily indicate an allergy to sugar. It may instead be related to the child's inability to properly regulate blood sugar after ingesting excessive quantities of this food material. After eating sugary foods some children may produce inappropriate quantities of adrenaline or cortisol — hormones that the body uses to regulate blood sugar which may also have powerful effects on the brain.

In some cases it isn't that important to differentiate between food allergies and food intolerances. If simply eliminating the offensive food alleviates the symptoms and poses no significant difficulties or nutritional challenges it may not matter whether the individual suffers from a food allergy or other non-allergic food reactions. For example, if you have noticed that your child becomes grumpy, miserable or hyperactive after eating junk foods it probably doesn't really matter whether this is due to a food allergy or a food intolerance. Simple wisdom would suggest that the best thing to do in this case is to simply limit your child's intake of junk food by working hard to find healthy and tasty snacks as replacements. On the other hand, if your child reacts adversely to nutritionally important foods such as eggs, soy, meats or fruits it may become very important to try and distinguish whether or not this is a food allergy or food intolerance. Depending upon the nature of the adverse reaction, specific treatment may or may not be available which could allow that food to eventually be eaten once again.

WHAT WE KNOW, WHAT WE THINK WE KNOW AND WHAT WE WISH WE KNEW ABOUT FOOD ALLERGY

Several decades ago scientists discovered that there are four different reactions that explain how the immune system responds when a threatening foreign antigen is encountered. If the antigen in question belongs to a potentially harmful microbe, it is quite appropriate and necessary for the immune system to react in such a way as to eliminate this potential threat. On the other hand, allergy or hypersensitivity occurs when an otherwise harmless antigen is mistakenly classified as threatening by the immune system.

A great deal of the controversy surrounding food allergies exists because of a lack of agreement amongst scientists and healthcare practitioners as to what actually constitutes an allergic reaction to food. On one hand, the majority of medical allergy specialists in North America define food allergy as arising from only one out of the potential four hypersensitivity reactions — the reaction which is known to cause serious food allergies or anaphylaxis. On the other hand, many medical allergy specialists in Europe along with the majority of alternative healthcare providers recognize that food allergy may actually come about from at least three out of the four potential hypersensitivity reactions.

The scientific position taken on this matter by a physician or other healthcare provider may greatly influence how the practitioner goes about diagnosing and treating food allergies. Unfortunately, in many cases, if a patient's symptoms do not fit neatly into a physician's narrow definition of food allergy, their symptoms may be dismissed as simply psychosomatic. On the other hand, some practitioners regard nearly every illness as arising in some way from food allergies without properly evaluating the cause of the patient's difficulties. The risk in this case is that the suffering person may spend an inordinate amount of time, money and trouble following rigid, nutritionally marginal diets without ever really finding true relief from their symptoms.

In order to determine whether or not food allergies are indeed a significant cause of an individual's medical problems (including ADHD) some basic understanding of the physiological mechanisms of food hypersensitivity is a must.

TYPE I HYPERSENSITIVITY

This is the class of immune reaction, which is responsible for immediate allergic reactions and is the primary reaction involved in respiratory allergies such as allergic rhinitis (hay fever), and in more severe food allergies including those which are potentially life threatening (anaphylaxis). Type I hypersensitivity is also thought to play a significant role in defending the body against parasitic infections. This reaction is also known as immediate hypersensitivity and is part of the body's surface defense system. In Type I hypersensitivity, antigens that break through the barrier of the skin or penetrate through the mucous membranes of the respiratory and digestive tracts may be greeted by an immediate and explosive reaction from specialized cells that live just under these surfaces. These remarkable cells, known as mast cells, line every potential entrance to the body like land mines waiting for just the right trigger to set off a violent explosion.

When an individual has an immediate hypersensitivity (Type I) allergy, their mast cells are covered with high amounts of allergy promoting antibodies known as IgE. Antibodies are large protein molecules manufactured by immune cells. Each antibody molecule is designed to attach to one specific antigen. There are five different classes of antibodies: IgA, IgD, IgE, IgG and IgM. Each class of antibody has a different role in immune system function. The IgE molecules on the surface of mast cells are manufactured by other types of immune cells, which, in turn, transfer the IgE to the surface of mast cells until they are completely covered with IgE — like thousands of tiny antennas. Each allergy-generating antigen is specific to only one IgE molecule; that is, it will stick to only one specific IgE as precisely as a key fits a specific lock. This means that the mast cells of allergic individuals are covered with high amounts of specific IgE molecules that are designed to stick to only those antigens to which they are allergic. These allergy-generating antigens are known as allergens. If a high enough number of allergens attach to the IgE molecules on any given mast cell, a chain reaction will be set off and the mast cell will violently explode — releasing thousands of tiny packets full of alarm substances such as histamine and leukotrienes. These substances then initiate an immediate and powerful inflammatory reaction.

These potent molecules of inflammation are responsible for the swelling, redness, irritation and mucous production so typical of an allergic response. If this process takes place in the skin, hives are likely to occur; in the nose, nasal congestion, sneezing and increased mucus production are experienced; on the surface of the eyes, redness and itching are the result; and in the lungs, wheezing and coughing may occur. These are referred to as local effects. Since the chemical mediators of inflammation are also released into circulation, allergic reactions may include more widespread effects – referred to as systemic effects. For instance, individuals with allergic rhinitis (hay fever) suffer from local allergic effects such as nasal congestion and sneezing, but they also may experience systemic effects such as fatigue or "brain fog" during their allergy season. This is due to the impact of various molecules of inflammation on the brain and other organs. However, because of the relatively minute amounts of allergen that can enter the body through the skin or respiratory tract, the potential for predominant systemic effects in these types of allergies is usually not very great. The exception to this is in the case of serious anaphylaxis; a severe and immediate allergic reaction such as those from bee sting or peanut. In such cases, even an extremely tiny amount of allergen can rapidly initiate massive systemic effects and can even result in death if not treated promptly. All of this occurs because these individuals have a very large number of mast cells equipped with a dense concentration of IgE antibodies specific to their particular allergens.

Mast cells also line the digestive tract and, in allergic individuals, are fully equipped to respond immediately upon exposure to an allergen. However, for several reasons, the effects of allergens within the digestive tract are quite different than elsewhere in the body. First of all, the amount of allergen, which enters the body in the case of food allergy, is vastly greater than respiratory allergies. This means that after eating food that contains allergens, huge amounts of those allergens may cross the mucous membrane of the gut. These allergens can then travel throughout the body activating mast cells and other immune cells in locations quite distant from the digestive tract. As a result of these circulating allergens, food allergies are commonly accompanied by symptoms like hives on the skin and various systemic symptoms such as fatigue, malaise (generally feeling awful), headaches, muscle pain, irritability, hyperactivity and cognitive problems. (Kitts, 1997)

Furthermore, the immune system of the digestive tract is more complex than in the rest of the body. (Theodorou, 1996) Following exposure to an allergen, mast cells and other immune cells may release a much wider variety of inflammatory molecules than would tend to occur in other regions. The allergic response in other areas, such as inside the nose, tends to be fairly simple and symptoms are primarily due to result of the release of histamine from mast cells. This is why antihistamines reduce the symptoms of hay fever so effectively. In contrast, histamine is only one out of the many different inflammatory mediators released during an allergic response in the gut. Thus, antihistamines have virtually no place in the treatment of food allergy.

Additional important differences between food allergies and other types of allergies are the result of the complex community of cells that exist within the GALT (gut associated lymphoid tissue). Nowhere else in the body are the immune cells so intricately interconnected as they are within the GALT. Because of this complexity, many of the rules that govern allergy in other parts of the body are just too simple to apply to the gut. For example, mast cells in the respiratory mucous membrane only release their inflammation generating contents when specific allergens attach to specific IgE molecules on the surface of the cell. This is, by definition, a true Type I hypersensitivity reaction. In contrast, recent research has suggested that the highly connected mast cells within the GALT may release their contents under circumstances that are not considered to be a part of the Type I hypersensitivity reaction. For example, gut mast cells may release their contents when directly stimulated by nerve endings, or when communicated to by neuropeptides (released from nerves or absorbed from the diet if digestion is inefficient or the gut is leaky) or a variety of inflammatory mediators released from other immune cells. This is very confusing and even quite disturbing for immunologists and allergy specialists who have been taught that food allergy only exists when specific IgE molecules on the surface of mast cells are stimulated by specific allergens. It is certain that in the next few years, the official definitions of food allergy will be expanded greatly as science clarifies this complex phenomenon.

Overall, classical Type I hypersensitivity based food allergies have remained the focus of attention in medicine since they are responsible for the most serious forms of food allergy and are the easiest to identify with specific laboratory or skin tests. Current estimates suggest that between 3 and 5 percent of children (some experts have estimated as high as 8 percent) and approximately 1 to 2 percent of adults have significant Type I hypersensitivity based food allergies. Since adverse reactions to food occur in a much higher percentage of the population than these statistics suggest, classical Type I hypersensitivity may only explain a rather small fraction of the negative responses that people may have to food. This is certainly true in ADHD. Research suggests that only a minority of kids with ADHD have clearly identifiable Type I food allergies (perhaps higher than the general population but still a minority nonetheless). However, several studies, including one recently conducted in our facility, suggests that 75 percent or more more of children with ADHD who are placed on a high-quality, low allergy potential diet experience a significant improvement in overall health and often demonstrate striking improvements in behavior and cognitive performance. This cannot be explained by Type I hypersensitivity reactions alone. There must certainly be other immunological and non-immunological reasons for dietary factors to have such a significant impact on ADHD.

TYPE II HYPERSENSITIVITY

Although this class of immune reaction is very important in the body's defense systems, it is not likely to play a major role in food allergies. This is a type of immune reaction that occurs when a cell inside the body is judged to be foreign and then antibodies are produced against antigens on the surface of that cell. Once the cell is coated with antibodies, immune cells either engulf it or the antibodies set off immune reactions that cause the cell to explode. This type of reaction is the reason why blood types must be matched before a transfusion is administered. Unlike Type I hypersensitivity reactions, Type II hypersensitivity does not involve specific IgE antibodies. Instead, the immune system manufactures specific IgA, IgG and IgM antibodies to carry out this defensive strategy. Type II hypersensitivity reactions are probably occurring to some extent in individuals with increased intestinal permeability (leaky gut). In such cases whole cells, such as those from bacteria, yeasts or undigested food, cross the mucous membrane of the gut and then may have to be destroyed and eliminated through Type II hypersensitivity reactions. The end result of the Type II hypersensitivity reaction is the release of inflammatory mediators from immune cells. This could contribute to a wide variety of symptoms. Much more research will be required to determine the significance of Type II hypersensitivity in food allergy. Dealing with the causes of increased intestinal permeability is the primary way to reduce this type of hypersensitivity phenomenon.

TYPE III HYPERSENSITIVITY

Many experts believe that this class of immune reaction may soon prove to be the most important mechanism to predominate in the majority of individuals with adverse reactions to foods, particularly in adults and children with hard-to-pinpoint, delayed rather than immediate, food allergies. (Kitts, 1997; King, 1998; Joneja, 1998; Paganelli, 1986; Marinkovitch, 1996) Type III hypersensitivity occurs when antibodies and antigens combine together within the bloodstream to form very large molecules called immune complexes. These immune complexes are capable of stimulating immune cells to release molecules of inflammation, which in turn can lead to an extraordinary variety of symptoms.

The textbook description of Type III hypersensitivity occurs as a side effect of therapies that involve the injection of foreign protein into the bloodstream of a sick person. For example, if a venomous snake bites a person, they might be treated by an injection made from the blood of an animal that has been made immune to the snakebite (usually a horse). Although this anti-snakebite serum may save the person's life by neutralizing the snake venom, the individual may become very ill several days later. This sickness occurs because their immune system develops antibodies against the injected horse blood serum. These antibodies combine with the horse antigens to form immune complexes. Immune complexes may grow until they form large clumps, which can clog up tiny blood vessels and deposit in soft tissues where they cause various destructive inflammatory changes. This severe form of Type III hypersensitivity is known as **serum sickness**. (Virella, 1990; Virella, 1993)

Another textbook example of Type III hypersensitivity occurs when foreign protein is injected under the skin of an individual who has already been exposed to that foreign protein. In this case, antibodies rapidly combine with the foreign antigens and immune complexes are formed in the soft tissues. Because these immune complexes are too large to simply slip into blood vessels and be carried away in the circulation they remain in the region of the injection. Within four to six hours of the injection, immune cells migrate into the region of the injection and a local inflammatory response takes place, resulting in pain, redness and swelling of the area of injection. This more rapid and local form of Type III hypersensitivity is known as the **Arthus reaction**. In situations where an individual has a leaky gut, it is very likely that both local (Arthus reaction) and more widespread (serum sickness) related Type III hypersensitivity reactions are occurring to some extent on a frequent and varying basis.

Eating a meal is, in some ways, similar to being given an injection of foreign antigens. (Husby, 1988) Under completely normal circumstances, about 1/1000 of all protein eaten will actually cross the gut wall undigested or partially digested and it is then capable of provoking an immune response. For example if your intestine is entirely healthy and you eat a big steak dinner containing 100 grams of beef protein, about 100 mg of undigested or partially digested protein will end up getting across the gut wall and will be met by the immune cells of the gut (GALT). This is actually thought to be a normal mechanism by which the GALT cells sample microbial and food antigens and survey for any threatening invaders. If this process detects hostile antigens, immune defenses can be activated to protect the body from the intruder.

This flow of antigenic material across the gut wall is also important in the development and maintenance of immunological tolerance. (Granstein, 1994) In this normal process, small amounts of antibodies (IgA and IgG) are produced which are specific to microbial and food antigens present within the gut. In particular, IgA antibodies are used by the immune system to capture food antigens, to promote tolerance to those antigens and to provide a mechanism for the immune system to rapidly clear these antigens from circulation without promoting inflammation. When small quantities of antigens combine with the antibodies specific to them, immune complexes are then formed. These immune complexes are then rapidly recognized and captured by specialized engulfing cells within the gut and liver. Some of these immune complexes will escape capture by the gut and liver engulfing cells and instead, will end up in circulation for a short period time until they are captured by engulfing cells in the skin, lungs and other organs. Because of this, under normal circumstances small amounts of antibodies such as IgG or IgA, which are specific to certain foods, can be found in the blood of healthy individuals. In small quantities, antibodies against specific foods do not reflect any disease process and do not indicate an allergy to any particular food.

Unfortunately, there are common circumstances, which can result in malfunctioning of these normal processes. For instance, if an individual develops increased gut permeability (leaky gut), very large quantities of antigenic material (proteins and peptides) will readily cross the gut wall and enter the bloodstream and lymph vessels of the gut. Engulfing cells within the gut and liver will capture some of this antigenic material. The GALT (gut associated lymphoid tissue) will also increase its production of antibodies specific to the antigens that are leaking across the gut wall and immune complexes will be formed when antigens and antibodies combine together. Once these immune complexes exceed a certain concentration, they may surpass the capacity of the engulfing cells and then escape into the general circulation in high quantities. Once immune complexes have reached a certain concentration within the GALT, liver or circulation they have the potential to turn on a very powerful part of the immune system known as the complement system. Complement is a team of over one dozen different proteins that circulate continuously everywhere in the bloodstream. In the presence of immune complexes of a certain size and concentration, a chain reaction is triggered in which complement molecules "explode" violently around the immune complex like a string of firecrackers on the Fourth of July. In this situation, complement has the potential to cause damage to cells in the area of the immune complex. Activated complement also powerfully attracts immune cells and causes them to release inflammatory mediators. Although this food related effect probably never develops to the point where full-blown serum sickness takes place, diffuse, low-grade Type III hypersensitivity may be a very frequent occurrence in individuals who experience adverse reactions to food.

TYPE III HYPERSENSITIVITY AND DELAYED FOOD REACTIONS

Susceptibility to Type III hypersensitivity is amplified when gut permeability is increased and when an individual's immune system reacts excessively when exposed to particular food antigens. Since Type III hypersensitivity reactions are somewhat delayed (not fully manifested for four to six hours) it can be difficult to recognize that ill health is coming from specific foods if the problems are related to this type of immune response. Nevertheless, affected individuals may have numerous symptoms related to immune complex formation and the subsequent release of various inflammatory mediators. As well, Type III reactions tend to result in prolonged adverse effects. Therefore, if a person regularly eats foods which provoke Type III hypersensitivity reactions, they may never associate specific foods to specific adverse symptoms. Instead, they may simply experience poor health with no apparent cause.

TYPE III HYPERSENSITIVITY AND FOOD ADDICTIONS

It has often been observed that when individuals begin a specially prescribed diet in which all commonly allergenic, foods are eliminated, they may feel quite sick for several days before they begin to experiencing significant benefits from the diet. It has been proposed by experts in the field of food allergy that these "withdrawal symptoms" occur because of a transient serum sickness-like event that occurs after allergenic foods are withdrawn suddenly from the diet. Immune complexes can vary in size from tiny to very large. When a person daily eats a food to which they are allergic the immune complexes formed tend to be small and numerous. High numbers of small immune complexes tend to create vague and hard to define symptoms. However, if that person suddenly stops eating the allergenic food, smaller numbers of very large immune complexes tend to form for a few days until they are cleared by the immune system. Large immune complexes tend to provoke more severe symptoms by stimulating a very strong inflammatory response.

Thus, until all these large immune complexes are cleared from the body and the immune complex stimulated inflammation has subsided, the individual experiences a serum sickness-like event, which may leave them feeling like "death warmed over" for a few days. Headaches, muscle and joint pain, malaise, abdominal pain, skin rashes as well as emotional, mood, behavioral and cognitive problems commonly occur during this withdrawal phase. Anyone who works with those who they suspect are suffering from food allergies should be aware of the high likelihood of this "allergen withdrawal syndrome" occurring during the first 3 to 10 days of an allergy elimination diet. In fact, this Type III hypersensitivity mediated withdrawal syndrome is so common that, if it is not experienced to some extent within the first few days of an allergy elimination diet, the health-care practitioner may wonder if the patient really has food allergies at all.

This same phenomenon may help to explain why food allergies might share other similarities with addiction. It has been frequently noted by healthcare practitioners that food allergic individuals frequently eat and often crave the very foods that they eventually are proven to be allergic to. The theory behind this relationship is that the person with a primarily Type III mediated food hypersensitivity obtains momentary pleasure by eating foods to which they are allergic. This momentary pleasure may be partly caused by the release of stress hormones like adrenaline and cortisol, or an increase in sympathetic nervous system activity secondary to the physiological stress that accompanies the eating of an allergenic food. Alternatively, this short term "high" may be caused by the release of opioid peptides (morphine - like protein fragments) from nerve endings or immune cells within the gut — all immediately following the eating of a food to which that person is allergic. Even though the individual feels poorly later on, unpleasant symptoms are delayed long enough that they may never make the association between the allergenic food and their ill health. Furthermore, if the individual is feeling poorly during a time that they have been abstaining from their allergenic food, they may quickly feel relief, and perhaps even euphoria, if the allergenic food is eaten again. All of this tends to reinforce the desire to eat the allergenic food regularly, and may also be why food allergic people can be quite reluctant to eliminate favorite foods from their diet. Food addictions seem to be most common with dairy or wheat allergy. Perhaps this is because these food also contain opioid peptides which might add to their addictive potential.

TYPE IV HYPERSENSITIVITY

This final category of hypersensitivity reaction does not likely play a significant role in most adverse reactions to foods. In Type IV hypersensitivity, specialized immune cells become highly sensitized to specific antigens and then attack those antigens directly without the need for the production of any antibodies. These specialized cells, referred to as "natural killer cells", are extremely powerful predatory cells that spend their lives seeking out and destroying foreign invaders. Type IV hypersensitivity is a very slow reacting process, which is responsible for the inflammation seen in the skin after exposure to poison ivy, or the irritation of the skin from wearing cheap earrings. Type IV hypersensitivity has been implicated as a cause of celiac disease (gluten intolerance) and may be contributing factor in Crohn's disease, an inflammatory bowel disease. At this point it is really not known if Type IV hypersensitivity is involved to a lesser extent in more common manifestations of food allergy.

WHERE IN THE WORLD DO FOOD ALLERGIES COME FROM?

By now you should certainly understand how complex the relationship is between our bodies and our diets. Our constant need for nutrients must be kept in balance with our need to be protected from potentially harmful food molecules, toxins and microbes in our gastrointestinal tracts. Early in life, our immune systems become educated; learning the difference between molecular friend and foe. Ideally, our immune system learns to be tolerant of all harmless self and non-self antigens while developing appropriate defensive strategies to deal with all potentially harmful antigens. Unfortunately, mistakes can be made in this cellular educational process and the immune system can inappropriately lose tolerance to otherwise harmless food antigens.

There are several reasons why food allergies develop. From a Functional Medicine perspective, food allergies can be viewed as being physiological disturbances (triggers) resulting from predisposing factors (antecedents) that leave an individual vulnerable to the physiological disturbance. Remember that antecedents are factors that precede the onset of symptoms and predispose the individual to the development of physiological disturbances.

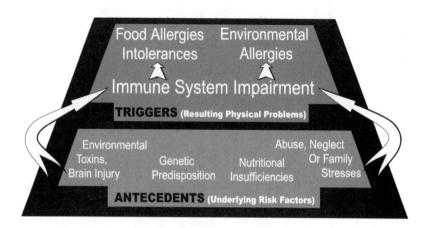

The following list of factors are antecedents, which play a significant role in the development of environmental and food allergies:

· **Genetics** is an important factor in the risk of developing food allergies. This is particularly true of Type I hypersensitivity (immediate) allergies and is probably true for other types of food allergies and non-allergic food intolerances as well. Our research has suggested one potentially positive aspect to the genetics of food allergy. In a recent research project we placed fifty children with attention deficit disorder on a prescribed allergy elimination diet. Their parents attended weekly nutrition classes and were encouraged to use the recipes they were learning in order to change the diet of the child as well as their whole family. At the end of this study not only did the majority of kids with ADHD benefit from the allergy elimination diet but so did many of the parents and siblings as well. This is quite likely because children with ADHD who have food allergies are also likely to have parents and siblings with similar problems. It certainly is a lot easier for a whole family to change to a more wholesome way of eating and to avoid certain allergenic foods than for one family member to be singled out and put on a special diet.

· **Nutritional factors** undoubtedly play a role in the development and severity of all forms of allergy and inflammation. When a person has less than optimal nutrition, their immune system cannot function in an ideal fashion and is more likely to act inappropriately when faced with various molecular stresses. For instance, individuals with deficiencies of omega-3 fatty acids are more likely to experience inflammation and allergy than those with optimal omega-3 status. Deficiencies of magnesium and zinc are also known to increase the irritability of cells and may promote allergic responsiveness. Having poor antioxidant protection will also contribute significantly to the likelihood of experiencing inflammation and allergy. As well, the overall quality of the diet probably plays a tremendous role in determining the health of the immune system and the likelihood that it will respond inappropriately to dietary components. Overly processed, stale, chemically altered, or nutritionally depleted foods will be more likely to elicit an adverse response than fresh, unprocessed food.

· **Toxicological stresses** also play a significant role in determining the health of the immune system and how it will respond to foreign antigens. For instance, if a person is regularly exposed to immunotoxic pesticide residues through dietary or other sources, their immune system will never be able to function optimally and will be more likely to respond in an inappropriately hostile fashion to food antigens. Other immunotoxins such as heavy metals, PCBs, plastic residues and solvents are very common components of our day-to-day environment and some individuals may be affected by many of these substances inadvertently and insidiously. Of course children are especially vulnerable to toxicological influences, which may leave their mark on their immune systems and may cause them to be more prone to allergies.

· Developmental factors play a highly significant role in the risk of acquiring food allergies. Breastfeeding is a protective factor, which significantly reduces the risk of subsequently developing food allergies. Ideally, an infant should be breast-fed exclusively until at least six months of age — perhaps as long as one year. The healthy infant naturally has a leaky gut. The reason for this is so large molecules, such as antibodies in the mother's milk, can easily cross over into the baby's bloodstream to protect the infant from infection while his immune system is immature. During this vulnerable period, antigens other than those from the mother's milk may be viewed by the developing immune system as threatening and it may be instructed to become non-tolerant towards these antigens. There is actually a fairly high level of awareness of this fact amongst the medical profession. Mother's are usually encouraged to breastfeed as long as possible and to carefully and slowly introduce solid foods one food at a time, starting with the foods least likely to generate an allergic response. This process gradually educates the infant's immune system and promotes the development of tolerance towards the foods that are introduced. Unfortunately, the manufacturers of infant formula have highly aggressive marketing strategies and their efforts have made it very easy for mothers to opt out of breast-feeding and use formula instead. Most of these contain cow's milk proteins and are as allergenic as milk. Infants who are intolerant to cow's milk formulas are often switched to soy formula and then almost half of these infants will develop allergy to soy. It is certainly true that interrupting the natural order of things can make life much more complicated.

· Anything that irritates or damages the intestinal mucous membrane will lead to increased intestinal permeability (leaky gut) and an increase in the absorption of intact antigens. If a person develops a leaky gut they will often become sensitized to several foods. Once the leaky gut has healed, many of the Type III hypersensitivity reactions will gradually dissipate or even disappear altogether. However, in the absence of a leaky gut, Type I hypersensitivity reactions may lessen but do not disappear. In fact, if an individual without a leaky gut eats a food to which they have a Type I food allergy, the allergic reaction will damage the intestinal mucous membrane and a leaky gut quickly develops. If the individual continues to eat this food, they are more likely to develop adverse reactions (probably Type III hypersensitivity) to other foods as well. Likewise, other causes of a leaky gut such as ingestion of alcohol, nonsteroidal anti-inflammatory drugs and antibiotics may also lead to the development of food hypersensitivities.

· The presence of intestinal parasites is especially likely to turn on the Type I hypersensitivity system and lead to an increase in allergic responsiveness. The immune system uses the Type I hypersensitivity system to defend against parasitic infestations. However, there is also mounting evidence that microscopic parasites (protozoans like Giardia) within the intestine can also increase allergic responsiveness. (DiPrisco, 1998; Cuffari, 1998; Veraldi, 1991) This could mean that an individual with specific allergies might experience worsening of those allergies if they are also infected with intestinal parasites. It may also mean that an individual without any allergies at all may develop allergies for the first time following an intestinal parasitic infection. Recently, we examined stool samples from seventy-five children with ADHD and were startled to find that nearly half of these children had intestinal parasites. This is certainly a higher percentage than has been found in other studies looking for the presence of parasites in normal children.(Kabani, 1995; Kappus, 1994) It is quite possible that these unwanted guests may be responsible for increased allergic disease in these children.

· The presence of non-food allergies such as hay fever can impact the severity of food allergies. If these types of allergies are particularly active, as often occur in spring and early summer, pre-existing food allergies may become more predominant at the same time. The reason for this is that non-food allergies can activate the allergy systems of the body and cause the number of allergy producing mast cells to increase significantly. If there are more mast cells around and higher levels of inflammatory mediators in the blood, exposure to allergenic foods can bring about a greater response than in other seasons when allergies are not prominent.

WHAT ELSE CAN LEAD TO ADVERSE REACTIONS TO FOODS BESIDES FOOD ALLERGIES?

Thus far I have described a view of food allergies that goes beyond the recognition of only those adverse reactions to food which are mediated by Type I (immediate) hypersensitivity. This expanded view is in keeping with the classical understanding of how the immune system operates and helps to explain why so many people experience adverse reactions to foods which do not appear to have a strong Type I component. In the opinion of a growing number of researchers and physicians, the more narrow view of food allergy, which only recognizes allergies as resulting from Type I hypersensitivity reactions, is not consistent with the wealth of scientific literature and clinical experience, which strongly suggests that food allergies are mediated by multiple mechanisms.

It is also recognized that individuals can react adversely to foods through processes that do not primarily involve the immune system. These kind of reactions are referred to as food intolerances. It is not always easy to distinguish between food allergy and food intolerance but knowing the difference may have a tremendous impact on the success of treatment. Food intolerance can occur secondary to a number of mechanisms:

· INADEQUATE DIGESTION

Perhaps the most common example of food intolerance secondary to inadequate digestion is lactose intolerance. Lactose or milk sugar is a minimally sweet sugar, which is actually composed of two simple sugars or monosaccharides (glucose and galactose) that are stuck together to form a double sugar or disaccharide. Your intestinal cells can only absorb simple sugars and therefore lactose must be completely digested into simple sugars before it can be absorbed. Infants are almost always born with an adequate ability to digest lactose. However, children after weaning and adults of most races, except for those of Northern European descent, often lose their ability to efficiently digest lactose. If an individual who cannot digest lactose efficiently consumes dairy products containing more lactose than they are able to properly digest, they may experience abdominal pain, gas, bloating and diarrhea within a short period of time. The reason for this is that undigested lactose is not absorbed through the small intestine and it ends up in the colon where bacteria ferment the lactose, producing gas and irritating acids. Although the immune system is not directly affected by lactose intolerance, this maldigestion problem may encourage the overgrowth of bacteria within the small intestine. This overgrowth can, in turn, lead to the production of substances which can irritate intestinal cells resulting in poor absorption and a leaky gut. This, of course, leads to excessive passage of food and microbial antigens through the gut wall and over stimulation of the immune system. This may be why research has shown that individuals who are lactose intolerant but not milk allergic will often become milk allergic if they persist in drinking milk.

Inadequate digestion of other nutrients, particularly proteins, may actually be fairly common. Hypochlorhydria, or inadequate stomach acid production, can contribute to inefficient protein digestion as well as overgrowth of bacteria in the small intestine. Stomach acid production can be measured by swallowing a device called a Heidelberg capsule. In an, as of yet, unpublished study conducted by an Australian researcher, seventy-five percent of children with ADHD were found to have significant hypochlorhydria (low stomach acid). The reason for this is currently not well understood but it is probably related to excessive immune system activity within the intestinal immune system (GALT). If protein digestion is slow or inefficient, as would occur if stomach acid is low, larger than normal quantities of intact protein or peptides would end up crossing the wall of the gut and stimulating an immune response. In this case, hypochlorhydria could significantly increase the risk for the development of food allergies. Protein maldigestion may also lead to food intolerance because undigested and unabsorbed protein will end up in the colon where it putrefies — a process that releases irritating and toxic chemical byproducts. Some of these putrefactive chemicals may have their effects locally, leading to cramping, gas, diarrhea or constipation, while others may inflame the GALT or circulate throughout the body with various toxic consequences.

· POOR DETOXIFICATION CAPABILITIES

Several years ago Dr. Benjamin Feingold popularized the theory that food additives and certain naturally occurring food chemicals, known as salicylates, were the primary cause of attention deficit disorder in children. Dr. Feingold reported that over three-quarters of the children that he placed on an additive and salicylate free diet would show marked improvements in their behavior and cognitive performance. In the hands of other, perhaps less enthusiastic researchers the success rate of the Feingold diet has been reported to be closer to a maximum of about 10 percent. It is most likely that Dr. Feingold was describing a real phenomenon that is present in a minority of those with ADHD as the primary cause of their problem. The main reason why a person would react adversely to certain chemicals found in food is most often related to inherited or acquired inefficiencies in that individual's ability to detoxify and eliminate these chemicals efficiently. Many chemicals that enter the body through food (both naturally occurring as well as artificial food additives) must be detoxified within the gut wall and liver by changing the molecular structure of the chemical. The gut wall and liver are equipped with hundreds of different enzyme systems each designed to effectively detoxify a certain type of chemical substance. If any particular enzyme is genetically absent or has been impaired through lack of certain nutrients, then chemicals specific to that enzyme will be more likely to accumulate in the body and exert toxic effects. Many different drugs and toxins are also able to impair the function of certain detoxifying enzyme systems.

Salicylates are naturally occurring chemicals related to aspirin. They are found in a wide variety of fruits and vegetables in various concentrations. Under normal circumstances, if a person eats foods containing salicylates their liver will rapidly detoxify these chemicals and remove them before they have a chance to exert any toxic or drug like effects. However, if a person inherited a low concentration of salicylate detoxifying enzymes or if they lack certain nutrients, which are necessary for these enzymes to work, their body may not be capable of detoxifying even the small amounts of salicylates found in many foods. Once salicylate levels reach a certain concentration in that person's blood the salicylates may exert drug like effects and may provoke a reaction in the immune system.

Another common cause of food intolerance is from food additives. Artificial colors, especially colors derived from tartrazine (used to impart yellow, orange, green and brown color to food) are the most likely in this category to cause problems. Preservatives such as BHA, BHT and benzoic acid (sodium benzoate) are also common causes of food intolerance. Unfortunately, if an individual is sensitive to the sodium benzoate listed on food labels they may also be sensitive to benzoic acids found naturally in certain foods. Sulfites are another type of preservative commonly used in dried fruits, beverages, and several other categories of food. Intolerance to sulfites can be particularly harmful because it can induce serious asthmatic attacks in susceptible individuals. Nitrates are common additives to meats and are used to maintain the food's color, flavor and prevent the growth of bacteria. These agents may be carcinogenic (cause cancer) and may be a significant cause of headaches and other problems.

Histamine, the main molecule of inflammation released from mast cells (the explosive "land mines" under the skin and all mucous membranes) is also commonly found in some foods. Histamine is actually derived from a common amino acid called histidine. If a food containing histidine begins to spoil or is fermented purposefully, such as occurs in the making of cheese, significant quantities of histamine may accumulate in that food. For those who are unable to efficiently detoxify histamine, or already have elevated histamine levels because of preexisting allergies, these histamine-containing foods may cause significant symptoms.

An increase in various toxic symptoms may also occur secondary to inefficient liver detoxification of byproducts of the microbial fermentation (breakdown of sugar or starch) or putrefaction (breakdown of protein or fat) of undigested foods within the colon.(Hunter, 1991) This type of food intolerance is most likely to occur after overeating, eating junk food or in individuals with poor digestive activity. Inefficient detoxification of microbial metabolites, as is true for many drugs and chemicals, may be secondary to genetic enzyme deficiencies, overload of detoxification enzymes or an inadequate supply of nutrients necessary to allow efficient detoxification to take place.

· SENSITIVITY TO EFFECTS OF DRUGS IN FOODS

Certain chemicals, which can be easily classified as drugs, are added to foods or are naturally present in those foods. Naturally occurring salicylates, having already been mentioned, are related to aspirin. Caffeine is naturally present in coffee, tea and chocolate and is an additive to colas and "Mountain Dew". Some studies have suggested that caffeine increases the activity level of children and promotes aggressiveness and other undesirable behaviors. It is certain that caffeine increases anxiety levels and causes insomnia in susceptible individuals at certain doses. Although cognition can be enhanced by low dose caffeine in adults, it has not been shown to improve behavior or cognition in children. (Durlach, 1998;Hughes,1998) Monosodium glutamate (MSG) can be considered to be a flavor-enhancing drug added to an extraordinarily wide variety of foods. It works by dramatically increasing the activity of sensory nerves in the tongue and thus increasing the flavors of foods. Although it is manufactured from a naturally occurring amino acid, it has drug-like effects and may lead to over activation of brain cells. Many adverse symptoms have been reported by those who are sensitive to monosodium glutamate.

In addition to the drugs that might be added to foods during processing, large quantities of hormones, antibiotics and drugs are administered to animals being raised using "modern" commercial agricultural methods. Residues of many of these drugs are undoubtedly present in the final products consumed by humans. As was reported in a previous chapter, pesticides contaminate most commercially grown fruits and vegetables. Some adverse reactions to food may, in fact, be related to the toxic effects of these contaminants.

FOOD ALLERGIES, FOOD INTOLERANCES AND ADHD

When I graduated from medical school 1985, the field of psychoneuroimmunology was a fringe discipline and few serious scientists would risk their careers endeavoring to promote the idea that the immune system, the brain, and the mind were any more than casually connected. Since then psychoneuroimmunology has revolutionized medicine and has uncovered more surprises than perhaps any other field in medicine. Psychosomatic illness or illness originating in the mind is not a new concept. It has been known for centuries that the mind can have tremendous effects upon the body. However, what we are now beginning to understand through the science psychoneuroimmunology is that the body has a tremendous effect upon the brain as well.

Many scientists describe the immune system as our "mobile brain" because immune cells have receptors for virtually every neurotransmitter produced by the brain cells. As well, immune cells secrete an extraordinary variety of communication molecules including neurotransmitters and neuropeptides. The molecules of inflammation released during an allergic response have extraordinarily complex and varied activities. Many research papers prove that food allergies are accompanied by an increase in the release of cytokines and other inflammatory mediators which may have a profound influence upon brain function. These types of observations of psychoneuroimmunology have taught us that the immune system carries on a constant conversation with the brain through the continual release of communication molecules. When the immune system is in distress the brain can respond instantly and powerfully. In light of such profound discoveries, it is not hard to imagine that food allergies and intolerances may indeed have a significant impact on brain function and could easily be one of the most significant factors in the development of ADHD.

Our most recent research project certainly supports this view. We were able to clearly demonstrate that eliminating junk foods, improving the overall quality of the diet and eliminating a number of potentially allergenic foods can have a remarkable effect upon the overall health as well as the behavior and cognition of a significant proportion of children with ADHD.

I have known for years that I am highly sensitive to a number of different foods including dairy, wheat, and most every kind of junk food. If I eat more than a small amount of any of these foods my sense of wellness, energy, mood and cognitive performance deteriorates dramatically and it sometimes takes me days to fully recover. I have learned through the school of hard knocks that it is much easier to deprive myself of these tasty foods than to enjoy them for a few moments and then live in misery for days. Over last couple of years I have also pinpointed my son's food allergies and have eliminated these from his diet. He had always hated to read and was a very slow reader. After several months of being on a proper elimination diet his reading was tested and found to be several levels above his actual grade. Since then, he has also learned to love reading without any pushing on our part. This is truly a remarkable change in such a brief period of time and without any therapy specific for reading skills. At our research facility, we have observed similar and even more dramatic improvements in academic skills and behavioral factors in numerous children who have been treated simply by discovering their food allergies and intolerances and placing them on a suitable diet. This is one of the primary areas that Functional Medicine Practitioners have learned to focus on when beginning to work with any child or adult with ADHD. There are now plenty of good reasons to make the effort to identify and eliminate allergy provoking and intolerant foods in everyone with ADHD. (Carter, 1993; Boris, 1994; Kaplan, 1987; Kaplan, 1989; Salzman, 1976; Egger, 1985; Schulte-Körne, 1996; Williams, 1978; Egger, 1992; Joneja, 1996) Upcoming chapters will provide practical solutions to the problem of food allergies and adverse reactions to foods, as well as common sense principles which can be used to optimize the diet in those with ADHD.

Chapter 12

The Universe Within; Bacteria, Yeast and Parasites in ADHD

THE REMARKABLE UNIVERSE WITHIN

We have all, at one time or another, pondered the wondrous nature of our universe. Ever since I was a young boy, I become overwhelmed with reverence and awe whenever I consider the incomprehensible vastness of space. It is really impossible to truly grasp the idea that trillions of stars like our own sun reside in millions of separate galaxies some of which are millions of light years away from us. It is easy to feel very small when contemplating such lofty realities. Yet, on the other hand, there is an equally vast universe in the opposite direction, within the vast domain of cells, molecules, atoms and even tinier subatomic particles. From this microscopic perspective, our bodies are equally as vast. Every cell in our body is like an immense and complex world, far beyond the complexity of the world that we see with our eyes. Although each individual cell is tremendously complex, the human body contains approximately 100,000,000,000,000 of these highly sophisticated cells.

This microscopic view also reveals an enormous world of bacteria, yeasts and viruses, which inhabit our skin, respiratory tract, urinary tract and gastrointestinal system. If we were to take a census of the cells inhabiting our body, bacteria would actually be (numerically) the predominant form of life, outnumbering all human cells by ten times (1,000,000,000,000,000 bacterial cells). In fact, on average, there are more bacteria in our bodies than there are stars in the known universe. Under ideal circumstances we happily coexist with our bacterial inhabitants and actually benefit tremendously from their presence. In states of good health, the immune system expends a great deal of energy in selectively "farming" beneficial bacteria while making life more difficult for unfriendly bacteria, yeasts, protozoans, worms and viruses.

WHAT GOOD ARE MICROBES?

Why in the world do we need microbes anyway? The fact is that without them the world would be a terrible mess. We think of ourselves as trendy and responsible citizens if we are diligently involved in recycling our garbage. However, microbes are way ahead of us. They have been recycling since the beginning of life on Earth. These tiny creatures specialize in making something out of almost nothing. All living things generally resist being eaten by microbes. However, once something is dead, microbes go to work breaking up its complex molecules into other simpler chemicals, which can then be used by plants to create life all over again. Without microbes nothing would decay: we might end up having to build our houses on piles of garbage miles high. In reality, life could not exist without the harmonious relationship we now have with the microbial world.

Our bodies also have an important and mutually beneficial relationship with specific kinds of microbes. In the gastrointestinal tract of an average person, approximately 400 species of bacteria and several species of yeast can commonly be found. Many of these organisms play important roles in the optimal function of our digestive and immune systems. Other species may be neither beneficial nor harmful, while some have the potential to be downright nasty.

Can Intestinal Bacteria Contribute to Disease?

Since the turn-of-the-century a small but very stubborn group of physicians and scientists have maintained the position that certain species of intestinal bacteria play a tremendously important role in the maintenance of human health and longevity. In fact, by the early 1900's this idea was well ingrained in the views of many of the world's leading medical professors. The basic idea behind this hypothesis was that particularly undesirable intestinal bacteria rot or putrefy undigested food materials in the colon. When this occurs, putrid bacterial byproducts are absorbed through the colon and then circulate throughout the body creating stress upon tissues and organs, leading to disease. A strong segment of the medical profession responded to these ideas by encouraging their patients to avoid constipation at all cost and to regularly use enemas to purge the colon. Some physicians took this idea to such an extreme that surgery to remove a portion of the colon for the treatment of constipation became one of the most common operations of that era. Gradually, as the practice of medicine became more and more dependent on the use of symptom suppressing drugs, doctors began to scoff at the idea that gut bacteria could have anything to do with health or disease except in the obvious cases of infectious diarrhea. But, as is often true with new ideas, the pendulum is swinging back once again as physicians and scientists around the world are beginning to recognize the tremendous importance of gut ecology in the function of the human organism. Microorganisms inhabiting the gut are now thought to play a significant role in stomach ulcers, gastritis, stomach cancer, Crohn's disease, ulcerative colitis, rheumatoid arthritis, ankylosing spondylitis, and colon cancer. There is also mounting evidence that abnormal gut organisms may contribute significantly to the development of chronic fatigue syndrome, autism and to the worsening of AIDS. Most recently, research conducted at our facility has demonstrated significant abnormalities in the microbial ecology of the gut in the majority of children with ADHD.

Probiotic Bacteria – Farming the Friendly Flora

Research examining the importance of intestinal bacteria has expanded tremendously in the past few years and now an extensive body of scientific literature supports the hypothesis that specific bacteria truly are important participants in human health as well as in many illnesses. Numerous species of bacteria and a few forms of yeasts have been studied for their ability to prevent and treat illnesses, and to bring about beneficial physiological changes in humans and animals. Specific microbial species that have been demonstrated to have health-giving properties are known as "probiotics" a term that means they are beneficial to life.

Soon after birth, probiotic bacterial species can be identified in high numbers in the gastrointestinal tract of infants who are breast-fed. Specific components of the breast milk suppress the growth of harmful microbes while promoting the growth of beneficial bacterial flora. Breast milk contains specific antibodies (secretory IgA) as well as certain enzymes (lactoferrin and lactoperoxidase) which are designed to target and kill a variety of undesirable microbes while leaving the friendly flora completely alone. Breast milk also contains oligosacharides (short chains of rare sugars) which suppress the growth of disease bacteria, encourage the growth of friendly flora and stimulate the infant's immune system. In a very real sense, the mother's immune system is "farming" the flora of her child's gastrointestinal tract by weeding out undesirable organisms while encouraging the growth of probiotic bacteria. Within a few months the infant's own immune system takes over this role. In a healthy infant, after the age of weaning, nearly all of the important immune components found in breast milk can then be found in the child's tears, saliva, intestinal juices, stool and urine.

As a general rule the beneficial bacteria found in the breast-fed infant are various types of Lactobacilli and Bifidobacteria which are initially acquired by the baby at birth as she passes through her mother's vagina. Later on, other species become established as resident flora through food, beverages, intimate human contact and, in some cases, by taking nutritional supplements containing probiotic bacteria. Several hundred different varieties of these bacterial species have been identified and many have been studied for their potential role as probiotic bacteria. The relative presence or lack of these types of intestinal bacteria may reflect significantly upon the health or lack of health of an individual. People who are chronically ill or very elderly usually have a relative lack of these beneficial bacteria and, instead, have a predominance of less desirable organisms. On the other hand, healthy individuals generally have an abundance of friendly flora. A great deal of research has now been done to determine the variety of benefits derived from probiotic organisms as well as the possible links between human disease and more unfriendly gut bacteria.

INTESTINAL MICROBES — THE GOOD, THE BAD, AND THE UGLY

In general, the 400 or so species of microbes residing within the gastrointestinal tract of the average weaned child or adult can be classified into three basic groups:

· Group 1 — Those which are known to be beneficial and are never responsible for disease (probiotic).

· Group 2 — Those that have no known benefits and which cause or contribute to disease processes only under certain circumstances.

· Group 3 — Those that have no known benefits and which are known to readily cause or contribute to disease processes (pathogenic or parasitic).

The relative balance of these various organisms within the intestinal tract may have a tremendous influence on a person's health. Those who have insufficient Group 1 organisms or who have a predominance of Group 2 or Group 3 organisms are said to suffer from intestinal dysbiosis. Intestinal dysbiosis means literally "bad life forms in the intestine". Identifying and treating intestinal dysbiosis is an important part of the practice of Functional Medicine.

Group 1 organisms primarily consist of Lactobacilli and Bifidobacteria along with a several other types of bacteria and even perhaps a few species of yeast. Some of these friendly flora are the same kind of organisms that are used to make fermented foods like yogurt, cheese, kefir and sauerkraut. These foods have been revered for centuries for their health giving benefits. As I'm sure you probably realize, we ingest billions of harmless probiotic bacteria every time we eat these types of foods.

In states of optimal health, Lactobacilli are usually the predominant organisms in the small intestine, whereas Bifidobacteria should predominate in the large intestine or colon. Dozens of different species of Lactobacilli and Bifidobacteria are known to exist. Although none of these have been shown to be harmful, only a few specific species have been shown to be most useful when administered for medical purposes. The other bacterial species which have also been proven to be probiotic in nature include certain species of Streptococcus, Enterococcus, Bacillus and E coli. These Group 1 organisms are the upright citizens of the intestinal tract — they work hard, pay their taxes and never get into trouble with the law. These bacteria are well adapted to the human gastrointestinal tract and are not destroyed by the body's immune defenses. They provide a wide range of services to the body in exchange for a secure and nourishing environment..

Group 2 organisms consist of a wide array of bacteria and a few species of yeasts. These are organisms which have only limited benefits to the body and under certain conditions may over populate the intestine or turn aggressive and contribute to ill health. They primarily include organisms, which are known to cause serious disease elsewhere in the body, or when people have seriously suppressed immune systems. Examples include bacteria, which cause pneumonia (such as Streptococcus pneumoniae), and yeasts that cause vaginal infections (Candida albicans). One benefit to these types of organisms is that if they are present in modest numbers, they may help to maintain the immune system in a vigilant state thus improving the body's resistance to infection. Group 2 organisms are the shadier characters of intestinal society. When present in smaller numbers and scattered throughout a population of more upright citizens they do some work and generally stay out of trouble. However, if they ever get together in large crowds or if they feel threatened or deprived of their basic needs they can turn aggressive and end up causing havoc.

Group 3 organisms include those bacteria, viruses, protozoans and worms, which readily cause disease once present within the intestine. These organisms include those that cause food poisoning (like Salmonella or enterotoxigenic E coli — the "hamburger disease"), those that cause severe diarrhea or dysentery (like cholera or rotavirus) or those that cause chronic gastrointestinal disease, such as Helicobacter pylori (the cause of ulcers), or Giardia lamblia ("beaver fever"). Many of these organisms are known to be associated with serious disease outside of the gastrointestinal tract. For example, the bacteria Klebsiella, when present in the colon, has been associated with an increased risk of ankylosing spondylitis, a painful arthritic condition of the spine. Another example can be found in the parasitic protozoa, Giardia which has been associated with growth retardation in children. Group 3 organisms are the truly criminal element of intestinal society. Even small numbers of these bad actors can create serious and widespread problems for the body. Intestinal society is better off without them altogether.

THE ANTIMICROBIAL DEFENSE SYSTEMS OF THE GASTROINTESTINAL TRACT

The food we ingest is usually loaded with microbes. This is why food spoils so quickly when left unrefrigerated. Food would spoil even more quickly in the warmth of our digestive tract if the body did not have a number of mechanisms to delay the growth of microorganisms until digestion and absorption was complete. As soon as food enters your mouth, it is mixed with saliva that contains molecules designed to kill microorganisms (lysozyme, lactoferrin and lactoperoxidase), and antibodies (secretory IgA) which stick to microbes and prevent them from growing or adhering to the mucous membrane of the gut. Once food hits the stomach, highly concentrated acids are produced which helps to kill all living microbes while digestion begins. Although the stomach is not a perfect sterilizer, it does a pretty good job of killing most microbes. Because of this, when food leaves the stomach and enters the small intestine, it should be relatively free of bacteria, yeasts and parasites. Once the liquefied food empties into the small intestine, bile from the gallbladder is mixed with the food along with digestive enzymes from the pancreas. Bile contains antibodies (secretory IgA) as well as bile acids (a natural detergent) and other substances, which effectively inhibit the growth of most microbes. Intestinal cells also secrete large amounts of antibodies (secretory IgA) and they manufacture a mucous layer, which acts like an impenetrable moving conveyer belt that prevents most organisms from adhering to the intestinal cells. The intestine also emits significant amounts of fluid and is in constant motion, mixing the food with digestive juices and moving it along toward the colon so that digesting food is never permitted to stagnate.

Because of all these defensive factors, the amount of bacteria present in the small intestine is normally very modest. However, if there is a breakdown in any of these antimicrobial factors, overgrowth of bacteria may occur within the small intestine. This can result in food material fermenting or putrefying in the small intestine rather than being properly digested and absorbed. Small bowel bacterial overgrowth or the so-called "auto-brewery syndrome" results when bacteria populate the small intestine to such an extent that the intestine becomes a living "brewing vat". (Pignata, 1990; Bouhnik, 1999) Alcohols like ethanol, and D-lactic acid (an unmetabolizable form of lactic acid) are just two of the many fermentation byproducts that can be generated withing the small bowel in the auto-brewery syndrome. (Batt, 1996) This condition is the focus of a considerable amount of research and many clinicians are beginning to suspect that it is a causative or contributing factor in some cases of ADHD and autism. It is easy to imagine that if your intestine has become a "brewing vat" and is producing various toxic acids, alcohols, and gases instead of efficiently digesting and absorbing nutrients, that there may be some considerable effects upon the brain.

SOME OF THE MANY BENEFITS OF PROBIOTIC BACTERIA

Certain species of probiotic organisms are highly adapted to the human gastrointestinal tract and are able to survive all of the defensive strategies used by the GALT to suppress microbial growth within the gut. Over the millennia, certain organisms have adapted to life inside human beings. In exchange for a warm secure environment with plenty of food, they provide their human host with a long list of significant benefits. (Goldin, 1998; Batt, 1996; Bengmark, 1998; Salminen, 1998) These organisms are able to populate the mucous layer of the small intestine and, once they become stable residents, they will assist the intestine and the intestinal immune system in many important ways.

These friendly flora produce enzymes which assist in the digestion of protein, carbohydrates and fats. Thus, when plenty of these organisms are present, absorption of food occurs more rapidly and less undigested food is left behind for bacterial fermentation and putrefaction. For these and other reasons, probiotics are able to prevent and treat bacterial overgrowth in the small bowel (auto brewery syndrome). (Vanderhoof, 1998) As well, since probiotics improve the digestion protein, they may decrease the absorption of neuropeptides from foods such as dairy and wheat products. Of particular importance in ADHD is the fact that probiotic intestinal bacteria may significantly improve the absorption of brain-critical fatty acids and the building blocks of neurotransmitters (amino acids). Another amino acid, glutamine, is largely generated by the work of probiotic bacteria upon protein in the gut. This amino acid is the principle food of the small intestinal cells and is vital to their normal function. Probiotic organisms also improve the absorption of minerals and vitamins and they actually synthesize a number of vitamins needed by the body. In addition, friendly flora in the last part of the small intestine and first part of the colon digest and ferment dietary fiber and from this produce the primary food for the colonic cells (short chain fatty acids).

Probiotics may also play a highly significant role in the prevention of allergic diseases including food allergies. Because these friendly flora help to break protein down until it is composed of non-antigenic amino acids, probiotics are able to decrease the allergic potential of food. They also have a profound effect upon the immune system and have been found to decrease gut inflammation and allergic responsiveness towards food antigens. Recent research suggests that regular administration of specific probiotic bacterial species can actually diminish or even reverse serious food allergies in children. (Majamaa, 1998; Kirjavainen, 1999) In fact, many researchers now consider that normal populations of probiotic bacteria must be resident within the small intestine in order for the development and maintenance of tolerance toward food antigens to take place. In other words, the GALT (gut associated lymphoid tissue) simply cannot function adequately without the assistance of adequate populations of friendly intestinal flora. Importantly, probiotics do not simply suppress immunity to decrease allergic states. Instead, these friendly flora remarkably diminish gut inflammation and food allergies, while improving immune responsiveness toward infectious organisms.(Pelto, 1998; Sudo, 1997)

These organisms also act as living antioxidants protecting the intestine from free radical damage and neutralizing various toxins produced by other microbes within the intestinal tract. Furthermore, they carry on a continual dialog with the GALT, instructing the immune cells to focus upon healing and the production of appropriate defensive materials while decreasing inflammatory activity. Because these friendly flora have so many healing properties, it is of no surprise that research has now demonstrated that the administration of certain probiotics can accelerate the repair of a leaky gut. (Bengmark, 1995)

Of great importance is the fact that probiotic bacteria have been shown to produce antimicrobial substances referred to as biocins. These natural agents inhibit the growth of a variety of unfriendly bacteria, yeasts and parasites and help to maintain an ideal balance of organisms throughout the gastrointestinal tract. In the small intestine, friendly flora inhabit the thin mucous layer covering intestinal cells and they assist the GALT in the general suppression of microbial growth. Once the remains of food enter the colon, bacterial growth proliferates immensely. In fact, stool is approximately one-third bacteria by weight. The immune defenses within the large intestine are not as formidable as they are within the stomach and small intestine. Because of this, the body depends even more heavily upon probiotic organisms to predominate and by doing so reduce the numbers of hostile microbes within the region of the colon.

GUT ECOLOGY IN ADHD

Unfortunately, a number of factors very common to our modern lifestyle can contribute to the depletion or even eradication of friendly flora within the gut. In recent research, we tested stool samples from 63 children with

ADHD. In 46 percent of these children, absolutely no Lactobacillus or Bifidobacteria species were found. In addition, over 80 percent of these children were discovered to have significant quantities of various Group 3 bacteria which are known to be pathogenic (disease causing) in humans. In this same study, 32 percent of the stool samples tested were found to have dense populations of the yeast organism Candida albicans or other related fungi. Particularly surprising was the fact that in 41 percent of cases, protozoal parasites were found on microscopic analysis. In some cases as many as five species of parasites were found in one stool sample. Previous research looking at the frequency of parasites in North American children has suggested that parasites can be found in no more than 5 or 10 percent of the normal childhood population. Our research certainly suggests that children with ADHD are very likely to have serious disturbances of their gastrointestinal ecology. There is a microscopic war being fought and lost within the gastrointestinal tracts of those with ADHD, a war that may very well be a principle factor in the development and maintenance of this disorder.

THE DARK SIDE OF THE MICROSCOPIC WORLD

It would be foolish for us to underestimate the power of the microbial world or be lulled into thinking that we have somehow conquered infectious disease because we have discovered antibiotics. Microbes, in spite of their small size, are incredibly sophisticated and have adapted to some of the most amazing circumstances. Consider the difference in size between the lowly bacteria and the human. A bacterium can weigh as little as 0.00000000001 gram. A human on the other hand can easily weigh 150,000 grams. Yet, one bacterium of the wrong species has the potential to multiply and kill a large population of humans. It has happened many times before and will likely happen many times again especially with the emergence of increasing numbers of antibiotic resistant strains of bacteria. Although we are seldom aware of this fact, it is clear we are presently, as humans always have been, in the midst of a constant and raging battle against the dark side of the microbial world.

HEPATIC ENCEPHALOPATHY — EVIDENCE THAT COMMON GUT BACTERIA PRODUCE POTENT BRAIN TOXINS

One of the most vivid proofs that common gut bacteria have the potential to exert an extraordinary influence upon the brain can be seen by considering the condition known as hepatic encephalopathy. Hepatic refers to the liver, encephal refers to the brain, and pathy means disease. Therefore, hepatic encephalopathy is a brain disease caused by problems with the liver. This condition is commonly seen in individuals with severe liver disease, such as cirrhosis of the liver. Once their liver function becomes so poor that it is no longer able to detoxify the poisonous substances that are constantly generated by unfriendly gut bacteria, the individual will become confused, forgetful and emotionally disturbed. If the condition continues to progress, they will eventually be overcome by a state of severe delirium in which they become psychotic and have horrid hallucinations and mental anguish. If it progresses beyond this point, death is certain due to total collapse of brain function. All of these symptoms are the result of gut-derived toxins ending up in the brain instead of being rapidly detoxified by the liver!

There are few things as shocking and puzzling as seeing someone overcome by hepatic encephalopathy. Several of these cases are still etched in my mind from medical student days. I recall when I first saw a person admitted to the hospital with hepatic encephalopathy. This poor man was "completely out of his mind" and appeared to be right at death's doorstep. To my amazement, when I entered his room the next day, he was sitting up eating breakfast and looking quite alert. With a friendly smile, he reached over to shake my hand and introduced himself. Needless to say, I almost fell over backwards with amazement at his rapid recovery. Immediately after making his acquaintance, I raced to the nurses station to find out what miracle drug had brought this man out of such a profound state of delirium so quickly. "Oh, we didn't need to give him any drugs", said the charge nurse, "we just gave him a good case of diarrhea". Now I was really confused! At my first opportunity, I headed to the medical school library and read everything I could about hepatic encephalopathy.

The explanation for hepatic encephalopathy is actually rather straightforward. Under normal circumstances, bacteria within the colon ferment and putrefy undigested food materials. Many of these bacterial breakdown products are potentially poisonous to the brain, immune system and other organs if they were to enter the general circulation. However, everything that is absorbed from the large and small intestines filters through the liver rather than just entering the circulation directly. When the liver is functioning normally, most of these toxic bacterial byproducts are captured and detoxified by the liver. However, when the liver is severely damaged, many of these toxins bypass the liver and end up in circulation where they can have a profound influence on the brain and even cause death. Decades ago it was discovered that if you simply administer a powerful laxative and give these patients a "rip-roaring" case of diarrhea, the colon will be temporarily cleared of toxin producing bacteria and the patient often regains their full mental functions within several hours. Although this doesn't solve the underlying liver problems, it is able to buy some time and help ease the patient's suffering if only for a while.

Research into hepatic encephalopathy has proven definitively that microbes within the intestinal tract produce some very significant toxins. It should also suggest to us that the brain has the potential to be affected significantly by gut microbes under other circumstances where unfriendly Group 2 and Group 3 microbes begin to predominate in the gastrointestinal tract. Similarly, if intestinal permeability increases significantly, the quantity of toxic material presenting itself to the liver may increase beyond the liver's capability to efficiently detoxify this material. Even when the liver has not severely failed as it does in cirrhosis, its ability to detoxify various substances can be diminished significantly due to various genetic, nutritional or environmental factors. It is likely that, even in the absence of obvious illness, the brain is affected somewhat by gut derived toxins on a regular basis. Most importantly, there is mounting evidence that disturbances in gut ecology, digestive efficiency, intestinal immune function, gut permeability and liver detoxification capability all work hand in hand as principle factors in ADHD and related conditions such as autism. Pondering the implications of hepatic encephalopathy will help to convince even the most skeptical physician that there may indeed be a significant gut-brain connection.

THE NATURE OF MICROBIAL TOXINS

The basic purpose of a microbe is to eat and perpetuate its species. Competition for food and for habitat explains a great deal about microbial behavior. Microbes are amazing chemical manufacturing experts. Although some of these chemicals are simply harmless breakdown products of the foods consumed by the microbe, thousands of other chemicals are produced by microbes for malicious purposes. Some of these chemical substances are used by the microbe to inhibit the growth of other microbes that might be trying to compete in their chosen habitat. For example, yeasts derive energy for their growth and reproduction by consuming sugars and converting them to alcohol through the process of fermentation. Yeasts have a strong tolerance for alcohol and can thrive in an alcohol-enriched environment that is toxic to most other organisms. Thus, yeasts are able to eat, drink and be merry while all other organisms are left out in the cold. In a similar manner, probiotic bacteria consume carbohydrates and produce lactic acid, which inhibits the growth of most other organisms.

Thousands of more sinister microbial toxins have now been identified. Undoubtedly, a far greater number of these substances are still yet to be discovered. Each of these toxins serves specific purposes for the organism and can have an extraordinarily wide range of effects on the human host. One of the most common strategies used by microbes is to produce toxins, which impair the function of other microbial species by impairing their ability to make energy. Unfortunately, bacteria and human cells have some striking similarities, which can make them both susceptible to similar microbial toxins. Within every human cell, numerous tiny energy generating stations known as mitochondria are found. Every human cell, without exception relies on its mitochondria to produce the energy that it needs to survive and do work. These mitochondria are remarkably similar to bacteria in many ways. Firstly, they contain many of the same enzymes that bacteria use to produce energy from food derived molecules. Therefore, if a gut microbe produces a toxin which is designed to shut down energy production within other bacteria, this same toxin has the potential to shut down energy producing enzymes within the mitochondria of human cells as well. It is certain that some bacteria take advantage of this phenomenon for their own purposes. For example, in order for some bacteria to survive inside the human gut, they might purposefully produce chemicals which weakens the immunity of its human host. (Fasano, 1998; Popoff, 1998)

Researchers have begun to identify this very phenomenon at work in certain disease processes. A well-known research pathologist, Dr. William Shaw, has identified high levels of tartaric acid in the urine of many children with autism in contrast to normal children who do not have this substance in their urine. (Shaw, 1996) Dr. Shaw's research has determined that tartaric acid is actually a fermentation byproduct resulting from the overgrowth of the yeast organism Candida albicans within the gut of children with autism. There are scientific reasons to believe that tartaric acid may be purposefully produced by Candida albicans to prevent competitive microbes from manufacturing energy. Tartaric acid has been demonstrated to be a potent inhibitor of certain microbial enzymes, which are used to generate energy from food materials. Unfortunately, tartaric acid also strongly inhibits energy production within human mitochondria. Since brain cells contain the highest number of mitochondria and have the highest requirements for energy production of any cell in the body, it is not unimaginable that this toxin could affect brain function in susceptible children. In keeping with this finding, numerous Functional Medicine practitioners have demonstrated that clinical improvements can be achieved in some of these children by reducing the quantity of yeast from the gut and thus lowering tartaric acid levels in the body. Our own research demonstrated heavy overgrowth of Candida albicans and other similar fungal species in the stool of over one third of children with ADHD. It comes as no surprise then that Dr. Shaw's laboratory and other labs performing similar work, commonly find high levels of tartaric acid in the urine of children with ADHD. Interestingly, many clinicians have noted that high levels of tartaric acid can also be commonly found in the urine of adults with fibromyalgia, a condition characterized by muscle pain, stiffness, fatigue and "brain fog". Perhaps in such cases, tartaric acid accumulates in muscle cells and inhibits energy production in the muscles as well as causing some inhibition of brain function.

Recently, researchers from Australia, directed by Dr. Hugh Dunstan, discovered a substance in the urine of individuals with chronic fatigue syndrome. This chemical substance, referred to as chronic fatigue syndrome urinary marker number one (CFSUM1), has been detected in approximately 85 percent of those with chronic fatigue syndrome and only very rarely in those who are unaffected by this condition. (McGregor, 1996a, McGregor, 1996b) CFSUM1 is a potent neurotoxin, which inhibits energy production in human mitochondria. The molecular structure of CFSUM is though to be similar to that of a common neurotoxic pesticide known as N-methyl proline. This nasty substance is known to come from the overgrowth of certain undesirable gut bacteria. Although no research has been done to look for this gut derived toxin in those with ADHD, the finding of this substance helps to further establish the reality of a gut-brain connection.

Because analytical chemistry technology has improved so tremendously, researchers have begun to identify several other gut-derived toxins in the urine of individuals with various brain disorders. One example is arabinose, another yeast metabolite, which disturbs brain cell function and may cause structural damage to neurons. Another neurotoxin is referred to as DHPPA, a metabolite of certain unfriendly Clostridium bacteria (relatives of the botulism bacteria). Perhaps the most intriguing of these recent findings was recently described to me by Dr. Woody McGuiness, an autism researcher whom I know personally and greatly respect. In personal communication he has described the fact that various researchers have detected a gut derived toxin in the urine of autistic kids, which is the same molecule as the neurotoxin used by Amazonian Indians as a blowgun dart toxin. Again, although this toxin is thought to derive from unfriendly gut bacteria it is the same substance acquired by the Amazonians from the skin of poisonous frogs!

However, not all of the bacterial toxins being discovered recently are complex or esoteric substances. Even lactic acid can have a significant neurotoxic influence under certain circumstances. The form of lactic acid is produced by the body is called L-lactic acid (left handed shape). However, many bacteria produce both L-lactic acid and its mirror image, D-lactic acid (right handed shape). Unfortunately, the body cannot utilize or metabolize D-lactic acid very well at all. Therefore, if bacteria that produce D-lactic acid overgrow in the human gut, the person's blood will become acidic and their brain will work very poorly. (Spillane, 1994; Gurevitch , 1993; Traub, 1983; Haan, 1985) Since so many bacteria, good and bad, produce lactic acid, it is possible that D-lactic acid is a common neurotoxic stressor in ADHD. And, since probiotic bacteria all produce plenty of lactic acid, it is important to only use those bacteria which produce L-lactic acid exclusively. Several species are now known to fulfill this criteria.

Besides producing chemicals that inhibit the function of other cells, microbes utilize a number of different strategies to improve their status in intestinal society, or to increase their population and improve the chance that their kind will continue to thrive on the Earth. (Popoff, 1996) Some unfriendly microbes produced toxins that markedly increase gut permeability. This can increase the amount of fluid expelled by intestinal cells into the gut and provide more nutrients for these aggressive organisms. As well, if the human host has a leaky gut, the intestinal immune system will be weakened and less capable of eradicating the undesirable microbe. Certain microbial toxins will markedly decrease the ability of the liver to detoxify a wide range of substances. Perhaps the bacteria are using this as a strategy to weaken their human host so that the immune system will be less able to expel these nasty organisms. In some cases, the organism prefers to live in the soil or in the aquatic environment. If this is the case, it is to the organism's advantage to create diarrhea in its human host so that it is likely to be released into a more preferred environment.

JEKYLL AND HYDE MICROBES

One the most interesting topics of research in this area involves the recent discovery that gut microbes can markedly alter their state of aggressiveness depending upon the nature of their intestinal environment. (Alverdy, 1998) Numerous gut organisms are virtually harmless as long as they are provided with optimal nutrition and their environment is free from certain threatening factors. However, if the organisms sense that their survival is threatened they may undergo marked changes in their structure and function which allow them to become aggressive invaders. For example, if an otherwise healthy individual is placed on a diet in which certain nutrients (such as vitamins, minerals or various phytochemicals) are lacking, previously harmless species of gut bacteria may undergo changes allowing them to colonize the surface of the intestine or even invade intestinal cells. Insufficient dietary fiber and a lack of oligosacharides (short chains of rare sugars found in many plant foods) have been shown to be particularly likely to provoke gut bacteria to mutiny against their intestinal host. Rather than wait around starving to death, these bacteria go looking for their dinner inside the cells of their human host! This is certainly one of the perils of the junk food diet and may be why junk food has such a tendency to create abnormal changes in gut flora and problems like a leaky gut.

Similar changes may occur when gut microbes are threatened by toxins such as antibiotics or heavy metals. Following a course of antibiotics, a person's intestinal tract may become populated by a collection of angry and vengeful microbes with behaviors that are far more aggressive than their predecessors. In a similar way, it has been shown by researchers at

University of Calgary (where I attended medical school) that placing mercury containing amalgam fillings in a person's mouth results in the development of numerous aggressive, antibiotic resistant intestinal bacteria within just a few weeks. (Lorscheider, 1995) Researchers have even shown that high levels of stress hormones (such as would occur if an individual were on drugs like Ritalin® or Dexedrine®) can significantly increase the aggressiveness of intestinal bacteria. (Alverdy, 1998)

Interestingly, research shows that some gut pathogens may cause little or no harm when there is a relative absence of competitive gut pathogens. However, if other potentially harmful species begin to proliferate within the gut, these pathogens may declare war and start fighting aggressively for dominance in the intestinal environment. This principle may be of particular importance in ADHD since our research has demonstrated that most of these individuals have more than one potential pathogen in a single stool sample. Thus, organisms which are normally considered relatively benign may actually be more pathogenic (disease causing) in this highly competitive environment.

If previously harmless intestinal bacteria become hostile and begin to invade host cells, a great deal of stress is placed upon the gut and immune system. Leaky gut is very likely to result along with diminished capability for nutrient absorption. With a leaky gut comes an increased burden upon the immune system and the detoxification mechanisms of the liver. The immune system, in turn, becomes activated by these changes and then releases various alarm substances into the bloodstream, leading to adverse symptoms in the brain and organs.

SUPERANTIGENS AND IMMUNE SUPPRESSORS

One of the most profound discoveries to come out of gut flora research relates to the ability of certain organisms to profoundly affect the immune system in a variety of ways. Several organisms have now been identified as having the ability to act as "superantigens". Remember that antigens are larger molecules (usually proteins or protein breakdown products called peptides) which are recognized by the immune system as either self or non-self. The immune system should have tolerance toward all antigens it deems as self. This tolerance normally extends to all food antigens as well as all antigens from normal gut flora (Type 1 and some Type 2 organisms). However, numerous organisms that commonly inhabit the gut have the potential to cause disease or death if the immune system does not keep the population of these organisms very low (some Type 2 and many Type 3 organisms). If these organisms were to escape into the bloodstream and begin to proliferate, they could cause death within hours. Therefore, the immune system recognizes certain microbial antigens and responds to them in an extremely aggressive fashion. In some cases, these superantigens can aggravate the immune system and result in increased allergic responsiveness. The presence of high amounts of the yeast, Candida albicans in the gut has been shown to markedly increase the likelihood that an individual will suffer from allergic diseases such as eczema. (Morita, 1999) As well, intestinal parasites (such as the protozoan Giardia or intestinal roundworms) can also act as superantigens and greatly increase the likelihood that a person will develop allergic diseases including food allergies. (DiPrisco, 1998)

Other microbes are able to act as immune suppressors. These organisms are able to transmit chemical messages to immune cells, which diminish certain aspects of their function and allow the microorganism to proliferate. Thus, when a variety of unfriendly flora flourish within the intestinal tract, the immune system can be both over activated in some ways by antigens and superantigens, and weakened in other ways by toxic immune suppressors. These effects will be particularly prominent if the individual also suffers from inadequate quantities of probiotic bacterial flora.

As mentioned before, in our research, we found the presence of potential superantigens and immune suppressors in a very high percentage of the 63 children with ADHD. Stool samples gathered for this study revealed Candida albicans in over one third of subjects, protozoal parasites in nearly one half and many Group 3 bacteria such as Klebsiella,

Pseudomonas, Proteus and Citrobacter in the majority of children. Perhaps the presence of gut superantigens is partly to blame for the high incidence of food allergies and intolerances in these children. It may also be responsible for immune system over activation resulting in the release of alarm substances with directly adverse effects upon brain function. As will be discussed in the following chapter, we also found evidence of suppression of intestinal immune function in nearly half of our study subjects.

WHAT LEADS TO THE DEVELOPMENT OF DYSBIOSIS?

Ideally, humans should maintain a healthy balance of intestinal flora throughout their lives. Unfortunately, this may not be the case as many factors in our modern lifestyle can lead to a reduction or eradication of normal gut flora and their subsequent replacement by less desirable organisms (intestinal dysbiosis). Dysbiosis can begin at birth in infants who are not breast-fed. It is also a common occurrence after the administration of antibiotics, especially after repeated courses of the very broad-spectrum antibiotics usually required to combat today's antibiotic resistant infections. As mentioned previously, the placement of mercury containing amalgams has been shown repeatedly in animal and human studies to destroy friendly gut flora and to promote the growth of aggressive, antibiotic resistant strains. Junk foods and fast foods are also tremendous stimulants for the growth of abnormal gut flora. Not consuming adequate dietary fiber and having a diet, which is lacking in sufficient fruits and vegetables is one of the most common causes of intestinal dysbiosis in children. Emotional stress and various medications which induce a stress response or mimic stress in the body are also major contributors to depleted immunity and disturbed gut flora. These can include alcohol, tobacco, excessive caffeine, cortisone-like drugs, as well as the ADHD drugs, Ritalin® and Dexedrine®.

Most studies indicate that, outside of third world countries, intestinal parasites are relatively uncommon in healthy adults and children. Factors which suppress immunity or which lead to an increased exposure to these organisms have been shown to increase the likelihood that these harmful inhabitants will be found. Intestinal parasites can include various worms as well as single celled protozoa. Very young children who regularly attend large daycare centers are more likely to harbor intestinal parasites. Presumably, this is because they are in very close contact with many other children in diapers and fecal contamination of their environment makes for easy transmission of parasites. It may also be, in part, because children who attend daycare experience frequent respiratory infections and spend considerable time on antibiotics, which then destroys normal gut flora and increases their susceptibility to parasitic infection. Several studies have indicated that there is a very high incidence of intestinal parasites amongst homosexual men with or without HIV infection. Most likely, anal intercourse leads to a very high rate of parasitic transmission and can be significantly immune suppressive even in the absence of HIV. Our research found intestinal parasites (protozoa) in nearly half of the 63 children we examined with ADHD. This is certainly a much higher incidence of parasites than has been found in other studies of North American children. Since the water quality in our city is excellent and there has never been any reported outbreaks attributed to this source, it is most likely that the majority of these parasites were present secondary to some degree of immune suppression. The evidence for this possibility will be discussed in the next chapter.

FUNCTIONAL MEDICINE RESPONSE TO THE PATIENT WITH DYSBIOSIS

When significant forms of dysbiosis are detected through Functional Medicine testing in individuals with chronic illness, these people often benefit greatly by properly correcting their internal ecological disturbances. In Functional Medicine, intestinal dysbiosis is considered a common trigger or physiological disturbance contributing to the signs and symptoms of many chronic disease processes and developmental disorders. Although this area of Functional Medicine science is in its infancy and will mature dramatically over the next few years, many practical tools for the evaluation and treatment of intestinal dysbiosis are now available. These principles will be covered in detail in Chapters 16 and 24.

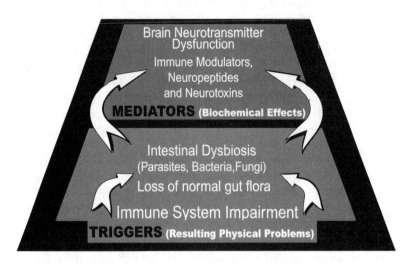

Intestinal Dysbiosis in ADHD

Chapter 13

Debilitated Defenses; Immune System Impairment in ADHD

THE IMMUNE SYSTEM RULES

By this time, it should be very clear that the immune system plays an extraordinarily important role in every aspect of body and brain function, both in its role as a communications network and as a defense organization. Through the release of its molecules of emotion, inflammation and communication, the immune system has the power to elevate us into realms of joyous ecstasy or cast us into a bottomless pit of despair. It has the ability to faithfully defend us from the most hideous plague or kill us in minutes for simply eating a bite of the wrong food. The immune system demands respect and science is finally starting to give it some of the respect it deserves. It seems that if medical science looks closely enough, there are highly significant immunological factors below the surface of almost every human malady. The revolutionary field of psychoneuroimmunology has opened up a whole new world of understanding and is inspiring completely new possibilities in the treatment of a wide range of disorders. Many conditions, such as ADHD, autism, fibromyalgia and depression, have by and large been regarded by the medical profession as "mysterious chemical imbalances" and then simply treated with symptom suppressing drugs. Now, with the breakthroughs that have occurred in the fields of immunology, nutritional biochemistry, microbiology and psychoneuroimmunology, there are strong reasons to believe that immune system impairment may be at the very heart of these and countless other disorders. Because of such breakthroughs, approaches to treatment will increasingly reflect this developing understanding.

IMMUNE SYSTEM IMPAIRMENT IN ADHD

Over the past decade, evidence has been accumulating which supports the concept that there are significant immune system abnormalities in individuals with ADHD. In 1995, a research team headed up by Dr. R.Warren of Utah State University demonstrated that children with ADHD had significantly lower levels of a critical immune factor known as complement C4B as compared to normal, age matched children.(Warren, 1995) Complement C4B is the captain of a team of over one dozen different proteins that circulate continuously in the bloodstream. As mentioned in Chapter 11, when complement encounters a foreign antigen which has been coated with antibodies, a chain reaction is triggered in which complement molecules "explode" violently around the foreign invader like a string of firecrackers on the Fourth of July. Because of the explosive action of complement, even the most aggressive virus, bacteria or yeast organism is quickly destroyed. In a sense, antibodies that have attached themselves to foreign antigens in the blood serve as antennas to guide the complement, like "smart bombs", into their intended target. If the members of the complement team are not all present and accounted for, foreign intruders have a much greater chance of succeeding in their attempts to invade the body. Insufficient complement activity may help to explain why children with ADHD tend to experience more frequent infections than their non-ADHD peers and are more likely to end up on repeated courses of antibiotics.

Further research by Dr. Warren's team, suggests that the form of complement deficiency found in ADHD may be due in part to a genetic factor. (Warren, 1996; Odell,1997) Interestingly, the same immune abnormality, as well as the genetic basis for this problem, has been found in autistic kids and those with dyslexia. It is also quite possible that in addition to a genetic weakness in complement production, complement is being consumed excessively in those with ADHD who have Type III mediated food allergies. If you will recall from Chapter 11, when immune complexes are formed from the combination of antibodies and food antigens, complement can be activated. If this is occurring continually, complement supplies may be depleted just as the cruise missiles were depleted after the NATO invasion of Yugoslavia. Although we cannot yet correct a genetic weakness in complement production, we may be able to improve ADHD sufferers' immunity by reducing immune depleting factors such as food allergies, leaky gut and overgrowth of gut pathogens. This should leave more complement around to perform the important role for which it was intended.

Recently, researchers at the National Institutes of Health (Mittleman, 1997), examined the blood of children with ADHD and found significant abnormalities in the quantity of a wide range of inflammatory mediators known as cytokines. These important molecules of information form the words and sentences of the molecular dialogue that goes on continuously between the immune and nervous systems. These researchers provided evidence for both inflammation and immune system depletion in children with ADHD. Essentially, this data suggests that the immune system of the ADHD sufferer is angry, exhausted and confused. In turn, the messages being sent to the brain by such unhappy immune systems tend to set off alarm bells in the brain's own immune system leading to cognitive and behavioral problems. This is, in fact, the very picture that one would expect in a body, which has been enduring the kinds of physiological stresses and imbalances that have been discussed in previous chapters. It certainly gives strength to the argument that we should be searching for and addressing the underlying causes of ADHD rather than just modifying the symptoms with powerful drugs.

GUT IMMUNE DEFENSES IN ADHD

Although it should come as no surprise, our facility has demonstrated that diminished gut immunity may also be a significant factor in ADHD. As has been previously discussed, significant quantities of bacterial pathogens, yeast organisms and protozoal parasites were found in a high proportion of stool samples from children with ADHD. These findings are quite suggestive that these children suffer from impairment of gut mucosal immunity. However, in the same study, more direct evidence for this possibility was found. Every stool sample was tested for the presence of a critical antibody known as secretory IgA. In 44 percent of 63 cases, secretory IgA, was either absent or present in quantities significantly lower than normal values. This finding is of vital importance as it demonstrates that a significant proportion of children with ADHD suffer from a form of immune deficiency, which places them at much higher risk of respiratory infection, gastrointestinal infection and food allergies.

Secretory IgA is arguably the most important immune factor produced by the body. It is certainly produced in much higher quantities than any other component of the immune system. Under normal circumstances approximately 3 grams of secretory IgA is manufactured by the gut associated lymphoid tissue (GALT) of every person and transported into the intestine every day. (Mestecky, 1991) This means that the daily worldwide production of human secretory IgA is over 18 million kilograms per day. Specific GALT cells are assigned the task of producing one specific type of secretory IgA molecule designed to attach to one specific antigen. Since there is an enormous variety of antigens to which the immune system is familiar, thousands of different versions of secretory IgA must be produced every day. Secretory IgA is manufactured by GALT cells as well as cells which were born in the GALT and then migrated away to produce secretory IgA in other parts of the body. Tear ducts, salivary glands, nasal and respiratory mucous membranes, and the tissues that line the urinary and reproductive tracts all contain a collection of immune cells whose sole purpose in life is to produce secretory IgA. Therefore, under normal circumstances, every fluid secretion of the body is endowed with this vital immune component.

Secretory IgA is a large antibody molecule made up of two separate antibody molecules glued together at their base with a joining protein molecule. Immune cells manufacture the secretory IgA and then transfer this molecule to gut mucous membrane cells. Gut cells then wrap another protein around the secretory IgA which serves to prevent the secretory IgA from being digested. Because of this special wraparound molecule, secretory IgA is one of the few proteins that cannot be digested at all by the enzymes of the intestinal tract. Therefore, virtually every bit of secretory IgA released into the digestive tract can be found later in the stool. This is the reason that stool can be used to accurately measure the adequacy of secretory IgA production.

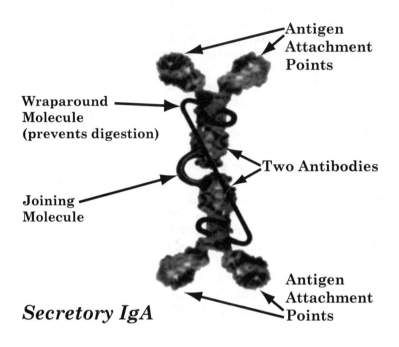

Secretory IgA

Secretory IgA also has four separate places for antigens to attach; each attachment point being specific for one antigen — like a key that fits only one lock. Once released, secretory IgA wanders around in the digestive tract until it finds and attaches to four antigens of the same type. Some secretory IgA is intended to attach to antigens from unfriendly microbes whereas other secretory IgA is designed to stick to food antigens. Normally, secretory IgA is produced in such high quantities that virtually every undesirable antigen ends up finding itself attached to secretory IgA. The enormous immune complex formed by secretory IgA and its four captive antigens is now more likely to stay within the digestive tract until the antigens are fully digested into harmless nutrients (amino acids). The size of this immune complex prevents it from crossing the gut wall and causing trouble with the immune system. Secretory IgA also prevents microbes from sticking to the gut wall, which they must be able to do before they can invade. This important antibody also sticks to and neutralizes a wide array of microbial toxins. Clearly, we all need adequate levels of secretory IgA!

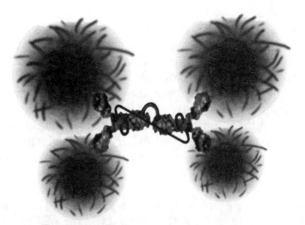

Immune Complex: composed of 1 secretory IgA molecule attached to 4 bacteria.

If secretory IgA levels are inadequate, harmful microbial species are more likely to establish their unwelcome presence in the gastrointestinal tract. In such cases, parasites such as those found in our study group as well as bacterial pathogens and yeast organisms will be more likely to flourish in numbers and will more readily stick to and colonize the gastrointestinal mucous membrane. Studies have also shown repeatedly that in the absence of secretory IgA, high numbers of gut microbes will invade right through the intestinal lining and place tremendous stress upon the GALT and liver. As well, individuals with insufficient secretory IgA production are more likely to suffer from the "autobrewery syndrome", which is characterized by overgrowth of fermenting microorganisms in the small intestinal tract and the release of toxic fermentation byproducts into the bloodstream. Since the respiratory and urinary tracts are also protected from infection by this same mechanism, deficiency of secretory IgA will also lead to higher rates of infection in these regions. Additionally, food allergies are more likely to develop in such individuals because deficient secretory IgA results in higher quantities of food antigens leaking across the gut mucous membrane and provoking an immunological reaction.

A number of factors have been shown to diminish the production of secretory IgA. About one in every four hundred people are born with an inability to manufacture all forms of IgA (there is a blood form as well as a secretory form). This is considered to be an inherited disorder, which results in a high risk of respiratory and gastrointestinal infections as well as food allergies and other unusual immunological problems. More commonly, secretory IgA can become depleted through a number of reversible factors.

Fortunately, secretory IgA does not limit the growth of probiotic bacteria within the mucous layer of the gastrointestinal tract and, in fact, their presence is a major stimulus for secretory IgA production. If gut flora is diminished or destroyed for whatever reason, secretory IgA production will go down. Studies have also shown that if certain probiotic species are administered as a dietary supplement, secretory IgA levels will significantly increase. (Bengmark, 1998; Fukushima, 1998; Buts, 1990) On the other hand, numerous other unfriendly microbes have immune depleting effects and their chronic presence may lead to a marked reduction in secretory IgA. Other factors such as food allergies, leaky gut, nutritional insufficiencies, certain drugs and stress may all play a role in the depletion of secretory IgA.

IMMUNE SYSTEM MUTINY

One of the most important findings of researchers looking into the immunology of ADHD relates to the fact that children with ADHD and other neuropsychiatric disorders often have antibodies in their blood directed at their own brain tissue. (Swedo, 1994; Kiessling, 1994) This phenomenon, referred to as autoimmunity occurs when the immune system loses tolerance for certain self antigens and begins to form antibodies against body tissues. Autoimmunity is responsible for a wide range of illnesses including juvenile onset diabetes, rheumatic fever, lupus, and rheumatoid arthritis. According to one of the most enduring explanations for autoimmunity, the immune system occasionally reacts against certain foreign antigens (from microbes or food) which happen to have significant similarities to certain self antigens. This is called "cross reaction". For example, individuals with celiac disease have a strong immunological intolerance to gluten from grains and their immune systems produce various antibodies against gluten. Unfortunately, although antigluten antibodies react or stick to gluten, they also cross react with antigens in the blood brain barrier. Thus, untreated celiac patients with high amounts of antigluten antibodies in their blood, may experience brain problems because of autoimmune damage to their blood brain barrier. (Pratesi, 1998)

Similarly, autoimmunity may also result when the immune system produces antibodies against microbial antigens which cross react with tissue antigens. For example, antibodies against the yeast organism Candida albicans have been shown to cross react with tissues from several organs in the body, including the brain. (Vojdani, 1996) Thus, an individual whose immune system must fight an overgrowth of Candida albicans may also experience symptoms secondary to autoimmune damage to their body. Since high quantities of Candida albicans were found in the stool of over 30 percent of our subjects, the possibility of secondary autoimmunity from yeast overgrowth should be considered as a possible factor in ADHD. Since autoimmune cross reactions between microbial antigens and human tissue have been described extensively it makes the leaky gut syndrome of particularly concern if it is found to be present in addition to low levels of probiotic organisms, high quantities of potential gut pathogens and low levels of secretory IgA. Unfortunately, many of those in our recent study were demonstrated to possess all of these undesirable factors.

FIGHTING THE FOOD THAT FEEDS YOU

As we described in Chapter 11, food allergies or intolerances may be a common accompaniment of ADHD. The potential immunological reasons for adverse reactions to foods are complex and may go well beyond that of a simple (Type I) allergic reaction. In our most recent research, we found evidence that the majority of children with ADHD indeed react adversely to a number of commonly allergenic foods. Blood samples from 75 children were gathered and examined for the presence of antibodies against over 90 different common foods. Only a few of these children showed elevated levels of IgE antibodies to food. Recall from Chapter 11 that IgE antibodies are responsible for immediate (Type I) hypersensitivity reactions such as those which result in dangerous anaphylactic reactions to foods. Therefore, few children in our study showed evidence of significant Type I food allergies. However, a very high percentage (over 80 percent) of our study subjects demonstrated very high levels of IgG antibodies to various commonly allergenic foods. Remember that IgG antibodies form immune complexes with food antigens and result in the activation of complement and the release of inflammatory molecules from immune cells. The type of allergic reaction resulting from immune complex formation is called delayed (Type III) hypersensitivity. Small quantities of IgG antibodies towards food are completely normal and are probably present to help clean up the small amount of food antigens that normally leak through a healthy gut. However, high quantities of IgG anti-food antibodies reflect leakage of excessive quantities of food antigens through a damaged intestinal lining and probably reflect an excessive immune response to those antigens. Interestingly, the majority of children in our study had an excellent response to a program of dietary modification in which commonly allergenic foods and junk food were eliminated. As well, by the end of the study period, the amount of IgG antibodies toward foods diminished to negligible levels. This may provide further evidence that children with ADHD suffer from Type III mediated hypersensitivity reactions to commonly allergenic foods and that these adverse changes can be largely reversed by some simple dietary changes.

Several other studies have also demonstrated that the majority of children with ADHD respond favorably to dietary changes in which commonly allergenic foods are eliminated. (Kaplan, 1989; Egger, 1985; Schulte-Korne, 1996; Williams, 1978) A combination of improvement in overall nutritional status along with reduction in Type I and especially Type III hypersensitivity responses likely explains the benefits of these dietary changes.

Although research defining the role of the immune system in ADHD is currently in its infancy, there are now clear reasons to believe that immune dysfunction plays a primary role in this disorder. Fortunately, enough is known about the potential reasons for these immune system problems that Functional Medicine can now offer very practical help to those who suffer or who have a loved one who suffers from ADHD.

Section Four

Solving the ADHD Puzzle through the Functional Medicine Method

Chapter 14

The Patient Centered Diagnosis

LET'S NAME THAT DISEASE

No one can deny that medicine has made enormous scientific progress over the last one hundred years. Much of that progress rests upon a foundation, which relies upon the accurate classification of disease. Back in the middle of the 1700s, Carolus Linnaeus, develop a system of assigning names to plants and animals according to similarities in their structure. Linnaeus, was actually a practicing medical doctor and he relied on Latin, the language of medicine, for his system of biological classification. Because of the meticulous method of classification developed by Dr. Linnaeus, we will never have to worry about mistaking a Gallus gallus (broiler chicken), for a Scarabaeus sacer (dung beetle). By the 1800s, medical science had adapted the Linnaean system of classification for its own purposes and a race began to accurately classify every disease. Important advancements were made when medicine took over this system of classification. For instance, specialists in disease classification known as pathologists decided that it would be helpful to name diseases after their lunch. Thus, pathology textbooks are loaded with diseases like nutmeg liver, oat cell carcinoma, prune belly syndrome and cauliflower ear. Later, when one could achieve significant notoriety for discovering a disease, physicians like Dr. Alzheimer, Dr. Parkinson and Dr. Crohn decided to be immortalized in the name of the disease, which they discovered. Fresh out of high school, I discovered a previously unclassified bacterium while working in the department of pathology. Although I didn't get to name it after my lunch, or myself, I had a small taste of why science people get so excited when they discover and then classify some new thing.

On a more serious note, without an accurate language of medicine and an orderly system of classification, medicine would have remained in the stone age forever. In many cases, accurately identifying and classifying a disease process leads to an effective cure. For instance, if a person experiences intermittent episodes of extremely high blood pressure accompanied by sweating, rapid heartbeat and a sense of panic there is a small chance that they may have an adrenaline producing tumor called a pheochromocytoma. If a smart doctor detects and accurately determines the name of this disease, the patient's life can be saved by removing this benign but deadly tumor. However, if the doctor decides instead that this is simply high blood pressure or a neurotic condition, the person is likely to die from a stroke. In this case, the pheochromocytoma can be considered a "disease entity" which must be accurately identified so it can be removed from the body. In some cases, the system of classifying diseases as distinct "entities" and then using specific "weapons" to remove or destroy the disease entity is effective and often life saving.

DISEASE CENTERED MEDICINE

Medical doctors are trained on the front lines where they learn to make life and death decisions day in and day out. At 2 a.m. in the emergency department, halfway through a grueling thirty-six hour shift, every intern learns that medicine is war. When your pager has gone off for the 25th time in one night you must learn how important it is to identify, classify and triage (prioritize) every "case" you are called to see. In this war-zone environment, you learn that "real medicine" involves working with clearly identifiable illness. Every disease must show up on an x-ray, appear under a microscope or be revealed by a lab test or simply does not exist. At least it doesn't exist according to the hospital admitting office and it certainly doesn't exist as far as the patient's insurance company is concerned.

In this setting disease is often so serious that it takes precedence over the more humane needs of the patient. As the knowledge and experience of a physician matures, their skill in accurately identifying and classifying disease becomes sharper and more accurate. Even in the more routine practice of medicine, physicians must deal with plenty of serious illness. It is not hard to imagine why good physicians often become disease centered in their style of practice, focussing more upon the correct diagnosis and the the most acceptable treatment than on the highly individualized needs of a complex and very human patient.

Unfortunately, it is becoming quite clear that the disease centered approach lacks effectiveness in the management of many chronic conditions. Not every human ailment can be placed neatly into a classification system, which then automatically dictates an appropriate method of treatment. For example, ADHD is not a specific disease "entity" with a single, identifiable cause that needs to be poisoned, removed or suppressed. The disease centered approach often fails to appreciate that certain conditions like this one are an expression of symptoms resulting from a collection of underlying medical problems exerting their effects upon a highly unique individual. In fact, because ADHD cannot be neatly classified as a distinct disease entity by specific and objective diagnostic tests, there are still some mental health authorities who question whether or not it actually exists at all! Certainly these disease centered experts have not grown up with ADHD nor have they experienced what it is like to raise a child with this very real condition.

In a disease centered approach, it is common for the practitioner to make a rapid diagnosis followed by a specific prescription. Although this makes for quick office visits, it often leaves the needs of the patient unmet. This is certainly a common occurrence in the treatment of ADHD. In many cases, the school requests that a child be evaluated for ADHD and then he or she is seen by a pediatrician over a few brief visits. Various questions are asked and perhaps a questionnaire or two is administered until a "conclusive diagnosis" is made. Once the "disease" has been properly identified and classified as ADHD, a prescription for Ritalin® or Dexedrine® is often given. The child is then seen on follow-up and if their behavior has improved, the treatment is considered a success. If their behavior has not improved either the dosage is increased or a new drug is tried. Although this disease centered approach effectively improves certain symptoms in the majority of children, it has some very real limitations and, in will probably be viewed as obsolete in years to come.

PATIENT CENTERED MEDICINE

One of the core principles of Functional Medicine is that healthcare practitioners must become patient centered rather than disease centered — focussing where appropriate upon the needs of the patient more than on the name of the disease. Patient centered practitioners must view health as the presence of wholeness and vitality rather than just the absence of a definable disease. This has some very important implications. For example, studies indicate that stimulant drugs are effective in about 75 percent of children with ADHD. However, if these "successfully treated" children were examined more closely it might be clear in some cases that their behavior and school performance may be improved but their quality of life may be no better or even worse. A patient centered approach would give high priority to the side effects of medication and the long-term implications of its use. As well, the overall wellness of the child on the medication would be an important criterion for judging its success rather than just being satisfied that his behavior and school performance has improved. The fact that only a minority of children are willing to stay on stimulant medications over the long-term suggests that from the the child's point of view, the treatment is not always a success.

It is also consistent with the patient centered approach to help those individuals who seek help even if they do not fit the strict criteria for the diagnosis of a specific disease process. Many individuals suffer with some of the troubling features of ADHD but may not have a sufficient number of symptoms or their symptoms may not be severe enough to accurately establish a diagnosis. In a disease centered approach, these individuals would simply be reassured that there is nothing really wrong and then told that they will have to live with their problems. However, such people might have underlying physiological problems similar to those with ADHD and their function and quality of life may improve significantly by identification and correction of these problems. For instance, we have a daughter who has always had a tendency to be aggressive and hyperactive. She has never fit the strict criteria for ADHD but her aggression and hyperactivity has repeatedly caused problems in her life. Many years ago, we discovered that she has significant food allergies and intolerances. Since then, we have found that as long as she abstains from junk foods and the foods to which she is allergic or intolerant and gets regular exercise, her hyperactive and aggressive tendencies are greatly minimized. Whether she does or does not have ADHD is irrelevant if her function and quality of life is excellent. Unfortunately, for every child or adult who clearly has ADHD there are probably two or three others who suffer with some of the features of this disorder but never receive help because they are told that they really have no problem or that they will just have to learn to live with it.

In the disease centered approach, you either have a "disease entity" or you do not. Although this principle certainly holds true when it comes to the diagnosis of pregnancy or an infestation of tapeworms, it is not often so clear-cut in conditions like ADHD. Individuals with ADHD are suffering from various underlying problems, most of which can be considered to be somewhere along a spectrum of severity rather than completely present or completely absent.

THE WONDERFUL UNIQUENESS OF HUMANS

One of the most important concepts in Functional Medicine is that all individuals are all biochemically unique. In fact, humans have more biochemical individuality than they have differences in facial features or fingerprints. The power of biochemical individuality has been recognized in the science of criminology where one hair or one drop of blood can be used to separate one person from every other human on the planet. Our uniqueness is now known to extend to thousands of different biochemical processes and physiological functions. There are many important implications for this concept of Functional Medicine. For example, individuals may vary as much as perhaps 100 fold in their ability to effectively excrete toxic metals. Thus, a level of exposure that would be completely harmless to one person may be seriously toxic to another. Similarly, an individual's need for various nutrients may differ significantly from the Recommended Dietary Allowances (RDA's) adopted to suit the needs of the average healthy individual. Research is increasingly demonstrating that nutritional requirements vary enormously from person to person especially in individuals who are suffering from a disease or disability.

In recognition of this concept of biochemical individuality, the Functional Medicine practitioner should always ponder two questions when dealing with a patient:

· Does this person lack something for which he or she has an unusually high requirement in order to thrive?

· Does this person have something in his or her body that is preventing them from experiencing optimal wellness and vitality (i.e. a stressful or toxic influence)?

These two questions require that the Functional Medicine practitioner evaluate each patient as biochemically unique with a set of special nutritional needs and a distinctive list of stressful or toxic influences underlying their condition. Through the process of careful interviews, skillful examination and selected testing, the Functional Medicine practitioner gradually formulates a clear picture of the underlying factors which eventually led to the signs and symptoms for which the patient is seeking assistance.

PATIENT AS TEAM CAPTAIN

Another unique aspect of Functional Medicine is the recognition that we now live in an age of unprecedented information. Because of this, healthcare practitioners must become accustomed to dealing with informed, educated and sophisticated patients. Rather than being threatened by knowledgeable, proactive patients, the Functional Medicine practitioner prefers to work with the patient who is a full participant in the process of getting well. In Functional Medicine, the patient is ideally the captain of the healthcare team with the practitioner functioning as the coach. Many of the therapeutic interventions used in Functional Medicine are natural, nutritional or involve modifications of a person's lifestyle. This is why it is common for a

Functional Medicine practitioner to first encounter a patient after they have already identified a number of underlying problems or tried various therapeutic interventions. The Functional Medicine practitioner is there to act as a resource person and coach; helping you or your child to move forward towards wellness.

For a healthcare provider, deciding to utilize a Functional Medicine approach in the treatment of ADHD is certainly not the path of least resistance. It is much simpler to make a "definitive diagnosis" of ADHD and then prescribe an "appropriate" medication. The principles which are fundamental to Functional Medicine are not currently taught in medical school curriculums. If a healthcare practitioner decides to effectively utilize the principles of Functional Medicine they will not be able acquire this knowledge by visits from pharmaceutical representatives or the occasional drug company sponsored seminar. Functional Medicine practitioners must have a sincere commitment to academic excellence and must have a true hunger for knowledge. They must be willing to dedicate a significant amount of personal time to studying new concepts; reacquainting themselves with scientific subjects, like biochemistry, which may have been long forgotten. Fortunately, the resources to make this educational adventure possible have been made available through the pioneering work of the scientists and clinicians associated with the Institute for Functional Medicine in Gig Harbor , Washington (www.fxmed.com). This organization has also taken a leadership role to bring the revolutionary concepts of Function Medicine to medical school curriculums.

PATIENT CENTERED DIAGNOSIS

Coming to an accurate patient centered diagnosis is much like detective work. This process involves the step by step gathering of information to establish the underlying antecedents (risk factors), triggers (resulting physical problems) and mediators which have resulted in the signs and symptoms of ADHD in that unique individual. By taking an organized, systematic approach to the ADHD patient, finding effective and lasting answers is often relatively straightforward. It is helpful to think of this as similar to solving a large jigsaw puzzle. The key to the puzzle is to persist and have hope that, with time and effort, the puzzle will eventually become a clear picture.

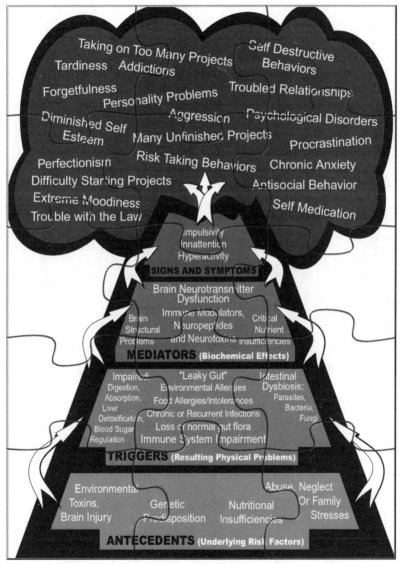

Solving the ADHD Puzzle

Chapter 15

Clinical Assessment of the ADHD Patient

SOLVING THE ADHD PUZZLE

Successful management of ADHD begins by gathering and organizing relevant information pertaining to the ADHD sufferer. This can be likened to gathering up all the pieces of the ADHD puzzle. There are rarely any real shortcuts when it comes to solving a complex puzzle. If you simply start randomly grabbing puzzle pieces and try to force them to fit together you will probably just end up frustrated.

Successfully solving a puzzle starts by carefully studying the picture on the puzzle box and then placing all the pieces in full view on a large table. As you carefully scan the pieces eventually, you begin to see how certain pieces belong together. With persistence, small sections of the picture come become clear until the whole puzzle is solved. I have observed many people who have successfully assembled their ADHD puzzle. With few exceptions, this process requires patience, persistence and often requires the assistance of one or more competent healthcare professionals to be fully successful.

The most skillful puzzle masters will always assemble a puzzle using a proven method; a systematic approach. For instance, they may start from the top of the puzzle and then work down. Likewise, when efforts are being made to uncover the significant factors which are contributing to the signs and symptoms of ADHD, it is critical that this process be conducted in an organized, systematic fashion. Too often, individuals with ADHD are subjected to a random series of visits to different professionals followed by this or that medication. Perhaps a test will be thrown in here or there and maybe a couple of nutritional supplements will be tried. Then there might be a consultation with an alternative practitioner followed by a special diet for a while. At the end of all of these efforts, there may be little improvement in the ADHD symptoms and not much has been discovered about the real factors that are contributing to the patient's condition. In our own facility, we have observed the value in approaching each ADHD subject in an organized and systematic fashion. This is much like starting a successful business by first compiling and then sticking to a well researched business plan instead of simply opening your doors and trying to "make a go of it". Those with an organized plan will always have a greater chance of success.

Properly Defining the Current Disabling Problems
The puzzle assembling process should begin by first properly defining the primary problems, which have led to difficulties in the person's life. It is important to develop a full understanding of the problems affecting the person's func-

tion, quality of life as well as the quality of life of those who have to deal with that person. In other words, how are the symptoms of impulsivity, hyperactivity and inattentiveness manifesting in that person's life in ways that are harmful to them or to those around them?

This exercise helps to determine the seriousness of the person's problems and gives some indication of the prognosis if these symptoms are left unmanaged. For example, a child whose primary problem is daydreaming in class can be considered differently than a child who often punches other kids in the face. The two problems may both have serious implications but they need to be dealt with in a very different way. All relevant authorities recommend that a thorough evaluation be done before the person is labeled as having ADHD. Too often, a child with behavioral problems or an adult with cognitive or organizational problems is quickly given the ADHD label, which implies that they have a lifelong neuropsychological disorder. Not only does this often result in them being placed on medication prematurely or unnecessarily, but it also may give them and those who deal with them the notion that they are bound with a handicap. The neuropsychological function of a person is highly complex and affects every aspect of a person's life. If there are suspicions that a child or adult has problems in this realm, it makes sense to have the individual properly evaluated early on in the intervention process.

Ideally, clarification of the ADHD related problems should begin with an evaluation by a competent psychologist or other professional who is qualified to perform learning, behavioral and neuropsychological evaluations. These tests can be used as a gauge to assess the severity of ADHD symptoms and to look for learning disabilities, psychological, neurological or psychiatric problems. Such testing may also reveal some real surprises. For example, as a child, a friend of mine was labeled as a "slow learner" and was placed on Ritalin® for hyperactivity. However, when neuropsychological testing was done he was found to have an IQ over 140! Today he is a brilliant and successful computer programmer working for a successful, worldwide organization. If he had not had neuropsychological testing, he may never have had the confidence to excel at anything and might not have been encouraged to pursue a highly academic path. It is not uncommon for potentially gifted kids, with or without ADHD, to be identified as disruptive, hyperactive or pathologically inattentive when they are primarily under-stimulated and bored out of their minds. In other cases, kids may be labeled as lazy or stupid when they actually have a very definable learning disability. Many of these problems can be minimized or effectively eliminated with proper treatment. Likewise, it is tragically too common for children with visual or hearing problems to be labeled as "slow" when, in fact their sensory deficits are the primary cause of their problems.

Some of the methods for objectively assessing learning and neuropsychological function are complex and must be performed by a highly trained specialist. There are other tests that are relatively simple and can be conducted by non-psychologists such as a medical doctor or naturopathic physician. The Conners' Questionnaires are a series of feedback forms which are completed by parents, teachers, or by the adult ADHD sufferer. There are versions of these questionnaires designed to evaluate both children and adults. The Conner's Questionnaires are very useful in assessing the severity of an array of ADHD related symptoms. All healthcare practitioners who work with ADHD patients will find the Conner's Questionnaires to be an invaluable resource for following the progress of ADHD patients. Some of the other methods for evaluating neuropsychological function are simple enough for the patient to perform. For instance, one of the most effective tests to evaluate certain aspects of brain function is called the Stroop Color-Word Test. This test is often abnormal if a person has significant problems stemming from inadequate function of the pre-frontal cortex regions of the brain. Recall from Chapter 1 that these are the brain regions that exert executive control over brain function. (If you would like to see how your executive centers are working, you can take the Stroop Color-Word Test by going to the Internet location: www.PureLiving.com. Remember, this is just for fun and should not be taken as a diagnosis of any medical condition.)

Formal neuropsychological testing conducted by a qualified psychologist can help to objectively determine if the individual truly has any degree of brain dysfunction or if their problems might be purely behavioral. Individuals with ADHD usually have measurable deficits in memory and executive center function which can be readily assessed. Some of these tests can also form a baseline against which comparisons can be made later to help judge the outcome of various treatments. It can certainly be helpful and encouraging to have objective evidence of the progress being gained by the efforts you are making.

THE MEDICAL WORKUP

The next step in the assembly of your ADHD puzzle should involve an organized method for gathering relevant medical information. Conducting a proper medical history and physical examination followed by performing pertinent medical tests is referred to as the "medical workup". A properly conducted medical workup is the primary means by which a healthcare provider is able to determine the antecedents, triggers and mediators which are contributing to the symptoms of ADHD in each individual. It is also important to note that a thorough medical workup is necessary to "rule out" highly serious medical problems which could lead to symptoms typical of ADHD. For instance, if a home has faulty ventilation, carbon monoxide may pollute the air inside the home and family members may suffer from some degree of carbon monoxide poisoning. In less severe cases, children may develop cognitive and behavioral problems identical to ADHD and may be quite inappropriately put on symptom suppressing drugs instead of being treated for the medical problem responsible for the symptoms. Similarly, lead poisoning, thyroid disease and several other potentially very serious medical problems should be considered in the medical workup and, if indicated, appropriate tests conducted to rule out these possibilities. In some cases, such as lead poisoning, there is a high chance that symptoms can be largely reversed if the problem is detected and treated early on. However, if detection and treatment is delayed too long, permanent brain damage may take place.

EXAMPLES OF SERIOUS MEDICAL PROBLEMS WHICH CAN RESULT IN ADHD SYMPTOMS

· **Toxic exposure to:**
  · *Lead*
  · *Mercury, cadmium, manganese, aluminum, arsenic*
  · *Pesticides*
  · *Carbon monoxide*
  · *Fumes from glue and other solvents*

· **Seizure disorders**

· **Sleep apnea (periodic interruption of breathing)**

· **Congenital heart disease**

· **Hyperthyroidism**

· **Celiac disease**

· **Drug abuse**

· **Head injury (even minor, repeated concussions)**

· **Genetic disorders such as Marfan's syndrome, fragile X syndrome, Turner's syndrome, sickle cell anemia**

TIME HONORED ROLE OF THE STANDARD MEDICAL HISTORY

Some of the most important innovations of modern medical practice as we know it today were the result of work conducted by the Canadian born physician Sir William Osler during the latter part of the 19th-century. Although he developed many advancements to the process of medical education and the practice of medicine, his most enduring contribution was in the methods still used today to gather and organize medical information about a patient. The basic methods of gathering a medical history and conducting a physical exam developed by Sir Osler, continue to be taught to and used by medical doctors, chiropractors, naturopathic physicians and many other healthcare professionals. In the field of Functional Medicine, the time honored methods for gathering a medical history and conducting a physical examination still form the basis of clinical assessment and an important foundation upon which to formulate a patient centered diagnosis.

SUMMARY OF THE STANDARD MEDICAL "WORKUP"

- *Presenting Problem* (disabling symptoms associated with ADHD)
- *History of Present Condition*
- *Past Medical History*
- *Family History*
- *Review of Systems* (symptoms arising from all the body's systems)
- *Physical Examination*
- *Laboratory Tests*
- *Assessment and Summary of Problems*
- *Treatment Plan*

KEEPING TO AN ORDERLY PLAN OF INVESTIGATION

Once the ADHD related behavioral and cognitive problems have been properly identified and evaluated, it is time to begin the search for important factors contributing to the individual's problems. Unfortunately, many physicians will consider the next step to be a prescription for stimulant medication once the symptoms of ADHD have been properly considered and the "disease" has been identified and labeled. Some will even prescribe a "therapeutic trial" of Ritalin® or Dexedrine® with the thought that this will help to establish a diagnose ADHD. Unfortunately, most authorities consider this "therapeutic trial" to have little value in making such a judgement since almost everyone will be more attentive and many will be less hyperactive on prescribed doses of these drugs even if they do not suffer from ADHD.

In Functional Medicine, establishing a "diagnosis" of ADHD is not a sufficient end point. Instead, the Functional Medicine practitioner will delve deeply into the patient's medical history, and will search for valuable clues by considering the symptoms originating from various systems of the body. They will then conduct a pertinent physical exam and will often order laboratory tests to help assemble the pieces of the ADHD puzzle. Many of the lab tests used in Functional Medicine are highly advanced and are usually only used in sophisticated research settings. All of these efforts are based on the view that there are many definable and treatable causes for the symptoms that we conveniently call ADHD. This approach is in no way an abandonment of the principles of good medicine. Instead, it is a methodology, which places great value on each patient, and which asserts that all people have a right to achieve their optimum potential in life.

THE FUNCTIONAL MEDICINE DETECTIVE

If an individual is suffering with ADHD, a great crime is being perpetrated against a priceless victim. The victim is the ADHD sufferer's brain and the factors that are committing this offense are the criminals. The Functional Medicine practitioner is the detective and you, the parent or adult ADHD sufferer are the investigative assistant. In this case, the detective simply cannot succeed without his or her assistant. You will be the one that goes behind the scenes and digs out many valuable clues, some of which may eventually solve the crime. Your role as the investigative assistant cannot be emphasized strongly enough. There are innumerable cases of ADHD, autism and other developmental disorders in which the unrelenting efforts of inquisitive parents "cracked the case" and "solved the crime" giving normal life back to a captive child. In fact, some of the most important breakthroughs in the treatment of developmental disorders have come through the efforts of individual sufferers, loving parents or parent support groups from around the world who brought their observations and ideas to an open minded physician or researcher. As was explained in Chapter 14, you are the Captain of the Healthcare Team in Functional Medicine. Your best chance of success is to remain assertive and proactive; realizing that your persistence may very well make the difference between success and failure.

If you want to play a key role in helping to solve your personal "crime against the brain", you should begin by organizing information about the case in an order that is familiar to all healthcare professionals. They will likely have you fill out their own forms and will ask you many more questions. However, if you present them with pertinent historical information in the order to which they are accustomed, it can be easily incorporated into the healthcare record, which they are required to develop. Your efforts may significantly shorten the time it takes to gather this information and by taking the time to remember various details in the leisure of your home, you may recall more accurate and detailed information. All of this begins by gathering and organizing all the data you have about the presenting problem including any developmental, learning or neuropsychological evaluations. Be sure to obtain copies of all test results or report summaries conducted up to that date. You may want to use the questions below as a guide to compile a summary of responses to take with you when you see your healthcare provider or Functional Medicine practitioner. Since ADHD is a developmental disorder, these questions have a strong emphasis upon events in the early stages of the patient's life.

HISTORY OF THE PRESENT CONDITION

Summarize the history of the present condition including:

- *What are the primary ADHD related problems that you (if you are the patient) or your child have experienced?*

- *When were these problems first apparent and how did they develop?*

- *Why have you needed to seek out medical help for these problems?*

- *How and in what settings have these problems been an impairment to you or your child's life?*

As well, try to recall any important events, which may have occurred prior to or coincidental to the onset of symptoms. For example, the "symptoms began after he fell off his bike and hit his head", or "things seemed to get worse after her third ear infection that year".

Also, note anything, which seems to provoke a worsening of symptoms such as, "he seems fine until he comes back from his father's house" or "she bounces off the wall anytime she gets candy or ice cream".

Finally, summarize the efforts that have been made to treat this problem including any medical doctors that have been consulted, drugs that have been used or alternative treatments that have been tried.

Past Medical History

Now, answer the following pertinent questions:

Pregnancy and Birth History

- *Did patient's mother smoke, drink, or use any drugs during pregnancy?*

- *Did patient's mother suffer from any sicknesses or complications during the pregnancy?*

- *What were the dietary and exercise habits of the patient's mother in pregnancy?*

- *Did patient's mother have dental amalgams put in or replaced during pregnancy?*

- *Were there any occupational or home exposures to toxic chemicals during pregnancy?*

- *Was the patient's mother living a home built prior to 1979 while pregnant?*

- *If yes, were renovations done to the home during pregnancy?*

- *Was this home ever tested for the presence of leaded paint?*

- *How many weeks along was the mother when she gave birth?*

· *Were there any problems with the delivery (either mother or infant)?*

· *Did the infant experience any problems in the first days or weeks of life?*

Childhood

· *Was the child breast fed?*

· *How long?*

· *Briefly describe the quality of the mother's diet during breast feeding.*

· *Did the infant experience colic, eczema or other problems during the breast feeding or bottle feeding period?*

· *When was solid food introduced, what foods, how was it introduced, any problems with food introductions?*

· *Did the child experience any feeding problems?*

· *Describe the infections suffered by the child.*

· *On how many occasions has the child been on antibiotics?*

· *Has the child suffered any head injuries or other injuries?*

· *Has the child suffered from allergies or related problems (eczema, asthma, cough, recurrent fluid in the ear, hay fever, itching eyes, hives, food allergies)?*

· *Has the child had any problems related to immunizations?*

· *When did the child roll over, show eye contact, smile, coo, sit, crawl, stand, walk, speak words, talk sentences, potty train, tie shoe laces, dress themselves, recognize colors, name animals, count, read numbers, read words, read sentences?*

· *Has the child been slow to speak or had speech problems?*

· *Has the child been clumsy or prone to injuries?*

· *Describe the child's environment (air pollution, water quality, living in an older home, breathing second hand smoke, pets in the house, older carpets, excessive dust, unpleasant smells, plastic window shades, insecticides used in home, play environment)*

· *Does or did the child eat plenty of foods which are known to be highly contaminated with pesticides? (see pesticide chart in chapter 6)*

· *Has the child suffered from any known poisonings or accidental exposures to toxic cleaners, solvents, pesticides or other chemicals?*

· *Has the child had the habit of eating or chewing on such things as dirt, paper, or other unusual items?*

· *Describe child's social environment (violence, tension, alcohol or drug use in home, divorce, abuse)*

· *What were the first signs of behavioral problems (tantrums, screaming, oppositional behavior, impulsive behavior, aggression, hyperactivity, excessively talkative, easily distractible, soiled their underwear)*

· *Describe childhood school performance and behavior.*

· *Has the child had sleep problems such as frequent awakenings, breathing problems, bed wetting, loud snoring, night terrors, do they stop breathing, do they awaken well rested?*

· *Describe the child's diet (strong preferences, strong refusals, overall quality of diet, junk foods, vegetables and fruits, organic or regular produce, how much fluid consumed, what beverages consumed, size, makeup and timing of meals, vitamins, suspected or confirmed food allergies, excessive thirst, frequent bad breath, noted ill effects from specific foods)*

Adolescent and Adult History

· *Describe academic performance and behavior at school.*

· *Has he/she been expelled from school, fired from a job, arrested or charged with a crime?*

· *Have there been problems with oppositional or aggressive behaviors?*

· *Has there been any known or suspected history of smoking, drinking, use of street drugs or addictions?*

· *Has there been a problem with gambling, sexual behavior, pornography or any compulsive or destructive or behavior?*

· *Has there been any involvement in extreme sports, dangerous driving or other high risk behaviors?*

· *Has there been a problem with extremes of mood or any psychological problems?*

· *Have there been problems with close relationships or family responsibilities?*

· *Have there been problems with money management or business failures?*

· *Have there been any exposures to toxic chemicals at home or work such as solvents, pesticides, herbicides, cleaners, welding fumes, or smoke?*

· *Have there been any accidents, injuries, serious burns, infections or operations?*

· *Briefly, summarize the quality of the person's diet, exercise and other lifestyle habits.*

Family History

· *Are there signs of ADHD in parents, siblings or close relatives?*

· *Are there learning disabilities in parents, siblings or close relatives?*

· *Are there psychiatric or psychological illnesses in parents, siblings or close relatives?*

· *Are there addictions or problems with alcohol or drug use in parents, siblings or close relatives?*

· *Are there allergies in parents, siblings or close relatives?*

· *Is there a history of adverse drug reactions, or chemical sensitivities in parents, siblings or close relatives?*

· *Are there illnesses like chronic fatigue syndrome, fibromyalgia or autoimmune diseases like lupus or rheumatoid arthritis in parents, siblings or close relatives?*

REVIEW OF SYSTEMS

The next part of the medical history is referred to as the review of systems. This process involves the answering of questions pertaining to the health or dysfunction of the various systems of the body. A properly conducted review of systems can often raise suspicions about certain problems which can then be confirmed or ruled out by physical examination or laboratory tests. The review of systems is often conducted when the healthcare provider reviews a questionnaire completed by the patient (or parent) prior to or on their first visit. The questions in the review of systems are usually grouped into logical areas such as the cardiovascular, neurological, gastrointestinal and urinary systems. Functional Medicine practitioners may also add to the review of systems by utilizing questionnaires which help to define a patient's function or which suggest that particular problems may be predominant. For example, the Childhood Symptom Questionnaire is a helpful tool to assess overall wellness and to suggest problems arising from certain body systems. This questionnaire and a version for adults are both available from the Institute for Functional Medicine in Gig Harbor Washington (www.fxmed.com).

THE PHYSICAL EXAMINATION

The historical interview is generally followed by a pertinent physical examination. Functional Medicine practitioners are familiar with important physical features which can give clues to the underlying medical problems of the ADHD sufferer. Because the Functional Medicine assessment can be a very time consuming process, you should not be surprised or offended if the physical examination is scheduled for a separate visit or visits. Every practitioner has their own scheduling challenges and limitations and they usually have to make some very real sacrifices to practice with the kind of thoroughness demanded by Functional Medicine. Again, it takes time, patience and persistence to assemble a complex puzzle.

After completing a routine examination of the ADHD subject, much of what the practitioner will look for on physical examination will be related to the growth and nutritional status of the child. For instance, if a child has a short stature for her age, the practitioner may consider the possibility of an infection with an intestinal parasite. Essential fatty acids may also give telltale signs if deficient. Dry skin, dry hair, dandruff, brittle nails and small bumps on the back of the arms may all suggest essential fatty acid deficiencies, especially in children with excessive thirst and frequent urination. There are many other telltale signs of nutritional inadequacy that can be detected by a good physical examination. The practitioner will also look for suggestions of allergy in the child such as dark circles under the eyes, a crease across the end of the nose from continual nose wiping, reddened cheeks or ears, pale complexion and swollen nasal mucous membranes.

There is no substitute for a thorough medical history and physical exam. They are the foundation upon which to build a patient centered diagnosis. Through a properly conducted clinical assessment, the pieces of the puzzle start to come together and some parts of the picture may become clear. However, there are also many factors that cannot be detected by history and physical exam alone. Sophisticated laboratory testing may provide further invaluable information.

Chapter 16

Functional Testing in the Assessment of the ADHD Patient

LOOKING THROUGH THE FUNCTIONAL MEDICINE MICROSCOPE

In the years before the sophisticated science of forensic medicine, crimes were solved almost entirely through the observations of witnesses and the work of brilliant detectives. Today, things have changed considerably. Advancements in technology have brought about amazing capabilities to solve crimes, which in years past would have remained forever a mystery. The ability to detect minute amounts of residual toxins and to identify a person from the DNA found within a few skin cells are some of the ways that technology is helping to unlock unsolved mysteries even from crimes committed decades ago. Similarly, medicine is experiencing a technological revolution. Most notably, diagnostic instrumentation has seen some very impressive progress over the past few years, leading to increasingly sophisticated ways to look into the unseen realms within the body. Without such technological advancements, the ability to search for the underlying causes of many illnesses would be impossible.

Healthcare providers trained in the concepts of Functional Medicine are on the leading edge of this technological revolution and are familiar with diagnostic methodologies that are often years ahead of widespread use. In many cases, the usefulness of certain diagnostic procedures is well described in the scientific literature decades before the methods come into common use in the mainstream medical world. For instance, there are now hundreds of studies published in reputable medical journals pointing to the great importance of intestinal permeability (leakiness of the gut) in health and disease. There are also numerous papers describing the validity of certain technologies used to measure gut permeability. Nevertheless, few physicians consider investigating whether or not a patient has a leaky gut and very few labs are even aware of how to perform this assessment. Perhaps this is because there is no simple drug treatment available for a leaky gut and therefore no drug company is marketing this concept to physicians. Nevertheless, identifying and treating a leaky gut through the principles of Functional Medicine can have extraordinary benefits in the treatment of numerous illnesses. Functional Medicine trained practitioners are aware of how to perform this test and how to manage and follow a patient with this highly important gut abnormality.

Many other advanced diagnostic methodologies are in common use by those practicing Functional Medicine. Although they are familiar with and may often use the more commonly available tests, Functional Medicine practitioners must also become accustomed to working with laboratories which provide highly sophisticated analyses not usually available in the local medical labs. Because the tests that are unique to Functional Medicine are highly valid scientifically, most of these will likely become commonplace some day. However, at this point in time, only those practitioners familiar with the advanced concepts of Functional Medicine will be able to provide their patients with the kind of diagnostic sophistication needed to establish a true patient centered diagnosis in conditions such as ADHD. Uncovering the causes underlying a particular disorder can certainly be more complex and challenging than simply giving the disease a name. For the Functional Medicine practitioner, a thorough history and physical examination provides valuable clues. Sophisticated laboratory testing may be required then to provide important evidence to help "crack the case".

In the Functional Medicine assessment of ADHD, several unique laboratory tests are often performed. The clinical judgement of the healthcare provider and the unique nature of the patient will determine which tests should be done and in what order they ought to be performed.

GASTROINTESTINAL ASSESSMENT

Intestinal Permeability Testing is one of the most common tests performed in Functional Medicine. This test is simple, inexpensive and easy to perform even on children. As we have discussed in previous chapters, numerous problems can result in increased intestinal permeability or a leaky gut. As well, if an individual has a leaky gut it indicates that there are serious stresses upon their gastrointestinal tract and immune system. It also suggests that their nutritional status is likely impaired. Intestinal permeability testing is often one of the first tests performed in the Functional Medicine "workup" of the ADHD patient. As our research has demonstrated, the majority of children with ADHD will be found to have a leaky gut. If this is indeed detected, it suggests that it is worth the effort to establish the underlying reasons for the leaky gut. It also suggests that treatments focused upon improving nutrition and gastrointestinal function will likely be a significant benefit to the patient. Since this test is inexpensive and easy to perform it is commonly repeated on different occasions, especially after the diet has been altered or specific treatments have been administered. By repeating the intestinal permeability test, the Functional Medicine practitioner can gauge the success of the efforts being made to improve the patient's health.

Although the scientific literature describes several different methods of measuring intestinal permeability, the most common method used is the lactulose-mannitol technique. To perform this test, the subject skips breakfast, empties the bladder and then drinks a sweet tasting solution containing two completely harmless sugars — lactulose and mannitol. Since it tastes much like sugary water, most kids will drink this solution without hesitation. Over the next six hours every drop of urine must be collected in a large container provided by the laboratory. The amount of urine produced is recorded and a small sample is placed into a test tube which is shipped to the lab.

The laboratory then measures the quantity of lactulose and mannitol in the urine. Lactulose is a sugar which is not normally digested or absorbed by the intestine. Only a small trace of lactulose (less than 0.8 percent of that ingested) should be present over the six hour urine collection if the individual has normal gastrointestinal function. However, if the gut is leaky, significant quantities of the lactulose will leak across the mucous membrane of the intestine and circulate freely in the blood. Since the human body cannot metabolize lactulose, it ends up being excreted by the kidneys as waste material. Therefore, the amount of lactulose in the urine reflects the leakiness of the intestinal mucous membrane. Mannitol, on the other hand, is a sugar which is normally absorbed by the intestinal mucous membrane. However, it is one of the more challenging substances for the intestine to absorb. If the intestinal cells are functioning poorly or if the mucous membrane of the intestine is damaged and there is a loss of surface area for absorption, only small amounts of mannitol will be absorbed into the bloodstream. Like lactulose, the body cells are unable to utilize mannitol, therefore, it circulates around until it is excreted by the kidneys as waste material. Low levels of mannitol in the urine suggest that there is some degree of malabsorption. This might indicate that important nutrients (such as fatty acids, minerals and certain vitamins) are not being absorbed adequately either.

Three measurements are reported by the laboratory when an intestinal permeability test is done — lactulose level, mannitol level, and the urinary lactulose/mannitol ratio.

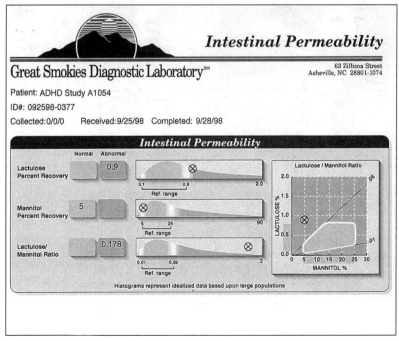

High lactulose levels are indicative of a leaky gut:

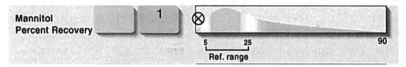

Low mannitol levels suggest poor absorption of nutrients:

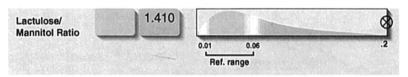

If the ratio, which is calculated by dividing the amount of lactulose by the amount of mannitol, is elevated, this indicates a leaky gut. The scientific literature most often relies upon the lactulose/mannitol ratio as the most sensitive indicator of a leaky gut:

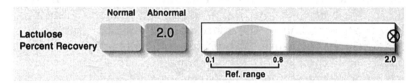

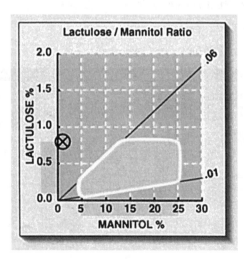

Comprehensive Digestive Stool Analysis (CDSA) with Comprehensive Parasitology is also one of the most commonly performed tests in Functional Medicine. This extensive analysis is comprised of over 20 individual laboratory tests performed upon a single stool sample.

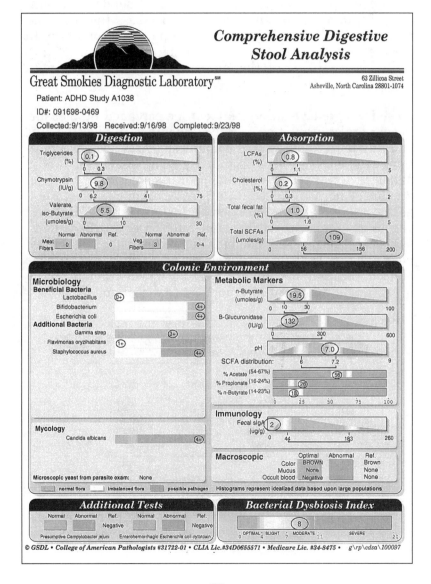

Analyses are performed on the stool sample for evidence of inadequate digestion, inadequate absorption, bacterial overgrowth in the small intestine, excessive fermentation or putrefaction, gut immune function and abnormal intestinal flora. The comprehensive digestive stool analysis with comprehensive parasitology can provide a tremendous amount of useful information that can help to assess the contribution of gastrointestinal problems in a patient's condition. In our research, this analysis proved to be one of the most clinically useful tests in the management of patients with ADHD.

Basic digestive adequacy can be screened by measuring several parameters. Triglycerides are undigested fats and any more than a trace amount suggests poor fat digestion. Chymotrypsin is a protein digesting enzyme. Lowered amounts of this factor suggests poor pancreatic enzyme production. Valerate and iso-Buterate are produced when undigested protein enters the colon and is fermented. Meat and vegetable fibers are visible under microscope when digestion is inefficient. Any combination of low stomach acidity, poor pancreatic enzyme production or overly rapid passage of food through the small intestine (often from bacterial overgrowth) may result in inadequate digestion.

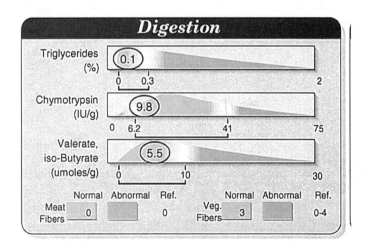

Serious malabsorption problems can be detected when certain fatty substances are elevated in the stool. Long chain fatty acids (LCFAs) are the products of fat digestion. If excessive amounts are found, it suggests that fat is being digested but not properly absorbed. Excessive quantities of cholesterol or total fecal fat also reflect poor small intestinal absorption. Short chain fatty acids (SCFAs) are produced by the bacterial fermentation of dietary fiber within the latter part of the small intestine and the colon. If these are elevated, it suggests overly rapid passage of food through the intestine, which can result in poor absorption of nutrients.

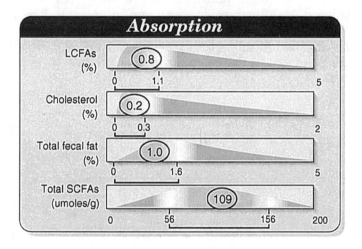

Certain chemical substances or **metabolic markers** in the stool provide an indication of the health of the colonic environment. N-butyrate is a short chain fatty acid produced by bacterial fermentation of dietary fiber in the colon. This important substance is the primary fuel for colonic cells and inadequate quantities suggests that the colon is undernourished and overstressed. Inadequate dietary fiber or overgrowth of harmful microbes may result in deficient quantities of short chain fatty acids. beta-glucuronidase is an enzyme produced by harmful colonic microbes, which can result in poor detoxification of hormones and environmental chemicals. Elevated quantities of this substance have been associated with increased aggression in animals. The pH of the stool is a measurement of colonic acidity. If the pH is high (alkaline), it indicates excessive putrefaction (rotting of protein and fat) in the colon, or lack of friendly (acid loving) bacteria.

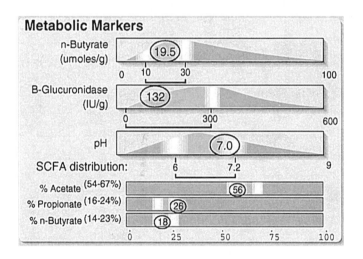

The stool can be used as an indicator of gut **immune system function**. As was mentioned in previous chapters, secretory IgA (sIgA) is produced in large quantities by the immune system of the gut and is then secreted into the intestine by the small intestinal cells. This important antibody is the primary defense mechanism used by the GALT to protect the body from food antigens and potentially harmful microbes. Since secretory IgA is not digested, it is normally found in high quantities in the stool. The level of secretory IgA in the stool has been shown to correlate very well to the level of secretory IgA found in saliva. Excessive quantities of secretory IgA may be found in the stool for relatively brief intervals during and after gastrointestinal infections. Depressed levels of secretory IgA are indicative of gastrointestinal immune deficiency. In relatively rare cases, this can result from a genetically inherited absence of IgA production. More commonly, secretory IgA deficiency is a result of chronic gastrointestinal stress related to overtraining in sports, emotional stress, poor nutrition, poor nutrient absorption, food allergies, intestinal parasites, infection with harmful bacteria or yeasts, or chemical damage from ingestion of toxins or drugs. Our research has indicated that stool secretory IgA levels are commonly depressed in children with ADHD.

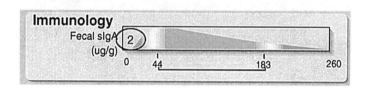

Microbiological flora within the stool is assessed by various methods. First, the specimen is tested for the presence of various beneficial bacteria by culturing the stool (seeing what organisms can be grown from the stool). By measuring how many bacteria of a certain species grow on a specific nutrient source, the specific species and their quantity can be determined. The same process is used to test the stool for potentially harmful bacteria and yeasts. Any potential pathogens found are then tested for sensitivity to various natural and pharmaceutical antimicrobial agents.

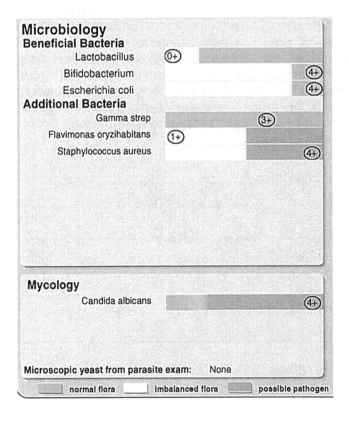

Parasitology examinations are performed by highly experienced technicians who can visually identify a wide range of parasites using sophisticated microscopes. The accuracy of parasitology examinations depends to a very large extent upon the skill and experience of the technician. In our research we used Great Smokies Diagnostic Laboratory in North Carolina for this test. At this lab, if a parasite is encountered with the microscopic analysis, it is identified and photographed. All photographs of parasites are included with the test report. In addition to microscopic examination, highly accurate immunological tests are performed in search of the most serious intestinal parasites — Giardia, Cryptosporidium, and Entamoeba histolytica.

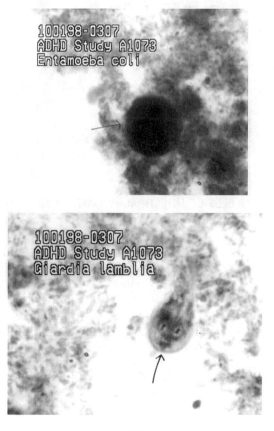

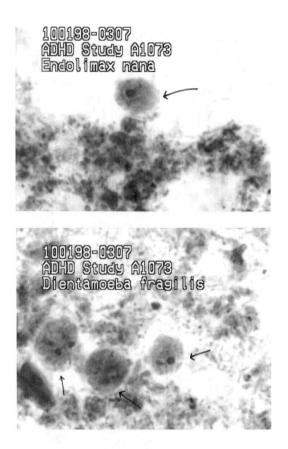

100198-0307
ADHD Study A1073
Endolimax nana

100198-0307
ADHD Study A1073
Dientamoeba fragilis

EXAMPLES OF INTESTINAL PARASITES FOUND IN A CHILD WITH ADHD

Few labs conduct the volume of parasitology examinations that are carried out at Great Smokies Diagnostic Laboratory. Because of this, they have developed a reputation for being one of the most reliable parasitology labs in the world. Comprehensive parasitology examinations may also be ordered separately from Great Smokies Diagnostic Laboratory. If parasites are ever found, they must be treated with specific therapies and testing should be conducted on all family members. Testing should be repeated until all parasites are completely eradicated.

Candida Albicans and other potentially harmful yeast (single celled fungi) within the gut are assessed when the comprehensive digestive stool analysis is performed but may also be assessed separately through a fungal (mycology) culture. Most of these organisms are normal inhabitants of the gut and probably pose no significant threat when their numbers are small. However, if certain yeasts or fungi overgrow, they can become primary factors in chronic disease processes. This is particularly true if a person also has an allergy or hypersensitivity to the fungal organism. Certain fungal species generate potent toxins known as mycotoxins. Fungi may also markedly overactivate the immune system by acting as "superantigens". In addition to fungal cultures, practitioners may order a blood test looking for the presence of antibodies against yeast organisms (usually Candida albicans). These tests help to determine if yeast is a cause of significant immunological stress. Again, Functional Medicine practitioners often rely upon the Great Smokies Diagnostic Laboratory for the performance of these tests.

Helicobacter pylori are bacteria which are proven to be the primary cause of stomach ulcers and other stomach problems, including stomach cancer. However, these same unfriendly bacteria may be found in the stomach of children with a variety of gastrointestinal problems. In addition to being a major cause of ulcers, Helicobacter can result in a marked decrease in stomach acid production. This, in turn results in poor protein digestion, poor absorption of minerals and a high likelihood of bacterial overgrowth of the small intestine (auto-brewery syndrome). Since preliminary research suggests that a high percentage of children with ADHD have hypochlorhydria (low stomach acid), healthcare providers may determine that it is important to look for Helicobacter in these individuals. Recurrent abdominal pain is also one of the most common symptoms of ADHD in children, and although this has been largely considered psychosomatic by the mainstream medical community, it may often have a very real physical cause, including such things as chronic infection with Helicobacter. The presence of this highly undesirable microbe can be detected by directly culturing stomach contents during an endoscopy procedure. However, measuring antibodies in the blood formed against Helicobacter is much simpler and is a highly reliable testing method.

Urinary organic acid testing is a highly sophisticated method to detect the type and quantity of toxic byproducts being produced by gut microbes. A number of toxic microbial metabolites have now been identified and associated with various disease processes, including ADHD and autism. Since these substances are absorbed by the intestines and sent into circulation, bacterial, protozoal (parasitic), and yeast byproducts can all be assessed by urinary organic acid testing. This is a simple test involving the collection of a urine specimen gathered first thing in the morning. This test can be easily repeated after treatments have been given to improve the gastrointestinal ecology in order to evaluate the success of therapy. Testing for microbial metabolites in the urine is going to undergo tremendous advances in the next few years and this technology may become increasingly invaluable in the assessment of the ADHD patient.

Breath testing has long been used as a means to detect lactose intolerance or an inability to digest milk sugar. In this test, the patient is given a drink containing lactose (milk sugar) and then a series of breath samples are collected similar to the "breathalyzer" used to catch drunk drivers. If the patient cannot digest lactose, instead of being digested and absorbed, the lactose will be fermented by bacteria in the latter parts of the small intestine and the colon. As a byproduct of lactose fermentation, these bacteria produce hydrogen gas, which is then absorbed into the bloodstream. Since hydrogen is not a normal byproduct of human cells, any found in the breath will be from bacterial fermentation. Excess breath hydrogen after a lactose drink is therefore diagnostic of lactose intolerance.

Breath testing is also now used to detect other problems related to abnormal gut fermentation. Fermentation of fiber and other remnants of food is a normal and necessary process occuring all the time in the large intestine (colon). Normal fermentation here produces short chain fatty acids, lactic acid and a certain amount of gases. However, if an individual suffers from overgrowth of bacteria or yeast in the nutrient rich environment of the small intestine, a variety of toxic fermentation byproducts will be produced. As described in Chapter 12, bacterial overgrowth of the small intestine (also known as the auto-brewery syndrome) results in abnormal fermention of starches and other carbohydrates in the small bowel. These fermentation products can include various alcohols, acids (like D-lactic acid), as well as gases like hydrogen and methane. In the most serious cases, these people have significant neurotoxic effects because their gut has become a veritable brewing vat. The frequency of gut fermentation syndromes in children with ADHD is currently unknown although certain British researchers suggest that is actually quite common in both ADHD and autism. If this is the case, it is quite feasible that some children produce enough alcohol in their small intestine after eating a load of candy or junk food to be intoxicated. Hypochlorhydria (low stomach acid), poor digestion, poor absorption, chronic overeating, junk food diets, food allergies, intestinal parasites and low secretory IgA levels are some of the conditions associated with the auto-brewery syndrome. Individuals who have significant bloating, belching or flatulence or "brain fog" soon after meals as well as those with chronic diarrhea are particularly likely candidates for this problem. People with markedly unusual or aggressive behavior within one to three hours after meals should also be considered as candidates for the auto-brewery syndrome.

Breath testing for gut fermentation syndromes typically involves swallowing a solution containing some type of sugar (usually glucose or lactulose) and then gathering breath samples in sealed test tubes at various intervals. The breath samples are sent to a laboratory to be analyzed for hydrogen and methane gas (yes, methane, like the natural gas that heats your home). If the production of these gases increases markedly within the first hour following ingestion of the carbohydrate, auto-brewery syndrome is indicated. Although it is not yet available in North America, British researchers have also been measuring blood alcohol levels after carbohydrate ingestion as a method of assessing gut fermentation. Breath testing for gut fermentation syndromes can be conducted through Great Smokies Diagnostic Laboratory.

Urinary peptide testing is being used extensively by many Functional Medicine practitioners who treat children with autism and by some who treat those with ADHD. Testing has now been developed to look for the presence of neuropeptides such as the opioid peptides (morphine-like protein fragments) that cross a leaky gut following the inadequate digestion of casein protein from milk or gluten protein from wheat. High levels of food-derived neuropeptides in the urine suggests that the patient has protein digestive problems, as well as damage to the intestinal mucous membrane with a resulting leaky gut. Such individuals usually benefit from a diet, which is completely free of gluten and dairy products. Probiotic supplementation, digestive enzymes and other digestive aids may also be used in such cases. Since a completely gluten and dairy free diet can be very difficult for some people to maintain, urinary peptide testing can provide strong evidence that such dietary restrictions are worth the trouble. Unfortunately, there are no labs in North America currently conducting urinary neuropeptide testing. At the time of this writing all samples must be sent to Norway to the principle researcher in this field, Dr. K. Reichelt of the Pediatric Research Institute of Oslo. However, the good news is that the processing and shipping are quite simple and the test is being run in a nonprofit University laboratory and it is not very expensive. Information about how to obtain this test will be posted on the website: www.PureLiving.com.

NUTRITIONAL ASSESSMENT

Nutrient minerals play a vital role in virtually every bodily process. Minerals may combine with protein to form structural components such as teeth and bone. Minerals are also involved in the transport of information through the body. Nerve impulses for instance are carried along by the flow of electrically charged minerals in and out of nerve cell membranes. Muscle contraction occurs when minerals suddenly flow into a muscle fiber activating the contraction machinery inside the muscle cell. Minerals are also powerful catalysts housed within protein enzymes. These enzyme catalysts are responsible for virtually every chemical reaction that takes place within the body. Magnesium, zinc, selenium, chromium, manganese, molybdenum and copper are some of the minerals that form the active catalytic region for numerous enzymes. In a sense, enzymes are the engines that do the work inside the body and minerals are the sparkplugs that make these engines run. For example, magnesium is a critical factor in the function of over three hundred different enzymes. It is not hard to imagine why magnesium deficiency can result in such an amazing variety of symptoms. Inadequacy of nutritional minerals not only leads to deficiency related problems, it also increases a person's susceptibility to toxic metals. As was mentioned previously, there is evidence to suggest that mineral deficiencies (especially magnesium, zinc, and iron) may play a significant role in ADHD. Therefore, a reliable method for evaluating the status of minerals can be invaluable in establishing a patient centered diagnosis.

Depending upon the mineral in question, and the preference of the healthcare provider, four different kinds of methods are used to evaluate nutrient mineral status:

· **Whole blood (or red blood cell) analysis** provides a reasonably reliable method of evaluating most nutritional minerals. Blood generally reflects the adequacy of mineral absorption that has taken place in the recent days to weeks prior to testing. In long standing, stable deficiencies, blood levels are usually quite accurate. However, if a person has optimal levels of certain minerals in their tissues but has only recently experienced inadequate absorption, blood levels may be lower than their actual body stores. As well, if a person has experienced a long-standing mineral deficiency, but has recently been absorbing adequate quantities of that mineral, their blood levels may wrongly suggest adequacy of minerals.

· **Urine element analysis** is used to assess the amount of certain minerals that are being excreted. For example, urinary calcium levels may reflect the amount of calcium loss compared to daily intake. Urine testing is used in one method of evaluating the adequacy of tissue magnesium stores. In this technique, a set dose of magnesium is given intravenously and urine is then gathered for a set number of hours. If the amount of magnesium in the urine is low following intravenous magnesium, it indicates that the cells are starving for magnesium and they have absorbed most of the magnesium given. On the other hand, if a high percentage of the magnesium given intravenously is detected in the urine collection, the patient's tissues have adequate magnesium stores and their kidneys eliminate most of the magnesium given intravenously.

· **Hair element analysis** is a widely utilized test used to screen for deficiencies of several minerals. This test is inexpensive, and samples are easy to collect. Hair mineral levels are more reflective of long term mineral absorption and tissue stores than are blood levels. Although hair does not precisely reflect the level of every mineral in all tissues, it is an economical way to generally evaluate mineral adequacy. Hair analysis also provides a reasonable method to screen for many toxic metals as well. Unfortunately, hair element analysis has developed a bad reputation because several labs have performed this analysis with little quality control. To be an accurate and reliable test, the testing laboratory must follow meticulous methods to avoid contamination of the sample and to obtain accurate results. As well, the lab must use techniques to differentiate between environmental contaminants that have been deposited on the outside of the hair from minerals that came from within the body as the hair was being manufactured. Great Smokies Diagnostic Laboratory is one of the few laboratories using this more accurate methodology.

· **Intracellular mineral analysis** is the most accurate method for the assessment of magnesium tissue stores.

This test is performed by obtaining a scraping of live cells from the mouth, in the region next to the tongue. These cells are then smeared on a special slide and then sent to Intracellular Diagnostics Laboratory in Foster City, California. X-rays are beamed at the cells under a special electron microscope. The reflected spectrum indicates the level of magnesium in the cells. Research conducted by NASA on this technology suggests that these levels correlate very well to the level of magnesium inside other tissue cells including the heart muscle. (It can also be used to screen for elevated calcium levels in cells, which has been associated with several diseases.) Although this test is quite expensive, it may prove very useful in certain situations where serious magnesium deficiency is suspected in the ADHD patient. For instance, if an ADHD patient has irregular heartbeats, it may simply be the result of magnesium deficiency. Treatment of the magnesium deficiency may eliminate the heart problem and may help numerous other bodily functions besides.

Amino acid analysis is performed on urine or plasma (the liquid part of blood minus the blood cells) and is used to detect the balance of these vital protein breakdown products. Besides being the building blocks for proteins, amino acids form the basis for the construction of several neurotransmitters, including dopamine, norepinephrine and serotonin; all of which have been strongly implicated as mediators of ADHD symptoms. Inadequacy of certain amino acids may reflect upon poor protein digestion and absorption. It may also be a result of the destruction of amino acids in the gut by certain gut microbes. As well, low levels of particular amino acids may indicate the excessive consumption of these molecules by cellular processes. In other cases, elevated levels of certain amino acids may indicate problems related to amino acid biochemistry. Toxic amino acid metabolites (byproducts) can also be detected by this method. If amino acids are not properly metabolized due to inherited or acquired problems with certain enzymes, toxic byproducts can accumulate. Although amino acid analysis is not often performed early on in the evaluation of an ADHD patient in certain difficult cases it may prove to be invaluable.

Essential fatty acid analysis is one of the tests which is often performed in the evaluation of the ADHD patient. Several studies, including our own recent study, have now demonstrated the usefulness of measuring the fatty acid status in those with ADHD. Performing this testing can determine if fatty acid supplementation is likely to be of benefit to these patients. It also allows a higher degree of precision in determining what kind of supplementation would be most suitable for a given patient.

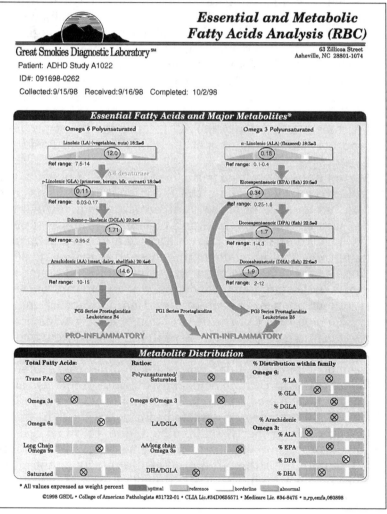

ALLERGY ASSESSMENT

Airborne allergies are relatively common in those with ADHD. Apart from the nasal congestion, runny nose, itchy eyes, coughing and wheezing that may result from airborne allergies, other symptoms such as fatigue, "brain fog", irritability and aggression may occur in susceptible persons as well. In some cases, the nasal obstruction accompanying allergies can result in the very serous condition known as sleep apnea. People who snore loudly and then periodically stop breathing for thirty to ninety seconds or more probably have sleep apnea. Because this repeated interruption of breathing deprives the brain of oxygen, it can cause harm to the brain and result in a lowering of the intelligence, as well as headaches, fatigue and behavioral problems. Sleep apnea is a serious problem and must be properly treated in all cases. It is not uncommon to discover sleep apnea in a child with allergic rhinitis (hay fever) and significant nasal obstruction. It is also seen in children with markedly enlarged tonsils.

In other cases, sleep apnea may not occur but the allergic individual still suffers from allergy-generated fatigue, cognitive difficulties, and behavioral problems. Certainly, airborne allergies are not the primary cause of ADHD, at least not in most cases. However, if undetected and untreated, they may add to the person's overall misery and amplify many ADHD symptoms.

Airborne allergies are largely caused by tiny particles such as pollen, mold spores, animal dander and the remnants of tiny bugs that live in carpets known as dust mites. Airborne allergies are the result of Type I (immediate) hypersensitivity reactions to these tiny particles when they land on the mucous membranes of the eye, nose and bronchial tubes. Mast cells, which line mucous membranes, are covered with IgE antibodies specific to an individual's allergens. When enough of the allergen particles are attached to a given mast cell, it explodes and releases histamine and other inflammatory mediators.

There are two primary ways that airborne allergens are detected. In one method, a tiny drop of fluid containing one specific allergen is placed on the patient's skin. The skin under this fluid drop is then pricked to introduce the allergen to the awaiting mast cells. If the individual is allergic to that particular allergen, a red and swollen spot will develop on the skin. If done properly by a meticulous physician (usually an allergy specialist), skin prick testing can be a reliable method for determining many airborne allergens. The second method is a blood test in which the laboratory searches for IgE antibodies specific to various potential allergens. RAST, MAST, and ELISA are the initials for three different techniques used to detect IgE antibodies to airborne allergens. Of these, ELISA testing is gaining in popularity because of its low cost per allergen and high degree of accuracy. ELISA testing is also readily available to nonspecialists.

Food allergies and intolerances can pose a much more difficult diagnostic challenge than that of airborne allergens. Because of the complex and controversial nature of this problem, food allergy detection will be addressed as a separate topic in the next chapter.

TOXICOLOGY ASSESSMENT

Chemical sensitivities can be suspected when people experience marked changes in their sense of well being, cognitive performance or behavior when in certain environments or when exposed to particular chemical fumes or odors. Sick building syndrome is now a widely recognized phenomenon and is thought to occur when susceptible individuals are exposed to high levels of certain chemicals in the air. Sick school syndrome has also been well described. In some cases, this may result from a collection of environmental challenges including airborne allergens such as mold spores or dust, along with toxic chemicals coming from carpets, shop classes, industrial cleaners or pesticides. There is little doubt that certain children are particularly vulnerable and may have ADHD symptoms at least in part because of a sick school or home environment. Adults with ADHD may also be highly sensitive to certain environments and may be significantly affected by chemicals in their home or workplace. Identifying chemical sensitivities requires some very intelligent detective work starting with a meticulous historical interview. In addition, laboratory testing is now available to detect specific anti-chemical antibodies. This may be of help in cases where a person suffers from puzzling chemical sensitivity problems or where it is suspected that certain chemicals have caused immunological problems.

Functional detoxification testing is one of the most important tests in Functional Medicine. This testing provides a means to gauge a person's susceptibility to various environmental and gut derived toxins. The body spends a significant portion of its hard-earned energy in the work of neutralizing thousands of different chemical substances each day. The liver is the primary site where this detoxification takes place, although the gut wall, kidneys, skin and lungs also take on a small proportion of this activity. Hundreds of different enzymes comprise the body's detoxification machinery. Even in a perfectly natural, pollution free environment, detoxification of internally derived poisons must take place constantly. In our modern world, even a very efficient liver faces enormous challenges to protect our body from the constant ravages of a multitude of different toxins.

As was mentioned in a previous chapter, if the liver is seriously damaged, such as occurs in cirrhosis, gut derived toxins can rapidly accumulate until the brain becomes poisoned and a life threatening delirium takes place (hepatic encephalopathy). Although the livers of most people are not in this bad of a condition, individual detoxification capabilities vary greatly from one person to the next. Some of these differences may be genetic and others may be based upon various aspects of a person's nutritional status. Research has now demonstrated that people with a high susceptibility to adverse drug reactions, who have chemical sensitivities, or suffer with chronic fatigue syndrome, often have some degree of impairment in their liver's detoxification capability. Importantly, recent research has also demonstrated that autistic children are likely to suffer from impaired liver detoxification. This means that such individuals may have a much greater susceptibility to gut and environmentally derived neurotoxins than others with normal liver detoxification. Although formal research has not yet been done, clinicians who are performing liver detoxification testing in their practices are reporting that those with ADHD commonly have detoxification problems as well.

Drugs or toxins exert their effects by having a very precise molecular structure. The liver detoxifies most of these molecules through a two-phase process. In the first phase, enzymes in the liver (called cytochromes) change the molecular structure of the drug or toxin by oxidizing it. In most cases, phase one of the detoxification process creates a molecule which is less toxic and more water soluble. Water-soluble molecules are easier to excrete through the kidneys or gut and they are less likely to penetrate through cell membranes and end up accumulating in tissues and organs. In the second phase of the detoxification process, enzymes in the liver connect other molecules to the oxidized toxin. The molecule which has been attached to the oxidized toxin increases its water solubility even further and it acts like kind of a handle, allowing cells to grab on to it in order to discard this toxic complex. Phase one and phase two detoxification systems must remain in harmonious balance in order for efficient detoxification to take place.

A simple analogy may help to explain the importance of balanced detoxification. Imagine working in a giant warehouse that has become infested with thousands of rats (the rats are like toxins in our body). If the rats are not eliminated, they can result in terrible disease. The first step in getting rid of the rats is to set all kinds of traps (the traps are like phase one detoxification). If a rat is killed in a trap, it is no longer as harmful as it was when it was alive and running around. However, if the warehouse was eventually filled with hundreds of dead rats in traps, the accumulation of dead rats would begin to cause bigger problems for the warehouse than existed before the traps were set. To correct this problem, the workers would have to stay alert for dead rats. Every time a worker finds a dead rat, he would place a stick with a flag on the end in the dead rat (the stick with a flag on the end is like phase two detoxification). The flags would then make it easy for cleaners to roam about the warehouse and quickly find and dispose of the rats. As long as there are enough traps and an equal number of flags, the rats do not accumulate and they are efficiently eliminated from the building. In a simplistic way, this analogy reflects accurately the importance of balanced phase one and phase two detoxification activities within the liver.

Functional liver detoxification testing can be used to assess the adequacy of both phases of detoxification. In this test, three different common substances (caffeine, acetaminophen, and aspirin) are given by mouth at different times of the day. (Dosages of these substances are adjusted down for children.) Once ingested, each of these substances must undergo phase one and phase two detoxification in order to be rapidly and safely eliminated from the body. After several hours, measurements are made of the saliva and the urine to judge the efficiency of several aspects of phase one and of phase two detoxification activity. If detoxification is decreased or imbalanced, the specific nature of the abnormality helps to determine what strategies, nutritional or otherwise, can be used to correct the problem. People who have chronically inadequate detoxification may accumulate high amounts of environmental toxins in their organs. As well, such individuals may experience amplified toxicity from gut derived or externally acquired drugs and toxins.

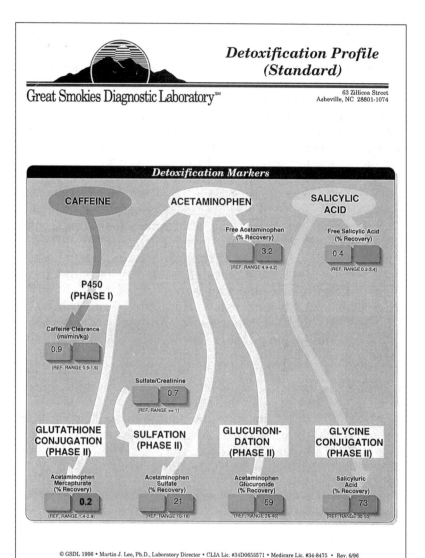

Detoxification Profile (Standard)

Great Smokies Diagnostic Laboratory℠

63 Zillicoa Street
Asheville, NC 28801-1074

Detoxification Markers

CAFFEINE

ACETAMINOPHEN

SALICYLIC ACID

Free Acetaminophen (% Recovery)
3.2
(REF. RANGE 4.9-9.2)

Free Salicylic Acid (% Recovery)
0.4
(REF. RANGE 0.2-3.4)

P450 (PHASE I)

Caffeine Clearance (ml/min/kg)
0.9
(REF. RANGE 0.5-1.6)

Sulfate/Creatinine
0.7
(REF. RANGE >= 1)

GLUTATHIONE CONJUGATION (PHASE II)

SULFATION (PHASE II)

GLUCURONI-DATION (PHASE II)

GLYCINE CONJUGATION (PHASE II)

Acetaminophen Mercapturate (% Recovery)
0.2
(REF. RANGE 1.4-2.9)

Acetaminophen Sulfate (% Recovery)
21
(REF. RANGE 10-18)

Acetaminophen Glucuronide (% Recovery)
59
(REF. RANGE 26-46)

Salicyluric Acid (% Recovery)
73
(REF. RANGE 30-53)

© GSDL 1996 • Martin J. Lee, Ph.D., Laboratory Director • CLIA Lic. #34D0655571 • Medicare Lic. #34-8475 • Rev. 6/96

Functional Detoxification Testing

Toxic metal testing can play a pivotal vital role in pin-pointing significant neurotoxic influences, especially on the brains of children. One of the greatest tragedies is when heavy metal poisoning goes undetected in a child until permanent damage is done. Low grade, toxic metal poisoning probably plays a significant role in number of neurological disorders in both children and adults.

Lead, mercury, cadmium, aluminum, and arsenic are all highly neurotoxic and have become common contaminants of the human environment. Additionally, manganese, although it is a required nutrient in trace amounts, if inhaled, is actually one of the most neurotoxic of all metals. Toxic metals are amongst the most persistent contaminants in our environment due to their resistance to biodegradation. Rather than being broken down and destroyed when released into the environment, toxic metals are simply passed up the food chain, accumulating in increasing quantities at every step in the chain. Because toxic metals are present in extremely minute quantities in the natural environment, organisms are not equipped with efficient mechanisms to excrete these poisons. Thus, it is very easy for a person to absorb more of any particular metal than they are able to excrete. On top of this, the ability to excrete toxic metals may vary greatly from one person to another due to genetic differences and nutritional factors. Not only do individuals commonly suffer for years without ever discovering that they are poisoned with heavy metals, they may even transfer some of these insidious neurotoxins to their child during fetal development. We have observed several cases of children with severe ADHD whose mothers were eventually proven to have very high levels of toxic metals — especially mercury. In many cases, these mothers themselves have fibromyalgia or chronic fatigue syndrome. Further research looking into these possible connections is urgently needed.

Every child with ADHD should have a minimum level of toxic metal testing. At the very least, this should include a measurement of blood lead levels. Elevated blood lead levels in children are so common that it is foolish not to look for this invisible brain killer in every child with behavioral or cognitive problems. Blood lead testing is inexpensive and can be easily ordered by any physician. In older children or adults, blood lead levels are not highly reflective of overall tissue lead burden. Blood lead levels primarily reflect the level of recent exposure (past few weeks to months only) and are really only useful in people who are working with lead or living in a high lead environment. Blood levels of most other toxic metals are likewise of little value in the assessment of actual body burdens.

Hair elemental analysis is a simple and useful method to screen for most of the toxic metals. Hair also has the advantage that it more closely reflects the actual tissue burden of many of the toxic metals. As previously mentioned, it is critical that only a lab with meticulous methodologies be used for hair analysis. This should include methods to differentiate external contamination on the hair from internally acquired metals. Hair analysis is more likely to be accurate in children who are unlikely to use hair dyes or work in highly contaminated environments, both of which can externally contaminate the hair to the extent that its diagnostic usefulness is considerably reduced.

Urine elemental analysis is commonly used in industrial medicine to monitor toxic metal exposure to workers in dirty industries. Urine represents a person's level of excretion of various toxic metals and is a simple way to monitor workers for overexposure to these toxins. However, urine metal levels are of little value in those who may be chronically exposed to minute quantities of heavy metals. The exception to this is when urine metal levels are measured after the administration of a metal chelating drug. Chelating drugs are agents that have been developed as antidotes for heavy metal poisoning. Following the oral or intravenous administration of a chelating agent, heavy metal excretion is dramatically increased through the kidneys.

Toxicology research has determined that the amount of metals excreted after a chelating agent is given more closely reflects the amount of metals stored in tissues and organs than any other testing method. This method is referred to as **post provocative urine testing or chelation challenge testing**.

In order for this method to be accurate and useful, the correct chelating agent must be given to test for a particular metal. For instance, the intravenous administration of the chelating agent DMPS is the most well researched agent used to test for body burdens of inorganic mercury acquired from dental fillings. It has been used for decades in Europe for the treatment of acute and chronic mercury poisoning. DMPS has been evaluated by the FDA and because of its high degree of safety and effectiveness it was approved for use by physicians in 1999. It is a generic drug and is available from compounding pharmacists. Some practitioners use the oral drug DMSA as an agent for mercury challenge testing. DMSA is approved by the FDA for treating lead poisoning in children. However, there are no standardized values or methods for the use of this agent in challenge testing and therefore, its reliability for diagnostic purposes is not currently established.

Stool testing for toxic metals is becoming increasingly available. Although it has not yet been well established how stool levels compare to tissue burdens, methods of measurement involving stool testing are evolving and will likely become very important in the future, especially for the measurement of mercury. Under normal circumstances, over 80 percent of the mercury, which leaves the body, is excreted through the stool. Techniques are currently being developed to stimulate metal excretion through the stool and then measure stool metal levels. This may eventually prove to be a more accurate method of assessing body burden than chelation challenge testing.

TESTING FOR BODY BURDENS OF MERCURY

Mercury found in hair analysis is primarily organic (methyl mercury) acquired from seafood, breast milk or placental transfer from the patient's mother during fetal development. Therefore, hair analysis is primarily useful to assess mercury burdens in children without amalgams and in anyone who has eaten a great deal of fish.

Mercury directly acquired from dental fillings is a fat soluble vapor which enters the body through the lungs and is quickly absorbed by cells. Mercury vapor preferentially enters fatty tissues like the brain and liver, and does not end up in the hair in significant quantities. Once mercury enters cells, it is oxidized into ionic mercury, which is not fat soluble, and it is therefore "locked up in the cell". Only a small percentage of this mercury will be changed to fat soluble methyl mercury which can end up in the hair. This is why chelation challenge testing (with DMPS) is a more accurate method to test for mercury acquired from dental amalgams than is hair analysis.

Because mercury remains so transiently in the blood, it is of no value to measure blood or urine mercury levels in people who have been exposed to very low levels of mercury over long periods of time. It is possible to suffer from chronic mercury poisoning and still have normal blood and urine levels.

Since 80% of the mercury excreted by the body leaves through the stool, some labs have begun stool mercury testing. Although this does reflect the amount of mercury the body is excreting, it may not accurately reflect body burdens in many cases. If a person's ability to excrete mercury is impaired, they may have very high organ levels of mercury even if stool mercury levels are low. Post provocative (chelation) challenge testing remains the only method to assess mercury body burdens which can currently be supported by the scientific literature. (Aposhian, 1983; Aposhian, 1992; Aposhian, 1995; Aposhian, 1996)

Doctor's Data, Inc.
P.O. Box 111
170 West Roosevelt Road
West Chicago, Illinois 60185-9986
CALL TOLL FREE (800) 323-2784
Fax: (630) 231-9190
E-mail: inquiries@doctorsdata.com
Web site: www.doctorsdata.com

James T. Hicks, M.D., Ph.D., FCAP
Medical Director
CLIA ID # 14D0646470, Medicare Provider # 148453

Urine Toxic Elements

Lab #:	T
Patient:	Age: / Sex:
Doctor:	Acct #:
c/o:	Collection Type: Random
Collection Date:	Time:
Date In:	Date Out:

ELEMENTS REGARDED AS TOXIC

Elements	Result (µg/g creatinine)	Reference Range (µg/g creatinine)	Expected Range	Elevated	Very Elevated
		Per gram Creatinine			
Aluminum	< dl	< 35			
Antimony	< dl	< 5			
Arsenic	59	< 140	******		
Beryllium	< dl	< .5			
Bismuth	< dl	< 30			
Cadmium	< dl	< 2			
Lead	20	< 15	******************		
Mercury	85	< 3	***		
Nickel	5.7	< 12	*******		
Platinum	< dl	< 2			
Thallium	< dl	< 14			
Thorium	< dl	< 12			
Tin	15	< 6	**************************		
Tungsten	< dl	< 23			
Uranium	< dl	< 1			

OTHER TESTS

	Result (mg/dl)	Reference Range (mg/dl)	2 SD Low	1 SD Low	MEAN	1 SD High	2 SD High
Creatinine	77.8	75 - 200		*******************			

Methodology: Analyzed by Induction Coupled Plasma Mass Spectrometry (ICP-MS). Creatinine by Jaffe method.

"dl" = detection limit.

Comments:
[Post provocative challenge.]

Example of a post provocative urinalysis (chelation challenge test) on an adult ADHD patient following IV injection with 250 mg of DMPS. A urine sample was collected 1½ hours after DMPS. Chronic mercury poisoning is suggested if the post provocative urine mercury level is greater than 50 micrograms mercury per gram of urinary creatinine.

Intravenous calcium disodium EDTA is the most well established agent to test for long standing burdens of lead. The use of chelating drugs to perform urine challenge testing requires considerable knowledge and should only be undertaken by medical doctors with special training in the use of these agents. Like all drugs, chelating agents have the potential for side effects, especially when administered by inadequately trained persons. However, many practitioners have the skill and experience to use these agents with a very high degree of safety. If properly used, chelating agents may provide invaluable evidence of heavy metal toxicity, one of the most pervasive neurotoxic factors in the human environment.

Urinary porphyrin analysis is used to detect direct evidence of toxic metal effects on the blood. Porphyrins are molecules used in the manufacturing of heme, a complex ring which is the business part of hemoglobin, the oxygen carrying red pigment of blood. Heme is also a vital component within the energy producing enzymes of the mitochondria, the power stations of every cell, and it forms the working part of the phase one detoxifying enzymes in the liver (cytochromes). Heme is manufactured in our cells in an eight-step assembly line, which involves a different enzyme and a different porphyrin molecule at each step. Porphyrin manufacturing enzymes are highly sensitive to the toxic effects of lead, mercury and to a lesser extent aluminum and arsenic. If these metals are present at toxic levels within cells, specific porphyrins will accumulate just like partly finished products would pile up on an assembly line if one of the workers had fallen asleep on the job.

Urinary porphyrin analysis is used to detect abnormal quantities of certain porphyrins. Because different metals affect porphyrin synthesis in specific ways, the pattern of porphyrin accumulation can be analyzed to suggest an accumulation of a specific metal or group of metals. Some toxicologists believe that porphyrin analysis is one of the most objective ways to determine if a person is actually being adversely affected by lead or mercury. Since it is non-invasive, and involves no drugs, it has some significant benefits, particularly when assessing the toxicological status of children. Many practitioners are beginning to use this technology as a routine part of the evaluation of all patients with neurological or immunological disorders. Quantitative and fractionated urinary porphyrin analysis is performed by MetaMetrix Laboratory.

Non-metallic toxicity testing is used to assess the level of organic toxins stored in body tissues. Pesticides, herbicides, solvents, petrochemicals, PCB's and other non-metallic toxins may accumulate in organs and exert significant toxic effects upon the brain, immune and reproductive systems. A high level of exposure or an increased susceptibility due to genetic or nutritional factors can lead to an accumulation of these undesirable substances. In early childhood, most overexposures to non-metallic toxins is inadvertent and occurs either because their environment is unknowingly contaminated (such as pesticides in food, home or school) or because they are accidentally exposed. Later in adolescence and adulthood, this class of toxins can be acquired in excess through careless handling of chemicals or from occupational exposure. For individuals whose liver detoxification systems are inadequate, toxins may accumulate to high levels even with normally safe levels of exposure.

Indirect evidence for exposure to non-metallic toxins is suggested by high levels of general detoxification byproducts in the urine, **D-glucaric acid and mercapturates**. These two substances are the result of phase two liver detoxification activities and, if elevated, they indicate that the liver is working overtime to detoxify one or more unidentified toxins. Urinary D-glucaric acid and mercapturate measurements are relatively inexpensive and only require a single, first morning urine specimen. This test may be helpful as a starting point to determine if a person is under a significant degree of toxic stress. This test is performed at Doctor's Data Laboratory in Chicago.

Direct measurements of non-metallic toxins can also be performed. Since there is such a large number of different toxins that can accumulate in the human body, it is not practical or economically feasible to measure the level of every possible contaminant. Based upon the suspicions of the practitioner, a group of toxins within specific chemical classes is ordered. For instance, since children are so commonly exposed to pesticides, a practitioner may order an organochlorine pesticide panel in which twenty-one of the most common organochlorine pesticides (DDT and related agents) are measured. Similar panels exist for organophosphate pesticides, solvents, herbicides, and PCB's. Before ordering these tests, it is important to have some clue as to which agents might be elevated. It is important to also know how to gather the samples correctly. For instance, organochlorine pesticides will often be present at levels five hundred times greater in fat than in the blood. Therefore, a fat sample has to be acquired to accurately measure the burden of these toxins. Organophosphate pesticides, on the other hand, will be most concentrated in the urine; therefore, a twenty-four hour urine sample is used to measure these toxins. Other chemicals may be most readily detected in the blood. This sophisticated toxicology testing can be invaluable in uncovering key factors underlying neuropsychological conditions such as ADHD. If levels of toxins are found to be elevated, testing can be repeated to assess the success of detoxification efforts (as outlined in Chapter 24). Accu-Chem Laboratories in Richardson, Texas is a worldrenowned facility for the performance of this highly sophisticated toxicology testing.

FOCUSSING THE FUNCTIONAL MEDICINE MICROSCOPE

The laboratory tests that have been discussed in this chapter by no means constitute an exhaustive list of every investigation that might prove valuable in putting together the pieces of the ADHD puzzle. As well, this is a rapidly expanding science and new investigational methods are being developed all the time. The tests that are described in this chapter are all based upon current scientific knowledge and many of these tests will be unfamiliar to physicians who are not educated in the principles of Functional Medicine.

Of course, there is no situation where most or all of these tests are done on any given individual. Good clinical judgement, based upon the practitioner's knowledge, experience and the suspicions derived from a thorough medical history and physical exam, will determine which tests should be performed. In some cases, tests are done one or two at a time until several are performed over a period of many months. Even one or two well-chosen tests might uncover some very important causative factors, which could then lead to highly effective treatments. In any case, a laboratory test should only be performed if the results of that test are likely to significantly influence the way a patient is treated. Otherwise, the test is only of academic interest and will provide little tangible benefits for the ADHD sufferer. When appropriately chosen, the laboratory testing unique to Functional Medicine can reveal hidden problems and causative factors that can greatly assist in the establishment of a highly effective treatment program.

LABORATORIES PERFORMING FUNCTIONAL MEDICINE TESTING

Great Smokies Diagnostic Laboratory
800-522-4762
Doctor's Data Laboratory
800-323-2784
MetaMetrix Clinical Laboratory
800-221-4640
Immunosciences Laboratory
800-950-4686
IntraCellular Diagnostics Inc.
800-874-4804
The Great Plains Laboratory
913-341-6207
Accu-Chem Laboratories
800-451-0116

Links to laboratory web sites can be found at
www.PureLiving.com

Chapter 17

An Intelligent Approach to Food Allergies and Intolerances

DIETARY CHANGES AND ADHD

Food allergies and other adverse reactions to foods are an important piece of the puzzle in most individuals with ADHD. Several studies have demonstrated that the majority of those with ADHD respond very positively to a well-designed diet, in which common food allergens, additives and junk foods are eliminated. (Carter, 1993; Boris, 1994; Kaplan, 1989; Egger, 1985; Schulte-Körne, 1996; Williams, 1978) In recent research, our facility was able to document the effects of dietary changes in a group of fifty children with ADHD. Nearly three quarters of the children who underwent modifications of their diet (elimination of common food allergens, food additives and junk food) showed significant improvements in their behavior and cognitive performance. In some cases, the improvements were dramatic. Several children became completely different people on the optimized diet, showing dramatic improvements in their school performance, their behavior, their attitude and their overall health. In contrast, a control group of twenty-five children with ADHD who were not placed on a diet, showed virtually none of these improvements.

In order for dietary modifications to have a positive effect in a person with ADHD, several changes must occur. First, the diet should be as nutrient dense as possible. Junk foods are generally high in calories and low in nutrients such as vitamins, minerals, fiber and other beneficial phytochemicals (natural plant chemicals). These foods are termed "empty calories". Such foods are detrimental to everyone, especially if eaten regularly. They are particularly harmful to children and to those with ADHD of all ages whose brains are more sensitive to toxic influences and are more demanding of many nutrients. A nutrient dense diet, on the other hand, is composed of foods that are rich in vitamins, minerals, phytochemicals and fiber. A nutrient dense diet is largely made up of whole foods, rather than processed, canned and packaged foods, and is ideally selected to have minimal contamination with brain damaging pesticides and herbicides. This diet must also avoid, as much as possible, rich deserts, candies, sweet baked goods and other foods, which taste wonderful but overload the sensitive person's body with fat, and sugar while providing little real nutritional value. All of these principles can do no harm and can benefit everyone. Many of our modern diseases are linked to dietary excesses or nutritional inadequacy and we should all be striving to improve the overall nutritional quality of our diets.

In addition to improving the nutritional density of the diet, properly identifying and eliminating intolerant or allergic foods can have a remarkable impact upon the ADHD brain. If an individual suffers with significant food allergies or intolerances, even the most natural and healthy diet can still be a source of brain altering biochemical confusion. However, the precise identification of food allergies and intolerances can be a frustrating process. It seems that there are more opinions as to how to identify food allergies than there are people with food allergies! Fortunately, Functional Medicine offers a highly rational and systematic approach to the identification of adverse food reactions. Since no single test or method has ever been shown to be failsafe, Functional Medicine relies upon the combination of laboratory tests along with an organized method of observation to eventually establish a dependable list of foods that should be avoided.

Testing for Food Hypersensitivity – Conventional Medical Approaches

Conventional allergy specialists usually depend upon one of three different methods to identify food allergies:

· **Skin prick tests** are used by some allergy specialists to detect food allergies. This method is similar to that used to detect allergies to airborne allergens. However, according to the scientific literature, there are a number of reasons why this methodology is probably of little value in establishing the presence of most food allergies and intolerances.

Skin testing only detects allergies that are mediated by Type I or immediate hypersensitivity reactions involving mast cells and specific IgE antibodies. However, as explained in Chapter 11, there is mounting evidence that the majority of food allergies are actually mediated by Type III or delayed hypersensitivity reactions. These types of reactions occur primarily as a result of immune complexes formed between IgG antibodies in combination with certain food antigens. Skin testing is of little or no value in the detection of Type III hypersensitivity reactions. For this and other reasons, there is little scientific evidence to support the use of skin testing in the detection of food allergies, except in cases of Type I mediated (immediate hypersensitivity) reactions. Unfortunately, many people have been erroneously reassured that they have no food allergies because of negative skin testing, when in fact they actually suffer greatly from some kind of adverse response to food.

· **RAST** is a method of blood testing commonly used by conventional allergists and medical specialists in the detection of food allergies. RAST is used to identify IgE antibodies specific to certain food antigens in the blood of the allergic person. Although this form of testing has a reasonably high degree of reliability in the detection of food allergies mediated by Type I or immediate hypersensitivity reactions, it has no value in the detection of Type III or delayed hypersensitivity mediated food reactions. Again, it is common for an individual to be erroneously reassured that they have no food allergies on the basis of RAST alone. This reassurance is quite misleading if the person indeed suffers from delayed food allergies or other adverse food reactions.

· **Double blind food challenge testing** is another method occasionally used by conventional allergists. In this test, the patient is given a handful of capsules containing a powder made up of either the specific food in question or a presumably inactive substance (placebo) like glucose. Neither the doctor nor the patient is supposed to know whether it is the food or the placebo that is given. After the capsules are swallowed, the patient is instructed to record how they feel over the next few hours and any symptoms such as abdominal pain, diarrhea, hives, or breathing problems are noted. The test is then repeated until all foods in question have been tested. As is true for the skin prick and RAST tests, this test is a good method to screen for Type I (immediate hypersensitivity) food allergies. However, the quantities of food which are usually given by this method is less than is frequently required to provoke a clear Type III (delayed hypersensitivity) reaction or a non-immunological food intolerance. Some food allergies require the ingestion of at least twenty grams of the offending food in order to provoke a clear-cut adverse response. This is certainly more capsules than many people, especially children, are able to easily swallow. As well, taste and smell may be important factors in the initiation of some adverse food reactions. Taking test foods in capsules of course does away with any reactions which require taste or smell in order to fully occur. The other drawback to the double blind food challenge method is that it is time consuming and complicated for medical practitioners to perform and it usually requires highly trained support staff to administer this testing properly. For these and other reasons it is uncommon to find this method of testing being used outside of the research setting.

TESTING FOR FOOD HYPERSENSITIVITY – ALTERNATIVE APPROACHES

The domain of alternative medicine is vast and varied with no specific definition other than that it encompasses every healing practice that is considered "unconventional" by those in mainstream medicine. Within the alternative medicine realm are a number of methods intended to diagnose food allergies. Some of these, such as the ELISA antibody test are based on well-described scientific principles, whereas other methods are highly esoteric and cannot be explained in current scientific terms. The most common esoteric methods of testing for allergies are biokinesiology (applied muscle testing) and Vega or (electrodermal testing).

· A specially trained healthcare provider may elect to perform **biokinesiology testing** in search of allergic or intolerant foods. In this test, the practitioner starts by testing the patient's muscular strength, often by pushing down on an outstretched arm. Then, the patient holds a particular food in their hand, often within a glass container, and places it up against their body. The practitioner then tests their muscle strength once again. Sometimes this test is conducted blinded so that neither the patient nor the the practitioner can see what food is being tested. A food is considered suspect if it results in a significant decrease in muscle strength when it is held up against the body. This method is said to work by the food's "energetic effects" upon the body's "energy fields". Although this may sound like nothing more than foolishness to a scientific thinker, there is actually a limited amount of well-designed research, which seems to indicate that this method can be reasonably accurate when performed by experienced practitioners. (Schmitt, 1998; Garrow, 1988) Further research will hopefully clarify the reliability of this mysterious technique and, if it does prove authentic, provide us with a scientific explanation for the mechanisms by which it works.

· **Vega or electrodermal testing** is based upon concepts derived from homeopathic medicine. In this test, an electronic instrument is used to determine a baseline measurement of "energy" from the subject's body. Vials containing minute quantities of food are then placed in a sensing unit and the instrument is used to detect the response of the body to each substance. Typically, the patient finishes the testing session with a list of foods to avoid. Unfortunately, there have been no good studies on this method (at least none which are available through the major scientific literature databases). Many practitioners utilize and seem to have confidence in this method, however, valid research is needed to properly evaluate this technique.

· **Provocation / neutralization** is a method used by many physicians in which extracts containing allergens (the same as are used in conventional skin testing) are injected under the skin to detect allergic responses. The difference with this technique from conventional skin prick testing is, firstly, that only one allergen is tested at one time, as opposed to conventional methods in which multiple skin sites are injected during the same session. Secondly, the physician not only observes changes in the skin after the injection, he also looks for changes in mood, behavior, handwriting, speech and physical symptoms such as hay fever, headaches or wheezing after the injection. Thirdly, if an adverse response occurs, the physician "neutralizes" the reaction by injecting a very dilute solution of the same allergy extract. The major drawback to this method is that it is very time consuming and requires painstaking effort by the physician and patient to establish a reasonable list of allergens. Because research supporting this method is still somewhat lacking, and perhaps because it can be impractical to perform in the context of a busy practice, it has not yet been well accepted in conventional medical circles.

· **ELISA testing** is a blood test, which is quite similar to the RAST testing used by conventional allergy specialists. However, unlike RAST testing, which is usually limited to testing specific IgE antibodies, ELISA testing is used to detect both specific IgE and IgG antibodies formed against food antigens. Although it is considered normal to have a small quantity of specific IgG antibodies to some foods, high amounts of IgG are probably indicative of an abnormality. Such results suggest that the patient has a leaky gut and may be experiencing significant Type III (delayed) hypersensitivity reactions to certain foods.

In our research, we performed ELISA testing on seventy-five children with ADHD. High quantities of specific IgE antibodies to foods were only found in a small minority of the children (less than 10 percent), indicating that only a few of these children likely experience significant Type I (immediate) hypersensitivity to foods. However, over eighty-five percent of these children were found to have very high levels of IgG antibodies specific to certain foods.

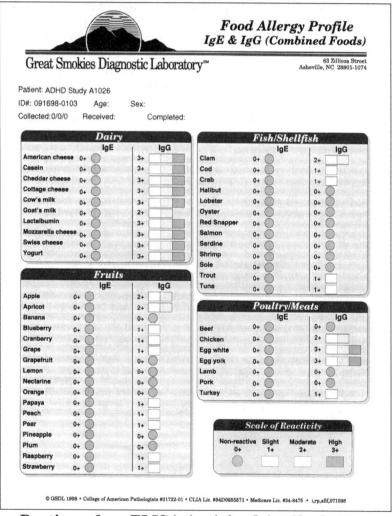

Portion of an ELISA Anti-food Antibody Test

This suggests that these children were probably experiencing significant Type III (delayed) hypersensitivity to these foods. Interestingly, most of the elevated antibodies were towards foods that are considered to be the most commonly allergenic foods such as dairy, wheat, eggs, soy, peanut, shellfish, yeast, and oranges.

The major drawback to this testing has been the relative lack of good quality controls by many laboratories performing this test. A few years ago, in an independent study conducted by Bastyr University in Seattle, several popular labs were found to generate inconsistent values for ELISA food allergy testing. Since then, several labs have apparently gone to great lengths to improve the accuracy and reproducibility of their ELISA food allergy testing. At our center, ELISA testing is commonly performed through Great Smokies Diagnostic Laboratories. The results from this lab have been clinically useful and seem to correlate well with the results of other methods used to help determine food allergies.

FUNCTIONAL MEDICINE APPROACH TO THE DETERMINATION OF FOOD ALLERGIES AND INTOLERANCES

Although some of the tests just described can provide important clues to help establish which foods are potentially contributing to adverse food reactions and the symptoms of ADHD, they should be considered as only clues and not as an absolute determination of the person's adverse food responses. There is currently no perfect test that can, by itself, accurately determine all forms of food allergy and intolerance. However, determining which foods are truly responsible for significant adverse responses can be of immense value in helping to solve the ADHD puzzle. In many cases, food allergies and intolerances will prove to be the single largest trigger (physiological disturbance) contributing to the person's ADHD symptoms. In such cases, it is certainly worth the time and trouble that is required to confidently establish a list of offending foods and gradually change the person's diet to accommodate these restrictions.

Functional Medicine provides an organized, step-wise and rational approach to the determination of food allergies and intolerances. This approach is similar to that taught by the noted immunologist, Dr. Janice Joneja. (Joneja, 1998)*

*Healthcare professionals who wish to gain a high level of competence in the management of food allergies and intolerances are advised to obtain the home study course and clinical manuals produced by Dr. Janice Joneja, Ph.D., R.D., adjunct professor in the School of Family and Nutritional Sciences at the University of British Columbia in Canada. Dr. Joneja is also the head of the Allergy Nutrition Program at the Vancouver General Hospital and Health Sciences Center and is a worldwide authority in the field of food allergies. The content of her course materials is compatible with the principles of Functional Medicine. These are probably the most comprehensive teaching materials ever produced on this topic. Lecture cassettes, manuals and workbooks are available through the web site: www.PureLiving.com.

Relevant Historical Information

Step 1 begins by gathering historical information that may be relevant to food allergies or intolerances. The patient or parent may have made observations about the effects of certain foods that may be highly significant. For instance, if a child develops an ear infection whenever they consume more than a small amount of dairy foods, this could be a clue that they indeed have a significant dairy allergy. Any of these suspicions or observations should be recorded and presented to the healthcare provider. Any strong food preferences, food habits or addictions should also be noted. Strongly preferred foods are often found to be allergenic or intolerant.

Conducting and Noting the Results of Diagnostic Tests

Step 2 involves the performance of laboratory tests or related diagnostic methods such as provocation-neutralization testing. The choice of test or tests used will vary depending upon the preferences, training and experience of the practitioner. For several reasons, the ELISA IgE and IgG food antibody testing provides useful and objective information to help establish a list of foods which are likely to prove allergenic. This same data can also be looked at later to help to determine whether or not a food allergy is primarily caused by Type I or Type III hypersensitivity. This can make a great deal of difference as to how the food allergy is treated.

The Use of a Diet and Symptom Diary

Step 3 requires that the patient or parent complete a diet and symptom diary for one week or more. In this diary, the patient or parent should record:

· Every food eaten (including all ingredients for recipes and packaged foods), the approximate quantity, the time of day and the location.

· Any symptoms noted after each meal such as behavioral, mood, or cognitive problems; abdominal pain, nausea, diarrhea, or constipation; itching skin, hives, wheezing, coughing, stuffy nose, sneezing, or runny nose; joint or muscle pains, and headaches.

· The quality of sleep that night and how the person feels in the morning.

· Energy levels, sense of exhaustion.

· Any strong food preferences, food habits or possible food addictions noted during this time.

The diet and symptom diary will be reviewed by the healthcare provider to look for clues as to which foods may be causing adverse effects. It is important for the patient or parent to become accustomed to keeping careful records of foods and associated symptoms. Many food allergies and intolerances will only be uncovered through the process of careful and recorded observation.

Formulating and Following an Elimination Test Diet

Step 4 involves the (temporary) prescription of an elimination test diet. This diet is used to see what degree of improvement occurs in the patient's ADHD symptoms when they are on an idealized diet, which has low allergy potential, is very nutrient dense and has a minimal amount of chemical additives. The exact composition of the elimination test diet is based upon several factors:

· It should be similar to the composition of diets that have been used with success in past research. All of these diets eliminate junk foods, processed foods, food additives and several specific foods or food types that are associated with a high allergic potential.

· Eliminated foods include all dairy products (<u>including goat milk products</u>), wheat, corn, bakers and brewers yeast, egg, peanut, soy, chocolate, apple, orange, tomato and refined sugar.

· Other foods may also be eliminated if they are suggested by the medical history, the food and symptom diary or allergy testing.

Guidelines for a standard elimination test diet are found at the end of this chapter. The restrictions in this diet may seem overwhelming at first. However, with planning and a few good allergy cookbooks, the required changes are not as difficult as they may seem. Food addictions or strong food preferences can make the transition to the elimination test diet more difficult. It is important to remember, however, that the foods eaten most often or for which the person has a particularly strong fondness are often the allergic or intolerant foods. Therefore, it is especially important to make every effort to exclude these foods from the elimination test diet.

The elimination test diet requires the least amount of sacrifice when tasty new recipes are used to substitute for previously eaten foods. Healthy snacks and main meals can be perfectly "legal" and yet be very enjoyable. Learning new recipes requires a commitment of time and the purchase of a few good cookbooks (an updated list of recommended allergy cookbooks can be found at www.PureLiving.com). Health food markets are often an excellent resource for people needing to make these difficult dietary changes. Most of these markets have knowledgeable staff who are familiar with the needs of people with food allergies. They also stock a wide range of books and products, which are useful for allergy free cooking.

If an elimination test diet has been properly designed to remove significant food allergies and intolerances, the patient must be aware that they may feel worse before they feel better. As described in Chapter 11, this allergy "withdrawal" effect probably occurs when large antibody-food antigen complexes (immune complexes) form as the amount of food antigens is dropping while the amount of antibodies is still very high. This withdrawal phenomenon may be accompanied by headaches, fatigue, malaise (feeling awful), muscle pain, "brain fog", worsening behavior, moodiness and other symptoms. These symptoms generally last from three to ten days before the person starts feeling progressively better. If the elimination test diet has been chosen correctly and the person sticks closely to the diet, behavior, cognitive performance and general health should be significantly improved after aproximately three to four weeks.

Completing the Conner's Questionnaires before and after the four weeks on the elimination test diet is a helpful way to monitor the effects of the diet on ADHD symptoms. Questionnaires to assess physical symptoms may also be administered before and after to gauge the physical effects of these changes. As well, it may be very helpful to perform the lactulose-mannitol intestinal permeability test before and then again after four weeks in order to determine if the diet has resulted in a resolution of the patient's leaky gut.

If the elimination test diet has not resulted in significant improvements in ADHD symptoms after four weeks of careful dietary observance, it may be that:

· The ADHD sufferer has been "cheating" and has not correctly adhered to the diet consistently enough for benefits to be seen. In this case, more effort should be placed into finding acceptable food substitutions. In our experience, a face-to-face talk with the healthcare practitioner can often convince a difficult child or adolescent that the sacrifices required on this diet are worth the trouble. If kids realize that their behavior will likely improve and they may do better in school because of these changes, many will accept the commitment and not cheat any longer.

· There is also a possibility that the composition of the diet was incorrect for that person and some significantly allergic or intolerant foods are still being consumed. In this case, further allergy testing may be required. In some instances, it is also worthwhile trying another, more restrictive diet referred to as a "few foods elimination diet" for about two weeks. This diet, consists only of foods which are very rarely a cause of allergy or intolerance. This is a very sparse diet with few food choices, but it provides an opportunity to see if foods really are significant factors in the person's ADHD symptoms. Since this diet is not nutritionally complete, it should only continue for two to three weeks. There are a number of variations of the few foods elimination diet. An example of a few foods elimination diet is found at the end of this chapter.

· Finally, there is a possibility that food allergies or intolerances are not a significant factor in the person's ADHD problems. Alternatively, there may be other, more pressing problems which have to be addressed before such dietary changes will positively impact the ADHD sufferer. (e.g. intestinal parasites, heavy metal toxicity, severe essential fatty acid deficiencies, gut fermentation syndrome)

The Open Food Challenge Process

Step 5 involves the identification of allergic or intolerant foods by a careful and systematic reintroduction process. This method of food allergy identification is also known as the open food challenge (as opposed to the double-blind food challenge explained above). The foods that are to be tested through the food challenge process should include all of those foods specifically eliminated in the elimination test diet. The order of food challenges is not important as long as all foods are eventually tested through the challenge process.

The open food challenge process begins once the patient has been carefully following the elimination test diet for approximately four weeks. If, after this period of time, the patient has experienced substantial improvements in ADHD symptoms, the diet is then considered a success. The next goal is to carefully and systematically determine which foods are problematic and which ones can be safely reintroduced back into the diet once again. This is accomplished through the open food challenge process.

Food challenges are conducted by testing only one food on one particular day. The challenged food is generally eaten during breakfast, lunch and supper in increasing quantities at each meal. The patient or parent must keep careful records of the foods eaten, the quantity consumed, the time of day and any symptoms that are experienced following the eating of those foods. For instance, on the day that milk is to be tested, the patient might consume half a glass of milk for breakfast, one glass for lunch and two glasses of milk for supper. Any physical symptoms, bad behaviors, mood swings or cognitive problems experienced by the patient during that day are recorded along with the time the symptoms occur. The patient or parent should also record the quality of sleep that night and how the patient feels and behaves the next day. Fatigue, bad breath, stuffy nose, headaches, moodiness, aggressiveness or other bad behaviors the day after a food challenge should all be recorded. If the patient gets sick with a cold or ear infection following a food challenge, this should be noted and further challenges should not occur until the patient has fully recovered from the infection.

In addition, prior to eating the test food, the patient should sit quietly and measure their pulse rate (in heart-beats per minute). After the challenge food is eaten, the patient should remain still and the pulse rate should be measured again after five and then ten minutes. Food allergies or intolerances may result in the release of the stress hormone adrenaline, which usually causes the pulse rate to rise ten beats per minute or more.

As mentioned previously, it is important that only one food is challenged on a particular day. As well, *following a food challenge the challenged food must be completely withdrawn again until all foods are challenged, even if no adverse effects are noted from the food.* In addition, a full day without food challenges should elapse before another food challenge is done. If a food challenge results in significant adverse symptoms, no further food challenges should be done until the symptoms have subsided for at least twenty-four hours.

Obviously, the food challenge process is a lengthy task, which requires a high level of commitment on the part of the patient and any other supportive member. In most cases this is only possible if the parent or patient has taken the time to make the elimination test diet as pleasant as possible by having the courage to try a variety of creative and tasty recipes. There are many completely "legal" recipes that are quite delicious and might even become family favorites. It is also far better for the whole family to be at least following the basic elements of the diet and consuming the same main recipes. It is very difficult to prepare special meals for only one family member. In our experience, other family members are often surprised at how good they feel when they have eliminated junk foods and potentially allergenic foods. Since food allergies and intolerances can be hereditary, it is not surprising that certain food restrictions will benefit several family members.

To carry out food challenges properly and with a high degree of accuracy, several weeks are often required. In some cases, the results of a given food challenge are not clear and the challenge may have to be repeated two or three times. As well some foods, such as dairy can be challenged in more than one step. For instance, milk can be challenged on a separate day from other dairy products such as yogurt, and cheeses. In some cases high lactose dairy foods will not be tolerated, whereas low lactose products will be well tolerated. In other cases milk protein allergy will be evident to milk or cheeses but not to yogurt. Similarly, separate challenges can be conducted for egg white and egg yoke; wheat and yeast etc. The most important key to accurate food challenge testing is patience, persistence and good record keeping. There are no short-cuts to this process and, unfortunately there is currently no better way to accurately determine all manner of food allergies and intolerances than the open food challenge method. For those that take the time and make the effort to follow this system, the information obtained can change an individual's life in a tremendously positive way.

Putting it all Together
Step 6 involves the formulation of long-term dietary recommendations. The open food challenge is the primary way that suspected foods are confirmed to be the source of food allergy or intolerance reactions. Those foods, which are found to be problematic through the open food challenge process are, of course, not included in the long-term diet. In some cases, problem causing foods may have to be permanently removed from the diet (usually those foods which cause Type I (immediate) hypersensitivity reactions or food intolerances such as lactose intolerance). Other foods may only need to be removed for a few months and can then be reintroduced in small quantities as long as they are only eaten every few days (usually foods that cause Type III (delayed) hypersensitivity reactions).

Results from ELISA IgE and IgG food antibody testing (done prior to starting the elimination test diet) can be helpful in making such determinations. Those foods which were shown to be problematic with the open food challenge and which were associated with high levels of IgE antibodies are most likely responsible for Type I (immediate) hypersensitivity reactions. Except in infants and very young children, one has to assume that these foods should be eliminated completely and often permanently. In many cases, Type I hypersensitivity food allergies will be lifelong and must always be avoided even in small amounts. The exception to this rule are infants and young children who often grow out of Type I hypersensitivity reactions.

On the other hand, those foods that are confirmed to be problematic by the open food challenge and were associated with high levels of IgG antibodies on ELISA testing, are most likely responsible for Type III (delayed) hypersensitivity reactions. If they are eliminated for several months and other efforts are made to heal the leaky gut, these foods can often be reintroduced in small amounts every few days. Such reintroductions should, of course be done only after a properly recorded open food challenge has shown that adverse reactions to this food no longer take place.

Once the allergic and intolerant foods have been identified with a high level of confidence, it is important to remain watchful for adverse food reactions on an ongoing basis. For instance if your child has a particularly bad day in terms of behavior and mood, it is well worthwhile to recollect the foods that were eaten over the past few days.

Make a record of these foods and when symptoms worsen again, see if a finger can be pointed at a particular food or combination of foods. Many people will note that their child has a particularly difficult time after events like Halloween, birthdays and other junk food binges. Eventually, when you become smart about the effects of dietary indiscretions you will decide that the few moments of pleasure may come with too high a price in poor health to make such indulgences worth the small pleasures that they bring.

All in all, the ADHD sufferer must come to accept that they have a highly sensitive physiology and a highly demanding brain. Even those without significant food allergies are wise to treat their bodies well and consistently choose the most nutritious diet possible consisting primarily of whole, unadulterated foods. Making the transition away from the standard North American diet to a diet of whole, natural foods can be difficult at first, especially when restrictions are also imposed by food allergies or intolerances. However, the benefits to following such a program can be truly remarkable and can prove to be one of the factors, which can turn ADHD into an asset rather than a disability.

Although the primary treatment for food allergies is long-term avoidance of the identified offending foods, a form of immunotherapy from Europe, known as Enzyme Potentiated Desensitization (EPD) is becoming increasingly available in North America. This remarkable therapy is holding up great hope as an effective way to reverse food allergies. One double blind, placebo controlled study has already confirmed that EPD is an effective treatment for children with ADHD who suffer with food allergies. EPD will be discussed in Chapter 22.

THE STANDARD ELIMINATION TEST DIET FOR ADHD

Foods to Avoid (elimination test diet continues for 4-8 weeks and then, if results are positive, open challenges begin):

Dairy

Exclude any type of milk, or dairy products including cheeses, ice cream, and cream cheese.

Avoid products that have casein, lactose, and whey on the label.

Limit butter use. Alternatives to butter are oils or ghee. (See butter alternatives page.)

Goat's milk or products made from goat's milk are not suitable substitutes (goat and cow milk are now known to be almost equal in allergic potential).

Wheat

Exclude all wheat pastas, spaghettis, and breads.

Avoid durham, semolina, whole wheat, white breads or flours. "Flour" on a label usually means wheat. (kamut, and spelt are too similar to wheat and may not be used on this diet)

Avoid products that have gluten or gliaden on the label.

Corn

Exclude all corn, corn meal, corn chips, cornstarch and other products containing corn.

Yeast	Exclude all yeast breads, cookies, and cakes (including sourdough and naturally risen breads).
	Read labels for yeast or yeast extract in prepared foods.
	Many salad dressings and packaged soups contain yeast. Read labels.
Eggs	Exclude all eggs, egg whites, and egg yolks, and any products with eggs in them.
	Many cookies, cakes, and breads have eggs in them, be sure to avoid.
	Avoid products with eggs, egg whites and lactalbumin on the label.
Peanuts	Exclude whole peanuts, peanut butter, and peanut oil.
Soy	Exclude all soy products: soybeans, soymilk, soy yogurt, tofu, soy sauce, miso, tempeh, margarine, and soybean oil.
	Avoid products with soy protein isolate, texturized vegetable protein (TVP), or any type of soy on the label. Read labels carefully, many products contain soy.
Chocolate	Exclude all cocoa products, chocolate bars, chips, cookies and cakes.
	Avoid products with cocoa, cocoa beans or chocolate on the label.
Oranges	Exclude whole oranges, orange juice, and orange flavoring.
	Check juice labels for oranges, orange juice concentrate and added sugars.

Apples	Exclude all apples, apple juice, apple sauce and other products containing apple.
Tomato	Exclude all tomato, tomato sauces and pastes, ketchup, salsa and other products with tomato.
Sugar	Exclude all refined white sugar.
	Avoid products with added sugar, glucose, fructose, and sucrose on the label. Check all labels, especially juice and salad dressings.
Food Additives	Exclude added artificial preservatives, flavorings, and colorings including:
	Sodium benzoate, sulfites, nitrates, BHA, BHT, artificial sweeteners such as aspartame or nutrasweet, yellow dye #5, tartrazine, or other dyes, monosodium glutamate or MSG.
	Avoid Jell-O, Kool-aid, fruit punch and all beverages containing sugar or artificial favors or sweeteners, cereals with preservatives and added sugars, packaged foods containing these additives. Read labels.
Oils/Fats	Avoid all trans-fatty acids (hydrogenated or partially-hydrogenated oils, vegetable oil shortening).
	Check labels of cookies, crackers, cakes, and chips! Most of these foods contain hydrogenated oils.
	Avoid margarine and products containing margarine. Avoid vegetable oil shortening which is mostly hydrogenated vegetable oil.
	Avoid all oil fried or deep fried foods.

Beverages	Avoid coffee or alcoholic beverages. Small amounts of black or green tea and unlimited herbal teas allowed. Avoid sugary drinks including juices. Unsweetened juices are acceptable in small amounts if they are diluted with twice as much water as called for on can.

Foods You May Eat:

Cereal	**Hot:** Cream of rice, oatmeal, or any hot cereals which do not contain wheat or corn.
	Cold: puffed rice, puffed millet, Natures Path makes many cereals with no wheat, added sugar or additives.
Grains	Rice: preferably brown, brown basmati, jasmine, rice pasta, plain rice cakes, rice bread.
	Flat breads and rye crisps, millet, quinoa, amaranth, teff, oats, barley, rye.
Flours	Rice, millet, quinoa, amaranth, teff, bean flours, oat, barley, and rye.
Fruits	All (EXCEPT oranges and apples) Preferably fresh. **Organic is best!** Dried fruit should be free of sulfites.
Vegetables	All except tomato. Eat lots of fresh veggies. If possible, fresh and organic is best.

Protein	Meat: all types are acceptable, except all processed meats including cold cuts, hams and wieners.
Poultry	All types are acceptable.
Fish	All ocean water types are acceptable. Try to include salmon, sardines, occasional tuna, and halibut.
Bean/legumes	You can have all beans and legumes EXCEPT peanuts and soy products.
	Check labels of canned beans, dips, and soups for sweeteners and additives.
Nuts	Cashews, pistachios, almonds, brazil nuts, walnuts, pine nuts.
	All nuts are acceptable EXCEPT peanuts, soy nuts, and all roasted and salted nuts.
	Use nut butters such as almond butter or cashew butter. Great for sauces, salad dressings, and butter/peanut butter alternatives. No peanut butter!
Seeds	All are acceptable and encouraged. Sunflower seeds and pumpkinseeds are great.
	Tahini, a sesame seed butter, is great for dressings and sauces!
Oils/Fats	Olive, canola, sunflower, safflower, sesame, flax, or coconut oil. Ghee.
	Store flax oil in a dark bottle in the refrigerator and use as dressing or in smoothies; do not heat this oil.

Sweeteners In general, use sparingly. Acceptable sweeteners include molasses (unsulfured), pure maple syrup, honey, stevia (herbal sweetener you can get at natural food store, very sweet so use a very small amount (use ½ to 1 packet), brown rice syrup.

Beverages Drink lots of water! Filtered water or bottled spring water is best.

Herbal teas including green tea, jasmine, chamomile and Oolong (read labels), rice milk.

All juice EXCEPT orange or apple juice. Use fruit juice sparingly and dilute with twice the recommended quantity of water. NO juice, tea, or soft drinks with added corn syrup, sugar, fructose, glucose, or colorings. Kids can learn to enjoy herbal tea including small amounts of green tea.

Condiments Salt, pepper, garlic, lemon, fresh parsley, chives, and other herbs. Spike is very tasty and nutritious (contains a small amount of nutritional yeast which is OK in very small amounts).

Vanilla (pure), unsweetened carob, baking powder with NO aluminum, baking soda.

HELPFUL DIET GUIDELINES

1. Use only those foods which are allowed. READ LABELS!

2. Bring your list of foods to avoid and foods allowed grocery shopping with you.

3. Get some good allergy cooking recipe books. Read, study, plan and experiment before embarking on an elimination test diet!

4. Withdrawal symptoms may occur during the first week on the diet. Some or all of your symptoms may increase temporarily, but these usually subside within 10 days.

5. Children imitate their parents, so set good examples by eating well.

6. Children tend to like food they recognize. It takes a child approximately 5 times to become familiar with a food. If your child does not like a food the first time he/she sees it, keep trying; they may like it better as the food becomes more familiar. Always provide at least one dish at each meal that you know your child enjoys.

7. Encourage your children to take at least one bite of everything on their plate. If they do not like it they do not have to eat it. Trying food encourages familiarity with the food.

8. Provide your child with healthy, allergy-free choices. Children like to be given a choice, but not junk food.

9. Take the junk food out of the cupboards! Substitute with healthy, good tasting snacks.

10. Smoothies made from a base of rice based powders such as Ultracare for Kids™ (children up to ten or twelve years), or UltraClear™ or UltraClear Plus™ (for adolescents or adults) combined with frozen fruit and a natural sweetener (stevia powder) and other nutritious ingredients. Smoothies are one great way to replace unhealthy snacks with healthy nutrition. See example of smoothie recipe below:

Ultracare for Kids™ Smoothie

Mix the following ingredients in a blender until completely liquefied:

6 ounces of filtered water

1 level scoop Ultracare for Kids

1-2 handfuls of frozen strawberries and/or blueberries

1 tsp. of flax seed oil (optional)

½- 1 package of stevia or a small amount of honey or molasses to taste

A small amount of allowable nut butter, whole nuts or seeds may be added for nutty flavor and extra protein.

2-4 Ice cubes for slushy texture.

*This is great to provide for your children as an afternoon and late night snack.

*It may be used for breakfast if you are in rush, or in addition to other breakfast items.

*Make up your own variations; try freezing them into popcicles.

EXAMPLE OF A FEW FOODS ELIMINATION DIET*

*(Adapted from Joneja, 1998)

Introduction
A few foods elimination diet may be prescribed if the standard elimination test diet for ADHD has failed to provide significant improvements and no other other causes for the failure of the standard elimination test diet can be discerned. If significant improvements do not occur on this very limited diet, it is highly unlikely that food allergies or intolerances are a significant cause of the ADHD symptoms.

In some cases, the few foods elimination diet will bring about marked improvements in the patient's condition and will give strong evidence that there is significant dietary componant to their problems. If successful, foods allowable on the standard elimination test diet may be added one at a time with careful observations. Eventually, all of the food restricted on standard elimination test diet may be tested using the open food challege process.

Only those foods listed below are permitted on the few foods elimination diet. This is a highly restrictive diet, which should only be continued for a maximum of three weeks. The ability to successfully carry out this diet is improved if an adequate number of suitable recipes are available which only utilize the permitted foods. The book entitled "Dietary Management of Food Allergies And Intolerances: A Comprehensive Guide" by Dr. Janice Joneja, Ph.D., R.D. is the most useful resource available for properly carrying out a few foods elimination diet. This book can be ordered from: www.PureLiving.com.

Allowable Foods include ONLY the following:

Protein allowed includes lamb or turkey.

Grains allowed include rice, and tapioca including the whole grains as well as flour made from these products.

Fruits allowed include pears (fresh or canned in glass jars in pear juice), cranberries and cranberry juice.

Vegetables allowed include squash of any kind, parsnips, sweet potatoes, yams and lettuce.

Condiments include sea salt.

Beverage includes only filtered water.

Deserts allowed include puddings made from tapioca, or rice combined with allowable fruits.

Oils allowed include safflower, sunflower and flax oil.

Smoothies allowed include those made from rice protein and rice carbohydrate. Ultracare for Kids™ is a palatable powder made from rice, which also contains a number of important nutrients. For older children or adults, UltraClear™, or UltraClear Plus™ is a more suitable base for low allergy potential smoothies. One or two scoops of Ultracare™ or UltraClear™ are placed in a blender with chopped pear and ice cubes. Water or rice milk is added and the mixture is blended. This provides an easy, high nutrition snack or meal replacement while on the few foods diet.

Section Five

Functional Medicine Approach to the Treatment of ADHD

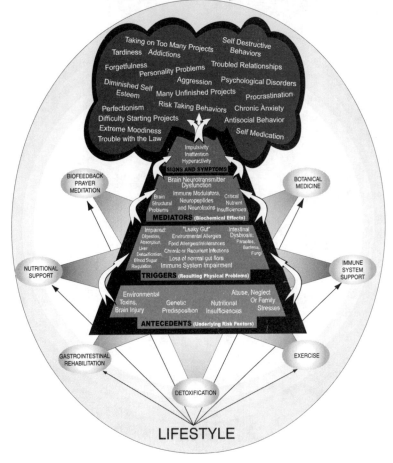

Taking on Too Many Projects Self Destructive Behaviors
Tardiness Addictions
Forgetfulness Troubled Relationships
Personality Problems
Diminished Self Aggression Psychological Disorders
Esteem Many Unfinished Projects Procrastination
Perfectionism Risk Taking Behaviors Chronic Anxiety
Difficulty Starting Projects Antisocial Behavior
Extreme Moodiness Self Medication
Trouble with the Law

Impulsivity
Inattention
Hyperactivity
SIGNS AND SYMPTOMS

BIOFEEDBACK
PRAYER
MEDITATION

Brain Neurotransmitter
Dysfunction
Brain Immune Modulators, Critical
Structural Neuropeptides Nutrient
Problems and Neurotoxins Insufficiencies
MEDIATORS (Biochemical Effects)

BOTANICAL
MEDICINE

NUTRITIONAL
SUPPORT

Impaired: "Leaky Gut" Intestinal
Digestion, Environmental Allergies Dysbiosis,
Absorption, Food Allergies/Intolerances Parasites,
Liver Chronic or Recurrent Infections Bacteria,
Detoxification, Loss of normal gut flora Fungi
Blood Sugar Immune System Impairment
Regulation
TRIGGERS (Resulting Physical Problems)

IMMUNE
SYSTEM
SUPPORT

Environmental Abuse, Neglect
Toxins, Genetic Nutritional Or Family
Brain Injury Predisposition Insufficiencies Stresses
ANTECEDENTS (Underlying Risk Factors)

GASTROINTESTINAL
REHABILITATION

EXERCISE

DETOXIFICATION

LIFESTYLE

Chapter 18
Patient Centered
Treatment of ADHD

TREATING LABELS OR TREATING PEOPLE?

In conventional (disease centered) medicine, establishing the diagnosis of ADHD is generally sufficient to justify a specific course of therapeutic action. Most often this course of action is a prescription for stimulant medication and perhaps a limited amount of counseling or behavioral therapy. This approach assumes that the millions of people with ADHD are a relatively uniform group who are all afflicted with the same "disease entity". Imaging technology is helping to demonstrate that there is some truth to this point of view in the sense that those with ADHD may share common patterns of brain dysfunction. As mentioned in previous chapters, this research has suggested that most individuals with ADHD suffer, for example, from diminished size and activity of brain centers responsible for executive control and a sense of reward or pleasure. Powerful drugs like Ritalin® and Dexedrine® influence the function of these brain centers and thus modify symptoms in the majority of those with ADHD.

However, even though they may share similar patterns of brain dysfunction, each and every person with ADHD symptoms has developed these problems secondary to an entirely unique collection of underlying antecedents, triggers and mediators. Is unlikely that ADHD ever exists in the absence of various underlying medical problems and developmental stresses. In other words, there is no evidence of "pure" ADHD, or ADHD as a specific "disease entity". Even if it is true that some of those with ADHD have inherited an "ADHD wired brain", this unique "neurological wiring" probably does not result in disability unless other underlying stresses are applied to the brain and immune system. It is my view that the inherited neurological aspects of ADHD may actually hold the promise of unique abilities and even giftedness in the absence of neurotoxic stresses.

The key to effectively managing ADHD and turning what is so often a formula for failure into a blueprint for success can be found by solving the ADHD puzzle for each unique individual, and then treating each person based upon their distinctive and changing needs. Instead of an approach to treatment which focuses upon the name of the disease (disease centered), Functional Medicine is patient centered and places the focus of treatment upon the unique requirements of each patient. Although this approach may depend to some extent upon sophisticated laboratory technologies and a range of unique therapies directed at the underlying causes, the most important factor which empowers this patient centered approach is the time and care taken by the healthcare practitioner.

The patient centered approach of Functional Medicine is really a call to return to the basic principles of concern and compassion for each patient. There are few shortcuts to this approach; it simply takes time to be this thorough. In contrast, the disease centered approach to ADHD is quick and easy — make the diagnosis and write the prescription. This fits nicely into the modern pattern of 5 or 10 minute office visits which seems to prevail under the influence of managed care organizations (HMO's) and under-funded government insurance schemes. However, an increasing number of healthcare practitioners are finding creative ways to work around these limitations in order to compassionately serve their patients the way they intended to do when they entered their chosen profession.

STRIVING TO ACHIEVE EVIDENCE BASED MEDICINE

Most people are under the impression that nearly everything that belongs to modern medicine is based upon proven science. Particularly, the majority of our populace trust that the drugs and surgical procedures prescribed by medical doctors are all thoroughly studied for their safety and effectiveness. Unfortunately, this is often not the case. Many surgical procedures become widely used before these basic questions have ever been answered. In some cases, decades pass before it is finally shown that a procedure actually causes more harm than good. Similarly there are hundreds of drugs which have been studied in small clinical trials and then released into the marketplace before their real effects are truly known. There are now dozens of examples of drugs which were in widespread use for years, only to be pulled from the market due to their danger or ineffectiveness. In other cases, drugs were developed many years ago when the drug approval process was even less rigorous than it is today. There are certainly drugs that have been in common use for many years, which would never be approved today based on the minimal amount of safety testing that resulted in the original drug approval. Ritalin® and Dexedrine® are examples of two drugs that have never undergone long-term safety testing even though they have been in use for many decades.

Because there is a growing recognition that so much of modern medicine is actually quite unscientific and based upon "convention" and marketing influences, more and more leaders in healthcare are promoting a practice of medicine which utilizes treatments which are supported by real scientific evidence. As surprising as it may seem to some, much of conventional medicine, as it is currently practiced, has a very long way to go before it becomes truly "evidence based".

Most physicians base their prescribing habits to a large extent upon personal experience with individual patients rather than sound medical literature or official scientific recommendations. Studies have also shown that the majority of physicians are greatly influenced by the marketing efforts of drug companies and they may obtain as much as 90 percent of their continuing education through pharmaceutical representatives and drug company sponsored educational programs. On top of this, medicine is tremendously influenced by convention and tradition. Once a particular treatment has become widely accepted, it can become quite unfashionable to question the correctness of this therapy. The use of powerful amphetamine stimulants for the treatment of ADHD is certainly one of those traditions. One is sure to offend a good proportion of the medical world if even basic questions about the safety and efficacy of these drugs is called into question. Although the majority of those in the mainstream medical world are quick to show their bitter opposition to any form of "alternative" or "complementary" medicine, they fail to recognize that only a small proportion of what is really practiced by conventional physicians is based on solid scientific evidence.

There are two primary ways that a given therapy can be evaluated and then said to be "evidence based". One method is known as the **randomized controlled trial**. This research technique involves the study of a particular therapy by randomly assigning a group of people to either a control group (where no treatment, or else an inactive placebo, is given) and a treatment group (where the treatment in question is given). The effectiveness and safety of the therapy is then examined in this carefully selected group of people. The randomized controlled trial is used primarily to determine the likelihood that a particular therapy will be effective when given to a person with a specific condition and to observe the range and frequency of its side effects. This method is especially important in the evaluation of drugs. Since most drugs have the potential for serious side effects, it would be unthinkable to start giving new drugs to patients before their risks are weighed against their benefits in randomized controlled trials.

There are now numerous herbal medicines which have also been evaluated by randomized controlled trials, primarily in Europe where herbal medicine is taken quite seriously. It is also possible to evaluate more complex treatments, such as dietary changes, through a randomized controlled trial. For example, our facility has recently conducted a randomized controlled trial which compared the changes in ADHD symptoms in those following a low allergy potential diet to the changes in ADHD symptoms in a control group who made no dietary changes. As far as possible, the randomized controlled trial should be the standard which is upheld for the evaluation of all new therapies. Unfortunately, because this type of rigorous research is costly and requires considerable research expertise, it is largely market driven by drug companies looking to collect healthy profits for their research investments. More natural, cause oriented treatments receive almost no funding in comparison to the more lucrative drug and surgery industry.

The other method used to evaluate the evidence of a treatment's effectiveness is by properly assessing medical outcomes. **Outcome based research** is gaining strong support amongst leaders in medicine worldwide. Rather than simply predicting the probability that a certain therapy will be safe and effective when given to a patient, as is done with a randomized controlled trial, outcome based medicine is based on the concept that the success of a therapy needs to be assessed in real patients within real practice settings. In contrast to randomized controlled trials, which are carried out in the rather artificial environment of academic centers on a group of specially selected individuals, outcome based research is often carried out by looking at the outcome of treatments when they are applied to actual patients seeking help from healthcare providers in typical practice settings.

Many authorities consider the assessment of medical outcomes to be the most valid way to evaluate a given therapy. Medical outcomes assessment is also increasingly used by individual practitioners to evaluate the effectiveness of treatment programs in individual patients. The true evidence of a therapy's effectiveness comes when good medical outcomes are achieved in an individual patient. Much of current medical practice involves simply prescribing the "right drug" and then casually following the patient, often with little effort made to carefully evaluate the outcome of that treatment (including changes in symptoms, side effects and quality of life).

Important Differences in the Proper Evaluation of Drug Treatments and Natural Therapies

Since drugs and surgery often carry such a high risk of serious side effects, there should be ethical constraints to prevent practitioners from using such treatments before well designed randomized clinical trials have proven that the treatment has a high enough degree of safety and effectiveness to justify using it in clinical practice. To some extent, the current drug approval process accomplishes this goal, however, this system is far from perfect and it is greatly influenced by the profits that can be gained by obtaining official drug approval.

On the other hand, most natural therapies, such as nutritional supplements and herbal medicines, are already in common use and, apart from a few important exceptions, carry little or no risk of causing harm. There is also a tremendous scarcity of research dollars to support the study of treatments which cannot be patented. As well, there may be active opposition by the medical establishment toward those who wish to conduct research into non-conventional treatments, making the personal price too high for most researchers (I have learned this by personal experience). These limitations and differences are helping to shape the evolution of Functional Medicine and are promoting a greater use of outcome based assessments to determine the effectiveness of treatments used. After all, the real evidence of a treatment's effectiveness eventually boils down to how that treatment works in each and every patient being treated. Additionally, Functional Medicine typically involves several different therapies individualized to each patient. Such multimodal approaches may have too many variables to be properly studied with a randomized controlled trial and must be examined instead by assessing their medical outcome. With the right tools to assess the outcome of treatment efforts on each patient, the healthcare practitioner can fill the role of a true scientist and practice the highest form of evidence based medicine.

Our research facility is currently involved in the development of high-technology tools to help Functional Medicine providers more effectively practice evidence based medicine. By incorporating methods of assessing and tracking medical outcomes into a sophisticated, computerized medical record system, our goal is to provide a means for practitioners to track medical outcomes on every patient and to participate in the development of an evolving database which will assess the effectiveness of every protocol used in Functional Medicine. It is our view that every healthcare provider should also be a scientist who meticulously follows the successes, failures and adverse effects of every intervention used in their practice. Already, many of those who follow the principles of Functional Medicine use various medical outcome questionnaires and other means to more fully assess the overall effects that their treatment efforts are having on their patients. Striving to practice evidence based healthcare is a worthy goal and one fully supported by Functional Medicine.

THE UNIQUE GOALS OF TREATMENT IN FUNCTIONAL MEDICINE

The primary purpose of Functional Medicine is to help people to achieve optimal function and quality of life through therapies that seek to achieve more than just a suppression of symptoms. Although these lofty goals are not yet achievable for all human disorders, they are certainly possible in most people with ADHD. Some healthcare professionals who utilize the principles of Functional Medicine may still prescribe drug therapy for ADHD under certain circumstances, or they may be called upon to work with individuals who are already on medications. In Functional Medicine, if symptom suppressing medication is used at all, it is generally considered just a means to "buy some time" while a better, and more long lasting solution can be discovered for that patient.

To comply with the ideals of Functional Medicine, a given treatment or set of treatments should:

· Carry no risk of doing harm and should be free of unpleasant side effects.

· Improve symptoms as well as the overall function and quality of life.

· Help to correct the underlying causes of the disorder.

· Improve the long-term prognosis for the patient.

There are actually numerous therapies used by Functional Medicine practitioners which hold the promise of achieving these goals. Following a thorough Functional Medicine assessment, the practitioner will decide upon a basic treatment plan which may include such things as herbal medicines, nutritional supplementation, identification and elimination of allergenic or intolerant foods, other dietary changes, immune support, allergy desensitization, gastrointestinal rehabilitation, biofeedback, detoxification regimens and behavioral therapies. The choice of therapeutic interventions are determined by the specific needs of the individual patient based upon the clinical judgment of the practitioner. In some cases excellent results are seen early on with only one or two therapeutic interventions. In other cases, good results may take longer, require more in-depth investigations or require a greater number of treatments.

HARNESSING THE POWER TO HEAL

Central to Functional Medicine is a recognition of the awesome order and complexity of the human body. Ingrained in this philosophy is also an appreciation for the intelligent healing power which is intrinsic to every one of our trillions of cells. Essentially, Functional Medicine recognizes that our bodies want to be well and the therapeutic strategies used in this field reflect this recognition. Rather than focusing on killing disease with various chemical and surgical weapons, Functional Medicine seeks to remove the various chemical, biological and emotional stresses that are impairing the healing process while providing sophisticated nutritional, botanical, emotional and even spiritual support to assist the natural healing process. Many of the high-tech drugs and surgical procedures so revered today will be obsolete in the future. However, as research progresses, natural principles of hygiene, nutrition, lifestyle and spirituality will become permanently embedded in the doctrines of an increasingly evidence based healthcare system. Functional Medicine may be slightly ahead of its time right now, but in years to come these principles will likely overshadow virtually every aspect of healthcare.

Chapter 19

Why Worry About Ritalin®, Dexedrine® and Other ADHD Drugs?

IS THERE A NEED FOR MEDICATION IN THE TREATMENT OF ADHD?

As parents, we sincerely desire the best for our children. No one wants to see their kids suffer because of school failure or social rejection, and we certainly don't want them to end up as criminals or drug addicts. Anyone who has raised a child with ADHD symptoms knows how frustrating it can be to live with their misbehavior, moodiness; their seeming inability to accomplish the simplest tasks without getting distracted; their constant forgetfulness, and a host of other problems. Likewise, teachers with one or more ADHD kids on their hands can be tested to the limits of their patience. In fact, it is not uncommon these days for teachers to change careers altogether due to the incalculable stress they have to endure in classrooms that are increasingly encumbered with unruly, hyperactive students.

It is not just parents and teachers who suffer when dealing with an ADHD child. The child himself must often endure regular blows to his self-esteem as he senses the disapproval of peers, teachers and parents. These kids can grow up thinking that they were born to lose and their general lack of self respect can make them even more likely to live out everyone's worst expectations. Adults with ADHD can go through life in continual turmoil, never really able to "get it together" even with issues and responsibilities that are so simple for others.

Having ADHD, or having to deal with someone with this condition, can leave the sufferer, parent, or spouse feeling desperate and willing to take some tough measures to bring about order to the constant chaos. Likewise, teachers and school administrators may become highly assertive in their attitude towards kids whom they suspect have ADHD, and they may routinely insist that a child be medicated if they are to remain in school. Physicians as well, are often quite limited in their understanding of this condition. Since they might consider that drug treatment is so "safe and effective" they might bypass even the most rudimentary assessment; going straight for the prescription pad as they sense the urgency of those involved with the unfortunate patient.

We should certainly have compassion and empathy for the parents, teachers, and physicians who have to deal with the ADHD sufferer and who are responsible for finding real solutions for what is often a truly serious situation. Since medication can have such a rapid and definite effect on ADHD symptoms, it is not surprising that there are so many strong advocates for drug treatment of this condition. To many parents or teachers, Ritalin® can seem like a life preserver thrown to a drowning child and they will defend drug treatment of ADHD with great passion. On the other hand, there are also a growing numbers of parents, scientists, lawmakers and other groups who have serious apprehensions surrounding the use of powerful stimulant drugs in children. No doubt, this debate will continue for some time yet. In the meanwhile, the use of stimulant medication continues to increase with every passing day.

Conservative estimates still suggest that only 3 to 5 percent of the childhood population suffers from ADHD. If this were strictly a genetic disorder, as some authorities suggest, these rates would be unlikely to change more than slightly even over many generations. However, if the number of prescriptions for Ritalin® is any indication, the frequency of ADHD symptoms in our children is rising explosively. In a ground breaking study published in the September 1999 issue of the American Journal of Public Health, researchers from the Center for Pediatric Research at the Eastern Virginia Medical School examined thirty-thousand grade school children and found, to their surprise that 20 percent of Caucasian boys are currently on Ritalin®. (LeFever, 1999) Disturbingly, these same researchers examined children from the same area in 1996 and found the rate of Ritalin®® prescription to be only 8 percent in boys of the same age. Such statistics are certainly not isolated to a few areas in the back woods of Virginia. In their most recent annual report, the International Narcotics Control Board of the United Nations has stated that prescriptions for Ritalin® have risen explosively around the World. They claim that the U.S. and Canada lead this race to medicate our children with numbers of Ritalin® prescriptions increasing exponentially over the past decade. (www.incb.org) This important organization considers the dramatic rise in Ritalin® prescriptions to be of utmost concern to welfare of our society and to that of the whole world. Some may argue that the rise in Ritalin® prescriptions is simply proof that there is now widespread "over-diagnosis" of ADHD. However, this trend may instead reflect a rapidly growing crisis of disordered brain function in the very people who will soon be in charge of our world!

Will the apparent downturn in our children's behavior and cognitive performance be properly remedied by simply prescribing powerful drugs to more and more of those affected? Is the drug approach really getting to the root of this widespread and growing problem or is it just covering over a smoldering fire that will eventually explode into flame? If the incidence of ADHD has really risen by several hundred percent in not much more than a decade, and if this trend continues, all the Ritalin® on Earth will not prevent our society from facing a crisis of unprecedented proportions.

QUICK AND EASY ANSWERS FOR THE PUSH BUTTON CULTURE

There are many reasons why children and adults end up on Ritalin® or other ADHD drugs. Most often, frantic and frazzled parents come across no other reasonable answers in their quest to find help for their troubled child. The embarrassment of having a child sent home repeatedly from school with reports of misbehavior can be overwhelming. Oftentimes, these parents are presented with a clear ultimatum from the principal -- "either this child is placed on Ritalin® or he is not welcome at this school".

Children with oppositional behavior have an effective way of saving their worst moments for times when you are with them in public. Our daughter used to fly into a rage on a frequent basis, such as in the grocery store when she did not get the cereal she wanted. In her fury, she would scream, and spit until the blood vessels ruptured in her face. People just assumed that we were awful parents. Fortunately, we toughed it out and did not turn to drugs to help us cope with this frightful problem. Instead, we kept digging until we found some real and correctable reasons for this tendency and now she is a pleasant and polite teenager who has never been on Ritalin®.

Children who are severely inattentive may not be humiliating and infuriating, but their inability to stay with even the simplest task can lead to a serious degradation of their self esteem and leave parents grasping for straws to know what to do to help them avoid catastrophic failure. By the time our son reached grade 2, his mind seemed to always be off in outer space. He would spend hours daydreaming when he was supposed to be doing his schoolwork. I am very glad that we avoided turning to Ritalin®, and instead, uncovered and corrected a few significant antecedents and triggers at the heart of his cognitive problems. Now, at ten, he is able to focus and learn better than many other "normal" kids.

In the case of adults with ADHD, continual frustration with non-productivity, pathologic daydreaming, forgetfulness, impulsive behavior or chronic restlessness may drive a person to seek medical or psychological help. Ritalin® is most often presented as a completely safe and reasonable solution for a problem with absolutely no identifiable cause. Because it is such a "wonder drug", doctors fail to tell you that it is not even approved for use in adults with ADHD. More than this, they probably have not taken the time to study the toxicology of stimulant drugs and to consider what might occur in an aging brain or heart after years of taking this potent medication. After all, if renowned experts are promoting long-term Ritalin® use in adults, it must be safe, right? In spite of its clear record as being amongst the most abused and dangerous of drugs, according to drug enforcement agencies, Ritalin® is now being given to adults with the suggestion that they are as "safe as blood pressure pills" and that "you should expect to take them for the remainder of your life." Even adults with drug abuse histories are often given Ritalin® without a second thought, even though if taken abusively, it can be as addictive as any other amphetamine. (Parran, 1991; Volkow , 1999)

Once medication is started, its effects can reinforce a person's decision to accept the prescription as good. The effects of stimulant drugs are rapid and often dramatic. Children may suddenly slow down and become better behaved. Adults often report that taking Ritalin® is like "putting glasses on your brain" – everything comes into better focus. Because these impressive effects bring some much needed relief to countless suffering parents, teachers and ADHD sufferers alike, there is now a good-sized army of raving Ritalin® fans, some of whom think so highly of this drug that they might vote in favor of reclassifying it as a vitamin if they were given the opportunity. Unfortunately, not every fairy tale concludes with a happy ending. There remain some truly nagging concerns about Ritalin® and every other drug used to treat ADHD. These concerns relate primarily to unanswered questions about the long-term effects of these medications, particularly the stimulants. In essence, the question that begs an answer is: What price will be paid tomorrow for the relief of symptoms experienced today? If some people develop senile dementia in their fifties or heart disease in their forties because of the long-term toxic effects of these drugs, would they and their families still think so highly of these wonder drugs?

HISTORICAL LESSONS FROM TOXICOLOGY RESEARCH

Prior to the last few decades, the science of toxicology was amazingly primitive and had little to do with the lives of ordinary people. It is pathetically amusing to realize that as recently as thirty or forty years ago, cigarettes were still promoted as medicinal products. I recently viewed a documentary in which a medical specialist appeared on a popular game show touting a particular brand of menthol cigarettes as being good for the throat and lungs. In the late 1970's, I had an opportunity to work under one of the world's foremost cardiac pathologists as a research student studying arterial disease. This eminent scientist also happened to be a compulsive three-pack per day smoker, who claimed that there was not one shred of evidence that could scientifically prove that smoking was the cause of any human illness. My, how times have changed. Even my former supervisor quit smoking by the mid 1980's after finally realizing that his addiction would inevitably lead to premature death.

There are dozens of examples of drugs and chemicals, which were initially considered innocent and are now known to be highly toxic. For example, Coca Cola®, the world's favorite beverage got its start as a tasty "health drink" containing coca leaf (cocaine) and kola nut (caffeine) extracts. Promoted as a great nerve tonic by respected authorities such as Dr. Sigmund Freud, it took almost one hundred years to convince lawmakers that cocaine was addictive and potentially deadly. Numerous other drugs have started out their careers as illustrious wonder drugs, only to be pulled from the market for their dangers. Unfortunately, the safety of drugs is primarily evaluated by their short-term effects upon animals and then upon humans in brief clinical trials with a relatively small number of subjects. The sad reality is that there may be virtually no correlation between the short-term (hours to weeks) side effects of a chemical or drug and its long-term toxicity (years to decades). Time and time again modern toxicology has demonstrated that an absence of short-term side effects is no assurance that a substance is free of serious long-term consequences, even with exposures that are considered minute.

Over the past two decades, the field of toxicology has discovered a principle, which is proving to be true over and over again; if something is shown to have toxic effects upon the brain or heart at high doses, it will usually be seriously neurotoxic or cardiotoxic at much lower doses if the exposure goes on for long enough periods of time. For example, only a few years ago it was believed that lead was harmless to a child until their blood lead levels exceeded 75 micrograms/dl. As research looked closer and closer at the long term effects of lead it became clear that this metal was toxic to the brain at much lower levels than was previously imagined. Now, instead of waiting until blood levels exceed 75 micrograms/dl before action is taken, physicians and parents should all be aware that permanent neurological damage begins to occur at levels below 10 micrograms/dl. It took almost twenty years of fighting between scientists and industry influenced lawmakers before leaded gasoline was banned and some effort was made to reduce other forms of childhood exposure to this deadly brain killer. A similar battle is currently taking place over the use of neurotoxic pesticides. Toxicologists now estimate that the legally allowable levels of pesticides on foods can exceed known safe levels by as much a two or three hundred times (see Consumer's Report March 1999 or www.ewg.org for details). There are now hundreds of examples demonstrating that drugs and environmental chemicals are often far more toxic than they seemed when examined in short term studies. If we should learn one thing from the history of toxicology it should be this: any substance known to kill brain cells or damage the heart over the short term, must be highly suspect for long term toxicity with regular exposures that are even a small fraction of the amount which causes short term harm.

PREDICTING THE TOXIC EFFECTS OF STIMULANT DRUGS

Ritalin® (methylphenidate), Dexedrine® (dextroamphetamine), Adderall® (d-amphetamine and l-amphetamine), and Cylert® (pemoline) are all stimulant drugs used in the treatment of ADHD. Except for Cylert®, these agents are all in the amphetamine family of drugs and only minor differences separate one from another. All of these drugs have been around for a long time and were approved decades before there was much thought given to the long-term effects of prescription drugs. The widespread popularity of the amphetamine family amongst drug abusers has provided a sad opportunity to study the effects of these drugs on the brains and cardiovascular systems of young people. (McCann, 1991; Williamson, 1997; Lan, 1998; Robinson, 1986; Zahn, 1981) Unfortunately, the amphetamine family (and their close relative, cocaine) have proven themselves to be the most neurotoxic and cardiotoxic drugs in existence, with acute and long-term dangers exceeding that of heroin, alcohol, LSD and virtually all prescription drugs. Severe depression, frequent suicide, persistent psychosis, mania, and drug-induced dementia have been extensively reported in amphetamine abuse. Unlike many other drug addictions, successful addiction recovery from amphetamine abuse does not always result in significant improvements in brain function or psychiatric health in these unfortunate people. As well, death from cardiovascular collapse or chronic cardiac disease is also a common accompaniment of amphetamine abuse. Ritalin® is no exception to this rule. According to the Drug Enforcement Agency, Ritalin® is one of the most popular street drugs around, especially with teenagers. (www.ndsn.org/MARCH96/PRESCRP.html) Even though it might popularly be described as a "mild stimulant", when abused, it results in the same kind of devastating effects as any member of the amphetamine family. (Massello, 1999; Parran, 1991)

Extensive animal studies have now been conducted in order to determine the reasons why amphetamine family drugs possess such potent toxic potential. Importantly, it has been firmly established that the administration of amphetamines in even small doses virtually replicates the effects of severe stress on the body. (Peeters, 1994; Feeney, 1993; Nurnberger, 1984; Stewart, 1984) In fact, even modest doses of amphetamines result in the kind of hormonal and cardiovascular changes seen with severe physical trauma or tremendous emotional alarm. In both animal and human studies, amphetamine administration results in a marked rise in the stress hormones adrenaline and cortisol and serious abnormalities in the production of growth hormone. The appetite suppression and growth interruption seen so commonly in children taking Ritalin® may be related to the stress-mimicking effects of this drug. Although brushed off as only temporary, growth disturbances may have more far reaching implications than that of short stature. Stress hormones like adrenaline and cortisol are highly toxic to the cardiovascular and nervous systems. Recent research has now determined that overexposure to stress hormones may be a primary cause of rapid brain aging and early onset dementia. (Kirschbaum, 1996; Lupien, 1997; Seeman, 1997; Bremner, 1995) It has been known for years that individuals who have lived through torturous circumstances (such as plane crashes or the Holocaust) and suffer subsequently from post-traumatic stress disorder have significant and measurable losses in cognitive performance related to stress hormone induced brain cell death. Other animal and human studies have verified the neurotoxic potential of chronic exposure to excessive quantities of our own stress hormones. Since having amphetamines percolate daily through every brain and body cell is identical to other forms of severe stress, the long-term implications of Ritalin® and its other family members should be of grave concern. In addition to the indirect effects of drug induced stress, amphetamine family drugs, including Ritalin®, have also been shown to result in the production of toxic free radicals in the brain; stimulate direct brain cell death; result in direct damage to brain blood vessels and in cumulative and permanent damage to the cells of the heart. (Henderson, 1995; Boughner, 1997; O'Callaghan J, 1997; Appel, 1989; Huang, 1997)

Unfortunately, little effort has been made to assess the impact of amphetamine drugs at typically prescribed dosages in real humans for ADHD. There seems to be a complete lack of willingness in the medical community to associate the known devastating effects of amphetamine abuse with the "proper prescription" of the same agents. Numerous respected authorities have staked their good reputations on the assumption that Ritalin® is a mild, risk-free and ideal treatment for ADHD. Support groups, government organizations and medical associations have all stood in solidarity with the corporations that are reaping vast fortunes off this profitable product. To suggest that this drug may have profound ill effects over the long-term is tantamount to heresy. Few scientists are willing to seek research grants or an audience to speak their concerns over issues related to Ritalin® toxicity for fear of some modern form of burning at the stake. One brave researcher, Dr. H. A. Nasrallah, Chairman of the Department of Psychiatry at Ohio State University, conducted a study in 1986, which demonstrated that 25 percent of young men who were on Ritalin® for ADHD as youngsters showed generalized cortical atrophy (generalized brain shrinkage) by CT scan examination. When compared to non-ADHD controls, who all had normal brains, the Ritalin® treated adults had brain changes seen commonly in elderly men prior to the onset of Alzheimer's disease! Although this study should have sent shockwaves through the medical world and resulted in an explosion in new research, it was instead, quietly buried in medical school libraries without a single follow up study ever conducted in the years that have followed. Curiously, even Dr. Nasrallah, who expressed his clear concerns over the neurotoxic effects of the stimulant drugs used to treat ADHD, has not published another study having anything to do with the adverse effects of Ritalin® or other amphetamine family members. (Nasrallah, 1986)

Current estimates suggest that as many as 10 million children are now being prescribed Ritalin® in the U.S. and Canada. Since this is such a recent phenomenon, there is really no way of knowing how this pattern of drug use will impact the future of our society. If, in the end, the amphetamine family of drugs do prove to have serious long-term ill effects at prescribed dosages, the damage done to our society will be immeasurable. Further research to examine these concerns is obviously an urgent necessity.

Is There any Perfect Drug for ADHD?
Unfortunately, each one of the drugs used to treat ADHD carries both known and unknown risks. Cylert®, the non-amphetamine stimulant, has resulted in severe liver failure in a large number of children. (Adcock, 1998; Marotta, 1998) Norpramin (desipramine), and imipramine the antidepressants often used as an alternative to stimulants, have caused sudden death in many kids. (Riddle, 1991) Prozac and its close relatives are also commonly prescribed to kids, even though they have never been approved in this age group, and isolated reports of very serious harm have begun to emerge. (Garland, 1998) Each of the many drugs which can improve ADHD symptoms carry the potential for serious side effects and none of them have been properly examined for their long term safety. Although writing a prescription for the treatment of ADHD may be the path of least resistance for many reasons, it certainly does not provide any significant long term answers to the ADHD problem and such chemical solutions have the potential to make matters far worse in the long run.

There are certainly situations that can make the avoidance of drug treatments very difficult. Some people may feel like they have been pushed into a corner and they really have no other choice but to put their child on medication. Fortunately, growing research now indicates that there are natural, plant derived medicines which have the ability to rapidly bring about significant improvements in brain function with far greater safety than any synthetically manufactured drugs. When properly prescribed, combinations of specific herbal medicines may, in fact, be as effective as prescription drugs in improving behavior and cognitive performance in those with ADHD. In many cases, natural medicines can improve symptoms quickly and significantly enough as to "buy some time" while underlying causes can be identified and other natural, curative treatments instituted.

We, like a growing number of parents, have chosen to search diligently to find safe and lasting help for our kids rather than just medicating them. We have used our kid's health challenges as an opportunity to help them understand the importance of living healthy lifestyles that are suitable for their extra-sensitive brains and bodies. Rather than raising kids who learn to turn to drugs to solve their problems, we now have kids with sophisticated knowledge about nutrition, herbal medicine, fitness, spirituality and physical fitness. We have used their ADHD symptoms as an opportunity to teach them the importance of treating their brains and bodies with respect and to shun those things that can bring harm to their health and sorrow to their lives.

Chapter 20

God's Pharmacy
Therapeutic
Phytochemicals
in ADHD

THE EMERGING SCIENCE OF BOTANICAL MEDICINE

The use of plants for medicinal purposes has accompanied humankind throughout the progress of history. Complex traditions of herbal medicine can still be found in nearly every culture with roots in the ancient world. Until the last two decades, herbal medicine was largely based on tradition and folklore with little participation of science. Perhaps to the surprise of the majority in the medical world, many of the herbs, which have been handed down through the ages, have now withstood some very rigorous scientific investigation and are proving themselves to have several very important healthcare applications. Unfortunately, while botanical medicine research has literally exploded in universities throughout much of Europe and Asia, the North American scientific establishment has largely ignored or actively shunned investigations into most natural substances. (Wagner, 1999) The wheels of change grind very slowly in our medical establishment and they are fueled by a medical-industrial complex that has very little interest in non-patentable medicines. In contrast, perhaps because of cultural factors, governments, industry and research authorities across Europe and Asia are far more likely to actively support research into natural therapeutics.

Throughout much of the past century, the prevailing attitude within the medical world has been that real cures to human maladies can only be found though high tech drugs and surgery. This mind-set is starting to face some serious opposition as new discoveries point to the awesome potential for healing within the natural realm. Western medicine has just begun to wake up to the importance of exercise, stress management and a number of dietary factors in the prevention of many diseases. There has also been some very recent interest in the power of certain food components as adjuncts to the more conventional treatment of particular diseases. The anticancer properties of broccoli, soy products and dietary fiber are examples of food derived factors that have been given widespread recognition by medical journals and the popular press alike. However, unlike Europe, where numerous therapeutic plant extracts have risen to become

346

some of the most widely prescribed medicinal products, the vast majority of North American doctors remain highly reluctant to recommend any herbal medicines, even when herbal alternatives are far safer and more effective than conventional drugs.

The attitude amongst North American physicians remains that botanical medicine is inferior to synthetic pharmaceuticals and any research into herbal substances must be just "soft science" and not really worth taking seriously. Unfortunately, this attitude is often based upon a lack of knowledge and preconceived bias rather than scientific fact. In reality, the emerging science of botanical medicine has repeatedly demonstrated that natural herbal extracts can possess an incredible array of beneficial properties with an extraordinarily low risk of side effects. In fact, research has shown that there are numerous herbal substances that are equal to or significantly superior to approved drugs in the treatment of a variety of illnesses. Many predict that the day will come when most synthetic drugs will be replaced by safer and more effective natural remedies.

POINTS TO PONDER ABOUT DRUGS

The term "drug" generally refers to a substance composed of only one specific molecule, which exerts potent effects on physiological processes through highly targeted actions. This might occur by the drug blocking the function of a particular enzyme, attaching to a cell membrane receptor or binding to a membrane channel to prevent the uptake of a substance into a cell. Because drugs alter very narrow physiological processes in such profound ways, they will always create undesirable side effects in addition to their desired effects. Even though side effects cannot always be sensed by the recipient of the drug, there are probably no drugs that do not exert both good and bad effects in the body. Most drugs are actually poisons at some dosage beyond that usually given for therapeutic purposes and, in some cases, the difference between the effective dose and the deadly dose is very small.

Every drug must be detoxified and eliminated by the liver or kidneys in order to prevent it from accumulating to toxic levels. Unfortunately, there is a wide variation in the efficiency of drug detoxification between different individuals. Even the same person can eliminate a drug at a markedly different rate depending upon factors such as the state of their nutrition and other drugs that they are taking. Drugs may also create toxic byproducts that must be neutralized by robust antioxidant defenses, which some people may be lacking. As well, drugs can exert toxic effects in individuals who are deficient in certain nutrients. For instance, fatal cardiac arrhythmias (irregular heartbeats) may be more likely to occur with Norpramin (desipramine), a drug used in ADHD, if the individual is seriously deficient in magnesium. Because of these and other factors, serious and usually unpredictable side effects can follow the ingestion of almost any drug.

Lethal reactions to drugs are far more common than had been previously suspected. In fact, recent research published in the Journal of the American Medical Association revealed that adverse reactions to properly prescribed drugs given to hospital patients is between the fourth and the sixth leading cause of death in North America. (Lazarou, 1998) Since this study did not include deaths from improperly prescribed drugs, drugs prescribed outside the hospital setting, non-prescription drugs, or drug abuse, one can only speculate that drug related deaths might even be the leading cause of death in North America! Not only are drugs responsible for an enormous toll of needless deaths, there are also an even greater number of non-lethal adverse drug reactions and long-term undesirable drug effects occurring every day. It seems ironic that humanity has invested trillions of dollars and incalculable amounts of labor into medical research and yet, so many of the treatments used within modern medicine carry such great potential for harm. There are certainly strong reasons to support efforts to find safer, more natural solutions to human illness with less reliance on potentially harmful drugs.

BOTANICAL DRUGS AND PLANT POISONS

There are numerous plant-derived substances, which in all respects are correctly classified as drugs. To be classified as a drug, a botanical product should contain a single active chemical, which exerts potent effects on physiological processes. Even though it is a natural herb, marijuana contains the hallucinogenic drug THC. Cocaine is potent and addictive stimulant drug derived from a natural herb. Crack cocaine is perhaps the most deadly standardized herbal extract in existence. Coffee is a botanical product that contains a rich supply of the drug caffeine. Ma huang is a Chinese herb, which contains the potent stimulant ephedrine, a drug almost identical to adrenalin and quite similar to amphetamines. Foxglove contains the potent heart drug digoxin. Clearly, these and many other plant-derived chemicals are properly classified as drugs. As such, these plant-derived drugs have some therapeutic effects at lower doses and toxic effects at higher doses. They can also interact adversely with many other natural and synthetic drugs. Like synthetic drugs, some of these botanical drugs have also resulted in death, particularly in cases of abuse.

Pharmaceutical companies are beginning to exploit the fact that there are many botanical drugs in nature and they are combing the forests and soils of the world in search of such novel agents. For example, taxol, an extract from the Yew tree of the Pacific Northwest, was the first drug to show promise in the treatment of ovarian cancer. Lovastatin, a breakthrough cholesterol-lowering drug is actually found in high concentrations in the red yeast used to spice Peking duck. There are numerous other examples of sophisticated drugs that have been found in the natural realm. However, pharmaceutical company research into botanical drugs is not simply for the benefit of humankind. Their primary motivation is to look for potent natural chemicals to use as molecular templates for the synthesis of patentable new drugs.

HERBAL MEDICINES

Although there are good reasons to believe there are many more breakthrough drugs yet to be found in nature, there are also numerous very useful botanical products that have potent healing properties but lack most of the drawbacks of drugs. Unlike a drug, which is a single molecule that exerts potent effects on targeted physiological processes, the majority of herbal medicines contain dozens or even hundreds of active chemical components, which act together to produce a much wider range of physiological effects. The effects of a drug could be likened to an electric guitarist playing a loud solo as compared to a herbal medicine, which is like a philharmonic orchestra playing a soothing concerto. Since many herbal medicines have such a wide range of active chemical constituents, it may be impossible to isolate the active "drug" from the herbal product. As well, since herbal phytochemicals appear to act in an additive or synergistic fashion, isolating one specific active ingredient may weaken the product's medicinal potential while increasing the likelihood that it will cause side effects.

Largely thanks to research conducted in Europe and Asia, over one hundred botanical medicines have now been studied for their pharmacological properties, their usefulness in the treatment of disease and their potential for exerting toxicity. (Wagner, 1999) Apart from a small handful of well-identified herbal agents, most botanical medicines have virtually no toxicity and an extremely low rate of side effects when taken appropriately. Even if taken in massive overdose, many herbal medicines carry no risk of serious complications or death. Most importantly, unlike drugs which virtually always have side effects as well as desirable effects, most herbal medicines possess desirable effects as well as a wide range of side benefits. For example, Ginkgo biloba was used traditionally by the Chinese for the treatment of asthma. However, over the past several years, it has become clear that, when concentrated, this herb also has potent brain protecting and cognitive enhancing effects. (Clostre, 1999) In other words, instead of higher doses of Ginkgo producing side effects, it produces some very desirable side benefits.

Taking time to scan the scientific literature that has accumulated on various herbal medicines will verify that many herbal products have an extraordinary range of different beneficial properties and seldom any significant adverse effects.*

*To conduct this exercise in personal information gathering, go to the National Library of Medicine through the Internet at the address http://igm.nlm.nih.gov. Click on "Medline" and then type the word ginseng in the "Search for" box. Then click "Perform Search" and soon over 1000 titles of articles will then be available. To read the summary of any of these articles click on "Full Citation". The same search can be performed on ginseng, Hypericum (St. John's wort), proanthocyanidins (grape seed extract or Pycnogenol) and numerous other herbal medicines.

Although the use of herbal medicines has become increasingly popular with the North American public, most physicians are entirely unaware that an enormous volume of research even exists. When asked by a patient if they could recommend an herbal product for their particular malady, many physicians will simply warn their patient that these things are completely unproven and they should stick to "scientific" treatments instead. In contrast to this prevailing attitude, modern herbal medicine research is increasingly demonstrating that the most sophisticated medical technology by far is locked up within medicinal herbs, many of which were used even before Hippocrates, the "Father of Medicine".

IMPROVING THE RELIABILITY OF HERBAL MEDICINE
Most of the well-researched products belonging to modern herbal medicine are various forms of extracts, which concentrate the herb's numerous active and synergistic constituents. Significant breakthroughs have been made in the growing and processing of medicinal herbs leading to a considerable improvement in the reliability of many herbal medicines. Germany has lead the way in this regard by officially setting high standards for the manufacturing of

herbal medicine. Thanks to Germany's Commission E (a government regulatory body assigned to assure quality control of herbal medicines), several herbal products are now available as standardized extracts. Most of the herbal medicines now in use in North America are, in fact, manufactured from standardized extracts imported from Europe. The widespread availability of standardized extracts has made it possible for repeatable research to be conducted on herbal medicines and has resulted in the formal approval of several herbal extracts as treatments for various human disorders by Germany's Commission E. Since medical insurance providers only pay for officially approved medicines, such advancements have led to more access to herbal medicine by the European public, as well as a new generation of physicians who are highly experienced in the use of herbal medicine. Although we cannot yet benefit from the official sanctioning of botanical medicine as they have in Europe, we can certainly benefit from the knowledge and experience that they have gained through several years of scientific progress.

CHEMICAL STANDARDIZATION

In order to determine that an herbal extract is of an equivalent potency from batch to batch, manufacturers must repeatedly subject their products to a reliable method of standardization. There are now numerous herbal extracts that have been standardized by examining the product for the quantity of specific phytochemicals, which are known to be important in the medicinal activity of the herb. For example, standardized Ginkgo biloba extract is usually an 80 to 1 extract (meaning that it is 80 times more potent than the raw herb), and it contains a minimum of 24% Ginkgo flavone glycosides, a group of important Ginkgo phytochemicals. Chemical standardization has greatly improved the dependability of herbal extracts and has made it possible for North American supplement manufacturers to purchase consistent quality extracts, which they can then encapsulate and provide to the public.

Unfortunately, since there are very few regulations surrounding the reliability of herbs in North America, the consumer must rely on the integrity and quality control of the company that has encapsulated the extract to ensure that what is said on the label is actually inside the bottle. The consumer of herbal medicines should become familiar with trustworthy brands through the advise of their Functional Medicine oriented healthcare provider or through knowledgeable and trained healthfood store employees. I have found that most healthfood stores now have very knowledgeable people on staff who are aware of companies that maintain rigorous quality controls over the manufacturing of their products. A person will likely pay somewhat more for a product manufactured with rigorous quality controls, but unless a person is simply looking for a placebo effect from their herbal medicine, they are wise to avoid "bargain basement" and chain-store brands and pay the additional cost for a reliable pharmaceutical grade brand.

BIOLOGICAL STANDARDIZATION

Although chemical standardization has paved the way for a higher degree of reliability in herbal medicines, it is not a perfect method for insuring the potency of a botanical extract. Chemical standardization typically measures the concentration of between one and three different important plant chemicals. However, in reality, many herbal extracts can contain several dozen to several hundred active constituents. Because of this, it is possible for an herbal extract to have a sufficient quantity of the measured components to be properly labeled as standardized even if some of the other unmeasured but important phytochemicals are relatively lacking. Since it would be currently impractical to measure the level of each one of the potentially hundreds of chemical constituents, relying on chemical standardization alone leaves the door open for some degree of product inconsistency from batch to batch or from one factory to another.

Fortunately, one Canadian university has help to develop new standardization methods, which significantly increase the reliability of chemical methods of standardization for several herbal products. For the past several years, the Department of Physiology at the University of Alberta has had a very active herbal medicine research group made up of top scientists with an interest in the future of botanical medicine. These Canadian researchers have developed a method of herbal standardization, known as biological standardization, which will likely be soon adopted as a worldwide standard for quality control in the manufacturing of herbal medicines. In this technique, a dilute dosage of the herbal concentrate being tested is added to living cells or living organisms and physiological responses are measured. If the herbal extract generates a powerful enough physiological response, it is determined to be biologically active. For example, a minute dosage of American ginseng extract, which is first standardized by chemical methods, is added to a cell culture containing live but injured brain cells. If the ginseng extract has sufficient biological activity, the brain cells will begin to regenerate many new branches within a few days. This verifies that the ginseng extract has potent biological properties, not just that one or two key phytochemicals are present. Occasionally, a batch of American ginseng extract will appear to be acceptable by chemical standardization but it is found to have insufficient biological activity to pass the process of biological standardization.

The University of Alberta scientists who have developed this technology have now formed a company called HerbTech to provide herbal extracts, which have undergone both chemical and biological methods of standardization. This forward thinking group of researchers are helping to place North America in a position of leadership in the development of herbal medicines with the kind of reliability that will be required for them to be fully integrated into conventional Western medicine.

HERBAL MEDICINES AND ADHD

Our facility (Oceanside Functional Medicine Research Institute) recently completed an interesting study in which we examined the effectiveness of a product known as AD-FX™ on 37 children with ADHD. This product was developed though the research efforts of the Herbal Medicine Research Group at the University of Alberta and is manufactured by the biotechnology company, HerbTech. AD-FX™ is a product that was formulated after an extensive review of the scientific literature suggested that the standardized extracts of certain forms of ginseng would likely act synergistically (cooperatively) when combined with a standardized extract of Ginkgo biloba to improve brain function and behavior in persons with ADHD. Each capsule of AD-FX™ is composed of 96 mg of HT-1001 (a potent extract of American ginseng developed by the HerbTech scientists containing >15% total ginsenosides) and 29 mg of Ginkgo biloba extract (containing >24% Ginkgo flavone glycosides). Both the ginseng and the Ginkgo extracts are first chemically standardized and then biologically standardized to verify their potency within biological systems. Because of its unique American ginseng extract and because of the rigid quality controls utilized by this company, no other ginseng or Gingko products are likely to produce effects equivalent to AD-FX™.

Our research demonstrated that two capsules of AD-FX™ given twice per day on an empty stomach, significantly improved ADHD symptoms in approximately 90 percent of children between six and seventeen years of age. Importantly, most of the children in our study had quite severe ADHD symptoms and many of them had failed to improve on Ritalin® or other ADHD drugs. In some cases, the improvements seen were quite remarkable and in keeping the degree of change commonly seen with successful drug therapy. As well, no side effects were reported by any of the study subjects. The results of this study are currently awaiting approval for publication in a major medical journal. AD-FX™ is currently available at many health food stores and pharmacies. Further information about AD-FX™ can also be found at: www.PureLiving.com.

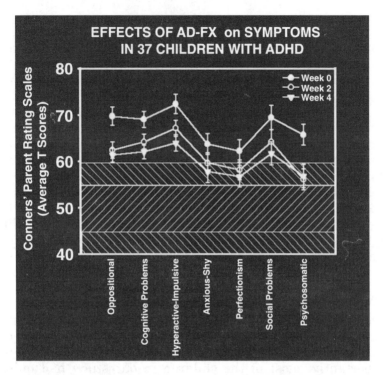

Ginseng extracts are among the most well studied of all medicinal substances. There are more than three distinctly different forms of ginseng, each having some properties unique from the others. Different types of concentrated extracts can be obtained from ginseng. One extraction method concentrates components of the ginseng known as ginsenosides. The American ginseng extract found in AD-FX™ is a highly potent and unique ginsenoside containing an extract known as HT-1001. Ginsenoside extracts have been shown to stimulate immune system function, to reduce inflammation, and to have anti-cancer properties. (Fan, 1995; Kenarova, 1990; Liu J, 1995; Matsuda, 1990; Rhee, 1991) Ginsenoside extracts have also been shown to bring about a general resistance to the negative effects of stress. (Lin, 1995) Animal studies have also shown that these extracts may help to improve sleep disturbances. (Lee, 1990) Importantly, ginsenoside extracts have potent antioxidant effects throughout the body, particularly in the brain and liver. (Deng, 1991; Sohn, 1993; Kim, 1996; Zhang, 1996) Thus, they help to defend the body against excessive oxidation caused by toxins, stress hormones and immune system over-activation.

The ginsenoside content of American ginseng is very high compared to other forms of Ginseng. Ginsenoside rich ginseng extracts have been shown to improve learning and memory, promote attention, heighten sensory-motor performance, and stimulate cognitive processes. (Nitta, 1995; Petkov, 1987; Petkov, 1990; Benishin, 1992; Abe, 1994) They have also been shown to increase brain glucose utilization, indicating that there is more efficient aerobic metabolism within the brain. (Samira, 1985) This effect may be important in light of recent imaging studies demonstrating inefficient brain glucose metabolism in subjects with ADHD. In animal models, ginsenosides have been shown to increase dopamine and norepinephrine in the cerebral cortex. (Itoh , 1989) This may explain why ginseng extracts have favorable effects upon attention, cognitive processing, integrated sensory-motor function and auditory reaction time in healthy human subjects. It may also be one mechanism to explain how ginsenosides can have some of the same benefits as stimulant drugs, yet without the side effects. (D'Angelo, 1986)

Besides its cognitive enhancing properties, ginsenosides have been shown to stimulate the repair and regeneration of brain neurons when they have suffered physical, chemical or oxidative injury. (Himi, 1989; Nishiyama, 1994) This property of ginseng extract suggests that long-term administration may have the potential to promote the growth of underdeveloped brain regions in those with ADHD. Each batch of American ginseng extract is biologically standardized for its neuron regenerating properties before it is mixed with Ginkgo biloba extract and encapsulated as AD-FX™. Over the long term, the nerve regenerative properties of AD-FX™ may be the most important aspect of this treatment. In strong contrast to Ritalin® and other amphetamine family drugs, which may have very negative long-term effects on the brain, AD-FX™ is quite likely to exert highly protective and even regenerative effects upon the brain over the course of time, especially when combined with nutritional support and efforts to decrease neurotoxic stress on the brain.

People should be very cautious when choosing a Ginseng extract. Because of its tremendous popularity, there are an extraordinary number of different ginseng extracts available with an extremely wide variety in quality and potency. Some are water extracts with no ginsenosides at all, while others are from Asian ginsengs with hormonal activities that are not desirable for children. Even though potent ginsenoside containing extracts are apparently popular in Europe, I have not encountered any extract that compares with the HT-1001 American ginseng extract found in AD-FX™.

Ginkgo biloba extracts have also been studied extensively in universities across Europe and Asia. (Clostre, 1999) Like ginsenoside extracts, ginkgo extract has been shown to possess adaptogenic properties, meaning that it helps to negate the undesirable effects of stress. It does this by protecting the body from the effects of excessive stress hormones such as adrenaline and cortisol and it actually helps to prevent excessive cortisol production when under stress. (Amri, 1997; Bolanos, 1995; Amri, 1996; Porsolt, 1990; Rapin, 1994) As well, ginkgo extract has mild calming and anxiety diminishing properties without having any sedating properties. (Hasenohrl, 1996; White, 1996) Since chronic elevations in cortisol may be one of the primary causes for memory loss and accelerated brain aging, reducing the brain's exposure to this internally generated neurotoxin is highly desirable.

Ginkgo is also well known to act as a potent antioxidant within the brain and the cardiovascular system, thus protecting these organs from the effects of toxic free radicals. (Oyama, 1994; Pietri, 1997; Sastre, 1998; Barth, 1991; Dumont, 1995; Gsell, 1995; Oyama, 1994; Barkats, 1995; Attella, 1989; Garg, 1995; Smith, 1996) Free radical damage occurs under many circumstances, such as exposure to neurotoxins like heavy metals, pesticides, and amphetamine family drugs. Excessive oxidation or free radical damage also occurs as a result of excessive stress hormones, head injury and immune system over-activation, such as occurs in chronic bowel infections or food allergy. Because many of these are common antecedents or triggers underlying ADHD symptoms, providing the brain with potent antioxidant protection may be one of the most important things that can be done for a person with ADHD. This may be especially important for individuals who take amphetamine family drugs like Ritalin® or Dexedrine® since these drugs generate potent neuron damaging free radicals. (Huang, 1997) Both the Ginkgo and the ginseng in AD-FX™ are highly neuroprotective and may help to diminish the adverse impact of amphetamines on the brain.

In addition to its brain protecting effects, Ginkgo extract has been found to significantly enhance learning and memory as well as concentration, mood and energy levels. It has been shown in numerous European studies to effectively improve memory and cognitive performance in subjects with brain disorders. (Gessner, 1985; Grassel, 1992; Itil, 1995; Rai, 1991; Allain, 1993) Only recently has a comparable study been carried out in North America. (Le Bars, 1997) Ginkgo has also been shown to significantly improve memory and other cognitive functions in normal adults. (Hindmarch, 1986; Subhan, 1984) One recent study demonstrated that ginkgo extract had particularly strong benefits on working memory in normal subjects. (Rigney, 1999) Recall from Chapter 3 that working memory is the immediate memory used to stay organized and on task, and is one of the most significant impairments in ADHD. Problems with working memory results in much of the day-to-day distress that people with ADHD experience as they struggle to achieve productivity in their lives. Poor sense of time, disorganization, difficulty with reading and staying on task are all manifestations of poor working memory. Anything that improves working memory is likely to have profound benefits in subjects with ADHD.

The cognitive enhancing effects of Ginkgo may be due in part to the effect that this agent has on brain neurotransmitters. Ginkgo has been shown to increase brain dopamine and norepinephrine activity, two key neurotransmitters involved in ADHD. (Ramassamy, 1992b; Ramassamy, 1993; Brunello, 1985)

Overall, there are considerable reasons to believe that the two extracts found in AD-FX™ should act synergistically to provide several significant benefits in the management of ADHD. As well, the safety of these two agents appears to be extremely high and, if anything, they are likely to have some very important long-term side benefits. It comes as no surprise then that our study produced such positive results in ADHD patients. Although this was a preliminary open label study (no control group was used), the results are very encouraging and we are hopeful that more research on this product will be forthcoming.

As a side note, I have been using AD-FX™ daily for the past two and a half years and I have found it to be one of the most important breakthroughs in my own personal struggle with ADHD. My son has also benefited immensely from this product. AD-FX™ first became available at a time when we were having a tremendous struggle with our son's inability to complete even the simplest schoolwork. Although he was home schooled by then, he still had a terrible time staying on task and would spend much of his day making silly sounds and fidgeting. He was also so grumpy and depressed that it was nearly impossible to be around him. Within four days of starting AD-FX™, his behavior had turned around completely. This improvement brought the whole family tremendous relief and encouraged us to persist with our decision to avoid drugs and to search for natural solutions to his problems. This was not the only piece of his ADHD puzzle, but it certainly helped to relieve some very significant symptoms without doing him any harm. He continues on AD-FX™ to this day and, now that we have found and corrected some important underlying antecedents and triggers, he is a bright, happy and very healthy boy with a very promising future. I am very thankful to the scientists who had the insight to develop this important product.

St. John's wort (Hypericum perforatum) standardized extracts of have not been studied in formal clinical trials for the treatment of ADHD. However, there are reasons to believe that this natural agent may be highly beneficial, especially in the improvement of impulsive and hyperactive behaviors, as well as mood problems, including depression, which commonly plague those with ADHD. Pharmaceutical antidepressants of the type known as tricyclics (e.g. imipramine and desipramine) have been shown to be effective in controlling hyperactivity and impulsivity and are often used as an alternative to stimulant drugs in the treatment of ADHD. (Gualtieri, 199; Riddle, 1991) However, these drugs have a high rate of unpleasant side effects and have been associated with several cases of sudden death due to heart arrhythmias, especially in children. In numerous double-blind studies, St. John's wort extract has been shown to be at least as effective as tricyclic antidepressants with a much lower rate of side effects. (Volz, 1997; Linde, 1996) In addition, some research has demonstrated that St. John's wort extracts result in greater activity of dopamine and norepinephrine in the brain. (Muller, 1998; Chatterjee, 1998) This strongly suggests that hypericum extract should have a significant influence upon the behavior of individuals with ADHD.

The remarkably high safety record of St. John's wort extract has been widely recognized. In a recent report based on data gathered by the World Health Organization and other official groups, St. John's wort extract was found to have a risk of side effects no higher than that of inactive placebo. (Ernst E, 1998) According to this same report, there have been no reports of serious side effects from this herbal medicine even though it has been used by millions of people worldwide for many years. Although it is often suggested that this agent can result in a rash with exposure to the sun this is also very rare and probably only occurs with very high doses. Although there are yet no reported cases of adverse interactions, it has been suggested that St. John's wort should not be taken with pharmaceutical antidepressants and should probably not be taken along with amphetamine family drugs. St. John's wort is even considered to be the safest of all antidepressants to give to the elderly or chronically ill heart patients. (Vorbach, 1994) The pharmacology of this herbal extract, composed of numerous different phytochemicals, suggests that it is likely to have several long-term benefits rather than long-term harm. In addition to its effects on mood and behavior, it has immune stimulating effects and is being looked at very closely because of its anti-viral properties. (Meruelo, 1988) European studies have demonstrated that it also has potent neuroprotective and antioxidant properties, both suggesting that it would have long-term benefits to the brain. (Bolshakova, 1997; Bork, 1999)

The effects of St. John's wort have been shown to improve when taken with other phytochemicals such as those found in grape seed extract, pine bark extract or Ginkgo biloba extract, suggesting that combinations of these herbs may be better than one or the other alone. (Butterweck, 1998) Of particular interest are the potential benefits of AD-FX™ when taken in combination with St. John's wort. Based on its known pharmacology, St. John's wort can be expected to exert its major effects on behavior and mood problems in those with ADHD, while AD-FX™ is known to be especially helpful in improving cognitive function. I have been in contact with many healthcare professionals who have obtained impressive results in some very difficult ADHD cases with the combination of AD-FX™ and St. John's wort. A sample protocol in common use by healthcare professionals is located in Section 6 at the back of this book.

A final mention should be made of **caffeine containing beverages** in ADHD. It is not uncommon to find an adolescent or adult with ADHD who has an exceptionally strong liking for caffeine. This often results in the consumption of large amounts of coffee and, as a result, very high daily caffeine intake. Higher doses of caffeine, such as would be common with the consumption of more than 3 or 4 cups of coffee per day are associated with an amplification of stress and the potential for diminished cognitive performance, heightened anxiety levels and exhaustion. For these and other reasons, it is probable wise for those with ADHD to significantly limit their coffee consumption.

Tea, on the other hand is proving itself to have many health benefits. Both green and black tea are now considered to possess potent antioxidant effects and are known to have significant anticancer properties. (Benzie, 1999; Lin, 1999) The moderate consumption of tea has also been studied and found to significantly improve many aspects of cognitive performance without causing rebound drowsiness which typically occurs after drinking coffee. (Hindmarch, 1999; Durlach, 1999) Avoiding coffee and regularly drinking tea (especially green tea) is a simple measure that can improve health and cognitive performance in those with ADHD. The drinking of low caffeine green teas such as jasmine or genmai (green tea with roasted rice) has been an integral part of most Asian societies for millenia. Even children in most of these cultures drink tea throughout the day rather than water with no apparent ill effects. In fact, studies have shown that children who regularly consume tea have a reduction in dental caries (cavities) by as much as 75 percent over children who do not drink tea. (Rasheed, 1998; Parajas, 1996).

THE FUTURE OF BOTANICAL MEDICINE IN THE TREATMENT OF ADHD

We are clearly at the threshold of some tremendous breakthroughs in the field of scientific botanical medicine. If the trend in Europe is any indication, it is only a matter of a few more years before a modernized form of herbal medicine will be commonly practiced even in the most conventional medical circles. Patented drugs will come and go, but as time goes on science is beginning to realize that the most incredible pharmaceutical technology is found right within God's Pharmacy -- the plants that have been with us since the dawn of humanity. Current research has only just scratched the surface and has given us a glimpse of the amazing healing potential found in natural phytochemicals.

Although herbal agents are not the whole solution to the ADHD puzzle, they can rapidly improve many symptoms without doing harm. Such improvements can relieve some of the urgency that is commonly associated with accelerating ADHD symptoms and may be a way of avoiding the use of drugs while underlying causes can be discovered and treated. Herbal medicines may also provide some welcome relief for those who cannot tolerate medications due to side effects or for those who have legitimate concerns about the long-term toxicity of ADHD medication. As well, many adolescents who are reluctant to take ADHD drugs because of the stigma they carry, will often readily try herbal medicines, which are viewed by themselves and their peers as completely natural. It is also my view that avoiding drugs if possible and teaching your children to rely on more natural approaches to healing helps to keep them from thinking that life's problems should be solved by taking drugs. For these and many other reasons, there certainly is a very real place for therapeutic phytochemicals in the management of ADHD.

Chapter 21

Gastrointestinal Rehabilitation - The 4-R Program™

BRINGING BACK ORDER TO THE CHAOS WITHIN

The world within the intestine is a violent realm abounding with concentrated acid, digestive enzymes, and molecules at various stages of breakdown. Within this hostile region, cultivation of desirable microbes occurs simultaneous with immunological warfare as hundreds of microbial species all struggle for a lead role in the intestinal ecosystems. Cellular events occur at a blinding pace within this invisible world. Although an intestinal cell lives an average of three days, it probably carries out more individual tasks than a person does in their entire lifetime. A healthy person loses and replaces about 3.3 billion intestinal cells every hour, a number greater than half the world's human population. The bacterial residents of our gut live at an even faster pace yet. The average bacterium lives 20 minutes until it divides and creates a whole new generation. From this perspective, one day in the bacterial realm is equivalent to about 3000 bacteria years. In the human world, kingdoms rise and fall over the span of decades to centuries, while the whole order of our intestinal world can change with just one meal.

The availability of functional gastrointestinal testing has revealed how common it is for individuals with ADHD to suffer with a variety of subtle, yet very real gastrointestinal problems. Signs of disordered gastrointestinal function may include one or more recognizable symptoms such as abdominal pain, belching, flatulence, "acid indigestion", constipation or diarrhea. However, as our research has indicated, conditions such as food allergy or intolerance, leaky gut, maldigestion, nutrient malabsorption, intestinal parasites, and overgrowth of yeast or potential bacterial pathogens, all occur commonly in those with ADHD, even though typical gastrointestinal symptoms may be completely lacking. Instead of experiencing direct sensations, many of these invisible disturbances result in activation of the intestine's resident immune system (GALT or gut associated lymphoid tissue). In turn, the GALT may release a wide range of alarm substances, which can create a myriad of potential symptoms. These immune modulators have the potential to directly affect brain function and may also "turn on" the brain's own immune system resulting in oxidative stress to the brain. In addition, maldigestion and a leaky gut can lead to the absorption of protein fragments (peptides), which have neurological activity (neuropeptides). As well, gut microbes, in addition to markedly activating the immune system, can also produce an extraordinary range of neurotoxic and immunotoxic molecules. In the end, disordered gastrointestinal function can be a primary cause of critical nutrient insufficiencies which may even contribute to structural problems within the brain. Restoring normal gastrointestinal function can pay big dividends in terms of overall health, behavior and cognitive function in a person with ADHD.

RESTORING GASTROINTESTINAL FUNCTION THROUGH THE 4-R PROGRAM™

Carefully evaluating the ADHD sufferer through clinical assessment and functional testing can help to clarify the specific nature of their gastrointestinal problems. Once gastrointestinal function has been reasonably assessed, rehabilitation of gastrointestinal function can be achieved through the application of an orderly set of principles. This approach to gastrointestinal rehabilitation, which has been adopted by Functional Medicine, is known as the 4-R Program™. Conceptualized and taught by the Institute for Functional Medicine in Gig Harbor Washington, the 4-R Program™ has become one of the most useful and practical approaches to the management of numerous problems related to gastrointestinal function. Although the 4-R Program™ is continually evolving as new discoveries are made, it currently provides a rational framework, which can be used to successfully rebuild healthy gastrointestinal function in those with many different chronic conditions, including ADHD.

The 4-R Program™ is comprised of a series of therapeutic steps, which relieve the gastrointestinal tract (and the GALT) from undue stresses and provide effective support for gastrointestinal function and tissue rebuilding:

1. **Remove** intolerant or allergenic foods, pathogenic gut microbes and damaging drugs or chemicals.

2. **Replace** factors required for adequate digestion of food.

3. **Reinoculate** the gut with desirable microscopic flora.

4. **Repair** damaged intestinal tissues.

The 4-R Program™ allows progress to be made by conducting a set of therapeutic interventions in logical steps rather than by just randomly trying different treatments to see what works. A "hit and miss" approach to restoring gastrointestinal integrity often ends in frustration; the patient and the healthcare practitioner concluding that gastrointestinal problems have little to do with that patient's problems. In contrast, the 4-R Program™ provides a comprehensive and multifaceted approach to restoring gut function, which leads to clear evidence of progress and a sense of direction. It is important to note that the 4-R Program™ does not necessarily proceed in a simple 1,2,3,4 order. Elements from different parts of the program may be used simultaneously or out of order depending upon the priorities dictated by the person's problem. However, with few exceptions, the first element of the program, the "remove" component, usually must be addressed successfully before further significant progress can be made.

REMOVE

This first step of the 4-R Program™ involves removing, or reducing as much as possible, all factors, which are placing stress upon the gastrointestinal tract and its associated immune system and liver. Eliminating junk foods, fast foods, food additives and food contaminants (such as pesticides, rancid fats and trans fatty acids) may reduce considerably, the total load of stresses upon the gut. Removal of gut damaging alcohol and drugs, such as non-steroidal anti-inflammatory agents (aspirin, ibuprofen and family) is also important. Essentially, the first part of the "remove" phase requires that the individual examine their diet and then make every effort to eat as exclusively as possible, natural, whole and uncontaminated foods. For many, this may require a period of study, and might include a few cooking classes and the purchase of some good natural foods cookbooks.

Secondly, what is food for one may be poison for another. Identifying and eliminating any foods to which the person is allergic or intolerant is an essential part of the "remove" step of the 4-R Program™. This can be a tremendously important aspect in the progress towards healthy gut function, especially in children. The means to identify and eliminate allergic or intolerant foods is described in Chapter 17.

Another very important part of the "remove" step is the identification and elimination of pathogenic (disease causing) or potentially pathogenic bacteria, yeasts and parasites. Chapter 16 describes in detail the use of tests such as the Comprehensive Digestive Stool Analysis with Comprehensive Parasitology Examination, Helicobacter pylori antibodies, Hydrogen-Methane Breath Testing and Urinary Organic Acid Analysis as a means to identify the species and quantities of potentially harmful microbes, as well as evidence of small bowel bacterial overgrowth. Once it has been determined that certain pathogens are present, targeted antimicrobial therapy can be instituted.

In many cases, natural agents can be highly effective in eradicating the offending pathogen, especially if used in synergistic combinations. A great many plants possess potent natural antimicrobial properties against gut pathogens. Quite a number of herbs used to add flavor to foods contain antibiotic (antibacterial), antifungal, antiprotozoal or antihelminthic (anti-worm) phytochemicals. In fact, the flavorful properties of onions, garlic, turmeric, oregano, rosemary, ginger, cinnamon, cloves and thyme are just few of the many flavorful herbs, which possess powerful antimicrobial properties. The inclusion of these herbs in traditional cuisine has probably helped to protect humans from gut infections over the millennia. The bland, North American fare, with its relative lack of natural herbs, is probably one open window for the intrusion of unwanted microscopic pests. This is probably true in particular for children who tend to shun spicy foods and choose plain, salt and pepper meals or chemically flavored foods instead. As well, those whose diets are lacking in natural herbs and spices are also being deprived of some of the most effective antioxidants, immune boosters and anti-inflammatory agents available. Beginning to expand the palate to accept more foods from spice-rich Asian cookery is one way to increase our exposure to these healthful substances. However, if these agents are required for therapeutic purposes, concentrates such as oil extracts of oregano or garlic concentrates may be prescribed.

Several other natural herbs, not usually used for food purposes, possess anti-infective properties and are commonly used to treat parasitic infestation as well as yeast and bacterial overgrowth or infection. Artemisia or wormwood is a herb that is undergoing intensive research because of its potent anti-malarial / antiparasitic properties. When used orally, it is a potent anti-parasitic agent and is often used in combination with other herbs for synergistic effects. Goldenseal is another herb with powerful anti-microbial and immune boosting effects. Grapefruit seed (not grape seed) extract, barberry bark extract, Pau D'Arco, and black walnut hull (green) extract are all examples of potent herbs that have effective action against certain gut pathogens.

Numerous products containing effective herbal combinations are readily available though health food stores. Healthcare providers who follow Functional Medicine principles usually recommend or stock advanced anti-parasitic and anti-microbial herbal formulas. Some network marketing companies have placed the whole focus of their company upon natural products designed to eradicate gut pathogens and parasites. Regardless of the approach used, it is best done under proper professional supervision and all treatment should generally be followed up by repeat laboratory testing to determine the success of therapy.

In addition to anti-infective herbs, other natural products can assist with the "remove phase" of the 4-R Program™. We have already discussed that breast milk provides a tremendously effective barrier to the growth of gut pathogens. Milk contains the important antibody, secretory IgA as well as antimicrobial proteins such as lactoferrin, and lactoperoxidase. Importantly, these immune factors effectively kill almost all pathogens while leaving the friendly gut flora completely alone. After weaning, under normal circumstances, these same anti-infective factors are produced by salivary glands and intestinal cells and these substances form the primary defensive system for the gut. However, as our research has pointed out, the majority of children with ADHD have inadequate secretory IgA production, which leaves a huge door open for pathogens to make their home in the ADHD sufferer's intestinal tract. Although there are means to boost the immune function of the gut, during the "remove phase" of the 4-R Program™, immune factors can be directly administered to the patient. Commercial products containing immune factors extracted from bovine colostrum (first milk from cows) or from the high immunoglobulin-containing cow's milk whey can greatly complement the administration of anti-microbial preparations in this phase of the 4-R Program™. The company Metagenics makes a very interesting product known as Probioplex Intensive Care™, which is a powder containing concentrated immunoglobulins (antibodies) from whey as well as the microbe killing enzymes lactoperoxidase and lactoferrin. This product also contains FOS (fructo-oligosaccharides), which are carbohydrates that selectively promote the growth of the friendly Bifidobacteria. Although caution needs to be used with people who have dairy allergies, many people who cannot tolerate dairy foods will tolerate this product without problems. Providing this type of "passive immune support" can help to bridge the gap until the patient's own immune system is functioning better.

In some cases, pharmaceutical agents (antibiotics, anti-fungals, antiprotozoal or antihelminthic) may be required to rid the gut of offending pathogens. This is particularly true if worms, protozoal (single-celled) parasites or persistent yeast overgrowth is detected or if natural agents have been tried and found to be ineffective. It is also commonly required in patients who are shown to have serious over-growth of bacteria in the small bowel. Such therapy should be highly targeted and if possible, an agent should be select-ed only after sensitivity testing has been done to test which anti-infective agent the pathogen is susceptible. The Comprehensive Digestive Stool Analysis provides sensitivi-ty testing to all potential bacterial and yeast pathogens found on stool culture. For protozoal pathogens, physicians utilize textbooks or manuals to select a suitable agent.

Proper eradication of gut pathogens can bring about remarkable benefits and is certainly worth the effort involved. Unfortunately, in some cases, such as chronic yeast overgrowth, protozoal parasites, or bacterial over-growth of the small bowel, the offending organisms come back to previous levels each time the anti-infective agent is stopped. This problem can be avoided by thoroughly apply-ing all of the elements of the 4-R Program™ rather than just eradication of pathogens in isolation. It may also suggest that the organism is resistant to the anti-infective agents used on first attempt. This is particularly true of bacteria and yeast which have been adapting and mutating over the past few decades in response to the widespread use of phar-maceutical antibiotics and anti-fungal agents. Ineffective eradication of gut pathogens can also be secondary to immune system problems. Except perhaps in cases of seri-ous acquired or inherited immune deficiencies, much can be done to improve immune system function. These principles will be discussed in the next chapter.

Poor hygienic habits can also commonly contribute to infection and re-infection, especially with parasites. If chil-dren and adults can simply be taught to wash their hands before they eat and before they put a finger in their mouth, nose or eye, the transmission of pathogens would be greatly diminished. Frequent hand washing has been shown to greatly decrease the risk of acquiring respiratory infections and will make it much less likely that children will pick up parasites from their peers or siblings. It is also important to note that if a parasitic infection is ever detected in one family member, all other members of that family should be treated, and retested until there is evidence that the parasite has been fully eradicated. Even pets should be considered as possible vectors (carriers) for parasitic infection and should be tested by a veterinarian if parasites are found in a family.

Removal of undesirable gut flora also involves the establishment of good elimination. Increasing dietary fiber, exercise and fluid intake are the basic steps that help to promote good elimination through the bowel. The **stool transit time** is a measurement of how long it takes food to be eliminated once it has been eaten. Most North Americans have transit times of 48 to 72 hours instead of the ideal, which is 18 hours, or less. Very prolonged transit times can be evident even if a person has a bowel movement every day because fecal matter can be backed up in the colon like a line of aircraft waiting to take off from the airport runway. When the transit time is increased, more time is available for putrefying organisms to become predominant. Making efforts to decrease stool transit time can dramatically change the gut flora for the better.

Although the administration of probiotic (friendly) bacteria is in the third step of the 4-R Program™, this intervention is often initiated at the outset of the 4-R Program™ because certain probiotic species have potent antimicrobial effects and can greatly assist in the "remove" step. (Elmer, 1996; Vanderhoof, 1998b)

REPLACE

The second step of the 4-R ProgramTM involves efforts to re-establish ideal digestive function through the provision of agents which either stimulate digestive function or replace digestive factors that might be lacking in the individual. If hypochlorhydria (low stomach acid) is suspected (e.g. meat fibers seen in microscopic stool exam or small bowel bacterial overgrowth) betaine hydrochloride is commonly given. Unpublished research from Australia has suggested that many children with ADHD have hypochlorhydria. If this is the case, these kids would be subject to poor protein digestion, insufficient mineral absorption, small bowel bacterial overgrowth (auto-brewery syndrome), and a tendency to harbor parasites and other gut pathogens. In such cases, administration of betaine hydrochloride may have an important role in re-establishing normal gut function. Traditional remedies such as gentian root or "stomach bitters" may also have some value, as may the administration of the amino acid, histidine. Histidine is a precursor to histamine, which acts as the major trigger of stomach acid production. In children, it is likely that hypochlorhydria is generally a secondary manifestation of GALT (gut immune system) over-activation due to infection in the stomach with Helicobacter or the growth of pathogens elsewhere in the gut. If the GALT is over-stimulated, it will result in the production of high levels of an inflammatory mediator known as nitric oxide. High levels of nitric oxide, in turn, can lead to a halt in stomach acid production. Treating the cause of low stomach acid in such cases is, of course, most important.

It is very common to consider the administration of digestive enzymes in the "replace" phase of the 4-R Program™. Digestive enzymes can assist with the efficient breakdown of protein and may result in a reduction of allergic hypersensitivity in those with a leaky gut. Depending upon the enzymes used, such supplementation can also improve the digestion of proteins, carbohydrates and fats with a resultant improvement in nutritional status and a lessening of gut fermentation (carbohydrate) or putrefaction (protein or fat) by intestinal microbes. Digestive enzyme supplements can be either an extract of animal pancreas (cow or pig) or can be derived from certain types of commercially harvested fungi. The fungal enzyme supplements often have a broader spectrum of activity and are active in a wider range of pH (acid levels). Health food stores and some pharmacies carry a selection of digestive enzyme products. As well, Functional Medicine oriented practitioners are familiar with reliable brands and the circumstances that would suggest that digestive enzyme supplementation would be appropriate. The addition of digestive enzymes should generally be considered as a stopgap measure until the cause of inefficient digestion is rooted out and treated. One of the most important bits of evidence that the 4-R Program™ has been successful is that digestive efficiency improves with a decrease in food intolerances and diminished problems with gut dysbiosis (unhealthy microbiological flora).

REINOCULATE

In the third element of the 4-R Program™, probiotic organisms are administered for specific therapeutic purposes and to help re-establish normal gut ecology. It is vital that an effective probiotic supplement is given and the quality of such products varies greatly. Fortunately, there has been a tremendous resurgence in scientific interest surrounding the use of probiotic supplementation and a great deal more is known about this field now than even ten years ago. It is now appropriate to insist that a therapeutic probiotic supplement contains very specific bacterial sub-species, which have undergone rigorous research and have been shown to possess a list of desirable characteristics. To obtain the full benefits from probiotic supplementation it is not acceptable to simply use any product containing "Lactobacillus acidophilus" since there are far more sub-species of this bacteria which are relatively ineffective than those which have clinically useful properties.

Traditionally, it has been assumed that the same organisms that are found in yogurt are the ones that provide useful probiotic benefits. Unfortunately, there is no guarantee that the bacteria used to make yogurt will have significant value as medical probiotics. Studies have repeatedly shown that consumption of the typical yogurt bacteria (e.g.

Lactobacillus acidophilus and Lactobacillus bulgaricus) does not alter gut flora significantly and any benefits from this are rather mild and transient. There are certainly some benefits to eating true "live culture" yogurt but this cannot replace the effects of taking a true medically proven probiotic supplement. In time this is likely to change, however, as public demand makes it worth the extra expense for companies to make yogurt with true medical probiotic species.

So what criteria are used used by scientists to judge whether or not a bacteria qualifies as being a true medical probiotic? There are now numerous sub-species of bacteria that have been shown to survive life within the human gastrointestinal tract and have a wide range of remarkable benefits. Although a common characteristic of beneficial bacteria is that they produce lactic acid as a primary fermentation byproduct, there are actually hundreds of different species and subspecies of lactic acid generating bacteria, only a few of which have been well characterized in terms of their suitability as a therapeutic probiotic organism.

Characteristics to look for when studying a bacterium for beneficial properties include:

· The bacteria must remain alive by the method used to store the organism (many "probiotic products" are largely dead by the time they are consumed).

· The organism should be proven to survive passage through the hostile environment of the stomach and intestines and it should possess properties allowing it to colonize the gut and become a reasonably long term resident of the human intestine.

· It should be able to ferment a wide selection of carbohydrates, insuring that it never goes hungry with the varied diet of its new human host.

- It should only produce the L form of lactic acid instead of both the D and L forms. D-lactic acid breaks down very slowly in the human body and can accumulate and result in neurotoxic stress.

- It should have a broad spectrum of anti-microbial activity and be proven to inhibit bacterial, yeast and protozoal pathogens.

- It should have definite immunostimulatory effects.

- It should promote the repair of damaged gut mucous membranes.

- It should have a clear record of significant and practical medical benefits when examined in both animal and human research.

- It should have a clear record of safety and should not be implicated as a potential pathogen even in immune deficient people.

There are just a few species thus far, which have been clearly shown to exert all of these benefits when used as probiotics. At the top of the list for accumulated research are presently Lactobacillus plantarum, Lactobacillus rhamnosus, and Lactobacillus GG (a particular variety of Lactobacillus rhamnosus). All three of these organisms have been proven to have a wide range of benefits and are commercially available as probiotic supplements. Lactobacillus plantarum is also considered the primary species present in properly fermented, unpasturized sauerkraut and certain other fermented foods. Traditionally, most human cultures probably consumed large quantities of this organism on a daily basis. (Bengmark, 1998)

In the near future, these organisms will be available in "functional food" products such as yogurts, juices and other beverages. Although these organisms are currently the major "stars" of the probiotic world, the human gut normally contains about 400 different bacterial species and it is logical to expect that in the days to come there will be other species that can be shown to be ideal probiotics possessing all of the desirable characteristics mentioned above. There are numerous other strains of bacteria which have been shown to possess at least some of the desirable features of probiotics. These include many varieties of Lactobacillus acidophilus, and various strains of Bifidobacterium. As well, Bacillus subtilis, Enterococcus faecium, Lactobacillus casei, Lactobacillus bulgaricus and Streptococcus thermophilus all have been researched to some degree and have been used extensively as probiotics. Saccharomyces boulardii, although a yeast, has also been shown to have a wide range of beneficial effects when given as a probiotic supplement.

The "reinoculate" component of the 4-R Program™ is often started simultaneously or even prior to the "remove" phase. Most probiotic organisms have significant antimicrobial effects and they can help to make the removal of pathogens more efficient. In addition, if antimicrobial agents are to be administered, it is also important to promote the re-establishment of desirable flora as soon as possible. This is like tearing out weeds from your yard and then immediately planting grass instead of just waiting to see what grows up after the weeds are pulled. In many cases, antimicrobial agents are administered at intervals in the day; separated by one or more hours from the administration of antimicrobials. Probiotics are also usually continued long after antimicrobial administration has ceased. Gut pathogens will likely make strong efforts to retake their lost territory within their intestinal host. Repeated course of probiotics or, in some cases, continual administration may provide some long-term insurance that friendly flora will continue to predominate in the gut. Periodically repeating functional gastrointestinal testing may help to determine the need for continued probiotics, especially if behavior, cognition or bowel function has deteriorated in any way.

A simple but not infallible means to determine when probiotics might be helpful is the "wallpaper test". If the person's bowel movements create such a stink that the wallpaper starts peeling off the bathroom walls, it is probably time to use probiotics! Of course, it never gets quite this bad but it is true that a person with significant gut dysbiosis (predominance of unfriendly gut flora) will most often have horribly smelling bowel movements. Gut pathogens produce all kinds of foul putrefactive byproducts with names like cadaverine (one of the the chemicals that makes dead carcasses stink) and putrescine. On the other hand, probiotics produce no putrefactive byproducts but instead produce simple fermentation byproducts like lactic acid, butyric acid and acetic acid. These beneficial byproducts have a mild odor, which should be almost non-offensive to others who have to use the bathroom next. This rule is not always true when chronic parasitic infections are present, especially if the parasite stimulates loose bowel movements and does not allow time for putrefaction to occur.

Lastly, the "reinoculate" phase can be made more effective if certain nutrients are provided which are favorite fuels for probiotic organisms. These special probiotic promoters are known as prebiotics. Fructooligosaccharides (FOS) are naturally occurring carbohydrates made from various sized small chains of fructose (fruit sugar). There are certain amounts of FOS in onions, asparagus and several other vegetables. FOS is also commonly added to probiotic supplements and other products designed to improve gastrointestinal health. Although there are a few gut pathogens that can use FOS as fuel, it is regarded as a delicacy by Bifidobacterium, the major friendly flora of the large bowel. As well, the highly researched probiotic species, Lactobacillus rhamnosus will thrive on FOS, as will many other beneficial lactic acid bacteria. Thus, administering FOS will help to promote the growth of friendly flora without supporting the growth of harmful microbes. (Sghir, 1998; Gibson, 1995a) FOS also improves nutrient absorption and inhibits the growth of unfriendly microbes, probably all by the promotion of probiotic species. (Buddington, 1996; Delzenne, 1995; Ohta, 1995; Morohashi, 1998) Inulin is another non-digestible carbohydrate, which has been well researched as an effective prebiotic with many beneficial properties. (Roberfroid, 1998; Gibson, 1995b) It is found in Jerusalem artichoke flour, a favorite thickener often used to replace more allergenic thickeners like wheat flour or cornstarch. It is also found in functional food products designed to improve gastrointestinal health. Oat bran is another prebiotic containing food, which is being studied as an ideal growth medium for many probiotic organisms. Because of this, don't be surprised if you see "oat bran yogurt" in your favorite food store in the next few years. (Bengmark, 1998)

For several years, I have been in the habit of using probiotics, and find them to be an important part of my overall health program. Every 3 or 4 days I make up a big batch of homemade yogurt using live culture yogurt and a 2 liter yogurt maker. After adding yogurt to the fresh milk as a "starter culture", I also add a few capsules of a powdered probiotic supplement. Although I have used many probiotics to "fortify" my homemade yogurt, I have found that Lactobacillus rhamnosus seems to have the most immediate and definite effects upon bowel function of any species I have tried. I eat at least one serving of this homemade yogurt every day added to oatmeal, bran or ground flax with some honey as a sweetener. This is a simple and economical way to get plenty of probitics in a nutritious and enjoyable manner.

I have a proven dairy allergy, but I have no problem eating a good live culture yogurt. This will hold true for many people with dairy allergies. In fact, one sub-species of Lactobacillus rhamnosus (Lactobacillus rhamnosus GG) has been shown to reverse dairy allergies if taken daily. (Majamaa, 1997; Kirjavainen, 1999a) However, while on the elimination test diet, yogurt or dairy-based probiotics are not permitted.

REPAIR

The last component of the 4-R Program™ involves the administration of nutritive factors, which are known to assist with the nourishment and repair of damaged or weakened gastrointestinal tissues. It should be noted that the interventions described in the "remove, replace and reinoculate" phases of the 4-R Program™ might also promote significant nourishment and repair of the dysfunctional gastrointestinal system. For example, probiotic bacteria are often administered because of their ability to bring about speedy recovery from a leaky gut following infection, antibiotic administration, surgery, or food allergy. (Salminen, 1996; Majamaa, 1997) However, there are also various nutritive substances that play an important role in nourishing intestinal cells and assisting in the repair of damaged intestinal mucous membranes.

· **L-Glutamine** is an amino acid, which is the primary fuel for the small intestinal cells. At least 80 percent of the energy generated in these rapidly metabolizing cells comes from L-glutamine. Although there is some L-glutamine in most protein containing foods, inefficient protein digestion or increased metabolic needs (such as in states of intestinal stress) can decrease the availability of, or increase the requirements for, this important nutrient. Several studies have demonstrated the effectiveness of supplemental L-glutamine in the treatment of people with a leaky gut. (van der Hulst, 1993; Klimberg, 1990; Noyer, 1998)

Rice protein is a very rich source of L-glutamine. When fortified with the amino acids L-lysine and L-threonine, it is also a balanced source of all essential amino acids (the UltraClear™ products are rice protein based medical foods that are fortified with L-lysine, and L-threonine). As well, rice protein is very unlikely to provoke an allergenic or intolerant response, and it is one of the most suitable foods for those on a low allergy potential diet.

L-glutamine is also often prescribed in supplement form (usually in quantities totalling between 500 and 10,000 mg per day). L-glutamine is a primary component of the the UltraClear line of medical food products which are available through healthcare professionals who utilize the principles of Functional Medicine.

· **Micronutrient support** of the gastrointestinal tract is a very important part of the "repair" phase of the 4-R Program™. Zinc, vitamin A, and the B vitamin pantothenic acid, all have a significant impact on the ability of the gut to heal.

Microbial toxins, immune activity and food itself can all place heavy stress upon the gut in the form of oxidation. Antioxidants like vitamin C, vitamin E, and bioflavonoids, such as those found in fruits and vegetables, can all provide significant antioxidant protection for the gut and allow more efficient healing. As well, the botanical medicinals such as Ginkgo biloba, rosemary, curcumin, rutin, and quercetin all possess both antioxidant and anti-inflammatory properties and can help to reduce gut inflammation and speed intestinal healing.

· **Essential fatty acids** are nutrients that can provide vital molecular building blocks for the repair and replacement of the cell membrane components of intestinal cells. The omega 3 fatty acids found in fish oils are important in intestinal cell repair, as well as playing an important role in decreasing gut inflammation and supporting the immune system of the gut (GALT). As well, Phospholipids such as phosphatidylcholine (lecithin) or phosphatidylserine (PS) can have a remarkable healing influence upon the gut wall. (Bengmark, 1998)

All of these fatty nutrients form the primary components of the intestinal cell membranes and since cellular turnover is so rapid on the surface of the gut wall, plenty of membrane fats are needed for optimal repair and cellular replacement.

· **Fiber** is a critical part of the "repair" phase of the 4-R Program™. Fiber plays many vital roles in normal intestinal function and is often markedly deficient in the diets of North Americans and Europeans. Children, especially those on junk food diets, are notorious for having gross inadequacy in their dietary fiber intake. By definition, fiber is any indigestible dietary carbohydrate. There are many different kinds of fiber, all of which are either water-soluble or water-insoluble. Water-insoluble fiber is like the fiber in wheat bran; it remains intact all the way through the digestive tract. Water-soluble fiber, on the other hand, is like that in oats, flax, legumes and apples; it turns gelatinous in water, and in the gut it gets broken down by bacteria before it is eliminated by the body.

Fiber provides an important medium to assist the growth of healthy gut bacteria and, in turn, these bacteria ferment fiber in the colon and produce short chain fatty acids as a byproduct. These short chain fatty acids, such as butyric acid, are the primary fuel for the large bowel cells. Without adequate amounts of these beneficial short chain fatty acids, the lining of the large will bowel become weak and susceptible to infection and inflammation. Adequate dietary fiber also helps to promote good elimination through two mechanisms. Firstly, it helps to decrease the stool transit time (the amount of time required for food to be eliminated once it is eaten). Secondly, fiber helps to absorb and neutralize toxins generated by gut organisms, as well as toxins that are being eliminated by the liver through the bile.

Increasing the amount of both water-soluble and water insoluble fiber should become a top priority for anyone going through the 4-R Program™. Eating whole grains allowable on the elimination diet as well as plenty of fruits, vegetables and, in many cases, fiber supplements, will help to insure that fiber intake is optimal. Pectin, from apple and banana, as well as oat bran are soluble fibers, which have been demonstrated to exert significant benefits upon gut function. Inulin and fructooligosaccharides are also very important fibers, which have numerous beneficial properties. Barley bran is a good alternative to wheat bran as a low allergy potential water insoluble fiber.

- **Detoxification support** is another important aspect of the "repair" phase of the 4-R Program™. Although it is normally recognized that the liver is the body's detoxification factory, the intestine that actually takes care of about 25 percent of this responsibility. If intestinal wall detoxification is inadequate or impaired, toxins will accumulate in the gut wall and will result in intestinal damage. In order to neutralize gut derived toxins and food contaminants, the intestinal cells require adequate amounts of specific nutrients. The amino acids methionine, N-acetyl cysteine, taurine, L-glutamine and glycine are particularly important in gut wall detoxification activity. Glutathione is a small peptide (protein fragment) made up of glycine, L-glutamine and cysteine. If glutathione is taken orally, it is used locally by intestinal cells for their own antioxidant protection and to enable detoxification activity to take place. Inorganic sulfate is also an important substance, which provides significant support for detoxification.

The **UltraBalance® line of products** are functional foods or medical foods available only through healthcare practitioners and a limited number of pharmacies. These are low allergy potential, rice based powders that contain a number of important ingredients, which are very helpful in the implementation of various aspects of the 4-R Program™. **UltraClear™ Sustain** (UltraClear GI in Canada) is the most commonly used intestinal support product in this line; containing high amounts of L-glutamine to nourish small intestinal cells. It also contains FOS and inulin, which are important prebiotics, supporting the growth of probiotic bacteria and increasing the production of colon nourishing short chain fatty acids. It also has a wide range of antioxidants and other important micronutrients. **UltraInflamX™** is a similar product, which also contains a large quantity of plant derived anti-inflammatory extracts, including curcumin, ginger, quercetin, rutin, hesperidin, limonene, and rosemary. This product is especially helpful for individuals with significant gastrointestinal inflammation, or pain and inflammation in other parts of the body. **UltraClear™** and **UltraClear Plus™** are powdered food products used primarily to assist the body in detoxification activities while the patient is undergoing an intensive detoxification regime. **Ultracare for Kids™** is a product designed for use in young children and it provides extra calcium, the important fatty acid DHA, the prebiotic nutrient FOS, as well as a wide selection of micronutrients.

All of these products are used to make up delicious smoothies and as a supplementary food while on a low allergy potential diet. These products are used around the world by Functional Medicine providers and have become an indispensable part of the 4-R Program™ for most clinicians in this field. For more information on these products, go to www.UltraBalance.com.

PUTTING IT ALL TOGETHER

When properly applied to individuals with ADHD, the 4-R Program™ can make a tremendous difference and can bring about lasting improvements in cognitive function, behavior, mood and physical health. If applied in a logical and scientific manner, under the supervision of a healthcare provider experienced in the principles of Functional Medicine, even some of the most difficult cases of ADHD, autism and other developmental disorders can be remarkably helped. In most cases, the effective application of 4-R Program™ is relatively simple and the benefits are seen in a reasonably short period of time. In other cases, factors such as persistent yeast overgrowth, recurrent parasites or small bowel bacterial overgrowth (auto-brewery syndrome) can make progress more difficult and will challenge even the highly astute healthcare provider. As a general rule, failure to see improvements on a properly applied 4-R Program™ suggests the presence of immune system impairment due to chronic, untreated infection, inadequate nutritional support, unmanaged stress or a significant toxic burden. Providing additional immunological support or having the patient undergo an effective detoxification regimen may bring success in these challenging situations. These topics will be covered in upcoming chapters.

Chapter 22

Restoring Strength to the Battered Immune System

WINNING THE SILENT WAR WITHIN

It has been emphasized throughout this book that the immune system plays a most significant role in ADHD. Disordered immune system function can result in inappropriate hypersensitivities to foods and environmental substances. Also, diminished immune defenses increase the likelihood that undesirable microbes will overgrow, colonize or infect the gut and respiratory tract. Infective or inflammatory processes, in turn, may result in the release of neurologically active immune-derived molecules and the production of neurotoxic microbial substances. As well, impaired gastrointestinal function, inefficient detoxification activities and other physiological problems, such as impaired blood sugar control, may accompany disturbances in immune system function; all of which can contribute to significant and persistent problems with brain function.

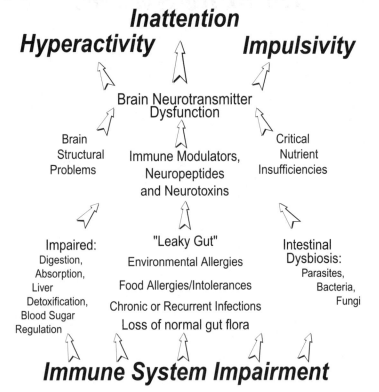

IF THE FOUNDATION IS WEAK THE WHOLE BUILDING IS WEAK

As described throughout Section 2 of this book, immune system impairment can begin early in life as a result of the additive effects of various antecedents or risk factors, which then weaken immune system function.

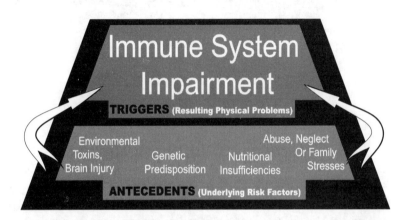

This is not to imply that disordered immune system function is solely to blame for the brain problems associated with ADHD. Factors such as neurotoxins, nutritional insufficiencies, genetic factors and abuse all can have a very direct effect upon brain function as well.

MANAGING IMMUNE SYSTEM STRESS

An alternative perspective from which to look at the factors that impair immune system function is to consider the **total underlying stressors** impacting the immune system. Emotional-psychological factors, toxic burdens, electromagnetic pollution, foreign antigen load (such as food allergens in the presence of a leaky gut), infectious agents, physical stresses (such as excessive exercise), and nutritional inadequacy may all contribute to the total underlying stressors which exert their ill effects upon the immune system.

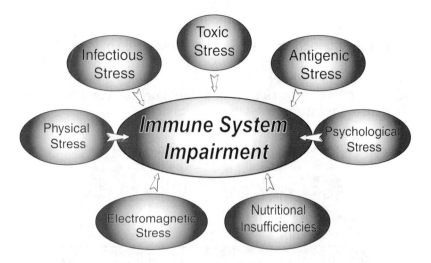

Total Underlying Immune Stressors

- **Emotional-psychological stresses** influence immune system function in a remarkably powerful way. Abuse, neglect or family stresses can precede the onset of ADHD and may contribute significantly as one of the factors underlying immune system impairment. Severe stresses of this sort will also directly shape the developing brain and may influence personality and behavior in a variety of ways. As well, emotional-psychological stresses may continue contribute to immune system depletion throughout the life of the person with ADHD.

Individuals with ADHD tend to be highly sensitive and easily impacted by stressful life events. Therefore, since the ADHD affected life is often burdened with plenty of trials and tribulations, stress levels can be extraordinary. The combination of high sensitivity to stress combined with a high frequency of stress producing events can place emotional-psychological stresses very high on the list of immune depleting factors in the ADHD sufferer's life. Such factors may become particularly predominant in the lives of adolescents and adults with ADHD who commonly find themselves having to deal with the consequences of impulsive decision-making, failures and other potentially catastrophic life events.

Emotional-psychological stresses lead to the production of high quantities of stress hormones such as adrenaline and cortisol. These "flight or fight" hormones are necessary and are normally produced cyclically at certain times of the day. They are also released in short bursts when tense or frightful events occur. In the proper context, these substances can increase mental alertness and can provide extra energy to perform demanding tasks. In fact, many people with ADHD will become drowsy and out of focus unless they are under a moderate amount of emotional stress.

Unfortunately, it is easy for those with ADHD to go over the threshold where the negative impact of excessive stress hormones far outweighs the benefits. Beyond a certain reasonable point, elevated stress hormones can greatly reduce mental performance, create physical exhaustion and lead to many harmful long-term effects. It is particularly important to remember that levels of the stress hormone cortisol, over time, have been shown to be directly correlated to the speed of brain aging, especially the part of the brain that is responsible for memory. If you cannot recall reading this fact from a previous chapter, then perhaps your stress hormone levels are too high!

As was mentioned in Chapter 19, stimulant medications have a potent ability to promote the release of stress hormones. When added to the already elevated stress hormone levels common to those with ADHD, stimulants may contribute to significant harm to the brain, cardiovascular and immune systems over the long-term. This certainly suggests that use of amphetamine family stimulant drugs (Ritalin®, Dexedrine®, Adderal) as well as high amounts of caffeine, and stimulant weight loss drugs should all be avoided if there is to be any improvement in the long-term prognosis for someone with ADHD.

Although many people with ADHD seem to thrive on stress because they actively seek out novel, risky or high pressure activities, they are also, more often than not, habitual worriers who are frequently overwhelmed by their internal sensations of nervous tension. Some have likened ADHD to living life inside a pressure cooker. Even children with ADHD have higher levels of muscle tension than their non-affected peers and they often experience stress related physical complaints. Because improperly managed stress can have such a weakening and debilitating effect, stress management must become a high priority for everyone with ADHD. Those with ADHD will either learn to be the master of their stress, or else their stress will certainly become the master over them. Stress management is both a science and an art requiring skills that must be learned and practiced. These principles will be covered in more detail in Chapters 25 through 27.

- **Toxic stresses** can also be a primary factor in immune system depletion. In Chapter 6, some of the most important sources of neurotoxic and immunotoxic stresses were described. Air, water, and food should all be considered as primary sources of toxic stress in those with ADHD. In children, pesticide contaminated foods may be a very predominant source of brain and immune depleting toxins. As well, chemicals in the home, school and work environments may add significantly to the total load of toxic stresses upon the ADHD affected brain and body. Drugs, including prescription drugs and substances of abuse can also be major sources of toxic internal pollution. It is unfortunate that the drugs most often used to treat ADHD are themselves potentially neurotoxic and they may add significantly to the toxic burden upon the brain and immune system. Smoking or breathing second hand smoke is a also major immune depleting stressor, which can result in a marked increase in childhood respiratory infection, asthma and other health problems in ADHD. Smoking also affects brain development. As many as 25 percent of children born to mothers who smoke during pregnancy end up suffering from significant behavioral problems. (Williams, 1998)

Importantly, dental amalgams provide an ongoing source of highly absorbable mercury vapor, which can pollute the brain and immune system. Mercury derived from dental amalgams can also be readily transferred from mother to child through the placenta during fetal development. (Vimy, 1990) In our facility, there have been several instances where the mother of a child with ADHD has been noted to suffer with chronic fatigue syndrome or fibromyalgia. These women usually have several dental amalgams, and on further assessment, it has been found that they generally have high body burdens of mercury. In such cases, their ADHD affected child may also have a significant body burden of mercury even if they have never had amalgam fillings or eaten much fish. Presumably, the child's mercury burden has come from their mother during fetal development. This is certainly an observation that needs to be investigated through further research. Strategies to deal with toxic stress will be addressed more fully in Chapter 24.

• **Electromagnetic pollution** is a largely neglected but increasingly important source of immune depleting stress. (Markov, 1994) Exposure to electronic equipment, including computer monitors, television sets, microwave ovens, high tension power lines, cellular phones, radio and satellite broadcasts are all an ever-increasing source of electromagnetic pollution in our high tech world. There is now accumulating data to suggest that electromagnetic pollution has immune depleting effects and may contribute to cancer and other disorders. Those with ADHD would be wise to avoid any unnecessary exposure to this invisible pollution.

Excessive exposure to ultraviolet radiation is another form of electromagnetic pollution, which may eventually become one of the most serious threats to human immune system function. There is clear evidence that the depletion of high atmospheric ozone is resulting in an increased exposure of humans to ultraviolet radiation. This has resulted in a marked increase in the incidence of skin cancers over the past decade. Excessive UV exposure can also cause immune system depression and an increased risk of infection. (Beissert, 1999) Everyone (especially children) should take precautionary measures to avoid excessive sun exposure and to use appropriate sun screens and protective clothing when outside.

- **Antigenic stress** refers to the excessive exposure of the immune system to substances that have the ability to create a specific immune response (primarily proteins or protein breakdown products). Antigens entering the mucous membranes of the respiratory tract have the potential to cause allergic responses like hay fever (Type I hypersensitivity). Severe allergies of this type can result in more generalized symptoms including behavioral and cognitive problems. In the condition commonly referred to as the "allergy-tension-fatigue syndrome", the allergy sufferer not only experiences the local effects of the allergen, such as itchy eyes, stuffy nose and wheezing, but also the impact of widespread immune dysfunction. Such individuals can suffer from fatigue, irritability, hyperactivity, cognitive problems and a wide range of ADHD-like symptoms – all secondary to the effects of antigenic stress.

In conventional medicine, airborne allergies are generally treated by avoiding or reducing exposure to the allergen, immunotherapy (allergy shots), and medication. In Functional Medicine, it is recognized that allergic inflammation can be significantly modified through such things as targeted nutritional interventions and the administration of certain botanical medicines with potent anti-inflammatory activities. The professional textbook, "Nutritional Management of Inflammatory Disorders" is an excellent review of this topic. This book has been produced by the Institute for Functional Medicine and can be acquired through the Internet at: www.fxmed.com. In addition to this, a new form of immunotherapy (allergy shots), known as EPD, has recently been imported from Europe. This therapy is safer and probably more effective than conventional immunotherapy. EPD will be discussed in more detail later in this chapter.

In Chapters 10-12, the impact of gut-derived antigens on the immune system and brain were described. It is clear that the immune system is exposed to a large quantity of antigens through the gut mucous membranes, even when gut function is normal. However, when a person has a leaky gut, food allergies or intestinal dysbiosis (overgrowth of unfriendly gut microbes), the load of antigens imposed upon the immune system can be vast. In such cases of antigenic stress, the immune system can easily become angry, exhausted and confused. The 4-R Program outlined in the previous chapter provides a rational means to greatly reduce the antigenic load upon the immune system. Once these primary stresses on the immune system are reduced significantly, it will be at liberty to focus its energies upon the appropriate protection and repair of the body.

- **Infectious stress** is a common factor underlying the immune depletion associated with ADHD. The AIDS epidemic has made society aware of the fact that infection can indeed be associated with serious immune dysfunction. Although few infectious agents are as deadly as the HIV virus responsible for AIDS, virtually every virus, bacteria or parasite capable of causing human infection will place the immune system under significant stress if that agent gains significant access to the body. In many cases, infection occurs largely because the immune system is already weakened by other antecedent factors such as toxic or emotional stress. As has been described at length in this book, gut dysbiosis (overgrowth of undesirable gut microbes) is a major source of infectious stress in ADHD. Chronic or recurring respiratory infections (including ear infection) are also an exceedingly frequent source of infectious stress in those with ADHD, especially in children. Undesirable microbes can place a tremendous antigenic load upon the immune system. These organisms may also produce a wide range of neurotoxic and immunotoxic substances; any of which can create an environment in which the immune system becomes angry, exhausted and confused, and where the dialog between the nervous system and immune system deteriorates into an exchange of very bitter "molecular words".

Although antibiotics are commonly prescribed to treat all manner of respiratory infections in children and adults, this approach is often ineffectual because antibiotics don't kill viruses, which are the cause of the majority of respiratory infections. As well, simply giving a prescription for an antibiotic does not improve the underlying immune system dysfunction responsible for recurrent respiratory infections. Although there are certainly times where antibiotics are appropriate and even necessary, they should not be used as indiscriminately as they are today. The overuse of antibiotics may cause disruption of the body's delicate ecosystems and the growth of aggressive, antibiotic resistant microbes. This means that the antibiotics used to eradicate immune depleting microbes can end up contributing to significant immune depletion. The impact of antibiotics on gut ecology, and thus the immune system, may be why recurrent ear infections in early childhood have been associated with a significantly higher risk of developing ADHD. In children suffering from recurring infections, rather than simply prescribing multiple courses of antibiotics, efforts should be made to reduce the stress upon, and provide support for, their ailing immune systems.

When properly applied, the 4-R Program can considerably reduce toxic, antigenic and infectious stress, and can result in a substantial increase in resistance to gastrointestinal and respiratory infections. As described in Chapter 13, our research has uncovered the fact that ADHD sufferers commonly have a marked decrease in their production of secretory IgA, the most important immune system factor protecting all surfaces of the body from allergy and infection. We were also able to demonstrate that even a partial application of the 4-R Program (removal of junk foods and commonly allergenic foods along with improvement in nutritional quality of the diet) can result in a significant rise in secretory IgA in these same people. Other research has demonstrated that secretory IgA can be increased by the administration of certain probiotic bacteria. (Fukushima, 1998; Malin, 1996; Buts, 1990) Many other elements of the 4-R Program also exert much of their beneficial action through the support of immune system function.

The incidence of respiratory infection can also be significantly decreased by following certain rules of hygiene. Principally, this means that an individual must be taught to wash his hands frequently, and should be instructed never to touch his hands to his mouth, nose or eyes unless he has just washed his hands. This simple measure can almost eliminate the transmission of respiratory infections such as colds and influenza between one person and another. In children, ear infections almost always begin as a simple viral infection (cold or flu). The simple virus is then followed by a secondary bacterial infection in the ear once the infectious stress of the virus has weakened immune defenses against the ear infection bacteria. Primary prevention of the initial viral infections would virtually eliminate ear infections in most children and almost abolish the need for antibiotics. Hand washing education programs have been used successfully in schools to reduce the rate of absenteeism due to respiratory infection. (Kimmel, 1996) Physicians who follow this simple but powerful hygienic principle of frequent hand washing rarely acquire a respiratory infection even though they are exposed to people with these conditions several times per day. Few respiratory infections are passed from person to person through the air, but are rather transferred to the hands, and then to the eyes, nose or mouth. Fastidious hand washing habits can also decrease the risk of bowel infections, especially with intestinal parasites, as these are often transferred from hand to mouth in the same way as respiratory infections.

Maintaining an adequate intake of water or other acceptable fluids is also a vital and often neglected element of immune system support. (Kleiner, 1999) Even mild dehydration can result in a marked increase in the risk of respiratory infections because of the drying effects of dehydration on respiratory mucous and other surface defenses. Dehydration can also significantly reduce the efficiency of waste elimination from the colon and kidneys, and it can result in diminished liver detoxification activities. All of these factors mean that dehydration may allow immune impairing toxic substances to accumulate in the body. Assuring optimal hydration is a simple and inexpensive intervention, which can play an important role in the establishment and maintenance of normal immune system function.

Those with ADHD often are particularly susceptible to dehydration. Food allergy, fatty acid abnormalities and a leaky gut all result in increased water loss through the kidneys. Studies in monkeys indicate that omega-3 fatty acid deficiency can double the daily fluid loss from the kidneys. (Reisbick, 1991) Children with ADHD are especially at risk for dehydration since they often neglect subtle thirst sensations and they lack the knowledge to know how to avoid dehydration. Unfortunately, many kids satisfy their fluid cravings with abundant quantities of fruit juices and sweet drinks, which exchanges the problem of dehydration for over-consumption of empty calories in the form of sugar.

- **Physical stresses** in the form of extremes of physical training can rapidly and markedly deplete immune system function. I have spent several years of my career working with a National Team and professional athletes, and it is clear that in these individuals the risk of over-stress from excessive physical exercise is very high. Although a moderate amount of exercise is very important for everyone with ADHD it should be made clear that extremes of exercise can backfire and result in a worsening of all immune system related problems. People with ADHD who become attracted to sports often develop obsessive training habits and can easily become over-stressed in their zeal to achieve excellence in their sport. This can be true even in children who excel in athletics, especially if they have a hard-driving parent with thoughts of gold medals or a lucrative professional career.

In my own case, as a young runner, I became so obsessed with my training that at one time I ran twice per day, often for 12 miles or more at a time. This continued until I shrunk down to a sickly 118 pounds (I am healthiest at about 165 pounds). Because of this compulsive running, I also developed bilateral stress fractures in my legs and knee injuries that eventually resulted in 3 knee operations. I still work out hard and nearly every day, but I am very careful to avoid over-training. Exercise done wisely can result in marked improvement in immune system function and can have many other benefits in ADHD. Athletes can excel more fully if they train smarter, not just harder. The National Bobsleigh Team that I worked with was ranked 27th in the world when I took over their medical care. They were often over-trained and spent much of the season fighting various overuse injuries and respiratory infections. Since that time, they have learned to train smarter and to avoid over-training. Subsequently, in the last Winter Olympics they took home a gold medal for Canada!

- **Nutritional Inadequacy** is a primary factor resulting in stress upon the immune system. The nutritional factors described in Chapter 8 all have a significant effect on brain and immune system function. Widespread nutritional inadequacy is quite characteristic of those with ADHD and is a certain accompaniment in those whose diets contain significant amounts of junk foods or fast foods. Inadequate provision of micronutrients such as the B vitamins and minerals (iron, calcium, magnesium, zinc, selenium, and chromium), plus dietary antioxidants and phytochemicals, can all result in immune system dysfunction. Skipping meals or eating nutritionally inadequate meals (especially breakfast) can be particularly deleterious, particularly for children or adolescents with ADHD. As has been discussed at length in Chapter 7, inadequate supply of essential fatty acids can result in problems with brain function, either directly or as a result of the stress that such deficiencies place upon the immune system. Ideally, these brain and immune system critical nutritional factors must be supplied in adequate quantities, even well before conception, to ensure that the developing child has an adequate supply of these vital molecular components. Later on, lack of breast-feeding and inadequacy of dietary essential fatty acid intake throughout childhood is a common factor in the immune system problems associated with ADHD.

POSITIVE SUPPORT FOR THE BATTERED IMMUNE SYSTEM

In addition to identifying removing the underlying stressors, which are adversely impacting the function of the immune system, specific actions can be taken to provide positive support for the immune system. Until recently, medical science has focused all attention upon factors that are known to impair immune system function, yet with little regard for interventions that directly promote optimal immune system function. This attitude is changing rapidly as research reveals that it is indeed possible to significantly improve immune system function through natural approaches, such as targeted nutrition factors and certain lifestyle practices.

- ***Exercise training*** has the potential to significantly improve immune system function. As explained above, excessive exercise is a significant immune suppressor. This is because exercise is such a potent source of physical stress. However, if exercise is not too extreme and an appropriate amount of time is provided to recover from an exercise session, the stress from the exercise acts as a stimulus to provoke an adaptive response by the body. This adaptive response can significantly strengthen the immune system and can result in many other benefits. (Nieman, 1997)

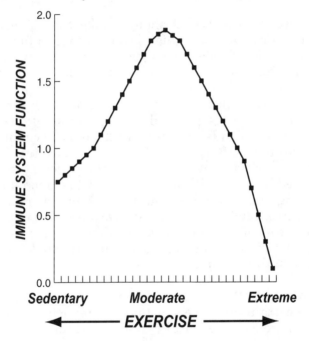

In other words, after exercise, the body must repair the damage incurred to millions of cells because of widespread microscopic and molecular trauma. If the exercise-caused damage is not too extensive, if enough rest time is provided for rebuilding, and if adequate quantities of various nutrients are available to the cells, the body will return to an even stronger state in the days after the exercise session. This is the basis of the training effect used by all athletes and fitness enthusiasts to improve their strength, speed and endurance through exercise.

Exercise also results in an improvement in the liver's detoxification capabilities and it strengthens the body's built-in antioxidant defenses. (Lew, 1991) These and many unmentioned facts suggest that those who achieve and maintain a high level of fitness (while avoiding overtraining) will reap tremendous benefits in terms of immune system health.

Everyone with ADHD should make the achievement and maintenance of a high level of physical fitness one of his or her fundamental goals in life. Parents should also make every effort to insure that their ADHD affected child develops athletically through regular participation in sports and recreation. Our son spent his first 8 years plagued with poor immune system function. He suffered from an extraordinary number of respiratory infections and was sick as often as was well. However, over the past three years we have helped him establish a commitment to personal fitness through mountain bike riding, BMX bicycle racing and plenty of family walks. This is certainly one of the reasons why his immune system function has improved dramatically; as evidenced by the fact that he rarely gets sick any more.

- *Immunonutrition* refers to the administration of a certain nutritive substances intended to specifically increase the vitality of the immune system. Immunonutrition is rapidly evolving as an important field of science and is beginning to play a major role in the management of many chronic illnesses. (Alexander, 1998; Alverdy, 1998; Bengmark, 1998; Levy, 1998) As was mentioned above, nutritional inadequacy places severe stress upon immunological functions. In contrast, making efforts to optimize nutritional status and to provide certain important nutrients can increase immune system function in a highly significant way.

▶ **Balanced macronutrients:** Immunonutrition should begin with the basics. Firstly, serving meals that are balanced in terms of their macronutrients (protein, carbohydrate and fat) provides the basic fuel for the immune system and avoids stressing the body's blood sugar control systems. Macronutrient balance means that a person should generally eat meals that contain protein, carbohydrate and fats in a reasonable balance, rather than overemphasis on one or two macronutrients only. Research suggests that breakfast is a very important meal, especially for children. Far too often, people start the day with a high carbohydrate, low protein breakfast (e.g. sugary cereal, donuts or muffins). This provides little support for the immune system during the time of day when stress hormones are the highest and the immune system is under the greatest workload. (Harbige, 1996) High fat meals also place the immune system under considerable stress and should be avoided.

▶ **Optimized micronutrients:** Providing optimal levels of micronutrients such as zinc, magnesium, selenium, and copper has been shown to have a significantly positive effect upon immune system function. (Levy, 1998) In children, athletes or women with heavy menstrual flow, iron is also often a highly beneficial immunonutrient, which may need to be provided in supplemental levels to achieve an adequate intake.

Several vitamins, including vitamins A, D, B6, and folic acid, can all affect immune system function. (Chandra, 1997) Vitamins E, and C, have important effects upon the immune system, primarily because of their antioxidant effects. As well, numerous plant bioflavonoids can have antioxidant potency equal to or greater than that of vitamins C and E. Oxidation damage is one of the most predominant factors exerting stress upon the immune system. Recent research also has shown that high doses of vitamin C can greatly reduce the amount of stress hormones secreted while under stress and can abolish immune depletion secondary to severe stress. (Campbell, 1999)

▶ **Essential fatty acids** are important components of immune cell membranes, which participate in a wide range of biochemical processes within these cells. Obtaining adequate quantities of the anti-inflammatory omega-3 oils (fish and flax oils) is an important aspect in the treatment of allergic disorders and other immune system related conditions, such as ADHD. (Kankaanpaa, 1999) Ideally, omega 3 oils should be consumed in combination with the unique omega 6 oils from evening primrose, black currant or borage seed. Such combinations are now commercially available and are being promoted for use in ADHD. In addition to insuring an adequate intake of the beneficial omega 3 and omega 6 oils, it is equally important to avoid ingesting excessive amounts of inflammation-amplifying animal and vegetable fats, as well as immune toxic trans-fatty acids (from hydrogenated vegetable oils).

It is also imperative that people become aware of the unhealthy nature of fats which have been damaged by heat or exposure to oxygen. Most of the cooking methods that involve heating oils to high temperatures result in severe molecular damage to those oils, rendering them toxic to the gut wall, immune system and brain. Perhaps the most insidiously toxic foods that we can put into our bodies are those that are deep fried. Most restaurants use vegetable oil shortening (pure hydrogenated fat) or lard (pure saturated fat) which is heated to extreme temperatures over and over again. The oils used in commercial deep fryers can be anywhere from several weeks to several months old. Studies have shown that these overused deep fryer fats contain numerous carcinogens and toxins. (Hageman, 1991; Warner, 1999) From this data, it seems clear that it would be wise to abstain completely from all deep fried foods. This rule would be especially important in those with ADHD. It seems ironic that the "kid's menu" of most restaurants is made up of a nauseating selection of some of the most unhealthy foods in the standard North American diet, including plenty of deep fried foods.

▶ **Dietary fiber** is one of the simplest, least expensive and most important components of immunonutrition. Unfortunately, most people are grossly fiber deficient and few have an awareness of the importance of this humble part of their diet. Children are especially prone to having diets that are seriously fiber poor. Not only can this result in bothersome constipation, it is also a primary factor in determining the quality of the gut microflora. Fiber can be either soluble or insoluble. Insoluble fiber is found in the indigestible component of most vegetables as well as corn, barley, rice and wheat bran. Insoluble fiber impairs the growth of harmful gut microbes and helps to reduce the time it takes for food to travel through the digestive tract (stool transit time). (Vanderhoof, 1998) As well, insoluble fiber acts to bind toxins within the gut, thus preventing their absorption and improving their excretion from the gut. (Rowland, 1986)

Soluble fiber is found in oat bran, legumes, psyllium, fruit pectin, seaweeds and vegetable gums like guar gum. Many soluble fibers are prebiotic, that is, they promote the growth of friendly probiotic gut microbes. This is especially true of inulin (from Jerusalem artichoke), fructooligosaccharides and oat bran. (Bengmark, 1995) Soluble fiber is fermented by gut flora to produce short chain fatty acids, the main food of the colonic cells. The prebiotic effects of soluble fiber promote the growth of beneficial microbes, which in turn, stimulate the immune system of the gut (GALT). This immune stimulation includes an increase in the production of the highly important antibody, secretory IgA. Soluble fibers also protect the gut and the GALT because they exert powerful antioxidant effects within the gut. (Bengmark, 1998) It also guards the gut wall and considerably reduces the stress upon the immune system by nourishing and helping to preserve the mucous layer covering the intestinal cells. This mucous layer forms a vital defensive shield against the adherence and penetration of allergens and pathogens. Many disorders of gastrointestinal function are associated with a decrease in the thickness and quality of this important mucous layer. As well, soluble fiber promotes an increase in liver detoxification activities. (Rowland, 1994) More efficient detoxification would result in a reduction of toxic stress upon the brain and immune system.

▶ **Probiotic supplementation** has been mentioned previously as an important part of the 4-R Program. Probiotics supplementation imparts several benefits including stimulation of the gastrointestinal immune system. Research over the past few years has concluded that probiotic organisms are, in fact, critical to the development of normal immune function in the gut and throughout the rest of the body. Studies have clearly shown that probiotic organisms are required for the development of normal immune responsiveness and the development of immunolgical tolerance towards food antigens. (Sudo, 1997) Children with allergic diseases tend to have a much lower level of probiotic intestinal bacteria and a high prevalence of potential intestinal pathogens. (Bjorksten, 1999) Intestinal parasites are especially associated with a high risk of allergic disorders. (DiPrisco, 1998) As mentioned previously, our research has demonstrated that children with ADHD usually have a diminished level of friendly gut flora and a high prevalence of potential gut pathogens and parasites. Therefore, it is not surprising that so many of these ADHD affected children showed evidence of food hypersensitivities.

One of the most exciting areas of the expanding knowledge emerging from recent research is the fact that the oral administration of certain probiotic organisms can effectively decrease or even eradicate food allergies. (Majamaa, 1997; Kirjavainen, 1999)

Importantly, probiotic supplements do not act simply by causing a decrease in immune response. Instead, they act by diminishing undesirable inflammation, while simultaneously bolstering many aspects of the desirable immune response. (Pelto, 1998) Of particular importance to those with ADHD is the fact that probiotic supplementation has been shown to increase the production of secretory IgA, perhaps the most important immune component in the body. (Fukushima, 1998 b; Buts, 1990; Tejada-Simon, 1999; Herias, 1999)

Overall, probiotic organisms play an indispensable role in the protection and nourishment of the gut wall, as well as the stimulation and coordination of immune system activities. The following diagram illustrates some of the many beneficial functions of probiotic organisms: (Bengmark, 1995)

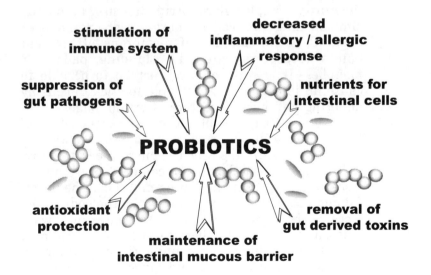

❯ **Glyconutritionals** (glyco meaning "sugar") refer to unusual complex carbohydrates (usually plant derived), which have the potential to dramatically improve immune system function. A number of naturally occurring products in this category are now undergoing intensive study for their ability to improve immune system function without imposing any degree of toxicity on the body. Glyconutritionals are thought to support immune function through one or more of these three primary mechanisms:

Firstly, certain complex, naturally occurring carbohydrates (known as oligosaccharides) have specific shapes and stickiness properties, allowing them to attach to receptors on the surface of immune cells. This attachment, in turn, may influence immune cell activity in a very potent way. Carbohydrates with this property can be found in plants such as Echinacea, Aloe vera, ginseng root, shitake mushroom and many others.

Secondly, complex glyconutritionals may mimic the sites on intestinal cell membranes where microbes stick. These intestinal cell membrane attachment points (receptors) are like "landing pads" for microbes. It is rare for any microbe to be able to cause an infection if it is unable to stick to cells by adhering to these receptors. Certain oligosaccharides, if ingested, are able to act as "receptor decoys" by mimicking the cell surface receptors and sticking to the microbe. In this way, the microbe becomes covered with oligosaccharide "receptor decoys" and it loses its ability to stick to intestinal cells. The harmful microbe then simply passes out of the body in the feces without ever colonizing the intestinal wall. Oligosaccharides with these properties are common constituents of breast milk and various plant medicinals such as Aloe vera, and ginseng root. (Alverdy, 1998)

Thirdly, it has been shown that certain rare gly-conutritionals are able to provide the fundamental building blocks for important cellular communication molecules. The cells of the immune system depend upon accurate communication to carry out their important activities. These cells produce a wide variety of information molecules to coordinate their activities and to alert the body when danger is detected. Some of these molecules provide for long-range communication; primarily the peptides, such as the opioids and cytokines, which have been described in previous chapters. These long-range molecules are kind of like a molecular "radio broadcast", which can be detected by the majority of the body cells.

In addition, immune cells depend upon a short-range system of communication — a sort of molecular "sign language", to communicate to cells in their immediate vicinity. The membrane surrounding all immune cells is covered with thousands of complex, branching molecules known as **glycoproteins** (molecules composed of sugars and protein together). Because of these glycoproteins, the surface of immune cells actually have a strange "fuzzy" appearance under a powerful electronic microscope. The exact size and shape of each glycoprotein determines its meaning in the "glycoprotein molecular language" spoken by all immune cells. Immune cells will display specific glycoproteins in order to communicate a vast array of "statements" ranging from identifying themselves, to shouting messages of alarm. In fact, all cells participate in this molecular dialog by displaying glycoproteins on their cell surface.

It is through this glycoprotein language that the immune system communicates, not only to its own members, but also to every other cell in the body. As well, all cells are able to "speak" to the immune system through this same language. For instance, if a cell turns cancerous and is unable to be repaired, it displays a set of glycoproteins on its surface to allow immune cells to detect and assist in the destruction of the malfunctioning cell.

Until recently, it was thought that the sugars required to make these important glycoproteins could be easily synthesized by the body from sugars such as glucose, which are readily available in the diet. However, some of the important glycoprotein sugars, such as mannose, fucose and xylose are rare in the modern diet and they must therefore be produced by the body through very complex biochemical processes. Unfortunately, because so many enzymatic steps are required to synthesize these rare sugars, their production can easily be impaired by toxicity, infection, stress or a lack of certain critical nutrients. This may explain why recent research has shown that immune system function improves dramatically when these unusual sugars are administered as a dietary supplement. (See, 1998) Interestingly, one recent study has shown that a glyconutritional product containing all eight of the sugars used in glycoprotein synthesis (Ambrotose™; Mannatech™, Inc.) improves behaviors in the majority of children with ADHD. (Dykman, 1998) It is likely that this supplement is able to improve ADHD behaviors secondary to an improvement in immune system function. This improvement would likely occur as a result of improved glycoprotein synthesis after these children were given the building blocks of these critical communication molecules. Ambrotose™ is the only product which is known to contain all of the eight rare sugars used by cells to manufacture glycoproteins.

It is likely that humans consumed many of these rare sugars at a more primitive time in history, when natural roots and leaves were a common part of the diet. Several plants that have been revered for their healing properties for millennia have now been shown to be good sources of some these important glyconutrients. The presence of rare glyconutrients in complex carbohydrates known as oligosaccharides (meaning a few sugars) and polysaccharides (meaning many sugars) is thought to be the primary reason why many herbal agents have now been shown to have immune stimulating properties.

Echinacea is perhaps the most popular herb used for its immune stimulating effects. Its immunological benefits have been shown to occur, at least in part, because of its polysaccharide constituents. (Tubaro, 1987; Luettig, 1989) Aloe vera has also been used for centuries for enhancement of wound healing and, recently, for several immunological disorders. (Stuart, 1997) Stabilized aloe carbohydrate, known as acemannan, contains the rare sugar, mannose, as its primary immune stimulating glyconutrient. Many types of mushrooms, used for centuries in traditional medicine, are also a rich source of immunologically active glyconutrients. (Chang, 1996)

Water-soluble extracts from various species of ginseng have been studied extensively for their immune-supportive properties. These herbal products have been demonstrated to contain a broad selection of glyconutrients relevant to glycoprotein synthesis, including mannose, fucose, xylose and others. (Tomoda, 1993; Tomoda, 1994; Shin, 1997; Gao, 1996) A carbohydrate-rich extract of ginseng has been shown to activate immune cells (macrophages) against the yeast, Candida albicans. (Abe, 1998) Ginseng carbohydrate extracts have also been shown to stimulate natural killer cells, one of the most important cell types in the immune system. (Kim, 1990; See, 1997) In human subjects with chronic fatigue syndrome or fibromyalgia, ginseng extracts have been shown to improve several parameters of immunity. (See, 1997)

At our facility, a glyconutritional extract of American ginseng has been found to be of significant value in the management of patients with immune system problems, including those with ADHD. This carbohydrate extract is water-soluble and possesses completely different properties than that of the oil soluble extract found in AD-FX™, the supplement that improves brain function. This extract, known as Cold-FX™, is the result of research conducted at the University of Alberta in their Herbal Medicine Research Group and is manufactured by the biotechnology company, HerbTech. Cold-FX™ is the result of extensive investigations directed at refining and amplifying the known immune supporting properties of ginseng glyconutritionals. Currently unpublished studies from HerbTech scientists indicate that Cold-FX™ is 20 times as potent as Echinacea in terms of its ability to increase immune system function. (Totosy de Zepetnick, 1999) Many clinicians are using Cold-FX™ as a primary immune supportive nutrient to help increase the success of the 4-R Program™, to reduce the risk of respiratory infections and to treat a wide range of immune related problems.

As the name suggests, Cold-FX™ has particular value in the prevention and treatment of respiratory infections such as colds and influenza. If a person starts to take Cold-FX™ at the first sign of a cold or flu, the infection often "stops in its tracks" or at least its duration is considerably shortened. This "cold busting" property makes Cold-FX™ especially useful for children when they develop a cold. Also, this product appears to help prevent secondary infections, such as ear infections, once a cold has developed. Taking vitamin C and zinc lozenges seems to amplify the effects of this product if taken at the same time as Cold-FX™.

Our facility participated in a preliminary study involving the Edmonton Oilers, a National Hockey League team, who were placed on Cold-FX™. The purpose of this study was to attempt to reduce the number and the severity of respiratory infections that often plague professional teams late in the season when their immune systems are run down. After one season on this product, the team members and coaching staff were highly enthusiastic about the results obtained. I always keep a box of it in my kitchen cupboard, and at the first sign of a cold, I start taking Cold-FX™ (letting it dissolve in the mouth before swallowing) along with vitamin C, zinc lozenges and lots of water. I have found that by starting this routine early enough in the progress of the cold, it can usually be beaten completely within 12 to 24 hours. Many other people have reported the same effects.

- *Immunotherapy* refers to the use of medical therapies to change the way the immune system responds to allergens. Another term for immunotherapy is allergy desensitization treatment. Three major forms of immunotherapy are currently being practiced throughout the world. Each form has advantages and disadvantages which will be discussed below.

▶ **"Conventional immunotherapy"** or "allergy shots" refers to the desensitizing injections most commonly used by North American allergy specialists. This form of immunotherapy involves the repeated injection of specific allergens under the skin. The concentration of the allergen is increased over time and the individual gradually develops increasing tolerance to the allergen. The success of this therapy depends upon accurate allergy testing in order to determine the exact allergens specific to the patient. The material used in these injections is individualized according to the person's allergies. Conventional immunotherapy works best in people with very specific allergies to airborne agents like grass pollen. It is especially helpful in those with hay fever (allergic rhinitis) and, if done correctly, can provide lasting improvement even years after the injections are stopped. (Durham, 1999) However, with few exceptions, it is of no value in the treatment of food allergy, pet allergies or in cases where multiple allergies exist. The injections must also be repeated weekly or monthly, and often for years. This form of immunotherapy also carries a significant risk of precipitating a serious allergic reaction (anaphylaxis). Because so many deaths have occurred from this therapy, it is essentially banned in some countries including Great Britain.

▶ **Provocation-neutralization** is a form of immunotherapy practiced by a minority of allergy specialists in North America as well as some physicians practicing Functional Medicine or Environmental Medicine. This technique begins by administering a single allergen by injection under the skin at a relatively high dose and then looking for adverse reactions that follow. Rather that just a skin reaction, the physician looks for all possible allergic symptoms such as wheezing, as well as behavioral, speech or cognitive problems. If a specific allergen does create a clear adverse response, progressively weaker dosages of the allergen are administered at various intervals until a dosage is found which appears to neutralize the adverse reaction. Once this "neutralization dosage" has been determined, the patient may return on subsequent occasions to have repeated neutralizing dose injections.

This technique has been shown in some double blind placebo controlled studies to be an effective method for both the diagnosis and treatment of allergic conditions, including food allergies. (King, 1988a; King, 1988b) Unlike conventional immunotherapy, which can take many months to begin working, patients receiving provocation-neutralization treatments can experience almost immediate benefits. The major disadvantages of this method are that it requires a considerable amount of special training and experience to perform accurately, and it is enormously time consuming since only one potential allergen can be tested or treated in any given session. Because fairly high doses of allergens are utilized, serious adverse reactions can occasionally occur with this therapy.

Some research has been done indicating that provocation-neutralization therapy can be successful in the
treatment of children with ADHD. (Rapp, 1979)
Although the effects of these injections are rather
short lived and must be repeated often to maintain
the benefits, many physicians suggest that patients
can be eventually switched to sublingual (under the
tongue) drops with near or equal success. This observation has been confirmed in one study of sublingual
drops in children with ADHD. (O'Shea, 1991) Currently,
only medical doctors (MD) or doctors of osteopathy
(DO) can undergo training and are legally able to
administer provocation-neutralization therapy. The
best resource to locate a physician performing this
therapy is thorough the American Academy of
Environmental Medicine at (316) 684-5500.

▶ **Enzyme Potentiated Desensitization (EPD)** is a
form of immunotherapy which has been used successfully across Europe for over twenty years for the
treatment of allergic disorders. This therapy is currently undergoing clinical testing for full approval in
the FDA although it has already undergone approximately 25 studies, including 10 double blind placebo
controlled trials. Convincing research now suggests
that EPD is an effective treatment for airborne allergies, chemical sensitivities and food allergies as well
as several conditions in which allergy may be a contributing factor.

EPD involves the injection of an extremely dilute
solution, containing allergens and an enzyme called
beta-glucuronidase. In this treatment, the beta-glucuronidase enzyme acts as a signaling molecule,
which turns on a mechanism in certain immune cells
(T-cells), enabling them to be completely "reprogrammed". (Ippoliti, 1997) When the beta-glucuronidase
is injected at the same time as the allergens, the
immune cells are reprogrammed to become tolerant
of each allergen presented in the injection.
Essentially, EPD works by re-educating the immune

cells, to enable them to more accurately know which dietary and environmental antigens to be tolerant towards.

There are several key advantages of EPD over other forms of immunotherapy:

☆ Firstly, because such tiny doses of allergens are used, the risk of serious side effects from EPD is extremely remote, even in people who have experienced episodes of severe anaphylaxis in the past. In over 30 years of total use, there has not been a single life threatening reaction to EPD. Because of its safety, EPD is permitted in Great Britain, whereas conventional immunotherapy, because of its dangers, is banned.

☆ Secondly, EPD can be used to desensitize a person from allergies to airborne agents such as dust and pollen as effectively as conventional immunotherapy. However, unlike conventional immunotherapy, EPD can also provide relief for those who are hypersensitive to chemical agents such as perfumes, car exhaust or solvents. It can also effectively treat all types of food allergies and many types of food intolerance.

☆ Thirdly, unlike conventional immunotherapy in which only a very few allergens in the same class can be desensitized at once, or provocation-neutralization in which only one allergen can be desensitized at once, EPD works best if the injected serum contains a very broad selection of allergens. Thus, EPD is able to desensitize patients from many different allergens all at once. This is particularly helpful for patients with food allergies and intolerances, since it is very hard to be certain as to the nature of all of the patient's sensitivities. Unlike conventional immunotherapy, which only treat Type I (immediate) hypersensitivities, EPD also appears to provide desensitization toward allergies mediated by Type I, II, III and IV hypersensitivities.

☆ Fourthly, unlike other forms of immunotherapy, which require very frequent injections that must be continued indefinitely, EPD is given quite infrequently. The typical treatment schedule for EPD is between once every four months and once per year. Although many people must continue to obtain infrequent EPD injections for decades, in some cases, they are able to completely stop all EPD within a few years.

In one double blind placebo controlled trial, EPD was shown to be effective in the treatment of ADHD in children who were previously diagnosed with food allergies. (Egger, 1992) In a more recent, yet unpublished study, EPD was found to be as effective as Ritalin® in the treatment of children with ADHD. (McEwen, 1999) This therapy is effective in those suffering from asthma, (Ippoliti, 1997) allergic rhinitis (Caramia, 1996; Di Stanislao, 1997) and other allergic diseases.

The primary disadvantages of EPD are, firstly, that there are not very many physicians currently trained to properly administer EPD in North America. Secondly, the success of EPD depends to some extent on the patient following a very carefully prescribed diet for the period of time surrounding each EPD injection (similar to the "few foods elimination diet" described at the end of Chapter 17). This diet is highly restrictive and some people will find compliance with it rather difficult, even for short periods of time. As well, significant gut dysbiosis (abnormal gut microflora) has been found to impair the success of EPD. Therefore, those with significant gut dysbiosis will have to be treated through the principles of the 4-R Program™ until their gut flora has become relatively normal before EPD can be started.

A list of physicians who are qualified for use of EPD in the U.S. and Canada can be obtained by sending a request along with a stamped, self-addressed envelope with a check or money order for $10.00 (US) to: The American EPD Society, c/o IRB Study: Physician Inquiries, 141 Paseo de Peralta, Santa Fe, NM, 87501. Only physicians who are currently participants in the North American EPD Study will be found on this list. There are other physicians, particularly in Canada and other countries, who have been trained in the use of EPD but who are not currently on this list.

In summary, restoring strength to the battered immune system is an important part of the comprehensive management of ADHD. The steps mentioned in this chapter should complement and reinforce the principles discussed in previous sections and in the chapters that follow.

Chapter 23

Feeding the Hyperactive Brain - Nutritional Management of ADHD

THE PURPOSE OF THIS CHAPTER

A good deal has already been mentioned thus far about the importance of nutrition in ADHD. In this chapter, some of the most important principles of nutrition will be summarized and clarified in order to make the application of these principles as simple and practical as possible.

HOW WELL ARE WE FEEDING OUR CHILDREN?

The diets of most children in Western societies are far from perfect. In the 1999 report of the Federal Interagency Forum on Child and Family Statistics, a large U.S. Government research agency, it was reported that most children and adolescents have a diet that is poor or needs improvement. In fact, dietary problems were found to increase significantly as children grew older. According to this research, 76 percent of children ages 2 to 5, 88 percent of children ages 6 to 12, and 94 percent of children ages 13 to 18 had a diet that was poor or needed improvement. This same report stated that 1 in 5 adolescents between 13 and 18 years of age had diets that were judged as "poor", that is, they were seriously malnourished. (www.childstats.gov) It seems rather ironic that at a time when record numbers of children and teenagers are now obese, the good majority of these same children are also malnourished.

BACK TO THE BASICS – THE FOOD PYRAMID

Improving a person's diet must start with the basics. The single biggest problem with the typical Westernized diet is an over-reliance upon packaged, processed, unnatural foods. Rebuilding the nutritional status of a child must first begin with a foundation of whole, natural foods. Junk foods, most processed foods and fast foods must be eliminated or kept to a minimum and the child must be encouraged to expand his or her palate to accept more nourishing whole foods. Constructing a family diet around the basic principles of the U.S. Department of Agriculture's Food Pyramid can provide a framework to help ensure that the diet consists of a reasonable balance of essential nutrients.

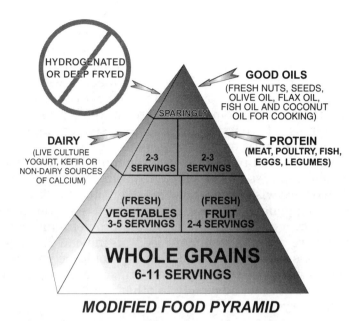

MODIFIED FOOD PYRAMID

Although the Food Pyramid provides basic direction for the construction of an optimal diet, there are some important areas which must be emphasized or modified to make this approach suitable for those with ADHD:

- **Bread, cereal, rice and pasta** should consist of whole grain foods with very few refined grain products. Sugary cereals, baked goods and white flour products, such as cakes and pastries, should be eliminated as far as possible. Whole grains provide the most important source of dietary fiber along with B vitamins, trace minerals and numerous important phytonutrients, all of which are vital for gastrointestinal, immune system and brain function. As opposed to refined flour products, which provide little more than empty calories, whole grains provide a nutrient dense source of energy. Because of their fiber, whole grains tend to fill the stomach, satisfy the appetite and help to prevent undesirable weight gain. The fiber in whole grains also slows down the absorption of sugar into the bloodstream, helping to prevent "roller coaster" blood sugar levels throughout the day.

It is important to recognize that grains can be a common source of food allergies and intolerances in those with ADHD. Wheat is the grain most commonly found to be a food allergen, probably because it is eaten with almost every meal in our culture, and perhaps because wheat is the most highly domesticated grain; having undergone hundreds of years of intensive breeding, and most recently, genetic engineering. Wheat gluten also breaks down into neurologically and immunologically active opioid peptides if not efficiently digested. Those with ADHD are wise to carefully consider the possibility that they may have a wheat hypersensitivity and should make every effort to identify this problem and reduce exposure to this common food if indicated. Related grains, such as spelt, and Kamut should be suspect as well if wheat allergy is present. In some cases, an individual will react adversely to other grains such as corn, oats, or rye.

In general, it is wise to consider using rice as a staple grain. Rice is a versatile grain that is rarely the cause of food allergy in North America. Several good allergy cookbooks provide numerous ways to add more rice to the diet. It may take time for some people to become fond of brown rice, but this is far healthier than white rice. As well, millet, quinoa, amaranth and teff are low allergy-potential grains, which are unusual to North American cuisine but can be used in many creative and delicious ways. Good old oatmeal is also a very healthy food for the intestine, especially if mixed with yogurt or probiotics.

Overcoming a reliance on breads can be one of the most difficult aspects of a restricted diet. Many people with wheat allergy will also be found to be sensitive to baker's yeast. It can be a challenge to find wheat-free, yeast-free bread with the kind of flavor and texture that most people can appreciate. Also, some of the breads which are sold as "yeast-free" are actually raised using naturally occurring yeasts which are virtually identical to baker's yeast. Flat breads, crisp breads and 100 percent sprouted grain bread are the most realistic bread alternatives for those with both wheat and yeast allergy.

Immunotherapy with enzyme potentiated desensitization (EPD) can be a tremendous benefit to those with multiple grain and yeast allergies. Multiple grain allergies can make it very difficult to maintain optimal nutritional status and to live a reasonably normal life. EPD has the potential to help many of these people to return to a diet with far fewer restrictions.(EPD is discussed in Chapter 22)

• **Vegetables** are typically the component of the diet most lacking in those with ADHD. Vegetables are an important source of fiber, vitamins, and trace minerals. As well, vegetables contain thousands of different antioxidants and other important phytochemicals, which provide protection for physiological processes and give the strength to the immune system. Many kids with ADHD are picky eaters who will shun many of the most important vegetables. Research has shown that many children and teenagers get the majority of their "vegetables" in the form of French fries and potato chips. This is certainly no substitute for fresh, nutrient dense vegetables. It is well worth making the effort to find creative ways of presenting vegetables to children; making them as attractive and tasty as possible. One of the best tricks to increase the intake of vegetables in a family is to get into the habit of setting out a tray covered with plenty of cut up vegetables, such as carrot, celery, broccoli and cauliflower, along with a tasty, nutritious dip. If this tray is placed on the kitchen table or counter after school and again after supper, kids (and adults) will soon get into the habit of snacking on healthy vegetables. As long as the junk food is either absent from the house or at least put well out of the way, the convenience of having vegetables within easy reach will eventually entice most family members to eat plenty of these healthy snacks.

- **Fruits** are also a very important part of a healthy diet, providing many vital micronutrients and phytochemicals. Unfortunately, many kids load up on sugary fruit juices and eat very little fresh fruit. Although small amounts of pure fruit juice are fine, children and adults also need plenty of fresh fruit.

To make matters more complicated, it is now becoming quite clear that fruits and vegetables are common source of neurotoxic pesticides and herbicides. If it is within a family's budget, consideration should be given for buying only organic fruits and vegetables. In most areas, there is now an excellent selection of organic produce in grocery stores as well as natural food markets. Going organic certainly costs more money but research has now shown that you do get what to pay for. Not only do you avoid toxic herbicides and pesticides when you buy organic, you also get produce that is tastier and loaded with micronutrients. For some time, our family has been on a program, which for a modest weekly fee, provides us with a great selection of organic fruits and vegetables all year round, delivered right to our door. The taste of fresh, organic produce is so good that our kids have increased their intake without much effort on our part at all. Similar programs are available in most North American towns and cities.

- **Dairy products** can be an important source of calcium, protein and certain vitamins. Unfortunately, a good proportion of children with ADHD will be found to have an allergy or intolerance to dairy foods. In some cases, dairy sensitivities will diminish once a leaky gut has been resolved and several months have passed in which dairy has been carefully avoided. At this point, many previously dairy intolerant people will be able to safely consume modest amounts of live culture yogurt or kefir. Yogurt is the least allergenic of all dairy foods and the probiotic bacteria may help to rebuild the immune system and could contribute to a reduction in allergic responsiveness over time. In Europe and Australia, yogurt is now available that has been fermented using proven probiotic species such as Lactobacillus rhamnosis

(GG). Hopefully, these "functional foods" will become available in North America in the near future. Until then, everyone can easily make their own yogurt fortified with proven probiotic species.

- **High protein foods** such as legumes, poultry, fish and meat are an indispensable part of the diet for those with ADHD. Lack of protein in a meal can contribute to wide swings of blood sugar and can affect mood and behavior quite significantly. Protein also supplies the amino acids which are used to manufacture neurotransmitters such as dopamine, norepinephrine and serotonin. Unfortunately, many children are sent to school after eating a high carbohydrate, low protein breakfast. This is certainly one of the most common contributors to behavioral and cognitive problems in children.

  As well, many kids end up eating junk food such as French fries, candy bars and pop for lunch. This can send their blood sugar on a roller coaster ride all afternoon. Protein should be evenly distributed throughout the day. Eating marginal amounts of protein for breakfast and lunch and then having huge amounts of meat for supper is not ideal. Excessive protein in one meal will not be properly digested and may result in excessive amounts of nitrogenous waste in the bloodstream and gut.

  Protein containing foods should also be fresh. Deli meats, wieners, and other prepared meats are quite unhealthy. Other than homemade or low-fat, preservative free sausages, meats should be fresh or fresh frozen and unprocessed. All meats should be low-fat and cooked with the least amount of fat possible. Deep-fried foods such as chicken fingers or battered fish should be avoided.

  Since meat may be a great reservoir for pesticides, herbicides and possibly hormone and antibiotic residues, eating organically grown poultry and meat is best. Fish is a highly nutritious source of protein, which can be very high in essential fatty acids. However, many fish are now contaminated with neurotoxic mercury, PCB's or other chemicals and should be eaten with caution. This is particularly true of most freshwater fish as well as large, predatory fish like tuna.

- **Fats and oils** are best consumed sparingly. The emphasis should be on avoiding excessive saturated fat, all hydrogenated fats and most vegetable oils if they are processed (flax and olive are exceptions). Supplementation of the low fat diet with sources of omega 3 essential fatty acids and smaller amounts of the omega 6 essential fatty acid, GLA (evening primrose, borage or black currant seed) is generally advisable in ADHD. Fresh nuts and seeds can make up a reasonable proportion of the fats consumed. High omega-3 flax seed oil (in dark bottles, stored in a refrigerator) can be mixed with olive oil as the base of a healthy salad dressing. Flax seed oil can also form the basis of a tasty vegetable dip. Fish oils and evening primrose oil are available in capsule form to supplement essential fatty acid intake. Carlson Laboratories makes a cod liver oil which is processed with special methods in Norway. This is the only cod liver oil I have ever encountered that would be palatable to many children. The best oil to use (in moderation) for light frying, such as for stir frys, is coconut oil. This is an easily digested and assimilated oil that does not spoil when heated. (Coconut oil is available at health food stores)

BREAKING BAD HABITS AND BUILDING GOOD ONES

The three primary symptoms of ADHD (hyperactivity, impulsivity and inattentiveness) can affect a persons nutritional status in a number of ways. ADHD affected people tend to be too busy to take the time to plan menus or prepare proper meals. When your life is a whirlwind, it is much easier to "fly by" the drive-through at your favorite hamburger joint than to plan ahead and bring a proper lunch to work. It is also easier to give your kids lunch money than to send them to school with nutritious homemade food. Kids with ADHD may also find it very hard to slow down long enough to eat a decent meal or drink enough water to avoid dehydration. People with ADHD can also make food choices impulsively, instead of using common sense to make decisions as to what they should eat. It is easy to pull into the fast food restaurant, order the "full meal deal", swallow it all in 5 minutes and then later wonder what compelled you to eat that awful stuff again.

People with ADHD are also prone to developing compulsive behaviors or addictions. This is commonly seen even in young children who seem to crave certain foods with an inordinate passion. Food preferences can easily become food addictions unless the behaviors are recognized and efforts are made to modify these potentially destructive habits. Unfortunately, food addictions are often towards unhealthy foods and they may be a manifestation of food allergies. Like any addiction, it is very unhealthy to have your life ruled by a compulsive behavior. Breaking bad eating habits and compulsive food behaviors is an important part of the nutritional management of ADHD. In children, food addictions are most often toward junk foods, dairy products or wheat products. Adults can share the same compulsions but are also prone to becoming hooked on drug containing foods and beverages such as chocolate and coffee. Like any addiction, breaking these habits can be a painful process for a while. However, the dividends in better health can make the sacrifices well worthwhile.

Several years ago, important research was conducted by Dr. W.E. Conner of the University of Oregon under the support of the National Institutes of Health. (Conner, 1986) The purpose of this research was to determine a means by which families could be motivated to improve their eating habits and then keep these good habits permanently. One of the interesting facts which emerged from this research was that the typical North American family consumes an average of ten favorite recipes to obtain the majority of their daily calories. Dr. Conner's research determined that by simply exchanging those ten, family-favorite recipes with ten new, completely healthy ones they all enjoyed, you could permanently change the whole family's eating habits without any sort of "special diet". This seems like such a simple principle and yet it makes all the difference in the world. I have adapted these same principles to the work that I have done with people suffering from all sorts of medical conditions in which dietary change is vital. People with heart disease, diabetes, food allergies, obesity, ADHD and any other medical condition, can all permanently change their eating habits if they simply learn to prepare a wide enough selection of acceptable snacks, main meals, beverages and deserts. With this new knowlege, they will be able to continue to enjoy eating and still be on the diet that is right for them.

In a recent research project, we worked with the parents of 50 kids with ADHD with the goal of helping them radically change their childrens' diets. This diet eliminated junk foods and a long list of potentially allergenic foods. It also required that their kids ate lots of fresh fruits and vegetables, increased their fiber intake and drank lots of water. I recall the evening that we first met with the parents to explain to them the dietary restrictions that would be necessary for participation in our study. There were a lot of gloomy looking faces as people began to imagine the difficulty they would have trying to make such drastic changes to their families' diets. At the end of that first session, I told people to relax about all of these restrictions over the next week and to trust me that things would work out. Their only requirement that first week was to make one recipe for the potluck dinner we would be having at the beginning of next week's class. As they left, I handed everyone a recipe. The next week, they all arrived and set out their dishes. We probably had at least 25 different recipes for everyone to try. Each person filled their plate and sat down. As they started to sample the food, the sound level in the room rose as people realized that they were enjoying a feast composed of delicious foods that were all perfectly "legal" on our restrictive diet. Within a few minutes, our glum crowd was transformed into a group of raving enthusiasts. For the next several weeks, we continued the same format with a potluck dinner at the beginning of each class. It was truly gratifying to see how, with a few simple tools, people were able to break their children's junk food habits, remove the most commonly allergenic foods and dramatically increase the nutritional quality of their family's diet. With a little knowledge and reasonable collection of tasty recipes, people were empowered to make genuine and lasting changes to their lifestyle. It is over a year later and we often encounter people from our study group who tell us that the dietary changes transformed their child's life and their whole family's health has improved.

THE "PERFECT" ADHD DIET

The process of identifying and avoiding allergic or intolerant foods is the most time consuming and difficult part of the individualized ADHD diet. This process is discussed in Chapter 17 and will not be reviewed here, but it should be emphasized that there is no one diet that is suitable for everyone with ADHD. However, a significant majority of ADHD sufferers will benefit immensely from a nutrient rich, whole foods based diet in which junk foods, food derived toxins (such as food additives and pesticides) and commonly allergenic foods are eliminated (the standard "elimination test diet" described in Chapter 17). If this highly restricted diet is shown to be of real benefit after 4-8 weeks, the "open food challenge" process can be used to help determine which restrictions are really needed. If conducted carefully, the open food challenge process should be able to make it clear which foods need to be avoided in the long term. Apart from avoiding allergenic or intolerant foods, everyone with ADHD should plan to remain on a junk food restricted, whole foods based diet for the rest of their lives.

Many of the best recipes you will encounter in your quest for the ideal ADHD diet will be derived from ethnic cuisines, which have followed cultures that are hundreds or thousands of years old. The basic staples of the traditional Mexican diet (not greasy "Tex-Mex" food) as well as the many different forms of Asian cooking (not Americanized Chinese food) can bring new and exciting flavors to the table, while being low in allergy potential and full of nutrition. Instead of relying on chemicals, fat, sugar and artificial flavors, authentic ethnic foods often have a perfect balance of macronutrients, lots of fiber, plenty of fresh vegetables and natural herbs and spices, which possess a wide range of medicinal benefits. Some of these flavors take a while to get used to, but even children can learn to love many ethnic foods if they are exposed to them often enough. Since children learn by imitating their parents, it is important for parents to set good examples by eating a healthy, nutrient rich diet themselves.

I have been on this sort of diet for the past 22 years and my wife and children eat the same foods as well. Although it used to be a sacrifice to avoid so many delectable treats and eat only wholesome, natural foods, we know that the benefits in terms of good health make this kind of eating worthwhile. It is not just the brain that benefits from wholesome eating; a diet that keeps your gut, immune system and brain happy and healthy is also one that wards off chronic disease and cancer, while slowing down the aging process. There may be some sacrifices to make in order to break bad eating habits and abandon the standard North American diet, but they are small in comparison to the improvements you and your family will experience in health, both now and in the decades to come. Taking the time to learn a new ways of cooking and eating is one of the best investments of your time you will ever make.

Everyone Needs Healthy Snacks

Snack foods are a multi-billion dollar industry in the Western world. We have all been saturated with a marketing campaign designed to promote snack foods, which is second to none (except, perhaps, that used by the tobacco industry). Unfortunately, not only are most snack foods just empty calories, most of them contain ingredients that are downright harmful. It is certainly worth the effort to find tasty, yet healthy alternatives to common commercial junk food. With a little effort, some study and some practice any family can have a wide selection of healthy snacks that will suit children and adults alike.

The first choice for healthy snacking should be fresh fruits and vegetables. Parents need to make the effort to find the fruits and vegetables that their children are willing to accept. Three things are necessary to increase the likelihood that children will eat plenty of fruits and vegetables for snacks. Firstly, they should be the most conveniently available foods especially at the times when children want snacks. Always having a full fruit bowl in the most visible area of the house is one step that will help. Even better, parents can prepare fruit by cutting it up in small pieces and placing it on the table with a tasty dip. Flavored yogurt is a great fruit dip for anyone who is not hypersensitive to this food. Nut creams are also a great fruit dip. These are made by blending fresh nuts or seeds with a little honey and some water to make a creamy treat for dipping fruit pieces. Vegetables should also be routinely cut up and placed on a plate beside a favorite healthy dip. A little flax oil mixed with some Spike® (a natural seasoning salt) is one of our family's favorite healthy vegetable dips. After school is a great time to put out cut up fruits, vegetables and dip.

Smoothies are also one of the best ways to give kids or adults a treat that is just loaded with good nutrition. A good smoothie starts with a healthy base. This is usually some sort of protein powder. Most protein powders are made from milk or egg protein, which have a high allergenic potential. Hydrolyzed whey protein is also made from milk but it is partially digested and is not as likely to be allergenic as undigested milk protein (casein). Soy protein is also available but many children with milk allergies will also have sensitivities to soy. The most suitable smoothie bases for most individuals with ADHD are powders made from rice protein. Plain rice protein is available from most health food stores but it is lacking in the amino acids L-lysine, and L-threonine and it is low in sulfur amino acids as well. Thus, unfortified rice protein is not a very high quality protein source either.

The UltraBalance® line of products, made by the company HealthComm, Inc. are the most useful and nutritious products that can serve as the base of a delicious smoothie. (www.UltraBalance.com) These products are powders made from purified rice protein and carbohydrate. Importantly the rice protein in these products has been fortified with the amino acids L-lysine, L-threonine and various sulfur amino acids. Thus, these products are a very high quality source of very low allergy potential protein. They also have additional vitamins, minerals and other important nutrients to increase their therapeutic potential. Ultracare for Kids™ is the product in this line which has been designed especially for children with allergies. Ultracare for Kids™ is a rice-based powder with added vitamins, and minerals that is designed to have an extremely low allergy potential and to be highly palatable for children. It also has added DHA (the brain critical omega-3 fatty acid), calcium (for kids who are allergic to dairy) and fructooligosaccharides (FOS, the pre-biotic carbohydrate which selectively promotes the growth of desirable intestinal bacteria).

In our research, we found that children readily except smoothies made from Ultracare for Kids™. The most acceptable way to prepare this is to place Ultracare for Kids™ in a blender and then add a generous serving of frozen fruit (blueberries, strawberries, raspberries, peaches, grapes or pears). Add some additional sweetener (either a small bit of honey or some powdered stevia, a natural calorie-free sweetener), and water, and blend to a smooth consistency. As an alternative, fruit juice could be added to provide liquid and additional sweetness instead of another sweetener. The frozen fruit not only adds flavor and additional nutrition; the ice crystals provide a slushy texture which kids really love.

Once kids begin to like these basic smoothies, additional nutrients can be "snuck in" to make this an even more nutrient dense snack. One of the best things to add to a smoothie is one of the powdered "green foods" such as freeze-dried barley, wheat or Kamut grass juice. Other than giving the smoothie a strange green color, these powdered foods take away only a little from the good taste while adding a tremendous source of healthy phytonutrients. Fresh vegetables such as a carrot or a piece of celery can also be added to the smoothie to provide additional nutrients and extra fiber. Ground flax seed is also another inexpensive way to add extra fiber to a tasty smoothie. Taking the time to experiment with different smoothie recipes is certainly worth while, and can be an easy way to dramatically increase the nutritional content of a child's (or adult's) diet while providing a delicious alternative to after school junk foods. Smoothies can also be used as a quick and easy meal replacement for busy people who don't have the time to prepare a proper meal. For years, I have used smoothies for snacks, before workouts and for meal replacements when I'm in a rush. I would guess that over the years I have probably saved myself from eating thousands of fast food meals because I am in the habit of grabbing a smoothie when I'm in a rush instead of stopping at the drive-through or eating some other sort of junk food.

NUTRITIONAL SUPPLEMENTS FOR THOSE WITH ADHD

As discussed in Chapters 7 and 8 there is evidence that those with ADHD commonly have marginal deficiencies of several nutrients. As well, because of their unique physiology and the stresses that their body must endure, these same people often have a need for a higher level of several key nutrients than those who are unaffected by ADHD. Many children with ADHD, when examined by an astute healthcare practitioner, will be found to have significant nutritional deficiencies that will need to be corrected through targeted nutritional supplementation. Many people may also choose to place themselves or their child on a reasonable nutritional supplement program as part of their efforts to optimize their nutritional status, and to help ensure that their brain and immune system have ideal levels of every nutrient required for optimal performance. Supplements can in no way replace the basic principles of nutrition that have been discussed earlier in this chapter. However, many of those with ADHD experience noticeable benefits when their nutritional status is boosted by a wisely chosen selection of supplements. A healthcare practitioner knowledgeable in the principles of Functional Medicine is your best resource to help construct an intelligent supplement program for you or your child. The basic elements of this program would generally include some of the following supplements:

(The amount of each supplement is a typical adult dosage. Dosages for children are generally less and will vary depending upon their age and weight. Please note that significant toxicity can occur with excessive doses of vitamin A, vitamin D, and with some minerals, including iron, zinc, selenium, chromium, copper, manganese, and molybdenum.)

BASIC NUTRITIONAL SUPPLEMENT PROGRAM FOR ADHD

- **Antioxidant support** using:
  - Vitamin C (500-3000 mg per day)
  - Vitamin E (200-400 IU per day)
  - Grape seed extract or Pycnogenol (50-200 mg per day)

- **Multivitamin/mineral supplement** should supply:*
  - Vitamin A or beta carotene (5,000 – 20,000 IU per day)
  - Vitamin D (100-400 IU per day)
  - B vitamins including B1 (thiamin, 20-100 mg per day); B2 (riboflavin, 20-100 mg per day); niacin (10-50 mg per day); B5 (pantothenic acid, 50-200 mg per day); B6 (pyridoxine, 20-75 mg per day); folic acid (500-1000 micrograms per day);
  - Minerals including zinc (5-50 mg per day); selenium (50-200 micrograms per day); chromium (50-200 micrograms per day); manganese (0.5-1 mg per day); molybdenum (50-100 micorgrams per day); copper (1-2 mg per day)

*Note that children with ADHD often have unusually high requirements for vitamins B1 (thiamine), B6 (pyridoxine), zinc and chromium. These children will also often benefit from supplemental iron (usually 15-30 mg per day is a reasonable level of supplementation for those who are not anemic). Adults with ADHD should generally not take iron supplementation.

- **Calcium supplementation** is often given in addition to any which may be contained in a multivitamin. People should generally avoid calcium carbonate, bone meal, dolomite, and oyster shell since these are often contaminated with lead. Certified lead-free calcium hydroxyapatite or most calcium citrates are generally safe, well-absorbed sources of calcium. Of course, children need plenty of calcium, especially if they are on a dairy free diet. Most people can safely take 400-750 mg of calcium per day in addition to their diet. More may be required for those who don't eat dairy products.

• **Magnesium supplementation** is often given in addition to that which may be supplied in a multivitamin. Magnesium citrate is a well-absorbed form of magnesium and should be given in dosages of 200-600 mg per day for children and 400-800 mg per day in adults (amount in mg refers to elemental magnesium).

• **Essential fatty acid supplementation** can be obtained from flax seed oil (omega-3 ALA) in dosages of 1-2 tablespoons per day. Find creative ways of adding this to food such as an ingredient in salad dressings, an addition to hot or cold cereal (don't cook with it), an addition to smoothies, or mixed 50-50 with butter as a spread. Additional brain-critical omega-3 fatty acids should be supplied through fish oil (salmon, sardines or tuna oil). Cod liver oil is a good source of omega-3 fatty acids but it is usually rancid and, as such, is probably not the best way to get fish oil (the exception is the cod liver oil from Carlson Laboratories). Fresh, non-rancid cod liver oil should be virtually tasteless and thus should be reasonably palatable for children. Cod liver oil also supplies high amounts of vitamins A and D so caution should be exercised to avoid toxicity from overdosing on these fat-soluble vitamins.

There is some evidence that those with ADHD may benefit from supplementation with the omega-6 fatty acid known as GLA. This fatty acid is found in evening primrose oil, black current seed oil and borage seed oil. These are usually taken in capsule form although they can be found in combination with flax oil in bottles for use on food. Perhaps the most intelligent way to supplement essential fatty acids is with new products containing a combination of fish oil and evening primrose oil. These products are usually in small capsules, which are easier for children to swallow. Most children with ADHD take 6-8 small capsules per day for the first 6 weeks and then decrease to 4 capsules per day.

The above description is a summary of some of the most basic and essential aspects of a supplement program to improve the nutritional status of those with ADHD. This is certainly not an all-inclusive list of every supplement that may provide benefits in ADHD. There are other supplements, such as the probiotics discussed in chapter 21 and the herbal medicines discussed in chapter 20, which are highly therapeutic and are used commonly in addition to basic nutritional supplements.

This chapter is intended to provide you with some common sense guidelines to help rebuild your or your child's nutritional status. Nutritional factors are certainly one of the most important pieces of the ADHD puzzle. Investments of time and effort made in this area are likely to have many very significant long-term benefits.

Chapter 24
Purifying the Toxic Brain

THE MILLENNIUM OF THE ENVIRONMENT

As we embark upon this new millennium, we leave behind a century of unprecedented environmental change. Over the past five decades, industrialization has expanded at a phenomenal rate while the human population has exploded. Over this same period, habitat destruction and environmental contamination has resulted in the mass extinction of hundreds of animal and plant species. As well, emerging diseases, fertility problems and malformations now threaten the survival of thousands of different species.

Humans have not escaped the impact of these changes. Global warming has contributed to catastrophic weather patterns, which have resulted in homelessness for tens of millions of people. While the rate of the world's human population continues to explode, it is the Earth's most impoverished citizens who are primarily contributing to this trend. Many predict this trend will soon be restrained by widespread famine, epidemics of infectious disease and a decrease in human fertility in the third world. (Nentwig, 1999)

Those of us who are fortunate enough to live in the prosperous nations of the developed world are also facing health challenges such as a dramatic rise in the incidence of cancer, migraine headaches, allergies and asthma. (Samet, 1995) The prescribing rate for ADHD has increased more rapidly than virtually any other disease. Recent research in the U.S. suggests that as many as 20 percent of boys are currently taking Ritalin® by the time they reach grade 5. (LeFever, 1999) These astounding figures sent shockwaves through the medical and psychiatric community with most authorities concluding that ADHD is being over-diagnosed. However, it is equally as probable that we have entered an era in which the human race is now being impacted by a century of environmental degradation and that this is partly to blame for the apparent deterioration of our children's brain function. It is vital that we each take steps to protect our brains from the very real threat imposed by our increasingly poisoned environment. We simply cannot wait until all of the "proof is in" before we take measures to guard our delicate brains from neurotoxic pollution.

THE NEUROTOXIC GENERATION

In Chapter 6, some of the many sources of common neurotoxins were described. Individuals may be at risk from the effects of neurotoxins because they are genetically susceptible, because they have a high level of exposure or because their nutritional status is sub-optimal. As well, neurotoxins seldom work in isolation. Most people who are affected by neurotoxic stress are actually experiencing the result of many toxic factors working together in an evil sort of synergy. It should also be recalled that microbes, stress hormones, electromagnetic fields and immunologically generated molecules also have the potential to impose additional toxic stress upon sensitive regions of the brain.

In the Functional Medicine model of ADHD, it is the additive effects of many potentially neurotoxic influences that lead to the disruption of brain neurotransmitters and may even result in impaired development of structural components of the brain. Neurotoxic stress upon the highly developed and very sensitive executive centers within the prefrontal cortex of the brain is the final common pathway leading to the various symptoms associated with ADHD.

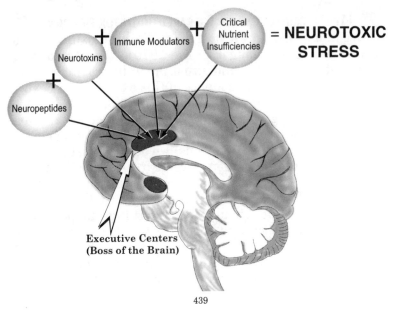

Effective and lasting treatment for ADHD must focus upon the identification and elimination of as many of these neurologically impairing effects as possible. Antioxidant and neuroprotective herbal medicines, along with the 4R-Program™ of gastrointestinal rehabilitation, nutritional optimization and other aspects of nervous and immune system support, all help to lessen the neurotoxic stress imposed upon the brain. However, further efforts can be made to lessen the impact of neurotoxins through a key Functional Medicine intervention referred to as **therapeutic detoxification**.

THE CONCEPT OF THERAPEUTIC DETOXIFICATION

Although foreign to conventional medicine, the concept of purification or detoxification has been central to almost every healing tradition throughout history. Only recently, have certain scientific thinkers begun to consider that there may be validity to some of these ancient concepts. As the evidence mounts, implicating accumulated environmental toxins in the rising incidence of many diseases, there are strong reasons to believe that therapeutic detoxification will likely become increasingly accepted as a vital component in the prevention and treatment of many disorders.

MY EXPERIENCES WITH THERAPEUTIC DETOXIFICATION

I have had a keen interest in therapeutic detoxification for many years. As a teenager in the 1970's, I began to study various methods that would assist me in improving my own brain function. As a consequence of this exploration, I experimented with numerous "cleansing programs" and different methods of fasting. On one occasion, I fasted for 21 days, drinking only water and eating no food at all during this entire period. On other occasions, I would subsist for 2 to 3 weeks on only diluted lemon juice or fresh fruit. Because of the very real benefits I experienced from these personal experiments, I came to believe strongly in the power of detoxification. Although many other things helped me to overcome my physical and cognitive problems, therapeutic detoxification made a very important contribution. Since that time, I have learned much more about the science of detoxification and I have been thankful that there are now methods of detoxification which are safer and more effective than traditional fasting programs and involve far less discomfort as well. Every few months, when my energy levels have ebbed low or my brain function seems diminished, I will spend a few days participating in a scientifically designed therapeutic detoxification program. Once this program is over, the lingering increase in vitality and clarity of mind makes the small sacrifice required to undergo this program well worthwhile. In addition to the benefits I have received personally from regular therapeutic detoxification, I have now witnessed, through the work that I have done at our clinical and research facility on Vancouver Island, the value of this approach in the lives of scores of people who suffer from various chronic illnesses.

FUNCTIONAL MEDICINE AND THERAPEUTIC DETOXIFICATION
Functional Medicine has contributed greatly to our current understanding of detoxification from a scientific perspective. Scientists at the Institute for Functional Medicine in Gig Harbor, Washington have been surveying the scientific literature and conducting clinical research into the practical application of therapeutic detoxification as a treatment for numerous medical conditions. Over the past couple of years, I have had the opportunity to participate in the education of physicians at this center as a visiting lecturer in the new field of **Functional Toxicology**. This new branch of Functional Medicine combines some of the valid principles used in traditional detoxification methods with what science has taught us about how the body is affected by toxins, and how we can support and assist the body's natural detoxification mechanisms. When properly applied, a scientifically designed program of therapeutic detoxification can bring about near miraculous improvements in patients with chronic fatigue syndrome, fibromyalgia, ADHD and a host of other chronic disorders.

BASIC PRINCIPLES OF FUNCTIONAL TOXICOLOGY

Many of the most puzzling conditions regularly encountered by healthcare practitioners could be helped significantly if the practitioner was aware of the contribution that toxicological factors can make in human illness. Making an effort to lessen the individual's exposure to all known toxic stressors and providing ongoing support for more efficient detoxification can be considered as a part of the standard approach to ADHD, even in the absence of specific toxicological test results. However, a thorough clinical assessment followed by selected toxicological testing can help to pinpoint the specific nature and severity of toxicological stresses in the individual ADHD sufferer and may allow for more effective interventions. Some of the basic principles of Functional Toxicology are presented below:

- **Identify and remove or reduce all significant sources of toxicity.** This should be the first phase of any therapeutic detoxification program. For example, reducing exposure to neurotoxic pesticides and other chemicals can be considered to be a prudent step that anyone can make, particularly for those with ADHD. In some cases, common sense can dictate some of the steps that should be taken in this regard. For instance, replacing pesticide contaminated produce with organically grown varieties is an example of how this principle might be applied. Similarly, if a person smokes or uses illicit drugs, the first step in their detoxification program should be a commitment to ending their self-destructive habits.

Other toxic stressors may only be apparent after reliable testing. For instance, if a child is found to have elevated blood lead levels, efforts must be made to identify the source of lead contamination and remove the child from the lead contaminated environment. Similarly, if a person is discovered to be mercury toxic, mercury-containing dental amalgams should be carefully removed by a dentist trained in the principles of "biological dentistry".

• **Optimize nutrition to provide support for the body's natural detoxification mechanisms.** Genetic factors result in a widespread variation in individual abilities to detoxify and excrete heavy metals and organic toxins. However, there are also several modifiable factors that can be adjusted to optimize a person's ability to deal with toxic stress:

Optimize the intake of nutritional minerals. For instance, toxic metals "chemically compete" inside the body with nutritional minerals. Poisonous elements such as lead, mercury, cadmium, arsenic, and aluminum tend to displace nutritional minerals from their positions on enzymes and other regions of the cell. (Goyer, 1997) Because of this, individuals whose intake of nutritional minerals (especially iron, calcium, zinc, selenium and magnesium) is sub-optimal or deficient are at a much greater risk of heavy metal toxicity than people whose intake of these nutrients is ideal. It is interesting to note that these are the same nutritional minerals that have been shown to have an important relationship to the severity of ADHD. Supplementation with these minerals has been shown to improve ADHD symptoms in a number of studies. This simple intervention may improve the symptoms of ADHD, at least in part, by helping the body to resist the absorption of various toxic metals as well as improving the efficiency of their excretion. Remember, however, that while iron supplementation can be of great value in children, athletes and women with heavy menstrual periods, it should be avoided in other groups because it can accumulate to excess and become a source of toxic stress.

Balancing macronutrients (carbohydrate, protein and fat) is important in the proper functioning of the liver's detoxification mechanisms. Efficient detoxification is an energy dependent process requiring a consistent and adequate intake of high quality protein. On the other hand, high carbohydrate, low protein diets tend to suppress liver detoxification and may contribute to a more rapid accumulation of organic toxins such as pesticides and solvent residues. (Guengerich, 1995) This is one more reason why those who regularly consume junk food, like refined carbohydrates, are likely to suffer the consequences of significant neurotoxic stress!

Increase fiber intake. Dietary fiber serves an important role in helping to make detoxification an effective process. Certain types of dietary fiber stimulate liver detoxification activity, making it more efficient. (Roland, 1994) Fiber also binds to various toxins in the gut, neutralizing them and preventing their absorption. Many of the toxins processed by the liver are put into the bile and then expelled into the small intestine. If there is inadequate fiber in the gut, many of the toxins present in bile will be reabsorbed back into the body through the small intestine. Dietary fiber minimizes this effect because it binds to and then escorts the toxins out of the body in the stool.

Eat lots of fruits and vegetables. Fruits and vegetables provide natural phytochemicals, many of which stimulate and support efficient detoxification. (Kitts, 1994) Compounds in onion and garlic, cruciferous vegetables (broccoli, cauliflower, cabbage, Brussels sprouts), citrus fruits, green tea, grapes and numerous other fruits and vegetables have a major impact upon the efficiency of detoxification processes.

•Optimize the lifestyle for efficient detoxification
Regular exercise actually results in a healthy enlargement of the liver with a resulting increase in the liver's capacity for detoxification. Exercise also increases the transport of toxins from the organs to the liver and kidneys where they can be excreted. Sweating also provides an efficient route of elimination for many toxins. Because of these and other factors, sedentary people are far more likely to suffer significant neurotoxic stress than those who maintain a high level of physical fitness. (Yiamouyiannis, 1992; Duncan, 1997) Stress management also diminishes the production of stress hormones which

place a great deal of toxic stress on the brain and immune system.

- **Optimize gastrointestinal function** through the 4-R Program. Food allergies, leaky gut and intestinal dysbiosis (overgrowth of harmful microbes) all place tremendous stress upon the liver and can result in a marked decrease in the efficiency of detoxification. (Veihelman, 1997; Salzman, 1995) On the other hand, supplementation with probiotic bacteria can greatly diminish stress upon the liver and may result in a significant improvement in detoxification activity. (Nanji, 1994)

POTENTIAL DRAWBACKS OF TRADITIONAL FASTING

Once the basic principles of Functional Toxicology have been successfully implemented and integrated into a person's lifestyle, consideration should be given for undergoing a more intensive therapeutic detoxification program. Some individuals may consider completing a traditional water fast, a juice fast or some other form of therapeutic detoxification. Although such programs may provide some real benefits, they also have some distinct limitations and may even prove harmful to certain people. Firstly, traditional forms of fasting are not advisable for children or growing adolescents, and therefore, are not a suitable aspect of treatment for youngsters with ADHD. As well, these forms of fasting rely on severe caloric deprivation and the absence of dietary protein and fat to bring about a rapid release of stored toxins from tissues, such as the fat cells, muscle and intestines. Within the first 24 hours of a traditional fast, lean body tissue starts to be consumed to keep blood sugar stable, and about 40 percent of all calories burned will come from muscle and organs like the liver, heart, and intestines. Since much more than fat is lost during a fast, it is not a suitable method for bringing about weight loss. I had to learn this the hard way. After my 21 day fast, I was so skinny that many people thought I was dying of cancer. It took 2 years of weight lifting to build muscle back onto my body after such a prolonged fast. My brain worked better than ever after this intensive water fast, but my body was really weakened.

Although traditional water or juice fasting may indeed help to mobilize stored toxins, getting them out of organs and into circulation, it provides no nutritional support for the liver's detoxification activities. Recall from Chapter 16 that liver detoxification is two-phase process, which is highly dependent upon the provision of energy and specific supportive nutrients. If toxins are released in high amounts from tissues and are then captured by the liver for detoxification, these toxins will place the liver under significant toxic stress with no dietary support to enable detoxification to proceed efficiently. In fact, the people who need the benefits of detoxification the most are the ones who are more likely to be harmed by traditional fasting. If an individual has very high body burdens of various toxic substances, the liver is already overburdened by toxic stress. If that person fasts and does not provide the liver with adequate nutritional support during this process, significant discomfort or serious illness is likely to result. I have had communication with researchers from an Australian university who have studied the effect of detoxification on patients with chronic fatigue syndrome. If such patients are admitted the hospital and placed on a complete water fast, their liver enzymes become markedly elevated with 24 hours, indicating that serious liver inflammation is occurring. If the same people are given specific nutrients to support liver detoxification, no liver inflammation occurs during their fasting program.

Having a good deal of personal experience with many traditional forms of fasting, I would say that if a person is well prepared and is willing to endure intense discomfort, traditional fasting programs may still be of benefit in some cases. However, for the past several years I have studied and become personally acquainted with a more scientific and sensible approach to therapeutic detoxification, which has been developed by researchers in the field of Functional Medicine. After having completed numerous Functional Medicine based detoxification programs and witnessing scores of people do the same, I can say with certainty that such an approach involves much less discomfort and provides superior benefits when compared to other forms of traditional fasting or cleansing.

The first few days of this scientific detoxification program can still be accompanied by some discomfort. This is particularly true in individuals with significant food allergies. Since this program involves the elimination of all commonly allergenic foods, people with food allergies may have withdrawal-like symptoms for up to 10 days when these foods are first removed from the diet. Enduring through these difficult few days and finishing the program can leave a person feeling far better than they have in many years.

A FUNCTIONAL MEDICINE BASED THERAPEUTIC DETOXIFICATION PROGRAM

•**Dietary Component:** The Functional Medicine approach to therapeutic detoxification begins with the prescription of a therapeutic medical food product known as UltraClear™ Plus. (Rigden, 1995; Bland, 1995; Bland, 1996) This medical food is made from a hypoallergenic purified rice protein, which naturally contains high amounts of glutamic acid, the nutrient most important for small intestinal cell function. It also contains rice-derived carbohydrate and several nutrients that are known to support liver detoxification activities, including N-acetyl cysteine, L-glutathione, glycine, taurine, inorganic sulfate and phytochemicals from green tea. This product contains high enough quantities of vitamins and trace minerals that most other food supplements can be stopped while therapeutic detoxification is taking place. UltraClear™ Plus is primarily available through healthcare practitioners and some pharmacies. (Further information about UltraClear™ Plus can be found at www.UltraBalance.com or www.PureLiving.com.)

In order for detoxification to take place effectively, all food that enters the body must be free of toxins and commonly allergenic substances. UltraClear™ Plus has been tested and found to be extremely low in its allergenic potential. It is even well tolerated by most people who suffer from multiple food allergies. UltraClear™ Plus is generally taken 2 to 5 times per day in water, juice or as the base of the smoothie blended with frozen fruit. Certainly most people will find this product most palatable if they make it up as part of a delicious smooth-ie. Other ingredients, such as flax oil, "green powders", hypoallergenic dietary fiber, probiotic powders and the natural sweetener, Stevia, can be added to enhance the flavor and therapeutic value of the smoothie. In our facil-ity, the low allergy fiber supplement known as UltraFiber™ is prescribed as an ingredient in the UltraClear™ Plus smoothies to increase fiber intake without adding any allergenic stress.

In most cases, the UltraClear™ Plus is consumed three times per day (breakfast, lunch and evening snack). Fresh, organic fruits or vegetables may be eaten as a mid-morning and mid-afternoon snack. Usually, a very simple evening meal is prepared with brown rice, steamed vegetables and lean broiled meat or cooked dry beans. People are free to use natural herbs, onions and garlic to season this meal. Other foods may be eaten for the evening meal, but they must be kept very simple and must all be very low in their allergenic potential. Booklets containing food suggestions usually accompany the UltraClear™ Plus.

Although the allowed evening meals are very simple, they can be made tasty enough that the whole family can participate in this part of the program. Those family members who don't wish to complete an intensive thera-peutic detoxification program may eat their regular meals for breakfast and lunch and then share a low aller-gy meal for supper. Parents, who wish to help their ADHD affected child undergo therapeutic detoxification, may elect to follow the full program themselves in order to empathize with and encourage their child while expe-riencing the benefits of this program as well.

Care should taken to avoid overeating while on this pro-gram. Although this is not a weight loss program, mild caloric restriction is advised in order to draw from the body's fat stores. A good deal of the body's stored toxins are bound up in fat cells and mild caloric restriction will help to draw from these stores. Interestingly, most people who need to lose weight will lose fat while on this program, whereas those who are underweight will maintain or increase their lean body weight. Because this program is so balanced nutritionally, any weight lost during this program is generally body fat rather than lean tissue.

Some people will decide to combine the elimination test diet described in Chapter 17 with the therapeutic detoxification program described here. In this way, detoxification as well as identification of food allergies and intolerances can both be accomplished. In this case, the person is permitted to eat those foods allowed on the elimination test diet as long as they consume UltraClear™ Plus smoothies 2 times per day as a meal replacement and one other time per day as a snack. The consumption of UltraClear™ Plus continues for 1-6 weeks, depending upon the advice of the healthcare practitioner. After 4-6 weeks on the elimination test diet, the open food challenge process can begin in order for food allergies and intolerances to be identified.

• **Exercise component:** While on the therapeutic detoxification program, individuals are encouraged to engage in regular exercise. For many reasons, daily exercise greatly enhances the effectiveness of detoxification. Unlike traditional fasting, which usually leaves a person exhausted much of the time and unable to exercise, the Functional Medicine detoxification program provides sufficient nutrition to allow a person to continue with virtually all of their normal activities including reasonably vigorous exercise. After having completed numerous fasting and cleansing programs, I had come to expect that one had to feel weak and spend lots of time in bed while undergoing intensive detoxification. The first time I went on a 7 day detoxification program, using UltraClear™ Plus, I was amazed at the level of energy that I had almost every day of the program. Although I had some pretty intensive symptoms such as headache and foul breath for the first two days, by the third day I felt wonderful and began to cycle vigorously 1 to 3 hours per day. By the end of that week, I had lost body fat, had tremendous clarity of mind and felt truly wonderful. That was about six years ago and I have never gone back to doing traditional fasting or cleansing again. I continue to complete a 1 to 2 week UltraClear™ Plus based therapeutic detoxification program about every six months and have found this to be one of the most important aspects of my personal health maintenance program, particularly in terms of its benefits to brain function and energy levels.

• **Hyperthermic therapy:** In our facility, individuals undergoing therapeutic detoxification complete a series of hyperthermic therapy sessions to accompany the nutritional and exercise components of the program. Hyperthermic (high temperature) therapy refers to the use of a sauna, steam bath or therapeutic whirlpool bath in order to raise the core body temperature and induce intensive sweating. Saunas, steam baths and sweat lodges have been used traditionally by many cultures for purification and restoration of health. More recently, science has begun to validate the cleansing benefits of hyperthermic therapies. Researchers from the Environmental Protection Agency (EPA) and other notable groups have demonstrated that saunas combined with exercise and nutritional support can significantly decrease body stores of non-metallic toxins such as PCB's, and pesticide residues. (Schnare, 1982; Schnare, 1986; Kilburn, 1994) As well, Russian and European researchers have shown that induction of sweating is an effective means to greatly increase the excretion of toxic metals such as mercury. (Fuzailov, 1992; Lovejoy, 1973) Sweating is a more direct route for the excretion of stored toxins than having to excrete them through the liver and kidneys. Because of this, hyperthermic therapies can help to relieve some of the stress placed on these detoxification organs during a therapeutic detoxification program. Each hyperthermic therapy session should be followed immediately by a cool shower or immersion into cool water. This promotes a tremendous sense of energy, and wakefulness and makes a person feel great. If the cool shower or immersion is not taken, it is common to feel quite exhausted after the hyperthermia session. This exhaustion may even persist into the next day in some people and should be avoided by a cold water or immersion.

Hyperthermic therapy can be safely undertaken by most people, including children, if certain precautions are taken. Firstly, one must be well hydrated before entering the sauna or steam bath and should drink water liberally while in the unit. Also, people should not try to be overly tough and should exit the unit before dizziness, headaches or severe weakness sets in. Children should always be accompanied by adults and should be allowed to exit if they are feel unwell or become drowsy or nauseated. Children are very prone to rapid dehydration while in a sauna or steam bath and great care must be taken to ensure that they drink plenty of liquids before and during the session.

Since it helps to promote the release of toxins from cells and into circulation, exercise has its greatest detoxifying benefits if it is undertaken just prior to the hyperthermic therapy session. As well, some practitioners prescribe the vitamin, niacin to be taken a few minutes before the treatment. Niacin creates a flushing of the skin, and an increase in blood flow through organs. This effect may help in the mobilization of toxins from the soft tissues. The practitioner may also recommend a tablespoon or two of oil (a mixture of flax and olive oil is often used) just prior to a hyperthermia session. The logic behind this is that the ingestion of oil might accelerate the turnover of fat from the fat cells and other fatty tissues such as the brain, and assist in the expulsion of fat-soluble toxins from these regions.(Information about an innovative and affordable steam sauna unit for home use can be found at www.pureliving.com)

- **Additional components of the therapeutic detoxification program:** Recall that providing optimal levels of **nutritional minerals** plays an essential role in the effective excretion of toxic metals. In our facility, patients who are undergoing therapeutic detoxification continue to receive high levels of calcium, magnesium, zinc, and selenium throughout their detoxification program in addition to the minerals which are contained in UltraClear™ Plus.

A standardized herbal extract prepared from the seeds of the **milk thistle** provides significant antioxidant protection to the liver during the therapeutic detoxification program. Milk thistle extract can help to diminish some of the unpleasant side effect of detoxification, especially in people who have not done much in the way of detoxification programs in the past. It may also assist the liver in detoxification and may accelerate the expulsion of toxin containing bile into the intestine.

Insuring adequacy of **bowel elimination** is essential during a therapeutic detoxification program. Greatly increasing dietary fiber is well advised as long as all fiber supplements are very low in their allergenic potential. Wheat bran, and psyllium seed husk are cheap and readily available, but they are commonly allergenic and are therefore unacceptable for the purposes of this program. UltraFiber™ is a low allergy potential fiber supplement composed of barley bran, rice bran, pea fiber, beet fiber, apple pectin, cellulose gum, xanthan gum, oat fiber and apple fiber. UltraFiber™ is an ideal fiber supplement to use during a therapeutic detoxification program. Like UltraClear™ Plus, UltraFiber™ is usually obtained from a healthcare practitioner who is applying the principles of Functional Medicine in their practice.

Most practitioners also prescribe various methods to flush or purge the bowel on a regular basis throughout the duration of the therapeutic detoxification program. Home enemas, colonics performed in a clinic or other methods may be recommended to thoroughly purge the bowel 3 to 5 times per week or more. This helps to ensure that toxins which have been excreted by the liver and into the gut (via the release of bile) exit the body rather than being reabsorbed back into the bloodstream.

Drinking plenty of **pure water** is a vital part of the detoxification program. Ideally, water purified by reverse osmosis or distillation should be used. The next best would be water purified with a carbon filter. Thirst may diminish during the therapeutic detoxification program and individuals must be careful to avoid even mild dehydration during this time.

WHAT ABOUT CHELATION THERAPY?

Chelation therapy refers to the administration of certain drugs, which bind strongly to metals inside the body and which have the ability to carry these metals out of the body, usually through the kidneys. Some chelating drugs (such as DMSA and penicillamine) may be administered orally whereas others (such as EDTA and DMPS) are given through the intravenous route. A number of practitioners who are trained in the principles of Functional Medicine also prescribe and administer chelating drugs in certain cases where heavy metal toxicity is determined to play a significant and prominent role in the individual's medical condition. If used wisely and appropriately, there are certainly circumstances in which chelation therapy can bring about a significant reduction in heavy metal burdens and a subsequent improvement in the patient's health. However, these agents are drugs and they have the potential to create a number of potentially significant side effects. Individuals with ADHD should be cautious before submitting themselves or their children to chelation therapy. Before agreeing to take chelation therapy, the patient should inquire about the practitioner's training and experience with such therapies. Generally, only medical doctors with formal training in the use of these agents should be involved in their administration. Even then, chelation therapy should only be used when there are clear indications that it offers distinct advantages over non-drug approaches to detoxification.

Chelation therapy is certainly not the only way that one can bring about an increase in the excretion of toxic metals from human body. The principles of Functional Toxicology along with the Functional Medicine approach to therapeutic detoxification described in the previous sections will greatly increase the excretion of toxic metals and will be an effective and adequate intervention to bring about a significant reduction in neurotoxic stress from both metallic and non-metallic sources in most people.

For those interested in reading more about the impact of our environment on the brains' of our children; the American Academy of Pediatrics has published an excellent book entitled, "Handbook of Pediatric Environmental Health". This outstanding publication can be ordered from the Academy's website at: www.aap.org.

Chapter 25

Empowering the Hyperactive Brain through Physical Exercise

WHY EXERCISE?

For many people, the only tangible benefits that might convince them to commit to a regular exercise routine is the appeal of a hard abdomen and a firm buttocks. Physical fitness certainly does have the potential to improve a person's appearance and to help them shed those unwanted pounds. However, the benefits of regular exercise extend far beyond weight loss and muscle toning. Decades of research have now accumulated examining the physical and psychological effects of exercise and the list of health benefits keeps growing on an almost daily basis. Improved immune function, reduction in the effects of stress, improved cardiovascular function, reduction in asthmatic symptoms, diminished risk of diabetes and obesity, as well as, a decreased risk of cancer are but a few of the many benefits to those who engage in a regular routine of moderate exercise.

EXERCISE AND EMOTIONAL HEALTH

For over twenty years, research evidence has supported the idea that regular exercise provides significant mental and emotional health benefits. (deCoverley, 1987) It is now considered by virtually all authorities to be one of the most important elements of an effective stress management program, and the stress reducing benefits of regular exercise are well established. (Steptoe, 1998; Broocks, 1998) Since virtually everyone is exposed to significant levels of stress, we all should make the time for exercise. The busier and more stressful our lives, the more we need to exercise. This is particularly true for those with ADHD, whose stress levels tend to increase with age. Unmanaged stress in anyone with ADHD will commonly lead to a anxiety disorders and stress related health problems; it is one of the most common causes of general misery in the lives of those with ADHD.

Exercise also has proven to be invaluable in the prevention and management of depression. (DiLorenzo, 1999; Singh, 1997) Depression in children and teenagers is a serious, yet often unrecognized accompaniment of ADHD that can lead to a higher risk of substance abuse, serious psychiatric problems and suicide. (Zeitlin, 1999; Runeson, 1998) Since ADHD is associated with such a high risk of depression, promoting regular exercise in children, adolescents and adults with ADHD helps to bring stability to moods and diminishes the risk of depression.

EXERCISE AND BRAIN NEUROTRANSMITTERS

Because of its proven benefits in mental and emotional health, it has long been suspected that exercise exerts specific effects upon brain the neurotransmitters central to the symptoms of ADHD. (Chaouloff, 1989) Research in this area of neurophysiology has expanded rapidly and it is clear that exercise indeed has an impact on virtually all of the brain's important neurotransmitter systems. The diminishing of depressive symptoms may be largely a result of an increase in serotonin activity within the brain. (Chaouloff, 1997) Numerous studies have now established that well-trained individuals experienced significantly greater dopamine production throughout their brains when compared to untrained individuals. (Gilbert C., 1995; Sutoo, 1996) Exercise also induces a rise in the quantity of dopamine receptors, resulting in a higher brain sensitivity to this ADHD-critical neurotransmitter. (MacRae, 1987)

EXERCISE AND THE ADHD BRAIN

The fact that exercise significantly improves brain dopamine activity has profound implications for the treatment of ADHD. Recall from Chapter 1 that diminished dopamine activity in the brain's executive centers within the pre-frontal cortex is the principle neurological defect leading to the symptoms associated with ADHD. As well, diminished dopamine activity within the brain's reward centers contributes significantly to the addictive, compulsive and risk-taking behaviors so commonly associated with ADHD. Clinical research is helping to confirm that the dopamine promoting effects of exercise have a targeted effect upon the regions of the brain most affected by ADHD. In a recent, groundbreaking study, University of Illinois neuroscientist, Dr. Arthur Kramer performed complex neuropsychological testing on individuals before and after participation in a brisk walking program over a period of several weeks. When compared to a group of control subjects, who did not exercise aerobically, the walking group showed significant improvements in brain executive center function. (Kramer, 1999) Other studies have demonstrated that regular exercise improves the behavior of hyperactive-impulsive children (Klein, 1977), as it does for those with more serious developmental disorders such as autism. (Celiberti, 1997; Kern, 1984)

In addition to its ability to increase neurotransmitter activity, exercise also brings about a transient rise in brain endorphins. The controlled rise in these important neuropeptides, along with the increase in dopamine activity, is thought to be the primary reasons why regular exercise is accompanied by a sense of well being. (MacRae, 1987; Goldfarb, 1997) It may also be why a commitment to exercise helps to prevent addictive behaviors and it can play an important role in the treatment of chemical dependencies. (Thoren, 1990; Burnham, 1998) In essence, exercise is one of the most important factors that can help to "satisfy the craving brain".

Perhaps one of the most intriguing facts recently uncovered by neuroscience research is the discovery that regular exercise results in the development of new brain cells as well as an increase in the number of new connections made by existing brain cells. (Gomez-Pinilla, 1998; van Praag, 1999) This research suggests that regular exercise has the potential to encourage repair and rebuilding in underdeveloped or damaged brain regions and to maximize the potential for cognitive improvement in the long-term for those with ADHD.

EXERCISE AND SELF ESTEEM

Under-achievement, inappropriate conduct, inconsistent performance and other behavioral traits contribute to low self-esteem in the majority of those with ADHD. Diminished self-esteem, in turn, contributes significantly to depression in children and adolescents and is thought to be a major risk factor for drug abuse, criminal behavior, sexual promiscuity and suicide. (Modrcin-Talbott, 1998) One very important thing that a parent can do for their ADHD child is to nurture the child's sense of self-worth in every way possible. An effective way to nurture self-esteem is to be sure that the child is involved in activities in which he will eventually be able to excel. Learning a musical instrument, developing artistic talent, or becoming very skillful in a particular sport or hobby can all build children's self-images and give them a sense of achievement and control in their lives. Such skills can provide a vital buffer to the self-esteem damaging impact of failure in the social and academic environment of the school.

Involvement in sports is an excellent way to build a child's confidence and self-esteem. Children should be encouraged to participate in different sports and parents should acknowledge their participation and willingness to practice and train in a very positive manner. Some children will excel in sports, and will build a confident self-image through their developing skills and achievements. (Saint-Phard, 1999) Other children do not have the ability to be highly competitive or to achieve winning status, yet they should be praised for their commitment to sportsmanship, participation and personal fitness. (Bell, 1998; Dykens, 1998) Because of the many benefits to a lifetime commitment to personal fitness, parents should encourage their children to be involved with the kind of sports and recreational activities that will likely remain as interests into their adult life.

TEACHING FITNESS BY EXAMPLE

The best way to encourage a commitment to personal fitness in children is by parental example. Parents, who participate with their children in healthy recreational activities, have an opportunity to build a strong bond of friendship and will be likely to succeed in helping their children to understand the importance of regular exercise. In our family, fitness is a way of life. Family walks and bike rides are a regular and much enjoyed activity. As well, I have spent a great deal of time helping my son to become a skillful bicycle rider by taking him off road cycling regularly. Prior to this, his self-esteem was very low and he had developed no skills to raise his self-image. He also tired very easily and lacked coordination: he seemed to continually trip over his own feet. Three years ago, I made a commitment to help my son become physically fit. We spent several months riding mountain bikes together and then I enrolled him in BMX (bicycle motocross racing). Because the BMX racing involved a great deal of coordination, I didn't expect him to excel. However, our months of off road cycling paid off and, to my surprise, his skills in BMX advanced rapidly. In his first season, he won the provincial championships and was voted the rookie of the year. Since then, he has become a confident, athletic boy who has a strong commitment to personal fitness. He remains one of the top local BMX racers and we continue to have a tremendously enjoyable time riding mountain bikes together. Regular participation in vigorous exercise has been one of the most important factors in minimizing the negative impact of ADHD in his life.

MY PERSONAL COMMITMENT TO EXERCISE

Regular exercise has been an indispensable part of my successful progress through the ADHD puzzle. I have maintained a commitment to fitness since I was 17 years old and, now that I am "40-something", I continue to find daily exercise to be one of the most helpful and enjoyable parts of my life. Even when I am "too busy to exercise", I have learned that I stay far more productive if I find the time to squeeze a workout into my schedule. I have come to depend on the rejuvenating, stress relieving value of a daily workout. I consider this to be my "daily vacation", where I can burn off stress, think through problems and recharge my batteries. With few exceptions, I have found that there is always time to exercise if it is really a top priority. To successfully stick with a fitness program you must be versatile and willing to fit exercise in any way you can. For instance, if I have a day off and the weather is nice, I will go for a long bike ride. If it's dark and rainy, I might lift weights inside or go running along a lighted path. If I'm stuck in a hotel room with no fitness center, I might just jump around and do calisthenics while watching the news. Making workouts varied can also help to break up the monotony of doing the same workout every day and it will reduce the risk that you will have to stop exercising because of an overuse injury. I can certainly say that my mind is clearer and more focused when I have been exercising regularly. On the other hand, two or three days without exercise and my mind becomes scattered, my nerves agitated, my mood drops very low and my body becomes sluggish. Exercise isn't always what I feel like doing, but I have come to accept that it is one of the things my body and brain need in order to function optimally.

PRECAUTIONS SURROUNDING EXERCISE

Although the benefits of exercise are manifold, if not done sensibly, it also has the potential to do harm. Almost all of the research demonstrating the benefits of exercise has shown these benefits occur when it is done in moderation. Exercising to excess is the quickest way to suppress the immune system and lead to increased susceptibility to infectious illness. Overtraining places the body under the severest form of stress and can result in osteoporosis, depression and anxiety disorders. After working with numerous Olympic and professional athletes, I have come to see how harmful overtraining can be. Athletes always walk a fine line between insufficient training, resulting in poor athletic progress, and overtraining, which results in an even greater decline in performance.

Although most people who pursue sports for personal fitness and recreation do not face much of a risk of overtraining, those with ADHD are more likely to be injured by athletic pursuits. Firstly, if a person with ADHD really likes their sport, they are more likely to experience exercise addiction or be driven to train compulsively. I have seen this tendency in many Olympic and professional athletes who have managed to avoid burnout and reach the pinnacle of success. I have also seen many hard-driven fitness buffs and "weekend warriors" who have ended up completely overtrained or suffering from needless injury because of compulsive overtraining. As well, I have witnessed many cases of parents taking on the role of the hard-driving coach and then pushing their child to be a sports star. There is a considerable difference between helping your child find self esteem and experience the joy of excellence, and driving him like a slave to become the best at any cost. The child should always be the primary person to decide if he wants to achieve excellence in sports. However, parents should be aware of the growing obsession with body image amongst adolescents, and the risk of potentially lethal eating disorders that may accompany compulsive exercise habits, especially in teenage girls. (Davis, 1999) Parents should also be aware of the increasing prevalence of anabolic steroid use amongst adolescents who are involved in weight training and who are seeking to achieve rapid gains in musculature. (Foley, 1993) These drugs present many long term dangers and may also seriously intensify problem behaviors in ADHD-affected adolescents who may already be facing problems related to aggression and oppositional behavior. The so-called "roid rage" phenomenon is very real, and has caused many "steroid juiced" teenagers and young adults to end up in jail on assault charges.

As long as it is taken in moderation, exercise has many benefits and few drawbacks. Adults with ADHD will also benefit greatly by increasing their fitness level and becoming regular exercisers. Few couch potatoes ever feel good. A sedentary person may have an excellent diet, take loads of nutritional supplements and still feel poor most of the time. There is just no getting away from the need for regular exercise, especially for those with ADHD.

Chapter 26

Focusing the Hyperactive Brain through Biofeedback, Meditation and Prayer

LIVING LIFE INSIDE A PINBALL MACHINE

For the majority of people in most situations, maintaining a reasonable degree of attentiveness is relatively easy. In contrast, for those with ADHD, staying attentive can seem like an insurmountable task. The ADHD brain is in continuous flight, fluttering about from one thought to the next for most waking moments of the day and night. This is often evident when talking to a person with ADHD — the topic of conversation may bounce around like the steel ball inside a pinball machine. Those who are afflicted with the primarily inattentive (non-hyperactive) form of ADHD may not seem, on the outside, like their hyperactive counterparts, but they often live their lives swirling around inside an ever-changing daydream, with little time spent actually concentrating on the tasks before them.

WHY IS THE BOSS ON VACATION?

In the first chapter of this book, ADHD was described as a disorder arising primarily because of diminished activity of the brain's executive control centers, the regions within the pre-frontal cortex which inhibit impulses, provide higher judgment and maintain one's thoughts in clear focus. In a sense, there is neurological anarchy in the ADHD brain because the boss of the brain is on an extended vacation. In subsequent chapters, evidence was presented indicating that many factors, both inherited and acquired, work in an additive fashion to impair the function of these highly sensitive brain regions. Genetic differences in neuronal function, neurotoxic stresses, and inadequacy of brain-critical nutrients may all lead to inadequate executive center performance.

Although potent stimulant drugs can be used to awaken these sleepy executive centers, it is far more sensible to uncover and then eliminate, as far as possible, the various factors which are keeping these sensitive brain regions subdued. Correcting these underlying causative factors can result in a remarkable improvement in ADHD symptoms, enhancements in other areas of health and a much brighter long-term prognosis for the ADHD sufferer. It only makes sense that a healthier brain will perform better and be far more amenable to positive change.

TAKING ADVANTAGE OF THE HYPER-FOCUSING TRAIT

In Chapter 3, it was mentioned that a substantial proportion of ADHD sufferers experience episodes of intensive focusing, particularly when they are engaged in pleasurable or interesting tasks. For example, children who may not seem capable of attending to math problems for more than a few seconds, can often spend endless hours, oblivious to their surroundings, while they are glued to a computer game. Adolescents with ADHD might not be able to stay in focus long enough to write a letter to their grandmother but they may have no trouble writing e-mail to friends half a day at a time. An adult who may not be able to sit still long enough to balance a checkbook might find themselves surfing the Internet until 3 AM. This phenomenon has been termed "hyper-focusing" and it is one of the hidden features of ADHD, which must be properly harnessed before a person can begin to triumph over their disabilities.

THE CONNECTION BETWEEN PLEASURE AND FOCUSING

As was described in Chapter 2, ADHD and addiction may share some common neurological features. Those with ADHD may be prone to addiction, in part, because of deficits in the activity of their brain's reward (pleasure) center. This reward center is intended to provide humans with a sense of pleasure and satisfaction after eating, resting, nurturing human contact and other natural pleasures. When adequately stimulated, these reward centers also cause the inhibitory executive centers of the brain to become activated through powerful lines of neurological communication. As described in Chapter 9, the pleasurable and loving bond between an infant and its mother may actually be the first important influence that stimulates the normal development of the executive centers through chemicals and nervous signals released from the reward center of the infant's brain.

In a sense, the brain's reward center is like the starting motor for the executive centers – the primary engines governing the most complex activities of the brain. This is probably why people with ADHD may find little difficulty maintain attentiveness if they are doing something interesting or pleasurable and why they usually find it so hard to even get started on tasks that are not very enjoyable. One strategy that can minimize this trait to some extent, is to help those with ADHD cultivate non-destructive interests and enjoyments – things that they can enjoy and focus upon but do no harm. Unfortunately, many of the essential responsibilities that everyone must face are not pleasurable and can be downright boring. For people with ADHD, boredom comes easily and can be intensely uncomfortable. Intolerance to boredom and other manifestations of diminished reward center activity is the reason why many ADHD sufferers end up using drugs, casual sex, gambling or other harmful behaviors to achieve that elusive sense of satisfaction and focus. It would certainly be of value to find other ways to increase the activity of these critical brain regions to enable those with ADHD to more easily achieve contentment and attentiveness.

CONTROLLING OUR BRAINS TO CONTROL OUR BODIES

We all take for granted the fact that we can think a thought, and in an instant, our hands will move or words will come out of our mouths. Since a specific brain activity is required for every action, word or thought, it is really quite an amazing mystery that we can activate our brains in such a diverse manner in order to execute so many complex tasks. Of course, most of what we do as humans requires learning and practice.

The reason why we are able to learn complex tasks, such as speaking, walking or playing a musical instrument, is because we have senses that let us know exactly what occurs when we activate our brains in certain ways as we attempt to perform specific tasks. For instance, you can learn to play specific notes on a piano because you can feel and see the movement of your fingers as they move over the keys, and you can hear the sound that results from this action. If you were blind, deaf and had no feeling in you fingers, it would be impossible to learn this skill. It is the constant feedback of sensory information following each specific action that allows you to adjust your brain activity until you can perform the desired action.

LEARNING TO CONTROL INVOLUNTARY FUNCTIONS THROUGH BIOFEEDBACK

If you could "see" your brain's electrical activity or "hear" the temperature of your fingers, would it be possible to control these involuntary processes? Yes, in fact many otherwise involuntary processes can be modified or controlled through a technological development known as biofeedback. Essentially, biofeedback is a technique, which uses an electronic device to measure a normally involuntary bodily function such as the heart rate, skin temperature, anxiety levels, degree of muscle tension or brain electrical activity. The biofeedback instrument then converts the measurement into a sound or image on a computer monitor, and the sound or image changes as the involuntary bodily process changes. This visible or audible signal allows the subject to clearly perceive changes in the particular bodily function being monitored and to rapidly learn how to modify what is normally an involuntary process.

Biofeedback research has been conducted for the past 30 years and various forms of this high-tech therapy have been established to play a significant role in the treatment of a number of different disorders. Three different types of biofeedback can play a useful role in the management of ADHD:

- **Galvanic skin response (GSR)** is the simplest and least costly form of biofeedback. GSR uses the same basic instrument as is used for lie detector tests. This instrument works by measuring the precise level of anxiety in the subject through a very simple principle. Essentially, the sweat glands open and close in various amounts, depending upon the moment-by-moment changes in the person's anxiety level. Everyone has experienced sweaty hands at times when they are very nervous or frightened. GSR biofeedback takes advantage of the fact that small changes in the output of the sweat glands occur with every thought we think, depending upon how the thought raises or lowers our anxiety level (the level of sympathetic nervous system activity).

GSR biofeedback is able to measures the moment-by-moment changes in sweat gland output by measuring how easily a small electric current passes through electrodes on two adjacent fingers. When anxiety levels rise, sweat gland output increases and electricity flows through the fingers more easily. When anxiety levels go down, less sweat is produced and electricity is less able to flow through the fingers. Essentially, the sweat glands open and close with changes in anxiety levels like a dimmer switch for a room light.

The changes measured by GSR are expressed by a change in the pitch of a sound emitted by the biofeedback instrument. Once the electrodes are attached to the fingers, the subject sits in a comfortable position, with their eyes closed and they then begin to relax. Usually deep breathing exercises are done and the subject tries to keep thoughts from entering their mind. Whenever a thought enters the subject's mind, which raises anxiety levels, a higher pitched is sound emitted by the instrument. The goal of GSR biofeedback is to learn to use the mind to control the pitch of the sound in order to greatly lower anxiety levels and to enter into a state of deep relaxation. Like all forms of biofeedback, it takes time and practice to become skillful enough to enter this deep state of relaxation.

GSR biofeedback is commonly used as an integral part of an effective stress management program. Once people have become skillful with GSR biofeedback, (usually 8 to 12 sessions) they can use this instrument to quickly enter into a deep state of relaxation. Sessions usually last between 20 minutes and 1 hour and are conducted at least 3 days per week. After the ability to quickly enter into a peaceful, relaxed state has been acquired, people usually find that this is a very pleasurable, peaceful and rejuvenating experience. GSR biofeedback has been shown to be useful in the management of stress-related medical and psychological disorders. (Collet, 1986) It has also been shown to improve focusing ability and academic performance in college students. (Valdes, 1985) Since individuals with ADHD are so prone to anxiety related problems, GSR biofeedback may have a valuable role to play in improving their health, quality of life and academic performance as well.

I began using GSR biofeedback when I was 19 years old and in university. I came across plans to build one of these devices out of commonly available electronic components and a friend of mine who was an electronics wiz helped me to build it. I used this machine regularly and found that GSR helped me to overcome a lifelong tendency to become easily overwhelmed by stress. After a session with the GSR machine I would feel highly energized, relaxed and more focused for about 24 hours. Although there are other forms of biofeedback that have been proven to be more effective for those with ADHD, using GSR is inexpensive and very good when stress is a major problem in any person's life. As well, home equipment and training programs are now available to enable people to utilize this technology in the comfort of their own home. Further information about these programs can be found on the Internet at: www.PureLiving.com.

- Electromyographic (EMG) is a form of biofeedback in which sensing electrodes are placed over specific muscles in the forehead or in the back of the neck. Even when not being actively used, all muscles have a certain degree of resting contraction or tension. Our ability to detect a muscle's tension level is not very sensitive unless the muscle is extremely tense. The EMG biofeedback instrument detects the precise level of tension in a muscle and then emits a tone corresponding to the degree of tension. The tone is low pitched if the muscle is very relaxed or high pitched if the muscle is very tense. People who are under stress tend to have higher levels of muscle tension, which can end up creating tension headaches, back pain, fatigue or just a general sense of "being tense". In EMG biofeedback, electrodes are placed over certain muscles that are prone to tension problems. The subject then sits in a comfortable position, with eyes closed, and begins to relax the muscles under the electrodes. After several sessions, the subject usually becomes quite skillful in the ability to bring about relaxation of the muscles and tension related problems usually diminish.

Children with ADHD have been found to have higher levels of muscle tension than their non-ADHD peers. Research has shown that EMG biofeedback effectively reduces muscular tension, hyperactivity, distractibility, irritability, impulsivity, explosiveness, aggression and emotional outbursts in hyperactive children. (Braud, 1978; Christie, 1984) EMG biofeedback has also been shown to improve academic performance in children with ADHD. (Denkowski, 1983; Denkowski, 1984) EMG biofeedback requires professional guidance and inexpensive home equipment is not available. Under qualified supervision, this form of biofeedback can be easily mastered by younger children, but it is currently not used as frequently to treat ADHD as neurofeedback; the subject of the following section.

- **Electroencephalographic (EEG) biofeedback (also called neurofeedback or neurotherapy)** is rapidly becoming recognized as one of the most effective single treatments for ADHD. Over the past decade, this most advanced form of biofeedback been increasingly adopted by university based ADHD treatment centers and, because of its safety and lasting effectiveness, it is likely to become far more popular in the coming years. Neurofeedback uses a highly sophisticated instrument to measure the actual electrical activity of the brain in specific locations. This information is then converted into varying sounds or images on a computer screen.

This instant sensory feedback allows the subject to gain control and then modify the brain's electrical activity in specific brain regions. Neurofeedback has also benefited from advancements in computer technology; sophisticated equipment and computer software has now been developed specifically for those with ADHD, including young children.

Rhythmic electrical activity (referred to as brainwaves) can be detected in the scalp overlying every region of the brain. This constantly changing pattern of energy reflects the coordinated activity of numerous brain regions, which generate complex electrical rhythms like the various sections of an orchestra all playing harmoniously together. When brain regions are working normally, one region will communicate and combine energies with other regions and their signals are then amplified through resonance (like the way sound from a vibrating string is amplified by entering into the inside of a violin). For example, the brain's reward center, when activated, will communicate and resonate with the executive centers, effectively amplifying the strength of electrical signals in both regions. (Lubar, 1997)

The frequency and strength of the brain's electrical rhythms are highly variable and depend upon the level of consciousness, the activity engaged in, an individual's state of health and other factors such as neurotoxic influences upon the brain. Sleeping and drowsiness is accompanied by a marked slowing in the frequency of brainwaves, whereas when a person is alert, the frequency of brainwaves becomes much faster and stronger. Researchers have discovered that the pattern of brainwaves in those with ADHD is much different from that of non-affected individuals. Those affected are typically found to have a marked slowing of brainwaves over the frontal part of the brain, the region which houses the brain's executive control centers. Normally, when alert, the whole brain generates high frequency brain waves called beta waves (15-30 Hz). During drowsy or meditative states, brainwaves may slow down to that of alpha waves (8-14 Hz). Light sleep is accompanied by slower theta waves (4-7 Hz) and deep sleep is characterized by very slow delta waves (1-3 Hz).

When brain waves are examined in those with ADHD while they are wide awake and alert, the frontal region of their brain is found to be generating a predominance of low frequency theta waves, the frequency of brainwaves that are normally found when people are sleeping. (Lazzaro, 1998) What this finding essentially means is that the executive centers in those with ADHD are asleep while the rest of their brain is wide-awake! As has been described repeatedly, the executive centers serve an important inhibitory role; helping a person to resist impulses, keeping them from moving excessively and giving them the ability to stay attentive. They also give a person the power to use moral reasoning and to act in a mature and responsible fashion. It is of no surprised then that there are serious consequences to being awake while your brain's executive centers are still fast asleep. This would almost be like trying to drive a car with no brakes and a defective steering wheel; controlling that car would be very difficult and accidents would most likely occur.

Neurofeedback is a remarkable therapy, enabling individuals with ADHD to voluntarily awaken their brain's executive centers by learning to gain control over the electrical activity in this region. During this therapy, electrodes are placed over the front of the head and the neurofeedback instrument precisely monitors the electrical activity of this region. These brainwave signals are then converted to a sound or an image on a computer monitor and the individual practices altering the frequency and strength of brainwave activity by learning to alter the sound or computer image. The primary goal of neurofeedback session is to learn to transform the weak, slow (theta) waves in the frontal region to strong, fast (beta) waves. Once the executive centers begin to produce a constant flow of beta waves, they begin to resonate with other brain regions. This results in a powerful increase in the electrical activity of the executive centers and other associated regions, such as the reward or pleasure centers. In a sense, neurofeedback works like a brilliant conductor who brings an out-of-tune orchestra back into perfect harmony, playing glorious melodies once again.

Once a person with ADHD becomes skillful with neurofeedback, each session is a highly pleasurable experience. Although subjects with ADHD have a very low tolerance to boredom, they usually find neurofeedback sessions to be enjoyable and rarely quit because of boredom. The pleasure experienced while in a neurofeedback session probably results from an intense activation of the brain's reward center along with a marked reduction in anxiety levels. Therefore, not only do neurofeedback participants learn to activate their brain's executive centers, they learn to activate their reward centers as well. This activation of the brain's reward centers probably explains why this therapy has been shown to be highly effective as a component in the treatment of addiction and depression. (Saxby, 1995)

Several studies indicate that neurofeedback can form an effective part of the treatment for ADHD. In one controlled study (40 sessions over 6 months), neurofeedback was shown to improve attentiveness and resulted in an average increase of 9 IQ points in ADHD affected subjects. In comparison, untreated controls demonstrated no improvements. (Linden, 1996) In another study, students suffering from ADHD who underwent 40 twice-weekly neurofeedback sessions experienced an average increase in IQ of 12 points! (Thompson, 1998) This magnitude of increase in IQ could make an enormous difference in a student's academic performance and might open up a whole different world of possibilities for their lives. In another study, a 2-3 month neurofeedback program was administered to students with ADHD during the summer. Computerized measurements of attentiveness, parent rating of behavior and IQ scores were all shown to improve significantly. (Lubar, 1995b)

Neurofeedback has also been compared to stimulant drugs like Ritalin® in two different studies. In one study, 10 sessions of neurofeedback were found to be superior to stimulants with regards to both the reduction in hyperactive behaviors and the reduction in muscle tension in students. (Potashkin, 1990) In the second study, 20 sessions of neurofeedback were determined to be as effective as Ritalin® and resulted in significant improvement in attention, impulse control, speed of information processing and consistency of attention. This was verified with computerized cognitive testing as well as parent rating scales. (Rossiter, 1995)

One feature of neurofeedback, which makes it clearly superior to drug treatment, is that its benefits linger long after the treatment sessions are completed. Unlike drug treatment, which provides absolutely no benefits once the drug is stopped, neurofeedback involves training the brain to work in a completely different way. In fact, once a successful series of neurofeedback sessions has been completed, the benefits may continue for many years or even throughout the rest of a person's life. (Tansey, 1993) In addition, unlike Ritalin®, which can seriously worsen tic disorders or Tourette's syndrome, neurofeedback may actually be a highly effective treatment for this disabling condition which sometimes accompanies ADHD. (Tansey, 1986)

On top of its ability to effectively reduce ADHD symptoms, neurofeedback provides the skills to enter into a state of deep relaxation or meditation at will. This can give an individual an effective stress management skill that will benefit them in many ways. Once the control of brain function is mastered with neurofeedback, deep relaxation or meditation can become a very satisfying part of life. Since people with ADHD suffer from a reward deficiency syndrome due to the lack of activity in their brain's reward center, continuing to practice deep relaxation or meditation can help to satisfy their "craving brains". This may reduce the risk that ADHD sufferers will turn to drugs or other high-risk activities in their search for satisfaction and serenity.

MY EXPERIENCE WITH NEUROFEEDBACK

One of the reasons I feel so strongly about neurofeedback is because it was one of the key factors that helped me to rise above my limitations as a young person with ADHD. By the time I was 19, I had spent a good deal of time experimenting with various ways to improve my ability to focus and learn. GSR biofeedback helped me to experience deep relaxation, which gave me a greater capability to handle the stress of university. However, after several months of using GSR biofeedback, I had worked hard and saved enough money to buy my own EEG biofeedback (neurofeedback) machine. I studied everything I could get my hands on about neurofeedback and then began to conduct my own neurofeedback sessions at home. After several weeks of regular practice, I was able to consistently increase the speed and power of the brainwaves emanating from the frontal part of my brain. With this new skill, I found that I was able to simply concentrate for a few minutes and voluntarily "awaken" the frontal part of my brain. After a while, I could reproduce this effect in a few seconds of quiet concentration at the beginning of classes or study sessions and my ability to focus and learn became far more effective. Over the course of the next year, I went from being a very marginal student with no hope of being accepted into medical school to one of the top students in the Faculty of Science. My marks stayed high enough that I received several thousand dollars per year in awards for academic performance and I ended up being accepted to medical school a year earlier than the usual 4-year premedical program. There were certainly other factors involved in this academic change, but I know that it was neurofeedback which trained my brain to work in a whole different way and gave me the ability to focus consistently and powerfully. Because it helped my brain to work so much better, I believe neurofeedback actually raised my IQ by several points and substantially improved my memory.

The skills I learned through neurofeedback in the 1970's are still at my disposal. I have come to accept that I must take the time each morning to consciously awaken the frontal part of my brain. For several years now, I accomplish this during a time of prayer and meditation which I enjoy every morning. I have learned that my brain is almost useless unless I start the day with this uplifting and energizing habit.

It has been 20 years since I underwent neurofeedback therapy and, since then, many advancements have been made in this field. Currently, anyone seeking to undergo neurofeedback should choose a professional who is either certified by or is in the process of obtaining certification from the Biofeedback Certification Institute of America (BCIA). This organization was formed in January 1981 to establish strict standards for biofeedback practitioners. Most of these professionals are either registered clinical psychologists, medical doctors or registered nurses who have taken extensive additional training to become certified in the provision of biofeedback. BCIA certified practitioners can be located through the Internet at: www.bcia.org. Alternatively, a printout of all BCIA certified practitioners can be obtained by sending a self-addressed, stamped, business sized envelope to: BCIA - 10200 W. 44th Avenue, #310 - Wheat Ridge, CO 80033-2840.

WHY MEDITATION?

Many people with ADHD have never experienced a waking moment of real peace. Some of these restless folks have learned to seek a false sense of peace through mind numbing drugs or alcohol. Opioids like heroin and sedatives like alcohol or Valium, numb the mind, slow down the thoughts and cover over inner suffering – for a short while. Stimulants like cocaine, "ecstasy" or methamphetamine (speed) awaken the brain's executive centers, charge up the reward center and give the ADHD sufferer a sense of euphoria, power and control – until it all comes crashing down a few hours later. Psychedelics or hallucinogens like marijuana, LSD or PCP ("angel dust") send a person on a short trip into an insane world of altered reality complete with delusions and hallucinations. The next day, true reality is just that much more gray and unpleasant. Unfortunately, all of these pharmaceutical shortcuts to peace and joy are really just dead end roads which often lead to tragic consequences and further deterioration in brain function.

Meditation can provide a way for those with scattered minds to find refuge from their inner turmoil and discover a world within themselves that is pleasant and inviting. I first turned to meditation as a teenager when I became tired of the life of parties and the emptiness of drug use. At first, my only real goal was to learn how to "get high" without having to smoke marijuana. Once I discovered the amazing tranquility and enjoyment that could be found by simply quieting my mind and body, I was hooked. In the typically extreme ADHD manner, I pursued the development of meditation skills with an obsessive passion. Most days, I would return from high school and would spend 2 or 3 hours in meditation. I came to realize that if I could achieve a deep enough state of relaxation that this pleasant state would linger for about a day. Soon after beginning this daily discipline, my interest in drug use began to fade. I was also able to finally quit smoking, a habit I had carried with me since I was 9 or 10 years old.

The changes that meditation brought about also seemed to awaken a newfound interest in studying natural medicine. Bit by bit, I revolutionized my diet (I became a complete vegetarian for a while), began to run every day and I studied herbal medicine, fasting, and many other interesting areas. Looking back, I believe that it was a simple meditation practice that started to awaken the sleeping executive centers in my brain, and helped me to venture down a road of maturity and responsibility in my life. In the space of about a year, I became a serious student and brought my marks up high enough to at least get into university. Later, biofeedback was able to significantly improve my meditation skills and my academic gains increased much more.

BASIC RELAXATION AND MEDITATION

The simplest form of meditation involves relaxation exercises intended to reduce stress levels and bring the mind into a place of tranquility. Many techniques have been advocated, and they often involve these few simple steps:

- Find a quiet location where you will not be disturbed by other people or telephone calls. Using foam earplugs is very helpful to prevent background noises from disturbing your quiet time.

- Try lying flat on your back on the floor with a pillow under your knees and a towel rolled up under your neck. Stretch your arms out with your palms up.

- Spend a few minutes gaining control over your breathing. Breath in as deeply as you can through your nose using your abdomen to inhale, followed by your chest. Exhale as slowly and evenly as possible squeezing all air out to completely empty your lungs. Breath control may sound simple, but it takes a considerable amount of practice to do well.

- Avoid thinking or worrying about anything. The goal of this experience is to expel all thoughts and to give the mind an opportunity to be wakeful but in a state of quiet rest. This is the most difficult skill to acquire but is vital in order to achieve benefits from relaxation exercises. Every thought entering mind during this time should be treated like a spark from a fire that lands on your arm. By quickly dismissing the thought as you would brush a spark off your arm, it immediately disappears from your consciousness. Entertaining the thought causes to grow in your mind (like a spark would burn), and it is much harder to return to a place of quiet tranquility.

- Each session generally requires at least 20 minutes to experience the full benefits. GSR biofeedback can be used to more rapidly acquire the skills to enter a deep state of tranquility through this method. GSR biofeedback essentially gives an audible indication whenever a thought enters the mind during the relaxation session and makes it much easier to enter and maintain a deep state of relaxation.

PRAYERFUL MEDITATION AND THE SPIRITUALLY CENTERED LIFE

Although relaxation exercises help to calm the mind and can leave one more focused and relaxed, many people will develop a longing for more spiritual meaning in their lives; something that simple relaxation exercises or biofeedback alone cannot satisfy. People with ADHD are often hurting and broken on the inside and will benefit greatly by developing themselves spiritually. If a person is spiritually crushed and his or her mind is full of guilt and turmoil, these issues must be addressed before they can really become focused and live a purposeful and productive life.

Meditation can be a place where this spiritual awakening can begin to take place and where a person can experience inner healing and transformation. Those who have a belief in God may find that daily prayerful meditation is a place where they can nurture a very personal and life-transforming relationship with their Creator. Others, who have no prior faith in anything beyond their senses, may find that the deeply mystical experience of prayerful meditation opens up new possibilities and may awaken them to spiritual realities.

I was an agnostic when I began to explore meditation back in the 70's. After a couple of years of intense devotion to this practice, studying many forms of meditation and later adding biofeedback, I began to sense an inner longing for deeper spiritual realities. In my quest, I began to read the New Testament of the Bible, not as a religious person, but as someone who was seeking to know if there was any real meaning to life. Instead of just reading, I would deeply contemplate meaningful passages, sometimes meditating on one sentence for several minutes. I found that something very powerful seemed to resonate with my spirit when I meditated on these passages and I found myself frequently caught up in a state of joyous awe that I had never experienced with any other form of meditation. Later, I began to incorporate prayer, thanksgiving and worship into this time of meditation. To this day, I have found great strength, healing and focus by starting each day with scriptural meditation, worship, thankfulness and prayer for myself and others. I really believe that a life of purpose and meaning must be built on a sound spiritual foundation. This is especially apparent for those with ADHD, whose lives can so easily end up broken, confused and meaningless. Over the years, I have seen scores of people who have risen above their apparent limitations and now have focused, productive and joy-filled lives by becoming spiritually centered and empowered.

Chapter 27

Keys to a Productive Life - ADHD as Friend and Ally

What's So Great About Having ADHD?

Most parents who have had to live with an ADHD child would find it challenging to see their child's inattentiveness, hyperactivity or impulsivity as anything positive. Particularly when a child is very strong willed or highly oppositional, a parent's patience can be stretched to the limit. Most adults with ADHD can easily end up wallowing in remorse over a life that has been tarnished by regretful decisions, and repeated failures. After all, how can anything good come out of such an insidious brain disorder? But, in fact, there are some truly beneficial qualities to the ADHD brain, qualities that can help a person find success and happiness if they are properly tapped and managed. Many authorities have observed that those with ADHD can often be highly creative, intuitive, decisive, and energetic. It is certain that many of the world's great leaders, artists, scientists, politicians and writers were able to be who they were and accomplish what they did by taking advantage of their peculiar ADHD traits.

Striking a Balance Between Discipline and Nurturing

Parents with ADHD children must nurture their self-esteem by helping them cultivate their gifts and talents. Every child has something that they can enjoy and do well – something that can give them a taste of excellence and accomplishment. Parents must also become sensitive to their child's need for recognition and affirmation. Kids with ADHD always hear about it when they have been bad or have failed in some way. These kids must also be smothered with affection whenever they do anything right. It takes effort for a parent to praise a child for doing well but it is energy well spent. Positive affirmation molds behavior in a much more powerful way than punishment.

On the other hand, letting hyperactive children get away with murder or allowing them to grow up as a spoiled brat is equally harmful. Spoiled kids will eventually face the consequences of unmanaged bad behavior. It is far better to help shape their behavior under the loving guidance of consistent parental discipline than to wait for the legal system to take over this responsibility. Parents need to be well equipped to deal with oppositional behavior through consistent, firm discipline without resorting to worthless nagging or the expression of anger. Nagging at a child only weakens a parent's authority and increases the likelihood that the behavior will continue. Children must learn that "no means no", and that disobedience brings definite and immediate consequences. Kids with no behavioral boundaries will be insecure and unhappy, even if they are defiant and act as if they want to completely "run their own show".

I have learned a great deal about positively molding behavior by training birds. Since I was a boy, I have raised and trained many intelligent birds such as crows, magpies, and parrots. Intelligent birds are often hyperactive and oppositional by nature but they can be molded into submissive, sweet and loving pets if trained correctly. Most bird behaviors can be shaped by praising them for good behavior and providing other appropriate rewards when those behaviors are exhibited. However, they must also learn that bad behaviors bring immediate negative consequences. For instance, if a parrot screams, it does no good to scream back at the parrot or to nag or threaten it. As well, you cannot hit, slap or act in anger toward the parrot — it will only express other bad behaviors and be emotionally (or physically) harmed. Instead, you might cover the bird's cage with a blanket or put the bird in an empty bath tub and shut the bathroom door for a few minutes. If the negative consequences are consistent, immediate and unpleasant, the bad behavior is eventually extinguished and you can spend your time focusing on love, nurturing and building a bond of trust. Once you have clearly established that you are above the bird in authority (higher on the "pecking order") the bird respects you and learns that no means no. Childhood behavior is, of course, far more sophisticated but many of the same principles apply.

The million copy best seller, "The Strong-Willed Child" by psychologist, Dr. James Dobson, is a classic work on child rearing that can be a lifesaver for parents with an ADHD child. My wife and I read this book over 12 years ago as we were grappling with some way to handle our very strong-willed daughter. Dr. Dobson provides principles that help to positively shape your child's will without breaking his or her spirit. These principles will help you to stay calm and collected as you establish and maintain authority with your child. It is essential for parents to establish the delicate balance between loving nurture and discipline that every child needs.

Avoiding the Most Common Parenting Mistakes

Being a good parent is always a tough job and one that is that much more difficult when your child has ADHD. Psychologists John and Linda Friel have written a brilliant book entitled *"The 7 Worst Things Parents Do"*. This book could be a lifesaver for parents with an ADHD child or adolescent, and it could make a great difference in the outcome of the child's life. In this book, the authors recount stories from their many years of family counselling that illustrate how some of the most well intentioned parents can make common sense mistakes which can end up seriously harming their child's development. Unfortunately, the pressures of today's society, combined with the changes in people's attitudes have tended made these parenting errors more common than ever before. In my opinion, this book is a "must read" for every parent with an ADHD child. This is a short summary of some of my own take-home lessons adapted from this excellent book:

1. Babying your child. Many of today's parents are afraid to discipline their child or set up clear boundaries of acceptable behavior. Rather than protecting their child's sensitive soul, a lack of parental discipline tends to create an insecure child with serious social disabilities. Children derive security and safety, in part, by learning submission to proper rules and authority figures rather than being allowed to run wild. There is nothing more obnoxious than a hyperactive, misbehaving child whose parents stand by and giggle at their rude behavior. As well, parents who continually coddle their children and try to protect them from every hurt are doing them a great disfavor. I know of families who still get up at night with five or six year old children every time they make a sound. Some of these kids have never learned to sleep through the night and will throw temper tantrums if one or the other parent does not immediately get up to attend them at any hour. Unfortunately, overly-coddled kids may be completely unprepared to face a very harsh and unforgiving world.

2. Don't put enough effort into your marriage. There is nothing more valuable you can do for your child than learning to sincerely and openly love your spouse. In contrast, broken or strife-filled marriages can lead to broken, anxious or psychologically scarred children. Research has clearly confirmed that children are the most seriously injured victims when there is marital strife. As well, parents who are divorced or otherwise single need to make every effort to create a loving and nurturing atmosphere in the home.

3. Forcing your child to be involved in too many activities. Some kids grow up without ever having a chance to just be kids. It is vital that kids have plenty of time to just play and have fun. Certainly it is good for them to learn to work hard and to do their best in everything they do, but it is not appropriate for children to be workaholics. Hard work, academic achievement or even extra-curricular activities should never crowd ordinary play out of a child's life. Healthy and happy children are those who grow up learning how to appropriately balance work, social activities and recreational pursuits.

4. Not putting effort into developing your emotional and spiritual life. Today, kids can easily grow up in an emotional and spiritual vacuum. This is the day of moral relativism where kids can easily come to think that there are no absolutes, no truth and no real purpose upon which to build their lives. The fact is that the strength of our society depends upon such basic principles as a respect for the lives of others, a commitment to our families, and a belief that our lives have purpose and meaning. Parents who are committed to developing their own moral, spiritual and emotional lives are also helping to build a strong foundation for the life of their child.

5. Trying to fill the role of your child's best friend. Parents need to be parents, first and foremost. So many people today are afraid to be tough with their kids when necessary because they are simply afraid that it will harm their friendship with their child. In some cases, parents even use their children as confidants, pouring out all of their problems onto the child or teenager as they would to a best friend. Although it is certainly important to be a friend to your child, and to develop open lines of communication, children need you to be a stable, strong parent far more than they need your friendship. This is an especially common problem for single parents, who might have little time for adult friendships, and who find it easy turn to their child to fill this void. Children or adolescents cannot bear the burden of being their parent's best friend or, even worse, their personal psychologist. Many parents who make this mistake will wake up in shock one day when their "best friend" betrays their friendship and runs the other way in rebellion.

6. Not building enough structure into your child's life. Even though there are many parents who turn their kids into workaholics or plan and structure every moment of their lives, there are also many parents who simply let their kids run their own lives. Most kids, if left to plan their schedule, will plan little or nothing at all. Apart from showing up at school, hanging out with friends and watching a few favorite TV shows, most kids who are left to manage their own time will spend much of it randomly drifting from one thing to the next. Although kids need a significant amount of unstructured play time, they also must learn time management, personal organization and ways to make productive use of their time. This is especially true of kids with ADHD who, without structure in their lives, are headed for personal disaster. Kids need to consistently clean their rooms, do their homework, keep track of their money, make progress in their personal reading and be involved in a reasonable amount of sports, music or other structured extracurricular activities. As well, parents should help their children to progressively develop their interests and aptitudes, and encourage them to set goals for their lives.

7. Expecting your your dreams to be fulfilled by your child. Although it is necessary for parents to believe in their kids and to hope the best for their futures, it is wrong for them to try to live out their own dreams through their children. I have seen how harmful this can be while working with many upcoming elite athletes who have hard-driving parents behind them, dreaming of gold medals and million dollar contracts. Although some of these kids turn out to be a Wayne Gretsky success story, in far more cases, they end up being square pegs in a round hole, having to suffer with sledge hammer parents. I know of cases where promising athletes did not make it at the world class level and ended up being disowned by their parents. Likewise, I have seen what can result from trying to force a child to become a physician, accountant or other professional, when all along, the child had other aspirations or aptitudes. I am very thankful that my parents believed in me and always encouraged me to do my best. They helped me look for my own interests and aptitudes, and poured their efforts into supporting and encouraging these, rather than pushing me to fulfill their own dreams.

THE IMPORTANCE OF STRUCTURE IN ADHD

Structure is a most necessary ingredient in every ADHD sufferer's life. Those with ADHD lack the internal mechanisms to conduct themselves in a structured and orderly manner. They will do much better in an environment in which external structure and organization is created. For children, this means regular schedules for meals, bedtimes, homework and extracurricular activities. Structure also means putting reasonable limits on things like TV viewing or video games; things that, in more than small quantities, can easily become a mind-numbing waste of time. College students with ADHD should take a course in effective study habits and live strictly by these principles. I took an effective study habits course in university and it helped my academic and personal life immensely. Based on the suggestions I learned in this course, I sat down each Sunday night and scheduled every event during my week into fifteen-minute blocks. Morning prayer and meditation, exercise, scheduled courses, after-lecture review sessions, meal breaks, new assignments and exam study times were all mapped out in a precise schedule. This system worked so well that I was able to take off one day per week to completely relax and yet maintained consistently high marks. Although such rigid structure may sound very inhibiting, under the circumstances, it was actually very freeing. Beneath an immense load of pressure in my pre-medicine courses, I was able to stay relaxed and focused, because all I had to worry about was completing what was on my schedule for the moment, and nothing else. Even though I am incredibly disorganized by nature, this experience taught me that structure and organization is very attainable if you take the time to create it externally.

Adults with ADHD must also make the effort to create appropriate structure and organization in their lives. Perhaps the most consistent trait of every successful ADHD adult is that they keep their lives ordered by an electronic or paper organizer. I have relied on various electronic organizers for years now and I would not want to live without this artificial extension to my brain. Currently I am completely sold on the Palm Pilot® electronic organizer, a personal digital assistant. This little gadget makes staying organized so simple that, if you use one, people might start thinking that you are the most organized person they know. It contains a great scheduler that can be programmed to beep you before appointments. I have also added a piece of software called "Bug Me" to my Palm Pilot®. This lets me set an unlimited number of alarms to remind me of important meetings, assignments and any other things on my "to do" list. There are many other features that make the Palm Pilot® one of the most useful items that adults with ADHD can use to help bring structure into their lives. I wear mine on my belt and, therefore, it never leaves my body. A less expensive version of the Palm Pilot®, called the "Visor®" is now available.

THE PRINCIPLE CENTERED LIFE

Many adults with ADHD have benefited from a program developed by Dr. Steven R. Covey and described in his book, "The 7 Habits of Highly Effective People". This book, which has been an international best seller for over 10 years, has helped millions of people to have more organized, productive and purposeful lives. Since this is such a practical and useful program, there are actually "7 Habits" workshops, specifically presented to groups of adult ADHD sufferers. These principles help ADHD adults to know how to take responsibility and make the most of their lives. More than just another positive-thinking program, the "7 Habits" provide a framework upon which to build an organized life, centered around personalized guiding principles. It is well worthwhile for every ADHD adult to study this book and take a "7 Habits" workshop if possible. There is even software to use the "7 Habits" program within the Palm Pilot® electronic organizer.

PRACTICAL SPIRITUALITY FOR THOSE WITH ADHD

Having ADHD is not a bed of roses. Most of us who carry this this insidious brain problem into our adult lives will face serious consequences. Unfortunately, many people never seek help or may not even know they suffer with ADHD until their lives are struck with disaster. So many people with ADHD live their lives like human bulldozers, plowing over every problem in life until they are suddenly faced with a mountain. For some, it will be a chemical dependency or addiction that finally brings them to their knees. For others, it might be a broken marriage or financial ruin, or maybe even all of these things at once, that will finally bring them to the place where they realize they just aren't able to get it together. For some people, ADHD unknowingly leads them down a long and treacherous trail that turns out to be a one-way trip into the "Valley of the Shadow of Death". Three of my rough and hyper school buddies never returned from that valley. They ended their lives before they were 20 years old. Regardless of the reasons, many with ADHD will one day find themselves at the bottom of life's barrel and in desperate need for a spiritual foundation upon which to rebuild their lives.

The spiritual practices of prayer, meditation and seeking to know God on a real and personal level are well-established essentials in the successful recovery from addictions. (Carter, 1998)

After many decades, the original 12-step program of spiritual recovery remains recognized as the only consistently successful approach to the management of all forms of serious addictive disorders. Because ADHD shares many common features with these disorders, there are strong reasons to consider incorporating spiritual practices into the treatment of ADHD. (F.I.R., 1996) The spiritual principles derived from the 12-step program are not just useful for the management of addictions; they are intended to help a person achieve balance, productivity and serenity – qualities of life, which are absent or deficient in the lives of those with ADHD.

Much like that of an addict, ADHD sufferer's often live their lives in a state of outward and inward chaos. Most grow up without ever living up to the expectations of parents and teachers, and often continue on to disappoint and frustrate their spouses and employers, as well as themselves. Impulsive decision-making often leaves a trail of regret, as well as a network of people who have, one way or another, fallen victim to the bad decisions made by the ADHD-affected person.

In search for some sense of control, many of those with ADHD succumb to workaholism, manipulative behavior or aggression. They may blame others for their misery and spend their lives seeking an elusive sense of happiness. They make resolutions to change but find that they are powerless to follow through with their good intentions. Many end up compulsively drawn into destructive habits, attempting to satisfy their inner cravings in order to experience some sense of pleasure inside a mind and body which is full of unpleasant thoughts and feelings. Unfortunately, for a significant proportion of those with ADHD, psychological illness comes to play a painful leading role in life.

Many people are repelled by the idea of exploring the 12-step program, thinking that it is only for alcoholics and drug addicts. In reality, the principles in this program can provide a spiritual foundation for anyone who is struggling with difficulties in life. These principles have given freedom to millions of people around the world and is being increasingly presented as a non-sectarian approach to genuine spirituality. One recent study indicated that a 12-step program was a successful and non-threatening way to introduce non-religious people to spiritual principles. (Winzelberg, 1999) Individuals who are agnostic or who do not come from any religious background can benefit from this program because it is practical, highly experiential, and can be adapted to a person's personal religious views. Many people, who begin this program as agnostic or atheistic, gradually become convinced of spiritual realities because of the potent and transforming effects of spirituality in their lives.

Essentially, the 12-step program involves coming to an experience of peace with God (first 3 steps), peace with ourselves (next 4 steps), peace with others (next 2 steps), and practicing spiritual disciplines intended to help us consistently maintain the spiritual gains that have been made (last 3 steps). These last steps include a commitment to prayer and meditation, with the intent to deepen our personal relationship with God and to come to a place where we can experience the powerful and joyous reality of God's presence. Rather than just a technique of spiritual escape for those with troubled lives, the 12-step principles compel people to come face to face with, and deal with, the issues that spiritually imprison them; separating them from a loving relationship with God, and other human beings, and keep them bound to a negative self-image. The book, "The Twelve Steps: a Guide for Adults with Attention Deficit Disorder" is an excellent resource for those who wish to explore this avenue of spirituality. (F.I.R., 1996)

THE TWELVE STEPS
A PRACTICAL SPIRITUAL PATH FOR THOSE WITH ADHD

GOAL	STEP
Peace **with** **God**	**STEP ONE:** We admitted that we were powerless over ADHD and that our lives had become unmanageable.
	STEP TWO: We came to believe that a power greater than ourselves could restore us to sanity.
	STEP THREE: We made a decision to turn our will and our lives over to the care of God as we understand Him.
Peace **with** **Ourselves**	**STEP FOUR:** We made a searching and fearless moral inventory of ourselves.
	STEP FIVE: We admitted to God, to ourselves and to another human being the exact nature of our wrongs.
	STEP SIX: We were entirely ready to have God remove all these defects of character.
	STEP SEVEN: We humbly asked God to remove our shortcomings.
Peace **with** **Others**	**STEP EIGHT:** We made a list of all persons we had harmed and became willing to make amends to them all.
	STEP NINE: We made direct amends to such people wherever possible, except when to do so would injure them or others.
	STEP TEN: We continued to take personal inventory and, when we were wrong we promptly admitted it.
Keeping **the** **Peace**	**STEP ELEVEN:** We sought, through prayer and meditation, to improve our conscious contact with God as we understood Him, praying for the knowledge of His will for us and the power to carry it out.
	STEP TWELVE: Having had a spiritual awakening as the result of these steps, we tried to carry this message to others, and to practice these principles in all our affairs.

PUTTING IT ALL TOGETHER

This book is intended to present a reasonably comprehensive and organized approach to ADHD in children and adults, using the concepts inherently unique to Functional Medicine. I have also included many of my own insights and experiences as an adult with ADHD and as the parent of a child with ADHD. My hope is that this book will prove to be a useful resource to help you put together your own personal ADHD puzzle. In reality, the puzzle is never completely solved. Successfully living with ADHD is a way of life and a continual process of discovery. To some people, the lifestyle that must kept in order to make ADHD a friend and ally may seem too limiting at first. Eating a certain way; taking herbal medicines and supplements; undergoing periodic detoxification; exercising regularly; getting organized; and learning to focus and recharge with meditation, biofeedback or spiritual practices all may seem overwhelming and just too restrictive. However, the freedom, joy and personal power that comes when a hyperactive brain begins to heal and to function optimally makes it all worthwhile.

I am regularly approached by people who have tried just one or two of the suggestions made in this book and have seen remarkable changes in themselves or their children. Perhaps they have simply tried an elimination test diet or used a couple of herbal medicines, and they are amazed at how much positive change has taken place. In other cases, a more comprehensive approach is required before real and lasting changes are experienced.

One of the keys to success with this program is to work under the guidance of a healthcare professional who is versed in the principles described in this book. As a whole, this program is somewhat new, and few professionals will be familiar with each step as it is presented. However, much of what is presented will be very familiar territory to many progressive healthcare providers. This is especially true of medical doctors or osteopathic physicians practicing Complementary Medicine, Alternative Medicine, Nutritional Medicine, Environmental Medicine or Functional Medicine. It would also be true of most naturopathic physicians (those who are certified by the American Association of Naturopathic Physicians) and some chiropractors who have taken extra training in Nutritional or Functional Medicine. There are also some dieticians and nurse practitioners who are qualified to supervise patients through much of what has been outlined in this book. I have been teaching these principles to healthcare professionals in various locations around the world for the past two years and I am amazed at how many professionals concur that much of what is presented in this book is what they have been using successfully for the treatment of ADHD in their own practices.

Some readers may wish to lend this book to their physician or purchase a copy for them. There is presently a great hunger amongst the medical profession for scientifically based information which would allow them to incorporate principles of natural medicine into their practices. For this reason, in the section that follows this chapter I have included the lecture notes that I use when teaching this information to healthcare professionals. This information is a rather concise discourse, in moderately technical language, covering many, but not all, of the same principles that are described in this book. A busy physician might consider reading this section first before attempting to read the remainder of the book.

For a list of some of the healthcare practitioners who currently utilize the principles of Functional Medicine, individuals should contact the Institute for Functional Medicine at (253) 858-4724 (www.fxmed.com). Another good resource is the American Association of Naturopathic Physicians at (206) 298-1026 (www.naturopathic.org).

Healthcare practitioners who are following the principles outined in this book are encouraged to submit their name and contact information to **www.PureLiving.com**. An expanding practitioner referal list will be posted at this web site for the benefit of individuals who are searching for a practitioner familiar with the program outlined in this book.

Section Six

Functional Medicine Approach to ADHD – Referenced Overview for Healthcare Professionals

This section is provided for the benefit of healthcare professionals as a concise overview of the Functional Medicine perspective on the evaluation and management of ADHD. Those healthcare providers who would like to obtain further training in the emerging field of Functional Medicine are encouraged to explore the educational resources available through the *Institute for Functional Medicine* in Gig Harbor, WA. (**www.fxmed.com**)

This organization offers comprehensive full-credit courses such as "Applying Functional Medicine in Clinical Practice" as well as pertinent published material and audiovisual programs. "Functional Medicine Update" is a monthly audio program produced by Dr. Jeffrey Bland, Ph.D. which is heard by thousands of subscribers from around the world. As well, the fully (continuing medical education) accredited **International Symposium on Functional Medicine** is an annual scientific conference attended by well over 1000 professionals and features some of the world's most sought after scientists and clinicians.

INTRODUCTION AND BACKGROUND

Attention deficit hyperactivity disorder (ADHD) is defined by the *Diagnostic and Statistical Manual, Fourth Edition* **(DSM-IV)**, as a condition characterized by developmentally inappropriate **inattention** and **impulsivity** with or without **hyperactivity**. Depending upon the region and the investigator, ADHD has been found in 5-15% of school age children and is responsible for approximately 50% of the referrals to childhood diagnostic clinics. (Hallowell, 1994; Hechtman, 1996) Most authorities estimate that the prevalence of this disorder is three to ten times greater in boys than in girls. However, many no longer consider this to be a valid estimate. More recently, it has been found that the majority of girls with ADHD, and a minority of boys with the disorder have a form of ADHD in which inattentiveness is the predominant manifestation and hyperactivity is not a significant symptom. (Ernst, 1994; Gaub, 1997) Such children may evade diagnosis because their behavior is not disruptive, as is the case with children having ADHD with hyperactivity.

It is common to refer to those with the predominantly inattentive form of the disorder as having attention deficit disorder (ADD), whereas ADHD is commonly reserved for those with hyperactivity as a predominant feature. However, according to the DSM-IV all forms of the disorder are now referred to as ADHD with the

Signs and Symptoms of ADHD

additional acknowledgement of three main subtypes: predominantly inattentive, predominantly hyperactive, and combined type. (APA, 1994)

ADHD may place a child at risk for numerous challenges. If not intensively managed, a child with ADHD will likely experience academic underachievement, increased risk of injuries and problems with self esteem and socialization. (Brooks R., 1994; Pless, 1995, Johnston, 1993; Satterfield, 1994) Later in adolescence and adulthood, those with ADHD have a high risk of experiencing psychological disorders, substance abuse and addictions, traffic accidents, and trouble with the law. (Eyestone, 1994; Jensen, 1993; Lie, 1992; Mannuzza, 1993; Biederman, 1993; Rugle, 1993) Nevertheless, there are numerous examples of individuals with ADHD who have risen above their potential limitations to achieve a high level of personal success.

DEFINING THE CAUSES OF ADHD: A PATIENT CENTERED APPROACH TO ADHD BEGINS BY GAINING AN UNDERSTANDING OF THE UNDERLYING ETIOLOGY.

General Principles

The prevailing approach to the treatment of ADHD relies almost entirely upon pharmacological manipulation of neurotransmitters to bring about a desirable symptomatic response. Efforts to treat this disorder by addressing underlying causation have been largely overlooked. Perhaps this is because many clinicians are under the impression that ADHD is the result of an immutable genetic defect or they may believe that the prevailing approach to treatment is satisfactory. However, data attributing a multifactorial etiology to ADHD has accumulated considerably in recent years along with numerous studies demonstrating benefits derived from addressing several of these underlying factors. The considerable challenge to clinicians wishing to take a more cause-oriented approach in treating ADHD is in trying to organize and implement a widely diverse range of investigational and therapeutic possibilities based upon a more cause-oriented approach. Functional Medicine provides a rational framework or an intellectual methodology, which enables a clinician to approach ADHD in an organized and effective manner. Firstly, the Functional Medicine practitioner maintains a **patient-centered** rather than

disease-centered perspective focussing away from the taxonomy of the patient's disease and focussing instead upon the patient's function. Each person is regarded as biochemically unique and the practitioner should strive through clinical skills and appropriate testing to uncover the underlying unique causes of the patient's disorder. Rather than just "attacking the disease" with a standard pharmaceutical "armamentarium", the Functional Medicine practitioner should make a sincere effort to understand the antecedents (risk factors), triggers (physiological disturbances) and mediators (neurotransmitter disturbances) which underlie the individual patient's condition. (Galland, 1997)

The Functional Medicine Model of ADHD

This approach dictates a priority of treatment (antecedents > triggers > mediators > signs and symptoms) but not necessarily an order of intervention. For instance, the clinician may elect to prescribe treatments, which improve the symptoms of ADHD (modify neurotransmitter mediators) while beginning to explore the underlying antecedents and triggers underlying that patient's symptoms. If underlying antecedents and triggers are identified and corrected, usually in time, there will be less reliance upon symptom suppressing therapies and the long-term prognosis will likely be significantly improved.

DISRUPTION OF NEUROLOGICAL MEDIATORS: PATHOPHYSIOLOGICAL FACTORS RESULTING IN THE SIGNS AND SYMPTOMS OF ADHD

ADHD – A Disorder of Executive Control

Knowledge of the basic mechanisms resulting in ADHD symptomatology has grown considerably over the last decade. Currently, the leading hypothesis explaining the behavioral and cognitive manifestations of ADHD suggests that in such cases there is diminished function of polysynaptic dopaminergic circuits belonging to executive centers within the brain's pre-frontal cortex. (Giedd, 1994; Levy, 1991; Baker, 1991) These executive centers are largely inhibitory in nature and are responsible for impulse control and the ability to maintain sustained attention.(Barkley,1997; Barkley, 1992; Benson, 1991; Koziol, 1992)

Dopamine Activity at Synapse

Evidence from studies using MRI, PET scan and SPECT scan imaging as well as EEG studies now suggests that the brains of those with ADHD exhibit differences both morphologically and metabolically from normal controls, particularly with regards to the prefrontal executive centers.

(Swanson, 1998a; Castellanos, 1996; Amen, 1997; Ernst, 1998; Lazzaro, 1998) Various disturbances in dopaminergic activity within these brain centers have remained the primary molecular defects implicated in ADHD, although other neurotransmitters (particularly norepinephrine) have also been incriminated. Decreased sensitivity of the dopaminergic (D4) receptor as well as heightened dopamine reuptake by the presynaptic dopamine transporter have been suggested to be two variants which both result in diminished dopaminergic activity within executive centers. (Swanson, 1998a; Swanson, 1998b; LaHoste, 1996; Alsobrook, 1998)

ADHD – A Reward Deficiency Syndrome

In addition to the problems of executive control conferred by diminished dopaminergic activity, decreased dopamine activity has been implicated as a primary factor in addiction. (Nash, 1997) ADHD has been closely associated with addiction and some authorities support the notion that the neurological basis for both addiction and ADHD are largely shared. (Blum, 1995; Wilens, 1997)

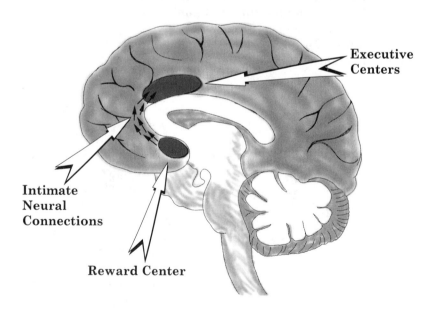

The dopaminergic system, and in particular the dopamine D2 receptor, has been clearly implicated as central to reward mechanisms in the brain (mechanisms which convey a sense of reward or satisfaction upon the individual). Dysfunction of the D2 dopamine receptors leads to aberrant substance seeking behavior (alcohol, drug, tobacco, and food) and other related behaviors (sexual addiction, pathological gambling, Tourette's syndrome, and ADHD). This need for "neurological satisfaction" may also help to explain why individuals with ADHD have a tendency to participate in high-risk sports, criminal activities or other euphoria generating behaviors and why ADHD sufferers typically have a very low tolerance to boredom. In light of accumulating evidence along these lines, ADHD has been called a "reward deficiency syndrome" with strong associations to addiction. (Blum, 1996)

ADHD – "Minimal Brain Dysfunction"

It has long been known that ADHD is often associated with other cognitive deficits. For example, memory deficits are commonly associated with ADHD suggesting that brain regions, such as the hippocampus, and neurotransmitters, such as acetlylcholine, may be involved in ADHD symptomatology. (Benezra, 1988; Felton, 1987; Douglas, 1990) Particularly disabling is the diminishment in nonverbal working memory exhibited by most ADHD sufferers. (Denckla, 1996; Barkley, 1997) This feature of ADHD results in a diminished sense of time as well as a decreased ability to hold events or tasks in the mind. Tardiness, missed appointments, procrastination, poor task planning, and failure to meet deadlines are all examples of how diminished working memory can result in serious consequences, particularly in adulthood.

Diminishment of serotonergic neuronal activity may also play a significant role in ADHD comorbid features such as depression or aggressive behaviors. This may explain why antidepressants have been shown bring about behavioral improvement in many cases. (Hornig, 1998; Cook, 1995)

ANTECEDENTS – INHERITANCE AND ENVIRONMENT

Genetics

Epidemiological data suggests that genetics may play a significant role as an antecedent in the etiology of ADHD. (Hechtman, 1996; Biederman, 1995) There is little doubt that the inherited predisposition to ADHD is polygenetic. Recent studies have identified differences in genes encoding for both the D2, and the D4 dopamine receptor in ADHD, which would create a state of relative dopamine insensitivity in affected brain regions. (LaHoste, 1996; Blum, 1996) Other studies have associated ADHD to genetic polymorphisms associated with increased activity of the pre-synaptic dopamine transporter (which would result in increased uptake of dopamine). (Cook, 1995) Other genetic factors contributing to ADHD may include inherited tendencies toward allergic states, decreased immune competence, and a variety of genetic polymorphisms encoding for diminished capacity to detoxify drugs, heavy metals and xenobiotics.

Environmental Neurotoxins

Because environmental contributions to the development of ADHD may begin at or even before conception, the genetic contribution may be difficult to differentiate from that coming from the environment. Maternal to fetal transport of various neurotoxicants can occur readily during pregnancy. (Needleman, 1995; Vimy, 1990; Lewis, 1992) A woman who has an ongoing exposure or a significant body burden of neurotoxic substances (metals, solvents, pesticides, PCB's, alcohol or other drugs of abuse) may herself exhibit features consistent with ADHD and she may give birth to a child who manifests symptoms of ADHD. In such cases it might be assumed that ADHD is inherited when it is actually acquired. (Milberger, 1997) Children remain susceptible to neurotoxicants following birth and some of these agents have been shown to be common amongst children in North America. (Minder, 1994; Eppright, 1996; Kahn, 1995; David, 1976; Jacobson, 1996)

Epidemiological and clinical data have identified a number of toxicological factors associated with ADHD. (Needleman, 1995; Minder, 1994; Eppright, 1996; Kahn, 1995; Schauss, 1981) Maternal tobacco and drug use has been associated with a higher risk of ADHD. One study suggested that as many as 25 percent of all behavioral disorders in children can be attributed to smoking in pregnancy. (Williams, 1998; Eyler, 1998) In addition, chronic, low-level lead intoxication in North American children is reported to exist in an alarmingly high incidence. Research has estimated that nearly one-fifth of American children under the age of six currently meet the criteria for lead toxicity at a level which has been associated with cognitive deficits and behavioral disturbances (>10 mcg/dl whole blood lead). (Needleman, 1993) Low-level lead intoxication has also been associated with addictive behaviors and impulsivity suggesting neurological changes consistent with a "reward deficiency syndrome". (Brockel, 1998) In keeping with this data, pilot studies have been done which have demonstrated improvement in ADHD behaviors in some children with moderate elevations in blood lead levels that have been treated with calcium edetate chelation. (David, 1976) It seems clear that all children with ADHD should be examined for lead toxicity early in the course of evaluation and treatment.

In addition to lead, other metal neurotoxicants such as mercury, cadmium, aluminum, as well as pesticides and PCB's are nearly ubiquitous contaminants arising from dental amalgams, food, air and drinking water and these agents may act synergistically to impair neurological function and development in susceptible children. (Vimy, 1990; Lewis, 1992) The Consumer's Union of the United States has recently conducted the largest study to date looking at the level of human exposure to a wide range of pesticides in the U.S. food supply. In this startling report, it was demonstrated that human exposure to pesticides is far greater than ever previously estimated and that children are at particularly high risk for neurotoxic effects from regular inadvertent pesticide exposure from common foodstuffs. (Kenney, 1999) A summary of this report has been published in the March 1999 U.S. edition of Consumer's Report Magazine.

Perhaps even more astonishing are the implications derived from a recent landmark study by S. Edelson , in which 56 autistic children were studied from a toxicological perspective. (Edelson, 1998; Edelson, 1999) In this study, post provocative urine challenge testing was performed on all children in which a chelating agent was given and a urine sample was then gathered to measure heavy metal excretion. This methodology demonstrated elevated body burdens of heavy metals in 100% of subjects. As well, highly significant elevations of a wide range of organic xenobiotics were also demonstrated in the blood in 95%. Functional liver detoxification testing (caffeine, acetaminophen, aspirin clearance) was markedly abnormal in 98%. Dr. Edelson postulates that autism is primarily a neurotoxicological phenomenon resulting from xenobiotic exposure of the fetus and infant (while the blood brain barrier is poorly developed) combined with an inherited insufficiency of liver detoxification mechanisms. Although this type of investigation has not yet been conducted in children with ADHD, many authorities believe that ADHD and autism are part of the same spectrum of disorders and may share many etiological features. (Myhr, 1998)

Nutrient Insufficiency — Essential Fatty Acids

Several workers have uncovered biochemical anomalies in children with ADHD, which may play a significant role in the morphologic and functional defects of this disorder. It has been repeatedly demonstrated that children with ADHD have a measurable reduction in tissue levels of the essential omega-six fatty acid gamma linolenic acid (GLA) as well as the omega-three fatty acid docosahexaenoic acid (DHA) when compared with age matched controls. (Crawford, 1993a; Crawford, 1993b; Neuringer, 1994; Stevens, 1995; Stevens, 1996; Colquhoun, 1981) Ongoing research at our own facility has demonstrated low levels of red blood cell DHA in 40 out of 50 children with ADHD. None of these children had elevated levels of any omega-three fatty acid. In the same series, low levels of arachidonic acid (AA) were found in only 1 subject and 10 out of 50 had modestly low levels of DGLA or GLA. Most of the subjects had elevated levels of one or more omega-six fatty acid. The ratio of total omega-six to total omega-three was elevated in 33 out of 50 subjects suggesting a need for a reduction in total omega-six fatty acids accompanied by supplementation of omega-three fatty acids. Our research would suggest that DHA supplementation is safe and beneficial in nearly all children with ADHD, whereas, omega-six supplementation, with GLA (evening primrose, borage or black current oils) is also necessary in a minority of children. EFA analysis can easily clarify a patient's EFA status. (Lyon, 1999)

Since brain EFA's are critical in neuronal structure and function, it has been frequently postulated that brain EFA dysregulation plays a key role in ADHD. DHA and AA are both important components of brain and peripheral neuron structure. They also play a vital role in the maintenance of normal immune responsiveness and in the regulation of allergy and inflammation. (Horrobin, 1990; Lee, 1991) As well, DHA has been shown to play a crucial role in fetal and childhood brain and retinal development. DHA is found in particularly high concentrations around synapses in the brain and it thus plays a vital role in impulse transmission across the synapse and in the maintenance of adequate neurotransmitter pools. (Horrobin, 1995; Liu, 1995) In fact, dopamine producing nerve endings are highly fluid and are composed of approximately 80% DHA. As well, DHA is found in high concentrations in the retina and it plays an important role in normal visual function. (Anderson, 1990; Carlson, 1993) Apart from this, DHA deficiency has been shown to result in an increased permeability of the blood brain barrier in animal studies and it is critical to the brain's defense against neurotoxic xenobiotics. (Hussain, 1994) EFA depletion may play an important role in the mediation of other toxic insults. Some researchers have suggested, in fact, that the primary effect of most xenobiotics occurs from oxidative destruction and subsequent depletion of membrane EFA's. (Horrobin, 1991)

Several studies have suggested that children who are bottle-fed are at twice the risk of developing ADHD as those who are breast fed. (Uauy, 1995) Currently, infant formulas in most of Europe and in North America do not provide supplementary DHA although breast milk has been repeatedly shown to contain DHA. (Makrides, 1995; Marked, 1994) In some countries, DHA is an additive to infant formulas and because of ethnic dietary composition, maternal intake of this EFA is also high throughout pregnancy and lactation. (Cant, 1991) Little effort has been made in North America or Europe to increase the intake of DHA during this critical period or during childhood when brain development is occurring. (Uauy-Dagach, 1995) Additionally, the typical diet of children throughout much of the developed world, including vegetarian children, is very low in EFA's. (Sanders, 1994; Simopoulos, 1991) Furthermore, children with ADHD have been reported to have impaired capabilities to synthesize DHA, AA and GLA from vegetable precursors found in the typical diet. (Stevens, 1995)

EFA deficiency has also been associated with diuresis and a marked increase in renal calcium loss. (Burgess, 1995; Claassen, 1995; Tulloch, 1994) Increased thirst and enuresis has been highly associated with ADHD (Biederman, 1995) and has been reported to be correctable through a reduction in food allergens. (Egger, 1992) This suggests that EFA deficiencies in ADHD may, at least in part, be the result of food hypersensitivity. Other data also suggests that atopic individuals and those with food allergies have an increased requirement for EFA's and normalization of EFA's may actually have a salutary effect upon atopic disorders. (Galland, 1986)

Trans fatty acids are common dietary constituents and are produced through the hydrogenation of vegetable oils. These agents are known to adversely impact health in many ways. (Ascherio, 1997) Trans fats may play a significant role in the impairment of fetal and childhood brain development. (Carlson, 1997) Amongst their many toxic effects, trans fatty acids block the enzymatic conversion of vegetable derived omega three and omega six fatty acids into the critical fatty acids DHA, EPA and GLA. In our recent research, 42 out of 50 subjects had significant levels of red blood cell trans fatty acids. (Lyon, 1999)

Nutrient Insufficiency – Other Nutrients

Besides fatty acids, inadequate provision of other nutrients during fetal development and early childhood may also play a significant role as antecedents to the development of ADHD. Magnesium levels in serum, red blood cells, and hair have all been shown to be low in the majority of children with ADHD. (Kozielec, 1997) These children also demonstrated improved behavior when administered magnesium supplements. (Starobrat, 1997) Both hair and serum zinc levels have been shown to frequently accompany ADHD. (Arnold, 1990; Bekaroglu, 1996) Those children with low serum zinc were also more frequently found to have lower free fatty acid levels suggesting that abnormalities in fatty acid metabolism may be, at least in part, a result of zinc deficiency. (Bekaroglu, 1996) It has also been shown that lower hair zinc levels correlate with a poorer response to treatment with amphetamines. (Arnold, 1990) Iron is known to play a role in the regulation of dopaminergic activity. One study demonstrated that iron supplementation in non-anemic children with ADHD resulted in diminished ADHD symptoms within 30 days. (Sever, 1997) Low levels of vitamin B1 (thiamin) have also been demonstrated in a group of children with ADHD. (Lonsdale, 1980) Although sucrose as a singular agent has remained a controversial contributor to ADHD, studies have shown improvement in behavior and school performance in children who are transferred to a diet in which "junk foods" high in sucrose, artificial flavors, artificial colors and preservatives are reduced and replaced by more nutrient dense foods. (Schauss, 1986) High refined carbohydrate diets have also been found to correlate with high tissue cadmium levels and poor cognitive performance in children. (Lester, 1982) Finally, it has been found that children with ADHD have impaired catecholamine control of blood sugar and they may exhibit worsening of behavior following a sucrose challenge. (Connors, 1986)

Other Antecedent Factors

Premature delivery, intrauterine growth retardation, neonatal sepsis and neonatal hypoxia have all been associated with a higher incidence of ADHD. (Allen, 1986; Geirsson, 1988; O' Callaghan, 1997; Matilainen, 1988) Providing excellent prenatal and obstetrical care as well as helping to improve patients' nutritional and toxicological status beginning prior to conception would likely reduce the subsequent incidence of ADHD considerably. Physical or sexual abuse, discord within the home or divorce may also have a significant impact upon the behavior of a child and their cognitive performance. Such stresses may exacerbate ADHD symptoms or promote ADHD-like behaviors in a child without ADHD.

TRIGGERS – FOOD ALLERGY, GASTROINTESTINAL FUNCTION AND THE BRAIN

Several workers have found a significant correlation between ADHD and atopic illness. (Marshall, 1989; Millman, 1976; Tryphonas, 1979) Others have linked ADHD to food allergy or food intolerances in at least a subgroup of affected children. (Carter, 1993; Boris, 1994; Krummel, 1996) In one study, demonstrable EEG changes were shown to occur immediately following the ingestion of previously identified sensitizing food. (Uhlig, 1997) Food allergies and other allergic disorders have been associated with a higher incidence of recurrent otitis media. (Nsouli, 1994; Fireman, 1988; Warshaw, 1975; Rapp, 1975) In turn, recurrent otitis media has been associated with an increased risk of ADHD. (Hagerman, 1987; Adesman, 1990; Funk, 1984; Arcia, 1983) Both food allergy and ADHD have been associated with sleep disturbances which may, in turn, contribute to a worsening of ADHD symptoms. (Marcotte, 1998; Kahn, 1987; McColley, 1997) Studies have demonstrated improved sleep in children with ADHD during an low allergy potential (oligoantigenic) diet. (Kaplan, 1987; Kaplan, 1989; Salzman, 1976)

In several studies, oligoantigenic or allergy elimination diets have been shown to be beneficial to children with ADHD (Kaplan, 1989; Egger, 1985; Schulte-Körne, 1996; Williams, 1978) and in one placebo controlled study, enzyme-potentiated desensitization (EPD) was used in an attempt to desensitize children from allergy to a broad range of potential food antigens. This treatment resulted in improved behavior in most children with ADHD. (Egger, 1992) In a recent study in England, EPD was compared to Ritalin® and to psychotherapy in three groups of children with ADHD. Although little benefit was obtained from psychotherapy, EPD and Ritalin® proved equally effective in the reduction of ADHD symptomatology. (McEwen, 1998)

Numerous mechanisms have been described to explain the immediate and longer term effects of food hypersensitivities on brain function. (Anderson, 1995) Mediators of inflammation such as histamine, bradykinins, interleukins, tumor necrosis factor alpha, prostaglandins of the PGE2 series and various neuropeptides have been shown to be present in the blood immediately after exposure to a sensitizing food. (Anderson, 1995; Carvajal, 1995) The vasoactive effects of these substances may influence cerebral vascular function and result in various symptoms, including migraine headaches. Thus, migraine headaches and even some seizure disorders in children have been shown to be highly responsive to an oligoantigenic diet. (Egger, 1983; Carter, 1985; Egger, 1989) Neuroactive peptides from food, as well as the endogenous opioids, have been demonstrated to play a significant role in the etiology of autism and other behavioral disorders. (Sher, 1997; Lucarelli, 1995) Neuroactive opioid peptides are common constituents of certain foods, such as cows milk or wheat gluten. (Teschemacher, 1991; Schick, 1985) Endogenous opioid peptides may also be released from immune cells following the administration of a sensitizing food. Neuroactive peptides may have increased access to the brain under certain pathological states such as allergy (Whitcomb, 1992; Weihe, 1991; Wahl, 1985) or essential fatty acid deficiency. As well, numerous gut derived inflammatory mediators have been shown to diminish the integrity of the blood brain barrier. (Wahl, 1985) Even in normal health, the blood brain barrier should not be considered a static barrier but should be recognized as a dynamic regulatory interface controlling the exchange of informational molecules, such as peptides, between the blood and central nervous system. (Banks, 1996) ADHD may, at least in part, be the result of a breakdown in the efficiency of this regulatory interface combined with an increase in the presence of certain neuroactive or neurotoxic substances.

Both immediate and delayed effects are possible from exposure to food antigens. Direct effects of sensitizing foodstuffs on gut mucosa may result in mucosal edema and poor digestive and absorptive functioning. (Eaton, 1995; van Elberg, 1992) Thus, numerous nutritional insufficiencies may result from chronic gut mucosal inflammation accompanying food allergy or intolerance. Additionally, inflamed gut mucosa becomes hyperpermeable resulting in a large increase in macro-molecular transport through the mesenteric lymphoid tissues and the portal circulation. (Laudat, 1994; Andre, 1987; Arvola, 1993; Bjarnason, 1995; Travis, 1992) Thus, gut lymphoid tissue and liver Kupffer cells must engage in the processing of high amounts of antigenically active debris. One of the end results of this antigenic stimulation is the release of cellular messengers and mediators of inflammation such as histamine, bradykinins and tumor necrosis factor, some of which, in turn, create increased permeability of the blood brain barrier. (Heyman, 1994) Macromolecular substances may also escape the first pass through the liver and may have direct physiological effects distant to the liver, including effects upon the brain. (Simon, 1995)

Several studies have pointed to the usefulness of intestinal permeability testing as a marker for food allergies. (Heyman, 1988; Tatsuno, 1989; Andre, 1987) This test may provide a practical means to follow the progress of patients undergoing treatment for food allergies. (Caffarelli, 1993)

Apart from food allergy, increased intestinal permeability has been associated with autism, atopic dermatitis, arthritis and numerous gastrointestinal diseases. Furthermore, a decrease in gut permeability may be accompanied by an improvement of the disease. (D'Eufemia, 1996; Forget, 1985; Jakobsson, 1993; Paganelli, 1991) Recent research at our facility has demonstrated elevated gut permeability in 49 out of 66 children (74%) with ADHD. (Lyon, 1999) Other research has been emerging which suggests that there may be a profound link between gastrointestinal function and behavior. Parenteral administration of the hormone secretin has resulted in a significant and prolonged improvement in the behavior and cognitive function of children with autism. (Horvath, 1998) The precise mechanism of action of secretin in this situation is not yet known. However, several clinicians who have been using IV secretin treatment in autistic children report evidence of improved gastrointestinal function and a concomitant decrease in microbial organic acid derivatives in the urine of these children suggestive of improved digestive function and gut mucosal immunity. (DAN Scientific Discussion Group, 1999) There are not yet any published reports of IV secretin in children with ADHD.

TRIGGERS — GASTROINTESTINAL MICROFLORA AND GASTROINTESTINAL FUNCTION

Increased intestinal permeability has been associated with the use of antibiotics. As well, frequent ear infections with repeated courses of antibiotics are common historical features of ADHD. (Hagerman, 1987) This data suggests that disruption in normal gut flora may have far reaching consequences and may be a significant factor in the etiology of ADHD.

Maintenance of normal gut flora probably plays a key role in the preservation of the mucosal barrier of the gut. (Salminen, 1996; Majamaa, 1997) Several species of Bifidobacteria and Lactobacilli have been associated with normal gut function and supplementation with these organisms may assist in the restoration of altered gut permeability. (Salminen, 1996) These organisms function as part of the first line of defense in gut immunity and may play a vital role in the development of normal immune responsiveness as well as immune tolerance to dietary components. Efforts to promote the growth of these desirable organisms may be important in the treatment of ADHD. In our current study of ADHD children, Lactobacilli or Bifidobacteria were absent in 29 out of 63 stool samples (46%). (Lyon, 1999) Appropriate quantities of secretory IgA result, in part, from adherence of adequate populations of beneficial bacterial species to the gut wall. Secretory IgA then, in turn, prevents the adherence of potential pathogens to the gut wall. Adequate amounts of secretory IgA also prevents passage of potential antigens across the gut mucosal epithelium. (Albanese, 1994) Depressed production of secretory IgA may be a significant factor in ADHD. Stool samples from our current study group demonstrated markedly depressed secretory IgA in 28 out of 63 subjects (44%). This may be due, at least in part, to diminished quantities of lactic acid fermenting bacteria adherent to the gut mucosa. A strategy to increase secretory IgA production such individuals may include administration of species specific probiotic (live bacteria) supplements. (Malin, 1996) Symbiotic gut bacteria have been recently found to carry out other important functions. Following the digestion of food, certain bacterial species which are adherent to the small intestinal mucosa may provide signaling molecules to the gut associated lymphoid tissue and through this mechanism, tolerance to food antigens is increased. Recent studies in Finland have shown that promotion of specific intestinal bacteria in food allergic children (by providing species specific probiotic supplementation) can markedly ameliorate the effects of food allergy and result in a desensitization of the child to the offending foods. (Majamaa, 1997) Certain species of small intestinal bacteria may modify immunomodulatory properties of native food proteins through enzymatic hydrolysis and this processing of antigens may be a primary factor in the development and maintenance of tolerance to potential food antigens. (Sutas, 1996a; Sutas, 1996b) Since restrictive diets may be difficult for some to comply with and may be nutritionally inadequate, efforts to restore immunological tolerance may be an important part of the long term management of food allergic patients. (Isolauri, 1995; Isolauri, 1998)

Symbiotic microbes have numerous other beneficial properties including neutralization of microbial toxins and carcinogens, (El-Nazami, 1998; Goldin, 1996) inhibition of pathogenic bacterial growth, including helicobacter pylori. (Midolo, 1995) In contrast to the numerous physiological benefits derived from adequate populations of symbiotic intestinal bacteria, overgrowth of potentially pathogenic bacteria, fungi or protozoans may have a wide range of deleterious consequences. Numerous putrefactive or fermentative metabolites can be produced in vivo by intestinal microbes. Some of these agents (such as d-lactic acid, tartaric acid, ethanol, arabinose, dihydroxyphenylpropionic acid (DHPPA), ammonia, benzo-diazepine receptor ligands, and methane) are significantly neuro-toxic and can be demonstrated in the urine or breath of individu-als with neuropsychological disorders. (Shaw, 1996; Yurdaydin, 1995) Other microbial components may significantly impact ADHD. For example, the bacterial enzyme beta-glucuronidase results in deconjugation of steroids intended for excretion via the stool. High amounts of this bacterial enzyme may result in heightened blood levels of certain steroids, (Martin, 1977) which, in turn, may con-tribute to aggressive behavior in children with ADHD. (Scerbo, 1994) Other bacterial, fungal, protozoal or helminthic enzymes or endo-toxins may result in a direct degradation of the gut epithelium and result in the translocation of microbes across the gut wall, gut inflammation and increased permeability. (Alexander, 1990; Northrop, 1987; O'Dwyer, 1988)

Our recent study revealed the presence of protozoal parasites in single, random stool samples in 26 out of 63 subjects (41%) as well as heavy growth of Candida albicans in 20 out of 63 (32%) and significant quantities of potential bacterial pathogens in almost every child studied. The presence of intestinal protozoans in near-ly half of our study subjects was somewhat unexpected and may be of particular clinical significance. Based on research evaluating the accuracy of single vs. multiple stool samples, the actual inci-dence of intestinal protozoans in our study group was likely about 23% higher than reported because we only utilized one sample per subject. (Hiatt, 1995) Many of our subjects had multiple species of protozoans; some as many as five species. The incidence of intes-tinal protozoans in our study group was much higher than that found in other studies of North American children with or without diarrheal diseases (Kabani, 1995; Kappus, 1994) and in keeping with the incidence found in children of lower socioeconomic groups in Third World countries (Cancrini, 1988; Jarabo, 1995; Brannan, 1996) Several studies have shown that the presence of intestinal protozoans in children increases allergic responsiveness and can be a primary cause of atopy. (Di Prisco, 1993; Di Prisco, 1998; Cuffari, 1998; Veraldi, 1991) Intestinal pro-tozoans have also been implicated in cases of reactive arthritis, synovitis as well as autoimmune colitis. (Gato, 1998; Russo, 1988; Shein, 1983; Lee, 1990; Letts, 1998; Burnstein, 1983) In addition, certain bacterial pathogens are known to significantly increase the pathogenicity of protozoal parasites. Thus, the high frequency of protozoal parasites found in our study group may be of even greater significance in the presence of the intestinal bacterial pathogens that were found so frequently in these children. (Gomes, 1995)

Known bacterial pathogens may have many other deleterious effects. As mentioned above, numerous intestinal bacterial metabolites are being increasingly identified as neurotoxic and immunotoxic. In our recent research, many of the stools samples from children with ADHD had large quantities of known pathogens such as Klebsiella pneumoniae, Citrobacter freundii, and Pseudomonas. Small intestinal overgrowth of these bacteria have been shown to play a central role in the pathogenesis of tropical malabsorption syndrome or tropical sprue and, thus may contribute to poor nutrient absorption in ADHD. (Tomkins, 1980) Certain bacterial species, such as Klebsiella have been found to exist in association with autoimmune disorders. (Cooper, 1988) Since ADHD has been associated with higher titres of antineural antibodies, the possibility exists that ADHD may be due, in part, to autoimmune cross reactivity between bacterial and neuronal antigens. (Swedo, 1994; Kiessling, 1994)

TRIGGERS — IMMUNE SYSTEM IMPAIRMENT

It has been shown that subtle immune dysfunction may be a prominent problem in ADHD. Both cellular and humoral immunity have been shown to be abnormal in children with ADHD as compared to age matched controls. (Mittleman, 1997) Plasma complement levels have been found to be lower in children with ADHD. (Warren, 1995; Warren, 1996) Immune dysfunction in ADHD may be either directly inherited (Odell , 1997) or it may be a result of nutritional, toxicological or atopic factors. ADHD may also be, in part, an autoimmune disorder. Antineural antibodies have been found in the blood and cerebrospinal fluid in ADHD. (Swedo, 1994; Kiessling, 1994) Maternal autoimmunity may also contribute to the development of ADHD. Maternal immune hyper-responsiveness to the increased antigenic potential of male vs. female fetuses may explain, in part, the higher incidence of ADHD in male children. (Gualtieri, 1987; McAllister, 1997)

Gut mucosal immunity may also be significantly impaired in ADHD. Our recent investigation has demonstrated low levels of secretory IgA in the stool of the majority of children with ADHD.

This finding is suggestive of diminished gut mucosal immunity, and a concomitant increased susceptibility to gut pathogens and food allergies. (Lyon, 1999)

THE FUNCTIONAL MEDICINE APPROACH TO THE ADHD PATIENT: PART I

The Patient Centered Diagnosis

The Functional Medicine practitioner has a unique opportunity to utilize core principles of this discipline to invoke significant and lasting improvements in the function of individuals with ADHD. The first step in working with individuals who have been previously diagnosed, or who are suspected to have ADHD is to develop a ***patient centered diagnosis***. This approach does not negate the necessity for carefully defining the patient's disorder taxonomically but once this is done, the focus is placed upon defining the patient functionally. Establishing a patient's functional status is critical in following the ***medical outcome*** of the treatment program. Carefully tracking medical outcome in a regular and systematic fashion elevates the practice of Functional Medicine to the level of ***evidence-based medicine***. It can be easily argued that demonstrating a satisfactory outcome of a treatment program in an individual patient is better evidence of the efficacy of that particular treatment, or set of treatments than a randomized double-blind placebo controlled trial on a group of individuals who may differ considerably from that individual patient. Ultimately, treatments proven to work in placebo-controlled trials must still be proven to produce a satisfactory medical outcome when used in the context of a multimodal treatment program on an individual patient.

As well as defining the patient's functional status, patient centered diagnosis also requires that the clinician seek to uncover as clearly as possible the underlying antecedents, triggers and mediators contributing to the individual patient's condition. Systematically addressing these underlying factors will help the clinician to develop an organized, individualized and priority driven treatment program adjusted to the needs of that individual patient.

FUNCTIONAL ASSESSMENT OF ADHD PATIENTS: DEFINING, QUANTIFYING AND TRACKING CHANGES IN ADHD SYMPTOMATOLOGY.

Complex neuropsychological testing, vocational testing or examination for learning disabilities is beyond the scope of practice for most practitioners of functional medicine. However, confirming the basic diagnosis of ADHD and grading the severity of symptoms is a reasonably simple and clinically essential starting point. This starting point also forms a vital baseline for tracking medical outcome, which is, in turn, necessary to objectively quantify the success of any treatment strategy. We have developed a basic diagnostic questionnaire for children based upon the strict DSM-IV criteria. This questionnaire can be viewed on the Internet at: www.PureLiving.com. Another instrument, which is very useful to confirm the diagnosis and to rate a child's degree of functional impairment, is the Conners' Parent Rating Scale (revised version, Long Form). This is an 80-question scale, which rates ADHD symptoms according to several categories. It can be marked and interpreted in a few minutes and it provides an excellent method for quantifying clinical outcome. Questionnaires for teachers are also available (Conner's Teacher Rating Scale – Revised). An interpretation manual (which is essential) and quick score forms can be obtained from www.PureLiving.com.

To confirm the diagnosis in adults suspected of having ADHD, a questionnaire based upon the DSM-IV criteria can also be found at www.PureLiving.com. As well, Conners' questionnaires for adults are also now available.

FUNCTIONAL ASSESSMENT OF ADHD PATIENTS: DEFINING, QUANTIFYING AND TRACKING CHANGES IN SOMATIC SYMPTOMATOLOGY.

Both adults and children with ADHD commonly experience a wide range of somatic symptoms related to underlying physiological disturbances. Although this correlation has not been made in the scientific literature, experience at our facility has suggested that ADHD, chronic fatigue syndrome and fibromyalgia all share many common features and that individuals who have ADHD as a child may be more likely to experience chronic fatigue syndrome or fibromyalgia as an adult. We have found it quite important to track somatic symptomatology in ADHD patients using the Symptom Inventory Checklist for Children or, in the case of adolescents or adults, the Symptom Questionnaire. These questionnaires are simple to complete and score and they provide additional data enabling the clinician to practice evidence based Functional Medicine through the tracking of medical outcomes. These questionnaires can also be found at: www.PureLiving.com.

FUNCTIONAL ASSESSMENT OF ADHD PATIENTS: DEFINING, QUANTIFYING AND TRACKING CHANGES IN UNDERLYING ANTECEDENTS, AND TRIGGERS.

Determination of Antecedents

Genetic assessment of ADHD patients is currently relegated to the realm of research. In the near future genetic testing may be available to demonstrate polymorphisms in D2 and D4 dopaminergic receptors as well as the dopamine transporter. This testing would enable infants or young children to be tested and, if appropriate, placed in a high-risk category for early behavioral intervention. In such cases efforts could also be made to optimize phenotypic expression through nutritional and environmental interventions. In a similar manner, genetic testing will likely soon be widely available to define risk for allergy and diminished capability to detoxify organic xenobiotics and heavy metals.

Perinatal factors should be determined in the initial assessment of the ADHD patient. Birth trauma, hypoxic birth injury, preterm delivery, neonatal sepsis, severe jaundice are all important to note. Other factors in pregnancy such as maternal smoking, drug, or alcohol use, hyperemesis gravidarum, level of physical activity and major life stress events should be noted.

Social assessment of the child with ADHD is an important aspect of the initial clinical encounter. Children who have suffered physical or sexual abuse, or who have endured severe parental strife in the home may exhibit behaviors, which can mimic ADHD or such stresses may exacerbate ADHD symptomatology. Counseling or referral to an appropriate professional or social service agency may be an important aspect of treatment. As well, children with learning disabilities or sensory problems may exhibit ADHD-like behaviors, which may respond to treatment of the underlying sensory or learning disorder. Finally, gifted children may act out and exhibit behaviors much like a child with ADHD. Such children may be acting out in response to extreme boredom with their non-challenging school environment and their behavior may improve markedly in an enriched learning environment adjusted for gifted children.

Toxicological assessment of the ADHD patient should be considered in all cases. Toxicological assessment should begin with a careful interview to determine potential toxic exposures. This should include a review of maternal habits (smoking, drug or alcohol use) as well as maternal occupation and home environmental factors (e.g. solvents at work, renovation of an older home with lead paint, exposure to air pollution). The interviewer should consider the maternal exposure to neurotoxicants through eating fish as well as a maternal dental history (e.g. total amalgam surfaces, adding or removing amalgams during pregnancy). The environment of the child (e.g. home with leaded paint or proximity to polluting industry) as well as a dental history and history of accidental toxic exposures should be considered.

An essential test for all children with ADHD should be a whole blood lead level. Whole blood lead levels above 10μg/dl are sufficient to cause neurological impairment and this should be addressed as an important part of the treatment program. Numerous labs now provide low cost whole blood lead analysis and portable, finger stick units are now available for immediate whole blood lead levels in the clinician's office (ESA Inc. 978-250-7000). If the lead status of the home environment is questionable, the clinician should supply the parents with a lead test kit to screen their house dust and painted surfaces for lead. A simple and reliable home test kit is the Acc-U-Test Kit (781-337-5546).

Provocation testing (administration of a dithiol chelating drug followed by measurement of urinary metal excretion) to assess body burden of mercury and other neurotoxic metals should be considered in the assessment of adults with ADHD but may impose too great a medico-legal risk to perform in children in certain jurisdictions. Post provocative urine testing following oral administration of DMSA is often used, however, no normative values have been established for this procedure as a diagnostic intervention. Hair analysis may provide a useful indication of toxic metal burden except in the case of inorganic mercury. The clinician should consider utilizing a lab, which uses a reliable methodology to differentiate external contaminants on the hair from endogenously derived elements (www.gsdl.com). Provocation testing with DMPS may be currently the only reliable means to assess inorganic (amalgam derived) mercury body burden. The clinician should also inspect the mouth of the child and the mother to assess the number of amalgam surfaces and their relative size. Toxicological assessment of the ADHD patient may also include functional liver testing using the caffeine, acetaminophen, and aspirin clearance test (www.gsdl.com). This test is helpful to assist in the determination of a patient's susceptibility to toxic stress. Other tests may indicate the current level of xenobiotic exposure. One such test is urinary d-glucaric acid and mercapturate levels (www.metametrix.com). These urinary markers are often elevated if a patient has a high exposure to one or more organic xenobiotics. In some cases a clinician may wish to identify the body burden of specific organic xenobiotics. Many of these can be identified through organic xenobiotic panels using blood, urine or fat aspiration (Accu-Chem Laboratories, 800-451-0116). All available laboratory data, together with information derived from the historical interview, will help the clinician to decide if a detoxification protocol should be placed as a high priority in the treatment of the ADHD patient. Urinary porphyrin assessment is another method often used to look for evidence of heavy metal toxicity (www.metametrix.com).

Nutritional assessment of the ADHD patient is a challenging and important part of the patient evaluation. The Functional Medicine practitioner should pay particular attention to gathering a detailed nutritional history, inquiring about the mother's nutritional habits before conception, during pregnancy and during breast feeding. The nutritional history of the patient during infancy, early childhood and beyond is also very important. The length of breast feeding, the methods used by the parents to introduce solids, the kinds of foods preferred and shunned, food habits or addictions, the use of food supplements and the intake of junk foods are all important points to clarify. As well, the clinician should become intimately familiar with the physical signs and symptoms of nutritional inadequacies, paying particular attention to signs and symptoms of magnesium, zinc and essential fatty acid deficiencies. Hair analysis may provide useful data about the adequacy of certain nutrient elements, particularly zinc. Red blood cell elemental analysis is also readily available and may be clinically useful in certain cases. Perhaps the most important nutritional test for the ADHD patient is the red blood cell fatty acid profile (www.gsdl.com). This test may provide some very useful data to guide specific dietary recommendations, which are highly important to the ADHD sufferer.

DETERMINATION OF TRIGGERS

General Principles

The antecedent factors just reviewed may render the patient susceptible to a wide range of physiological disruptions or states of altered function. These changes, which can occur in several organs or systems of the body, are referred to as *triggers*. Triggers do not result in symptoms in and of themselves but rather, they lead to disturbances in mediators, which then generate the signs and symptoms of illness. For example, fatty acid deficiencies (antecedent) may lead to allergic hypersensitivity (trigger), which in turn may lead to the release of cytokines (mediators), which in turn may lead to alterations in neurotransmitters and thus, brain function (signs and symptoms). When possible, antecedent factors should be corrected as an important part of the treatment regimen. In some cases (such as history of birth trauma), this is not feasible. In other cases, such as toxic exposure, the antecedent factors can be gradually diminished (through detoxification strategies) simultaneous to the treatment of triggers and mediators. In conventional allopathic medicine, the majority of treatments are focussed upon the direct manipulation of mediators to bring about a rapid change in signs and symptoms. However, if the underlying antecedents and triggers remain unaffected by the treatment intervention, its effects are usually transient and are rapidly extinguished if the treatment is interrupted. This is certainly true in the treatment of ADHD using stimulant drugs. The effect of these drugs remains only as long as the drug is present at therapeutic blood levels. No long-term amelioration of the disorder has ever been demonstrated with this treatment method. (Barkley, 1990) In this regard, Functional Medicine is distinctly superior to the allopathic approach which usually considers suppression of symptoms alone to be an adequate end point in treatment often without regard to long term adverse effects of the treatment or the impact of the treatment upon the eventual prognosis of the disorder. In contrast, while providing treatments, which ease the symptoms of ADHD, the Functional Medicine practitioner develops a patient centered diagnosis and then strives to treat the underlying antecedents and triggers responsible for the individual patient's condition.

Gastrointestinal assessment of patients with ADHD will likely uncover multiple, highly important triggers which may impact significantly upon ADHD symptomatology. Gastrointestinal triggers can be divided into the following categories:

· Increased intestinal permeability

· Malabsorption

· Digestive impairment

· Hypochlorhydria

· Adverse changes in oral, gastric, small intestinal or colonic microflora

· Impairment of gastrointestinal immune defenses

· Food allergies or intolerances

· Gastrointestinal motility problems

· Impaired hepatic detoxification

Assessment of gastrointestinal function should begin with a relevant historical review. Clinicians should inquire about such symptoms as presence, frequency and timing of abdominal pain, diarrhea or constipation, as well as burping, flatulence or excessively foul smelling bowel movements. History of pinworms, travel history, history of daycare attendance, hygienic habits, antibiotic usage, and suspected food allergies or intolerances should also be points of inquiry. In some cases, the poor quality of the diet alone may strongly suggest that gastrointestinal disturbances are likely present. Based upon our recent research findings, overt gastrointestinal symptoms are commonly absent in ADHD patients, especially in children, even though, with further testing, highly significant functional abnormalities can often be found.

Lactulose-mannitol (small) intestinal permeability testing (www.gsdl.com) is one of the least expensive and most clinically useful tests available to the Functional Medicine practitioner. If this test is abnormal, it generally indicates that gastrointestinal function is significantly impaired and that the underlying causes of this impairment should be vigorously pursued. In all cases where the lactulose–mannitol ratio is found to be abnormal, patients should be fully assessed and treated for possible food allergies or intolerances and should be examined for intestinal parasites and other disturbances in gastrointestinal microflora. Recent antibiotic use should be considered in all cases. In adolescents or adults with ADHD, other causes of increased intestinal permeability such as NSAID use, alcohol consumption, or smoking should also be considered. Apart from increased small intestinal permeability, as evidenced by an elevated lactulose-mannitol ratio, very low urinary mannitol recovery may be suggestive of some degree of malabsorption. In our recent research, overt malabsorption, as suggested by significant steatorrhea (fat in stool) was seen in only a few of our 75 subjects. However, low urinary mannitol recovery was seen in several patients, suggesting that subclinical malabsorption is a frequent occurrence in ADHD. Conditions such giardiasis, celiac disease and small intestinal bacterial overgrowth (bacterial sprue) may be responsible for various degrees of malabsorption.

The intestinal permeability test may be repeated at regular intervals as a simple means to help gauge the success of treatment interventions upon gastrointestinal function. Restoration of intestinal mucosal integrity as evidenced by the lactulose-mannitol test, is usually accompanied by significant clinical improvement and it will likely have a positive long-term impact upon the patient's prognosis.

Comprehensive digestive stool analysis (CDSA) with parasitology examination (www.gsdl.com) is also likely to yield a good deal of useful data. The CDSA is a compilation of numerous tests, which reflect upon digestive and absorptive efficiency, stool transit time, as well as the ecological environment of the colon. The quantification of several metabolic markers can help to gauge the presence of both beneficial as well as harmful bacterial metabolites. The level of fecal secretory IgA (sIgA) is an important indicator of the adequacy of gut mucosal immune function. This complex molecule is a dimer, is composed of two IgA molecules joined by a "J-chain". Another protein, known as a secretory piece, extends the length of sIgA and prevents its digestion. (Joneja, 1990) This enables sIgA to survive passage through the gut and to bind to microbes and food antigens, thus preventing their absorption. It also binds to microbial pathogens, preventing their adherence to the gut wall.

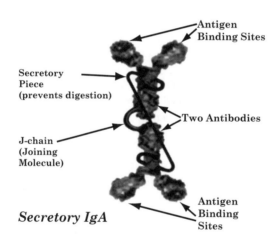

Antigen Binding Sites

Secretory Piece (prevents digestion)

Two Antibodies

J-chain (Joining Molecule)

Antigen Binding Sites

Secretory IgA

The CDSA also provides culture proven evidence of the adequacy of normal colonic flora as well as a quantification of potentially pathogenic bacterial or fungal species. As well, bacterial and fungal pathogens are subjected to sensitivity testing which includes both pharmaceutical and natural antimicrobial agents to guide therapeutic decisions. Another highly important addition to the basic CDSA is a microscopic and immunological assay for protozoal parasites and helminthic organisms. As discussed previously, the majority of ADHD subjects in our recent study were found to have protozoal parasites, which are known to have far reaching physiological effects including the promotion of allergic disease.

Urinary organic acid testing is becoming widely recognized as an important tool in the identification of byproducts of pathological intestinal microbial metabolism. (www.metametrix.com; www.autismandpdd.com) This test may compliment and provide additional information not provided by the CDSA by identifying and quantifying several potentially toxic bacterial or fungal metabolites. Many such substances have been identified in temporal association with several neuropsychological disorders.

Urinary peptide testing (K.L.Reichelt@rh.uio.no) has not yet been formally studied in ADHD. However, with increasing data demonstrating high levels of neurologically and immunologically active peptides in the urine of autistic children, as well as individuals with other neuropsychological disorders, this may prove to be an important functional test. Urinary peptide assays may assist in the identification of those children who would benefit from a strictly gluten or dairy free diet. Improper protein digestion combined with increased gut permeability can result in the absorption of large quantities of these highly potent molecules. Peptides such as the potent opioid casomorphin from casein and the opioid gliadinomorphin from gluten as well as various immunomodulating peptides from casein may play a significant role in the etiology of ADHD in certain cases. As well, as comorbid conditions such as addiction may be related to this factor.

Functional liver detoxification testing (www.gsdl.com) using the caffeine, acetaminophen, and acetylsalicylic challenge acid test may be used in select patients with ADHD, particularly where somatic symptomatology is pronounced and the patient does not respond favorably to dietary modification or where toxicological factors appear to be predominant in their disorder.

Detection of food allergies and intolerances – conventional approach.

Most conventional allergists limit their search for adverse food reactions to those events which are mediated through IgE (type I immediate hypersensitivity) and a few easily defined adverse food reactions, such as lactose intolerance. Such clinicians generally limit their investigation for food allergy to skin testing, RAST testing for anti-food IgE antibodies and, in some cases, double blind food challenge trials. The skin test and RAST test methods lack both specificity and sensitivity even in the detection of type I (IgE mediated) food hypersensitivity. Furthermore, they completely neglect adverse food reactions from type III (delayed hypersensitivity involving IgG, IgM, antibody-antigen complexes and the complement cascade) and type IV food hypersensitivity (cell mediated, contact allergy) that have been demonstrated to mediate many adverse food reactions. The highly revered double blind food challenge may not provide a sufficient quantity of food to elicit a reaction in many people with true food allergies. As well, an adverse food response may only occur when offending foods are eaten in combination with certain other foods or when the subject tastes or smells the offending food (conditioned response). Delayed food reactions are also usually not looked for following the double blind food challenge and it tends to be very complex to implement.

In addition, all of these techniques fail to determine a wide range of adverse responses to food due to non-immune mediated phenomenon associated with reactive chemicals (e.g. salicylates, benzoates, amines, tartrazine, MSG, lactose and other disaccharides). Any combination of immune and non-immune mechanisms, as well as complex neuropsychological triggers may be acting in any given adverse reaction to food. Because of the highly variable nature of this problem, a simplistic, reductionist approach to food allergies and intolerances will usually yield unsatisfactory clinical outcomes in a large number of patients experiencing legitimate adverse reactions to foods. Many patients who suffer from adverse food reactions are not helped by conventional allergists and are often dismissed as psychosomatically afflicted. This attitude does not recognize the highly complex nature of the problem and the fact that true physiological and immunological effects, including mast cell degranulation or even anaphylaxis can occur from a conditioned response alone.

Detection of food allergies and intolerances – alternative medical approaches.

In contrast to most conventional allergists, clinicians that practice various forms of alternative medicine may choose to utilize a wide array of methods to detect food allergies. Such methods may include electrodermal (VEGA) testing, ELISA, ALCAT, muscle testing, or provocation/neutralization injections. The intent of all of these methods is to extend the detection of food allergies beyond just IgE mediated immediate hypersensitivities. All of these methods are controversial in allopathic circles and none of these methods have been fully defined through rigorous research. Financial considerations, training and clinical experience usually dictates which of these tests are used and in what clinical context they are useful. Experienced practitioners will recognize that none of these tests are failsafe and they will use the data from such tests as a general guide or a basic starting point in the investigation of a patient's food allergies and intolerances. Clinicians will also realize that such tests provide them with "leverage" to help motivate patients to change.

Detection of food allergies and intolerances – Functional Medicine approach.

The Open Food Challenge

In addition to the above tests, Functional Medicine practitioners may utilize elimination diets followed by open (unblinded) food challenges to determine adverse food reactions. Although conventional allergists would argue that open food challenges are inaccurate due to placebo effects, there are actually distinct advantages to this approach over double blind food challenges. Firstly, this method is inexpensive and technically much simpler to conduct. Secondly, the quantity of food given in an open challenge can be assured to be sufficient enough to provoke an adverse effect, unlike the small quantity of foods usually administered in a blinded trial. Thirdly, an open trial brings into play all of the potential mechanisms which may be responsible for the adverse food response, including the sensations of taste and smell as well as conditioned responses. Rather than dismissing a conditioned response as invalid, the clinician should realize that sensory-neural triggers might play a very important role in the establishment and maintenance of an adverse food response (including IgE mediated allergy). In all likelihood, adverse food reactions are probably never brought about through a single mechanism alone. If we were able to examine in detail the subtleties of cellular and molecular changes taking place during an adverse food response we would likely observe a wide range of combined immunological effects (type I, type III and types IV) as well as highly diverse biochemical and neuropsychological effects. The open food challenge uses the patient's own cognitive and sensory systems to carry out, in a sense, a sophisticated bioassay reflecting upon all of these complex variables.

The major weakness of the open food challenge is usually that the process is not conducted in a systematic fashion. If not performed in a meticulous and scientific fashion, the open food challenge process can be frustrating and time consuming for both the clinician and the patient. Also, the data derived from a poorly organized open food challenge can be inaccurate and may even exacerbate the patient's pre-existing food anxieties.

A SYSTEMATIC APPROACH TO FOOD ALLERGIES AND INTOLERANCES

An approach to the identification and management of food allergies and intolerances consistent with the principles of Functional Medicine is covered in detail in Chapter 17 of this book and will not be repeated in this section.

THE FUNCTIONAL MEDICINE APPROACH TO THE ADHD PATIENT: PART II

Patient Centered Treatment

Clinicians who make the effort to develop a *patient centered diagnosis*, focusing on the underlying antecedents, triggers and mediators responsible for the signs and symptoms of an individual patient's condition, may be confronted with a staggering array of therapeutic possibilities. Functional Medicine practitioners should avoid the temptation to use a "shotgun approach" in which various treatments are prescribed randomly in the hope that a pathological target is hit in the process. Instead, clinicians should undertake a rational and organized approach to treatment of each patient. The order of treatment intervention should be based upon clinical judgment utilizing historical details, physical findings, results of testing, accumulated clinical experience and financial practicalities.

First and foremost, practitioners should retain a compassionate and concerned point of view, considering the tremendous impact that ADHD has upon the individual and their family. Although the Functional Medicine approach does not rely solely upon symptom suppressing therapies, providing improvement in ADHD symptoms may be an urgent and compassionate necessity. Many parents have become highly distressed over their child's behavior or school performance and they may be under pressure from school authorities to place their child on medication. In some cases, the child or adult ADHD sufferer has been placed on medication and the improvement in symptoms has been very impressive. In other cases, medication has been used and was ineffective or it resulted in intolerable side effects. In still other cases, parents or adult patients are very reluctant to use powerful medication and they may prefer to use more natural therapies instead.

In all cases, the clinician should educate the patient about the Functional Medicine model and should discuss the importance of assessing and treating the underlying antecedents, triggers and mediators underlying the signs and symptoms of ADHD. Most patients will want to address underlying causes and will be very happy to try more natural approaches to control ADHD symptoms. In those patients whose symptoms are well controlled on medications, clinicians may suggest that the process of Functional Medicine assessment and treatment be initiated and that medications be continued until a vacation period, when medication is often stopped. Symptom modifying natural therapies may then be initiated during this time off medication. Some patients would prefer to initiate natural, symptom modifying therapies while simultaneously reducing the dosage of medication. In most cases, success will require a comprehensive approach to treatment brought about gradually as various underlying factors are addressed and natural agents are utilized in a highly individualized fashion.

IMPACTING MEDIATORS (NEUROTRANSMITTERS) — CONVENTIONAL TREATMENT

Functional Medicine practitioners should be familiar with the prevailing allopathic approach to treating ADHD. Currently, the prevailing approach to the treatment of ADHD is monotherapy with stimulant drugs such as methylphenidate, dextroamphetamine or pemoline . Stimulants improve ADHD symptoms primarily by blocking dopamine reuptake in nerve endings via the dopamine transporter. (Cook, 1995)

These medications reportedly improve behavior and cognitive functioning in approximately 75% of children in formal placebo controlled trials. (Greenhill, 1992) However, the success of treatment when studied in a double blind, placebo controlled trial within actual clinical practice may be significantly lower. (DiTraglia, 1991) Furthermore, follow-up studies have failed to demonstrate an improved prognosis for children treated with stimulant medications. (Brooks, 1994; Lie, 1992) Additionally, these drugs are associated with a high prevalence of adverse effects and their long term safety has not been adequately studied. (Greenhill, 1992; Ahmann, 1993; Elia, 1991; Fox, 1993)

Dextroamphetamine (Dexedrine®) and methylphenidate (Ritalin®) are amphetamines and they have the same basic physiological effects as other amphetamines and amphetamine derivatives. Amphetamines are known to enhance catecholamine production, (Vogel, 1984; Seiden, 1993) and they have a profound effect upon the cardiovascular system, leading to increases in heart rate and blood pressure. (Goldstein, 1983; Caldwell, 1996) This suggests that the stimulants used to treat ADHD may significantly increase the risk of cardiovascular disease especially in higher doses given over long periods of time. Other amphetamine derivatives have been implicated in causing damage to the heart in as many as fifty percent of subjects even after short-term use at dosages commonly prescribed for appetite suppression. (Boughner, 1997)

Amphetamines also have a profound effect upon cortisol secretion. Administration of amphetamines has been used for many years as a model to study the physiological effects of stress. Giving moderate doses of amphetamines has been shown to produce the same degree of cortisol release as severe physical stresses such as major trauma or hypothermia. (Peeters, 1994; Feeney, 1993; Nurnberger, 1984; Stewart, 1984) The effect of amphetamines upon cortisol secretion may have serious implications for the long term health of the brain. It has been recently demonstrated that mean serum cortisol levels are directly correlated to the speed of brain aging, and even a moderate elevation in serum cortisol levels may markedly increase the risk of memory loss and dementia. (Kirschbaum, 1996; Lupien, 1997; Seeman, 1997; Bremner, 1995) In addition to the potential influence upon brain aging, amphetamines have been shown to increase the permeability of the blood brain barrier, which results in greater susceptibility to neurotoxic agents. (Murphy, 1985) Amphetamines are also known to result in acute and chronic psychosis if given in high doses. (Robinson, 1986; Zahn, 1981) They can also induce mania at therapeutic doses in susceptible individuals. (Masand, 1995; Jacobs, 1986) Other amphetamine derivatives have been shown to cause permanent loss of serotonin producing neuronal structures in the brain. (O'Callaghan J, 1997; Appel, 1989) This suggests that the use of amphetamine derivatives may lead to a higher risk of clinical depression especially with long-term use. The less frequently used stimulant, pemoline (Cyclert) has now been shown to carry the risk of serious hepatotoxicity and, for this reason, is no longer considered a first line agent. (Marotta, 1998)

All of this data suggests that there is an urgent need to study the long-term physiological impact of stimulant drugs in patients with ADHD. In one disturbing study, CT scans were used to examine the brains of men in their twenties who had all been treated for ADHD with stimulant drugs in childhood. In most cases, significant cerebral atrophy was detected in these men. Similar findings were absent from aged match controls. (Nasrallah, 1986) It is quite surprising that there is such a scarcity of similar studies particularly in light of the recent explosion in the rate of prescribing of stimulant drugs for the treatment of ADHD.

Several other drugs, primarily antidepressants, have been shown to have efficacy in the management of ADHD but are also limited by side effects and concerns regarding their long term safety and efficacy. (Riddle, 1991; Barrickman, 1991; Gualtieri, 1991; Jankovic, 1993; Huessy, 1983)

IMPACTING MEDIATORS (NEUROTRANSMITTERS) –

NATURAL PHARMACOLOGICAL AGENTS

In the past decade, there has been increased attention upon the pharmacology and clinical utility of botanical extracts and derivatives in the treatment of neurologic, behavioral and psychiatric disorders. In Europe and Asia, and more recently, in North America, several herbal extracts have become widely utilized for these and other conditions as methods of standardization have advanced and the safety and efficacy of botanical derivatives has been increasingly demonstrated. (Stoppe, 1996; Eliason, 1997)

There are important differences in the nature of herbal medicines and western pharmaceuticals in the treatment of illness. Unlike western medicine, where single molecules are administered for highly targeted effects, herbal medicines often contain dozens or even hundreds of potentially active constituents many of which can be demonstrated to act in a synergistic and perhaps superior manner than any particular botanical constituent alone. (Liu, 1992; Wojcicki, 1995) Furthermore, botanical medicines frequently exhibit a wide range of physiological benefits, such as antioxidant protection, which may greatly increase their utility beyond their symptom modifying effects.

Our facility recently completed an open trial examining the effects of a nootropic (cognitive enhancing) agent derived from American ginseng in combination with an extract from Ginkgo biloba on the behavior of 37 children with ADHD. This product, known as AD-FX (HerbTech, Inc.; 1-888-843-7239), significantly improved ADHD symptomatology in over eighty percent of the children studied with no reported side effects. (Lyon, 1998) Each capsule of AD-FX™ is composed of 96 mg of HT-1001 (an extract of American ginseng developed by the HerbTech scientists containing >15% total ginsenoside saponins) and 29 mg of Ginkgo biloba extract (containing >24% Ginkgo flavone glycosides). In our study, children took two capsules twice per day on an empty stomach. This dosage effectively improved ADHD symptoms in approximately 85% of the children studied.

Ginseng extracts from have been widely studied. One fraction obtained from the processing of ginseng contains saponins known as ginsenosides. These extracts have been shown to possess immune stimulating (Fan, 1995; Kenarova, 1990; Liu J, 1995) as well as anti-inflammatory, (Matsuda, 1990) and anti-carcinogenic properties. (Rhee, 1991) Ginseng saponin extracts have also been shown to bring about a general resistance to the negative effects of stress (Lin, 1995) and may help to normalize disturbances in the sleep-wake cycle. (Lee, 1990) Additionally, ginsenosides have been demonstrated to possess diverse antioxidant activity. The ginsenosides Rg1 and Rb1 have both been shown to inhibit lipid peroxidation within liver and brain by causing a potent upregulation of the critical antioxidant enzymes, catalase, glutathione peroxidase, and superoxide dismutase (Deng, 1991; Sohn, 1993; Kim, 1996) as well as through direct free radical scavenging activity. (Zhang, 1996)

Of particular interest are the diverse effects that ginsenosides exert upon the central nervous system. These effects can be classified into three categories: nootropic, neurotrophic, and neuroprotective. Nootropics are those drugs or botanical agents which facilitate learning, improve memory, promote attention, heighten sensory-motor performance, and stimulate cognitive processing. Several drugs and a few botanical extracts, including ginseng and Ginkgo biloba extracts, are now correctly classified as nootropic agents. Ginseng extracts have been shown to improve memory, (Nitta, 1995; Petkov, 1987; Petkov, 1990; Benishin, 1992) and enhance learning through the stimulation of activity dependent synaptic plasticity. (Abe, 1994) As well, ginsenosides have been shown to increase brain glucose utilization while simultaneously reducing lactate and pyruvate, indicating increased and more efficient aerobic metabolism within the brain. (Samira, 1985) This effect may be important in light of recent imaging studies demonstrating inefficient brain glucose metabolism in subjects with ADHD. In rodent models, ginsenosides have been shown to increase dopamine and norepinephrine activity in the cerebral cortex. (Itoh, 1989) This may explain why, ginseng extract has favorable effects upon attention, cognitive processing, integrated sensory- motor function and auditory reaction time in healthy human subjects. (D'Angelo, 1986)

Besides nootropic (cognitive enhancing) effects, ginsenosides have been shown to possess neurotrophic effects. An agent is said to be neurotrophic if it causes neurite outgrowth and repair when a neuron has undergone physical, chemical or oxidative injury. The ginsenosides Rb1 and Rg1 have been shown to greatly potentiate the effects of nerve growth factor, which is a critical endogenous neurotrophic substance. (Himi, 1989; Nishiyama, 1994) This property of ginseng extract, suggests that long-term administration may have the potential to promote the growth of hypodeveloped brain regions in ADHD.

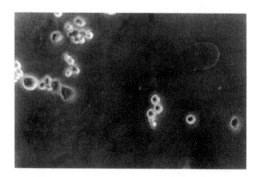

Neuronal Cell Culture after 2 Weeks in Nutrient Media

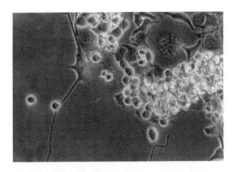

Neuronal Cell Culture after 2 Weeks in Nutrient Media Plus HT-1001 American Ginseng Extract

Ginkgo biloba extracts have also been studied extensively. The properties of ginkgo are manifold. Like ginseng saponin extracts, ginkgo extract has been shown to possess adaptogenic properties (ameliorates the effects of stress). Stress results in chronic glucocorticoid excess, which then leads to immunosupression, neurotoxicity and loss of neuroreceptor sensitivity. Ginkgo extract has been shown to decrease these pathogenic effects of glucocorticoid excess, (Amri, 1997; Bolanos, 1995) and it also results in a decrease in adrenal glucocorticoid release with ACTH stimulation. (Amri, 1996) As well, ginkgo possesses anxiolytic effects, (Hasenohrl, 1996; White, 1996) and it modifies pathologic behaviors typical of a stress response. (Porsolt, 1990; Rapin, 1994)

Ginkgo exerts widespread antioxidant effects. Both the terpenoid and the flavonoid components of ginkgo exert antioxidant effects in the brain and the cardiovascular system. (Oyama, 1994; Pietri, 1997) Furthermore, ginkgo extract diminishes mitochondrial aging by decreasing mitochondrial glutathione depletion and by protecting mitochondrial DNA from oxidative damage. (Sastre, 1998) It also prevents neuronal oxidative injury and thus prevents apoptosis (programmed cell death) by this same mechanism. (Ni, 1996) An unusual, but highly desirable property of an antioxidant is to remain active as an antioxidant in the presence of transition metals such as iron or copper. Ginkgo has been shown to remain stable and prevent lipid peroxidation when exposed to an iron rich oxidative environment. (Barth, 1991; Dumont, 1995) In the brain, ginkgo has been shown to induce the activity of the antioxidant enzyme, superoxide dismutase, (Gsell, 1995) and to protect brain cells from oxidation due to hydrogen peroxide. (Oyama, 1994)

Ginkgo has been shown to exert potent neuroprotective effects in animal and human models. (Barkats, 1995; Attella, 1989; Garg, 1995; Smith, 1996) It has also been shown to have significant neurotrophic potential. Rats, which undergo traumatic motor nerve damage, show rapid reinnervation under the influence of ginkgo extract as compared to untreated controls. (Bruno, 1993)

Ginkgo has been found to have significant cognition enhancing or nootropic effects. It has been shown in numerous European trials to effectively enhance memory and cognitive processing in subjects with dementia. (Gessner, 1985; Grassel, 1992; Itil, 1995; Rai, 1991; Allain, 1993) Only recently has a comparable trial been carried out in North America. (Le Bars, 1997) Ginkgo has also been shown to significantly improve memory and other cognitive functions in normal adults. (Hindmarch, 1986; Subhan, 1984)

Ginkgo extract has been shown to affect brain neurotransmitters and receptors in several ways. Ginkgo has been shown to reverse the reduction in 5-HT1A receptors as well as noradrenergic receptors in the aging rat. (Huguet, 1994; Huguet, 1992; Racagni, 1986) It has also been found to increase 5-hydroxytryptamine uptake in the cerebral cortex of mice. (Ramassamy, 1992a) Recently, it has been demonstrated that ginkgo extract produces reversible inhibition of both MAO-A and MAO-B within the brain. This mechanism may underlie the anxiolytic and mild antidepressant of ginkgo extract. (White, 1996) Most importantly, in relationship to a possible effect upon ADHD, is ginkgo extract's effect upon dopamine and noradrenergic systems in the brain. Ginkgo has been shown to prevent the loss of dopamine and serotonin activity, which occurs when brain synaptosomes are exposed to oxidative stress. (Ramassamy, 1992b) Additionally, it has been shown that oxidative stress results in peroxidation of the highly fluid polyunsaturated fatty acids in the neuronal membrane, which, in turn, results in loss of membrane fluidity, and a reduction in the neuron's ability to release dopamine. This mechanism, which is inhibited by ginkgo extract, may be a highly important in the pathophysiology of ADHD. (Ramassamy, 1993) As well, ginkgo extract has been shown to increase noradrenergic activity in the cerebral cortex of animals. (Brunello, 1985)

Overall, there is considerable evidence for the efficacy of both extracts of ginseng as well as from Ginkgo biloba in the general enhancement of brain function. Because of their diverse mechanisms, there is also a basis to expect that these agents might provide significant benefits in the management of ADHD. There is also a rational basis to expect considerable synergistic effects when ginseng saponin extracts and ginkgo extracts are used in combination. To our knowledge, the pilot study carried out by our facility is the first attempt to examine these agents in the management of ADHD. Controlled studies of these agents in the treatment of ADHD are warranted.

Other botanical extracts may hold promise in the symptomatic management of ADHD. Although controlled trials in subjects with ADHD have not yet been performed, standardized extracts of **St. John's wort** (Hypericum perforatum) may be helpful in the management of behavioral and mood problems in this disorder. The safety and efficacy of Hypericum extract has been well described as an alternative to antidepressant drugs in the treatment of depression. (Volz, 1997; Linde, 1996) Hypericum extract has been shown repeatedly to be at least as effective as tricyclic antidepressants with a similar mechanism (increased production of serotonergic receptors. (Teufel, 1997) After extensive use of Hypericum extracts throughout Europe, they have been shown to have minimal side effects and a markedly improved cardiac safety profile as compared to tricyclic antidepressants. (Czekalla, 1997) Tricyclic antidepressants, such as desipramine and imipramine have been used for years to successfully manage ADHD. (Gualtieri, 1991) Anticholinergic side effects and sudden cardiac deaths in ADHD children have limited the popularity of these agents. (Riddle, 1991) Hypericum may have the same degree of efficacy as the tricyclic drugs with lower side effects and no risk of sudden death. (Vorbach, 1994) In addition, recent research has demonstrated that hypericum extracts significantly inhibit dopamine reuptake, leading to greater cortical dopamine activity. (Muller, 1998; Chatterjee, 1998) This suggests that hypericum extract should have a significant influence upon the behavior of individuals with ADHD. As well, the pharmacological effects of hypericum are synergistically potentiated in the presence of the proanthocyanidin bioflavonoids. This group of phytochemicals is found in high concentrations in grape seed extract, pine bark extract and Ginkgo biloba extract, suggesting that hypericum may be more effective in ADHD if given in combination with these other agents. (Butterweck, 1998) Hypericum has also been shown to have significant antiviral effects, which may provide additional benefits in ADHD. (Meruelo, 1988) Clinical trials on this agent in ADHD are warranted.

PHYTOPHARMACOLOGY IN THE TREATMENT OF ADHD

Based upon their known actions, as well as the growing experience of healthcare providers utilizing these agents, the following protocol is being utilized with increasing frequency:

Step 1—American ginseng/Ginkgo biloba combination:

Based upon our research, this is often successful as a first line therapy to safely improve symptoms in children with ADHD. Many adults also use this product with reported success. Each capsule of AD-FX™ is composed of 96 mg of HT-1001 (an extract of American ginseng developed by the HerbTech scientists containing >15% total ginsenoside saponins) and 29 mg of Ginkgo biloba extract (containing >24% Ginkgo flavone glycosides). The usual dosage of ADFX is 2 capsules twice per day on empty stomach at least 20 minutes before meals (total of approx. 400 mg American ginseng extract and 120 mg. Ginkgo extract per day). Two before breakfast and two after school is a common dosage schedule. Very small children may do well with 1 to 2 per day given before breakfast and later in the day as needed. Absorption may be improved further if it is allowed to dissolve for a few minutes in the mouth before swallowing. However, the taste of this product is so bitter that only a few very hardy adult ADHD sufferers will be able to tolerate this method of administration.

Step 2 – Additional Ginkgo biloba

If 4 ADFX per day does not control symptoms adequately then additional standardized ginkgo extract up to 300 mg per day total Ginkgo may be of benefit. Ginkgo extract should be standardized to contain 24% ginkgo flavone glycosides. (4 capsules of ADFX provide 120 mg of ginkgo. Adding 3 additional 60 mg capsules of Ginkgo per day would make the total daily dose equal 300mg). The addition of extra Ginkgo is often needed for optimal effects in adolescent or adult ADHD sufferers. Ginkgo is best taken before meals to ensure maximum absorption and to provide antioxidant and anti-inflammatory effects in the gut prior to meals. Quercetin, one of the major bioflavonoids of Ginkgo is analogous to cromalyn glycate a drug commonly given before meals to food allergic children to reduce allergic responsiveness. (Andre, 1987)

Step 3 – St. John's wort (Hypericum perforatum)

St. John's wort (Hypericum perforatum) extract may also be highly useful in ADHD. Although it has been used primarily for its antidepressant effects, it often improves behavior and stabilizes labile moods in those suffering with ADHD. A highly effective combination has been found to be St. John's wort with ADFX and, in some cases, additional ginkgo. Dosage of St. John's wort usually begins at 300mg per day of the standardized extract and is gradually increased to as much as 1200 mg per day (under the supervision of a qualified healthcare practitioner). St. John's wort can usually be taken once per day in the morning, although some find that it works better if it is taken twice per day. St. John's wort should always be taken with plenty of liquid and should never be allowed to come into direct contact with the mouth because it can irritate mucous membranes. Higher doses may cause burning or itchy skin in certain people after sun exposure (especially if adequate sun screens are not used). If photosensitization occurs, interrupt St. John's wort for a couple of days or use a lower dose. St. John's wort extract should be standardized to contain .3% hypericin.

IMPACTING MEDIATORS (NEUROTRANSMITTERS) –

NEUROLOGICAL AND BEHAVIORAL TREATMENTS

Behavioral and neuropsychological treatments are often very helpful in the management of ADHD, particularly if the underlying physiological and toxicological antecedents and triggers are being addressed simultaneously. Electroencephalographic (EEG) biofeedback, also known as **neurotherapy or neurofeedback**, is particularly effective in the treatment of ADHD. (Lee, 1991; Lubar, 1991; Tansey, 1993) In two studies, EEG biofeedback was found to be *as effective as methylphenidate* in improving cognition, behavior, psychopathology and school performance in children with ADHD. (Rossiter, 1995; Potashkin, 1990) However, unlike all drug treatments, which are only effective as long as the drug is administered, the effects of neurofeedback are permanent or should persist for at least a decade or more. Rather than chemically inducing an increase in the activity of prefrontal executive centers, as occurs with stimulant drugs, neurofeedback enables the subject to gain volitional control over the activity of these same brain regions. Overall, there is an increasing body of evidence to support the premise that EEG biofeedback, particularly when delivered in the context of a multimodal treatment program, leads to "normalization" of behavior and can enhance the long-term academic performance, social functioning, and overall life adjustment of the ADHD patient. A series of 20-40 treatments is usually required for lasting results to take place. Clinicians who are willing to undergo extra training can obtain nationally recognized certification as biofeedback technicians through the Biofeedback Certification Institute of America (BCIA). Further information about EEG biofeedback certification as well as a current practitioner list can be obtained from: www.bcia.org.

It is widely accepted that other **behavioral and learning management** is critical in the treatment of ADHD. (Hallowell, 1994) Children with ADHD function best in a highly structured environment under parents and teachers with training in the appropriate behavioral management of ADHD. A particularly effective approach to improving the learning capabilities of the child with ADHD (with or without learning disabilities) has been developed by the psychologist J.P. Guilford. This approach, known as the

Structure of Intellect System, is currently being used in schools, prisons and other institutional settings with a high degree of success. An excellent review of the basic concepts of this system can be found at: www.soisystems.com.

Exercise comprises one of the most critical and most often neglected aspects of treatment for the individual with ADHD. Regular vigorous exercise has been shown to be highly beneficial in the treatment of behaviorally disturbed children and adults. (Celiberti, 1997; Elliott, 1994; Quill, 1989; Kern, 1984) Exercise has been shown to have a profound influence on the balance of neurotransmitters in the brain. Vigorous physical activity has been reported to reduce depressive symptoms and anxiety, and to improve coping with stress. (Ransford, 1982) It has been repeatedly shown that exercise increases the production of brain dopamine, noradrenaline and serotonin activity. (Chaouloff, 1989; Meeusen, 1995; Dluzen, 1995)

Many well adapted individuals with ADHD report that exercise is the most important aspect of their successful lifestyle. Exercise and sports participation can build self esteem, give the subject a keen sense of "focus" and can even open up scholarship and career possibilities for academically challenged individuals. Enthusiastic participation in sports has been used for millennia to keep the minds and bodies of young people away from self destructive and illegal behaviors. In my city, one sport (BMX racing) has been used to rehabilitate dozens of troubled youth in foster care, and through dedication to this sport many kids have gained self esteem and confidence.

Exercise also helps to address underlying antecedent and triggers of ADHD. Vigorous exercise has been shown to improve the efficiency of endogenous detoxification and antioxidant systems. This suggests that in individuals subjected to neurotoxic stress, regular exercise may be an important factor in reduction of toxic burdens over time. (Lew, 1991; Marin, 1993) Apart from over training, exercise also improves immune system function and inceases digestive efficiency. (Shinkai, 1997; Jonsdottir, 1997; Oliveria, 1997)

IMPACTING ANTECEDENTS AND TRIGGERS —

DIETARY AND GASTROINTESTINAL MANAGEMENT OF ADHD

General Principles

Through the process of the Functional Medical Assessment (thorough history, physical examination and appropriate laboratory testing), the clinician may uncover several specific nutritional factors, which may play a role in the individual patient's condition. As well, certain nutritional principles apply in general to all patients with ADHD and clinicians should be prepared to assist patients with these first steps. Many children and some adults with ADHD have very poor diets and clinicians should be prepared to encourage the patient improve the general quality of their diet. This may include breaking true addictions to junk foods and fast foods. Increasing the vegetable content, fiber and basic macronutrient and micronutrient composition of the diet should also be addressed. Overall, the patient should be encouraged to eat a whole foods diet with minimal exposure to processed foods including all foods with artificial colors, preservatives, deep fried fats and hydrogenated oils.

To begin the process of dietary optimization, the clinician should have the patient (or parents) complete the food and symptom diary as described in Chapter 17. If clinicians conduct a diet history and utilize the food and symptom diary they will find that many ADHD sufferers have very marginal diets with a high proportion of daily calories coming from foods with very low nutrient density. By simply increasing the nutrient density of the diet, and ensuring that the subject eats a good breakfast before school, significant behavioral improvements may occur.

Gastrointestinal Rehabilitation – The "4-R™ Program"

The Functional Medicine practitioner must become familiar with a core methodology in the treatment of chronically ill patients known as the 4-R™ Program of gastrointestinal support. As described in the above sections, disruption of the gastrointestinal milieu is of critical importance in the etiology of ADHD. If a clinician conducts a thorough Functional Medicine assessment of the ADHD patient, numerous potential triggers will likely be uncovered. The 4-R™ Program is a rational methodology, which enables the practitioner to assist in the rehabilitation of the patient's gastrointestinal system in a stepwise and organized fashion. Once the patient's gastrointestinal milieu has been rehabilitated and their nutritional status optimized, the number and quantity of neurotoxic and immunotoxic substances may be considerably reduced.

The 4-R™ Program results in the reduction of microbes, which produce endotoxins or exotoxins, that have an extraordinarily wide range of damaging effects. In turn, beneficial gut flora is reestablished through this therapeutic method, resulting in a numerous benefits. This program also results in an improvement in the gut associated lymphoid tissue (GALT), which is critical in the maintenance of normal gut ecology. As a part of this process, allergic or intolerant foods are eliminated which may be a major source of toxic stress and immunological exhaustion. The 4-R™ Program also results in improved digestion, lessening the quantity of neurologically and immunologically active peptides. Improved digestion will also result in better nutrient availability and will lessen the amount of nutritive material available for microbes to ferment or putrefy. Gut permeability is also diminished through this approach, a key factor in the reduction of toxic stress and improved nutrient availability. A critical benefit of this program is the improvements it affords to the patient's detoxification systems. With improved xenobiotic processing and excretion, toxic tissue burdens of both organic and metallic substances will be gradually diminished, as long as the source of such toxicants are removed from the patient's environment. With decreased toxic stress upon the brain and immune systems and with improved nutrient availability, somatic, cognitive, and behavioral progress should become evident and morphological improvements in the brain are very likely to occur.

The 4-R™ Program consists of the following interventional steps:

REMOVE

· Pathogenic microflora and /or parasites found through the comprehensive digestive stool analysis with parasitology examination. Depending upon the pathogens found, a wide range of botanical or pharmaceutical agents may be utilized.

> › Botancal agents with antimicrobial activity include the common spices garlic, onions, ginger, oregano, curcumin (from turmeric), rosemary, cinnamon, cloves and thyme. Other antimicrobial botanicals include Artemisia annua (wormwood), Hydrastis canadensis (goldenseal root), grapefruit seed extract, tea tree oil, Juglans nigra (black walnut) and pumpkin seed.

> › Clinicians may choose to use pharmaceutical agents such as metronidazole, nystatin or other agents in certain cases. Client services at the Great Smokies Diagnostic Laboratory in North Carolina (www.gsdl.com) is a valuable resource for clinicians unfamiliar with the range of therapeutic agents utilized in this phase of the 4-R™ Program.

· The Remove phase of the 4-R™ Program also should include a thorough attempt to identify the source of pathogens, especially in the case of protozoal or helminthic parasites. The patient's water supply, their food sources, and their outside environment should all be considered. A recent example is that of an local outbreak of intestinal worms in a school where children played in a sandbox where animals frequently defecated. Hygienic habits of the patient should also be considered. A simple program of hand washing education can greatly reduce the transmission rate of infectious organisms. (Hall, 1995)

· The Remove phase of the 4-R™ Program also focuses upon foods, which generate an allergic or intolerant response. This process was covered in detail in Chapter 17. This also refers to overall improvement in the quality of the diet and the removal of junk foods and fast foods whether or not there is a clear adverse response to such foods.

> › Supplementation of the diet with oligoantigenic medical food products may of significant value in this process. In our recent research, children with ADHD were placed

on an elimination test diet as well as the medical food product, Ultracare for Kids™ (www.UltraBalance.com). This is a highly palatable rice-based powder containing numerous nutrients of benefit in the 4-R™ Program. This powder was used as the base for a frozen fruit "smoothie". The acceptability of this product was very high and it made the transition to the elimination test diet much easier as healthy "smoothies" were used as a substitute for unhealthy snack foods.

REPLACE

· Factors important in the digestive process may be used in the initial stages of treatment and until gastrointestinal function is optimized.

· Betain hydrochloride may be used to augment gastric acid secretion in cases where hypochlorhydria is suspected. Poor nutrition, as well as infection with helicobacter, giardia and other pathogens are common accompaniments of hypochlorhydria in children. (Mahalanabis, 1996; Judd, 1992; Solomons, 1982) Unpublished data from Australia suggests that approximately 75% of children with ADHD have hypochlorhydria by Heidelberg capsule testing. (McGuiness, 1998) Augmentation of gastric acid may assist in the improvement of digestion as well as the eradication of pathogens but the clinician should be vigilant to identify the causative factors and ensure their eventual removal, rather than persist with betaine hydrochloride while giving no thought as to the cause.

· Plant or animal derived digestive enzyme supplements are commonly given to children with ADHD. Increased gut permeability and dysbiosis leads to decreased efficiency of pancreatic enzyme function, diminished bile production and release as well as damage to mucosal disaccharidase enzymes. A broad range of enzymes can be administered via the oral route. Again, if the other clinical interventions are adequate this should be a temporary intervention only.

· Fiber is nearly absent in the diets of many children, particular those with a taste for junk foods. Fiber is critical in the maintenance of normal gut flora and in the elimination of gut derived toxins. As well, toxins processed by the liver and excreted through the bile require the presence of adequate fiber to pass through the gut quickly while being sequestered onto the surface of the fiber to prevent their reabsorption. Increasing the consumption of fruits and vegetables, legumes, brown rice and other permitted whole grains and adding an oligoantigenic fiber supplement such as UltraFiber (www.UltraBalance.com) to nutritional "smoothies" can all increase the fiber content of the ADHD patient's diet.

REINOCULATE

This phase refers to the reestablishment of desirable GI microflora through:

· The use of live bacterial supplements (**probiotics**). Various species of Lactobacillus and Bifidobacteria are the major organisms involved. Several factors are used to determine whether or not a particular species, subspecies or strain is suitable as a probiotic:

› Firstly, the bacteria must maintain its viability under normal conditions of storage for a reasonable amount of time.

› Secondly, the organism must survive the passage through the acid environment of the stomach, and should stay viable in the presence of intestinal bile acids.

› It should also become readily incorporated into the "anaerobic paste", the thin layer of mucous covering the intestinal cells, and it should become adherent to the intestinal mucosa colonizing and remaining there.

› It should ferment a wide range of carbohydrates.

› It should produce only L-lactic acid (not both the D and L isomers) as its major by product.

› Finally, it should have an accumulating record of scientifically verified physiological benefits.

› This far, a few species have come at the top of their class for providing most or all of these benefits. These include Lactobacillus plantarum, Lactobacillus rhamnosus and Lactobacillus GG. The yeast, Saccharomyces boulardii is another probiotic supplement, which has proven, benefits, including the stimulation of secretory IgA production in the gut. (Buts, 1990)

· In addition to probiotic supplementation, specific agents may be given to selectively promote the growth of beneficial bacterial flora. Some of these agents, referred to as **prebiotics**, form a preferred food source for desirable flora.

› Fructooligosacharide (FOS) is a naturally occurring, indigestible carbohydrate, which promotes the growth of beneficial Bifidobacteria and Lactobacilli within the colon. (Sghir, 1998; Gibson, 1995a) FOS has been shown to improve intestinal mineral absorption (Delzenne, 1995; Ohta, 1995; Morohashi, 1998) and reduce the production of toxic bacterial and yeast metabolites within the gut. (Buddington, 1996) In our research, the product Ultracare for Kids™ was used to administer significant quantities of FOS to ADHD children. This proved to have significant beneficial effects upon gut flora and related parameters.

› Inulin is another carbohydrate found in chicory, onions, asparagus and Jerusalem artichoke. It has prebiotic properties, which promote the growth of bifidobacteria. (Roberfroid, 1998; Gibson, 1995b) It also promotes the production of beneficial short chain fatty acids through bacterial metabolism (Levrat, 1994) and it results in an augmentation of xenobiotic detoxification enzymes. (Nugon, 1996) Inulin is a component of the oligoantigenic medical food product UltraClear Sustain (www.UltraBalance.com).

- **Non-toxic inhibitors** of intestinal pathogens may also be administered as part of the both the remove and the reinoculate phase. These are primarily derivatives from bovine colostrum. Dairy cattle are exposed to a wide range of potential human pathogens in the "barnyard environment" and they mount an extensive immune response against most of these pathogens to provide passive immunity to their offspring. Such factors can be isolated from milk or colostrum and made into stable products for human consumption. Such factors may include:

  › Immunoglobulins (primarily sIgA), which binds to pathogens and prevents their adherence to GI mucosa. (Shield, 1993)

  › Lactoferrin, a protein which binds to iron making it unavailable for bacteria, protozoans and yeast. Although Lactobacilli and Bifidobacteria do not require iron, most gut pathogens do. Thus lactoferrin has very potent, and very broad-spectrum antimicrobial effects. (Teraguchi, 1995; Okutomi, 1997; Naidu, 1994) Lactoferrin also aids in the absorption of iron through the gut (Schulz, 1991; Chierici, 1992) and has general immune stimulating properties. (Yamauchi, 1998; Zimecki, 1998)

  › Some milk allergic individuals will be intolerant to these products, however they are derived from whey which is the least allergenic component of milk. Thus, many milk allergic individuals tolerate these products without difficulty.

REPAIR

This phase refers to the provision of specific nutritional factors, which aid in the regeneration and repair of the gastrointestinal mucosa. The above steps of the 4-R™ Program are often carried out simultaneous to the repair phase. Some of the nutrients used in this process include:

- L-glutamine is an amino acid, which is the primary source of energy for intestinal mucosal cells. L-glutamine has been shown to be highly effective in helping to restore normal mucosal integrity in patients with increased intestinal permeability or a "leaky gut". (van der Hulst, 1993; Klimberg, 1990; Noyer, 1998) Rice protein is an excellent source of L-glutamine and when fortified with L-lysine, L-threonine it is also a balanced source of all essential amino acids. Since rice protein is also rarely allergenic, it is an ideal base for medical food products intended for nutritional support of the GI mucosa. All of the UltraClear™ products, as well as Ultracare for Kids™ are fortified rice protein/carbohydrate based products. (www.UltraBalance.com) UltraClear Sustain™ (UltraClear GI in Canada) is fortified with additional L-glutamine and several other nutrients to aid in the repair process.

· The vitamins ascorbic acid (vit C), pantothenic acid (B5), vitamin E, and vitamin A all play a significant role in the repair of damaged GI mucosa. The overall quality of the diet, including calories, macro and micronutrient composition and adequacy of phytonutrient antioxidants is vital in the repair of damaged GI mucosa.

· The sulfur amino acids N-acetylcysteine, cysteine and the tripeptide glutathione are critical nutrients, which support detoxification of xenobiotics within the intestinal mucosa and liver and contribute significantly to gut mucosal repair in state of toxic stress. (Pollack, 1996; Aw, 1992)

· Ensuring an adequate supply of essential fatty acids is also important in the repair of damaged gut mucosa. (Miura, 1993; Ohtsuka, 1997; Kaur, 1996; Horie, 1998) EFA'a also assist in the absorption of minerals and in the function of the immune system. (Calder, 1998; Cartwright, 1995)

IMPACTING ANTECEDENTS AND TRIGGERS — IMMUNOLOGICAL SUPPORT

Consideration should be given for immune support in all ADHD patients. This consists of three basic elements (more elements are described in Chapter 22):

· Relief from antigenic overload: When increased intestinal permeability is present, a large antigenic load, composed of partially digested food material as well as microbial debris is continuously entering the mesenteric lymphatic structures and the capillaries belonging to the portal circulation. This imposes a great deal of stress upon the gut associated lymphoid tissue (GALT) as well as the liver macrophages (Kupfer cells). Immunological responses to these antigens are varied and may include type I, III and IV immune responses. (Joneja, 1990) Immune complexes may be formed in high quantities in the GALT. Some of these are cleared on first pass through the liver and others escape into the general circulation leading to deposition of immune complexes and a wide array of adverse effects. Immunological support of the patient with increased gut permeability should begin by reducing the antigenic load via the processes discussed above in the 4-R™ Program.

· Nutritional optimization: Many nutritional factors greatly influence immune system function and should be considered in all ADHD patients. Many children with ADHD have markedly sub optimal nutrition, which undoubtedly has a significant impact upon their immune function. Subjects with ADHD are commonly very picky eaters who thrive on "junk food" and shun many nutrient dense foods. This problem is clearly exacerbated by stimulant drugs, which can markedly suppress appetite. Basic protein calorie adequacy is the most fundamental requirement for immune competence. (Levy, 1998) Essential fatty acids are also important (Alexander, 1998) along with vitamins A, E, D and pyridoxine, (Klasing, 1998) and the trace elements magnesium, iron, zinc, copper and selenium. (Harbige, 1996; Konig, 1998) Glutamine, arginine, taurine and sulfur amino acids all have a potent immunomodulatory effects, especially in chronically ill patients or those with infection. (Wilmore, 1998; Redmond, 1998; Evoy, 1998; Grimble, 1998) Supplementation with specific types of dietary fiber as well as probiotic and prebiotic supplementation has a profound affect upon the immune competence of the gut and the resultant GI microbiological environment. (Bengmark, 1998; Cunningham, 1998) It is important to note that chronic infection, including infection of the gut or respiratory tract, can affect nutritional status and lead to nutritional inadequacies. Conversely, nutritional inadequacy is probably the primary factor leading to chronic infection. Both must be addressed.

· Specific immune stimulants: An important category of nutritive substances, composed of various short chain carbohydrates, have been shown to significantly influence immune function and have been shown to modulate immunity in various way. Various medicinal mushrooms, (Chang, 1996) yeast extracts, (Penna, 1996) aloe vera (Stuart, 1997) and other herbal substances such as echinacea have all been demonstrated to increase immune responsiveness in a variety of ways. (Burger, 1997) In our facility a water extract from American ginseng (not the same as a ginsenoside extract) is often utilized and has been found to be a well-tolerated adjunct to the 4-R Program™ when significant immune dysfunction and gastrointestinal dysbiosis is detected. This product (Cold-FX™; 1-888-843-7239) is a fraction composed of complex, water soluble polysaccharides and oligosaccharides. This fraction has been primarily studied for its immune stimulant properties as well as its ability to provide gastric mucosal protection. The base sugars which make up these unusual carbohydrates include L-arabinose, D-galactose, L-rhamnose, D-galacturonic acid, D-glucuronic acid, and D-galactosyl residues. (Tomoda, 1993; Tomoda, 1994) This carbohydrate fraction of ginseng has been shown to activate macrophages against Candida albicans, (Akagawa, 1996) induce the production of interferon-gamma and tumor necrosis factor-alpha in lymphocytes and peritoneal macrophages, (Gao, 1996; Jie, 1984) potentate anti-complement activity, (Tomoda, 1994) stimulate phagocytosis in polymorphonuclear leukocytes, (Hu, 1995) stimulate natural killer cell activity, (Kim, 1990) induce interleukin-2, (Ma, 1995) and activate several other components of cell mediated immunity. (Scaglione, 1990) It has been shown to be particularly useful in improving parameters of immunity in human subjects with AIDS or chronic fatigue syndrome. (See, 1997) It has also been shown to reduce bacterial load and lung pathology in animal models of cystic fibrosis (Song, 1997) and to potentiate the effectiveness of antibiotic therapy in children with bacterial dysentery. (Vereshchagin, 1982) This same carbohydrate fraction has been shown to exert potent gastric cytoprotective and anti-ulcer effects. (Kiyohara, 1994; Sun, 1991)

IMPACTING ANTECEDENTS AND TRIGGERS — ADJUNCTS TO NUTRITIONAL MANAGEMENT OF THE ADHD PATIENT

Even if the patient makes their best effort to be compliant with the oligoantigenic diet, nutritional challenges may hinder the effectiveness of the diet. Important nutrients, such as calcium, may be inadequate after dairy products, are eliminated. In children with ADHD, high metabolic acid production, high catecholamine production and, potentially, sympathomimetic drugs may all contribute to calcium and magnesium wasting. Caloric intake may also be low in children with restricted diets and intense hunger or hypoglycemic episodes between meals may tempt the child to consume unhealthy snack foods. Clinicians may find the oligoantigenic medical food product, Ultracare for Kids™ (www.UltraBalance.com), a very helpful and well-accepted addition to the diet of the ADHD child. In a recent study we compared the effectiveness of an oligoantigenic diet alone or in combination with the medical food product Ultracare for Kids™. This product is used as the basis of a tasty fruit "smoothie" drink twice a day as an alternative to unhealthy snack foods. It was found to be a convenient way to significantly increase dietary nutrient density and to provide several nurients which are important in ADHD.

There are a number of potential benefits of Ultracare for Kids™, which make it a highly useful adjunct in the dietary management of ADHD. Firstly, it is a palatable source of low allergy potential nutrients. Many children with ADHD, especially those on stimulant medications have impaired appetites and delayed growth and they will benefit from a highly nutritious, oligoantigenic calorie source. If used as the base for a fruit "smoothie", it can be used to increase a child's intake of fruit, fiber, vegetable juice, essential fatty acids and other nutrients, depending upon the composition of the "smoothie". Ultracare for Kids™ is also an excellent source of calcium for children unable to consume dairy products and it is a good source of highly bioavailable micronutrients for children with potentially compromised absorptive capacities and pre-existing micronutrient insufficiencies. Because algae derived DHA is present in Ultracare for Kids™, it is an excellent source of this critical omega three fatty acid. Ultracare for Kids™ is also an excellent source of fructo-oligosacharides (FOS) which encourage the growth of desirable intestinal microbes.

For older children or adults, UltraClear Sustain™ (UltraClear GI™ in Canada) is highly useful in implementing the "repair" phase of the "4-R Program". Essential fatty acids must also be optimized in both adults and children with ADHD. DHA may be added through fish oil. Flax oil is a rich source of ALA and it is a useful means of increasing the overall omega three fatty acid content of the diet. GLA supplements may be of benefit in some cases of ADHD (evening primrose, borage or black current oils). Fatty acid testing would clarify this need.

IMPACTING ANTECEDENTS AND TRIGGERS — TOXICOLOGICAL THERAPIES

In the months or years to come, it will likely become increasingly evident that the most important antecedent factors increasing the risk of ADHD are environmental neurotoxins and immunotoxins. Both increased xenobiotic susceptibility as well excessive exposure to toxicants has now been clearly demonstrated in autistic children, and the same will likely hold true in those with ADHD. These toxic influences set the stage for a wide range of physiological disruptions, which play out as the triggers, and mediators of ADHD. To be effective, the Functional Medicine practitioner must become intimately familiar with the theoretical and practical principles of Functional Toxicology. Some of these basic principles will be briefly summarized below. More detailed information about the principles and practice of Functional Toxicology can be obtained from the Institute for Functional

Medicine (www.fxmed.com).

· The treatment of a patient suspected to suffer from toxic stress should begin with an appropriate toxicological assessment.

· The foremost treatment principle in Functional Toxicology is to remove the patient from the source of toxicity. For example, lead toxic patients should be removed from homes with leaded paint until professional lead abatement is completed and mercury toxic patients should have amalgams should be removed by a dentist following protocols of "biological dentistry".

· Any safe and effective detoxification strategy should:

> › Increase mobilization of xenobiotics and heavy metal from cells.

> › Maximize excretion of the toxins from the body.

> › Minimize the redistribution of mobilized toxins back into cells and organs.

Chelating drugs, nutritive substances and physical interventions such as hyperthermic therapy all have the capacity to increase mobilization. Whether or not these interventions result in an acceptably high level of excretion and acceptably low level of redistribution depends upon numerous factors. Special caution must be used especially in the case of chelating drugs or very high doses of natural chelating substances such as lipoic acid, or N-acetyl cysteine. Clinicians utilizing such agents must be aware of their capability of creating very serious redistribution problems and should be thoroughly trained in their use.

· The foundation of any detoxification strategy must be optimal support of the body's natural detoxification mechanisms. The capability of a optimally functioning liver and intestinal tract for excreting large quantities of organic and inorganic toxicants is far greater than that of any pharmaceutical or nutritive substance alone in megadoses.

› "Enterohepatic resuscitation" using UltraClear Plus™ combined with an oligoantigenic diet is a clinically safe and practical approach to the detoxification of both children and adults. Information about this program can be obtained through the Institute for Functional Medicine. (www.fxmed.com)

› The addition of xenobiotic and heavy metal binding substances, nutritional supplements, exercise, heat depuration (saunas, steam baths or hydrotherapy), and massage therapy may all play an important adjunctive role in the reduction of toxic stress.

References

Abe K, Cho S, Kitagawa I, Nishiyama N, Saito H. Differential effects of ginsenoside Rb1 and malonylginsenoside Rb1 on long-term potentiation in the dentate gyrus of rats. Brain Res. 1994;649:7-11.

Abe S, Tansho S, Ishibashi H, Inagaki N, Komatsu Y, Yamaguchi H. Protective effect of oral administration of a traditional medicine, Juzen-Taiho-To, and its components on lethal Candida albicans infection in immunosuppressed mice. Immunopharmacol Immunotoxicol. 1998;20:421-31.

Adcock K, MacElroy D, Wolford E, Farrington E. Pemoline therapy resulting in liver transplantation. Ann Pharmacother. 1998;32:422-5.

Ascherio A, Willett W. Health effects of trans fatty acids. Am J Clin Nutr. 1997;66:1006S-1010S.

Adesman A, Altshuler L, Lipkin P, Walco G. Otitis media in children with learning disabilities and in children with attention deficit disorder with hyperactivity. Pediatrics. 1990;85:442-6.

Ahmann P, Waltonen S, Olson K, Theye F, Van Erem A, LaPlant R. Placebo-controlled evaluation of ritalin side effects. Pediatrics. 1993;91:1101-6

Akagawa G, Abe S, Tansho S, Uchida K, Yamaguchi H. Protection of C3H/HE J mice from development of Candida albicans infection by oral administration of Juzen-taiho-to and its component, Ginseng radix: possible roles of macrophages in the host defense mechanisms. Immunopharmacol Immunotoxicol. 1996;18:73-89.

Albanese C, Smith S, Watkins S, Kurkchubasche A, Simmons R, Rowe M. Effect of secretory IgA on the transepithelial passage of bacteria across the intact ileum in vitro. J Am Coll Surg. 1994;179:679-88.

Alexander J, Boyce S, Babcock G, et al. The process of microbial translocation. Ann Surg. 1990;212:496-512.

Alexander J. Immunonutrition: the role of omega-3 fatty acids. Nutrition. 1998;14:627-33.

Allain H, Raoul P, Lieury A, LeCoz F, Gandon J, d AP. Effect of two doses of ginkgo biloba extract (EGb 761) on the dual-coding test in elderly subjects. Clin Ther. 1993;15:549-58.

Allen M, Jones MJ. Medical complications of prematurity. Obstet Gynecol. 1986;67:427-37.

Alsobrook Jn, Pauls D. Molecular approaches to child psychopathology. Hum Biol. 1998;70:413-32.

Alverdy J, Stern E. Effect of immunonutrition on virulence strategies in bacteria. Nutrition. 1998;14:580-4.

Amen D, Carmichael B. High-resolution brain SPECT imaging in ADHD. Ann Clin Psychiatry. 1997;9:81-6.

Amri H, Drieu K, Papadopoulos V. Ex vivo regulation of adrenal cortical cell steroid and protein synthesis, in response to adrenocorticotropic hormone stimulation, by the Ginkgo biloba extract EGb 761 and isolated ginkgolide B. Endocrinology. 1997;138:5415-26.

Amri H, Ogwuegbu S, Boujrad N, Drieu K, Papadopoulos V. In vivo regulation of peripheral-type benzodiazepine receptor and glucocorticoid synthesis by Ginkgo biloba extract EGb 761 and isolated ginkgolides. Endocrinology. 1996;137:5707-18.

Anderson G, Connor W, Corliss J. Docosahexaenoic acid is the preferred dietary n-3 fatty acid for the development of the brain and retina. Pediatr Res. 1990;27:89-97.

Anderson J., Mechanisms in adverse reactions to food. The brain. Allergy. 1995;50:78-81.

Andre C, Andre F, Colin L, Cavagna S. Measurement of intestinal permeability to mannitol and lactulose as a means of diagnosing food allergy and evaluating theraputic effectiveness of disodium cromoglycate. Ann Allergy. 1987;59:127-30.

APA. (American Psychiatric Association) Diagnostic and Statistical Manual, Fourth Edition (DSM-IV). : Psychiatric Press, Inc.; 1994.

Aposhian HV. DMSA and DMPS - water soluble antidotes for heavy metal poisoning. Annu. Rev. Pharmacol. Toxicol. 1983;23:193-215.

Aposhian H, Bruce D, Alter W, Dart R, Hurlbut K, Aposhian M. Urinary mercury after administration of 2,3-dimercaptopropane-1-sulfonic acid: correlation with dental amalgam score. FASEB J. 1992;6:2472-6.

Aposhian HV, Maiorino RM, Gonzalez-Ramirez D, et al. Mobilization of heavy metals by newer, therapeutically useful chelating agents. Toxicology. 1995;97:23-38.

Aposhian MM, Maiorino RM, Xu Z, Aposhian HV. Sodium 2,3-dimercapto-1-propane-sulfonate (DMPS) treatment does not redistribute lead or mercury to the brain of rats. Toxicology. 1996;109:49-55.

Appel N, Contrera J, De SE. Fenfluramine selectively and differentially decreases the density of serotonergic nerve terminals in rat brain: evidence from immunocytochemical studies. J Pharmacol Exp Ther. 1989;249:928-43.

Arcia E, Roberts J. Otitis media in early childhood and its association with sustained attention in structured situations. J Dev Behav Pediatr. 1993;14:181-3.

Arnold L, Votolato N, Kleykamp D, Baker G, Bornstein R. Does hair zinc predict amphetamine improvement of ADD/hyperactivity?. Int J Neurosci. 1990;50:103-7.

Arvola T, Isolauri E, Rantala I, et al. Increased in vitro intestinal permeability in suckling rats exposed to cow milk during lactation. J Pediatr Gastroenterol Nutr. 1993;16:294-300.

Ascherio A, Willett W. Health effects of trans fatty acids. Am J Clin Nutr. 1997;66:1006S-1010S.

Attella M, Hoffman S, Stasio M, Stein D. Ginkgo biloba extract facilitates recovery from penetrating brain injury in adult male rats. Exp Neurol. 1989;105:62-71.

Aw T, Williams M. Intestinal absorption and lymphatic transport of peroxidized lipids in rats: effect of exogenous GSH. Am J Physiol. 1992;263:G665-72.

Baker G, Bornstein R, Rouget A, Ashton S, van Muyden J, Coutts R. Phenylethylaminergic mechanisms in attention-deficit disorder. Biological Psychiatry. 1991;29:15-22.

Banks W, Kastin A. Passage of peptides across the blood-brain barrier: pathophysiological perspectives. Life Sci. 1996;59:1923-43.

Barkats M, Venault P, Christen Y, Cohen -SC. Effect of long-term treatment with EGb 761 on age-dependent structural changes in the hippocampi of three inbred mouse strains. Life Sci. 1995;56:213-22.

Barkley R, Grodzinsky G, DuPaul G. Frontal lobe functions in attention deficit disorder with and without hyperactivity: a review and research report. Journal of Abnormal Child Psychology. 1992;20:163-88.

Barkley R. Attention deficit hyperactivity disorder: a handbook for diagnosis and treatment. . New York: Gulford Press; 1990.

Barkley R. Attention-deficit/hyperactivity disorder, self-regulation, and time: toward a more comprehensive theory. J Dev Behav Pediatr. 1997;18:271-9.

Barkley R. Behavioral inhibition, sustained attention, and executive functions: constructing a unifying theory of ADHD. Psychol Bull. 1997;121:65-94.

Barrickman L, Noyes R, Kuperman S, Schumacher E, Verda M. Treatment of adhd with fluoxetine: a preliminary trial. Journal of the American Academy of Child & Adolescent Psychiatry. 1991;30:762-7.

Barth S, Inselmann G, Engemann R, Heidemann H. Influences of Ginkgo biloba on cyclosporin A induced lipid peroxidation in human liver microsomes in comparison to vitamin E, glutathione and N-acetylcysteine. Biochem Pharmacol. 1991;41:1521-6.

Batt RM, Rutgers HC, Sancak AA. Enteric bacteria: friend or foe? J Small Anim Pract. 1996;37:261-7.

Bekaroglu M, Aslan Y, Gedik Y, et al. Relationships between serum free fatty acids and zinc, and attention deficit hyperactivity disorder: a research note. J Child Psychol Psychiatry. 1996;37:225-7.

Benezra E, Douglas V. Short-term serial recall in ADDH, normal, and reading-disabled boys. J Abnorm Child Psychol. 1988;16:511-25.

Bengmark S, Jeppsson B. Gastrointestinal surface protection and mucosa reconditioning. JPEN J Parenter Enteral Nutr. 1995;19:410-5.

Bengmark S. Immunonutrition: role of biosurfactants, fiber, and probiotic bacteria. Nutrition. 1998;14:585-94.

Benishin C. Actions of ginsenoside Rb1 on choline uptake in central cholinergic nerve endings. Neurochem Int. 1992;21:1-5.

Benson D. The role of frontal dysfunction in attention deficit hyperactivity disorder. Journal of Child Neurology. 1991;6:S9-12.

Benzie IF, Szeto YT, Strain JJ, Tomlinson B. Consumption of green tea causes rapid increase in plasma antioxidant power in humans. Nutr Cancer. 1999;34:83-7

Biederman J, Faraone S, Mick E, et al. High risk for attention deficit hyperactivity disorder among children of parents with childhood onset of the disorder: a pilot study. American Journal of Psychiatry. 1995;152:431-5.

Biederman J, Faraone S, Spencer T, et al. Patterns of psychiatric comorbidity, cognition, and psychosocial functioning in adults with attention deficit hyperactivity disorder. American Journal of Psychiatry. 1993;150:1792-8.

Biederman J, Santangelo S, Faraone S, et al. Clinical correlates of enuresis in ADHD and non-ADHD children. J Child Psychol Psychiatry. 1995;5:865-77.

Beissert S, Schwarz T. Mechanisms involved in ultraviolet light-induced immunosuppression. J Investig Dermatol Symp Proc. 1999;4:61-4.

Bell CC, Suggs H. Using sports to strengthen resiliency in children. Training heart. Child Adolesc Psychiatr Clin N Am. 1998;7:859-65.

Bjarnason I, Macpherson A, Hollander D. Intestinal permeability: An overview. Gastroenterology. 1995;108:1566-81.

Bjorksten B, Naaber P, Sepp E, Mikelsaar M. The intestinal microflora in allergic Estonian and Swedish 2-year-old children. Clin Exp Allergy. 1999;29:342-6.

Bland J, Barrager E, Reedy R, Bland K. A medical food-supplemented detoxification program in the management of chronic health problems. Alternative Therapies in Health and Medicine. 1995;1:67-71.

Bland J. Nutritional modulation of the detoxification process. In: Alexander M, ed. New Perspectives in Nutritional Therapies. Improving Patient Outcomes. Gig Harbor, WA: HealthComm; 1996.

Blum K, Sheridan P, Wood R, Braverman E, Chen T, Comings D. Dopamine D2 receptor gene variants: association and linkage studies in impulsive-addictive-compulsive behaviour. Pharmacogenetics. 1995;5:121-41.

Blum K, Sheridan P, Wood R, et al. The D2 dopamine receptor gene as a determinant of reward deficiency syndrome. J R Soc Med. 1996;7:89:396-400.

Bolanos -JF, Manhaes dCR, Sarhan H, Prudhomme N, Drieu K, Fillion G. Stress-induced 5-HT1A receptor desensitization: protective effects of Ginkgo biloba extract (EGb 761). Fundam Clin Pharmacol. 1995;9:169-74.

Bol'shakova IV, Lozovskaia EL, Sapezhinskii, II. [Antioxidant properties of a series of extracts from medicinal plants]. Biofizika. 1997;42:480-3.

Bork PM, Bacher S, Schmitz ML, Kaspers U, Heinrich M. Hypericin as a non-antioxidant inhibitor of NF-kappa B. Planta Med. 1999;65:297-300.

Boris M. Foods and food additives are common causes of the attention deficit hyperactivity disorder in children. Annals Allergy. 1994;72:462-68.

Boughner D. A dangerous duo? A combination of common diet drugs (fen-phen) may lead to heart valve disease [editorial]. CMAJ. 1997;157:705-6.

Bouhnik Y, Alain S, Attar A, et al. Bacterial populations contaminating the upper gut in patients with small intestinal bacterial overgrowth syndrome. Am J Gastroenterol. 1999;94:1327-31.

Brannan D, Greenfield R, Owen W, Welch D, Kuhls T. Protozoal colonization of the intestinal tract in institutionalized Romanian children. Clin Infect Dis. 1996;22:456-61.

Brandtzaeg P. Development and basic mechanisms of human gut immunity. Nutr Rev. 1998;56:S5-18.

Braud LW. The effects of frontal EMG biofeedback and progressive relaxation upon hyperactivity and its behavioral concomitants. Biofeedback Self Regul. 1978;3:69-89.

Bremner J, Randall P, Scott T, et al. MRI-based measurement of hippocampal volume in patients with combat-related posttraumatic stress disorder. Am J Psychiatry. 1995;152:973-81.

Brockel B, Cory -SD. Lead, attention, and impulsive behavior: changes in a fixed-ratio waiting-for-reward paradigm. Pharmacol Biochem Behav. 1998;60:545-52.

Broocks A, Bandelow B, Pekrun G, et al. Comparison of aerobic exercise, clomipramine, and placebo in the treatment of panic disorder [see comments]. Am J Psychiatry. 1998;155:603-9.

Brooks R. Children at risk: fostering resilience and hope. American Journal of Orthopsychiatry. 1994;64:545-53.

Bro-Rasmussen F. Contamination by persistent chemicals in food chain and human health. Sci Total Environ. 1996;188 Suppl 1:S45-60.

Brunello N, Racagni G, Clostre F, Drieu K, Braquet P. Effects of an extract of Ginkgo biloba on noradrenergic systems of rat cerebral cortex. Pharmacol Res Commun. 1985;17:1063-72.

Bruno C, Cuppini R, Sartini S, Cecchini T, Ambrogini P, Bombardelli E. Regeneration of motor nerves in bilobalide-treated rats. Planta Med. 1993;59:302-7.

Buddington RK, Williams C, Chen S, Witherly S. Dietary supplement of neosugar alters the fecal flora and decreases activities of some reductive enzymes in human subjects. Clinical Nutrition. 1996;63:709-16.

Burger R, Torres A, Warren R, Caldwell V, Hughes B. Echinacea-induced cytokine production by human macrophages. Int J Immunopharmacol. 1997;19:371-9.

Burgess N, Reynolds T, Williams N, Pathy A, Smith S. Evaluation of four animal models of intrarenal calcium deposition and assessment of the influence of dietary supplementation with essential fatty acids on calcification. Urol Res. 1995;23:239-42.

Burnham JM. Exercise is medicine: health benefits of regular physical activity. J La State Med Soc. 1998;150:319-23.

Burnstein S, Liakos S. Parasitic rheumatism presenting as rheumatoid arthritis. J Rheumatol. 1983;10:514-5.

Buts J. Stimulation of secretory IgA and secretory componant of immunoglobulins in small intestine of rats treated with Saccharomyces boulardii. Digestive Diseases and Sciences. 1990;35:251-56.

Butterweck V, Petereit F, Winterhoff H, Nahrstedt A. Solubilized hypericin and pseudo-hypericin from Hypericum perforatum exert antidepressant activity in the forced swimming test. Planta Med. 1998;64:291-4.

Cadet JL, Ordonez SV, Ordonez JV. Methamphetamine induces apoptosis in immortalized neural cells: protection by the proto-oncogene, bcl-2. Synapse. 1997;25:176-84.

Caffarelli C, Cavagni G, Menzies I, Bertolini P, Atherton D. Elimination diet and intestinal permeability in atopic eczema: a preliminary study. Clinical and Experimental Allergy. 1993;23:28-31.

Calder P. Dietary fatty acids and the immune system. Nutr Rev. 1998;56:S70-83.

Caldwell JJ. Effects of operationally effective doses of dextroamphetamine on heart rates and blood pressures of army aviators. Mil Med. 1996;161:673-8.

Campbell P. Effect of high dose vitamin C administration on cortisol secretion and immune parameters in stressed rats. American Chemical Society Annual Meeting. New Orleans; 1999.

Cancrini G, Bartoloni A, Nunez L, Paradisi F. Intestinal parasites in the Camiri, Gutierrez and Boyuibe areas, Santa Cruz Department, Bolivia. Parassitologia. 1988;30:263-9.

Cant A, Shay J, Horrobin D. The effect of maternal supplementation with linoleic and gamma-linolenic acids on the fat composition and content of human milk: a placebo-controlled trial. J Nutr Sci Vitaminol (Tokyo). 1991;37:573-9.

Caramia G, Franceschini F, Cimarelli ZA, Ciucchi MS, Gagliardini R, Ruffini E. The efficacy of E.P.D., a new immunotherapy, in the treatment of allergic diseases in children. Allerg Immunol (Paris). 1996;28:308-10.

Carlson S, Clandinin M, Cook H, Emken E, Filer LJ. trans Fatty acids: infant and fetal development. Am J Clin Nutr. 1997;66:715S-36S.

Carlson S, Werkman S, Rhodes P, Tolley E. Visual-acuity development in healthy perterm infants: effect of marine-oil supplementation. Am J Clin Nutr. 1993;58:35-42.

Carter C, Egger J, Soothill J. A dietary management of severe childhood migraine. Hum Nutr Appl Nutr. 1985;39:294-303.

Carter C, Urbanowicz M, Hemsley R, et al. Effects of a few food diet in attention deficit disorder. Arch Dis Child. 1993;69:564-8.

Carter TM. The effects of spiritual practices on recovery from substance abuse. J Psychiatr Ment Health Nurs. 1998;5:409-13

Cartwright -SJ, Dodge J, McMaster C. A complex biochemical modulation of intestinal ion transport in rats fed on high-fat diets. J Pediatr Gastroenterol Nutr. 1995;20:36-43.

Carvajal S, Mulvihill S. Intestinal peptides and their relevance in pediatric disease. Semin Pediatr Surg. 1995;4:9-21.

Castellanos F, Giedd J, Marsh W, et al. Quantitative brain magnetic resonance imaging in attention-deficit hyperactivity disorder. Arch Gen Psychiatry. 1996;53:607-16.

Celiberti D, Bobo H, Kelly K, Harris S, Handleman J. The differential and temporal effects of antecedent exercise on the self-stimulatory behavior of a child with autism. Res Dev Disabil. 1997;18:139-50.

Chandra R. Nutrition and the immune system: an introduction. Am J Clin Nutr. 1997;66:460S-463S.

Chang R. Functional properties of edible mushrooms. Nutr Rev. 1996;54:S91-3.

Chaouloff F. Physical exercise and brain monoamines: a review. Acta Physiol Scand. 1989;137:1-13.

Chaouloff F. Effects of acute physical exercise on central serotonergic systems. Med Sci Sports Exerc. 1997;29:58-62.

Chatterjee S, Bhattacharya S, Wonnemann M, Singer A, Muller W. Hyperforin as a possible antidepressant component of hypericum extracts. Life Sci. 1998;63:499-510.

Chierici R, Sawatzki G, Tamisari L, Volpato S, Vigi V. Supplementation of an adapted formula with bovine lactoferrin. 2. Effects on serum iron, ferritin and zinc levels. Acta Paediatr. 1992;81:475-9.

Christie DJ, Dewitt RA, Kaltenbach P, Reed D. Using EMg biofeedback to signal hyperactive children when to relax. Except Child. 1984;50:547-8.

Claassen N, Coetzer H, Steinmann C, Kruger M. The effect of different n-6/n-3 essential fatty acid ratios on calcium balance and bone in rats. Prostaglandins Leukot Essent Fatty Acids. 1995;53:13-9.

Clostre F. Ginkgo biloba extract (EGb 761). State of knowledge in the dawn of the year 2000. Ann Pharm Fr. 1999;57 Suppl 1:1S8-88.

Collet L, Cottraux J, Juenet C. GSR feedback and Schultz relaxation in tension headaches: a comparative study. Pain. 1986;25:205-13.

Colquhoun I, Bunday S. A lack of essential fatty acids as a possible cause of hyperactivity in children. Medical Hypotheses. 1981;7:673-9.

Conner S, Conner W. The New American Diet. New York: Simon and Schuster; 1986:410pp.

Connors C, Caldwell J, Caldwell L. Experimental studies of sugar and aspartame on autonomic, cortical and behavioral responses of children. . Proceedings of interactions in psychology. Lubbock, TX: Texas Technical Press; 1986.

Cook EJ, Stein M, Ellison T, Unis A, Leventhal B. Attention deficit hyperactivity disorder and whole-blood serotonin levels: effects of comorbidity. Psychiatry Res. 1995;57:13-20.

Cook EJ, Stein M, Krasowski M, et al. Association of attention-deficit disorder and the dopamine transporter gene. Am J Hum Genet. 1995;56:993-8.

Cooley JD, Wong WC, Jumper CA, Straus DC. Correlation between the prevalence of certain fungi and sick building syndrome. Occup Environ Med. 1998;55:579-84.

Cooper R, Fraser S, Sturrock R, Gemmell C. Raised titres of anti-klebsiella IgA in ankylosing spondylitis, rheumatoid arthritis, and inflammatory bowel disease. Br Med J (Clin Res Ed). 1988;296:1432-4.

Crawford M, Doyle W, Leaf A, Leighfield M, Ghebremeskel K, Phylactos A. Nutrition and neurodevelopmental disorders. Nutr Health. 1993;2:81-97.

Crawford M. The role of essential fatty acids in neural development: implications for perinatal nutrition. Am J Clin Nutr. 1993;5:703S-709S.

Crook TH, Tinklenberg J, Yesavage J, Petrie W, Nunzi MG, Massari DC. Effects of phosphatidylserine in age-associated memory impairment. Neurology. 1991;41:644-9.

Cuffari C, Oligny L, Seidman E. Dientamoeba fragilis masquerading as allergic colitis. J Pediatr Gastroenterol Nutr. 1998;26:16-20.

Cunningham -RS, Lin D. Nutrition and the immune system of the gut. Nutrition. 1998;14:573-9.

Czekalla J, Gastpar M, Hubner W, Jager D. The effect of hypericum extract on cardiac conduction as seen in the electrocardiogram compared to that of imipramine. Pharmacopsychiatry. 1997;30 Suppl 2:86-8.

Defeat Autism Now ([RTF annotation: fixit]DAN) Professional Autism Discussion Group; Personal Communication, 1999.

D'Angelo L, Grimaldi R, Caravaggi M, et al. A double-blind, placebo-controlled clinical study on the effect of a standardized ginseng extract on psychomotor performance in healthy volunteers. J Ethnopharmacol. 1986;16:15-22.

David O, Hoffman S, Sverd J, Clark J, Voeller K. Lead and hyperactivity. Behavioral response to chelation: a pilot study. Am J Psychiatry. 1976;133:1155-58.

Davis C, Katzman DK, Kirsh C. Compulsive physical activity in adolescents with anorexia nervosa: a psychobehavioral spiral of pathology. J Nerv Ment Dis. 1999;187:336-42.

de Coverley Veale DM. Exercise and mental health. Acta Psychiatr Scand. 1987;76:113-20.

Delzenne N, Aertssens J, Verplaetse H, Roccaro M, Roberfroid M. Effect of fermentable fructo-oligosaccharides on mineral, nitrogen and energy digestive balance in the rat. Life Sci Date of Pub. 1995;17:1578-87.

Denckla M. Biological correlates of learning and attention: what is relevant to learning disability and attention-deficit hyperactivity disorder? J Dev Behav Pediatr. 1996;17:114-9.

Deng H, Zhang J. Anti-lipid peroxilative effect of ginsenoside Rb1 and Rg1. Chin Med J (Engl). 1991;104:395-8.

Denkowski KM, Denkowski GC, Omizo MM. The effects of EMG-assisted relaxation training on the academic performance, locus of control, and self-esteem of hyperactive boys. Biofeedback Self Regul. 1983;8:363-75.

Denkowski KM, Denkowski GC. Is group progressive relaxation training as effective with hyperactive children as individual EMG biofeedback treatment? Biofeedback Self Regul. 1984;9:353-64.

D'Eufemia P, Celli M, Finocchiaro R, et al. Abnormal intestinal permeability in children with autism. Acta Paediatr. 1996;9:1076-9.

DiLorenzo TM, Bargman EP, Stucky-Ropp R, Brassington GS, Frensch PA, LaFontaine T. Long-term effects of aerobic exercise on psychological outcomes. Prev Med. 1999;28:75-85.

DiPrisco PM, Hagel I, Lynch N, Barrios R, Alvarez N, Lopez R. Possible relationship between allergic disease and infection by Giardia lamblia. Ann Allergy. 1993;70:210-3.

DiPrisco PM, Hagel I, Lynch N, et al. Association between giardiasis and allergy. Ann Allergy Asthma Immunol. 1998;81:261-5.

Di Stanislao C, Di Berardino L, Bianchi I, Bologna G. A double-blind, placebo-controlled study of preventive immunotherapy with E.P.D., in the treatment of seasonal allergic disease. Allerg Immunol (Paris). 1997;29:39-42.

DiTraglia J. METHYLPHENIDATE PROTOCOL: FEASIBILITY IN A PEDIATRIC PRACTICE. Clinical Pediatrics. 1991;30:656-60.

Dluzen D, Binjun L, Chen C, DiCarlo S. Daily spontaneous running alters behavioral and neurochemical indexes of nigrostriatal function. J Appl Physiol. 1995;78(4):1219-24.

Douglas V, Benezra E. Supraspan verbal memory in attention deficit disorder with hyperactivity normal and reading-disabled boys. J Abnorm Child Psychol. 1990;18:617-38.

Dumont E, D AP, Nouvelot A. Protection of polyunsaturated fatty acids against iron-dependent lipid peroxidation by a Ginkgo biloba extract (EGb 761). Methods Find Exp Clin Pharmacol. 1995;17:83-8.

Duncan K, Harris S, Ardies C. Running exercise may reduce risk for lung and liver cancer by inducing activity of antioxidant and phase II enzymes. Cancer Lett. 1997;116:151-8.

Durham SR, Walker SM, Varga EM, et al. Long-term clinical efficacy of grass-pollen immunotherapy. N Engl J Med. 1999;341:468-75.

Durlach PJ. The effects of a low dose of caffeine on cognitive performance. Psychopharmacology (Berl). 1998;140:116-9.

Dykens EM, Rosner BA, Butterbaugh G. Exercise and sports in children and adolescents with developmental disabilities. Positive physical and psychosocial effects. Child Adolesc Psychiatr Clin N Am. 1998;7:757-71, viii.

Dykman KD, Dykman RA. Effect of nutritional supplements on attentional-deficit hyperactivity disorder. Integr Physiol Behav Sci. 1998;33:49-60.

Eaton K, Howard M, Howard J. Gut permeability measured by polyethylene glycol absorption in abnormal gut fermentation as compared with food intolerance. J R Soc Med. 1995;88:63-6.

Edelson S, Cantor D. Autism: xenobiotic influences. Toxicol Ind Health. 1998;14:553-63.

Edelson S. The Neurotoxic Etiology of Autistic Spectrum Disorders (56 Patients): Personal Communication. ; 1999.

Egger J, Carter C, Graham P, Gumley D, Soothill J. Controlled trial of oligoantigenic treatment in the hyperkinetic syndrome. Lancet. 1985;1:540-5.

Egger J, Carter C, Soothill J, Wilson J. Effect of diet treatment on enuresis in children with migraine or hyperkinetic behavior. Clin Pediatr (Phila). 1992;31:302-7.

Egger J, Carter C, Soothill J, Wilson J. Oligoantigenic diet treatment of children with epilepsy and migraine. J Pediatr. 1989;114:51-8.

Egger J, Carter C, Wilson J, Turner M, Soothill J. Is migraine food allergy? A double-blind controlled trial of oligoantigenic diet treatment. Lancet. 1983;2:865-9.

Egger J, Stolla A, McEwen L. Controlled trial of hyposensitisation in children with food-induced hyperkinetic syndrome. Lancet. 1992;339:1150-3.

El -Nazami H, Kankaanpaa P, Salminen S, Ahokas J. Ability of dairy strains of lactic acid bacteria to bind a common food carcinogen, aflatoxin B1. Food Chem Toxicol. 1998;36:321-6.

Elia J. Stimulants and antidepressant pharmacokinetics in hyperactive children. Psychopharmacology Bulletin. 1991;27:411-5.

Eliason B, Kruger J, Mark D, Rasmann D. Dietary supplement users: demographics, product use, and medical system interaction. J Am Board Fam Pract. 1997;10:265-71.

Elliott RJ, Dobbin A, Rose G, Soper H. Vigorous, aerobic exercise versus general motor training activities: effects on maladaptive and stereotypic behaviors of adults with both autism and mental retardation. J Autism Dev Disord. 1994;24:565-76.

Elmer G. Biotherapeutic agents. A neglected modality for the treatment and prevention of selected intestinal and vaginal infections. JAMA. 1996;275:870-6.

Eppright T, Sanfacon J, Horwitz E. Attention deficit hyperactivity disorder, infantile autism, and elevated blood-lead: a possible relationship. Mo Med. 1996;3:136-8.

Ernst E, Rand JI, Barnes J, Stevinson C. Adverse effects profile of the herbal antidepressant St. John's wort (Hypericum perforatum L.). Eur J Clin Pharmacol. 1998;54:589-94.

Ernst M, Liebenauer L, King A, Fitzgerald G, Cohen R, Zametkin A. Reduced brain metabolism in hyperactive girls. Journal of the American Academy of Child & Adolescent Psychiatry. 1994;33:858-68.

Ernst M, Zametkin A, Matochik J, Jons P, Cohen R. DOPA decarboxylase activity in attention deficit hyperactivity disorder adults. A [fluorine-18]fluorodopa positron emission tomographic study. J Neurosci. 1998;18:5901-7.

Evoy D, Lieberman M, Fahey Tr, Daly J. Immunonutrition: the role of arginine. Nutrition. 1998;14:611-7.

Eyestone L, Howell R. An epidemiological study of attention-deficit hyperactivity disorder and major depression in a male prison population. Bulletin of the American Academy of Psychiatry & the Law. 1994;22:181-93.

Eyler F, Behnke M, Conlon M, Woods N, Wobie K. Birth outcome from a prospective, matched study of prenatal crack/cocaine use: II. Interactive and dose effects on neurobehavioral assessment. Pediatrics. 1998;101:237-41.

Fan Z, Isobe K, Kiuchi K, Nakashima I. Enhancement of nitric oxide production from activated macrophages by a purified form of ginsenoside (Rg1). Am J Chin Med. 1995;23:279-87.

Fasano A. Cellular microbiology: how enteric pathogens socialize with their intestinal host. J Pediatr Gastroenterol Nutr. 1998;26:520-32.

Feeney S, Goodall E, Silverstone T. The effects of d- and l-fenfluramine (and their interactions with d-amphetamine) on cortisol secretion. Int Clin Psychopharmacol. 1993;8:139-42.

Fell P, Brostoff J. A single dose desensitization for summer hay fever. Results of a double blind study-1988. Eur J Clin Pharmacol. 1990;38:77-9.

Felton R, Wood F, Brown I, Campbell S, Harter M. Separate verbal memory and naming deficits in attention deficit disorder and reading disability. Brain Lang. 1987;31:171-84.

F.I.R. (Friends in Recovery). The Twelve Steps: A Guide for Adults with Attention Deficit Disorder. San Diego: RPI Publishing; 1996:264 pp.

Fireman P. Otitis media and its relationship to allergy. Pediatr Clin North Am. 1988;35:1075-90.

Foley JD, Schydlower M. Anabolic Steroid and Ergogenic Drug Use by Adolescents. Adolesc Med. 1993;4:341-352

Forget P, Sodoyez-Goffaux F, Zappitelli A. Permeability of the small intestine to [51Cr]EDTA in children with acute gastroenteritis or eczema. J Pediatr Gastroenterol Nutr. 1985;4:393-6.

Fox A, Rieder M. Risks and benefits of drugs used in the management of the hyperactive child. Drug Safety. 1993;9:38-50.

Friberg L. Inorganic Mercury. In: Organization WH, ed. Environmental Health Criteria 118. Geneva: WHO; 1991.

Fukushima Y, Kawata Y, Mizumachi K, Kurisaki J. Effect of whey hydrolysate formula on the transfer of beta- lactoglobulin into serum and milk in mice. J Nutr Sci Vitaminol (Tokyo). 1998;44:723-8.

Fukushima Y, Kawata Y, Hara H, Terada A, Mitsuoka T. Effect of a probiotic formula on intestinal immunoglobulin A production in healthy children. Int J Food Microbiol. 1998;42:39-44.

Funk J, Ruppert E. Language disorders and behavioral problems in preschool children. J Dev Behav Pediatr. 1984;5:357-60.

Fuzailov I. The role of the sweat glands in excreting antimony from the body in people living in the biogeochemical provinces of the Fergana Valley. . Gig Tr Prof Zabol. RUSSIA; 1992:13-5.

Galland L. Increased requirements of essential fatty acids in atopic individuals: A review with clinical descriptions. J Am Coll Nutr. 1986;5:213-28.

Galland L. The Four Pillars of Healing. . New York: Random House; 1997:330.

Gao H, Wang F, Lien E, Trousdale M. Immunostimulating polysaccharides from Panax notoginseng. Pharm Res. 1996;13:1196-200.

Garg R, Nag D, Agrawal A. A double blind placebo controlled trial of ginkgo biloba extract in acute cerebral ischaemia. J Assoc Physicians India. 1995;43:760-3.

Garland EJ. Pharmacotherapy of adolescent attention deficit hyperactivity disorder: challenges, choices and caveats. J Psychopharmacol. 1998;12:385-95.

Garrow JS. Kinesiology and food allergy. Br Med J (Clin Res Ed). 1988;296:1573-4.

Gato MR, Banez SF, Pascual GJ, Fernandez CC, Garcia JC. [Reactive arthritis due to Giardia lamblia in a patient with IgA deficiency (letter)]. An Med Interna. 1998;15:398-9.

Gaub M, Carlson C. Gender differences in ADHD: a meta-analysis and critical review. J Am Acad Child Adolesc Psychiatry. 1997;36:1036-45.

Geirsson R. Birth trauma and brain damage. Baillieres Clin Obstet Gynaecol. 1988;2:195-212.

Gessner B, Voelp A, Klasser M. Study of the long-term action of a Ginkgo biloba extract on vigilance and mental performance as determined by means of quantitative pharmaco-EEG and psychometric measurements. Arzneimittelforschung. 1985;35:1459-65.

Gibson G, Beatty E, Wang X, Cummings J. Selective stimulation of bifidobacteria in the human colon by oligofructose and inulin. Gastroenterology. 1995;108:975-82.

Gibson G, Roberfroid M. Dietary modulation of the human colonic microbiota: introducing the concept of prebiotics. J Nutr. 1995;125:1401-12.

Giedd J, Castellanos F, Casey B, et al. Quantitative morphology of the corpus callosum in attention deficit hyperactivity disorder. American Journal of Psychiatry. 1994;151:665-9.

Gilbert C. Optimal physical performance in athletes: key roles of dopamine in a specific neurotransmitter/hormonal mechanism. Mech Ageing Dev. 1995;84:83-102.

Gilbert S, Grant -WK. Neurobehavioral effects of developmental methylmercury exposure. Environ Health Perspect. 1995;103 Suppl 6:135-42.

Gochfeld M. Factors influencing susceptibility to metals. Environ Health Perspect. 1997;105 Suppl 4:817-22.

Goldfarb AH, Jamurtas AZ. Beta-endorphin response to exercise. An update. Sports Med. 1997;24:8-16.

Goldin BR. Health benefits of probiotics. Br J Nutr. 1998;80:S203-7.

Goldin B, Gualtieri L, Moore R. The effect of Lactobacillus GG on the initiation and promotion of DMH-induced intestinal tumors in the rat. Nutr Cancer. 1996;25:197-204.

Goldstein D, Nurnberger JJ, Simmons S, Gershon E, Polinsky R, Keiser H. Effects of injected sympathomimetic amines on plasma catecholamines and circulatory variables in man. Life Sci. 1983;32:1057-63.

Gomes M, Martins M, Costa A, Silva E. Influence of bacteria upon cytopathic effect and erythrophagocytosis of different axenic strains of Entamoeba histolytica. Rev Inst Med Trop Sao Paulo. 1995;37:197-200.

Gomez-Pinilla F, So V, Kesslak JP. Spatial learning and physical activity contribute to the induction of fibroblast growth factor: neural substrates for increased cognition associated with exercise. Neuroscience. 1998;85:53-61.

Gottschalk LA, Rebello T, Buchsbaum MS, Tucker HG, Hodges EL. Abnormalities in hair trace elements as indicators of aberrant behavior. Compr Psychiatry. 1991;32:229-37.

Goyer R. Toxic and essential metal interactions. Annu Rev Nutr. 1997;17:37-50.

Granstein R. Oral tolerance: a biologically relevant pathway to generate peripheral tolerence against external and self antigens. Chem Immunol. 1994;58:259-90.

Grassel E. [Effect of Ginkgo-biloba extract on mental performance. Double-blind study using computerized measurement conditions in patients with cerebral insufficiency]. Fortschr Med. 1992;110:73-6.

Greenhill L. Pharmacologic treatment of attention deficit hyperactivity disorder. Psychiatric Clinics of North America. 1992;15:1-27.

Grimble R, Grimble G. Immunonutrition: role of sulfur amino acids, related amino acids, and polyamines. Nutrition. 1998;14:605-10.

Gsell W, Reichert N, Youdim M, Riederer P. Interaction of neuroprotective substances with human brain superoxide dismutase. An in vitro study. J Neural Transm Suppl. 1995;45:271-9.

Gualtieri C, Keenan P, Chandler M. Clinical and neuropsychological effects of desipramine in children with attention deficit hyperactivity disorder. J Clin Psychopharmacol. 1991;11:155-9.

Gualtieri C. Fetal antigenicity and maternal immunoreactivity. Factors in mental retardation. . Monogr Am Assoc Ment Defic. United States; 1987:33-69.

Guengerich F. Influence of nutrients and other dietary materials on cytochrome P-450 enzymes. Am J Clin Nutr. 1995;61:651S-658S.

Gurevitch J, Sela B, Jonas A, Golan H, Yahav Y, Passwell JH. D-lactic acidosis: a treatable encephalopathy in pediatric patients. Acta Paediatr. 1993;82:119-21.

Haan E, Brown G, Bankier A, et al. Severe illness caused by the products of bacterial metabolism in a child with a short gut. Eur J Pediatr. 1985;144:63-5.

Hageman G, Verhagen H, Schutte B, Kleinjans J. Biological effects of short-term feeding to rats of repeatedly used deep-frying fats in relation to fat mutagen content. Food Chem Toxicol. 1991;29:689-98.

Hagerman RJ, Falkenstein MA. An association between recurrent otitis media in infancy and later hyperactivity. Clinical Pediatrics. 1987;Vol.26.

Hall H. Handwashing in medicine: infrequent use of an ancient practice. Int J Psychosom. 1995;42:44-7.

Hallowell E. Driven to distraction: recognizing and coping with attention deficit disorder from childhood through adulthood. . New York: Touchstone; 1994.

Harbige L. Nutrition and immunity with emphasis on infection and autoimmune disease. Nutr Health. 1996;10:285-312.

Hasenohrl R, Nichau C, Frisch C, et al. Anxiolytic-like effect of combined extracts of Zingiber officinale and ginkgo biloba in the elevated plus-maze. Pharmacol Biochem Behav. 1996;53:271-5.

Hechtman L. Families of children with attention deficit hyperactivity disorder: a review. Can J Psychiatry. 1996;6:350-60.

Henderson TA, Fischer VW. Effects of methylphenidate (Ritalin) on mammalian myocardial ultrastructure. Am J Cardiovasc Pathol. 1995;5:68-78.

Herias MV, Hessle C, Telemo E, Midtvedt T, Hanson LA, Wold AE. Immunomodulatory effects of Lactobacillus plantarum colonizing the intestine of gnotobiotic rats. Clin Exp Immunol. 1999;116:283-90.

Heyman M, Darmon N, Dupont C, et al. Mononuclear cells from infants allergic to cow's milk secrete tumor necrosis factor alpha, altering intestinal function. Gastroenterology. 1994;6:1514-23.

Heyman M, Grasset E, Ducroc R, Desjeux J. Antigen absorption by the jejunal epithelium of children with cow's milk allergy. Pediatr Res. 1988;24:197-202.

Hiatt R, Markell E, Ng E. How many stool examinations are necessary to detect pathogenic intestinal protozoa? Am J Trop Med Hyg. 1995;53:36-9.

Himi T, Saito H, Nishiyama N. Effect of ginseng saponins on the survival of cerebral cortex neurons in cell cultures. Chem Pharm Bull (Tokyo). 1989;37:481-4.

Hindmarch I. [Activity of Ginkgo biloba extract on short-term memory]. Presse Med. 1986;15:1592-4.

Hindmarch I, Quinlan PT, Moore KL, Parkin C. The effects of black tea and other beverages on aspects of cognition and psychomotor performance. Psychopharmacology (Berl). 1998;139:230-8.

Horie T, Nakamaru M, Masubuchi Y. Docosahexaenoic acid exhibits a potent protection of small intestine from methotrexate-induced damage in mice. Life Sci. 1998;62:1333-8.

Hornig M. Addressing comorbidity in adults with attention-deficit/hyperactivity disorder. J Clin Psychiatry. 1998;59 Suppl 7:69-75.

Horrobin D, Glen A, Hudson C. Possible relevance of phospholipid abnormalities and genetic interactions in psychiatric disorders: the relationship between dyslexia and schizophrenia. Med Hypotheses. 1995;6:605-13.

Horrobin D. Is the main problem in free radical damage caused by radiation, oxygen and other toxins the loss of membrane essential fatty acids rather than the accumulation of toxic materials? Med Hypotheses. 1991;35:23-6.

Horrobin D. Post-viral fatigue syndrome, viral infections in atopic eczema, and essential fatty acids. Med Hypotheses. 1990;32:211-7.

Horvath K, Stefanatos G, Sokolski K, Wachtel R, Nabors L, Tildon J. Improved social and language skills after secretin administration in patients with autistic spectrum disorders. J Assoc Acad Minor Phys. 1998;9:9-15.

Hu S, Concha C, Cooray R, Holmberg O. Ginseng-enhanced oxidative and phagocytic activities of polymorphonuclear leucocytes from bovine peripheral blood and stripping milk. Vet Res. 1995;26:155-61.

Huang NK, Wan FJ, Tseng CJ, Tung CS. Amphetamine induces hydroxyl radical formation in the striatum of rats. Life Sci. 1997;61:2219-29.

Huessy H. Imipramine for attention deficit disorder. Am J Psychiatry. 1983;140:272.

Hughes JR, Hale KL. Behavioral effects of caffeine and other methylxanthines on children. Exp Clin Psychopharmacol. 1998;6:87-95.

Huguet F, Drieu K, Piriou A. Decreased cerebral 5-HT1A receptors during ageing: reversal by Ginkgo biloba extract (EGb 761). J Pharm Pharmacol. 1994;46:316-8.

Huguet F, Tarrade T. Alpha 2-adrenoceptor changes during cerebral ageing. The effect of Ginkgo biloba extract. J Pharm Pharmacol. 1992;44:24-7.

Hunter, J Food allergy – or enterometabolic disorder? Lancet. 1991;338:495-496

Husby S. Dietary antigens: uptake and humoral immunity in man. APMIS Suppl. 1988;1:1-40.

Hussain S, Roots B. Effect of essential fatty acid deficiency & immunopathological stresses on blood brain barrier (B-BB) in Lewis rats: a biochemical study. Biochem Soc Trans. 1994;3:338.

Ippoliti F, Ragno V, Del Nero A, McEwen LM, McEwen H, Businco L. Effect of preseasonal enzyme potentiated desensitisation (EPD) on plasma-IL-6 and IL-10 of grass pollen-sensitive asthmatic children. Allerg Immunol (Paris). 1997;29:120, 123-5.

Isolauri E, Sutas Y, Salo M, Isosomppi R, Kaila M. Elimination diet in cow's milk allergy: risk for impaired growth in young children. J Pediatr. 1998;132:1004-9.

Isolauri E. The treatment of cow's milk allergy. Eur J Clin Nutr. 1995;49 Suppl 1:S49-55.

Itil T, Martorano D. Natural substances in psychiatry (Ginkgo biloba in dementia). Psychopharmacol Bull. 1995;31:147-58.

Itoh T, Zang Y, Murai S, Saito H. Effects of Panax ginseng root on the vertical and horizontal motor activities and on brain monoamine-related substances in mice. Planta Med. 1989;55:429-33.

Jacobs D, Silverstone T. Dextroamphetamine-induced arousal in human subjects as a model for mania. Psychol Med. 1986;16:323-9.

Jacobson JL, Jacobson SW. Intellectual Impairment in Children Exposed to Polychlorinated Biphenyls in Utero. N Eng J Med. 1996;335:11:738-89.

Jakobsson I. Intestinal permeability in children of different ages and with different gastrointestinal diseases. Pediatr Allergy Immunol. 1993;4:33-9.

Jankovic J. Deprenyl in attention deficit associated with tourette's syndrome. Archives of Neurology. 1993;50:286-8.

Jarabo M, Garcia -MN, Garcia -MJ. Prevalence of intestinal parasites in a student population. Enferm Infecc Microbiol Clin. 1995;13:464-8.

Jensen P, Shervette Rd, Xenakis S, Richters J. Anxiety and depressive disorders in attention deficit disorder with hyperactivity: new findings. American Journal of Psychiatry. 1993;150:1203-9.

Jie Y, Cammisuli S, Baggiolini M. Immunomodulatory effects of Panax Ginseng C.A. Meyer in the mouse. Agents Actions. 1984;15:386-91.

Johnston B, Wright J. Attentional dysfunction in children with encopresis. Journal of Developmental & Behavioral Pediatrics. 1993;14:381-5.

Joneja J, Bielory L. Understanding Allergy, Sensitivity and Immunity. . New Brunswick and London: Rutgers University Press; 1990:332.

Joneja, J. Diet and behavior – myth or science? Canadian Child Psychiatry Bulletin; 1996;5(1):4-17

Joneja J. Dietary management of food allergies and intolerances: a comprehensive guide. : J.A. Hall Publications; 1998

Jonsdottir I, Hoffmann P, Thoren P. Physical exercise, endogenous opioids and immune function. Acta Physiol Scand Suppl. 1997;640:47-50.

Joseph R. Environmental influences on neural plasticity, the limbic system, emotional development and attachment: a review. Child Psychiatry Hum Dev. 1999;29:189-208.

Judd R. Helicobacter pylori, gastritis, and ulcers in pediatrics. Adv Pediatr. 1992;39:283-306.

Kabani A, Cadrain G, Trevenen C, Jadavji T, Church D. Practice guidelines for ordering stool ova and parasite testing in a pediatric population. The Alberta Children's Hospital. Am J Clin Pathol. 1995;104:272-8.

Kahn A, Rebuffat E, Blum D, et al. Difficulty in initiating and maintaining sleep associated with cow's milk allergy in infants. Sleep. 1987;10:116-21.

Kahn CA. Lead Screening Children With Attention Deficit Hyperactivity Disorder and Developmental Delay. Clinical Pediatrics. 1995:498-501.

Kankaanpaa P, Sutas Y, Salminen S, Lichtenstein A, Isolauri E. Dietary fatty acids and allergy. Ann Med. 1999;31:282-7.

Kaplan B, McNicol J, Conte R, Moghadam H. Sleep disturbance in preschool-aged hyperactive and nonhyperactive children. Pediatrics. 1987;80:839-44.

Kaplan BJ. Dietary replacement in preschool-aged hyperactive boys. Pediatrics. 1989; 83:7-17.

Kappus K, Lundgren RJ, Juranek D, Roberts J, Spencer H. Intestinal parasitism in the United States: update on a continuing problem. Am J Trop Med Hyg. 1994;50:705-13.

Kaur M, Kaur J, Ojha S, Mahmood A. Dietary fat effects on brush border membrane composition and enzyme activities in rat intestine. Ann Nutr Metab. 1996;40:269-76.

Kenarova B, Neychev H, Hadjiivanova C, Petkov V. Immunomodulating activity of ginsenoside Rg1 from Panax ginseng. Jpn J Pharmacol. 1990;54:447-54.

Kenney J, Groth E, Benbrook C. Worst First: High Risk Insecticide Uses, Children's Foods and Safer Alternatives. . Washington, D.C.: Consumer's Union of The United States; 1999.

Kern L, Koegel R, Dunlap G. The influence of vigorous versus mild exercise on autistic stereotyped behaviors. J Autism Dev Disord. 1984;14:57-67.

Kiessling L, Marcotte A, Culpepper L. Antineuronal antibodies: tics and obsessive-compulsive symptoms. J Dev Behav Pediatr. 1994;15:421-5.

Kilburn K, Warsaw R, Shields M. Neurobehavioral dysfunction in firemen exposed to polycholorinated biphenyls (PCBs): possible improvement after detoxification. Arch Environ Health. 1989;44:345-50.

Kim J, Germolec D, Luster M. Panax ginseng as a potential immunomodulator: studies in mice. Immunopharmacol Immunotoxicol. 1990;12:257-76.

Kim Y, Park K, Rho H. Transcriptional activation of the Cu,Zn-superoxide dismutase gene through the AP2 site by ginsenoside Rb2 extracted from a medicinal plant, Panax ginseng. J Biol Chem. 1996;271:24539-43.

Kimel L. Handwashing education can decrease illness absenteeism. J Sch Nurs. 1996;12:14-6 18.

King H, King W. Alternatives in the diagnosis and treatment of food allergies. Otolaryngologic Clinics of North America. 1998;31

King WP, Fadal RG, Ward WA, et al. Provocation-neutralization: a two-part study. Part II. Subcutaneous neutralization therapy: a multi-center study. Otolaryngol Head Neck Surg. 1988;99:272-7.

King WP, Rubin WA, Fadal RG, et al. Provocation-neutralization: a two-part study. Part I. The intracutaneous provocative food test: a multi-center comparison study. Otolaryngol Head Neck Surg. 1988;99:263-71.

Kirjavainen PV, Apostolou E, Salminen SJ, Isolauri E. New aspects of probiotics—a novel approach in the management of food allergy. Allergy. 1999;54:909-155

Kirjavainen PV, Gibson GR. Healthy gut microflora and allergy: factors influencing development of the microbiota. Ann Med. 1999;31:288-92.

Kirschbaum C, Wolf O, May M, Wippich W, Hellhammer D. Stress- and treatment-induced elevations of cortisol levels associated with impaired declarative memory in healthy adults. Life Sci. 1996;58:1475-83.

Kitts D. Bioactive substances in food: identification and potential uses. Can J Physiol Pharmacol. 1994;72:423-34.

Kitts D, Yuan Y, Joneja J, et al. Adverse reactions to food constituents: allergy, intolerance, and autoimmunity. Can J Physiol Pharmacol. 1997;75:241-54.

Kiyohara H, Hirano M, Wen X, Matsumoto T, Sun X, Yamada H. Characterisation of an anti-ulcer pectic polysaccharide from leaves of Panax ginseng C.A. Meyer. Carbohydr Res. 1994;263:89-101.

Klasing K. Nutritional modulation of resistance to infectious diseases. Poult Sci. 1998;77:1119-25.

Klein SA, Deffenbacher JL. Relaxation and exercise for hyperactive impulsive children. Percept Mot Skills. 1977;45:1159-62.

Kleiner SM. Water: an essential but overlooked nutrient. J Am Diet Assoc. 1999;99:200-6.

Klimberg V, Salloum R, Kasper M, et al. Oral glutamine accelerates healing of the small intestine and improves outcome after whole abdominal radiation. Arch Surg. 1990;125:1040-5.

Konig D, Weinstock C, Keul J, Northoff H, Berg A. Zinc, iron, and magnesium status in athletes—influence on the regulation of exercise-induced stress and immune function. Exerc Immunol Rev. 1998;4:2-21..

Kozielec T, Starobrat -HB. Assessment of magnesium levels in children with attention deficit hyperactivity disorder (ADHD). Magnes Res. 1997;10:143-8.

Koziol L, Stout C. Use of a verbal fluency measure in understanding and evaluating adhd as an executive function disorder. Perceptual & Motor Skills. 1992;75:1187-92.

Kramer AF, Hahn S, Cohen NJ, et al. Ageing, fitness and neurocognitive function [letter]. Nature. 1999;400:418-9.

LaHoste G, Swanson J, Wigal S, et al. Dopamine D4 receptor gene polymorphism is associated with attention deficit hyperactivity disorder. Mol Psychiatry. 1996;1:121-4.

Lan KC, Lin YF, Yu FC, Lin CS, Chu P. Clinical manifestations and prognostic features of acute methamphetamine intoxication. J Formos Med Assoc. 1998;97:528-33.

Laudat A, Arnaud P, Napoly A, Brion F. The intestinal permeability test applied to the diagnosis of food allergy in paediatrics. West Indian Med J. 1994;3:87-8.

Lazarou J, Pomeranz BH, Corey PN. Incidence of adverse drug reactions in hospitalized patients: a meta- analysis of prospective studies. JAMA. 1998;279:1200-5.

Lazzaro I, Gordon E, Whitmont S, et al. Quantified EEG activity in adolescent attention deficit hyperactivity disorder. Clin Electroencephalogr. 1998;29:37-42.

Le Bars P, Katz M, Berman N, Itil T, Freedman A, Schatzberg A. A placebo-controlled, double-blind, randomized trial of an extract of Ginkgo biloba for dementia. North American EGb Study Group. JAMA. 1997;278:1327-32.

Lee M, Rawlins S, Didier M, DeCeulaer K. Infective arthritis due to Blastocystis hominis. Ann Rheum Dis. 1990;49:192-3.

Lee S, Honda K, Rhee Y, Inoue S. Chronic intake of panax ginseng extract stabilizes sleep and wakefulness in food-deprived rats. Neurosci Lett. 1990;111:217-21.

Lee S. Biofeedback as a treatment for childhood hyperactivity: a critical review of the literature. Psychological Reports. 1991;68:163-92.

Lee T, Arm J, Horton C, Crea A, Mencia-Huerta J, Spur B. Effects of dietary fish oil lipids on allergic and inflammatory diseases. Allergy Proc. 1991;12:299-303.

LeFever GB, Dawson KV, Morrow AL. The extent of drug therapy for attention deficit-hyperactivity disorder among children in public schools. Am J Public Health. 1999;89:1359-64.

Lester M, Thatcher R, Monroe-Lord L. Refined carbohydrate intake, hair cadmium levels and cognitive functioning in children. J Nutr Behavior. 1982;1:1-14.

Letts M, Davidson D, Lalonde F. Synovitis secondary to giardiasis in children. Am J Orthop. 1998;27:451-4.

Levrat M, Favier M, Moundras C, Remesy C, Demigne C, Morand C. Role of dietary propionic acid and bile acid excretion in the hypocholesterolemic effects of oligosaccharides in rats. J Nutr. 1994;124:531-8.

Levy F. The dopamine theory of attention deficit hyperactivity disorder (ADHD). Australian & New Zealand Journal of Psychiatry. 1991;25:277-83.

Levy J. Immunonutrition: the pediatric experience. Nutrition. 1998;14:641-7.

Lew H, Quintanilha A. Effects of endurance training and exercise on tissue antioxidative capacity and acetaminophen detoxification. Eur J Drug Metab Pharmacokinet. 1991;16:59-68.

Lewis M, Worobey J, Ramsay D, McCormack M. Prenatal exposure to heavy metals: effect on childhood cognitive skills and health status. Pediatrics. 1992;89:1010-15.

Lie N. Follow-ups of children with attention deficit hyperactivity disorder (ADHD). review of literature. Acta Psychiatrica Scandinavica. 1992;368:1-40.

Lin J, Wu L, Tsai K, Leu S, Jeang Y, Hsieh M. Effects of ginseng on the blood chemistry profile of dexamethasone-treated male rats. Am J Chin Med. 1995;23:167-72.

Lin JK, Liang YC, Lin-Shiau SY. Cancer chemoprevention by tea polyphenols through mitotic signal transduction blockade. Biochem Pharmacol. 1999;58:911-5.

Linde K, Ramirez G, Mulrow C, Pauls A, Weidenhammer W, Melchart D. St John's wort for depression—an overview and meta-analysis of randomised clinical trials. BMJ. 1996;313:253-8..

Linden M, Habib T, Radojevic V. A controlled study of the effects of EEG biofeedback on cognition and behavior of children with attention deficit disorder and learning disabilities. Biofeedback Self Regul. 1996;21:35-49.

Liu C, Xiao P. Recent advances on ginseng research in China. J Ethnopharmacol. 1992;36:27-38.

Liu J, Wang S, Liu H, Yang L, Nan G. Stimulatory effect of saponin from Panax ginseng on immune function of lymphocytes in the elderly. Mech Ageing Dev. 1995;83:43-53.

Liu X, Kao Y, Chi S, Chang T, Pei Y, Lee D. The effects of omega-3 fish oil enriched with DHA on memory. . 2nd International Congress of the ISSFAL International Society for the Study of Fatty Acids and Lipids; 1995.

Lonsdale D, Shamberger R. Red cell transketolase as an indicator of nutritional deficiency. Am J Clin Nutr. 1980;33:205-11.

Lorscheider FL, Inorganic mercury and the CNS; genetic linkage of mercury and antibiotic resistance. Toxicology. 1995;97:19-22.

Lorscheider FL, Vimy MJ. Evaluation of the safety issue of mercury release from dental fillings. FASEB J. 1993;7:1432-33.

Lovejoy H, Bell ZJ, Vizena T. Mercury exposure evaluations and their correlation with urine mercury excretions. 4. Elimination of mercury by sweating. J Occup Med. 1973;15:590-1.

Lubar J. Discourse on the development of eeg diagnostics and biofeedback for attention-deficit/hyperactivity disorders. Biofeedback & Self Regulation. 1991;16:201-25.

Lubar JF. Neocortical dynamics: implications for understanding the role of neurofeedback and related techniques for the enhancement of attention. Appl Psychophysiol Biofeedback. 1997;22:111-26.

Lubar J, (a) Neurofeedback for the management of attention-deficit/hyperactivity disorder. In: Schwartz MSAE, ed. Biofeedback: A Practitioners Guide (2nd ed.). New York: Guilford Press.; 1995:493-522.

Lubar J, (b) Swartwood M, Swartwood J, O DP. Evaluation of the effectiveness of EEG neurofeedback training for ADHD in a clinical setting as measured by changes in T.O.V.A. scores, behavioral ratings, and WISC-R performance. Biofeedback Self Regul. 1995;20:83-99.

Lucarelli S, Frediani T, Zingoni A, et al. Food allergy and infantile autism. Panminerva Med. 1995;37:137-41.

Lupien S, Gaudreau S, Tchiteya B, et al. Stress-induced declarative memory impairment in healthy elderly subjects: relationship to cortisol reactivity. J Clin Endocrinol Metab. 1997;82:2070-5.

Luettig B, Steinmuller C, Gifford GE, Wagner H, Lohmann-Matthes ML. Macrophage activation by the polysaccharide arabinogalactan isolated from plant cell cultures of Echinacea purpurea. J Natl Cancer Inst. 1989;81:669-75.

Lundin L. Allergic and non-allergic students' perception of the same high school environment. Indoor Air. 1999;9:92-102.

Lyon M, Cline J, Totosy de Zepetnick J. Effects an extract of American ginseng in combination with ginkgo biloba extract on children with ADHD. In press. 1999.

Lyon M, Cline J. The effect of an oligoantigenic diet with or without a prescribed medical food product on the behavior and physiological parameter of children with attention deficit hyperactivity disorder. : Unpublished data; 1999.

Ma L, Zhou Z, Yang Q. Study on effect of polysaccharides of ginseng on peripheral blood mononuclear cell induced interleukin-2 production and activity of its receptors in vitro. Chung Kuo Chung Hsi I Chieh Ho Tsa Chih. 1995;15:411-3.

MacRae PG, Spirduso WW, Cartee GD, Farrar RP, Wilcox RE. Endurance training effects on striatal D2 dopamine receptor binding and striatal dopamine metabolite levels. Neurosci Lett. 1987;79:138-44.

Mahalanabis D, Rahman M, Sarker S, et al. Helicobacter pylori infection in the young in Bangladesh: prevalence, socioeconomic and nutritional aspects. Int J Epidemiol. 1996;25:894-8.

Majamaa H, Isolauri E. Probiotics: a novel approach in the management of food allergy. J Allergy Clin Immunol. 1997;99:179-85.

Makrides M, Neuman M, Simmer K, Pater J, Gibson R. Are long-chain polyunsaturated fatty acids essential nutrients in infancy? The Lancet. 1995;345.

Malin M, Suomalainen H, Saxelin M, Isolauri E. Promotion of IgA immune response in patients with Crohn's disease by oral bacteriotherapy with Lactobacillus GG. Ann Nutr Metab. 1996;40:137-45.

Mannuzza S, Klein R, Bessler A, Malloy P, LaPadula M. Adult outcome of hyperactive boys. educational achievement, occupational rank, and psychiatric status. Archives of General Psychiatry. 1993;50:565-76.

Marcotte A, Thacher P, Butters M, Bortz J, Acebo C, Carskadon M. Parental report of sleep problems in children with attentional and learning disorders. J Dev Behav Pediatr. 1998;19:178-86.

Marin E, Kretzschmar M, Arokoski J, Hanninen O, Klinger W. Enzymes of glutathione synthesis in dog skeletal muscles and their response to training. Acta Physiol Scand. 1993;147:369-73.

Marinkovitch V. Specific IgG antibodies as markers of adverse reactions to foods. Monogr Allergy. 1996;32:221-25.

Marked M, Neumann M, Byard R, Simmer K, Gibson R. Fatty acid composition of brain, retina, and erythrocytes in breast- and formula-fed infants. Am J Clin Nutr. 1994;60:189-94.

Markov MS. Biophysical estimation of the environmental importance of electromagnetic fields. Rev Environ Health. 1994;10:75-83.

Marotta P, Roberts E. Pemoline hepatotoxicity in children. J Pediatr. 1998;132:894-7.

Marshall P. Attention deficit disorder and allergy: a neurochemical model of the relation between the illnesses. Psychol Bull. 1989;3:434-46.

Martin F, Bhargava A, Adlerereutz H. Androgen metabolism in the beagle: Endogenous androgen metabolites in bile and feces and the effect of ampicillin administration. J Steroid Biochem. 1977;8:753-60.

Masand P, Pickett P, Murray G. Hypomania precipitated by psychostimulant use in depressed medically ill patients. Psychosomatics. 1995;36:145-7.

Massello W, 3rd, Carpenter DA. A fatality due to the intranasal abuse of methylphenidate (Ritalin). J Forensic Sci. 1999;44:220-1.

Mate G. Scattered Minds. Toronto: Alfred A. Knopf, Canada; 1999:348 pp.

Matilainen R, Heinonen K, Siren -TH. Effect of intrauterine growth retardation (IUGR) on the psychological performance of preterm children at preschool age. J Child Psychol Psychiatry. 1988;29:601-9.

Matsuda H, Samukawa K, Kubo M. Anti-inflammatory activity of ginsenoside Ro. Planta Med. 1990;56:19-23.

McAllister D, Kaplan B, Edworthy S, et al. The influence of systemic lupus erythematosus on fetal development: cognitive, behavioral, and health trends. J Int Neuropsychol Soc. 1997;3:370-6.

McCann UD, Ricaurte GA. Lasting neuropsychiatric sequelae of (+-) methylene-dioxymethamphetamine ('ecstasy') in recreational users. J Clin Psychopharmacol. 1991;11:302-5.

McColley S, Carroll J, Curtis S, Loughlin G, Sampson H. High prevalence of allergic sensitization in children with habitual snoring and obstructive sleep apnea. Chest. 1997;111:170-3.

McEwen L. A comparison between the effects of enzyme potentiated desensitization, methylphenidate and psychotherapy on the symptoms of attention deficit hyperactivity disorder in children. (personal communication); 1999.

McGregor NR, Dunstan RH, Zerbes M, Butt HL, Roberts TK, Klineberg IJ. Preliminary determination of the association between symptom expression and urinary metabolites in subjects with chronic fatigue syndrome. Biochem Mol Med. 1996;58:85-92.

McGregor NR, Dunstan RH, Zerbes M, Butt HL, Roberts TK, Klineberg IJ. Preliminary determination of a molecular basis of chronic fatigue syndrome. Biochem Mol Med. 1996;57:73-80.

McGuiness W. Heidelberg capsule testing in children with ADHD demonstrates hypochlorhydria in 75% of cases. (personal communication) ; 1998.

Meeusen R, De MK. Exercise and brain neurotransmission. Sports Med. 1995;20:160-88.

Meruelo D, Lavie G, Lavie D. Therapeutic agents with dramatic antiretroviral activity and little toxicity at effective doses: aromatic polycyclic diones hypericin and pseudohypericin. Proc Natl Acad Sci U S A. 1988;85:5230-4.

Midolo P, Lambert J, Hull R, Luo F, Grayson M. In vitro inhibition of Helicobacter pylori NCTC 11637 by organic acids and lactic acid bacteria. J Appl Bacteriol. 1995;79:475-9.

Milberger S, Biederman J, Faraone S, Chen L, Jones J. Further evidence of an association between attention-deficit/hyperactivity disorder and cigarette smoking. Findings from a high-risk sample of siblings. Am J Addict. 1997;6:205-17.

Millman M, Campbell M, Wright K, Johnston A. Allergy and learning disabilities in children. Ann Allergy. 1976;36:149-60.

Minder B, Das-Smaal E, Brand E, Orlebeke J. Exposure to lead and specific attentional problems in schoolchildren. Journal of Learning Disabilities. 1994;27:393-9.

Mittleman B, Castellanos F, Jacobsen L, Rapoport J, Swedo S, Shearer G. Cerebrospinal fluid cytokines in pediatric neuropsychiatric disease. J Immunol. 1997;159:2994-9.

Miura S, Imaeda H, Shiozaki H, et al. Attenuation of endotoxin-induced intestinal microcirculatory damage by eicosapentanoic acid. Am J Physiol. 1993;264:G828-34.

Modrcin-Talbott MA, Pullen L, Zandstra K, Ehrenberger H, Muenchen B. A study of self-esteem among well adolescents: seeking a new direction. Issues Compr Pediatr Nurs. 1998;21:229-41

Morita E, Hide M, Yoneya Y, Kannbe M, Tanaka A, Yamamoto S. An assessment of the role of Candida albicans antigen in atopic dermatitis. J Dermatol. 1999;26:282-7.

Morohashi T, Sano T, Ohta A, Yamada S. True calcium absorption in the intestine is enhanced by fructooligosaccharide feeding in rats. J Nutr. 1998;128:1815-8.

Muller W, Singer A, Wonnemann M, Hafner U, Rolli M, Schafer C. Hyperforin represents the neurotransmitter reuptake inhibiting constituent of hypericum extract. Pharmacopsychiatry. 1998;31 Suppl 1:16-21.

Murphy V, Johanson C. Adrenergic-induced enhancement of brain barrier system permeability to small nonelectrolytes: choroid plexus versus cerebral capillaries. J Cereb Blood Flow Metab. 1985;5:401-12.

Murray L, Fiori-Cowley A, Hooper R, Cooper P. The impact of postnatal depression and associated adversity on early mother-infant interactions and later infant outcome. Child Dev. 1996;67:2512-26.

Myhr G. Autism and other pervasive developmental disorders: exploring the dimensional view. Can J Psychiatry. 1998;43:589-95.

Naidu A, Arnold R. Lactoferrin interaction with salmonellae potentiates antibiotic susceptibility in vitro. Diagn Microbiol Infect Dis. 1994;20:69-75.

Nanji A, Khettry U, Sadrzadeh S. Lactobacillus feeding reduces endotoxemia and severity of experimental alcoholic liver (disease). Proc Soc Exp Biol Med. 1994;205:243-7.

Nash JM. Dopamine System May Be the Key to Addiction. Nature. 1997;386:827.

Nasrallah, H. A., J. Loney, et al.. Cortical atrophy in young adults with a history of hyperactivity in childhood. Psychiatry Res 1986; 17(3): 241-6.

Needleman H. Behavioral toxicology. Environ Health Perspect. 1995;103:77-9.

Needleman H. The current status of childhood low-level lead toxicity. Neurotoxicology. 1993;14:161-6.

Nelson EE, Panksepp J. Brain substrates of infant-mother attachment: contributions of opioids, oxytocin, and norepinephrine. Neurosci Biobehav Rev. 1998;22:437-52.

Nentwig W. The importance of human ecology at the threshold of the next millennium: how can population growth Be stopped? Naturwissenschaften. 1999;86:411-21

Neuringer M. The role of N-3 fatty acids in visual and cognitive development: Current evidence and methods of assessment. J Pediatr. 1994;125 (5/part 2):S39-47.

Ni Y, Zhao B, Hou J, Xin W. Preventive effect of Ginkgo biloba extract on apoptosis in rat cerebellar neuronal cells induced by hydroxyl radicals. Neurosci Lett. 1996;214:115-8.

Nieman D. Exercise immunology: practical applications. Int J Sports Med. 1997;18 Suppl 1:S91-100.

Nishiyama N, Cho S, Kitagawa I, Saito H. Malonylginsenoside Rb1 potentiates nerve growth factor (NGF)-induced neurite outgrowth of cultured chick embryonic dorsal root ganglia. Biol Pharm Bull. 1994;17:509-13.

Nitta H, Matsumoto K, Shimizu M, Ni X, Watanabe H. Panax ginseng extract improves the scopolamine-induced disruption of 8-arm radial maze performance in rats. Biol Pharm Bull. 1995;18:1439-42.

Northrop C, Lunn P, Wainwright M, Evans J. Plasma albumin concentrations and intestinal permeability in Bangladeshi children infected with Ascaris lumbricoides. Transactions of the Royal Society of Tropical Medicine and Hygiene. 1987;81:811-5.

Noyer C, Simon D, Borczuk A, Brandt L, Lee M, Nehra V. A double-blind placebo-controlled pilot study of glutamine therapy for abnormal intestinal permeability in patients with AIDS. Am J Gastroenterol. 1998;93:972-5.

Nsouli T, Nsouli S, Linde R, O MF, Scanlon R, Bellanti J. Role of food allergy in serous otitis media. Ann Allergy. 1994;73:215-9.

Nugon -BL, Roland N, Flinois J, Beaune P. Hepatic cytochrome P450 and UDP-glucuronosyl transferase are affected by five sources of dietary fiber in germ-free rats. J Nutr. 1996;126:403-9.

Nurnberger JJ, Simmons -AS, Kessler L, et al. Separate mechanisms for behavioral, cardiovascular, and hormonal responses to dextroamphetamine in man. Psychopharmacology (Berl). 1984;84:200-4.

O'Callaghan J, Miller D. Brain serotonin neurotoxicity and fenfluramine and dexfenfluramine [letter]. JAMA. 1997;278:2141-2; discussion 2142.

O'Callaghan M, Harvey J. Biological predictors and co-morbidity of attention deficit and hyperactivity disorder in extremely low birthweight infants at school. J Paediatr Child Health. 1997;33:491-6.

Odell J, Warren R, Warren W, Burger R, Maciulis A. Association of genes within the major histocompatibility complex with attention deficit hyperactivity disorder. Neuropsychobiology. 1997;35:181-6.

O'Dwyer S, Michie H, Ziegler T, Revhaug A, Smith R, Wilmore D. A single dose of endotoxin increases intestinal permeability in healthy humans. Arch Surg. 1988;123:1459-64.

Ohta A, Ohtsuki M, Baba S, Adachi T, Sakata T, Sakaguchi E. Calcium and magnesium absorption from the colon and rectum are increased in rats fed fructooligosaccharides. J Nutr. 1995;125:2417-24.

Ohtsuka Y, Yamashiro Y, Shimizu T, et al. Reducing cell membrane n-6 fatty acids attenuate mucosal damage in food-sensitive enteropathy in mice. Pediatr Res. 1997;42:835-9.

Okutomi T, Abe S, Tansho S, Wakabayashi H, Kawase K, Yamaguchi H. Augmented inhibition of growth of Candida albicans by neutrophils in the presence of lactoferrin. FEMS Immunol Med Microbiol. 1997;18:105-12.

Oliveria S, Christos P. The epidemiology of physical activity and cancer. Ann N Y Acad Sci. 1997;833:79-90.

O'Shea J, Porter SF. Double-blind study of children with hyperkinetic syndrome treated with multi-allergen extract sublingually. J Learn Disabil. 1981;14:189-91, 237.

Oyama Y, Fuchs P, Katayama N, Noda K. Myricetin and quercetin, the flavonoid constituents of Ginkgo biloba extract, greatly reduce oxidative metabolism in both resting and Ca(2+)-loaded brain neurons. Brain Res. 1994;635:125-9.

Paganelli R, Fagiolo U, Cancian M, Scala E. Intestinal permeability in patients with chronic uticaria-angioedema with and without arthralgia. Ann Allergy. 1991;66:181-4.

Paganelli R, Cavagni G, Pallone F. The role of antigenic absorption and circulating immune complexes in food allergy. Ann Allergy. 1986;57:330-6.

Parran TV, Jr., Jasinski DR. Intravenous methylphenidate abuse. Prototype for prescription drug abuse. Arch Intern Med. 1991;151:781-3.

Peeters B, Broekkamp C. Involvement of corticosteroids in the processing of stressful life-events. A possible implication for the development of depression. J Steroid Biochem Mol Biol. 1994;49:417-27.

Pelto L, Isolauri E, Lilius EM, Nuutila J, Salminen S. Probiotic bacteria down-regulate the milk-induced inflammatory response in milk-hypersensitive subjects but have an immunostimulatory effect in healthy subjects. Clin Exp Allergy. 1998;28:1474-9.

Pert C, Ruff M, Weber R, Herkenham M. Neuropeptides and their receptors: a psychosomatic network. J Immunol. 1985;135:820s-826s.

Penna C, Dean P, Nelson H. Pulmonary metastases neutralization and tumor rejection by in vivo administration of beta glucan and bispecific antibody. Int J Cancer. 1996;65:377-82.

Petkov V, Mosharrof A, Petkov V, Kehayov R. Age-related differences in memory and in the memory effects of nootropic drugs. Acta Physiol Pharmacol Bulg. 1990;16:28-36.

Petkov V, Mosharrof A. Effects of standardized ginseng extract on learning, memory and physical capabilities. Am J Chin Med. 1987;15:19-29.

Pietri S, Maurelli E, Drieu K, Culcasi M. Cardioprotective and anti-oxidant effects of the terpenoid constituents of Ginkgo biloba extract (EGb 761). J Mol Cell Cardiol. 1997;29:733-42.

Pignata C, Budillon G, Monaco G, et al. Jejunal bacterial overgrowth and intestinal permeability in children with immunodeficiency syndromes. Gut. 1990;31:879-82.

Pless I, Taylor H, Arsenault L. The relationship between vigilance deficits and traffic injuries involving children. Pediatrics. 1995;95:219-24.

Pollack P, Rivera AJ, Rassin D, Nishioka K. Cysteine supplementation increases glutathione, but not polyamine, concentrations of the small intestine and colon of parenterally fed newborn rabbits. J Pediatr Gastroenterol Nutr. 1996;22:364-72.

Popoff MR. Interactions between bacterial toxins and intestinal cells. Toxicon. 1998;36:665-85.

Popova EI, Mikheev VF, Shuvaev VT, Ivonin AA, Chernyakov GM. Functional rearrangements in the human brain during emotional self- regulation with biological feedback. Neurosci Behav Physiol. 1998;28:8-16.

Popper CW. Antidepressants in the treatment of attention-deficit/hyperactivity disorder. J Clin Psychiatry. 1997;58 Suppl 14:14-29; discussion 30-1.

Porsolt R, Martin P, Lenegre A, Fromage S, Drieu K. Effects of an extract of Ginkgo Biloba (EGB 761) on "learned helplessness" and other models of stress in rodents. Pharmacol Biochem Behav. 1990;36:963-71.

Potashkin BD, Beckles N. Relative efficacy of ritalin and biofeedback treatments in the management of hyperactivity. Biofeedback Self Regul. 1990;15:305-15.

Quill K, Gurry S, Larkin A. Daily life therapy: a Japanese model for educating children with autism. J Autism Dev Disord. 1989;19:625-35.

Racagni G, Brunello N, Paoletti R. [Neuromediator changes during cerebral aging. The effect of Ginkgo biloba extract]. Presse Med. 1986;15:1488-90.

Rai G, Shovlin C, Wesnes K. A double-blind, placebo controlled study of Ginkgo biloba extract ('tanakan') in elderly outpatients with mild to moderate memory impairment. Curr Med Res Opin. 1991;12:350-5.

Ramassamy C, Christen Y, Clostre F, Costentin J. The Ginkgo biloba extract, EGb761, increases synaptosomal uptake of 5-hydroxytryptamine: in-vitro and ex-vivo studies. J Pharm Pharmacol. 1992;44:943-5.

Ramassamy C, Girbe F, Christen Y, Costentin J. Ginkgo biloba extract EGb 761 or trolox C prevent the ascorbic acid/Fe2+ induced decrease in synaptosomal membrane fluidity. Free Radic Res Commun. 1993;19:341-50.

Ramassamy C, Naudin B, Christen Y, Clostre F, Costentin J. Prevention by Ginkgo biloba extract (EGb 761) and trolox C of the decrease in synaptosomal dopamine or serotonin uptake following incubation. Biochem Pharmacol. 1992;44:2395-401.

Ransford C. A role for amines in the antidepressant effect of exercise: a review. Med Sci Sports Exerc. 1982;14:1-10.

Rapin J, Lamproglou I, Drieu K, DeFeudis F. Demonstration of the "anti-stress" activity of an extract of Ginkgo biloba (EGb 761) using a discrimination learning task. Gen Pharmacol. 1994;25:1009-16.

Rapp D, Fahey D. Allergy and chronic secretory otitis media. Pediatr Clin North Am. 1975;22:259-64.

Rapp DJ. Food allergy treatment for hyperkinesis. J Learn Disabil. 1979;12:608-16.

Redmond H, Stapleton P, Neary P, Bouchier -HD. Immunonutrition: the role of taurine. Nutrition. 1998;14:599-604.

Reichelt K. [Biochemistry and psychophysiology of autistic syndromes]. Tidsskr Nor Laegeforen. 1994;114:1432-4.

Reichelt K, Seim A, Reichelt W. Could schizophrenia be reasonably explained by Dohan's hypothesis on genetic interaction with a dietary peptide overload? Prog Neuropsychopharmacol Biol Psychiatry. 1996;20:1083-114.

Reisbick S, Neuringer M, Connor WE, Iliff-Sizemore S. Increased intake of water and NaCl solutions in omega-3 fatty acid deficient monkeys. Physiol Behav. 1991;49:1139-46.

Rhee Y, Ahn J, Choe J, Kang K, Joe C. Inhibition of mutagenesis and transformation by root extracts of Panax ginseng in vitro. Planta Med. 1991;57:125-8.

Rigden S. Entero-hepatic resuscitation program for CFIDS. CFIDS Chronicle. 1995; Spring Edition.

Rigney U, Kimber S, Hindmarch I. The effects of acute doses of standardized ginkgo biloba extract on memory and psychomotor performance in volunteers. Phytother Res. 1999;13:408-15

Riddle M, Nelson J, Kleinman C, et al. Sudden death in children receiving norpramin: a review of three reported cases and commentary. Journal of the American Academy of Child & Adolescent Psychiatry. 1991;30:104-8.
Roberfroid M, Van LJ, Gibson G. The bifidogenic nature of chicory inulin and its hydrolysis products. J Nutr. 1998;128:11-9.

Robinson T, Becker J. Enduring changes in brain and behavior produced by chronic amphetamine administration: a review and evaluation of animal models of amphetamine psychosis. Brain Res. 1986;396:157-98.

Rossiter T, LaVaque T. A comparison of EEG biofeedback and psychostimulants in treating attention deficit hyperactivity disorders. Journal of Neurotherapy. 1995:48-59.

Roland N, Nugon-Baudon L, Flinois JP, Beaune P. Hepatic and intestinal cytochrome P-450, glutathione-S-transferase and UDP-glucuronosyl transferase are affected by six types of dietary fiber in rats inoculated with human whole fecal flora. J Nutr. 1994;124:1581-7.

Rowland I, Mallett A, Flynn J, Hargreaves R. The effect of various dietary fibres on tissue concentration and chemical form of mercury after methylmercury exposure in mice. Arch Toxicol. 1986;59:94-8.

Rugle L, Melamed L. Neuropsychological assessment of attention problems in pathological gamblers. Journal of Nervous & Mental Disease. 1993;181:107-12.

Runeson BS. Child psychiatric symptoms in consecutive suicides among young people. Ann Clin Psychiatry. 1998;10:69-73.

Russo A, Stone S, Taplin M, Snapper H, Doern G. Presumptive evidence for Blastocystis hominis as a cause of colitis. Arch Intern Med. 1988;148:1064.

Saint-Phard D, Van Dorsten B, Marx RG, York KA. Self-perception in elite collegiate female gymnasts, cross-country runners, and track-and-field athletes. Mayo Clin Proc. 1999;74:770-4.

Salminen S, Bouley C, Boutron-Ruault MC, et al. Functional food science and gastrointestinal physiology and function. Br J Nutr. 1998;80 Suppl 1:S147-71.

Salminen S, Isolauri E, Salminen E. Clinical uses of probiotics for stabilizing the gut mucosal barrier: successful strains and future challenges. Antonie Van Leeuwenhoek. 1996;70:347-58.

Salzman A. Nitric oxide in the gut. New Horiz. 1995;3:352-64.

Salzman L. Allergy testing, psychological assessment and dietary treatment of the hyperactive child syndrome. Med J Aust. 1976;2:248-51.

Samet JM. Asthma and the environment: do environmental factors affect the incidence and prognosis of asthma? Toxicol Lett. 1995;82-83:33-8.

Samira M, Attia M, Allam M, Elwan O. Effect of the standardized Ginseng Extract G115 on the metabolism and electrical activity of the rabbit's brain. J Int Med Res. 1985;13:342-8.

Sanders T, Reddy S. Vegetarian diets and children. Am J Clin Nutr. 1994;59(suppl):1176s-1181s.

Sastre J, Millan A, Garcia dlAJ, et al. A Ginkgo biloba extract (EGb 761) prevents mitochondrial aging by protecting against oxidative stress. Free Radic Biol Med. 1998;24:298-304.

Satterfield J, Swanson J, Schell A, Lee F. Prediction of antisocial behavior in attention-deficit hyperactivity disorder boys from aggression/defiance scores. Journal of the American Academy of Child & Adolescent Psychiatry. 1994;33:185-90.

Saxby E, Peniston EG. Alpha-theta brainwave neurofeedback training: an effective treatment for male and female alcoholics with depressive symptoms. J Clin Psychol. 1995;51:685-93.

Scaglione F, Ferrara F, Dugnani S, Falchi M, Santoro G, Fraschini F. Immunomodulatory effects of two extracts of Panax ginseng C.A. Meyer. Drugs Exp Clin Res. 1990;16:537-42.

Scerbo A, Kolko D. Salivary testosterone and cortisol in disruptive children: relationship to aggressive, hyperactive, and internalizing behaviors. Journal of the American Academy of Child & Adolescent Psychiatry. 1994;33:1174-84.

Schauss A. Diet, crime and delinquency. Berkely, CA: Parker House; 1981:110.

Schauss A. New York City public school dietary revisions 1979-1983. Positive effects on 800,000 students acedemic achievement. International J Biosocial Res. 1986;8:2-5.

Schick R, Schusdziarra V. Physiological, pathophysiological and pharmacological aspects of exogenous and endogenous opiates. Clin Physiol Biochem. 1985;3:43-60.

Schmitt WH, Jr., Leisman G. Correlation of applied kinesiology muscle testing findings with serum immunoglobulin levels for food allergies. Int J Neurosci. 1998;96:237-44.

Schnare D, Denk G, Shields M, Brunton S. Evaluation of a detoxification regimen for fat stored xenobiotics. Med Hypotheses. 1982;9:265-82.

Schnare D, Robinson P. Reduction of the human body burdens of hexachlorobenzene and polychlornated biphenyls. IARC Sci Pub. 1986;77:596-603.

Schulte-Körne G, Deimel W, Gutenbrunner C, et al. Effect of an oligo-antigen diet on the behavior of hyperkinetic children. Z Kinder Jugendpsychiatr. 1996;3:176-83.

Schulz -LG, Dorner K, Oldigs H, Sievers E, Schaub J. Iron availability from an infant formula supplemented with bovine lactoferrin. Acta Paediatr Scand. 1991;80:155-8.

See D, Broumand N, Sahl L, Tilles J. In vitro effects of echinacea and ginseng on natural killer and antibody-dependent cell cytotoxicity in healthy subjects and chronic fatigue syndrome or acquired immunodeficiency syndrome patients. Immunopharmacology. 1997;35:229-35.

See DM, Cimoch P, Chou S, Chang J, Tilles J. The in vitro immunomodulatory effects of glyconutrients on peripheral blood mononuclear cells of patients with chronic fatigue syndrome. Integr Physiol Behav Sci. 1998;33:280-7.

Seeman T, McEwen B, Singer B, Albert M, Rowe J. Increase in urinary cortisol excretion and memory declines: MacArthur studies of successful aging. J Clin Endocrinol Metab. 1997;82:2458-65.

Seiden L, Sabol K, Ricaurte G. Amphetamine: effects on catecholamine systems and behavior. Annu Rev Pharmacol Toxicol. 1993;33:639-77.

Sever Y, Ashkenazi A, Tyano S, Weizman A. Iron treatment in children with attention deficit hyperactivity disorder. A preliminary report. Neuropsychobiology. 1997;35:178-80.

Sghir A, Chow J, Mackie R. Continuous culture selection of bifidobacteria and lactobacilli from human faecal samples using fructooligosaccharide as selective substrate. J Appl Microbiol. 1998;85:769-77.

Shaw W. Experience with organic acid testing to evaluate abnormal microbial metabolites in the urine of children with autism. National Conference on Autism. Milwaukee, WI; 1996.

Shein R, Gelb A. Colitis due to Dientamoeba fragilis. Am J Gastroenterol. 1983;78:634-6.

Sher L. Autistic disorder and the endogenous opioid system. Med Hypotheses. 1997;48:413-4.

Schick R, Schusdziarra V. Physiological, pathophysiological and pharmacological aspects of exogenous and endogenous opiates. Clin Physiol Biochem. 1985;3:43-60.

Shield J, Melville C, Novelli V, et al. Bovine colostrum immunoglobulin concentrate for cryptosporidiosis in AIDS [see comments]. Arch Dis Child. 1993;69:451-3.

Shin KS, Kiyohara H, Matsumoto T, Yamada H. Rhamnogalacturonan II from the leaves of Panax ginseng C.A. Meyer as a macrophage Fc receptor expression-enhancing polysaccharide. Carbohydr Res. 1997;300:239-49.

Shinkai S, Konishi M, Shephard R. Aging, exercise, training, and the immune system. Exerc Immunol Rev. 1997;3:68-95.

Simon L, Shine G, Dayan A. Translocation of particulates across the gut wall—a quantitative approach. J Drug Target. 1995;3:217-9..

Simopoulos A. Omega-3 fatty acids in health and disease and in growth and development. Am J Clin Nutr. 1991;54:438-63.

Singh NA, Clements KM, Fiatarone MA. A randomized controlled trial of progressive resistance training in depressed elders. J Gerontol A Biol Sci Med Sci. 1997;52:M27-35.

Smith P, Maclennan K, Darlington C. The neuroprotective properties of the Ginkgo biloba leaf: a review of the possible relationship to platelet-activating factor (PAF). J Ethnopharmacol. 1996;50:131-9.

Sohn H, Lim H, Lee Y, Lee D, Kim Y. Effect of subchronic administration of antioxidants against cigarette smoke exposure in rats. Arch Toxicol. 1993;67:667-73.

Solomons N. Giardiasis: nutritional implications. Rev Infect Dis. 1982;4:859-69.

Song Z, Johansen H, Faber V, et al. Ginseng treatment reduces bacterial load and lung pathology in chronic Pseudomonas aeruginosa pneumonia in rats. Antimicrob Agents Chemother. 1997;41:961-4.

Spillane K, Nagendran K, Prior PF, Tabaqchali S, Wilks M. Serial electroencephalograms in a patient with D-lactic acidosis. Electroencephalogr Clin Neurophysiol. 1994;91:403-5.

Starobrat -HB, Kozielec T. The effects of magnesium physiological supplementation on hyperactivity in children with attention deficit hyperactivity disorder (ADHD). Positive response to magnesium oral loading test. Magnes Res. 1997;10:149-56.

Stevens L, Zentall S, Abate M, Kuczek T, Burgess J. Omega-3 fatty acids in boys with behavior, learning, and health problems. Physiol Behav. 1996;59:915-20.

Stevens L, Zentall S, Deck J, et al. Essential fatty acid metabolism in boys with attention-deficit hyperactivity disorder. Am J Clin Nutr. 1995;62:761-8.

Stewart J, Quitkin F, McGrath P, et al. Cortisol response to dextroamphetamine stimulation in depressed outpatients. Psychiatry Res. 1984;12:195-206.

Stoppe G, Sandholzer H, Staedt J, Winter S, Kiefer J, Ruther E. Prescribing practice with cognition enhancers in outpatient care: are there differences regarding type of dementia?—Results of a representative survey in lower Saxony, Germany. Pharmacopsychiatry. 1996;29:150-5..

Steptoe A, Kimbell J, Basford P. Exercise and the experience and appraisal of daily stressors: a naturalistic study. J Behav Med. 1998;21:363-74.

Stuart R, Lefkowitz D, Lincoln J, Howard K, Gelderman M, Lefkowitz S. Upregulation of phagocytosis and candidicidal activity of macrophages exposed to the immunostimulant acemannan. Int J Immunopharmacol. 1997;19:75-82.

Subhan Z, Hindmarch I. The psychopharmacological effects of Ginkgo biloba extract in normal healthy volunteers. Int J Clin Pharmacol Res. 1984;4:89-93.

Sudo N, Sawamura S, Tanaka K, Aiba Y, Kubo C, Koga Y. The requirement of intestinal bacterial flora for the development of an IgE production system fully susceptible to oral tolerance induction. J Immunol. 1997;159:1739-45.

Sullivan V, Burnett F, Cousins R. Metallothionein expression is increased in monocytes and erythrocytes of young men during zinc supplementation. J Nutr. 1998;128:707-13.

Sun X, Matsumoto T, Kiyohara H, Hirano M, Yamada H. Cytoprotective activity of pectic polysaccharides from the root of panax ginseng. J Ethnopharmacol. 1991;31:101-7.

Sutas Y, Hurme M, Isolauri E. Down-regulation of anti-CD3 antibody-induced IL-4 production by bovine caseins hydrolysed with Lactobacillus GG-derived enzymes. Scand J Immunol. 1996;43:687-9.

Sutas Y, Soppi E, Korhonen H, et al. Suppression of lymphocyte proliferation in vitro by bovine caseins hydrolyzed with Lactobacillus casei GG-derived enzymes. J Allergy Clin Immunol. 1996;98:216-24.

Sutoo DE, Akiyama K. The mechanism by which exercise modifies brain function. Physiol Behav. 1996;60:177-81.

Swanson J, Castellanos F, Murias M, LaHoste G, Kennedy J. Cognitive neuroscience of attention deficit hyperactivity disorder and hyperkinetic disorder. Curr Opin Neurobiol. 1998;8:263-71.

Swanson J, Sunohara G, Kennedy J, et al. Association of the dopamine receptor D4 (DRD4) gene with a refined phenotype of attention deficit hyperactivity disorder (ADHD): a family-based approach. Mol Psychiatry. 1998;3:38-41.

Swedo S, Leonard H, Kiessling L. Speculations on antineuronal antibody-mediated neuropsychiatric disorders of childhood. Pediatrics. 1994;93:323-6.

Tan G, Schneider S. Attention-deficit hyperactivity disorder. Pharmacotherapy and beyond. Postgrad Med. 1997;101:201-4

Tansey MA. A simple and a complex tic (Gilles de la Tourette's syndrome): their response to EEG sensorimotor rhythm biofeedback training. Int J Psychophysiol. 1986;4:91-7.

Tansey M. Ten-year stability of EEG biofeedback results for a hyperactive boy who failed fourth grade perceptually impaired class. Biofeedback & Self Regulation. 1993;18:33-44.

Tatsuno K. Intestinal permeability in children with food allergy. Arerugi. 1989;12:1311-8.

Tejada-Simon MV, Lee JH, Ustunol Z, Pestka JJ. Ingestion of yogurt containing Lactobacillus acidophilus and Bifidobacterium to potentiate immunoglobulin A responses to cholera toxin in mice. J Dairy Sci. 1999;82:649-60.

Teraguchi S, Shin K, Ogata T, et al. Orally administered bovine lactoferrin inhibits bacterial translocation in mice fed bovine milk. Appl Environ Microbiol. 1995;61:4131-4.

Teschemacher H, Koch G. Opioids in the milk. Endocr Regul. 1991;25:147-50.

Teufel -MR, Gleitz J. Effects of long-term administration of hypericum extracts on the affinity and density of the central serotonergic 5-HT1 A and 5-HT2 A receptors. Pharmacopsychiatry. 1997;30 Suppl 2:113-6.

Theodorou V, Fioramonti J, Bueno L. Integrative neuroimmunology of the digestive tract. Vet Res. 1996;27:427-42.

Thompson L, Thompson M. Neurofeedback combined with training in metacognitive strategies: effectiveness in students with ADD. Appl Psychophysiol Biofeedback. 1998;23:243-63.

Thoren P, Floras JS, Hoffmann P, Seals DR. Endorphins and exercise: physiological mechanisms and clinical implications. Med Sci Sports Exerc. 1990;22:417-28.

Thorn A. Building-related health problems: reflections on different symptom prevalence among pupils and teachers. Int J Circumpolar Health. 1998;57:249-56.

Tomkins A, Wright S, Drasar B. Bacterial colonization of the upper intestine in mild tropical malabsorption. Trans R Soc Trop Med Hyg. 1980;74:752-5.

Tomoda M, Hirabayashi K, Shimizu N, Gonda R, Ohara N. The core structure of ginsenan PA, a phagocytosis-activating polysaccharide from the root of Panax ginseng. Biol Pharm Bull. 1994;17:1287-91.

Tomoda M, Takeda K, Shimizu N, et al. Characterization of two acidic polysaccharides having immunological activities from the root of Panax ginseng. Biol Pharm Bull. 1993;16:22-5.

Totosy de Zepetnick J, Shan J. Comparative Effects on Immune Parameters of Cold-FX and Several Botanical Medicinals. Personal Communication; 1999.

Traube M, Bock JL, Boyer JL. D-Lactic acidosis after jejunoileal bypass: identification of organic anions by nuclear magnetic resonance spectroscopy. Ann Intern Med. 1983;98:171-3.

Travis S, Menzies I. Intestinal permeability: functional assessment and significance. Clinical Science. 1992;82:471-88.

Tryphonas H, Trites R. Food allergy in children with hyperactivity, learning disabilities and/or minimal brain dysfunction. Ann Allergy. 1979;42:22-7.

Tubaro A, Tragni E, Del Negro P, Galli CL, Della Loggia R. Anti-inflammatory activity of a polysaccharidic fraction of Echinacea angustifolia. J Pharm Pharmacol. 1987;39:567-9.

Tulloch I, Smellie W, Buck A. Evening primrose oil reduces urinary calcium excretion in both normal and hypercalciuric rats. Urol Res. 1994;22:227-30.

Uauy R, De AI. Human milk and breast feeding for optimal mental development. J Nutr. 1995;125:2278S-2280S.

Uauy-Dagach R, Mena P. Nutritional role of omega-3 fatty acids during the perinatal period. Clin Perinatol. 1995;1:157-75.

Uhlig T, Merkenschlager A, Brandmaier R, Egger J. Topographic mapping of brain electrical activity in children with food-induced attention deficit hyperkinetic disorder. Eur J Pediatr. 1997;156:557-61.

Valdes MR. Effects of biofeedback-assisted attention training in a college population. Biofeedback Self Regul. 1985;10:315-24.

Vanderhoof J. Immunonutrition: the role of carbohydrates. Nutrition. 1998;14:595-8.

Vanderhoof J. Treatment strategies for small bowel overgrowth in short bowel syndrome. Journal of Pediatric Gastroenterology and Nutrition. 1998;27:155-60.

van der Hulst R, van Kreel B, von Meyenfeldt M, et al. Glutamine and the preservation of gut integrity [see comments]. Lancet. 1993;341:1363-5.

van Elberg R, Uil J, De Monchy J, Heymans H. Intestinal permeability in pediatric gastroenterology. Scand J Gastroenterol. 1992;27:19-24.

van Praag H, Kempermann G, Gage FH. Running increases cell proliferation and neurogenesis in the adult mouse dentate gyrus [see comments]. Nat Neurosci. 1999;2:266-70.

Veraldi S, Schianchi -VR, Gasparini G. Urticaria probably caused by Endolimax nana. Int J Dermatol. 1991;30:376.

Vereshchagin I, Geskina O, Bukhteeva E. [Increased effectiveness of antibiotic therapy with adaptogens in dysentery and Proteus infection in children]. Antibiotiki. 1982;27:65-9.

Veihelmann A, Brill T, Blobner M, et al. Inhibition of nitric oxide synthesis improves detoxication in inflammatory liver dysfunction in vivo. Am J Physiol. 1997;273:G530-6.

Vimy MJ, Hooper DE, King WW, Lorscheider FL. Mercury from maternal "silver" tooth fillings in sheep and human breast milk: a source of neonatal exposure. Biological Trace Element Res. 1997;56:143-52.

Vimy MJ, Lorscheider FL. Intra-oral air mercury released from dental amlgam. J. Dent. Res. 1985;64:1069-71.

Vimy M, Takahashi Y, Lorscheider F. Maternal-fetal distribution of mercury (203Hg) released from dental amalgam fillings. Am J Physiol. 1990;258:R939-45.

Virella G. Immune complex diseases. Immunol Ser. 1990;50:395-414.

Virella G. Hypersensitivity reactions. Immunol Ser. 1993;58:329-41.

Vogel W, Miller J, DeTurck K, Routzahn BJ. Effects of psychoactive drugs on plasma catecholamines during stress in rats. Neuropharmacology. 1984;23:1105-8.

Volkow ND, Wang GJ, Fowler JS, et al. Association of methylphenidate-induced craving with changes in right striato-orbitofrontal metabolism in cocaine abusers: implications in addiction. Am J Psychiatry. 1999;156:19-26.

Volz H. Controlled clinical trials of hypericum extracts in depressed patients—an overview. Pharmacopsychiatry. 1997;30 Suppl 2:72-6..

Vorbach E, Hubner W, Arnoldt K. Effectiveness and tolerance of the hypericum extract LI 160 in comparison with imipramine: randomized double-blind study with 135 outpatients. J Geriatr Psychiatry Neurol. 1994;7 Suppl 1:S19-23.

Wagner H. Phytomedicine Research in Germany. Environ Health Perspect. 1999;107:779-781.

Wahl M. Local chemical, neural, and humoral regulation of cerebrovascular resistance vessels. J Cardiovasc Pharmacol. 1985;7 Suppl 3:S36-46.

Warner K. Impact of high-temperature food processing on fats and oils. Adv Exp Med Biol. 1999;459:67-77.

Warren R, Odell J, Warren W, Burger R, Maciulis A, Torres A. Is decreased blood plasma concentration of the complement C4B protein associated with attention-deficit hyperactivity disorder? J Am Acad Child Adolesc Psychiatry. 1995;34:1009-14.

Warren R, Singh V, Averett R, et al. Immunogenetic studies in autism and related disorders. Mol Chem Neuropathol. 1996;28:77-81.

Warshaw S, Unger L. Allergy and secretory otitis media. IMJ Ill Med J. 1975;147:43 90.

Weihe E, Nohr D, Michel S, et al. Molecular anatomy of the neuro-immune connection. Int J Neurosci. 1991;59:1-23.

Weingarten H. Cytokines and food intake: the relavence of the immune system to the student of ingestive behavior. Neurosci Biobehav Rev. 1996;20:163-70.

Weiss G. Controversial issues of the pharmacotherapy of the hyperactive child. Can J Psychiatry. 1981;26:385-92.

Weiss G, Kruger E, Danielson U, Elman M. Effect of long-term treatment of hyperactive children with methylphenidate. Can Med Assoc J. 1975;112:159-65.

Whitcomb D, Taylor I. A new twist in the brain-gut axis. Am J Med Sci. 1992;304:334-8.

White H, Scates P, Cooper B. Extracts of Ginkgo biloba leaves inhibit monoamine oxidase. Life Sci. 1996;58:1315-21.

Wilens T, Biederman J, Mick E, Faraone S, Spencer T. Attention deficit hyperactivity disorder (ADHD) is associated with early onset substance use disorders. J Nerv Ment Dis. 1997;185:475-82.

Wilens TE, Biederman J, Spencer TJ, Prince J. Pharmacotherapy of adult attention deficit/hyperactivity disorder: a review. J Clin Psychopharmacol. 1995;15:270-9.

Williams G, O' Callaghan, M, Najman J, et al. Maternal cigarette smoking and child psychiatric morbidity: a longitudinal study. Pediatrics. 1998;102(1):e11.

Williams J, Cram D, Tausig F, Webster E. Relative effects of drugs and diet on hyperactive behaviors: an experimental study. Pediatrics. 1978;61:811-7.

Williamson S, Gossop M, Powis B, Griffiths P, Fountain J, Strang J. Adverse effects of stimulant drugs in a community sample of drug users. Drug Alcohol Depend. 1997;44:87-94.

Wilmore D, Shabert J. Role of glutamine in immunologic responses. Nutrition. 1998;14:618-26.

Winzelberg A, Humphreys K. Should patients' religiosity influence clinicians' referral to 12-step self-help groups? Evidence from a study of 3,018 male substance abuse patients. J Consult Clin Psychol. 1999;67:790-4

Wojcicki J, Gawronska -SB, Bieganowski W, et al. Comparative pharmacokinetics and bioavailability of flavonoid glycosides of Ginkgo biloba after a single oral administration of three formulations to healthy volunteers. Mater Med Pol. 1995;27:141-6.

Yamauchi K, Wakabayashi H, Hashimoto S, Teraguchi S, Hayasawa H, Tomita M. Effects of orally administered bovine lactoferrin on the immune system of healthy volunteers. Adv Exp Med Biol. 1998;443:261-5.

Yiamouyiannis C, Sanders R, Watkins Jd, Martin B. Chronic physical activity: hepatic hypertrophy and increased total biotransformation enzyme activity. Biochem Pharmacol. 1992;44:121-7.

Youdim MB, Ben-Shachar D, Ashkenazi R, Yehuda S. Brain iron and dopamine receptor function. Adv Biochem Psychopharmacol. 1983;37:309-21.

Yurdaydin C, Walsh T, Engler H, et al. Gut bacteria provide precursors of benzodiazepine receptor ligands in a rat model of hepatic encephalopathy. Brain Res. 1995;679:42-8.

Zahn T, Rapoport J, Thompson C. Autonomic effects of dextroamphetamine in normal men: implications for hyperactivity and schizophrenia. Psychiatry Res. 1981;4:39-47.

Zhang D, Yasuda T, Yu Y, et al. Ginseng extract scavenges hydroxyl radical and protects unsaturated fatty acids from decomposition caused by iron-mediated lipid peroxidation. Free Radic Biol Med. 1996;20:145-50.

Zeitlin H. Psychiatric comorbidity with substance misuse in children an teenagers. Drug Alcohol Depend. 1999;55:225-34.

Zimecki M, Wlaszczyk A, Cheneau P, et al. Immunoregulatory effects of a nutritional preparation containing bovine lactoferrin taken orally by healthy individuals. Arch Immunol Ther Exp (Warsz). 1998;46:231-40.

Index

A

AA (arachidonic acid): 91; brain and: 91

Abuse: ADHD and: 124

Adderall®: 340

AD-FX™: 94, 354; benefits in the management of ADHD: 360

ADHD: abdominal pain and: 48; ADD vs.: 25; addictions and: 34, 36; asthma and: 50; brain executive centers: 27; brain's reward center and: 34; breast feeding and: 90; chronic fatigue syndrome and: 49; dietary management of: 429; ear infections and: 50; emotional-psychological stresses and: 390; entrepreneurial risk taking and: 38; "extreme" sports and: 34; fatigue and: 49; fibromyalgia and: 49; food allergies and: 185-187; genetics of; gut ecology and: 192, 199; headaches and: 48; imaging technologies and: 27; medical problems with symptoms similar to: 242-243; memory deficits and: 42; muscle pain and: 48; muscle tension and: 392; positive aspects of: 482; pre-frontal cortex and: 27; and secondary psychological disorders: 45; and psychosomatic disorders: 48; reward deficiency syndrome and: 36; standard medical workup in: 244; three sub types of: 24; varied characteristics of: 24; working memory and: 42

Adverse drug reactions: 348

Agricultural soil contamination: 68; heavy metal and: 68; organochlorine pesticides and: 68

Allergens: 157

Allergies: ADHD and: 58, 275; assessment of airborne: 275; sleep apnea and: 275

Amalgam fillings: 80-82, 90, 393; chronic fatigue syndrome and: 393; fibromyalgia and: 393; intestinal bacteria and: 208; placental transfer of mercury and: 393

American Psychiatric Association definition of ADHD: 24

Amino acid analysis: 273

Amphetamines: emotional-psychological stresses and: 391; toxicity: 340-341

Antecedents, definition: 18

Antecedents, triggers and mediators: 18

Auto-brewery syndrome: 219, 267, 374; breath testing and: 268-270

Autoimmunity: ADHD and: 220-221; Candida albicans and: 221; cross reaction with microbial antigens and: 221

B

B vitamins: 434

Bacteria: classification of gut organisms: 194; definition of probiotic: 192; hepatic encephalopathy and: 201; neurotoxins derived from: 203-207; number of species in gut: 191

Beta-glucuronidase: 262

Bifidobacteria: 194

Biochemical individuality: 232

Biofeedback: ADHD treatment using: 471; electroencephalographic (EEG) biofeedback (also called neurofeedback or neurotherapy): 470; electromyographic (EMG) for muscle tension: 469; EMG biofeedback and ADHD: 470; galvanic skin response (GSR) for stress management: 467

Biofeedback Certification Institute of America (BCIA): 476

Bioflavonoids: 115; Ginkgo biloba and: 116; green tea and: 116

Bland, Dr. Jeffrey: 5, 9

Blood brain barrier: 26; toxins: 26

Blum, Dr. Kenneth: 105

Botanical medicine: AD-FX and: 354; ADHD and: 354; biological standardization and: 353; botanical drugs: 349; current science in Europe and North America: 346, 351; Germany's Commission E and: 352; herbal medicines: 350; history of: 346; in contrast to drugs: 347-348; standardized extracts and: 352

Brain: oxygen and: 26

Breakfast: learning problems and inadequate: 112

Breast milk: lactoferrin and: 192; lactoperoxidase and: 192; oligosacharides and: 193; secretory IgA and: 192

Breastfeeding: mercury vapor from amalgam fillings and: 90; neurotoxins and: 90

Breath testing: 268

C

Calcium: 110, 434; factors causing loss of: 110; lead contamination and: 110; microcrystalline hydroxyapatite and: 111, 435; non-dairy sources of: 110; Ultracare for Kids and: 110

Candida albicans: 267, 411

Car exhaust and neurotoxicity: 64

Casomorphins: 140

Cells: number of bacterial: 190; number of human: 190

Chelation therapy: 453

Chromium: 110; immune system and: 111; insulin sensitivity and: 111

Cocaine: history: 339

Coconut oil: 97, 426; cooking and: 97

Cod liver oil: 426, 435

Cold-FX: 117, 412; Edmonton Oilers and: 412

Complement: ADHD and deficiency of: 214-215

Comprehensive Digestive Stool Analysis (CDSA) with Comprehensive Parasitology: 259

Conners' Parent Rating Scales: 241

Corporate exploitation of consumers: 102; marketing junk food to children: 102

Covey, Dr. Steven: "The 7 Habits of Highly Effective People": 488

Cruciferous vegetables: 116

Cylert®: 340; liver toxicity from: 343

D

Dairy products: 424

Dehumanization of medicine: 16

Dehydration: 118, 398; ADHD and: 118, 398; fatty acid deficiencies and: 119

Detoxification support: 384

Dexedrine®: 340

DHA (docosahexaenoic acid): 85; algae derived: 90; micronutrient support and: 94, 98; nerve endings and: 85; neuron processing speed and: 85; retina and: 86; sources of: 90; Ultracare for Kids and: 91

Digestion: immune system and: 154

Digestive enzymes: 374

Discipline: ADHD and the importance of: 482; ineffectiveness of nagging: 483; positively molding behavior: 483

Disease Centered Medicine: 324; ADHD and: 230; definition: 229; limitations in the treatment of ADHD: 239, 244; treatment of ADHD using: 324, 325

D-lactic acid: neurotoxicity of: 377

DMPS: 284, 453

DMSA: 453

Dobson, Dr. James: "The Strong-Willed Child" by: 483

Dopamine: 29; amphetamines and: 30; re-uptake of: 29

Drugs: safety: 339

Dysbiosis: 194, 395; causes of: 210-211

E

EDTA: 286, 453

Electroencephalographic (EEG) biofeedback (also called neurofeedback or neurotherapy; ADHD treatment using: 471; brainwaves in ADHD: 471; compared to Ritalin® as a primary treatment for ADHD: 474; improved attentiveness following: 473; increase in IQ following: 473

Electromagnetic pollution: 393

Elimination test diet for ADHD: 310-317

ELISA testing: importance of quality control in: 299; Type III hypersensitivity and: 297-299

Emotional-psychological stresses: 390

Enzyme Potentiated Desensitization (EPD): 309, 415; advantages over conventional "allergy shots": 416; as a treatment for ADHD: 417; food allergies and: 416; safety of: 416

Essential fatty acids: analysis of: 274; immune system and: 400, 404; supplementation: 435

Evidence-based medicine: 325-328; Functional Medicine and: 328-329

Executive centers: dopamine and: 29; function: 27; inhibition and: 28; neurotoxic influences upon: 439; Ritalin® and: 31; susceptibility to toxins and stress: 28

Exercise: 401; ADHD and: 457; anabolic steroid abuse and: 462; brain neurotransmitters and: 457; detoxification and: 449, 450; eating disorders and: 462; executive center function and: 458; mental and emotional health benefits: 456; personal fitness and ADHD: 459; precautions regarding: 461; repair of brain cells and: 458; self-esteem and: 458

F

Fasting: 7

Fats and oils: choosing proper: 426

Few foods elimination diet: 318

Fiber: 117, 382; detoxification activities and: 406; immune system and: 405

Flax oil: 89, 90, 97, 426

Food additives: amines: 74; benzoates: 74; caffeine: 74; monosodium glutamate: 74; salicylates: 74; sulfites: 74; tartrazine: 74; trans-fatty acids: 74

Food allergies: ADHD and: 185-187, 222; biokinesiology testing: 296; causes of: 175-180; double blind food challenge testing and: 294; ELISA testing: 297-299; food addictions and: 173, 427; food intolerances as opposed to: 163; Functional Medicine Method of assessment: 300-309; intestinal bacteria and: 406; intestinal parasites and: 179; leaky gut and: 178; most common foods causing: 159; open food challenge process for detection of: 305; provocation / neutralization testing and: 297; RAST and: 294; reasons for contoversy: 159-160; skin prick tests and: 293; symptoms associated with: 161; treatment in ADHD: 292; treatment of: 309; Type I hypersensitivity (immediate type food allergy) : 165-169; Type III hypersensitivity (delayed type food allergy): 169-174, 222; Vega or electrodermal testing: 296

Food intolerance: food additives and: 183; inadequate digestion and: 180; poor detoxification capabilities and: 182; salicylates and: 183

Food Pyramid: adapted for those with ADHD: 421

4-R Program™: anti-infective herbs and: 370; Comprehensive Digestive Stool Analysis in: 372; definition of: 367; detoxification support in: 384; digestive enzymes and: 374; essential fatty acids and: 382; fiber and: 382; fructooligosaccharides (FOS): 379; homemade yogurt and: 380; hypochlorhydria and: 374; inulin and: 379; L-Glutamine and: 381; micronutrient support and: 382; oat bran and: 380; pharmaceutical agents in: 372; phospholipids and: 382; probiotic bacteria and: 375; reinoculate phase of: 375; remove phase of: 368; repair phase of: 380; replace phase of: 374; stool transit time and: 373; therapeutic steps within: 368; UltraClear and: 381

Friel, Dr. John and Linda: "The 7 Worst Things Parents Do" by: 484

Fructooligosaccharides (FOS): 379

Fruits: 424

Functional Medicine: biochemical individuality and: 232; definition: 17; patient as "team captain" in: 233; patient centered medicine and: 231; principles of treatment: 17, 330; respect for the natural healing process and: 331

Functional Toxicology: basic Principles of: 442-445

G

Genetic basis of ADHD neurology: 57

Genetics: allergy and: 58; neurotoxins and: 58; optimizing genetic potential: 61

Ginkgo biloba: 116

Ginkgo biloba extracts: antioxidant effects within the brain and heart: 358; cognitive effects of: 359; increased dopamine production and: 359; stress ameliorating effects of: 358

Ginseng extracts: American ginseng and: 358; cognitive effects of: 357; increased dopamine production and: 357; properties of: 356-358

GLA (gamma linolenic acid): 92, 426

Glyconutritionals: 117; acemannan and: 411; ADHD and: 410; Aloe vera and: 408; Ambrotose™ and: 410; Candida albicans and: 411; chronic fatigue syndrome and: 411; Cold-FX™ and: 412; ginseng and: 411; glycoproteins and: 409; immune system function and: 408; Mannatech™ and: 410; oligosaccharides and: 408; receptor decoys: 408

Government health insurance: 16, 325

Grape seed extract: 94

Green tea: 116; antioxidant effects: 362; effects on cognitive performance: 363; reduction in dental caries from: 363

Gut associated lymphoid tissue or GALT: 137; ADHD and: 137; brain and: 137; normal intestinal defenses and: 196-197

Gut ecology: ADHD and: 199-200; competition between pathogens: 208; dental amalgams and: 208; immune suppressors and: 209; nutrition and: 207; superantigens and: 208

H

Hair element analysis: 272

Heavy metals: food supply and: 68

Helicobacter pylori: 267

Hepatic encephalopathy: 201

Human genome, size: 55

Hyper-focusing: 43-45, 465; pleasure and: 465

Hyperthermic therapy: Environmental Protection Agency (EPA) and: 450; pesticide residues and: 450; saunas and: 450; steam baths and: 450; toxic metals and: 450

Hypochlorhydria: 374

I

Immune system: activation by superantigens: 208-209; alarm molecules and: 135; antigenic stress and: 394; autoimmune disorders and: 156; cytokines: 135; electromagnetic pollution and: 393; emotional-psychological stresses and: 390; essential fatty acids and: 400; exercise (excessive) and: 399; exercise training (moderate) and: 401; hand washing and: 397; infectious stress and: 395; intake of water and: 398; memory: 155; microglia and: 135; micronutrients and: 400; neurotransmitters and: 134; nutritional inadequacy and: 400; self antigens: 155; superantigens and immune suppressors in ADHD: 209-210; suppression by microbes: 209; the "mobile nervous system": 134; tolerance and: 155, 158; total underlying stressors impacting the immune system: 389-399; toxic stresses and: 392; ultraviolet radiation and: 394

Immunonutrition: 402-413; balanced macronutrients and: 403; dietary fiber and: 405; essential fatty acids and: 404; glyconutritionals and: 408; optimized micronutrients and: 403; probiotic supplementation and: 406

Immunotherapy: 413; "allergy" shots and: 413; Enzyme Potentiated Desensitization (EPD) and: 415; provocation-neutralization and: 414

Institute for Functional Medicine: 234, 251, 367, 395, 497

Intestinal permeability testing (using lactulose and mannitol): 255

Inulin: 379

J

Junk foods: 102; addictions to: 427; breaking addictions to: 428; malnutrition and: 103

L

Lactobacilli: 194
Lactobacillus GG: 377
Lactobacillus plantarum: 377
Lactobacillus rhamnosus: 377
Lactoferrin: 192, 371
Lactoperoxidase: 192, 371
Lead: discovery of low level poisoning with: 339
Leaky gut: ADHD and: 141-142; causes of: 146-149; effects of: 149-152
L-glutamine: 381; UltraClear and: 381
Linnaeus, Dr. Carolus: 228; Linnaean system of classification and: 228
Liver detoxification: 277-279

M

Magnesium: ADHD and: 107; DHA and: 107; hyperirritability and: 107; Intracellular Diagnostics Laboratory and: 108; Ritalin® and: 107; supplementation: 108, 435
Malnutrition: North American children and: 420
Managed-care organizations: 16, 325
Maté, Dr. Gabor: 126
Maternal-infant bond: 124-127; breast feeding and: 126; executive center development and: 125
Mediators, definition: 19
Meditation: 7, 476; relaxation and: 478
Mercury: testing for: 284
Metagenics: 371
Micronutrient malnutrition: 103
Micronutrients: 434; assessment of: 270-273; brain function and: 104, 105; colloidal minerals and: 114; cytochromes and: 106; immune system function and: 403
Multi-vitamin: 114

N

Nasrallah, Dr. H.A.: 342
Neurology of ADHD: benefits of: 57; drawbacks of: 57-58
Neuropeptides: 139; beta-endorphin and: 139; milk and: 140; substance-P and: 139; wheat gluten and: 141
Neuropsychological assessment, importance of: 240
Neurotoxicity: aluminum and: 66; amalgam fillings and: 80; cadmium and: 64; drinking water and: 65; fish and: 74-75; lead and: 64, 77; manganese and: 65; mercury and: 80-82; microbial toxins and: 204-207; sick building syndrome and: 76; violent criminals and: 65
Neurotoxicity: D-lactic acid and
Norpramin: toxicity from: 343
Nutritional supplements: ADHD and: 433

O

Oceanside Functional Medicine Research Institute: 354
Oligosacharides: 117

Omega-3 fatty acid: 85; ADHD and: 87; and susceptibility to oxidation: 86; antioxidants and: 94; breast feeding and: 90; cod liver oil and: 426; delta-six desaturase and: 88; fish oils and: 88; flax oil and: 88; genetic requirements for: 89; heavy metals and depletion of: 87; proanthocyanidins and: 94; sources of: 87; stress hormones and depletion of: 87; underdeveloped brain regions and: 85

Organically grown produce: 114

Osler, Sir William: 243

Outcome based medicine: 328; Functional Medicine and: 328

P

Palm Pilot®: 488

Parasites: examples of in ADHD (photos): 265-266; in children attending daycare centers: 211; in children with ADHD: 211; in homosexual men: 211

Parents: as "sculptors of the soul"; breakdown of traditional roles : 129

Patient Centered Medicine: ADHD and: 231; biochemical individuality and: 232; Functional Medicine and: 231; Patient Centered Diagnosis and: 234

Pesticides: 69-73, 340; history: 70-71; organophosphate toxicity: 71-72; worst offenders: 73

Prayer: 7, 479; ADHD and: 480

Probioplex Intensive Care: 371

Probiotic bacteria: 193, 375; allergic disorders and: 406; benefits of: 197-199, 407; characteristics of effective species: 375-378; food allergies and: 380; immune system and: 406; immune system development and: 406; intestinal inflammation and: 407; secretory IgA and: 407

Protein: 104; and neurotransmitters: 105

Protein foods: 425

Provocation-neutralization: 414

PS (phosphatidylserine): 93; memory, concentration and: 93

Psychoneuroimmunology: 214

Pycnogenol: 94, 116

R

Rancid fats: 95

Reward center: 34; amphetamines and: 36; cocaine and: 36; dopamine and: 35; executive centers connections to: 36; gambling and: 38; nicotine and: 36

Ritalin®: action of: 31; and cardiovascular toxicity: 340; and potential for abuse and addiction : 337, 341; cortical atrophy (generalized brain shrinkage) from: 342; dopamine reuptake and: 31; emotional-psychological stresses and: 391; free radicals in the brain from: 342; heart damage from: 342; International Narcotics Control Board of the United Nations and: 335; lack of long term safety studies: 338; neurotoxic potential of: 341; positive short term effects of: 337-338; predicting long term toxicity: 340; prescription rates for: 335, 343, 438; schools promoting prescriptions for: 336; stress hormones and: 341; Tourette's disorder and: 45

S

Saturated fats: 95

Sauna: 7

Seaweed: 114

Secretory IgA: ADHD and depletion of: 216-217; and ADHD: 371; causes of diminished production: 220, 263; results of depletion: 219-220; stool testing for: 263; structure and function of: 217-219

Selenium: 110, 112; glutathione peroxidase and: 112; mercury and: 113; thyroid function and: 112

Sewage sludge and agriculture: 67-68

Single parenting: 129

Small intestine: lifespan of cells within: 366; probiotic bacteria and: 144; structure of: 142-145; tight junctions and: 143

Smoking: history: 338; risk of ADHD and

Snacks, healthy: 430

Societal pressures and ADHD: 127-128

Spirituality: ADHD and: 489; 12-Step Program as a practical form of: 489-493

St. John's wort: 360; as a treatment for depression: 361; effects on behavior in ADHD: 361; efffects on mood: 361; in combination with other botanical medicines: 362; safety of: 361

Stroop Color-Word Test: 241

Structure: importance of in ADHD: 487; Palm Pilot® as a tool to maintain: 488

Suicide: 7; gambling addiction and: 38

Superantigens: 208

T

Therapeutic detoxification: chelation therapy and: 453; exercise and: 449; hyperthermic therapy and: 450; milk thistle extract and: 452; nutritional minerals and: 451; traditional fasting vs.: 445; UltraClear Plus and: 447

Toxicology assessment: 276-288; D-glucaric acid and mercaptures: 287; Functional detoxification testing: 277; non-metallic toxin assessment: 287, 288; porphyrin analysis: 286; toxic metal testing: 281-287

Trans-fatty acids: 95; hydrogenation and: 95; metabolism of omega-3 fattty acids and: 96

Triggers, definition: 18

U

UltraBalance® line of products: 384, 431

Ultracare for Kids™: 317, 385, 432; ADHD and: 91; delicious smoothies and: 91, 317; FOS (fructooligosaccharides) and: 91

UltraClear™: 381

UltraFiber™: 448

UltraInflamX™: 384

Ultraviolet radiation: 394

University of Alberta: 117, 353; biological standardization and: 354; Herbal Medicine Research Group at: 354; HerbTech and: 354

Urinary organic acid testing: 268

Urinary peptide testing: 270

Utah State University: 214

V

Vegetable oils: 96; hexane extraction and: 97; oxidation and: 97

Vegetables: 423

W

Warren, Dr. R.: 214

Water: purification of: 120

Whole grain foods: 421

Working memory: 42-43; chronic lateness and: 43; definition: 42; hyper-focusing and: 43-45; reading problems and: 43; sense of time and: 43

Z

Zinc: ADHD and: 109; omega-3 fatty acids and: 109; taste and: 108; toxic metal excretion and: 109